Praise for Psych

MW00462251

"*Psychstrology* is a unique guide to integrating psychology and astrology. Dr. Stacy Dicker clearly elucidates how the archetypes of astrology can support clinicians and clients alike in broadening their understanding of the dynamics of relationships, whether between parents, partners, families, or coworkers. She includes excellent examples of the synchronicities that led her to realize the universal applicability of this ancient archetypal system.

The book also discusses some of the major life cycles defined by astrology, such as the Saturn return. Dr. Dicker lays out an easily accessible use of the Sun, Moon, and rising signs as a method to unlock the wisdom available to those interested in increasing their therapy tools. Helpful charts are included for the reader to explore their primary astrological archetypes and those of others.

As an astrologer, I highly commend her work, which creates a much-needed bridge between the field of psychotherapy and the ancient practice of astrological counsel."

—Patricia Liles, Astrologer

"Dr. Stacy Dicker explores two complex disciplines, psychology and astrology, in a way that makes them approachable and relevant for everyone, then brings the two together in perfect harmony. Interweaving her personal journey throughout makes this read all the more compelling.

Stacy has bridged a gap that has been too wide for too long, and lets the reader get to know her along the way. Her courage will serve all seekers in unfolding self-awareness and joy."

—Lauren Skye, Director of Inner Connection Institute and author of *Spiritual Amnesia: A Wake Up Call to What You Really Are*

"Brilliant, lucidly written, and intimate in tone, *Psychstrology* is an extraordinary integration of healing wisdom from a variety of traditions. It is practical, educational, easy to use, and immensely valuable to those offering healing as well as those seeking it. Anyone can benefit from this gem."

—Dr. Heather LaChance, PhD, DCEP, owner of Compassion in Practice LLC, Licensed Clinical Psychologist, and CO State Representative for ACEP

"In *Psychstrology*, Dr. Stacy Dicker offers an intuitively appealing framework to describe individual personality traits and patterns and interpersonal interaction patterns that invites the reader to scrutinize and even challenge what they believe about themselves and why they act the way they do, especially with significant others.

Dr. Dicker presents her approach to using zodiac signs with sufficient recognition of the broader context of the many variables that impact a person's behavior that the reader is not required to assign specific validity to particular statements or predictions. Rather, the reader can simply choose to use her approach as an intriguing opportunity to consider the possibility that they may have overlooked some important aspects of themselves or others, and to treat themselves and others more compassionately.

The book provides a rich vocabulary to talk about needs, wants, fears, and motivations, which can help the reader consider how they may live with greater ease within themselves, understand the patterns they recognize, and grow through consideration of their shadow selves."

—Dr. Linda Craighead, PhD, Director of Clinical Training at Emory University and author of *The Appetite Awareness Workbook* and *Training Your Inner Pup to Eat Well*

"As someone who found a Jungian therapist through an astrologer, I was thrilled when I started reading *Psychstrology*. Dr. Stacy Dicker has a wonderful ability to weave the many principles of psychology and astrology together in a clear, informative, and fascinating manner.

While many astrology books include descriptions of the twelve astrological signs, Stacy's unique approach illuminates new facets of each sign. I immediately wanted to look up the signs of friends, family members, and clients for new revelations.

While this book works on many levels, including as an introduction to astrology and a helpful relationship guide, the insight and wisdom found in it transcend one simple category. I look forward to adding *Psychstrology* to my library, and plan to refer to its wise approach on a regular basis."

—Geri Bellino, Intuitive Astrologer

Psychstrology

Psychstrology

**Apply the Wisdom of the Cosmos to Gain Balance
and Improve Your Relationships**

STACY DICKER, PhD

Real Avenue Press

Psychstrology: Apply the Wisdom of the Cosmos to Gain Balance and Improve Your Relationships

Copyright © 2019, 2022 by Stacy Dicker, PhD

All rights reserved.

No part of this publication may be reproduced, distributed, or transmitted in any form or by any means, including photocopying, recording, or other electronic or mechanical methods, without the prior written permission of the author, except in the case of brief quotations embodied in critical reviews and certain other noncommercial uses permitted by copyright law.

ISBN: 978-1-7341356-0-2

Published by Real Avenue Press

For more information, visit www.psychstrology.com

Editing by Red Letter Editing, LLC, www.redletterediting.com
Book design by Christy Day, Constellation Book Services

Printed in the United States of America

To the two air sun-Leo moon men in my life, my husband and my dad, who have made me feel the most seen, cherished, and loved.

When I Heard the Learn'd Astronomer

When I heard the learn'd astronomer,
When the proofs, the figures, were ranged in columns before me,
When I was shown the charts and diagrams, to add, divide,
and measure them,
When I sitting heard the astronomer where he lectured
with much applause in the lecture-room,
How soon unaccountable I became tired and sick,
Till rising and gliding out I wander'd off by myself,
In the mystical moist night-air, and from time to time,
Look'd up in perfect silence at the stars.
—Walt Whitman

Contents

Therapists as Wounded Healers—The Need to Transform the Pain

Have you ever had the sense that you were different from people around you? Maybe you see things from a different vantage point, or your natural, inner responses don't seem to match up with the perspective of others, sometimes even those in your own family. Or maybe you just feel like you don't totally, or even mostly, fit in, even if you can't figure out how to put words to the feeling. It's not easy feeling like an outsider.

Throughout my entire life I have felt a little different from everyone else. For example, I skipped first grade and was significantly younger than the rest of my class for the duration of school, and I moved from northern New Jersey to a Colorado mountain town when I was eleven; both of these facts made me different, in a real way, from those around me. Much of the time, though, my sense that I'm different from those around me revolves around the particular lens through which I view the world. I have often had the feeling that I know or see too much for my own good.

I have often wanted so badly to just fit in, to see things the same way as everyone else, yet something in my very nature does not allow me to do it, or at least not completely. I feel like I can't do anything but speak the truth about reality as I see it. At times, this has been mostly welcome, like in my job as a therapist or as a friend to my friends, but overall, it's been a difficult nature to have. My dad told me early in my life that I was a truth-teller, and to expect that role to be a hard one to play at times; he couldn't have been more right.

It all started in the context of my family environment. When my mother was six months pregnant with me, her mother died of a massive heart attack. With all the perspective that psychotherapy and age can bring, I can now imagine not only what that must have been like for her, but also how much it must have affected me in my earliest experiences of the world.

Three years after our move to Colorado, which was hard enough in itself, my parents split up. I was fourteen, a sophomore in high school. The divorce was contentious, and my parents were, understandably though not ideally, absorbed by their own experience of the trauma and transition. No one paid enough attention to our experience as kids, and my younger brothers were much more willing and able than I was to fly under the radar and not make waves, so I certainly felt different within the context of my family.

This experience of feeling different has been replicated numerous times since then, as traumatic experiences typically are—therapists call it a *repetition compulsion*, where we unconsciously attempt to heal and process old, unfinished business by repeatedly casting the same characters so we can play out the scenes with them.

For example, after college, having majored in psychology, I mistook my interest in victims' rights to mean I should become a lawyer. While I don't fault my younger self for not knowing exactly what she wanted (why do they make us choose so early on?), it did mean that I spent three years in law school feeling isolated and different from most of my classmates.

Later, in my clinical psychology doctoral program, I found myself disillusioned by many of the ideas my classmates were excited about, and ultimately felt different from them, too. My graduate program was focused on research, which inevitably favors treatments that are easy to capture in a manual. *This can't be all there is to it*, I thought—but once again, I had inadvertently picked a program into which I did not fit very well. Thankfully, my graduate advisor was fluid, forward-thinking, and had a lot of faith in me.

I was also fortunate to have my first clinical supervisor, a brilliant man in his seventies, teach me some of the basic premises of a deeper form of therapy called *psychodynamic* or *depth* therapy; later, starting my own psychoanalysis and taking courses in psychodynamic therapy felt like a homecoming because of those seeds he had planted.

Alas, I even came to sense my difference from many of the people in the world of psychodynamic therapy. While I thrived in an environment where people talked about the nature of the unconscious and dream interpretation, my longstanding interest in cosmic forces like astrology didn't have a place there. Enter Carl Jung, who has a reputation for making we outcasts feel understood. One thing is for sure: it has taken me quite a while to find where I fit, both personally and professionally. I had to know myself really well first.

My interests in both psychology and astrology have stemmed from this feeling of being different. I have spent my whole life trying to feel seen and understood, not least of all by my own self. I want to understand why I am who I am and why others are who they are. The idea that there are reasons for this has always given me, and probably most therapists, a particular form of comfort.

Now my mission is to help self-aware people who struggle with feeling lost, having relationship problems, and wondering what's next. I have struggled with these same things, and I can now help because I have been a clinical psychologist in private practice who has seen clients for the last twenty years. I have been studying astrology for even longer. In my experience, combining psychology and astrology—what I call *psychstrology*—yields much more benefit than either method alone to get us through difficult times.

This book is the result of my deep desire to help others gain a greater understanding of themselves and others; to gain balance, find clarity, and have the healthiest relationships possible with everyone who touches their lives. I truly hope you find valuable insight and guidance as a result of reading it.

Introduction

Let's face it: astrology hasn't gotten the best rap over the years. When you think of astrology, you may think of fortune-telling via daily or monthly horoscopes based solely on people's sun signs—no wonder so many people think it's all nonsense! Astrologer and Jungian analyst Liz Greene has expressed her hope that astrology can be freed from this fortune-telling image. My experience has shown me that those of us who deeply understand its power would also like to see this change; we know how poorly astrology is still perceived, especially in academic circles.

The good news is, many people are feeling a nudge, an inclination to move astrology forward by making it part of the discussion. I see this every day online, in articles analyzing how different zodiac signs approach anything from fashion and diet to relationships and employment preferences. In many settings, including academically oriented ones, it seems that spiritual forces from the great beyond are nudging the people who deeply understand astrology's power. There is a mission underway, and it is gaining momentum.

Besides the criticism that astrology is too general to be helpful or valid, you may not know much about it because you have found it too vast to be useful—and I understand this. I felt that way when I first started to delve into astrology, and looking at all of the huge books at the bookstore just confirmed my sense that it was

1

overwhelming. It is ironic that astrology has been both over-reduced to its fortune-telling image and under-reduced in that it's much more digestible when broken into small chunks than one might think.

My goal with this book is to help facilitate greater balance in both of these areas by making an intellectual argument for the validity of astrology and by making it more accessible and constructive. I believe we should be using astrology to better understand ourselves and the important others in our lives, on par and in conjunction with our use of psychology for these same objectives. Astrology can help us find more balance, clarity, and ease in our relationship with ourselves, and it can also help tremendously in our efforts to better understand our most important others.

Maybe you are in the middle of a crisis of some sort, wondering what the next chapter of your life will look like, facing your own personal black hole of confusion, or maybe you're struggling to better understand your partner, child, or friend. Astrology provides a particular vantage point from which to see ourselves and others. My hope is that this book will resonate with you enough that you will want to dig deeper, to learn more about your astrological nature as well as the natures of those closest to you. If we are open to receiving its wisdom, astrology can help us uncover our own missing pieces. The stars have life lessons to teach us about finding more balance in ourselves and our relationships.

I am a clinical psychologist. In my world, we talk of nature and nurture, which, in some combination, account for everything about who we become as humans. In my own experience, both in my close relationships and with my clients over the last two decades, I have found astrology to provide a particularly helpful view into our own individual nature. Of course, throughout the lifespan, this nature interacts with the experiences we have in life—the nurture. *How* we experience our families and people in other environments (school, work, etc.) depends very much on our nature. Our nature determines whether we are sensitive or less so, for example, or whether we tend to crave structure or freedom. In other words, each of us, given our individual birth charts, responds to our particular environments in particular ways.

Psychology and astrology share a strong, mutually influential dynamic. (Think yin-yang, double helix, right hand-left hand.) When it comes to understanding who we are, using both lenses together yields much more insight than either one alone. Integrating the other also makes each field better; astrology can benefit from psychology's validity and legitimacy, and psychology needs to make more space for the idea that the universe is bigger than we think.

I am not the first person to see the value of combining psychology and astrology. While there have been many others, the most notable example is Carl Jung (1875–1961), who was a student and proponent of astrology for fifty years. In the anthology entitled *Letters*, he writes:

> As I am a psychologist I'm chiefly interested in the particular light the horoscope sheds on certain complications in the character.
>
> In cases of difficult psychological diagnosis I usually get a horoscope in order to have a further point of view from an entirely different angle. I must say that I very often found that the astrological data elucidated certain points which I otherwise would have been unable to understand. From such experiences I formed the opinion that astrology is of particular interest to the psychologist.

Jung saw dreams as containing symbolic language in the form of visual images that convey much additional meaning once explored and understood; it makes perfect sense that he would come to use and understand astrology in this same way. Given this, the fact that the idea for this book came to me in a dream is highly fitting and synchronistic. The only thing I can remember from the dream is that Jung was handing me the baton in a relay race, but what a dream fragment to have captured! That morning, I groggily told my husband that if I were ever going to write a book, I knew what it would be about: weaving together psychology and astrology. (One of my more intuitive friends had been telling me for more than twenty years that I would write a book, but I never believed her.)

I first learned about astrology as a young girl, when I found my dear aunt's copy of Linda Goodman's famous book *Love Signs*. My interest was piqued, and I remember studying that book every time I went to visit my aunt. Later, when I was seventeen, one of my close friends was interested in astrology and repeatedly encouraged me to read about my sun sign. When I did, I found that it fit me perfectly. I am a double-Capricorn—it is both my sun sign and rising sign, and I also have a number of other planets in Capricorn (but most of that discussion is beyond the scope of this book). I marveled at how well the descriptions captured my personality—my driven and serious nature, my dark sense of humor, my caretaking of my friends.

I say this to illustrate an important point about astrology: belief in its validity comes from resonance, or appreciating what Jung called *synchronicity*; namely, the acute awareness that something *has* to be valid or meaningful on a deeper level, that it can't just be random coincidence. Experiences of resonance are similar to the connections people make during psychotherapy: there are times when they know something is true because they feel it in their bones, when something just clicks and feels undeniably accurate. Such was my experience reading about Capricorns; it was like looking in a mirror, and a really wise one at that. I read about things I wouldn't have been able to see clearly without someone seeing them first and pointing them out to me.

As I became more interested in reading the descriptions of sun signs of people I knew, and especially as I began to look up people's moon signs (and comparing them if they were part of a couple), the more shocked I was by not only the accuracy of astrology but also the specificity of it. As these synchronicities unfolded, I increasingly believed in astrology's power to illuminate.

Eventually I became a psychologist. As a graduate student, my doctoral program was a rigorous, scientific, academic one whose favorite phrase was "empirically validated treatment." I learned a lot about research, statistics, and well-studied forms of treatment such as cognitive behavioral therapy. Shortly after I began practicing, though, I became drawn to the world of depth psychology and psychodynamic relational therapy.

I began my own personal journey of deep therapeutic work, and entered into relational psychoanalysis four times a week. This infused my personal and professional life with great insight and excitement about the work of personal growth. Much of my analysis focused on interpreting my dreams and developing a deeper appreciation for my unconscious. At this point, I had been to Jungian workshops because Jung focused a lot on these same areas.

Though I knew that Jung's interests could tend toward the cosmic realm, it was only in an astrology book that I learned about his strong and continual interest in the field. If I hadn't encountered that information, I'm not sure I would have had the confidence to go out on such a professional limb myself and use it with my own clients, and ultimately, write this book. Sigmund Freud discouraged Jung from being open about his interest in astrology lest it tarnish his reputation as a man of science, and as Capricorns are known to take their reputations especially seriously, I can certainly relate to this fear.

Fortunately, I did start using astrology with my clients. At first I used it surreptitiously (getting clients' birthdays from their intake forms, for example, or listening for them to mention a loved one's birthday), but eventually, I was more open about it. I found that knowing a client's sun sign and knowing and understanding their moon sign could have the effect of increasing my compassion for the ways in which they operate, especially when some of those ways were difficult to work with or deeply understand. It made me more objectively able to understand what I was seeing in them.

I also saw that my clients could use this same information to better understand their partners, kids, friends, and even enemies by developing more empathy and compassion for the other person's internal experience. The more I used astrology with my clients, the more synchronicities revealed themselves to me and to them, and the more helpful it proved to be, which perpetuated my use of it in my practice.

Over time, astrology has become woven into my thought process as a psychologist in a way that is now completely intractable from the other ways in which I think about the world and how we affect and are affected by it. When I hear about something that piques my interest, I frequently look up the birth information of the relevant people. Now that the internet allows us unfettered access to this information for public figures, I find these synchronicities everywhere, and I reference many of them in this book.

The topic of synchronicities brings up a minor warning: I will be using a little bit of math to explain probabilities. In clinical psychology, the validity of any idea is based on there being a high-enough probability that the observed effect is not just due to chance. I will be calculating some astrological probabilities as a means of illustration and comparison, essentially allowing us to see synchronicities empirically. I promise the math won't be complicated or extensive.

Astrology is not the only lens we can use to get a better view of your nature. There are obviously biological and genetic aspects of us that can be described as part of our nature in the nature versus nurture discussion. Additionally, there are other helpful typing systems that cleave, or sort, our basic psychological natures into categories, such as the Enneagram, Myers-Briggs Type Indicator (MBTI, which is also based on Jung's principles), and the Five Love Languages.

Astrology provides a unique vantage point that, like these other methods, can bring a sense of meaning and order as we attempt to understand ourselves and others. In fact, astrology has some things in common with MBTI, such as its focus on opposites and polarities, and not unlike the Enneagram, astrology conceptualizes people as expressing relatively healthy or unhealthy versions of each type. Thus, if you are already familiar with some of these other typing systems and have found them to be helpful, astrology shouldn't feel like much of a leap.

This book is divided into three parts. Part I discusses psychology, the nurture in the nature-nurture conversation, and the psychological principles I have leaned on most heavily in my work with my clients and my own personal work: attachment, empathy, attunement, and individuation. This part is about laying a foundation for what is to come.

Part II explains only enough about astrology to make it usable. Astrology is much more involved than the small slice presented here, and there is already a lot of quality information available that this book does not attempt to duplicate. You will be provided with a roadmap of my own path of understanding astrology to help you gain a deeper psychological understanding of the essential nature of the signs, instead of trying to learn the signs' individual descriptions (or never learning them at all). My goal is to help you learn how to think about and use astrology in your own life.

Part III delves more deeply into using these principles to assist in your personal growth, as well as to find more relational harmony in different types of relationships—romantic, parent-child, siblings, friendships, work relationships, and the therapeutic relationship. This approach can be used with people of various ages—a client and a girlfriend separately suggested that I include something about the fact that parents can use psychstrology with kids as young as elementary-school age in order to help the children understand themselves better.

Finally, you can find a table, known as an ephemeris, in appendix A. Use it to look up your moon sign. If you know your time of birth, use the chart in appendix B to find your rising sign. If you would rather use the internet to look up your signs, you can do so for free at www.cafeastrology.com, a great website for further exploring astrology. (If you are interested in receiving monthly astrology forecasts, which use the current and projected positions of the celestial bodies to provide insight into your experience and growth, I highly recommend you visit www.thepowerpath.

com and sign up on their email list. Their forecasts are incredibly informative.)

While you may already believe in the validity of astrology as well as psychology, there are those who believe in the power of psychology but who may question the validity or usefulness of astrology, and still others do not have strong opinions either way. I want to have a conversation with the enlightened skeptics, so I ask you to keep your mind "open enough" as you encounter the material. (Psychoanalyst Donald Winnicott coined the term "good enough mother" in 1953. The idea that things simply have to be just enough to be passable has had wide applicability in the minds of therapists ever since.)

As previously mentioned, Jung saw astrology as based on the principle of *synchronicity*, or meaningful coincidence. The synchronicities are how we know it is there, why we trust that there is an order to astrology. I had a conversation with my brother during which he pointed out that this way of framing astrology is the same way that astronomers and cosmologists view the concept of dark matter—it can't be seen in a literal sense, but we know it exists because its presence is implied by a number of things we can observe. In astrology, the things we can observe are the synchronicities; they provide a deeply resonating sense of accuracy, which leads to a sense that there has to be something true and valid about the astrological forces playing out in the cosmos. As Aristotle said, intuition is the source of scientific knowledge.

As you read this book, try to keep an open-enough mind. Let me plant the seed of astrology into the soil of your intellect, and see if it can grow over time into a tree with deeper roots. In your efforts to nourish it, after reading the foundational material, start by looking up your own signs and those of the people closest to you. Read the descriptions of the signs in chapter 5, and if you feel motivated to dig deeper, you can consult one of the many quality sources for astrological information that are available both online and in book form.

Give yourself space to see the synchronicities, to see if the descriptions resonate with you ("Wow, I never put those words to it, but that's exactly right!"). If you think astrology isn't valid or is at best just projection—in other words, that we see ourselves in the descriptions of the signs only because we want to—it is possible that you haven't yet had an experience that resonates deeply enough for you to think there has to be something to it. I am hopeful that will change.

The opportunity to connect with ourselves and others on a deeper level can lead to truly extraordinary shifts. Indeed, as Jung remarked to a young alcoholic, the only hope for true healing involves a "vital spiritual experience." (It was this comment that helped plant the seed from which AA sprouted; Jung was incredibly influential.)

In this day and age, making space for deeper healing with the parts of ourselves we don't know or understand well is especially important. The things we can't understand or make space for in ourselves are the exact things we see and dislike in others. If we can't understand ourselves and our loved ones well enough, how in the world are we supposed to understand people on the other side of life's most relevant issues? Empathy starts with the self and radiates outward. Therapists know this, meditation and mindfulness practitioners know this, and the most mindful and self-aware people know this. Empathy is the foundation of a healthier community and the only true path to healing, as individuals and as a people.

You may feel deeply disconnected from your true nature, or have no idea how to find your way back to it. You might feel that same disconnection in your most important relationships, leading to loneliness, resentment, and angst. Life is hard, and there are no quick fixes, but fortunately, there are approaches that can help us better understand ourselves and each other—even with all of our not-fully-conscious complexity.

Psychology and astrology are two of these approaches and though you may not appreciate it yet, they actually go together like peanut butter and jelly. In an interview for *The Atlantic,* Dr. Bertram Malle, a social-cognitive scientist at Brown University, had this to say about astrology: "Full-fledged astrology [that goes beyond newspaper-style sun-sign horoscopes] provides a powerful vocabulary to capture not only personality and temperament but also life's challenges and opportunities. To the extent that one simply learns this vocabulary, it may be appealing as a rich way of representing human experiences and life events, and identifying some possible paths of coping."

Please bring your open-enough minds on this journey with me, because I want you to see it for yourself. There really is something to this!

PART I
Lessons from Psychology: The Role of Empathy in the Search for the True Self

CHAPTER 1

Attachment, Empathy, and the Need to Feel Seen

I don't think anyone can grow unless he's loved exactly as he is.
—Fred Rogers (*Mister Rogers' Neighborhood*)

There's no doubt about it: we are relational creatures. Our relationships make up the structure of our entire experience, from both a big-picture perspective and a day-to-day one. All day long, most of us interact with other people, be they family members, co-workers, customers, friends, or strangers. How those interactions unfold tends to have a big impact on how we feel and function in the world.

We are all individuals, and we value that freedom intensely, and at the same time, most of us care deeply about the experience people are having of us, and we want things to feel harmonious in our relationships. When these two sets of needs come into conflict, the terrain can become tricky to navigate. We want to preserve ourselves, but we also want to preserve the connection. What do we do?

This is the crucial point at which we want to dig deep and cultivate more empathy, for the other person as well as ourselves. I like to think of empathy as keeping a split screen in our minds: one half of the screen has ourselves on it, while the other half contains the other person. Having empathy for both our own experience and the other person's requires that we keep an eye on both halves of the screen at the same time, which can be challenging.

In relationships between parents and children, romantic partners, bosses and coworkers—all relationships, really—we can't truly meet each other's needs when we don't understand the deeper nature of the other person, how they are put together, what it takes for them to feel secure. This is especially important in tougher relationships or rough patches, when the other person doesn't make complete sense to us. (Part III specifically addresses how to add astrology to your analysis of these relationships, after all of the psychological and astrological building blocks are in place.)

Parenting Is the Hardest Job

As a psychologist, I have seen many people suffer pain because their parents could not or did not understand their needs on a deep level. Obviously, this lack of understanding runs the gamut, from the exceptionally narcissistic parent who forced their child to shoulder their own burdens and didn't give the child's needs much space to the essentially good-enough parent who tried hard but struggled to understand their child, who showed up in ways that were different from them.

A parent's job is to figure out how to *see* their child, to understand their child's young, selfish, imperfect perspective. There is only one way for a child to learn empathy, and that is by being treated with empathy by their parent or trusted caregiver. There is no point in trying to admonish a child to be empathic; if they are treated with empathy, they will naturally become that way. For all of us, our understanding of relationships comes directly from the relationships we experience. Sadly, I have known numerous people, many of them clients, who did not experience true empathy until they became adults and took themselves to therapy.

Parents are in essence the first and most important mirror for their child to look into, to help them see themselves by reflecting back to them what the parent sees in them. We cannot come to know ourselves for our strengths, positive character traits, and potential without someone seeing those things in us first and reflecting them back—though unfortunately, if we get negative feedback or none at all, we will fill in the blanks with shame-filled stories about ourselves in an attempt to make sense of things. In other words, we need a compassionate mirror in order to temper our faults, too.

A parent who can *see* their temperamental child and more deeply understand their experience, known as *attunement*, can teach the child how to get help from others when anxious or afraid, which will improve their life tremendously. Psychoanalyst Heinz Kohut calls empathy *vicarious introspection*, and says that without it, "the mental life of man is unthinkable." Parents can help their child understand their innate responses better by first understanding them themselves. Attuned, empathic parenting therefore requires understanding a child's deeper nature, because different people have different needs—or more precisely, we all need different things in order to feel secure.

The good news is, even a difficult baby can develop favorably if given sensitive enough care. As psychoanalyst John Bowlby said, "The capacity of a sensitive mother to adapt to even a difficult unpredictable baby and thereby enable him to develop favorably is perhaps the most heartening of all recent findings in this field."

In parenting, getting frustrated is obviously a part of the process, but it is also true that if a child is pushed against his nature too much or too often, the bond between parent and child will eventually fray. If attachment research tells us anything, it is that the bond is the most important variable in the entire equation for the child to go on to have a good life and successful relationships—which is all a parent really wants, anyway. On an optimistic note, it's all about the repair, as therapists like to say. If you are thinking you wish you would have done some things differently as a parent—you still have time! (If you are the child of a parent who couldn't see you, you also still have time to heal and repair those wounds, as well.)

Romantic Relationships

For most of us, romantic relationships make up the core of our lives. As we become more separate from our families—or not, which causes big problems of its own—we look to our significant other to provide the mirror once held up by our parent. So it is that we need to be able to see the deeper nature of our significant others, because they will come to see themselves—even if not fully consciously—as we see them. If we can't see them in ways that make them feel decent about who they are and that allow the benefits of their nature to shine through, we will lose them eventually, whether they physically or emotionally retreat from us.

To get our partner to understand our own needs, it is helpful if we first understand ourselves through a compassionate lens. The more empathy we can have for ourselves, the more calmly we will be able to explain what it is that we need from our partner, which increases the chance that our partner will be able to hear us and meet our need well enough. In this way, as couples, we are better able to steer our relational cars off the shoulder and back onto the road. Using astrology to better understand ourselves as well as our partners can help us develop greater psychological understanding of our deeper natures.

Friendships and Workplace Relationships

Many of us also find great comfort and spend much time and energy in our friendships. Maybe you are someone who, like me, discovered early on the power and importance of friends to help you make it through life. My friends were like my life rafts during the turbulent waters of adolescence, and several of them are still close friends more than three decades later. For many of us, our friends see us through failed marriages, career changes, kids growing up and leaving home; they are some of the longest and closest relationships we will have.

While our friendships are usually supportive, they can also be challenging. For one thing, many long-term friendships experience bumps in the road, and some friends are more challenging for us. Sometimes we have friends who almost feel like siblings in terms of the complex dynamics that exist in the relationship. Using astrology to gain insight into the deeper psychological natures of our friendships can be helpful at crucial times.

The same is true for our workplace relationships, especially because we don't generally choose our coworkers or bosses the way we choose our friends. These relationships can become especially complicated when the lines blur between the two realms of work and friendship, such as when we become friends with people we work with or go into business with friends, which has become increasingly common in our mobile world.

Workplace relationships can also be much more challenging than friendships in the sense that you are trying to get something done together. In group interactions, and when efforts are focused on a joint goal, additional aspects of our natures come into play that don't usually have much reason to show themselves in our friendships. For these reasons, understanding the people with whom we have workplace relationships, and utilizing as much compassion for the innate validity of different natures as possible, can be very helpful.

Back to Basics

Understanding how we become who we are from an attachment-based perspective provides a microcosm of how to best move through our relationships. Attachment theory is a psychological model that looks at the dynamics of our interpersonal relationships. It teaches us that our earliest relationship dynamics become a template for our later relationships, and it helps to explain why the same patterns in our interpersonal relationships tend to repeat themselves over time, even with multiple different people.

Once we review the attachment research and you understand just how much attunement and empathy for someone's inner experience—including, and especially, their challenges—can help them feel and function better, you will then have a roadmap for navigating your relationships better. We will also use this roadmap when we start talking more about astrology. The translation of the roadmap from one field to the other will make more sense later, but for now, the short of it is this: if we can see ourselves and others through more empathic eyes, everything in our lives functions more smoothly.

In his seminal book *Becoming Attached*, psychologist Robert Karen asks, "What early experiences enable a child to feel that the world of people is a positive place and that he has value?" Bowlby, the founder of attachment theory, thought that our first relationship, with our primary caregiver (usually the mother, but a father or other non-related adult can also play this role), acts as a blueprint for our future relationships and thus determines much about how we will tend to fare in our lives.

This is not the only important factor in determining who we are to become, of course. In the realm of family dynamics alone, there are other factors at play—for example, the parents' relationship with each other, sibling relationships, birth order, and community and cultural values. But in the attachment world, no other factor is seen as having as much importance as the quality of our first relationship with our primary caregiver.

In the 1960s, psychologist Mary Ainsworth carried out a series of studies that led her to classify attachment as either *secure* or *insecure* (also known as anxious). Secure attachment was viewed as "a source of emotional health, giving a child the confidence that someone will be there for him and thus the capacity to form satisfying relationships with others." In contrast, insecure attachment "could reverberate through the child's life in the form of lowered self-esteem, impaired relationships, inability to seek help or to seek it in an ineffective way, and distorted character development."

Each parent has their own attachment with the child, meaning that a child may be securely attached to one parent but not the other, both parents, or neither parent. One secure attachment is unequivocally better than none, but not surprisingly, research has shown that children with secure attachments to two parents were notably superior on measures of empathy.

While it can be hard to pin down what makes for secure attachment, we know for sure that it is integrally related to empathy. We know from the attachment research that a parent's response to her child—including traits commonly referred to as "temperamental," whether through the lens of psychology, behavioral genetics, or astrology—determines much about how the child will go on to develop throughout life. Karen writes, "The baby's ability to regulate itself, especially in all those areas related to emotion, depends on parental attunement and empathy; and if the mother fails to attune to the baby emotionally, the baby's brain may exhibit lasting physiological deficits. These may show up early in the chronic dysregulation of a 'difficult child' and later in various personality deficits."

Indeed, this truth—that empathy enables us to grow—is what psychotherapy is based on. Such theories as humanistic and self psychology (developed by Kohut) have long stressed the point that in order for us to change, we first need someone to see where we are *right now*. Otherwise, moving forward forces us to leave a not-understood part of ourselves behind, which on some level we are unwilling and unable to do.

A Little Help from the Cosmos

We each have a birth chart (sometimes called a *natal chart*), which is a snapshot of the cosmos that tells us which signs and houses the celestial bodies were in at the exact moment of our birth. Using information from our own and others' birth charts can be extremely helpful to better understand our deeper psychological natures. We will look at this more closely in chapter 3, but for now, there is much more to know than just the sign the sun was in when you were born, also known as your *sun sign* or *sun placement*. This is the sign that most people already know about themselves because of magazines and internet horoscopes (e.g., "I'm a Pisces"). Another crucial piece of information (among many others) is to know which sign the moon was in when you were born, also known as your *moon sign* or *moon placement*, because the moon governs different aspects of your nature.

Using the birth chart can help immensely in a parent's process of seeing and understanding their child better, especially when the child is either 1) too young, or too much of an internal processor, to be able to explain what they need in order to feel secure (many adults have a hard time with this, as well), or 2) very different, by nature, from one or both parents. If the child is young, knowing their moon placement is especially important, because moon signs express themselves most strongly in childhood. Given that the moon shows what we need to feel secure in terms of both our home and our emotions, knowing the moon placement of people with whom we are closely connected is always important.

The idea that both attachment and astrology focus a lot on what people need in order to feel secure is no random coincidence. This is what Jung called a synchronicity, as exists when perceptions through different lenses align with one another. According to Jung, synchronicity refers to the *meaningful coincidences* that occur when things have no causal relationship yet seem to be significantly related. We will discuss the concept of synchronicity further in chapter 7.

If attachment research shows us that potentially difficult babies can develop favorably given sensitive enough care, we should see these same benefits as we better understand our important others' deeper psychological natures with the help of an astrological lens. All of us, when out of balance or struggling in our lives, are potentially difficult to be around, and feeling seen and understood can make a world of difference in terms of helping us recalibrate.

In my field, there is much hope that insecure attachment patterns can change, given enough corrective and reparative relational experience. This is true whether it happens earlier in life, as when a family goes to therapy and is able to make some important adjustments, or later, when an adult goes to therapy, or is healthy and lucky enough to find another secure attachment object with whom to have a relationship, though this is less common.

In the therapy I do with my clients, I try to figure out what they need on a deeper level so they can develop a secure attachment to me. If the person started out as insecurely attached, then good-enough therapy can actually lead to a state known as *earned security*, wherein the therapy relationship acts as a new template for the client's relationships, mitigating the negative effects of the older, dysfunctional template.

This is the kind of therapy I strive to do, and let me say again how important astrology has been in my quest to be a good-enough therapist to my clients, seeing them and understanding them well enough for them to be able to have faith and trust that other people can do so, as well. Besides my own deep therapy, my work with my clients is the thing that has most helped me to understand how deeply meaningful feeling seen is; when my clients experience it, knowing that I am witnessing healing in action is awe-inspiring.

Understanding Is Everything

All around us we see the idea that understanding each other more deeply is the way through our struggles in our closest relationships. Books like *The Five Love Languages* are based on the notion that we have different natures and different ways of feeling secure in our relationships. Emotionally Focused Therapy is a current and effective form of couples therapy, based on notions of attachment and attunement to each other's deeper needs for security.

Please note that attuning is not the same thing as enabling or overindulging someone in a way that impedes growth. In order to have a decent relationship, any person has to be healthy enough to do some work on their own path of growth. A relationship in which one or both people limit each other's growth and independence by enabling immature and dysfunctional behavior to continue without consequence is called *codependent*. Codependent relationships are based on insecurity and fear, moving people in the opposite direction of growth.

In sum, the attachment research shows us that we really need to appreciate the power of attunement and empathy to impact the relational process. When we understand what underlies secure attachment, we are clearer on the need to treat each other as individual beings with particular natures that deserve respect, compassion, and understanding. Here is some extra incentive: everything goes more smoothly for all of us, not just the person we are trying to understand, when we can attune. Isn't that what astrology, psychology, and other related fields are all about, anyway? Aren't we all just trying to see ourselves—and see and be seen by others—better?

Chapter 2, on individuation, follows naturally from this one. A parent can't help their child individuate—become their most whole, true selves—unless they can see the child first; as adults, we can't individuate until we can see ourselves first. Also, individuating from the secure base of a good-enough relationship, whatever form that relationship takes—parent, partner, therapist, boss, supervisor, and so on—is much easier. As we courageously move along on our own unique paths of individuation, it is the *seeing* of the different parts of ourselves, including the less developed or less understood parts, that lights the way for us to figure out the next right, authentic step on our path.

CHAPTER 2

Individuation—Becoming Your Most Whole, True Self

*The difference between the "natural" individuation process . . .
and the one which is consciously realized, is tremendous. . . .
In the second case, so much darkness comes to light that the
personality is permeated with light, and consciousness
necessarily gains in scope and insight.*

–Carl Jung

A man wanted to learn to meditate, so he asked his teacher how long he thought it would take for him to become enlightened. Ten years, the teacher told him. This answer prompted the man to ask if he could get there faster by working harder and more intensely to achieve the goal. No, the teacher told him, it would take twenty years.

Trying to individuate, or become our most whole and true selves, can feel like that, too. We somehow end up further away from our goal even as we attempt to move toward it, because the road twists and turns in ways we don't anticipate, and we don't even realize we are headed in a direction other than the one in which we assume we are going. Soon we are further away than ever, and don't even know how we got off track in the first place.

Or we may think we can pinpoint exactly where we took a wrong turn, all of our wrong turns, even—the wrong decision, job, partner—but given that we were almost certainly doing our best to stay awake at the wheel during that part of the journey, how do we explain the fact that we ended up so far astray in the first place? How do we explain feeling so much different than we thought we would once we got to where we thought we meant to go? Psychstrology, the blending of psychology principles and the wisdom gleaned from astrology, is a method of helping us to understand ourselves in ways that bring a consciousness to the decisions we make now, helping us to stay on the journey we want to be on.

Separate Souls

Parenting is the hardest job on earth, and we all want to do our best. However, in my work, I see over and over the desire for parents to mold and shape their children in the image they want, and not allowing the children to be their shining, unique selves. Is that really the best and highest good for our children?

Individuation is the process by which we become the most whole and true versions of our unique selves. It involves finding and integrating all of our various parts—including those aspects of ourselves that we don't yet fully understand, lost track of somewhere along the way, or haven't even met yet—but whose seeds live inside of us and beg for compassionate expression. Besides being important for ourselves and our families, who are much better off if we are on our right path of growth, individuation is important because each of us plays a crucial and unique role in our collective growth. If we aren't connected to ourselves or our paths well enough to express our unique natures, we are doing the world a disservice.

At the American Psychological Association's annual convention in 2016, I saw psychologist Alison Gopnik (author of the parenting book *The Gardner and the Carpenter*) speak about the importance of parents allowing their children to become the truest versions of themselves instead of who their parents would have them be. She writes, "The purpose is not to change the people we love, but to give them what they need to thrive. Love's purpose is not to shape our beloved's destiny, but to help them shape their own." It is deeply important, though often difficult, for a parent to see their child as an individual person who is separate from them—"a soul on a journey," as my friend and teacher Lauren Skye likes to say.

To realize that your child is different and separate from you is truly the greatest gift a parent can give to a child. Parenting pulls for the narcissism we all tend toward at times; we are tempted to see our child as "a chip off the old block." They are separate beings, of course, with different natures and different paths of growth and evolution. Since a birth chart is an astrological map of where the sun, moon, and planets were in the sky at the exact moment of one's birth, looking at your child's birth chart will help to drive home this point about separateness, making it more clear that they don't share your same chart or soul journey.

A parent's efforts to individuate and find their lost and unknown parts will greatly benefit their children, no matter their age. This is because we are unfortunately doomed to pass down, in some fashion, what we have not healed in ourselves. (This is true for everyone, whether or not they have children.) The healthier one is as a parent, the more they can tolerate their child being separate from them. If you are a parent, besides working hard to help and allow your child to individuate, work on your own path of self-improvement, as this is a huge part of being a better parent.

Many of us are significantly concerned with not being selfish, but in actuality, we can't give our gifts to the world if we don't heal and express our authentic selves first. Besides, in truth, we are all selfish beings in the sense that we are all just trying to be ourselves. Of course, we will collide with each other sometimes, given that we all have different paths, needs, and natures, but we can often get through rough patches without losing connection, especially if we can see and make space for each other. Being of service in the deepest ways possible—both large and small—can happen only when we are truly connected to ourselves as authentically and wholly as possible.

If we actively engage in the task of trying to be our most whole, true selves, we will be serving and fulfilling our highest possible purpose in this life in innumerable ways, some of which we will know, others of which only the people we affect will know about. If all of we souls work to individuate over the course of our lives, it will truly be a win-win situation for everyone. Ideally, the individuation process should last for our entire lives, meaning that we're never done growing, learning about ourselves, or figuring out the next right steps on our paths.

Lots of people tell us that we should try to become our truest, most authentic selves. Poet Mary Oliver wrote in *Wild Geese*, "You only have to let the soft animal of your body love what it loves." Author Sarah Ban Breathnach teaches that "the authentic self is the soul made visible," and Oprah tells us, "You have to find what sparks a light in you so that you in your own way can illuminate the world." We are told that the main purpose of both yoga and meditation is to bring us closer to our true nature, and that both practices are highly beneficial for us. When we are connected to ourselves, every living thing on the planet benefits. I consider it synchronistic when numerous people from different areas converge on the same basic truth; it gives me more faith in its validity.

This is great advice, as far as advice goes. I personally love the idea of letting my true self have authentic expression, as I think most of us do, but like all advice, it is not easy to follow—or at least, not by just being given that directive and told to achieve it. If it were enough to envision how we want to feel and move toward it, nothing new would have come after the book *The Secret,* and we would all be living our truest lives right now. We are nothing if not persistent in our quest for self-improvement, and the fact that you picked up this book means that you are probably struggling with how to get there, just like the rest of us.

How We Individuate

Most psychologically minded people see individuation as a process of active self-discovery. We need to reflect deeply on what is truly inside of us, which is much harder and more complicated than it sounds. In living our lives, as we try to get closer to our truest natures, we will usually have to start out by saying no to who we are not and what does not feel right to us in our cores, until eventually the beacons of who we *are*—the manifestations of our most authentic selves, the core truths that feel the most right to us, the parts of us we have never understood before—become brighter and more visible.

In addition to becoming more aware of these inner nudges or whispers from our deepest selves, also known as intuition, some of us also engage in efforts that are more concentrated and structured in order to realize our deepest and truest natures. Most commonly, this takes the form of psychotherapy, other psycho-spiritual pursuits (workshops, retreats, etc.), journaling, and self-help books, such as this one. Therapy can be especially important for helping us to see and understand parts of ourselves that are presently outside of our conscious awareness.

Individuating, or connecting with your whole and true self, requires that you try to live your life as authentically as possible, even when that means taking risks, going out on limbs, and upsetting the status quo in your life. Talking about the importance of living your life authentically but not actually doing it is okay as long as it is part of your journey toward actual change, but unless your talk is backed by brave action—such as changing or ending relationships or work that doesn't support your growth—such talk is only counterfeit individuation, not the real thing. Fortunately, the universe seems to reward our courage by removing or easing the obstacles that stand in our way.

The psychological concept of individuation involves more than just being authentic in the sense that is usually meant these days. Authenticity is certainly a highly important goal in itself and is part of what is required for us to individuate, but being authentic involves conscious awareness, and other aspects of the individuation process require us to access unconscious or less conscious material. Therefore, in addition to being authentic, individuation also requires us to become the most whole version of ourselves, which usually involves finding, understanding, and integrating previously unknown parts of ourselves so those parts can add their vital wisdom to our whole selves, paths, and ultimately, the world.

The Role of Astrology in the Individuation Process

Astrology provides us a unique and invaluable map to facilitate the process of individuation, whether we are working on our own path or helping another person navigate theirs. While it doesn't tell us who to marry or what to do for a living, our birth chart gives us an essential blueprint for this lifetime. As you will learn in later chapters, the birth chart points to our inner resources and helps us to see the potential of who we are meant to be, or more precisely who we chose to be before birth, in order to best survive and grow from the things we have to deal with in this life. We are much wiser to work with our natures instead of swimming against the current of who our deepest selves would have us be, and the birth chart helps us to see these possibilities for growth more clearly.

The birth chart also reflects what we are here to work on and cultivate in ourselves, in large part by showing us our shadow sides, or the parts of ourselves we are not fully conscious or aware of. Part III discusses how to use the birth chart for this purpose, but the point for now is that the unconscious parts of ourselves that are contained in our shadow are seen as the parts we most need to meet in order to achieve balance in ourselves and our lives. Our birth charts allow us more access to those unknown parts of ourselves by revealing the shadow sides of our most important astrological signs and by showing us what is underdeveloped and thus needing further cultivation. If we don't try to meet our shadow in a more conscious way, it will exert control outside of our awareness.

All of us have an innate drive to discover our uniqueness, but the path takes different forms for each of us based on our individual charts. This is why knowing your main astrological influences is helpful in providing you with order, meaning, and direction as you navigate your own right path through life. In a big-picture way, this translates into seeing your major life lessons and challenges more clearly; in a small-picture way, it means helping you get through your day-to-day challenges—including in your relationships with your most important others—with enough energy and optimism left over to be doing a good-enough job in your life.

If you want to feel less in the dark in your life, you need to shine your light into your own apparent darkness. You need to understand your whole, entire self; you need for your own light of compassion to comprehend the parts of you that are the hardest to own, love, and understand. Your birth chart can be profoundly helpful in this process because it can act as a flashlight, pointing the way to your underdeveloped parts and the healing that needs to be done.

Astrologers and psychotherapists alike know that under-standing and explaining things—especially things we don't fully comprehend—helps us to feel better, more self-aware, and more in control of ourselves and our lives. In other words, they understand this core truth: an honest relationship with our "darker" parts can often yield the most powerful experiences of growth.

Wherever You Go, There You Are

A famous Jung quote comes from *Dialogue with C.G. Jung*: "The acorn can become an oak, and not a donkey. A man or woman becomes that which he or she is from the beginning." Since I have long been a fan of dream interpretation, and because I often write in the mornings, I have been able and fortunate to capture many of my own dreams. In one, I saw a contraption that I eventually iden-tified as the electric shoe polisher I used to play with in my parents' walk-in closet when I was a child. It had a dark-green cloth covering on both sides, and it would spin when turned on so you could buff shoes by holding the shoes up to the spinning cloth.

In the dream, I didn't recognize it as the shoe polisher at first, but I saw that the cloth end of the device was coated with a pink, fluffy, sticky gunk (like hair gel). As it started to spin, all of the pink gunk came flying off, and I eventually recognized it as my dad's old shoe polisher with the fuzzy dark-green cover. Then the dream became a split screen, with the image of the shoe polisher on the left and the right-hand side of the screen scrolling like a slot machine. There were various images on the right, some of which involved the pink gunk. Then, just as if it were a slot machine, the image on the right came to a stop, directly aligning with the dark-green shoe polisher image on the left side. The image was . . . the exact same dark-green shoe polisher.

Given the image-based symbolic language of dreams, here is what I saw as the value: reality will always mirror the core truth. In other words, even if all the stuff we coat ourselves with hides or contradicts our true self, the true self will always find a way to express itself—for better or for worse. We may as well try to figure out who we really are and work to express the best versions of ourselves.

This is where the approach of psychstrology comes in. Coupling the wisdom of psychology and astrology can help us see ourselves and our paths much more clearly than either method alone by enabling us to unlock and access the hidden parts of ourselves that are begging for us to understand or express them.

If we don't try to consciously evolve and give our parts compassionate expression, eventually the worst, angriest, most stifled versions of ourselves will bust (or seep) out of us instead, often without our being consciously aware of it happening. As written in the *Gospel of Thomas*, "If you bring forth what is within you, what you bring forth will save you. If you do not bring forth what is within you, what you do not bring forth will destroy you." As psychologists are known to say, we express ourselves whether we mean to or not.

My dream also illustrates something helpful about dreams in general: by showing us visual images and symbols, dreams speak to us in a language of metaphor and analogy. As a therapist, all of my clients can attest to the fact that I use metaphors and analogies all the time—whenever I can, as a matter of fact. I love the generalization of insight that can take place as a result.

Unknown Parts of Ourselves

Jung described individuation as a process of integrating the opposite and multiple parts of ourselves while still maintaining their relative autonomy from one another. In other words, integration doesn't mean that the boundaries between our parts disintegrate and everything blends together; rather, we can still see that the separate parts of us are there, but the edges are softer, and all of the parts can coexist in a state of relative harmony.

Jung talked at length about our shadow side, which contains the parts of ourselves that we are not fully conscious or aware of. The parts of us that are contained in our shadow are the areas we most need to acknowledge and understand in order to achieve more balance and wholeness in ourselves, our relationships, and our lives. The goal is to hold within ourselves multiple parts that are often in apparent contradiction with one another—hence the focus on integration and balance between opposites.

As a natural extension, or projection, given his theory of the individual, Jung also believed that every growing person contributes to the healing and wholeness of all life by doing their own piece of the collective work. (This type of projection takes a different form from the traditional defense mechanism of lodging an unacceptable feeling in someone else.) I think of the Batman symbol or a movie screen when I think about this kind of projection, where something small has been made large. This is referred to again in chapter 3, when we discuss the zodiac wheel and birth chart being projected into the heavens at the time of birth.

Besides Jung, other psychologists have also stressed the importance of individuation. Psychoanalyst Margaret Mahler, for example, emphasized the need for infants to separate and individuate from their mothers in order to arrive at the self. Winnicott wrote at length about the *true self*, a sense of self based on spontaneous authentic experience and a feeling of being alive, in contrast to the *false self*, a defensive façade that, in extreme cases, can leave us feeling dead and empty inside, behind a "mere appearance of being real." He observed that other people's expectations can override or contradict the sense of self a child is born with, affecting the child's ability to be spontaneous and authentic.

Later, psychologist Alice Miller expanded on Winnicott's ideas in *Drama of the Gifted Child*, observing that depression usually results when a false sense of self leads to the loss of one's potential true self. In other words, depression can be viewed as a cutting off from oneself, a numbness or inability to access the things that bring a sense of aliveness or vibrancy to one's life. Unfortunately, many of these writers observe that parents can often unwittingly be the biggest forces behind their kids' lost connection to crucial parts of themselves. If you are a parent, this is probably not easy to hear, but thankfully, knowing is half the battle, and learning and applying psychstrology will empower you to make more space for your children and their needs.

Out of the Shadows

Individuation requires our active engagement in the task of discovering our most whole, true selves. If we heed its call, we will be serving and fulfilling our highest purpose in this life in the deepest possible ways—both large and small—which can happen only when we are truly connected to ourselves. In addition to living our lives authentically, individuation also requires us to find, understand, and integrate previously unknown parts of ourselves in order for those parts to add their vital wisdom to our paths.

Psychstrology helps with the individuation process, for ourselves and those in our care. In the coming chapters, I weave astrology together with psychological analysis, and you will see the importance of using the birth chart to help you better understand yourself and your most important others.

Before we dive more deeply into using astrology, however, we will discuss some basic astrological background to lay as a foundation, which will enable you to think more deeply about the information in the chapters to come. Then, in Part III, you will see more clearly that knowing your signs isn't an end in itself but rather a starting point for understanding your nature more deeply so that you can more consciously evolve.

PART II
Lessons from Astrology: A Brief Introduction to the Cosmos

CHAPTER 3

Your Sun, Moon, and Rising Signs

*Those who have even a nodding acquaintance with [astrology]
and are in any way affected by it obey the unwritten but
strictly observed convention: "One does not speak of such
things." They are only whispered about, no one admits them,
for no one wants to be considered all that stupid. In reality,
however, it is very different.*

—Carl Jung

Astrology can be extremely involved and complicated, but it doesn't have to be. Here, you will learn about how to use the most fundamental aspects of astrology, distilled into a simple-enough form that is easy to metabolize. I want to be clear: I am a psychologist, not an astrologer, but I will teach you, in the simplest way possible, what has worked for me to understand each sign on a deeper psychological level. My goal is to explain to you the basic, underlying principles of astrology so that you can use them in your own life. If you want to explore your birth chart further after reading it, all the better.

There are many complicated pieces to astrology. In my capacity as a professional therapist, I have spent many years trying to understand the human psyche, and astrologers have been doing the same thing with their craft. Besides the fact that there is much astrological information to learn and integrate, there is also the kind of knowledge that can be gained only by working with a system for a long time.

In other words, in an attempt to make it usable, what I am about to present to you is only a small slice of what astrology has to offer. It may seem paradoxical, but before I attempt to distill it into usable parts, I want to give you a feel for its complexity.

Understanding that everything in this discussion takes place within a larger context is extremely helpful. If you have your birth chart read by a professional astrologer, you will have a real appreciation for the ways in which all of the different astrological pieces fit together to make you who you are; everything plays its own role in the story of you. However, there are certain pieces that are more central to one's experience, especially one's deeply emotional experience, which has been my primary concern as a psychologist. Those are the pieces we will focus on once we ground all of this in its larger context.

The Multiple Layers of the Birth Chart

The zodiac is a belt in the sky that encircles the Earth, and the zodiac constellations lie on this belt. The sun, moon, and planets, collectively called the *celestial bodies*, travel along the zodiac, passing through each of the constellations as they orbit the Earth. Besides the sun and moon, astrologers look at where the planets (Mercury, Venus, Mars, Jupiter, Saturn, Uranus, Neptune, and Pluto) were at the time of your birth, as well as the midheaven point (known as the *Medium Coeli*, or middle sky) and lunar nodes (the two points at which the orbit of the moon intercepted the ecliptic). Some astrologers even look at additional cosmic factors.

Each celestial body was in one of the twelve zodiac signs when you were born, and each of those astronomical facts says something about your life. Each planet rules, or corresponds with, a particular zodiac sign and is thought to give the sign its power to imbue you with traits. Mars, for example, rules how you take action in your life, and it also rules Aries, which is the most action-oriented sign of the zodiac. Venus rules how you show up in love relationships, and it rules both Taurus and Libra, both of which are signs that are highly concerned with (and here to work on) their issues in love relationships.

In addition to this layer of complexity, there are also twelve *houses* (segments, like pizza slices, of the zodiac wheel, each of which is ruled by a different sign) that represent different areas of your life (e.g., home, relationships, career). Each celestial body has a position in one of the houses, so Mars, for example, is in both a sign and house at the time of your birth. Astrologers also talk about *aspects*, which are angles the celestial bodies form with each other. There is much important information contained in a birth chart. Figure 1 depicts a zodiac wheel showing the signs and houses but not the planets.

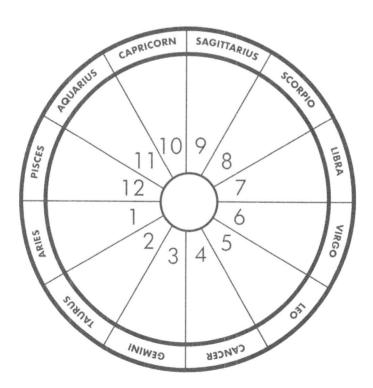

FIGURE 1. THE ZODIAC WHEEL

This section does not cover anywhere near the entirety of your chart; here we will discuss just two celestial bodies: the sun and the moon. We will also address the rising sign, which is the zodiac constellation that was rising on the eastern horizon at the time of your birth.

Since my goal is to provide an easy-to-understand basic overview of astrology, there are several areas of astrology that we will not be discussing. For example, I won't be addressing the planets or the houses, as there are so many of each that we would have to take them all on or omit them entirely—there is no way to cover that much information briefly. Nor will we discuss the fact that each sign rules a particular part of your body. There are many good books and websites that can take you deep into the nuances of your birth chart, but that is not our goal here.

We will focus on the zodiac signs that the sun and moon were in at your time of birth, as well as your rising sign. (The rising sign changes every two hours, so you must know what time you were born to determine yours.) While the planets' influence is certainly not small, and while astrologers differ on which components they see as most important in a birth chart, many believe (as I do) that your sun, moon, and rising signs are the three most influential factors. While they don't explain everything about you, your basic astrological nature comprises these three signs, and they give you the most value in terms of how much information they contain. *Psychstrology* is like the *Cliff's Notes* version of an astrology book.

In other words, if all you know about yourself is your sun and moon signs—even if you don't know your time of birth to find out your rising sign—you will learn some useful information about how you operate in the world, including aspects that you may not have been fully conscious of before.

Before we begin discussing your sun, moon, and rising signs, however, I want to briefly touch on the history of psychological astrology and give an explanation of how astrology works (as far as we know, although there are multiple theories put forth, including several by Jung himself).

Combining Psychology and Astrology

People have seen the wisdom in combining astrology and psychology since the turn of the twentieth century. Astrologers Alan Leo (1860–1917), Marc Edmund Jones (1888–1980), and Dane Rudhyar (1895–1985) were all instrumental in the shift from using astrology to predict events to using astrology for psychological purposes. Their work was what gave Jung his foundation to build upon.

Once Jung began using and writing about astrology, and seeing the heavens as a mirror for the soul, many other thinkers interested in both psychology and astrology began to follow suit. Renowned astrologers Stephen Arroyo and Liz Greene were especially prolific; Greene, also a Jungian analyst, co-founded the Centre for Psychological Astrology in London. Currently, a hospital in Buenos Aires, Argentina, uses therapeutic astrology to develop stronger mental health for patients who have been referred by their doctors.

Some writers have speculated about the possibility that there is a connection, or at least an overlap, between what astrology taps and what is gleaned by both the Enneagram and the Myers-Briggs Type Indicator (MTBI), which are commonly used psychological assessment measures. In their seminal book about the Enneagram, authors Don Riso and Russ Hudson give thanks for the capital-G "Guidance" they received in developing the measure: "As much as this work is the product of our own efforts, we can also truly say that it seems to come from something beyond us. There is a consciousness that wishes to manifest itself more clearly in the world." This does sound eerily similar to the "nudging from the great beyond," which I mentioned in the introduction, that is moving astrology forward.

In her book *Relating,* Greene noted that Jung's four function types of sensing, intuiting, thinking, and feeling (used in the MBTI) "fit hand in glove" with the ancient division of the four elements in astrology: earth, fire, air, and water, respectively—not that one is being explained by or derived from the other; rather, each is a particular way of describing the same observed phenomena, also known as synchronicity. (The four elements are discussed further in chapter 4.)

How and Why the Stars Affect Our Lives and Personalities

Nobody knows for sure exactly how and why astrology works. In an attempt to answer this question, Jung himself came up with no less than seven theories over the course of his lifetime. His evolving answers reflect two things about his thinking process: he didn't accept astrology outright, and he felt that something about it was fundamentally true.

Given that Jung initially saw astrology as entirely based on the projection of our own minds and psyches into the heavens via the collective unconscious, it took him some time to see astrology as valid and legitimate in its own right. This makes perfect sense, as any psychologist knows that we are bound to project ourselves into whatever we are looking at, especially if it is positive. However, Jung's personal and professional experiences with astrology—seeing all of its crazy, mind-blowing coincidences over and over again—eventually led him to realize that there was something more than simply projection at play.

The other idea that is reflected in Jung's continued effort to objectively explain the inner workings of astrology—seven times over—is that there is something that feels so true about it that it drives we science-minded types into an all-out frenzy to try to legitimize it, as if something in the gut is telling us something that the mind can't explain—but we try!

Perhaps you have experienced the feeling of just "knowing" something is true even though you couldn't prove it. Even if you never found a way to do so, that knowing has affected your way of moving through the world, sometimes even under the surface of your conscious awareness. I have been unconsciously following in Jung's footsteps, amassing synchronicities and calculating probabilities. I am not trying to prove *how* astrology works as much as *that* it does, but my underlying subjective experience is similar to what I imagine Jung's was: to draw out the objective proof for astrology so that my inner conviction of its validity makes sense.

Even though Jung never figured out how or why the heavens influence our personalities and lives, the theory he eventually landed on, a theory much more deeply powerful than his early, simple theory of astrology-as-projection, was his theory of synchronicity. More specifically, he saw astrology as "synchronicity on a grand scale."

Jung saw astrology as based on the concept of synchronicities, or *meaningful coincidences*, between external, objective facts—the position of the celestial bodies—and subjective, inner aspects of the human experience. This is why, or how, we see particular psychological traits in people when the celestial bodies are in certain positions in their charts.

While Jung wasn't sure how to conceptualize the astrological forces at play—in 1957, he wrote about the idea of a "transcendental arranger" to explain such synchronistic observations—it was clear that he didn't see it as simply the celestial bodies imprinting upon us at the time of birth. (At least, he eventually decided that there was more to it than just this but not before he made his famous statement, "Whatever is born or done at this particular moment of time, has the quality of this moment of time," to explain astrology.) Rather, like many astrologers, Jung believed in the mutual imprinting of the heavens upon the psyche and the psyche upon the heavens.

Remember that Batman-signal type of projection, where the interior of the psyche is seen as reflecting outward into the sky? This is the kind of projection that Jung, and classical astrology, invoke to explain how astrology works. The celestial sphere is reflected within each one of us; each of us is a microcosm, or miniature version, of the bigger-picture macrocosm of what was going on in the heavens at the time we were born. The chart is seen as a symbolic visual map in time and space of the planets at the moment of one's birth. It is our own personal snapshot of the heavens; our psyche is reflected in it, though not caused by it. The celestial bodies and our psyches are in a simultaneous occurrence of synchrony.

To take this one step further, many people—myself included—believe that we choose certain aspects of our lives before we (re)incarnate. The astrological chart is one such aspect. More specifically, we choose a particular moment in time to be born, and we choose an optimal birth chart to help us fulfill our soul's purpose. This is true in terms of choosing what we will have inside us to help us get through the challenges, via the strengths and resources of particular signs and also in terms of the lessons we are here to learn, since the signs have particular vulnerabilities and limitations we spend our lives trying to temper. Part III looks more closely at the growth part of the equation by posing the following question: given your chart, what should you be working to cultivate in order to develop more balance?

Your Sun, Moon, and Rising Signs

Psychologists and astrologers alike understand that we, as people, are made up of parts. Think of your sun, moon, and rising signs as separate aspects of yourself. Each part is likely to show up in some situations more than others, as each part rules how we feel and act in different realms of our lives. When you are reading descriptions of the signs, you need to understand that the placement of a sign—whether sun, moon, or rising—affects its expression. (Once you have more information about the basics of astrology, we will look at some examples of this to make it clearer.) For now, let's explore what each sign tells you about yourself.

THE SUN SIGN

Much like the sun is the source of life on Earth and the center of the solar system, your sun sign represents your basic self and personality. In many ways, it is synonymous with your identity, because it is how you consciously experience yourself and show up in the world. It organizes your approach to life in most situations (except those governed by the moon and rising signs), including what you are trying to achieve. It starts to show itself as you develop a sense of self that is separate from your parents (as discussed in chapter

1). It is the you that your friends and co-workers know. It is often described as your *daytime self*.

THE MOON SIGN

The moon does not emit any light of its own; we can see it only when the light of the sun illuminates it. The moon controls the tides and changes every day, so it makes sense that the moon rules the way you experience emotions. Your moon sign thus governs the deepest, most private, least conscious parts of your inner self. It is the first part of you that becomes active, as soon as you are born, so it is commonly associated with your relationship to your mother. Only the people closest to you, such as your family, partner, and closest friends, get to see this part, especially if you have lived with them or do so now, because the moon rules your home life, habits, and daily rhythms. These include your attitude toward food and eating, getting ready for the day, and going off to school or work—all the ways in which you nurture and take care of yourself on a foundational level.

The moon also rules your emotions and instincts—again, anything that is less available to your conscious control. This part of you also shows up when you are highly stressed or otherwise at your most vulnerable, because when you regress, your moon sign is your oldest part to regress to. Since it is less accessible to your conscious awareness, it holds many of the shadowy parts of you and is often referred to as your *nighttime self*.

The Particular Importance of Your Moon Sign

The moon holds all of your innermost parts that are more or less unconscious to you. This includes your deepest requirements and motivations in relationships, your approach to emotions, your underlying urges and longings, and your worst fears. Also included here are the parts of you that were repressed during childhood—recall the discussion in chapter 1 about the true versus false self and how we repress parts of ourselves to please our parents—or later, due to societal expectations and pressures.

Your moon sign contains the parts of your personality you are less aware of, because the traits operated on you at a time when you did not yet have words to describe anything. As adults, these traits come out under two sets of circumstances: 1) when you get close enough to someone to feel safe to show them the innermost parts of yourself, and 2) when you are regressed into those psychological states that make you feel the most vulnerable, such as during a crisis of some sort.

Given that we are relational creatures who spend our entire lives trying to get close to (or avoid getting close to) other people, and given that your moon sign represents how you deal with your emotions and how you show up in your closest relationships, learning more about this crucial sign in your (and your important others') charts is important. Liz Greene puts it perfectly in *Dark of the Soul* when she says, "The moon is the organ of contact with others." It is similar to your *Love Language* (from the popular book) in the sense that it shows how you give and receive nurturing as well as what you need to feel safe, secure, happy, and comfortable. Your moon sign also points to which emotions you feel especially uncomfortable expressing.

In psychological terms, we would say that your moon sign points to your defense mechanisms, attachment strategies, and security needs. Perhaps this makes clearer why Jung thought that psychologists needed to find out about their clients' birth charts. Speaking of Jung, having been especially interested in moon signs, he carried out an entire research study analyzing the moon place-ments of 483 couples. Though the study was methodologically flawed, it pointed to the frequency and importance of married cou-ples having a *beneficial conjunction* between their two charts, where the moon of one person is represented in the sun, moon, or rising sign of the other. There is a reason it is the moon that is involved in all beneficial conjunctions; one person speaking the language of the other's moon provides powerful glue in couple relationships.

It is for all of these reasons that knowing and understanding your own and others' moon placement is helpful in smoothing the fabric of your closest relationships. As spouses and family members, we experience our significant others' moon signs at least as much as their sun signs, and the same is true for them of us. If you learn nothing else, knowing your moon sign and appreciating its basic characteristics can take you far in itself.

THE RISING SIGN

Your rising sign, also called your *ascendant*, represents your outer-most layer. It is concerned with how you appear and come across to others when they first encounter you. Think of it as the first-glance, first-impression version of yourself that you consciously express. Your rising sign is developed last, as it requires more conscious control over yourself. It is often said that our rising sign represents the role we had to play, or mask we had to wear, in our family, so it can be seen as a response to psychological and social conditioning. It is the way you operate with both acquaintances and strangers, and is roughly synonymous with Jung's concept of the persona.

Figure 2 shows a graphic illustration of how the three signs fit together.

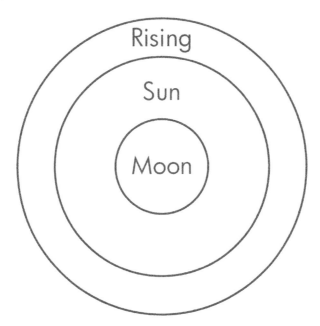

FIGURE 2. HOW RISING, SUN, AND MOON SIGNS FIT
TOGETHER

I have been struck by the synchronicity in how astrology and psychology describe the development of the personality. Both Freud and Jung described the personality as composed of parts that develop early and those that develop later. The moon sign, which is most prominent in childhood, sounds a lot like Freud's description of the *id*, which is present as soon as we are born and contains our deepest unconscious drives, needs, instincts, and impulses; as mentioned earlier, it contains the unconscious parts of us Jung called the shadow.

The sun sign, being your basic personality, displays most of the adaptations you have made to survive in the world—what both Jung and Freud referred to as the *ego*. Your rising sign is similar to your persona (Jung) and superego (Freud), the part of the self that develops last, representing the role we feel compelled to play and traits we think we *should* possess and express. Again, synchronicities such as this suggest that there is something valid to which both fields are pointing with separate arrows.

When you read about your own or someone else's sun sign and don't feel connected to the description, it is often because the moon or rising signs, or both, are of a completely different nature. This will become clearer when we discuss the elements and qualities of the astrological signs in chapter 4.

To summarize the relationship between these different parts of yourself: your innermost qualities become active first (moon), and you then develop your outwardly expressed traits once you have more control over yourself (sun, and eventually, rising). Another way of saying this is that your self-expression evolves from being mostly unconscious to being more conscious. When you are young, all you can focus on are your feelings and basic needs for comfort and safety; you don't yet understand who you are as a self separate from your parents, let alone the role you play in your family.

Figuring Out Your Sun, Moon, and Rising Signs

Determining your sun, moon, and rising signs is simple if you know your birthday, birthplace, and time of birth.

YOUR SUN SIGN

It is highly likely that you already know your sun sign, but if you are not sure, the relevant dates are shown in table 1. The exact dates the sun changes signs can vary by plus or minus a day, depending on the year.

TABLE 1. DATES FOR SUN SIGNS

Aries March 21–April 20	Taurus April 21–May 21	Gemini May 22–June 21
Cancer June 22–July 22	Leo July 23–August 21	Virgo August 22– September 22
Libra September 23– October 22	Scorpio October 23– November 21	Sagittarius November 22– December 20
Capricorn December 21– January 19	Aquarius January 20– February 18	Pisces February 19– March 20

If you were born on a date between the eighteenth and the twenty-third, your sun sign might be different here than in other sources. Since the sun's move into the next sign can change plus or minus a day, you have to know your time of birth so you could see where the sun was at that time on that day and year in order to know for sure which sign the sun was in when you were born. Regardless of which sign the sun was in, though, if you were born close to the "edge," you are said to be on the cusp of, or between, two signs.

For clarification, your moon and rising signs can also be on the cusp between two signs, not just your sun sign. Some astrologers say that the fact that your Mercury and Venus signs are never more than one or two signs away from your sun sign is why they influence the "cusp traits" that show themselves. Either way, realizing this is useful, especially if you are close to a dividing line, as you will be influenced by that sign as well as your actual sign.

Being on the cusp of two signs means that you possess characteristics of both. Each cusp has its own set of traits based on the signs it is straddling. I always say that I am envious of people who are born on a cusp, because they automatically possess an extra bit of balance, due to the fact that any two adjacent signs have natures that differ from one another, as their element and quality will both be different. The person born on a cusp has access to a wider set of traits, strengths, and adaptabilities from which to draw. (They have more access to the signs' negative traits and tendencies, too, but that doesn't mean that the negative traits are more influential than the challenges other people experience.)

YOUR MOON SIGN

Do you know your time and place of birth? If so, you can easily look up your moon sign in the table in appendix A. If you don't know your exact time or place of birth, you can still look up your moon sign in the table, but you may not be able to tell for sure which of two signs is your moon sign. This is because the moon moves through each sign over the course of a month, staying in each sign for roughly two and a half days.

If you were born on a day when the moon was definitely in a particular sign, you can be sure that is your moon sign; otherwise, if the moon changed signs on your birthday, you have to know your time of birth to know for sure on which side of the transition your moon sign falls. At least you will know that your moon placement is on the cusp between two signs, and that alone is useful information, because that particular cusp points to a particular set of traits.

If this applies to you, you can read the descriptions of both moon signs. Chances are you will identify more with one sign than the other, which should give you a better idea that the moon was in that constellation when you were born.

YOUR RISING SIGN

Your rising sign refers to the zodiac constellation that was rising on the horizon at the time of your birth. Rising signs change every two hours, which means that all twelve signs rise on the horizon over the course of a twenty-four-hour day. This means that you must know your time of birth to access this information. If you know your time and place of birth, you can easily look up your rising sign in appendix B.

If you don't know your time of birth, please don't fret. You can still find out the rest of your planetary placements and their relationships with each other, even if you can't determine your rising sign. While opinions differ on this point, if you can find out only one of the two signs besides your sun sign, you will get much more mileage knowing your moon sign, because your moon sign characteristics are usually less conscious to you than those of your rising sign. In other words, your rising sign description should be one that resonates with you on a conscious level, so while learning about it is definitely interesting and helpful, it won't likely provide you with any new information about yourself (other than validating why you show up to new situations in the way you do).

The moon sign descriptions, on the other hand, will likely not be as conscious to you, so there is a chance you will encounter something you never considered or had words to describe before. Since your moon sign shows itself in your closest relationships and during your most vulnerable moments, cultivating more self-awareness about these tendencies is especially important.

Though you likely know your sun sign already, and though you can look up your moon and rising signs at the back of this book, you can also go to a number of different websites to calculate this information, and more, for free. My favorite website in this regard is www.cafeastrology.com.

The Case of Twins

Let's address one last point before we move on to look at the characteristics that make up the essential natures of the signs. Being a psychologist who is also interested in astrology, I have been asked multiple times about how it is that twins are often so different from each other, even though they were born with most if not all of their signs in common. My answer has always been based in the psychology of differentiation. We are all born with a natural drive to differentiate ourselves from others (differentiation is a close cousin of individuation). Twins not only have the same innate, primal drive to separate from their parents that all of us do, they also have the deep psychological urge to differentiate themselves from each other and be seen as separate people.

I have known several sets of twins who, interestingly, have all had Gemini or Pisces—both of which are dual or twin signs (this will make more sense later when you see the signs' glyphs, or symbols)—as one of their three major signs. In my experience of knowing these sets of twins, I have found that they each express different aspects of the sign they share. (This is especially easy to see when the sign is a dual sign like Pisces or Gemini.) It is also the case that since twins are not born at exactly the same time, often their rising signs and houses will be different, especially if they were born with some time between each of their births.

The other thing I say when I am asked about twins who are so different is that much of the time, the two people are still much the same in fundamental ways. This can be hard to see, though, as the parts that are the same might be more shadowy for one or both twins—and repressed in an effort to be different—depending on their relationship with each other.

Before we move on to chapter 4 and discuss the qualities and elements of the astrological signs, please take a moment to look up your sun, moon, and rising signs and record them here.

WORKSHEET 1. YOUR SUN, MOON, AND RISING SIGNS

My sun sign is _____.

My moon sign is _____.

My rising sign is_____.

CHAPTER 4

Elements and Qualities of the Signs

I don't want to offend you but I should like to call your attention to astrology, which has dealt with such phenomena for about 5000 years.
—Carl Jung, *Letters II*

Since time immemorial, hundreds of traditions have utilized the elements of nature to describe humans. Astrology goes one step further and incorporates *qualities*, a classification that describes differences in temperament based on attitude, strength, and motivation.

The twelve signs of the zodiac are divided into four *elements* and three *qualities*. As you work to gain a deeper understanding of the essential nature of each sign, you will find that the best building blocks come from your developing a feel for the different elements and qualities. Once you understand them better, you will find it easier to get a feel for the nature of each individual sign, as each one represents a particular combination, or expression, of the two features of element and quality. (This will become especially clear when we look more closely at the twelve signs in chapter 5.)

My job as a psychologist involves trying to understand complex entities, such as people and family systems, more deeply over time. As will become clearer in a moment, the fact that I am made of the earth element—sun, moon, and rising—means that the way I get there is by building solid foundations, piece by piece, and increasing and refining my understanding over time as I get to know the landscape better. This is what I meant when I wrote in the introduction that I want to help you learn how to use the information yourself instead of just describing the signs to you; I am going to try to help you understand the signs in the same way I came to understand them myself.

The Four Elements of Earth, Air, Water, and Fire

Astrology uses the four ancient elements of earth, air, water, and fire to describe the signs. Since there are twelve signs and four elements, three signs fall under each element. As you read the following descriptions, try to keep the feel, or essence, of each element in your mind. For example, earth is constant, air is hard to pin down, water goes deep, fire is hot. This will help immensely to deepen your understanding of the nature of each sign.

Remember that we all have multiple signs in our birth charts, which means that *all of these descriptions are subject to modification by the other signs in your chart.* For example, if you have an air sun sign and an earth moon sign, you will be more down-to-earth than the typical air sign. If you have a water sun sign and a fire rising sign, you will show up as more extroverted than the average water sign. This is why we need to know which part of us is ruled by each of our three main signs of sun, moon, and rising. (We will discuss this further, with lots of examples, once more of the building blocks are in place.)

THE EARTH SIGNS—TAURUS, VIRGO, AND CAPRICORN

People who have the earth element strongly represented in their chart are reliable, sensible, practical, and concerned with concrete results. Think of the element of earth from a physical standpoint: it's there, you know it's there, and it's where it's supposed to be when you need it. People with this element have staying power, which makes them good people to have on your team. They mean what they say and say what they mean. If you know someone you would describe as grounded or down-to-earth, chances are that their sun, moon, or rising sign is an earth sign.

Earthy people slowly, methodically, and thoroughly build a deep sense of security and structure in their lives. This shows up in their support systems as they build deep, close, caring relationships with people over time. They tend to be mature; many earthy children have ways in which they seem like little adults. Earth signs can get too attached to their possessions and find it hard to let go of things, both physically and emotionally. Again, think of the element: when something gets lodged in the earth, it tends to stay put for a long while.

Earthy people find getting materially organized helpful because it helps their psyches feel clearer, as well. For them, restoring order to the physical world is a form of therapy, an opportunity to sort through thoughts and feelings by sifting through tangible items or working with the earth in some way (e.g., gardening, cooking). They are generally not trusting of things they can't touch, often preferring to keep a day planner over an electronic schedule. They experience the world in terms of observable facts.

In terms of their challenges—and challenging traits—earthy people can be too serious and lacking in spontaneity, having a hard time losing themselves in play or relaxation. They can be finicky and too focused on productivity and getting things done in the material world, given that everything gets filtered through the lens of practicality and concrete results. When they are out of balance, they feel "heavy" to the people around them. (All of these traits are mitigated when air and fire signs are mixed into the chart.) Fortunately, they are sensual people and appreciate earthly pleasures such as delicious food, luxurious comfort, and great music, so these avenues of self-care can do wonders to help them unwind and replenish themselves if they can allow themselves to take a break long enough to enjoy them.

THE AIR SIGNS—GEMINI, LIBRA, AND AQUARIUS

Air signs are quick-thinking, intellectual types, always up-to-date on the latest information that interests them. They are typically into some form of technology, or at least it comes easily to them, as communication travels through the airwaves. They like being privy to things as well as being known for knowing things; this is why many of them end up in the field of education. They often have the high-level perspective that can come only from being up in the air and looking down at the big picture. Were it not for their objectivity and level-headedness, our society would be doomed. Many times, their perspective is like a breath of fresh air, infusing cramped and polarized situations with a much-needed dose of elevated comprehension.

High-minded types that they are, air signs spend much time thinking, analyzing, and pondering the theoretical mysteries of the universe. They want to understand exactly how everything works. They are some of the least likely people to accept astrology because their mental natures can't easily make space for something they don't fully comprehend and can't explain with their minds.

Though not especially warm by nature, air signs are usually quite pleasant to be around. Airy people are the least likely to cause direct conflict or affect the energy of a social or group situation in a negative way. None of the three air signs want to be associated with causing a scene. To the contrary, they are invested in presenting themselves well and coming off as cool, calm, and collected. However, the flip side is also true; getting close to or discerning the true feelings of people who have a lot of air in their charts can feel hard to do.

Emotionally speaking, the words *cool* and *detached* are commonly used to describe them; however, they do have much kindness in their hearts, even if they are not the easiest people to get close to and aren't into sentimental displays of affection.

Air signs can be hard to pin down or get to commit to anything. Think of air: even when we think we have captured it in any kind of container, it can always seep out. Airy people want to be able to move about freely in any given situation, and commitment is restrictive in a particular way. During communication, they are able to easily avoid emotional material—which they tend to want to do, given that anything too upsetting will rattle their calm collectedness—by quickly flying away from it and moving into more comfortable realms of the intellect. Air signs' natural disdain for emotional displays provides a model to the rest of the world for holding on to our heads in stressful situations, which is a much-needed skill for functioning well as a society.

THE WATER SIGNS—CANCER, SCORPIO, AND PISCES

As ancient Chinese philosopher Lao Tzu said, "Water is the softest thing, yet it can penetrate mountains and the earth." Water signs are deeply powerful. They are highly emotional and intuitive, being the most open and receptive to psychic impressions (especially Pisces). In the introduction I mentioned a friend who told me I was going to write a book twenty years before I had the dream that made me decide to do it. She is double-water, meaning that two of her three major signs are water signs. Coincidentally, or should I say synchronistically, she has the same double-water combination as my book designer. Clearly, watery people possess a particular kind of vision.

Introverted and observant, watery people feel things very, very deeply. Think about the element of water: it runs deep, often containing aspects that can't be easily seen from the surface, and it absorbs and reflects everything it encounters.

I joke with my watery clients that they are like energetic Swiffers, often unconsciously picking up every sentiment in the room. Because of this trait, watery people are subject to anxiety and moodiness. Living in a constant state of involuntarily sensing everything that is going on around you is not easy, so please go easy on them. They feel especially anxious when their strong needs for family, home, and security (both emotional and financial) aren't being met. When hurt, they can be slow to heal, and when out of balance, they have been known to stew in victimhood and resentment toward others rather than growing themselves.

While airy people have a hard time believing in astrology because they can't understand it with their minds, watery people are the most likely to make space for astrology because they can *feel* its truth; it resonates with them on an emotional level, through their feelings, which is how they access their intuition.

Like my double-water friend (an artist by profession) and my book designer (also an artist), watery people tend to be drawn to music and other art forms, including writing. Water figures prominently in the charts of many poets and piano composers. Art is the most gentle and subliminal way to connect with others, and when we can truly appreciate it, we can receive the deep, often spiritual information that is channeled and expressed by the artist. Art makes us feel connected to the artist and the other people who appreciate it along with us, so it helps remind us of the interconnection between us all.

I have heard it said that water is here to heal the earth, and in my mind, this is how. Unfortunately, deeply sensitive artist types can end up living as tortured souls because of the difficulty of this nature. Robin Williams, Kurt Cobain, and Edgar Allan Poe were all double-water people (Robin Williams was triple-water). Their deep sensitivity and pain make them tend toward self-medication, and they are thus prone to addiction.

Fortunately, some people with a preponderance of water in their chart figure out how to temper the challenges of this nature, and even teach others how to do the same. Dr. Judith Orloff, for instance, is a double-water (Cancer sun-Pisces moon) psychiatrist and author whose most recent book, *The Empath's Survival Guide*, offers coping skills for sensitive people. The fact that highly sensitive, empathic people are Dr. Orloff's specialty is, of course, another synchronicity.

THE FIRE SIGNS—ARIES, LEO, AND SAGITTARIUS

Fire signs are known for being enthusiastic and inspiring to others. Young at heart, they possess much innate optimism and are absolutely passionate about all that moves them. Their optimism motivates others, which is why fire signs are known for getting things moving (though they are also known to leave many of the details for others, especially the earth signs, to finish). Think of the element of fire: to heat things up means to speed up processes. The fire signs light a proverbial fire under our butts to get us moving.

Fiery people are the innovative, pioneering types who come up with the highly creative ideas that blow your mind. They are entertaining and engaging, even intoxicating, to be around. They are great at thinking on their feet, have an abundance of natural wit and charisma, and are natural performers and public figures. Their good, quick instincts—lightning fast, as a matter of fact—mean that they experience the world in terms of intuitive hunches.

Fiery people are playful, and like younger people, they can see life as if it were a game and possess a certain amount of impulsiveness, restlessness, and unpredictability. Again, think of fire: it is not easily predictable or containable, and it can surprise us by quickly taking turns we never see coming. Depending on the situation, fire can be warm, generous, and nourishing—or it can burn down everything in its path. It is better when it is contained, as it is in a fireplace, than when it takes the form of a raging forest fire.

As is the case with everyone, the faults of fire signs tend to be the natural, albeit unintended, consequences of their strengths. Because their natural baseline state is charged, they tend to be hot-headed and hot-tempered. The same fiery lava that fuels their enthusiasm can be intense during a conflict, and they tend toward arrogance and narcissistic behavior when feeling insecure. Like all of us, they come by their flaws honestly; they have reason to believe they are special, given the crucial role they play in the zodiac.

As a nature, fire is not naturally the most empathic to the needs of others (though as always, it depends on what else is in the person's chart); its function is to inspire, not soothe. When out of balance, the anger of fiery people can cause much damage to those they love, and can leave their relationships looking like the charred remains of a wildfire.

If you draw a line connecting the three signs of each element on the zodiac wheel, they form a triangle, as seen in figure 3. In astrology, this relationship, or aspect, is known as *trine*.

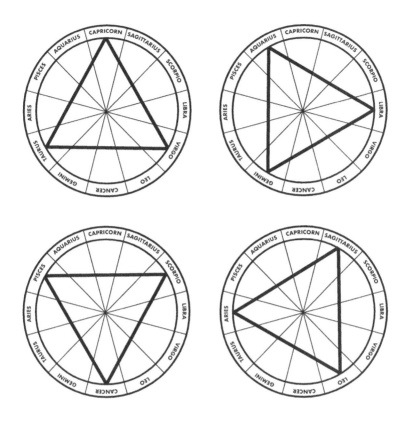

FIGURE 3. THE TRINE RELATIONSHIP BETWEEN THE ELEMENTS

Astrology pays much attention to the angles the different cosmic entities form with one another, called *aspects*. I am not going to cover aspects, but I do want to point out this triangular, or *trine*, aspect because it illustrates a point. Being in a trine relationship to one another, signs of the same element tend to understand each other and mesh well together because they are made of the same material and can speak the same language. If you venture into the online or print world to do more astrological research on your own, you might encounter the word *trine*, and you will know that this aspect indicates a harmonious relationship between any two cosmic entities (not just signs of the same element).

TENSION OF THE OPPOSITES

One last note about the elements. The ancient idea of opposites, as seen in the principle of yin and yang, shows up much in astrology. The idea is that each half of the whole contains part of the other half inside of it, and that each half is brought into a better state of balance through its contact with the other. Astrology divides the elements into two halves: the feminine half, made up of the water and earth signs, and the masculine half, consisting of the air and fire signs. The feminine signs are receptive, like yin energy, while the masculine sings are assertive, like yang. This is not a gender distinction, but rather, it signifies the idea that there are two balancing energies; the bee pollinates the flower, but the flower attracts the bee to it.

Within each half, the water and earth signs are polar opposites to each other, and the same is true of the air and fire signs. This is discussed further in Part III, but for now, you may be able to appreciate some basic truths, given what you already know. Earth and water, being polar opposites, have much to bring to each other in order to arrive at a better feminine balance; water can soften the harder surfaces of earth, and earth can help contain all the water. Similarly, air and fire are polar-opposite masculine forces, and in order to be more balanced, the molten fire needs to be cooled by the air, and the air needs to have its passion stoked by the fire.

The Three Qualities—Cardinal, Fixed, and Mutable

Like the elements, the term *quality* describes another classification of temperament in astrology. The signs fall into three categories of quality: cardinal (leading), fixed (stabilizing), and mutable (mediating). Given that there are twelve zodiac signs, this means that there are four cardinal signs, four fixed signs, and four mutable signs, and the four signs within each quality correspond with one of the four elements.

The quality is an important aspect of our temperament, or nature, as viewed through the lens of astrology because it determines the expression of the element in terms of attitude, motivation, and strength.

As you read the descriptions of the qualities, think of them as being superimposed over the elements such that there are three different versions of each element: one sign represents the cardinal version of the element, one sign the fixed version, and one sign the mutable version. Cardinal earth (Capricorn), for example, has a different presentation than fixed earth (Taurus) and mutable earth (Virgo).

The four cardinal signs are Aries, Cancer, Libra, and Capricorn. Cardinal signs are future-focused and goal-oriented. They are constantly looking forward, trying to develop their vision of what is to come. These signs are considered the "leader" signs of the zodiac because their function involves initiating projects and launching new endeavors, in business as well as on the home front. They have a near-constant desire to improve upon the current state of affairs, and they have a strong drive to be successful in all they undertake. Not surprisingly, cardinal signs tend toward impatience and do not do well to be held under anyone's control. Having their own ideas about how everything should be run, they are more naturally inclined to give orders instead of taking them, so they can sometimes steamroll and be bossy and critical.

The four fixed signs are Taurus, Leo, Scorpio, and Aquarius. Fixed, or stabilizing, signs are strong and steadfast. Known as the "power" signs of the zodiac, their sense of strength and stability comes from within themselves, which is why fixed signs can tend toward stubbornness, especially when pushed. They hate being or feeling controlled. Fixed signs are most likely to shut someone out or wall themselves off during conflicts, and they tend to be slow to forgive. They don't like change and usually feel inclined to stay put. Because they are able to hunker down and withstand forces that are pushing against them, they possess a certain form of stability in terms of their responses. Fixed signs are very independent and have a serious capacity for follow-through. They are also especially resilient survivors who can endure much pain.

The four mutable signs are Gemini, Virgo, Sagittarius, and Pisces. Mutable, or "mediator," signs are flexible and adaptable. They have a chameleon-like, shape-shifting quality and can go with the flow much better than the other two types. They are able to perceive exactly what is needed at any given moment depending on the apparent needs of others, which makes them good at being of service; however, this ends up being double-edged, as they have a tendency to lose themselves in their roles and relationships and not know who they are deep down. Their sense of self is yoked to the way others perceive them. Because their thinking is wider and more multidimensional than the cardinal and fixed signs, they are especially helpful during times of crisis, when multiple things are needed at once.

Mutable signs *appear* to not get angry very easily or often. If anger can be viewed as blocked movement in cardinal signs (since they are always trying to move things forward) and blocked freedom in fixed signs (since they hate being encroached on), it is clear that mutable signs tend toward covert aggression; a large number of serial killers are mutable signs. This is undoubtedly facilitated by the fact that mutable signs can easily find the places where they can slip through the cracks and stay hidden.

If you draw a line connecting the four signs of each quality on the zodiac wheel, they form a square, as seen in figure 4.

FIGURE 4. THE SQUARE RELATIONSHIP BETWEEN THE QUALITIES

Being in a square relationship with one another, signs of the same quality tend to have a harder time meshing with each other because they are driven by the same motivations in life—moving things forward (cardinal), bearing down to preserve things (fixed), and meeting the needs of others (mutable)—and can end up competing with each other or not arriving at the balance most situations require. It's the age-old problem of too many cooks in the kitchen. (One notable exception to this truth involves the relationship two polar-opposite signs have to each other. We will discuss this more in chapter 8.)

If you see the word *square* during your astrological research, you will know that this aspect indicates a more tense, challenging relationship between two cosmic entities. However, it is also the case that squares bring with them the highest potential for your growth, because challenges are what propel us to evolve.

ANALYZING THE ELEMENTS BY QUALITY

To increase my psychological understanding of the nature of each of the elements, I have thought often about the quality each element possesses. This may sound confusing, but stay with me. Even though there is a cardinal earth sign, a fixed earth sign, and a mutable earth sign, we could say that earth is the most fixed of all the elements because it is the element that is slowest to change. Similarly, we could say that air is the most mutable of all the elements because it moves around the easiest; this is why air signs can easily avoid direct confrontation. Fire is undoubtedly the most cardinal, given that its job is to inspire and initiate others to change the status quo.

Water is the element that is the most difficult to categorize. At first glance, water seems to fit somewhere between fixed (being deep and slow to heal) and cardinal (because it can "penetrate the mountains and the earth," catalytic processes, indeed). However, think of how mutable water can be, how quickly it can move and change shape. Of all the elements, it is the one that most easily changes form—it can be a fast-moving current, a deep lake, or a sprinkling of raindrops—and is also the element that most easily absorbs the energy around it. No wonder its job is to heal the earth—it boasts quite a resume.

Hopefully, using this lens can help you develop a better feel for each of the elements, which will in turn help you to understand your sun, moon, and rising signs better. If you find the extra layer of analysis more confusing than helpful, however, please feel free to ignore it.

A Note about Ayurveda

Ayurvedic medicine was developed in India over three thousand years ago and is one of the oldest holistic healing systems in the world. (If Ayurveda were a tree, you can think of yoga as one of its branches.) Like astrology, Ayurveda is about bringing everything into a state of balance by adding its opposite, so some overlap between Ayurveda and astrology would not be surprising.

While I have not encountered anything specific about this topic, it seems to me that the three *doshas* in Ayurveda correspond to the three qualities in astrology. (I have developed this sense over time but was initially confused in my understanding of the overlap, as Ayurveda involves the same four ancient elements of air, fire, water, and earth that astrology does. However, the most direct points of overlap between the two fields are clearer when we look at the qualities of the signs instead of their elements.) I want to briefly present a description of the three doshas in Ayurveda so that you can decide if you agree with me that this seems like another example of synchronicity in action.

Doshas are biological energies that govern the functioning of the body and mind. They tell us about our body's natural rhythms and what we experience when we are out of balance, both physically and emotionally. Ayurveda identifies three doshas—vata, pitta, and kapha—and like astrology, describes basic nature in terms of innate type, depending on baseline levels of each type of energy. According to Deepak Chopra in *Perfect Health,* "The Ayurvedic body type is like a blueprint outlining the innate tendencies that have been built into your system." Already this sounds like a more biologically based version of astrology.

But wait, there's more! Vata types are described as quick, changeable, unpredictable, imaginative, always moving, sensitive to change, and having quick and acute responses to the environment. When out of balance, they tend to feel restless and may act impulsively. Doesn't this sound similar to mutable signs?

Pitta types are known to be intense, ambitious, and bold, naturally taking command and responsibility in most situations.

Their intensity shows up in both positive and negative ways: when in balance, pitta types are quite warm, loving, and helpful, but when out of balance, they are more impatient than usual and can be irritable, demanding, and critical. This sounds a lot like the description of cardinal signs.

Finally, kapha types are described as solid and steady, with lots of endurance to withstand difficult situations. They are slow to move and dislike being rushed along. They tend to hold and store both physical and emotional aspects of their experiences inside. When out of balance, they tend toward stubbornness and complacency. Many of these are characteristics of fixed signs.

Now that you have the building blocks of element and quality, let's look in more detail at the specific natures of the twelve signs of the zodiac. It will be much easier to appreciate each sign as the

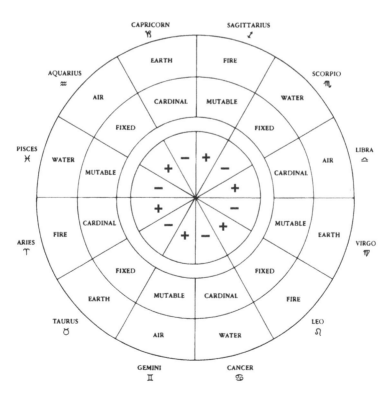

FIGURE 5. THE NATURE OF EACH SIGN
(+ DENOTES MASCULINE, AND—DENOTES FEMININE)

product of its element and quality because each sign embodies a particular combination or intersection of these two parts of astrological nature or temperament.

As a reference, the illustration in figure 5 shows the nature of each sign, depicting each of the layers we have discussed.

There is a worksheet at the end of chapter 8 where you will have the opportunity to record and synthesize all of the information about your three signs, including the life lessons indicated for you by your chart. For now, though, let's add to the information you recorded at the end of chapter 3.

WORKSHEET 2. THE ELEMENT AND QUALITY OF YOUR SUN, MOON, AND RISING SIGNS

My sun sign is _____.

This sign is made of _____(quality)

_____(element).

My moon sign is _____.

This sign is made of _____(quality)

_____(element).

My rising sign is _____.

This sign is made of _____(quality)

_____(element).

CHAPTER 5

The Twelve Signs of the Zodiac

Imagination is everything.
It is the preview of life's coming attractions.
—Albert Einstein, Pisces

W hat we see in astrology's symbolism is illuminated by our own intuition and inner imagination. If you are open to looking into it, astrology's mirror will reflect and reveal your own true self back to you, greatly enriching your life.

Along the zodiac wheel, the signs are ordered from youngest to oldest, or birth to death of the soul on a developmental or evolutionary level, with each sign representing its own particular piece of the journey. Each sign rules one of the twelve houses, corresponding with its position on the zodiac wheel. The process starts with Aries, which rules the first house, and ends with Pisces, which rules the twelfth.

The age of your soul is not necessarily determined by the signs you were born under, especially because most of us have a balance between younger and older signs in our birth charts, anyway. Rather, you can think about the *traits* the signs possess and give us the opportunity to cultivate over the course of our lives, as our maturity and wisdom increase by way of the lessons we have learned.

Pisces is the oldest sign of the zodiac, possessing all the wisdom of the others before it—when it is in a state of relative balance. This point, about balance, is an important one. We all exist somewhere along a continuum based on level of health, growth, and development no matter what our signs are. Having an idea of the range of functioning for each sign is helpful. As a shorthand way of describing it, this range of functioning will be referred to as the *degree of balance* we have at any given time. Balance can be thought of as a relative, dynamic, constantly shifting state, and one we will all find and lose a million times over.

The descriptions of the signs contain the highest potentials and darkest places as well as each sign's typical expression. As we move along on our paths of growth and individuation, we should see more of our signs' ideal expressions, but we will always be human, and we will always regress to an earlier stage of development at times, especially when things in our lives aren't going smoothly (such as when we are highly stressed or in crisis). When we are in this regressed state, the traits of our moon sign tend to show themselves.

As you read the descriptions of the signs, please keep in mind the differences between sun, moon, and rising, because the traits will be modified as a result of the position of the sign in your chart. For example, Leo as a moon sign greatly affects one's emotional expression, but if it is the rising sign, it doesn't impact behavior in one's closest relationships anywhere near as much. Rather, it governs the way one first shows up to new relationships and social situations.

You can read the descriptions of all three signs for yourself in this chapter: your sun, moon, and rising (if you know it) signs. When you read about your moon sign, please pay particular attention to the issues the sign causes in close relationships. Given that the moon rules our emotions and approach to intimacy and connection, it is in our closest relationships that our moon traits are most likely to emerge.

Please remember that the descriptions of your sun, moon, and rising signs are subject to modification from other parts of your chart, including the fact that these three signs temper and interact with each other. I cannot stress this point strongly enough. This is especially significant if your three major signs are of different natures in terms of element or quality. For example, if you have a Libra (cardinal air) sun and a Capricorn (cardinal earth) moon, you will be a much more grounded version of a Libra than if you didn't have earth represented so strongly in your chart. A fundamental truth in astrology, and psychology for that matter, is that each of us truly is a combination—and hopefully, integration—of all our parts. Specific examples of the ways in which signs can modify each other in your chart are discussed in chapter 8.

Another thing to keep in mind is that your attachment history and early experiences *act as modifiers* of your basic astrological nature. If you don't express many of the traits of your particular nature, it is likely because you had to repress those parts of yourself in order to survive your childhood.

I know two men who have the sun in Capricorn (cardinal earth) and moon in Scorpio (fixed water)—both very strong signs that are typically in touch with their anger. Recall, however, that the moon sign is the first part to emerge and corresponds with one's relationship with one's mother. Both of these men had fragile and needy mothers, so neither of them look much like their descriptions would suggest. Since both of these men have their moon in Scorpio, they have a need to control their strong emotions.

Because their mothers were fragile, these men especially needed to control and repress their anger toward their mothers because their mothers were unable to handle it. In their marriages, where moon signs express themselves, both of these men repressed all or most of their anger at their wives, instead showing up as overly mild and agreeable but driving their anger underground (a Scorpio tendency even in the best of circumstances, such as when Mom is hearty enough to take their anger).

Since I am a psychologist, my descriptions of the signs will naturally reflect my own (psychological) perspective. The essential questions guiding my descriptions are the same ones that are in the back of my mind guiding my work with my clients: I want to understand what is hindering them in their relationships and what they need to cultivate more of in order to grow. In my work with them, I do my best to show them empathy, which can admittedly be challenging at times. The reason I started weaving astrology into my work with clients in the first place was that I was trying to cultivate more empathy for them.

My sincere hope is that reading about the signs helps you to have more empathy—for yourself, if you are reading one of your own signs, and for any other person you want to improve your relationship with. Everyone has things to work on in themselves, and it helps tremendously if we all can have more empathy for the deeply ingrained nature each sign possesses, including the flaws. Just as we saw in the attachment research, empathy is the crucial ingredient we need in order to grow. We all need someone to witness and understand where we are *now* before we can move forward.

We need to have empathy for ourselves first and foremost so that we can calm down, explain our experience in a way the other person can hear, and hopefully get some empathy from them, as well. When we do receive empathy from others, we naturally feel moved to pay it forward by showing it back to them and to those we love most. This is what therapists call a *corrective relational experience*, and it is the only thing that can pave a path of true healing in ourselves and our relationships.

All of this is to say that when you read the descriptions that follow in order to learn more about one of your own signs, please remember that you will also read about some of your most difficult traits. If the descriptions feel a little harsh, see if you can make some space for astrology's mirror, and try to have some empathy for yourself. If someone has to see you where you are right now in order for you to grow, that person can be your own self at times (with some help from astrology).

I realize you will read many of the following descriptions with someone else in mind, and I initially struggled with how to word things: in terms of you or of them. I decided to keep almost everything in the second person, writing to you as though you are reading your own sign, even if you are looking up the description of someone who is currently driving you nuts. Besides the impossibility of accounting for the you/they distinction every step of the way, I kept the second person voice in the hope that it will help you cultivate more empathy for the experience of having that nature yourself. As the saying goes, we would all do well to walk a mile in someone else's shoes.

Each description of the signs includes four pieces:

1) Your essential nature. This involves looking at your sign's primary motivations, the benefits you bring, and the role you play in the collective whole. Jung believed that each zodiac sign represents a fundamental archetype (a recurrent mythological role or symbol), and the sum of all the signs—that is, the totality of the zodiac—represents a set of traits needed for the healthiest and most well-balanced individual or society. There's that projection process again, going from small to large.

2) At your best. This is what your nature looks like when you are at your best or in a state of relative balance; in other words, it is the highest potential of your sign in its imperfect human form. This is how you express yourself when you are feeling pretty good and secure in the world and your attachment needs are getting met well enough. It is more or less your sign's ideal expression.

3) Relationship challenges. When you read about your moon sign, please pay particular attention to this part because the moon rules our approach to emotions and has a large influence on us in our closest relationships. Within this section are two components:

    a) Your worst fear. This usually corresponds with what triggers you or makes you highly emotionally anxious and involves understanding your darkness, or shadow side. There are multiple ways to conceptualize this part of yourself: the primary fear that grips you, the main emotion you ward off, the biggest thing you are running from, or the thing you are most often preoccupied with (even if you don't realize it).

b) Your defense mechanisms. This refers to what you do when you get triggered and highly upset. We all try to avoid pain, but we do it in particular ways. Your defense mechanisms involve the way you express anger (including passive-aggressiveness) as well as the way you try to escape distress. Every sign has unhealthy behavior it tends toward when out of balance or highly upset. Chances are, these issues are playing out in your relationships in some way, and you may not be fully conscious of them.

You may notice some similarities across the masculine and feminine signs in terms of their defenses. For example, the masculine signs are more likely to engage in what therapists call the *narcissistic defense*, in which we elevate ourselves above others and condescend when we feel threatened. Feminine signs, on the other hand, are more likely to wallow and get stuck in victimhood. This makes sense, given our socialized roles.

4) How you grow. We all grow by cultivating traits that are less developed in us. In multiple ways, astrology can help us see what is lacking in ourselves. Every sign has polar-opposite traits that are part of its shadow side, and those are the traits to which this section will refer.

The discussion of this piece in each sign will point to the traits you can cultivate to be a more balanced version of yourself within the masculine or feminine role of the sign by looking to its polar-opposite sign on the zodiac wheel. However, keep in mind that because any two polar opposite signs are the same quality (see fig. 5), looking to the polar-opposite sign will not address any imbalance in quality in your chart; that is a separate analysis. Balance is discussed extensively in Part III.

Note that all three of your signs—sun, moon, and rising—have polar-opposite signs associated with them that point to how you can achieve more balance in the area of your life that particular sign rules (your basic self if sun, emotions if moon, or outer layer if rising; see fig. 2). At the least, I suggest that you read the description for both your sun sign and your moon sign.

If you haven't already done so, you can look up your moon sign in appendix A. For reference, table 2 shows the relevant dates for the sun signs.

TABLE 2. DATES FOR SUN SIGNS

Aries March 21–April 20	Taurus April 21–May 21	Gemini May 22–June 21
Cancer June 22–July 22	Leo July 23–August 21	Virgo August 22– September 22
Libra September 23– October 22	Scorpio October 23– November 21	Sagittarius November 22– December 20
Capricorn December 21– January 19	Aquarius January 20– February 18	Pisces February 19– March 20

(Please remember that the sun changes signs plus or minus a day, depending on the year.)

The Zodiac Signs

ARIES
CARDINAL FIRE

YOUR ESSENTIAL NATURE

Being both cardinal and fire, Aries is un-doubtedly the most cardinal sign of the zodiac. (Cardinal signs are leaders and catalyzers of action, and the element of fire has cardinal characteristics in that it is courageous and motivating to others.) You are first in line, kicking off the developmental trajectory of the zodiac signs and bursting forth into the world with your fiery enthusiasm—and this is true to form, because you love to be first for everything. Everyone else must work to forgive you for accidentally bumping into them or stepping on their toes in the process; you are truly on a mission, and attuning to minor details like toes when you are on a mission is hard to do.

The Aries symbol is the ram, charging forward with the fuel of its bravery and restless desire to initiate improvement. Your role is to shake others out of old, outdated belief systems, and you love a good challenge more than anyone. You are a warrior, pioneer, and catalyzer of change that needs to happen, and your vision is guided by the restlessness you feel. Females born with one of their major signs in Aries are said to have some degree of dissatisfaction with traditional feminine roles, and will naturally foster evolution by authentically living their lives.

Your warm-hearted, optimistic nature motivates others to go to their own edges in pursuit of growth and expansion. You not only want to inspire others with your enthusiasm, but like all cardinal signs, you are driven by a deep sense of responsibility to play your role in the world. Somebody's got to do it, you realize, and the rest of the signs aren't brave enough.

You are direct, honest, and good in a crisis because of your bravery and quick, instinctive emotional reactions; however, these quick reactions also contribute to your having a short fuse. Your lively, extroverted personality, highly original ideas, and faith in the future give others trust in your plans, even if you sometimes overestimate your abilities.

When your inner dissatisfaction with the status quo rises to a critical level, you charge forward into places that most others fear to tread in an effort to improve the current situation. This is true in your relationships as well as your professional life, where you are direct and not subtle. The restlessness you feel is supposed to stir inside of you, and that is why it is in your nature: because it is needed. You sense this truth on a deep level, which is why you take your responsibility to lead so seriously and carry it out with such conviction. It's not that you have no fear, it's that you must deny it in order to achieve your goals—and you are great at that.

AT YOUR BEST

You are adventurous, curious, and love to travel and experience new things. When in a state of relative balance, you move through the world in a way that is confident and assertive but still considerate, appreciating others' experience of you in addition to your own experience. Ideally, you are enthusiastic and outgoing but can share the space and time with others who also want to contribute. You are fun and can still be a bit of a rascal, but you are usually mindful of others' experience of your energy when you are at your best.

You enjoy active, engaging pursuits but also experience genuine pleasure having others in your life with whom to experience these things. You require space to move around in order to feel content, but when in balance, you can experience the genuine joy of feeling deeply connected to other people, as well. You can be a warm, caring parent who encourages your kids' independence by leading by example: you show them *I am me so you can be you.*

RELATIONSHIP CHALLENGES

Your biggest fear is going unnoticed or being forgotten. This can create several problems in your relationships, not the least of which is that you are unlikely to depend on others emotionally because you are then vulnerable to being hurt or left by them. Your strong drive to feel important, both in your relationships and in the world in general, can be difficult for others to deal with. You can take up a lot of space in your relationships at times, when you fear that you are not being seen unless you are the one running the show. Your quick, reactive nature makes you more impatient and irritable than any other sign, and there are times when you think you are being assertive in trying to get your needs met while others would call you abrasive or even aggressive.

You can grow bored and restless because relationships aren't as obviously beneficial and productive in your mind as direct action and movement toward some goal, because tracking results and progress in the growing intimacy of a relationship is harder to do. As a result of this strong cardinality, you are sometimes seen as indifferent to other people's need to connect with you, and they may experience you as selfish or dismissive of their experience. Depending on the personality of the other person, you may get into major conflicts about how time and energy are spent in the relationship, or you may be running the show and cultivating resentment in the other person even when they are going along with you.

Your primary defense when you are triggered is to get so intensely angry, mean, and pushy that you bully the other person into giving in and letting you have what you want. Feeling not seen makes you scared, and you detest the emotion of fear, so you lash out and try to turn the tables instead, making the other person feel not seen. You can minimize the importance of the other person in your life in a way that is very harsh, even if it is only in your mind. When you decide to do exactly what you want no matter how that choice impacts others, you can hurt people a lot.

You are capable of hurting others tremendously with your anger depending on how upset you are, especially if you are also dealing with other major life stressors (e.g., issues at work), because your fuse is naturally short to begin with. You see fighting as a form of connection, which is part of why you try to keep an argument going in that way. Ironically, as with all the signs, your defenses (here, bullying) can lead you directly to your worst fear if not kept in check—feeling alone, unimportant, and dependent because the people you love have distanced themselves from you. Working to develop more tolerance for vulnerable emotions that are harder to sit with, such as fear and sadness, instead of trying to get away from them as quickly as possible no matter the cost, would help you, even though doing so can be difficult and upsetting.

As is true with all signs, your family environment plays a significant role in who you are, as does the presence of receptive feminine signs elsewhere in your chart (especially water, which can tamp down fire). If there are beneficial, protective factors in your history, such as secure attachment to one or both of your parents, you will naturally have more empathy for others' experience of you, because your parents will have had empathy for your experience of them. If your parents treated you harshly, however, treating others harshly will be a hard habit to break in your darkest moments, because you will have gotten a double dose of it—from nature *and* nurture. Remember that a break can help during a fight, especially if you use it to exert yourself physically to burn off some of that anger.

HOW YOU GROW

Libra is your polar-opposite sign and possesses several important traits that can help you. Libra is the sign of relationships. Its symbol is the scales of justice, and Libras are concerned with making sure everyone is being treated fairly. They also care deeply about the experience other people have of them. The more you can work to let other people matter to you—even if it means they can hurt you—the more balanced you will become.

You could also benefit from Libra's higher-level perspective and emotional detachment from outcomes; being up in the air means you can see more sides of a situation, which makes decisions less clearly one-sided. Trying to see the other person's side of the situation, with a little more detachment from your own personal stance, will help to cool some of your fiery imbalance. Your restlessness and temper are also less of an issue in your relationships to the extent that you truly understand and appreciate the importance of others in your life as separate people with inner lives of their own, people with whom you can connect and share space while you are traveling through life. This connection is a highly important activity in and of itself.

If it is helpful, you can use the up-in-the-air detachment image of your polar-opposite air sign as a visualization strategy to try to get up above your fiery nature when it is getting you into trouble via anger, impatience, or selfishness. Not getting what we want is hard to tolerate, but we all have to deal with it if we want to have decent lives and relationships. An important part of maturity is learning how to do this with more grace and charm, which Libras value highly and tend to possess in spades.

TAURUS
FIXED EARTH

YOUR ESSENTIAL NATURE

Given the fixed nature of the earth element itself, being both fixed and earth makes Taurus the most fixed sign of the zodiac. You possess the fixed traits of stubbornness, loyalty, dependability, and independence, and being an earth sign makes you sensual, grounded, and down-to-earth. You have a deep inner sense of strength and stability, and you respect strength in others, as well. Your role is to teach others about building and preserving things in earth-based reality, including holding on to themselves in a relational sense.

If you were a tree, you would have a thick, sturdy trunk that would represent your self-concept, and it would be rooted deeply into the earth. (The symbol for Taurus is the bull, which is the animal form of this same idea.) Many therapists have Taurus as either their sun sign (like Freud, Mahler, and Kohut) or their moon sign (like Jung and me), so therapists spending so much time talking about our need to know exactly who we are, separate from others and their expectations of us, is a synchronicity. Taurus is all about being real and authentic, and carving out the space to be able to do so in the context of our lives and relationships.

For Taurus, what others see really is what they get, for better and for worse. You take your emotional commitments seriously and don't enter into relationships lightly, and once you care about someone, you want to hold on to them for as long as possible. Unfortunately, at times this desire to preserve things works against you, such as when a needed change is in order.

Being so earthy, you take in enjoyment of life through your physical body and your senses. You love food that tastes delicious and beauty in your surroundings, for example. You collaborate with nature to find spiritual connection in the realm of the physical world. You especially love music because you appreciate it with your entire body; it helps you feel more spiritually connected to your higher self and to other people. The simple pleasures and creature comforts of the material world make up the balm that nourishes your heart and soothes your soul.

Self-care is your specialty, and it can take many forms: beautiful surroundings, soft blankets and a warm cup of coffee or tea, a massage, taking it easy at home with a good book, or enjoying a long lunch when you can linger with a friend and not feel rushed. You like being able to run your own show and not be bossed around, so space and time can feel just as luxurious as the spa under the right circumstances.

AT YOUR BEST

When you are in balance, Taurus, you are absolutely wonderful to be around. You are so real that no one feels like they need to put on airs around you, and most people are grateful for that. You are warm and nurturing, and take care to ensure that those you love are having a comfortable experience of their own. At your best, you are confident but in a deeper sense, so you come off as less bullish because you don't always need to concretely show it. Your stubbornness is reflected positively in your endurance, especially when you are in a state of relative balance.

You are a caring parent who teaches your kids about strength, self-confidence, and setting appropriate boundaries to protect themselves from encroachment by others. As long as your needs are being met, you have space to truly give of yourself to other people, which you deeply enjoy and value. You are so grateful to have the space in which to feel generous that your heart can fully open up to others in a way that benefits both of you, not just the other person.

RELATIONSHIP CHALLENGES

You value earth-based security (financial, physical, and emotional) highly, so your biggest fear is unexpected change. This can make being in relationships with you, from the day-to-day level to the big picture one, more difficult. In a big-picture way, you can refuse to consider changes that need to be made, from sex and other relational dynamics to moving or changing jobs. Since you are naturally inclined to keep things the same, another person wanting change can feel like they are encroaching on your sense of self, and this can make you resentful and unwilling to give. However, to them, and in reality, you are stuck. Think about trying to move a tree or a bull, and this truth will become clearer.

On a micro level, keeping you comfortable can be hard for others, especially without them feeling like you are being possessive and keeping them stuck in a box with you. You can be very picky about things like where to go to dinner: it can't be too loud or crowded or hard to park, the food has to be really good, there has to be enough selection, and so on. Others can experience you as controlling, and depending on your moon placement, you may even like to go to the same places over and over again. All this fussiness means that you can be a serious resister when you don't want to do something, and people can see you as lazy. When you are too unwilling to try new things or go along with the majority vote, you can turn your fixed earth nature into a huge, annoying boulder in the middle of the room.

You are most triggered by anything that threatens your sense of emotional, physical, or financial stability, which means any time change is introduced as a possibility in the equation. Your biggest defenses are to dig in when pushed and to wall people off or shut them out if they won't stop trying to get you to change something (or if they refuse to change something for you, which usually means going back to some prior state of how things were before). You can act like a petulant child, trying to win by waiting the other person out and scaring them into giving up their own experience because they risk losing connection with you if they don't.

You may think your attitude is live and let live—"I don't tell you what to do, so you shouldn't lay down the law to me"—but you don't realize how much you can infringe on the freedom of others by being so heavy and intrusive with your communication and your unwillingness to grow or compromise. You stubbornly cling to roles, dynamics, items, and relationships that feel out-of-date compared to your present-time self. You do this in part because you hate change and because you don't want to have been wrong in the first place; giving up anything gracefully is not at all easy for you. The irony is, you are so focused on not being pushed into anything that you don't realize you are already stuck in a corner. Sorry if this seems harsh, Taurus, but real, honest language is the only thing you truly understand.

Your fearful refusal to evolve can cause disconnection in your relationships, leading you to feel lonely, angry, depressive, hopeless, and shut down. Like all the signs, your defense mechanisms can lead you straight into your most-feared situation: unexpected change in the form of a loved one wanting distance from you, or some other life change that gets forced on you because you won't make space for it any other way.

HOW YOU GROW

Scorpio, your polar-opposite sign, possesses some important traits that can help you. For one thing, Scorpios keep much more hidden than you do in terms of their reactions to situations. You can wear your feelings on your sleeve, and you need to work not only on compromising but also on handling your discomfort with more grace. (Can you see the trajectory of increasing maturity and refinement as the signs develop along the wheel from younger to older?)

Everyone shouldn't have to suffer so much just because something is not to your liking. You need to learn how to go along to get along and appreciate how much you are running the show by being so stubborn, even if you don't mean to be. What *can* you give, even if it's only trying to look less annoyed?

Another thing to learn from Scorpio is the calming power of going inward. This can come in the form of meditation, yoga, and journaling—and being Taurus, the more of it you can do outside, the better. Much of the time, your feeling like you can't give anything is because you don't have enough of what you need for yourself, especially in terms of time and rest. You have much to give to the world with all of your strength and tender caring for others, but you can also give yourself away and become angrily resentful if you are not careful. If you take care of yourself by resting and being more internal when needed, ironically, you will have more to give to others later.

One way to become better acquainted with your need for self-care is to acknowledge your pain and sadness when you feel out of balance—which is wisdom that Scorpio's watery nature brings to the equation—instead of using the anger that earth signs tend to feel more easily. If you can find your sadness and pain instead of just your angry resentment—which externalizes blame and is harder to sift through—you will be more inclined to nurture yourself back to a place of restoration and willingness to engage with others. On your journey to learn how to become more generous, starting with a gentler form of empathy for yourself will be helpful.

GEMINI
MUTABLE AIR

YOUR ESSENTIAL NATURE

Gemini, you are extremely flexible, mutable, and adaptable, especially given the highly mutable nature of the air element itself. You are the lightest on your feet, spontaneous in conversation, and the swiftest moving sign of the whole zodiac. Your versatility makes you delightful to interact with, especially in social situations. You have an uncanny ability to remain optimistic under even the darkest of circumstances, and your role in the zodiac involves lightening things up with your levity and humor. The natural communicator of the zodiac, you use words and language to connect others, and you tend to be great storytellers.

Naturally extroverted, you love chatting and having interesting conversations with others. Your mind is clever, and you can quickly and easily grasp complex ideas and conversational requirements. You are like a great social swing dancer, able to seamlessly follow along with the moves of the other person. Everyone likes interactions that feel that way, so you tend to be quite popular.

You are highly creative and an outside-the-box thinker, but being a mental air sign, you are also quite logical. You tend to collect a vast reservoir of all kinds of interesting pieces of knowledge. You like being up-to-date on everything, including interesting new ideas and the latest gossip. Known as the information gatherer, you tend to get bored without enough mental stimulation, so you often seek out others who like to operate at your same swift pace. At times, others see you as distractible, scattered, and unwilling to sit with emotional depth because it makes you uncomfortable.

Your ability to easily move around also helps immensely with your resilience to adversity. Many Geminis have had hard lives, and having this nature helps you cope better than most. Geminis are also quite funny, another trait that makes you so enjoyable to be around. We all need some levity and buoyancy to help us deal with the hardships we encounter, and without the light and fun energy you naturally bring and supply, life would just be too much to bear. In many situations, you are like a breath of fresh air.

AT YOUR BEST

When you are in balance, you are fun, chatty, and witty, yet you are able to find deeper points of connection with other people, especially the ones closest to you. In your relationships, you ideally want to fulfill the other person's needs because you love them, not just because you are seeking approval or see (in a more detached way) a need that you could fulfill. When you are in balance, you are sunny, friendly, and generous, and you bring people together by infusing every interaction with your intelligent, insightful, and witty perspective on just about any topic under the sun.

If you have a life that provides enough mental stimulation to ward off the sense of anxiety and restlessness that comes with too much inertia, you can feel a deeper sense of contentment and meaning in your work as well as your relationships. As a parent, you can enjoy teaching your kids about all the interesting things in the world and keep yourself entertained by experiencing everything all over again. You use your language gifts to help your children and those around you learn how to talk through and about their feelings logically, which is helpful because it enables them to better explain their feelings to others.

RELATIONSHIP CHALLENGES

Your biggest fear is feeling stuck in a routine or rut, and warding off this fear can create problems with those closest to you. People can find coldness in your extraordinary ability to compartmentalize anything emotionally difficult, and since you have an easy time moving off of pain yourself, you have little tolerance for sulking, in yourself and others. This can translate into others feeling that you lack empathy for their experience. This will be tempered to the extent that your parents showed you empathy or you received empathy later in life (as happens in good therapy).

Another way your need to have the freedom to constantly change gets you into trouble is that people can experience you as fickle; you are known to say whatever the situation calls for in a way that comes off as self-serving, opportunistic, and as though your loyalty goes whichever way the wind blows. The symbol for Gemini is the twins, which is why the sign is sometimes called two-faced; like Pisces, it is one of the signs known to have a dual nature.

All mutable signs, including Gemini, have a tendency toward codependence in relationships (though they are not the only ones). This is because you naturally look to the needs of others in determining your next move. You are also conflict-avoidant because you can easily move away from anything uncomfortable. You can get into a dynamic of enabling someone else's unreasonable behavior and then resenting it, which can come out only as passive-aggressiveness when a person is conflict-avoidant. When you are angry enough at someone, your high level of mental acuity combined with your popularity can enable you to turn the tide against them in a way that is subtle but deeply orchestrated.

Your primary defense when you get triggered is to immediately fly away or dissociate from whatever is uncomfortable by changing the course of the conversation, like an emotional ninja. Because you are so smart and quick-thinking, you can easily deflect anything you perceive as threatening your self-concept. You are able to steer and maneuver the conversation in whatever direction you choose, which makes you very hard to argue with. The other person can feel like you want to play only the well-liked parts in the relational play, and when you refuse to see anything less than positive in yourself, you force them to hold everything negative. With this mindset, getting you to consider painful feedback about yourself is hard to do, which is problematic because this is how you grow and how the other person gets their needs met.

Obviously, this means that when you are triggered and highly defensive about something, no one can possibly get you to talk about it until you are ready and willing, which can be deeply upsetting for the other person. You are a careful manager of your image, and the other person can feel like you always want to come out smelling like a rose. In a way, you can't really be blamed; you are an expert at outwitting the other person, and of course you would take advantage of your strength—as anyone else would—especially during a conflict. It helps, however, to consider that the other person's experience of you is designed to help you become a better version of yourself. Nothing gets resolved or learned, and no one grows, when conflict isn't resolved over the long term. Besides, just as with the other signs, all of your defensive maneuvers can lead you directly to your worst fear: being stuck in the painful routine of a disconnected and dissatisfying relationship, or being single.

HOW YOU GROW

Your polar-opposite sign is Sagittarius, and there are things you can learn from that sign that can help bring you into a better state of balance. For one thing, while Sagittarius tends toward restlessness as you do, it does need a secure base, and this is adaptive because it fosters deeper connection with others. Since Sagittarius is a fire sign, they tend to experience love more passionately than air signs; this can act as a connective glue in their relationships, even if they still need to be able to move about freely. (They are still mutable, after all.)

Like all air signs, Gemini, you are more interested in mental and intellectual ideas rather than the in-the-trenches nature of Sagittarius. Sagittarius cares more passionately about their causes than you care about yours. See if you can tap into and enlarge your own inner passion and enthusiasm about things instead of approaching them with detached intellectual interest. Be willing to get your hands dirty, emotionally speaking, when something or someone matters to you.

Sagittarius is higher-minded in the sense that they consider the needs of the collective whole to a greater extent than you do, Gemini. The lesson here is that gossip and other shallow forms of energetic expression are mostly a waste of time, and your energy is best spent on more worthwhile pursuits that have the hope of improving humanity's experience on a higher level, even if it is just in the context of your own personal or professional world. Sagittarius teaches others that life can be fun, but it should also be full of meaning. Committing to something you care about, and then working hard to achieve it, as passionate, fiery Sagittarius is known to do, would help you to grow.

CANCER
CARDINAL WATER

YOUR ESSENTIAL NATURE

Cancer, you are the natural mother of the zodiac. Being a water sign, you are highly sensitive to the emotional needs of those around you, and being cardinal, you are always looking for ways to improve anything that falls under your jurisdiction, so to speak. You are naturally protective and nurturing, and nothing makes you happier than tending to the needs of those you love most. Your symbol is the crab, and you prefer the safety of dark, contained spaces, such as your own home. Your thin but crucial outer shell protects your soft body.

You are incredibly intuitive and psychic, and you take great pleasure in meeting other people's needs even before they themselves are aware of the need. While you are deeply nurturing, being cardinal means that you are also a leader and ruler, as any mother needs to be in order to do her job well—and you know this on a deep, intuitive level. In other words, being nurturing does not mean that you are a doormat, as Pisces (the mutable water sign) can have a tendency to be. You get strong gut feelings about things, but unfortunately, this also leads to stomach problems, which is a form of what therapists call *somaticizing* (channeling psychological stress into the body, which causes it to manifest physically as symptoms).

You have strong personal security and attachment needs. You

love your home and like to stay close to it, and you need to be connected to your loved ones in order to feel secure. You have a hard time letting go of things because you get sentimentally attached, and you can often be a packrat. Though you do like to travel, your essential nature tends toward a quiet life. As the mother of the zodiac, it is likely that children have figured prominently in your life, especially if your moon is in Cancer. (I have known a number of Cancer women for whom this has become true in a less-than-traditional way, as happens when you marry someone with kids and end up with stepchildren.)

Being psychic and so much like an emotional Swiffer makes you tend toward anxiety and mood disorders. Your moods can change easily, either because you are having your own emotional experience or because you are picking up on someone else's bad mood; sometimes you can't even tell for sure. When I think of Cancer, one of the metaphors in my mind is that of being fair or thin-skinned; you get sunburned from the same exposure that leaves other people less affected because they are thicker-skinned. However, this is part of your nature, and you wouldn't be so intuitive if you weren't also so sensitive.

AT YOUR BEST

Cancer, when you are at your best, you are about as sweet and loving as can be. Your heart is full of love for all creatures, especially those you care about most, and you give of yourself with all that you have. Your maternal feelings for others translate into their feeling loved and well cared for. You make a great parent and an especially warm and attuned partner and friend. You are loyal and not at all likely to desert anyone close to you for any reason, especially if you consider them to be part of your family.

You value history, and your strong sentimentality makes you a keeper of old memories, sometimes for generations. Your intuition is a huge asset in many situations, and people routinely lean on you because they can tell you are kind and trustworthy. When you are in a relative state of balance and your emotional security needs are being met, you are absolutely lovely, and others are lucky to have you taking care of them in the myriad ways you do.

RELATIONSHIP CHALLENGES

It may seem paradoxical, but while you do make a wonderful caretaker, Cancer, you can also be fairly high maintenance when it comes to having close relationships. Your worst fear is not being needed by others, and because of this, you are constantly testing people (though not consciously) in an effort to see how much you matter in their lives. Your strong emotional security needs, coupled with your deep sense of intuition, can make for a difficult combination.

You can easily find things to worry about, even if nothing truly upsetting is taking place; you sometimes even border on being paranoid. When out of balance, you can be insecure, overly sensitive, and possessive in your closest relationships. Your frequently shifting moods can make the people who love you feel like they are walking on eggshells in order to avoid upsetting you.

Because you are so focused on feeling needed by others, you can tend toward codependence in your relationships. You can attract parasitic people who like that you take such good care of them, and you understandably feel hurt and resentful at their lack of reciprocal generosity. But you are just as much a part of the dance, because some part of you is drawn to externalizing the blame and playing the victim. It feels easier to focus on someone else's problems instead of looking more closely at and taking responsibility for your own.

Your tendency to externalize blame and lodge it in the other person makes you become mean and critical toward them. The symbol for Cancer is the crab, and those claws can pinch. At times you can be downright snarky and nasty, and you can brood and sulk about something for an inordinate amount of time. However, your complaining is positive in the sense that you are not as likely as the other two water signs to become resentful due to not speaking up about your needs. You may become resentful if they are not being met, but it won't be for lack of trying, because your cardinal nature means you will keep attempting to improve the situation by giving voice to your feelings.

As a parent, you may have a hard time letting go of your kids, which will hinder their ability to form secure attachments as adults if you don't work hard to keep it in check. Like all water signs, you have a tendency to self-medicate with food and substances, because you need to cope with your intense emotions.

When you get triggered, which happens when you feel criticized—the opposite of feeling needed, as you see it—your primary defense is to get profoundly emotionally upset, which can be scary for people. This can show up in the form of a tearful emotional display, an intense and emotional lashing out, or being so deeply injured by someone's criticism of you that you emotionally shut down and stop communicating altogether.

Since you have a tendency to take things too personally and feel everything so intensely, sometimes your emotions can completely overwhelm you, and you can't take in feedback that is constructive. You fear you can't handle taking it in, but if your defenses work too well, you will end up losing connection with your loved ones because they need you to hear them in order to feel seen themselves.

HOW YOU GROW

Capricorn is your polar-opposite sign, and it has some helpful traits to offer you in order to help you become more balanced. Since earth signs like Capricorn are deeply grounded in reality, Capricorn can help by asking you to look at things in a more reality-based way as opposed to using your own emotional yardstick to decide what's what. For instance, Capricorn says, *You can handle it, Cancer. You just have to harden up a little bit so you can contain your own sensitivity.* You don't have to be cold or insensitive, just tougher and thicker-skinned. Reality-based Capricorn says, *You can do that, Cancer—even if you think you can't.*

Another reality-based lesson from Capricorn has to do with your sensitivity level. Before you start worrying about everything under the sun, Capricorn asks you to consider the practicality of such worry, especially because much of it tends toward the paranoid. Look at the facts of the situation instead of your overly attuned instincts. They are like an antenna that is picking up a frequency you are sometimes better off trying to ignore.

Finally, because of Capricorn's strong focus on taking responsibility for one's actions, your polar-opposite sign can help you stop stewing in blame toward others and take the reins of your own life. It's not that Capricorn begrudges your being upset, it's that it is impractical to sit around and stew. It's better to get on with it so you can get back to improving things. Remember, the earth signs help balance the water signs by encouraging them to shore up and get tougher. As long as this comes from a place of love and compassion, it can be exactly what is needed.

LEO
FIXED FIRE

YOUR ESSENTIAL NATURE

Leo, your symbol is the lion, and just as the lion is king of the beasts, you are the king of the zodiac. Being fixed, you are determined, loyal, and stubborn; and being fiery, you are creative, courageous, and passionate. Warm, loving, radiant, and sunny (especially fitting because you are ruled by the sun), you are truly one of a kind, which is your most favorite thing of all to hear. You are proud as can be, even dignified, and your biggest wish in life is to be fully appreciated for all that you are. Your tag line is to proudly exclaim, "I am *that* one."

Your nature is youthful and playful, and you tend to like children and relate to them well. As much as you love to feel seen, you intuitively understand that all children have this need, and you make them feel important and respected when you shine your big, dazzling light upon them. Being a fire sign, you are naturally enthusiastic and encouraging of others.

You love to be in the spotlight (though this is not necessarily true when Leo is your moon sign), and you are naturally competitive and hard-working, so you tend to rise to the top of whatever field you are in. You get bored if you don't have enough going on to keep you engaged. Being naturally theatrical, you can create your own drama, in your relationships as well as your work life, if there isn't enough to feed your creative fire.

Most of all, you need to feel loved, appreciated, and respected by others. As generous as you are, when your generosity goes unnoticed or unappreciated, you become very upset indeed. This is one of the reasons Leos have a reputation for needing attention: it's really all about appreciation. If someone is fanning your inner fire with love, praise, or gratitude, you know you have done your job well, and you can contentedly bask in the warm glow of your sunny nature, much like a cat contentedly curls up and soaks in the sun coming through the window.

AT YOUR BEST

Leo, when you are at your best, you truly light up the room like the sun lights up the sky. You are engaging, friendly, and magnetic (as fire signs are known to be), and you evoke trust from others because you make them feel seen and inspired. You make everyone else feel as amazing as they think you are, just by being yourself.

You are passionate and loyal to those you care about, and you love with your whole heart. As a parent, you naturally inspire your kids to shine brightly, and you encourage their courage and independence. As long as you feel engaged and challenged enough in your life, whether at work or with your kids, or both, you give your all and are thrilled with all the appreciation and validation that comes back to you.

RELATIONSHIP CHALLENGES

Because you have such a strong personality, you can come off as bossy, domineering, and dogmatic. Others can find it difficult to work with you because they feel like you are laying down the law to them, like a king ruling. Being fixed, you don't easily back down or even see your mistakes because you have a hard time seeing the view from the other side of the wall you have built. Your fiery nature can be highly intimidating to others, and at times you can be possessive, jealous, and aggressive. When you are not feeling balanced, it is obvious, and people can feel the heat emanating off of you in a way that makes them anxious.

You are proud and need to feel appreciated, but the finer point to your worst fear is that you most dread being humiliated. This is probably because you always feel like you are in the spotlight and highly visible, and you feel like you are not performing well when you don't get the response you want from someone. You recoil in shame quickly when someone triggers something in you that makes you feel that way, and then you respond—which is equally as intense as your energy on your sunniest days, though in the opposite direction.

When you get triggered, your typical reaction is the narcissistic defense, which is why you have a reputation for tending toward narcissism. The narcissistic defense involves becoming superior, cold, and distant when you get hurt or scared, much like a cat or puffer fish pumps itself up to scare its enemy. You feel safer if you can intimidate the other person. Being a fixed sign, you much prefer this defense to lashing out at someone and will first try to control your anger; however, if you are pushed hard enough, you can blow up in a fiery explosion.

As warm and sunny as you are when feeling good, when you have been hurt and are angry at someone, being in your presence is like being in the coldest and darkest place imaginable. When you withhold all the love and generosity that you have previously given, people definitely feel it—it's like you turned off the sun. This is your intention, of course—you want them to hurt just as much as you are hurting—but your method can be way too harsh to do any good, and instead cause fire damage to parts of the house that compose your relationship. (I often think of relationships—and our psyches—as houses, with rooms that hold different parts of us and that we willingly enter or not, and that we can damage, restructure, and so on. I am made of earth, so I like to make everything tangible.)

Many people I know with their moon in Leo (also known as *lunar Leos*) have a fear of their own anger. I have seen them deal with this by various means—trying to talk themselves out of having anger, denying its existence, walling off and refusing to communicate because they would rather not say something that will burn down the barn. Many of the lunar Leos I know have a softer sun sign to help balance them out, like gentle Pisces or cooling Gemini or Aquarius (which is the polar opposite of Leo; more on this polar-opposite sun-moon relationship in chapter 8). If we do indeed choose our charts, it would make sense to set it up that way. Working to integrate our traits instead of having extreme versions that are needed to balance each other out is important. At the end of the day, we all need to make contact with our anger in order to find any resolution; the key is to do so in a way that isn't highly destructive.

HOW YOU GROW

Your opposite sign is Aquarius, and you could stand to take some pages from their book. Aquarius is known for keeping a cool head in all situations, and your fire could certainly use some cooling when you are at your most upset or unbalanced. Being up in the air, Aquarius is focused on the good of the collective because it can see the situation much more objectively from its detached perspective. Even though it is fixed and thus stubborn like Leo, because it is an air sign, Aquarius is more able to see what is on the other side of the wall during a conflict (eventually, at least).

You are not objective enough. Being so passionate, when you feel things strongly, remembering that the other person is also having a totally subjective, emotional experience of their own can be hard for you. You need to think about the good of the collective (which is made of individuals and their own experiences), or at least the relationship you are having, more than just your own needs. There is an adage in the couples therapy world—do you want to be right, or do you want to be happy?—and you are the primary exemplar of the person who needs to consider this question. You can get severely stuck in your own experience if you are not careful.

When you think of the experience someone might be having of you, consider how much damage you can do to the other person's ability to trust and feel safe with you in the future. You have a right to be angry and upset, but your challenge is to work to express those emotions in a way that is more constructive and less overwhelming to the other person. Fire can create lots of damage, but so can frostbite. There is a place in the middle where you can express yourself and also contain the damage, like a controlled burn in a fireplace or turning down the flame on the stove. Think of popcorn; it needs the right balance of heat and air in order to cook well. Approaching anger this way can prevent your defense mechanisms from leading you directly into the mouth of your worst fear: the deep humiliation and pain that comes from ruptured connection in a treasured relationship.

VIRGO
MUTABLE EARTH

YOUR ESSENTIAL NATURE

Virgo, you probably have it together more than any other sign. Naturally crafty, skilled, and resourceful, you have the MacGyver-like ability to effectively handle whatever crazy circumstances life throws at you and make it look easy. Being the mutable earth sign of the zodiac, your role and driving force is to be of service to other people in a practical way. Your symbol is the maiden, depicted holding an ear of corn to symbolize nurturance and daily ritual.

You can look like a cardinal sign because you are always on a mission to get something done, but the key is that your mission is defined by attending to the needs of others, making you mutable and flexible rather than a future-oriented leader sign. Being an earth sign, there is also a slightly fixed quality to you, and you are loyal, dependable, and responsible to those you care about.

You are highly competent, orderly, and dedicated to any duty you take on, so you are an especially great person to have around when anything needs to be done. You are productive and hard-working, but more specifically, you are a true efficiency expert. In just about any situation, you can't help but see a better way to do things. You are naturally good at discriminating and pay great attention to detail, and your fast-moving, mutable mind is able to grasp things much more quickly than average. You never accept at face value anything you are told without verifying it yourself first.

You are a perfectionist, which is part of your downfall. (Brené Brown, who calls herself a "recovering perfectionist," has her moon in Virgo.) Since life and people aren't ever perfect, you can experience—and cause others to experience—a lot of distress and irritation in life. You tend to be health conscious and perfection-istic when it comes to your body, and though you lack the intense rigidity of people with Scorpio in their chart, you can tend toward making healthy eating and exercise into something more rigidly disordered because of your drive to be perfect.

AT YOUR BEST

When you are at your best and in a state of relative balance, Virgo, you are like a busy little bee, happily buzzing around from one need to another and efficiently resolving them all. You definitely feel best being useful, and when this is reciprocated in a healthy way, you are content, go with the flow, and easy to be with. You are a natural parent, teaching your kids how to take care of themselves well and juggle life's many requirements efficiently.

Your need for healthy reciprocation is true whether it is in the context of a good relationship, where the other person is pulling their weight as well, or in a job, where you are valued, respected, and fairly compensated. (Not that you need to be overly wealthy; being so practical, you have a hard time indulging in anything too luxurious.) In healthy relationships, you can feel needed but still have time and space to figure out your own needs, separate from others, and you can allow others that space, as well. When you let yourself have and rely on a partner who is strong enough to contribute something to your life, too, you are calm, centered, and content.

RELATIONSHIP CHALLENGES

Your high competence level and perfectionistic tendencies can make you judgmental and critical of others. You can come off like a know-it-all. The irony is, especially if Virgo is your moon placement, you are actually filled with self-doubt, even though no one would believe it given how capable you are. You are truly your own worst critic. You can be utterly consumed by self-doubt and paralyzed by the constant swirl of self-deprecating thoughts in your head, especially when you are not feeling your best. You constantly feel like you are not good enough, that you haven't practiced or studied enough yet. You can tend toward being a workaholic, whether in your career or in the home, and this is mostly because you are constantly trying to stay ahead of your own critical mind. Either you work on others or your critical mind is directed inward and works on you, which you don't prefer.

Your biggest fear is not being good enough or not measuring up to your own or someone else's expectations of you. Though you never wear your emotions on your sleeve and highly value being reserved, in actuality you are hit harder by the experience of rejection than just about any other sign (other than your polar-opposite sign of Pisces). You will go out of your way to avoid it, preferring instead to play it safe, even if this means that your true self does not get to emerge. Rejection feels like it cuts to the core of your reason for being, and you instinctively think it is because you are not good enough. You feel so terrible that you want to tear yourself apart before anyone else has a chance to.

When you get triggered, your first instinct is to try to avoid or escape your emotional experience, as with all mutable signs (because they can move so easily). You are analytical and logical, even about your emotions, especially if Virgo is your moon placement. You avoid being overwhelmed by emotional material by compartmentalizing it, or putting it into a box in your mind, and thus mitigating its effect on you. Naturally contained and emotionally reserved, when you are upset you become especially cool and business-like. While you can be accused of being cold and unfeeling, the truth is that your feelings are strong but contained.

Like Gemini, at times you can seem unempathic because you can shore up and handle pain by such compartmentalizing. During an argument, it would not be unusual for you to get up and start cleaning or organizing something to help you cope with your overwhelming emotions. (Being earth, you busy yourself with routine, earth-based tasks; being mutable, you need to move around in order to process things.)

This avoidance can accumulate over the long term; you can avoid dealing with long-standing problems that need resolution, instead busying yourself with reality-based tasks and experiences to take your mind off of needed change and emotional issues that feel too overwhelming to contemplate (e.g., "I'll think about this after we get through the holidays").

Your mutability makes you tend toward codependent relationships; your competent nature makes you a magnet for those who are struggling. You think you can fix them, though of course you can't, and your sense of feeling overly responsible for them makes you understandably resentful. Part of what leads you into this pattern is that you don't know who you are separate from others; you have to confront your self-doubt if you want to find your own self in there.

HOW YOU GROW

While it may not look like it to you at first, you have much to learn from Pisces, your polar-opposite sign. Pisces scares and even repels you with its uncontained nature, but its water can benefit you by making you a softer, less rigid version of yourself. For one thing, you are not good at allowing yourself time to play and relax. When you are not sure who you are, space and time for yourself can be scary, and you can (not even consciously) avoid having it in the first place. Pisces knows the value of time to create and go inward, and it knows that is *how* to find yourself. For Virgo, this can take the form of something practical, like gardening or pottery to make functional objects. The point is, you could use an outlet like this.

Pisces can also help you get closer to your feelings, which is important given how much you tend to overthink things. This is another reason you can have a hard time finding yourself—your own wants and needs and drives—because much of the time, feelings such as sadness and anger are what provide the roadmap for us to figure those things out. You tend to be critical of your feelings ("I'm so emotional right now; I shouldn't be feeling this way") instead of allowing yourself to feel them. Getting more in touch with your feelings can help with your self-doubt and the paralysis that comes with it, because you will know better which way to go (or not) when life presents you with an opportunity for growth. Pisces sees the big picture, the forest, where Virgo tends to see the trees.

Finally, in addition to helping you with self-trust, Pisces can help soften you by teaching you about the importance of trusting others. Being so practical and competent, you easily attract broken birds who need fixing; because of this, you are one of those people who could, tragically, never allow yourself the luxury of a truly intimate and reciprocal romantic relationship. You can get so caught up in the details of your life, tending to others and ignoring your own needs and feelings—again, not even consciously—that you miss the big picture of what you could have if you grew enough to be able to find and trust a partner who is strong enough to have your back. The first step in that process is being more in touch with your feelings, because they provide the best roadmap you have.

LIBRA ♎

CARDINAL AIR

YOUR ESSENTIAL NATURE

Libra, your symbol is the scales, and you are concerned with justice, fairness, and balance. (Your sign ushers in the second half of the zodiac; these six signs are concerned with issues related to the collective.) Being cardinal, you are a leader and a ruler, and being an air sign, you are driven by principles and logic rather than emotions when making your decisions. Your role is to be the judge of the zodiac. You so abhor injustice that you take your responsibility, given your cardinality, especially seriously. You worry about any form of chaos emerging, and you try to ward it off if at all possible.

You have the deep conviction that whatever is soundly concluded in theory must govern in practice, and your job is to provide detached, objective analysis in order to arrive at the best course of action. You won't accept what anyone tells you without gathering your own proof first. You tend toward indecision, or at least slow decision-making, because you need to be able to see and carefully consider all sides of a situation. Think of the scales tipping back and forth.

You have a strong drive to keep in touch with the world and to keep your mind stimulated. However, you also have a deep need for peace, harmony, and balance in your home and work environment. You need to be surrounded by beautiful things and gentle sounds that make you feel calm inside. (You and Taurus have this in common because you are both ruled by the same planet, Venus.) Loving beauty, you tend to care a lot about your own looks and those of your partner and kids.

As the sign of the zodiac most associated with relationships, you naturally look to others to serve as a complement to yourself. (Given that air is the most mutable element, you are similar to the mutable signs in this way.) You need to feel connected to and at peace with your partner and those closest to you. This means that you will often use other people as your mirror, looking to see how they feel about you in order to know how to feel about yourself.

You hate discord of any kind and will serve as the peacemaker whenever possible. Even though you are concerned with the objective truth, you are also naturally people-pleasing and hate confrontation of any kind. In addition to the indecision that comes from trying to carefully discern the objective truth, you run into indecision when you realize that truth is likely to generate dissent in another person (which may then be directed at you). These are some of the fears that can lead you to have a difficult time putting theoretical ideas into practice.

AT YOUR BEST

When you are in a state of relative balance, Libra, you are diplomatic, determined, and never lose sight of your goals. You are charming, loving, and kind, and you can—and want to—see the good in everyone. You naturally build bridges between people, networking and connecting them with anything you intuit might help them solve their problems ("Here, read this book," or "Meet this person"). As a parent, you are naturally careful and gentle with your kids, teaching them how to see things objectively and not be too swayed by their fleeting emotions. You are known as "the iron fist in the velvet glove," yet strength and grace are two very important values after all.

While you always place high value on your relationships with other people and the way they see you, when you are in balance, you also have the willpower to stick to your own sound conclusions, even if someone important to you disagrees or is upset. You are connected to yourself as well as to others, and the deeper value you place on your relationship with yourself allows it to be a helpful guide in making decisions.

RELATIONSHIP CHALLENGES

Libra, your greatest fear is loneliness, and this is what you try to ward off through all your efforts to connect with others. Because of your aversion to chaos and confrontation, and the ultimate fear of being left by someone you love, you can be highly conflict-avoidant in your relationships, which then leads to a host of problems. You try to keep your emotions under the control of your mind in the hope that this will mitigate the difficulty of being in that dreaded place where you have to confront someone in order to find a compromise between your truth and theirs, but at times, you can end up just getting stuck in your own head and never making a move. You do anything you can to avoid being alone, because being alone makes you feel inadequate, and you hate to lose the mirror and validation that the other person provides—it's like your life blood.

Others can experience your need to control your environment as being rigid. In truth, as much as you love being in relationships with other people, you tend to enjoy the beginning of a romance—the idea of it, really—more than the later stages and real experience of it because you don't like to be emotionally fenced in by commitment, even if that means just having to do what someone else wants. Because you are focused on warding off chaos, you can tend toward rigidity in your eating, exercise, and neatness.

Your biggest defense when you get triggered is to dissociate—or fly away, as only air signs can—from anything that rattles your inner sense that things are in a state of peace and harmony. Because you don't like to see anything that goes against what you think should be the case, and because you can easily fly up in the air and lose sight of whatever is upsetting you, you have a tendency to be in denial about the unresolved issues in your life. In other words, because of your strong drive to preserve peace within yourself and in your relationships, you see what you want to see instead of seeing reality as it actually exists. This denial can take on a rigid quality, as well.

Like the four mutable signs and Cancer, you tend toward codependency in your relationships. You have a deep desire to be taken care of by others, and you often find other people to partner up with who are similarly afraid of being independent. You tend to ignore your own important needs for change and thus enable the other person to stay stuck in a state of non-growth, as well. Like the scales tipping back and forth, you can fixate on what others need to do when your own situation really needs your attention.

You have a difficult relationship to your anger, because it threatens to rustle the calm air. You try to avoid conflict at all costs, but this leads to passive-aggressiveness and resentment, which is often the glue of codependent relationships. Occasionally, despite your best efforts to control yourself and your anger, you blow your top in a way that is scary to others, as they are used to your naturally calm demeanor. When you get angry, you can be quite sarcastic and arrogant. At these moments, you fly right through the zone of balance in the middle of the zodiac wheel and act much like your polar-opposite sign of Aries when they are especially out of balance.

HOW YOU GROW

Your polar-opposite sign of Aries has some things to offer in terms of helping you achieve a greater degree of balance. Aries people are deeply connected to their own wants and needs in a visceral way, not caring anywhere near as much about what other people think. They are comfortable with conflict, and even prefer the need for change.

Libra, your journey of growth involves valuing and trusting yourself—including your deeper feelings, below the logical analysis—enough to have the courage to fully show up as yourself, even if it means walking into conflict. Aries's restlessness and desire for change provides the perfect antidote to your complacency. You need to dive below the cool, rational analysis to find your deeper desires and longings, and then you need to trust yourself enough to speak up and fight for those desires until they become a reality.

Opposite to Aries's fiery drive, which can leave others feeling singed, your emotional control can make you come off as chilly, distant, disingenuous, and aloof. You tend to keep people at arm's length because your dependence on them scares you, and because you worry about losing connection if they don't like something about you. They, in turn, can feel like they are not able to get close to the real you. Unfortunately, it is your charm, your not wanting to cause conflict, that can lead you to feel even more lonely. This is an example of your defense mechanisms working against you, protecting you but causing you to feel worse than you would if you weren't defending against pain in this way.

Contrary to your belief that others need to exist in a state of perfect harmony just as much as you do, healthier people would rather know what is really going on for you instead of coexisting in a state of feigned peace. Wanting to grow is human nature, and healthier people are grateful for the opportunity to look in the mirror you can provide for them (even if they may not fully realize it on a conscious level until later). When your own lack of growth in turn deprives others of the opportunity to do their part in the growth process, everyone suffers.

SCORPIO
FIXED WATER

YOUR ESSENTIAL NATURE

You have been called the most powerful sign in the zodiac, Scorpio. Being fixed, you are steady, reliable, determined, and independent; and being a water sign, you have strong, though restrained, emotions. The sign of Scorpio rules the underworld, the land of mystery, dreams, fantasies, and transformation. It also rules secrets, hidden meanings, and pretense, and you Scorpios have a wicked sense of intuition, especially for the secrets, hidden meanings, and pretenses of other people.

Yours is the kind of power that can influence others in ways that are not even part of their conscious awareness. You can seep in and really get under others' skin like no one else, for better and for worse. Your role is to transform others and their pain and disconnection from themselves with this quiet, hidden power, so it is synchronistic and funny that your description matches perfectly with the commercial jingle for the toy *Transformers*: "More than meets the eye." Your emotions are incredibly deep and intense, but it is your nature to be deeply internal and restrained; thus, you keep your active emotional life hidden from the rest of the world. In other words, your nature inherently contains a deep and intense need to maintain control.

There is a great metaphor to describe Scorpio: a duck, apparently calm and serene, glides along the surface of the water, but underneath, its feet are paddling furiously. You are a human paradox; internal conflict is the name of your game. You are slow and cautious but have a fast-moving current of intense emotions flowing deep inside you. Your survival instinct is strong and resilient, but you are also drawn to darker, more dangerous endeavors. (Alan Ball, creator of the HBO series *Six Feet Under*—an intense, darkly funny series about a family who runs a funeral business—has his moon in Scorpio.) Being a fixed sign, you like to stay in the same place, wanting constancy and stability, yet being ruled by the goddess of the underworld, you crave the edge, excitement, challenge, and mystery of the unknown.

Your intensity matches that of Aries in terms of how ambitious and driven you are; you will never allow anyone to get in your way. However, your power is much quieter than that of fiery Aries. You are known for being intensely sexual, similar to the sensuality of Taurus, your polar-opposite sign. Also similar to Taurus (which, like Scorpio, is fixed), you are slow, thorough, methodical, and hate being rushed. You can quickly assess someone's feelings and motives on meeting them. You never forget anything, which has both positive and negative sides: while you can retain a vast amount of knowledge, you can also be unforgiving, especially if you feel you have been treated unjustly. Whether centered on revenge or work, you are naturally exacting, and brilliant at anything that requires research or investigation. Loving power, you may also be drawn toward work in finance.

AT YOUR BEST

When you are at your best, Scorpio, you are deeply compelling and intense, yet you use your power for the benefit of others.

Your intuitive perceptions, when delivered carefully and allowed to seep in slowly, have the power to help others transform the deepest layers of their pain. When you are open enough to let your trustworthy others see your true feelings, you have the power to transform yourself, letting their perceptions and experience of you help you change and reshape yourself into a better version.

In your relationships, you are deeply loving, caring, and attuned to the feelings of those who matter to you. As a parent, you ideally work hard to give your kids space to develop their own unique personalities, trying not to smother them with your own intense power. You are more than happy to help your children as well as everyone else but only inasmuch as they are able to take over for themselves. You trust and respect them enough to let them have space to breathe freely and to grow in their relationship with you.

RELATIONSHIP CHALLENGES

If Scorpio is your moon placement, it is a challenging one, for you and the people you are closest to. Your biggest fear is true intimacy, being deeply vulnerable with another person, because letting yourself be fully seen feels like losing a struggle over power and control, even if it is only with yourself. When you feel activated—either positively or negatively—your instinct is to go inward because you feel safe to experience your strong emotions only when you are by yourself. This means that you require a lot of space in your relationships. However, you hold on tightly and don't like to give the other person a lot of space, particularly when you feel vulnerable; this is yet another one of your paradoxical tendencies.

If your emotional security feels threatened, you can become self-absorbed in a way that makes you jealous, obsessive, and possessive. You project onto the other person that they have the same need that you do to keep some part of themselves secret, and it can be hard for you to trust people.

Because you hate being vulnerable, you can put people in a position to have to read your mind when you have a need, which they experience as manipulative on your part. (Of course, it is manipulative because you are trying to get someone to do something but are being indirect in your approach.) Your deep internal conflict about being close to people can make being in a relationship with you feel like trying to stay on a bucking bronco. Being such a powerful—and power-hungry—sign, you can frequently get into power struggles in your relationships with others. You can be domineering and smothering, and this is something to be aware of particularly if you are a parent.

When you get triggered, which can happen when an interaction pushes you to your emotional edge, your first instinct is to retreat and go inward and underground. To the other person, you appear to have emotionally shut down or shut them out. As their anxiety leads them to keep pushing you to express yourself, you slowly boil under the surface until you lash out with an intensity that can only be matched by Aries. (Until Pluto was officially recognized as a planet in 1930, Mars ruled Scorpio as well as Aries, hence the unparalleled intensity of both signs.)

Your symbol is the scorpion, whose bites are known to be extremely painful, disorienting, and even deadly. You can become quite aggressive when you feel threatened, and since you are so intuitive, your knowledge of others' weak spots can make you a particularly hurtful and vicious opponent. However, your usual tendency, of course, is to bottle up your anger, forcing it downward so it can only seep into the underworld of your deep internal layers; your anger is so intense when it does come out because it has been festering for a while. As a water sign, you are like a deep alpine lake.

Being a water sign, you tend toward addiction to food and substances (especially alcohol), and as a Scorpio, you can overly rely on sex to change your mood. Your issues with food can manifest in two ways. As with all water signs, your emotional nature can be soothed by self-medicating with food, also known as emotional eating. Alternatively, and perhaps precisely because you know the intense power food has to soothe, you can channel your issues with power and control into your body, being obsessively rigid and exacting with it and thus developing an addiction to controlling your food intake. (Scorpios tend toward obsessive-compulsive disorder, or OCD, more than any other sign, and anorexia is like a form of OCD that is centered around food, eating, and weight.)

HOW YOU GROW

Scorpio, you could take a few lessons from your polar-opposite sign of Taurus, the sign that wears its emotions on its sleeve and whose motto is "What you see is what you get." Your biggest struggle is with shame, and this is the reason you have such a hard time being truly intimate. Your first instinct when you feel vulnerable is to go underground, and shame thrives in emotional secrecy the same way mold thrives in a moist environment. (Here is another fun synchronicity: Brené Brown, who has made her life's work studying and talking about vulnerability, shame, and true intimacy, has her sun in Scorpio. Here is a woman who has clearly made deep, intuitive contact with her life lessons and is trying to help others transform through her wisdom—the highest expression of Scorpio.)

In order to stop adding more shame to the amount that has already accumulated, you need to work to let your loved ones in when you are struggling. If you can let yourself be vulnerable with people who have proven to be trustworthy with your emotional safety, you can participate in your own transformation and healing by reducing your feelings of shame; you will also be helping to transform and heal your loved one, because it definitely hurts them deeply when you shut them out. You always require people to show effort before you let them into your heart, but when you can tell that they are working hard to get the entry code right, let that matter—in other words, do your part and work to emerge.

Finally, another lesson from Taurus (and a fundamental way earth balances water) is that you need to "shore up." Like all water signs, you can stew in your feelings, externalize responsibility for your own growth, and get stuck in victimhood. Because of the walls you build, Scorpio, you can have a tendency to become particularly bitter and isolated if you don't work to grow, especially if you also struggle with addiction. It goes against your natural defense mechanisms to come out of hiding, but as with all signs, your defenses start out being helpful and ultimately end up causing all your problems. Working to emerge will help to reduce the emotional turbulence that can be a part of your inner experience as well as your close relationships.

SAGITTARIUS
MUTABLE FIRE

YOUR ESSENTIAL NATURE

Sagittarius, your symbol is a centaur—half human and half horse—also known as the Archer, because he is drawing his bow and arrow. Sagittarius is also sometimes depicted as just the arrow. This is highly fitting, as you are the seeker and explorer of the zodiac, its most expansive sign. You shoot forward into new experiences and chart the territory so others can follow safely along and evolve, as well. Being a fire sign, you are naturally enthusiastic and motivating to others, and being mutable, you move swiftly through the world on your journey of mind, body, and spirit. High-minded and wise, you travel through the world in order to gain wisdom for the good of the whole. Your role is to help others grow and expand their horizons, to guide them so they can bravely move forward and never stop evolving.

Extroverted, confident, and sure of yourself, you see all the possibilities, even if you miss some of the limits. Loving travel and craving variety, you hate and fear being closed in or pinned down. You always need something to look forward to, and you are easily bored if you don't get enough stimulation from new experiences. You are constantly searching, never settling, never at peace. Because this nature is so restless, you can have a hard time sitting still, and you may have had attentional deficits and hyperactivity, especially as a younger person.

If you are a parent, you probably work outside the home at least part time, and this is especially beneficial for you if your job feels meaningful. The sign of Sagittarius rules philosophy and universities, so you have a broad thirst for knowledge and meaning as well as an interest in education and other high-minded pursuits. You love learning about other cultures and gleaning their wisdom so you can use it for your benefit and that of your family. Many Sagittariuses have traveled all over the world and often prefer to date culturally diverse people.

You are optimistic as can be, which, as with any trait possessed by any sign, is both a blessing and a curse. You are the sign of big ideas: your superpower is your exceptionally clear vision, even prophecy, in terms of being able to see to the heart of a problem— like an arrow hitting its mark—where others get lost in the smoke. Like many explorers and professors, your energy comes in bursts rather than a steady stream, and you (hopefully) rest in between.

AT YOUR BEST

When you are at your best and in a state of relative balance, Sagittarius, you are probably the most fun sign in the entire zodiac to be around. You are charming, charismatic, extroverted, and funny, but you are also quite wise and generous with your wisdom. Others feel like good fortune will befall them if they hang around you long enough. You are the life of every party and group in a way that feels truly magnetic. You organize complex thoughts and theories into systems that are meaningful and that lead others to wisdom. When something is important to you, you go after it like a horse, with great enthusiasm and tireless pursuit.

In your relationships, you need your personal freedom and independence, but you are also wise enough to know that you are best set up to go exploring only when you have a secure base at home. Your wisdom and clear vision are used for the good of others—including your own family unit—as well as for yourself. If you are a parent, you have a career or some part of your own separate life that feels meaningful. Your enthusiasm and optimism help those in your life (especially your children if you are a parent) to find the bravery to move out of their ruts and routines so that they never stop growing.

RELATIONSHIP CHALLENGES

Your greatest fear is being enclosed or having your freedom restricted. (The Sagittarius archer is half horse, so think of what would happen if you tried to put a wild horse in a stable.) This fear can be quite challenging in relationships with other people, since relationships by their very nature restrict certain aspects of our freedom. You are usually able to stay faithful as long as your partner gives you a lot of room to roam around and do your own thing. Paradoxically, as long as you perceive an open doorway, you don't actually want to exit; rather, it is the closed door, the encroachment on your freedom, that makes you want to bolt more than anything else—and bolt you will, if you want to. Containing you is about as easy as containing a brush fire in the wind.

One of the downsides to your optimism is that you can engage in irresponsible behavior, especially in the teens and twenties, or when you are out of balance, such as during times of extreme stress or crisis. You tend toward excess, impulsive escapism, overindulgence, and exaggeration in all its forms. Naturally impatient and a stimulation seeker, you can make impulsive spending decisions, but your desire to live the high life is more detached than Scorpio's is; yours is about having fun and meaningful experiences instead of acquiring possessions as status symbols.

As with all mutable signs, when you get triggered, you immediately avoid and deflect whatever you don't want to hear or see. Where Gemini will change the subject, Virgo will get busy, and Pisces will get dreamy and spaced out, Sagittarius will leave. You experience feeling sad or fearful as a restlessness and physical discomfort, and your urge is to literally flee the scene. If you can't leave, you have a wicked and explosive temper, like all the fire signs. You have a sharp and articulate tongue, and because you are highly skilled in seeing through the smoke to find your mark, like an arrow hitting the bullseye, you can be surprisingly hurtful and insensitive when you want to cut someone to the quick.

Fortunately, unlike Scorpio, you don't hold a grudge; one of the benefits of your optimism is that it helps you to look forward and move on after a conflict. You may find, however, that the other person does not share your optimism about the relationship or want to follow suit in moving on, either because the issue doesn't feel resolved for them or because they are not sure they want to continue the relationship at all. In this way, your defenses can lead you directly to your worst fear, when your freedom to spend time and energy with those you love most is restricted by the fact that they no longer want to spend time with you.

Also typical of the fire signs, you can tend toward narcissism. This can show up when you feel triggered in some way, such as when your freedom or ego are being threatened; in addition to having a temper, you can act superior and condescending. Like your polar opposite sign of Gemini, you are quick and clever, and you have the skill to be very efficient, but at times, you can focus too much on efficiency in a way that feels narcissistic.

You can also tend toward selfishness when you arrogantly take things over and push others out of your way, which is an unfortunate result of your innate resourcefulness. Finally, if you are a parent, your unpredictability (when extreme) can be narcissistic and hard for your kids to cope with. You can work tirelessly (like a horse), especially when you are uncomfortable, so you can also hurt those you love by not being around enough or having too little energy left over to spend quality time with them when you are home. All the wisdom you glean loses its impact if the close relationships in your life aren't connected enough for the others to truly absorb it.

HOW YOU GROW

Gemini is your polar opposite sign, and it possesses some wisdom of its own that can help bring you into a better state of balance. Being an air sign, Gemini can help you cool or turn down the flame of your fire in beneficial ways. You are both mutable, so there are certain traits that you have in common, but being different elements, you play your roles decidedly differently. Like you, Gemini gathers and communicates information, but it does so in a more detached and neutral way, with less investment in how it is used. As is typical of the fire signs, you have an ego, Sagittarius, and it can get in the way when you become too attached to the knowledge you try to instill in others.

Since you are so focused on finding meaning, you insert yourself into your conclusions more than neutral Gemini does; another way of saying this is that Gemini's neutrality gives it more tolerance. Your interpretation of the information you encounter naturally transmits your own beliefs and values along with it; in other words, rather than just neutrally delivering the information, you have definite opinions about which ideas are good and true. While there is absolutely nothing wrong with your nature—to the contrary, it is highly important—when you are too fiery, your job is to try to become more neutral and detached from the information and wisdom you are delivering.

Taking this lesson from Gemini, where you work to become more detached from your passionate feelings, can also help with cooling your anger during intense situations. Because Gemini is a mutable sign like you are, it can't do much to teach you how to stay put during conflict or discomfort, but at least it can help teach you how to chill out a little bit by adding a dose of its light, airy neutrality and detachment to your passionate, fiery nature. Try journaling, engaging in something creative, or going for a walk in order to calm down. As a mutable sign, you generally need to move in some way, but you also want to try to preserve your home base for when you are ready to reengage.

CAPRICORN
CARDINAL EARTH

YOUR ESSENTIAL NATURE

Capricorn, your nature is confusing. Your role is known as the father of the zodiac (polar opposite to mother Cancer), but being an earth sign, your nature is actually feminine. Your symbol is the goat, and while this goat is known to be able to climb the highest mountains, it has the tail of a fish and is actually a sea goat! The sea goat represents the evolution from the murky depths of the emotional sea to the practical, cautious skills needed to rise to the top of the earth world. In other words, while you are apparently restrained and down to earth, you intuitively understand the power of your emotions and draw on them as you climb. Think of Capricorn Martin Luther King Jr.'s "I Have a Dream" speech.

As an earth sign, you are practical, sensible, and dependable, and you have a deep appreciation for earthly pleasures like music, physical beauty, and comfort. Being cardinal, you feel a strong sense of responsibility to caretake others in your way by helping them use whatever is at their disposal to build their own structures and scale their own mountains. Like a wise parent with enough foresight to teach their kids how to be successful adults in the world, you see the potential in everyone and want those in your care to be well prepared for their own future endeavors.

As the zodiac's most goal-oriented sign, you are driven, determined, hardworking, and organized; you have a natural talent for calculating the best route to a destination and then methodically executing your plan. Nothing is ever enough, because there is always more to improve. You see life as serious business, and being an earth sign, you are focused on concrete manifestation. You place high value on integrity, reputation, and the respect of your peers. You have the maturity to set boundaries and delay gratification in order to achieve your goals.

There is a saying that if you want to make sure something gets done, give it to a Capricorn. You are comfortable with, and good at, playing roles, but true happiness comes from traveling your own path. Known as a wise elder, you have a sense of responsibility that is usually apparent from the time you are a young child. You are described as old for your age and have older friends throughout your life. You build relationships slowly and cautiously, but once someone matters to you, you will hold on to them for years.

As tenacious and competent as you are, you are also deeply emotional and vulnerable, even shy (which usually comes off as seriousness). Being the sea goat, you are full of hidden sensitivity, which means that people don't often see your true nature. I once read a description of Capricorns as unfathomable! Your inside and outside experiences don't match up well, much like the sea goat's top and bottom halves. (As a Capricorn myself, I am always surprised by how much the people in my life don't realize how much I struggle. We don't show it because of our reserved nature but also because we think we can fix it ourselves.)

Another paradox in your nature is that your seriousness is combined with a dry, witty, off-beat humor; people who are on your same wavelength find you quite funny, and you like being around humorous people, as well. You have learned to see the humor in even the hardest of circumstances, and you often rely on it to lighten the heaviness and darkness that is inherent in your nature. It is your main conscious defense mechanism.

AT YOUR BEST

When you are at your best, Capricorn, you are highly ambitious and determined, but like your polar opposite sign of Cancer, you are also deeply connected to those you love most, because you don't feel balanced unless those you care about are materially and emotionally content. You are loyal and caring, and you teach your loved ones about integrity, honesty, strength of character, and the importance of tradition by living those values in a way they can emulate.

You are a naturally gentle parent, and you treat your kids with dignity as you work to prepare them for their adult lives. You build and value your own career, as well, and having the natural ability to motivate and discipline yourself, you often enjoy running your own business. You can be described as a grounding force, such as when Capricorn Michelle Obama called herself a steady trunk for her family, or when photographer Charles Peterson called Capricorn Dave Grohl, the structure-providing drummer for Nirvana, an anchor for the band. (Both of these are synchronicities.)

RELATIONSHIP CHALLENGES

Your deep need for both material and emotional security leads to your natural state as an anxiety-ridden worrier (and warrior), wary of the unknown, waiting for the other shoe to drop. Since this state is compounded by your nearly obsessive sense of responsibility, you can be a workaholic. This is very hard for you as well as your loved ones, because you know when you are not giving them enough time and attention. You are ruled by Saturn, and being under Saturn's watchful eye means that you are highly aware of the mistakes you make and the times when you let people down.

Your worst fear can be described as fear of failure, but to put a finer point on it, you most hate and fear the feeling of powerlessness that accompanies failure. Your absolute darkest place is when you need to function well and have hope for those who depend on you but feel powerless to get there. Given how much you value your career and reputation, feeling as though you are failing at work is hard enough, but this is all the more horrible if you are a parent or a therapist because of the deep nature of your responsibility.

As a side effect of feeling like you have to keep your nose to the grindstone, you can become a bossy, critical, and sometimes even cruel taskmaster. Your workaholism leads you into a downward spiral of pessimism and negativity as you become more out of balance, and over time you can become increasingly harsh, hopeless, and cynical. Your pain is compounded by your sense of responsibility; it is one thing to fail, but it is another thing to feel like you are failing others to whom you have a duty. Small failures add up and seem to you like significant diminishments of your reputation, skill, and reliability.

This sense of powerlessness can lead you toward an angry expression of what is actually depression (as opposed to the more classic depression of Pisces, where they can't get out of bed), which is fueled by your natural tendency to go it alone. You don't easily reach out to people or ask anyone for help, especially when you feel your worst and most vulnerable, in part because you think you can fix it yourself. Instead of reaching out to anyone, you isolate and alienate yourself, and your hope of ever feeling better dwindles even further.

Being naturally restrained, you try to control your inner emotional experience of anger and sadness. As you work to keep yourself contained, you become increasingly rigid and intolerant. As triple-Capricorn (sun, moon, and rising) astrologer Jessica Lanyadoo puts it, "Capricorn has a funny way of turning water into ice ... and turning vulnerability into a job." Eventually, something triggers you enough that you break—especially common themes are feeling disempowered or embarrassed—and your primary defense is to be highly reactionary and dominating. Your anger can be so intense that it scares others; indeed, if you are regressed enough, you can be overpoweringly destructive. This only makes you feel worse because you judge yourself so harshly, and the cycle continues. Over time, if you don't figure out how to recover and find hope again, you become cold, hardened, and emotionally shut down, and your fears of powerlessness and failure become self-fulfilling prophecies.

HOW YOU GROW

Your opposite sign is Cancer, and just like the case when there are two parents in a household, you are better for incorporating some of the lessons learned from your other half. Cancer is the water to your earth, and it is especially essential when you have hardened up to the point that you have started to petrify. Cancer can soften you by helping you make contact with the sadness that accompanies your feelings of failure and powerlessness. Being in touch with your sad feelings when you are already depressed might not sound like much, but balancing out some of your anger and rigidity would help immensely, since those expressions are swollen with the sadness you do not allow yourself to be in touch with.

Another softening influence of Cancer is to encourage you to let yourself approach, need, and depend on other people more. While the goat is known as a solitary climber who naturally spends time alone, you don't always need to do it that way; it is lonely at the top of that mountain! Cancer values love and emotional purpose, and you could use some of this balancing influence, especially when you are struggling. Quality time and connection with those who love and understand you best are the only things that can help restore your hope; consistently shutting them out is harmful to your well-being. Being all alone with your dark, heavy pain is like sitting in a room full of carbon monoxide with a towel shoved into the crack under the door.

When you do spend time alone at home, let Cancer help make you softer and more compassionate with yourself. Slow down, take downtime, get cozy, take a bath, have a cup of tea to soothe yourself. There is a saying that solitude is the cure for loneliness; it is like taking a different approach to the whole endeavor so that you can become a softer version of yourself. Being with you in your sadness is easier for others than being with you in your anger; anger is a less vulnerable, more rigid emotion that keeps people out. You already know the power of humor in maintaining hope and optimism; the element of water and finding your softer, more vulnerable feelings of sadness and powerlessness can help balance your tendency to rigidly, though inadvertently, keep hope from making its way back into your heart.

AQUARIUS
FIXED AIR

YOUR ESSENTIAL NATURE

Aquarius, your symbol is the water bearer, so it is easy to get confused and think you are a water sign, but you are actually made of the air element. True to form for fixed signs, you are loyal, stubborn, hate feeling controlled, and have a strong inner sense of yourself. As an air sign, you have an excellent logical and philosophical mind; you crave intellectual stimulation and need your freedom like it is, well, air.

You are highly original, one of a kind—and that is exactly how you like it. You have an independent streak a mile wide and prefer to march to your own off-beat drum, sometimes going left just to not go right like everyone else. It is worth noting that Aquarius is ruled by Uranus, the only planet that is tilted almost 90 degrees relative to the plane of the solar system so that it "rolls" along almost on its equator, which is very different from how most of the other planets orbit the sun. You are a pace setter, innovative and imaginative, with a vast storage of wisdom and knowledge—and because you are a fixed sign, you have the follow-through to put your great ideas into practice.

You are a true humanitarian, hating corruption, exploitation, and taking advantage of the powerless in all its forms. You have high standards of integrity and honesty, naturally reflecting on history and the lessons of our predecessors to point us in the right direction of evolution, and your idealistic, universally inclusive way of seeing the world is a benefit to us all. Your role is to be our teacher, but you are also a student, learning as much as possible and synthesizing the information in clever new ways. Your quirky humor and way of seeing the world bring a much-needed dose of originality to any analysis, and even though you are a fixed sign, your airy nature and detached perspective give you the latitude to see multiple vantage points at the same time.

You are cool and emotionally reserved, friendly but not overly expressive. You are extremely observant, especially in social situations. You have a tendency to withdraw into your own mind, so you tend to be on the quieter side (unless you have a more extroverted rising sign). Like all air signs, your emotional detachment can make getting close to you difficult; in other words, you prefer to keep others—and your own emotions—at a slight distance. You discuss your feelings more than you feel them, placing high value on having control over your emotions at all times. You prefer an equal partnership in your relationships, and if necessary, you can wait a long time for the right person to come along before you settle down.

AT YOUR BEST

At your best, Aquarius, you have the freedom and independence to think in your own original ways, yet you also have deeper connections with others because you are able to be more vulnerable with them. You are kind, compassionate, and thoughtful with those closest to you and with the world in general. You are a helpful partner and parent and teach your loved ones (and the rest of us) how to rise above difficulties and maintain hope and compassion as you stoically lead by example.

If you are a parent, you are naturally good at parenting because of your sensitivity to the needs of children, especially when it comes to encouraging their autonomy and independence. The people you live with are grateful for the ingenious ways you find to fix things and solve practical problems (partly due to your fixed persistence on finding a solution).

RELATIONSHIP CHALLENGES

Because you keep to yourself so much, especially in terms of your deepest vulnerabilities, your worst fear is that no one will ever care enough or have the patience to dig you out from inside yourself. You fear no one will want to know who you *really* are badly enough to keep trying to help you emerge in your own way and time. Obviously, this poses some relational challenges, in addition to the others that come with your (or any) nature. You have a hard time letting people in emotionally or letting them deeply matter to you, because you place such high value on your independence and self-sufficiency, and also because you feel "above" others on some level (that you are an air sign is not coincidental). That is hard for the other person, who consequently feels they are not important to you.

My Aquarius clients—and Aquarius husband—have made me work very hard to draw them out because they don't like to be vulnerable, but the fact that they have attached themselves to me and keep working just as hard as I do to get through their resistance is a testament to the fact that something in them wants to be drawn out. This leads me to believe that you, also, deeply want to be drawn out. Assuming people really want to know you just feels too vulnerable and foolish, so you force those of us who are trying to know you to be patient as we straddle the line between drawing you out and making you feel controlled. You use your intellect and wit to deflect efforts to get closer to you. No wonder Aquarius ends up being known well by only a couple of other people.

Your resistance to relying on others is typically quite fixed; you think the people in your life should take you as you are, and this lack of adaptability leads to a pattern where the other person thinks you are not truly interested in maintaining the relationship. They may also lose interest themselves because they feel controlled, manipulated, and resentful, or the relationship feels empty to them because you are not fully participating. Basically, your need to not feel controlled in the relationship becomes, in its own way, controlling of the parameters of the relationship—and of course, the other person will come to resent this.

Your primary defense when you get triggered, which usually happens because you feel someone is trying to oppress you in some way, is to block the other person's efforts from reaching you. You disappear in that dissociative way only air signs (and Pisces) can, and like Scorpio, you go underground and withdraw into yourself. You have a hard time with emotional pain, your own and that of others. Polar opposite to fiery Leo, you become cold, distant, and unfeeling when you feel threatened. Any slight flame of passionate emotion that did exist in you, you turn down even lower. You do have the same tendency as Leo to act superior and judgmental when you feel threatened, however. You want to be back in control of the situation, and fear you will be engulfed if you give up any independence or cede to your emotions.

Over time, because your airy nature will avoid conflict and contact with your deeper emotions if possible, your relationships can quietly disintegrate into emotional disconnection and withdrawal, so that the relationship exists more in theory than in real life and you are in it without really being in it. You can end up being much kinder to and feeling more connection with strangers than the other person in the relationship, especially if you have become more detached from the other person over time. You can even become highly disconnected from your own true self; always observing the group, you can confuse social expectations with your own feelings and natural reactions.

The biggest challenge of your nature is that you can tend toward loneliness and isolation, even if you are theoretically connected to other people (and especially if you are not), which unfortunately feeds right into your worst fear of never having another person make space for the real, original you.

HOW YOU GROW

Leo is your polar-opposite sign, and while there are certain faults you share (both being fixed), Leo's fiery nature has much to offer to bring more balance into your life. For one thing, you could use a dose of Leo's passion. People know when a Leo is interested in them, but because you have a tendency to be aloof, people think you are not really interested, and they follow your lead and back away. In psychological terms, you project your own discomfort with being seen (or wanting to be) onto others, making them feel uncomfortable for wanting you to see them. Like Scorpio, you need to work on emerging earlier than feels comfortable to you. You are scared to change or let the other person in because you feel like you would not fully be you anymore if you do; the truth is that we are all supposed to be changed by our relationships with others—or what is the point of having them?

The heat Leo brings to relationships has other benefits for you, as well, including when it comes to anger. (As with all air-fire polarities, if relationships are like kernels of popcorn, air alone can't make them grow into their fullest expression; they need heat, as well!) Leos may tend toward blowing up, but Aquarius, your passive-aggressiveness isn't any better; it is still anger, and it still damages the relationship unless you deal with it constructively. Your typical ways of being passive-aggressive are to become even more blocking of the other person's efforts to get close to you, which can look like increasing emotional or physical detachment, or tuning out the other person's needs or deeper feelings, which is easy for you to do as the fixed air sign of the zodiac.

Fortunately, if you are committed to growing, your stubbornness can be an asset, as it is with my clients who persistently work through their own stubborn resistance for years. Watching someone fight themselves as much as an Aquarius can in long-term therapy is a lesson in contradictory forces. They force themselves to stay committed, and then fight to not be too vulnerable the whole time they are there. The great thing is that over time, Aquarius, you can definitely grow if you want to, and one path toward that end involves challenging and allowing yourself to feel more of your own heated feelings (as well as the heat of other people), such as anger and passion.

PISCES
MUTABLE WATER

YOUR ESSENTIAL NATURE

Pisces, your symbol is the twin fish, making you a dual sign. Being mutable, you focus on the needs of other people, go with the flow, and can process experiences on multiple levels at once. As a water sign, you are sensitive, live in a feeling-based world, and have a kind and soft heart. You are the oldest sign of the zodiac and have the potential to be our greatest healer. Being psychic and able to deeply sense the connectedness between all things, you can, not even consciously, plumb the depths and layers of the collective unconscious like no other sign; your role is to help others transcend and dissolve the boundaries that keep us all disconnected from one another. Pisces Ruth Bader Ginsburg provides a powerful example of someone playing this role.

You are deeply intuitive, even mystical, and you process emotions in part through your vivid dreams and imagination. If you are familiar with the Indian system of chakras (centers of spiritual power in the human body), you can think of Pisces as the sign with the most open seventh chakra (at the top of the head), the one most receptive to information from the spiritual world. You seek to find deeper meaning in a spiritual sense, and want to help others find it, as well.

Your receptivity makes you extremely creative. Being highly sensitive to both beauty and pain in all their forms, you take in information in your intuitive, emotional way and transform and synthesize it into music, poetry, creative writing, and visual and performance art. Your creative output represents your innate attempt to unify others on a feeling level, opening their hearts as they appreciate your contributions (especially when they do so along with other like-minded souls). Because you sense the interconnectedness of all things, you see yourself in everyone and can find anyone's pain inside of yourself; this imbues you with a passion to help the underdog. You are like the color black, which contains a bit of all the other colors. A quote from the Roman playwright Terence captures Pisces beautifully: "I am human; nothing human is alien to me."

Being a dual sign, you can go in two different directions. Your powerful imagination and ability to create is both your greatest gift and biggest curse, depending on which direction you channel it. (The fact that the dual signs are mutable is no coincidence, given that they can easily change.) You have the potential to be the oldest, wisest soul, a true visionary who unifies others with your compassionate ways if you can shore up and pull yourself together—or you can be an uncontained puddle of water, steeping in your pain like a helpless child lost at sea.

Because you are so highly imaginative, the inner and outer worlds blur for you, and you can't easily distinguish one from the other to discern subjective reality from objective reality. This also applies to the boundaries between you and other people, as your extreme sensitivity can make you soak up the moods and desires of others and not even realize they are not your own, like a radio tuning in to multiple frequencies. On a deep, spiritual level, your nature possesses an urge to merge.

AT YOUR BEST

If Scorpio has the power to transform others, Pisces, when you are in balance and at your best, you have the power to truly heal others. Your creative output and loving influence deeply acquaints others with and helps them dissolve all the limiting beliefs and blocks that need to be released or surrendered in themselves. Even your behavior in daily life seeks to unite those around you, as you are known to treat everyone with an abundance of kindness, gentleness, and compassion.

Your nature makes you deeply unable to tolerate injustice. You are especially loving toward children and animals, and you make a great parent because you are able to play with your kids; what is more, your romantic and idealistic view of the world encourages them to enjoy escaping into their imaginations through a love of reading and fantasy. (Fred Rogers of *Mister Rogers' Neighborhood* was a double-Pisces [sun and moon]. This example of synchronicity will be discussed more in the next chapter.)

RELATIONSHIP CHALLENGES

Pisces, your active imagination can get you into trouble in a myriad of ways. You can be dreamy and spaced out, especially during conflicts, and you tend to lie or exaggerate, or both, because of the blur between subjective and objective reality. Worse than that, you can be manipulative even when you don't consciously mean to be because you intuitively understand the soft spots of others and thus how to best get your own needs met in surreptitious and indirect ways. You may sense this power in yourself and even find it scary at times.

You can feel and imagine so much that you easily access the furthest edges of your multiple fears, and this makes you vulnerable, confused, and insecure in your relationships. You can be a constant worrier, not just about things related to your relationship (similar to Cancer) but also about the state of the world. As a child, you may have had characteristics that would currently be labeled as sensory integration issues because, like a sponge or an emotional Swiffer, you constantly absorb everything that is swirling around and can easily become overstimulated. Your worst fear is losing yourself completely, and as usual, you correctly intuit that there is a risk of this outcome.

Love relationships are hard for you because while you deeply enjoy and crave them, you are also intuitively aware of—and scared by—your own intense needs for love and emotional sustenance. You deeply believe in and long for unconditional love, which can lead you into codependent relationships. Your need to merge with the other person frequently takes the form of either caretaking or being taken care of in inappropriate ways. For example, you could become an enabler of an addict or an addict yourself. You can easily become a martyr or victim, making countless self-sacrifices in the futile attempt to find lasting contentment in a merged state with another person. You have a tendency to be taken advantage of, and your passive-aggressiveness piles up such that it is mostly self-destructive (although it can at times be externally focused—remember, many serial killers are Pisces!).

When you get triggered, which usually happens when you feel rejected or criticized, your primary defense is to dissociate from the pain because you become so emotionally overwhelmed. Inside, you feel like you are disintegrating into a puddle and losing yourself completely, or at least losing the container that holds you together. When providing a therapeutic container for my Piscean clients, at times I become a little anxious about my ability to contain all the material swirling around from their vivid dreams and imaginations; when I mentioned this to one of them, she astutely remarked, "Welcome to what it's like to be me."

To escape pain, you tend toward addiction and retreat into hazy denial. This tendency is compounded by the daily anxiety and overstimulation you experience, which you attempt to cope with by numbing your sensitivity. You also tend toward depression for multiple reasons. If you struggle with substance use, you are more likely to be depressed, and if you are stuck in a cycle of overwhelming anxiety for long enough, it naturally leads to hopelessness about being able to combat it and an urge to withdraw and give up.

Your idealistic nature often sets you up for disappointment, and your natural urge to withdraw and isolate in response can become a downward spiral of alienation from others. Finally, you tend toward depression because your tendency to give yourself over to others and lose yourself in their expectations of you means you can't tell your true self from your false self. In the worst case, your deepest fear of losing yourself completely becomes a reality, with your own defenses having led you straight into that abyss.

HOW YOU GROW

Pisces, you can become more balanced by incorporating some of the traits of your polar-opposite sign, earth-based Virgo. Virgo teaches you how to compartmentalize and shore up by having structure and boundaries and by focusing on facts, practicality, and organization. You need to live more in reality, Pisces—you can deny, distort, or refuse to face reality more than any other sign, even to the point of being delusional—and focus on what you can see and touch instead of focusing only on your emotional inner world, which can help you become more balanced in your responses to life's challenges. I know a number of people who have their sun sign in Pisces but their moon in Virgo (or vice versa), and while this combination leads to an internal conflict in their nature, it also makes them more down-to-earth and effective.

Like your polar-opposite sign of Virgo, you are highly sensitive to criticism and rejection, but unlike Virgo, the pain you feel causes you to withdraw because, deep down, you feel like a misunderstood outcast or misfit. (This, by the way, is why Pisces can become violent; as an outcast, you can feel as though society's rules and expectations don't apply to you.) Again, living in concrete reality can help you here. Focusing so much on the inner world of your fears can cause you to make something out of nothing, create needless drama, and become self-absorbed. You need to get out of your own way—Pisces is the sign of self-sabotage—and highly competent Virgo can help you with this.

Finally, in the vein of staying grounded in concrete reality (because earth has more staying power than water), you need to work on holding on to yourself and your own needs in your relationships instead of constantly trying to intuit who the other person wants you to be. You need to feel more entitled to air your grievances with the other person; typically, there is far too much passive-aggressiveness and not enough directness in your communication when you are angry because you are too worried about upsetting the other person. Your fear of being cut off from the other, while part of your nature, mustn't cut you off from yourself completely.

Growth, Development, and the Challenge of Saturn Return

As you can see, the zodiac wheel is naturally organized around the theme of growth and evolution of the soul. The first three signs of the zodiac represent the early expressions of each quality and element, symbolizing a time in our development when our intentions are good but our expressions could use balancing. As we mature, we naturally develop the ability to keep others in mind as we move through the world, and we take responsibility for caring for those in our inner circle. Eventually, we develop the capacity to look further out as we care for others in the world, keeping the good of the collective whole in mind as a matter of course.

To gain an even better understanding of the nature of each sign, think about the season or time of year during which the signs emerge. For example, if your sun is in Aries, you were born in the springtime; think about the energy it takes for a seed to shoot up and burst out of the ground, like the little shoots of grass in early spring, and you will have a good feel for Aries people. Scorpio, which encompasses Halloween, begins the transition into colder months when we need to burrow down under the layers to stay warm and safe, a behavior characteristic of Scorpio. The goal-setting and high-achieving sign of Capricorn contains the New Year, a time of making resolutions to work toward achieving our goals in the upcoming year, and so on.

Remember that every sign of the zodiac—including the older ones—has a range of functions associated with it, so they all have an equal tendency to be out of balance and unhealthy in their expression. It is typical for young and old signs to be paired together in our charts because that way we have a better chance of being able to grow.

The next chapter is about a particular planetary transit called *Saturn Return*. Saturn Return is such an important time in our lives—it occurs twice for most of us, and three times for those who live long enough—that it is important to know something about it. There are many important planetary transits in astrology, and their impact can certainly be felt in our lives, but none of them get our attention more than a Saturn Return.

CHAPTER 6

Saturn Return—Your Moving Walkway for Growth

Saturn brings to mind the two ancient Greek maxims,
inscribed at the Temple at Delphi: "Know Thyself"
and "Nothing in Excess."
—Elizabeth Spring

Crises are never easy, but most of us can attest to the fact that they usually lead to important shifts in our lives. They have a way of focusing us on the things we need to see but have probably been ignoring. A crisis draws out the growth-impeding factors of your life from down below, pulling them up to the surface like a magnet pulls all of the metal particles within its magnetic field. When Saturn completes an entire twenty-nine-and-a-half-year orbit and returns to the exact place it was in the sky when you were born, a crisis of identity known as your *Saturn Return* occurs. While nobody would describe it as easy or pleasant, a Saturn Return comprises some of the most critical experiences in your journey of individuation.

It can be torturous to see your dysfunctional patterns more clearly than usual, especially when they are attached to valued relationships, including the one you have with yourself. A Saturn

Return is a crisis of identity because it impacts your sense of who you are, or more accurately, who you have known yourself to be. Saturn Returns are times of challenge, reevaluation, change, and often, tumult. But just as petrified wood has fossilized and become stronger, your Saturn Return demands that you root down and find your center so that you can draw on everything deep inside of you that can make you more resilient and able to weather life's future challenges.

Planetary Transits

Planetary transits are the movements of the planets across the sky, and are part of the complex web of important information that astrology has to offer. Although I am not going address much on transits because of their complexity, this small section will be helpful for you to better understand Saturn Returns.

In its transit across the sky, Saturn moves slowly through each sign of the zodiac, averaging almost two and a half years in each sign and passing through all twelve signs over the course of almost thirty years. This means that you will have your first Saturn Return in your late twenties and early thirties; your second, roughly thirty years later, in your late fifties and early sixties; and your third (if you live that long), about thirty years after that, in your late eighties and early nineties. Your Saturn Returns are *natal*, meaning Saturn returns to the place it was when you were born. There are other aspects to transits, such as when a planet is in direct opposition to the place it was when you were born; one of these is your Uranus opposition, for example. The impact of the Saturn Return comes from the qualities and traits of the particular sign Saturn occupies in your birth chart as well as the house it is in; this is true for all of the transits and is where astrology becomes increasingly complicated.

Saturn Return is just one transit; there are several other difficult transits, as well. The first Saturn Return kicks off a series of challenging transits that occur between the late twenties and the mid-forties, and their effects overlap each other. For example, Pluto is *square* to your natal Pluto (where Pluto was where you were born) when you are around thirty-six to forty-two. Recall from chapter 4 that squares indicate tension, so without having any idea about what areas of your life Pluto rules, you know enough to know that a Pluto square isn't easy. The same is true for your Neptune square, which occurs when you are around forty, and is followed by your Uranus opposition (when Uranus's place in the sky is directly opposite your natal Uranus) around ages forty to forty-two. This series of transits is bookended by Saturn, with a Saturn opposition when you are around forty-two to forty-four.

No wonder this time period is notoriously full of growth, especially for those who are willing to take on the challenges and adapt accordingly. The time from your mid-twenties through your mid-forties encompasses not only the huge identity crisis of your first Saturn Return but also the notorious midlife crisis that so many, from Carl Jung to Brené Brown, have written about. (If you are around that age, I highly recommend reading Brown's blog entry called "The Midlife Unraveling." Visit www.brenebrown.com/articles/2018/05/24/the-midlife-unraveling.) This time, when you are not old but not young anymore, is filled with restless rumblings that are difficult or even impossible to contain but are crucial for your development.

Astrologers use transits to predict what certain times in our lives will be like and is an area where we can observe how well psychology and astrology line up with each other. Astrological and psychological events occurring at the same time provide us with examples of synchronicity, or meaningful coincidence, because having two of these events line up in a random fashion seems highly unlikely. For example, long before there were psychologists, astrologers were predicting that the time period from twenty-seven to thirty would be especially challenging—and psychologists have confirmed that this is true. These synchronicities, such as when the description of a sign correctly predicts the behavior or psychology of a person, are how we come to trust in the validity of astrology.

Most sources declare that the first Saturn Return lasts from twenty-seven to thirty, but all astrological events have a shadow period that encompasses the time leading up to the event and the time after it subsides. (Please note that the following applies to the second and third Saturn Returns as well, though their peak ages are fifty-seven to sixty and eighty-seven to ninety, respectively.) Different from Jung's shadow, which contains your unconscious material, the astrological shadow period in this context means that the effects of the transit tend to gradually increase during the time leading up to its peak, and then gradually subside during the time shortly after.

Think of your first Saturn Return as an earthquake, where the first rumblings begin late in the twenty-sixth year, especially if you are psychologically sensitive and self-aware. The peak of the earthquake occurs when you are around twenty-nine and a half years old. As a psychologist who has seen many clients during their first Saturn Return, I can confirm that the aftershocks are felt throughout the first year or two of our thirties, as we work to rebuild more solid structures and assimilate the lessons of our Saturn Return into our lives.

Saturn Returns as Concentrated Individuation Cycles

Saturn Return has had central importance in my work as a therapist because people often go to therapy during their first or second Saturn Returns, which is why I want to highlight that particular transit here. (This is similar to my giving you the *Cliff's Notes* version of your chart by pointing you to your sun, moon, and rising signs.) Saturn Returns provide critical periods during your journey of individuation, much like language and other learning is acquired most readily when you are young, during a critical period of your development. During Saturn Returns, you are especially porous to the effects of your choices and actions.

Because they usually happen at least twice in a lifetime, you can think of Saturn Returns as cycles, or rounds, during your lifelong individuation process. Though the content will vary based on your stage of life (some specific themes are discussed later), there are connective threads and themes across Saturn Return cycles, both as a collective and over the course of our individual lives. I often ask clients in their second Saturn Return specifically about what was going on in their lives during their first, to help us get a better idea of their lessons this time around. The earlier themes usually reemerge in different (and some of the same) ways, much like a recurring dream in which some of the details have changed.

Across cycles, the way in which your Saturn Return unfolds will depend on how well you have done at negotiating the developmental tasks of the previous thirty years. Anything you didn't learn well enough in your first cycle will come back around in later cycles for you to work on again. As a psychologist, I honestly don't think we ever fully work through anything. Rather, in the best-case scenario, we continue to chip away at the same few life challenges and make as much progress as we can each time they come back around. For example, if your first Saturn Return involved having children and trying to integrate becoming a parent into your identity, your second might involve your transition to being less centrally involved in your kids' lives as they work on their own journeys of individuation with their own families. In both cases, the issues involve making space for the new aspects of your identity to emerge, which is much harder than it sounds because you may be terrified to let go of the old one. However, it is in these new spaces that we grow, evolve, and individuate.

Saturn—Capricorn's Ruling Planet

In astrology, all the signs are said to be ruled by a particular planet, and each sign's ruling planet exerts more influence over it than the other planets. In other words, it is the ruling planet's influence and symbols that imbue each sign with its particular personality traits. Some astrologers believe that the dynamic between the planets and signs is better described by the concept of *domiciles*, in that planets make their homes in certain signs.

Saturn rules, or makes its home in, Capricorn. This means that the traits Saturn helps you strengthen are the same ones that

Capricorn people help you strengthen (because Capricorns feel the effects and demands of Saturn more than anyone else, and can't help but teach you these same lessons). I tell you this for two reasons. First, in addition to how much it has affected my life as a psychologist seeing clients, Saturn has also had an especially large impact on me personally, so it is no random coincidence that I address Saturn Return here. Not only is Capricorn both my sun and rising sign, but I also have multiple other planets in Capricorn, as well. My birth chart thus makes me intimately acquainted with Saturn's lessons and demands, all of which—growth, responsibility, discipline, and the limitations of reality and time, for example—are issues that are prominent during a Saturn Return.

Second, I mention the fact that Saturn rules Capricorn because thinking about the traits of Capricorn and what that sign teaches is helpful when learning about Saturn Return. Capricorn is focused on the structure of your life, like the frame of a house. It wants you to make sure you aren't building important experiences atop a house of cards but rather a solid foundation. Capricorn people, and Saturn's influence, focus you on your goals. They emphasize taking responsibility for your life and having integrity in your relationships with yourself and other people. Capricorns see life as serious business, so it is no coincidence that in your Saturn Return, you are forced to get down to business, as the saying goes.

Similar to what depression (which Capricorns are prone to) can do, Saturn helps you by holding up a mirror for your pain so that you may ultimately experience a fuller expression of yourself and your life. Both Saturn and Capricorn are known for helping you shed the self-defeating behavior that blocks your path. Capricorn is an earth sign, and like the bones of a house, there is not much bending that can happen before the structure breaks. Earth is not known for its flexibility. The problem is that when unstable things flat-out break, as often happens during a Saturn Return, the consequences can be enormous.

Commit to Evolution and Growth or Be Sorry

Saturn represents our struggle with time, the limitations of real life, maturity, and lessons often learned the hard way. For many years, astrologers talked about Saturn in exceptionally harsh terms; it wasn't until Liz Greene wrote the influential book *Saturn: A New Look at an Old Devil* that perceptions of Saturn changed to become more balanced. In it, she writes, "Saturn symbolizes a psychic process, natural to all human beings, by which an individual may utilize the experiences of pain, restriction, and discipline as a means for greater consciousness and fulfillment."

Saturn is known to be a harsh teacher at times but is also seen as a helpful force to guide you onto your right path of individuation if you are willing to work toward evolution and growth. The further off track you veer, the more harshly Saturn will remind you to stay conscious and be your true self. It turns up the pressure to the point that it becomes harder to avoid the obstacles on your path than it is to just face them. The obstacles become like unavoidable boulders that you can't get around anymore. There is much to be gained if you can delay gratification and have the maturity to resist the limitations you feel are being imposed on your freedom.

For example, if you become a parent during your first Saturn Return, you will be challenged to mature enough to subordinate your own needs for those of your child much of the time (especially early on, until the child naturally starts to become more independent). If you can rise to this occasion, you will do much important work on your own path of individuation during this time, and you will also launch your own child well, giving them a solid foundation on which to begin to travel their own path of growth.

As a mirror, Saturn shows you your fears and inadequacies. It helps you grow beyond your limitations by demanding that you have discipline, focus, and a willingness to see things as they are in earth-based reality. The process begins with the subtle but restless rumblings of a sense that something feels amiss or unsettled in your life. This is much like the way in which symptoms of an illness develop over time to let you know something is wrong with your body. Is this relationship or this job serving your growth? Are you truly happy with where things are, or did you think you would feel better than you actually do at this stage of your life? Is your need to belong blinding you to your true nature?

Saturn Return is like an audit or the black light detectives use: it illuminates whatever problems or cracks in your structure were there already. Almost always, it requires that you make some major adjustments in your relationships, attitudes, and lifestyle choices. Whatever is soundly built can survive the next thirty-year cycle, but modifications will undoubtedly be necessary to ensure this outcome. (While the topic is too complex to explore here, if you happen to be in your Saturn Return, you can look up which sign Saturn occupies in your birth chart as well as which house it was in when you were born in order to learn more about how your Saturn Returns will impact you and which area of your life will be most impacted—or you can consult a professional astrologer!)

During a Saturn Return, you might find yourself reflecting on your own true needs and desires more and experience a stronger push for fulfillment in your life. It is a time to think long and hard about your own individual destiny and the role you want to play in the world. Even if your external life is apparently in order, your internal structures will feel the strain of the audit. You may feel lonely and alienated from people and roles to which you previously felt connected, but this turning inward is necessary in order to find yourself on a deeply foundational level. You can only hear the whispers of your true self when you retreat from the distractions of the outside world. This is an example of how astrology and your free will powerfully interact with each other; you will go through your Saturn Returns, but how you do so is up to you.

You may feel resolved and ambitious one minute, and scared and insecure the next. Your own need for greater fulfillment scares you because you know that it can be the impetus for overthrowing aspects of your existing life. If you are being deeply honest with yourself, Saturn gives you an opportunity to course-correct and get more aligned with your true path. During Saturn Return, you may feel like you are on a moving walkway, for better or for worse. Whatever you choose will have strong consequences, either in the direction of setting you up with a solid foundation for the next thirty years or leading you to build your future on an unstable structure (and potentially shortening that future). Saturn is known for rewarding you when you grow and ruining you when you don't.

Your Saturn Return offers you a chance to sharpen your natural talents as well as the opportunity to heal your inherited wounds and temper your faults. Like the help offered by Capricorn people, your Saturn Return enables you to be well prepared for the future. It demands that you let go of your illusions and defenses and take responsibility for your actions. Your Saturn Return brings you face-to-face with the needed wisdom that your defenses may protect you, but they inevitably end up limiting you, and you will undoubtedly need to hone them so they do less needless damage to your life.

Concrete Manifestations of Saturn Return

Saturn Return is a time of endings and beginnings, or more specifically, endings leading to new beginnings, even if the new beginnings are just improved or reborn versions of previously existing structures. Saturn Return reminds me of a tarot card called the Tower. (If you are unfamiliar, tarot cards originated in fifteenth-century Europe and have been used to tell the future or read the energy surrounding a situation.) The Tower card symbolizes the prediction that disruption will occur but will bring enlightenment in its wake. The card indicates a restructuring that involves discarding inappropriate defenses, just like Saturn Return. In both cases, confusion lasts until the liberating reorientation becomes solid.

A Saturn Return shakes you to your core, and just like when a giant tree is deeply shaken, everything that is not attached well enough will be shaken loose and fall to the ground. A Saturn Return shakes loose everything that is not authentically you or relevant to your path. (Maybe this is part of why Saturn Return makes me think of the Tower tarot card; the picture on that card depicts people falling from a burning tower.) It is a time of pruning your life, just as deadheading, or removing dead flowers from plants, promotes future growth. Ultimately, your true path is more clearly revealed without the old, outdated debris cluttering up your vision.

During Saturn Returns, you will tend to experience many of your major life events. These include getting married or divorced, having kids, or losing a parent. One of my clients, who was adopted, reached out to her birth parents during her first Saturn Return. My husband moved across the country during his. Relationships begun during a Saturn Return tend to have a fated or karmic quality to them. It is a time of reckoning, focusing you on what you want—or are here— to accomplish in the material world.

Basically, your actions of earlier days bear their fruit during your Saturn Returns. Your career may take off; I finished school and started my private practice during mine. If you have been building steadily toward a goal that is right for you, it can be a time of great reward and achievement. Or, if you have been living a life disconnected from your true nature, this is the time that everything can come crumbling down around you. As I write this, a lawsuit against the Church of Scientology has recently been filed that alleges kidnapping, abuse, and human trafficking. Their membership is dwindling, and they seem to be in a full-fledged crisis and on the verge of unraveling. David Miscavige, the Church's leader, is fifty-nine; Tom Cruise, its most famous member, is fifty-seven. (Much of the time, when people make the news, it is during one of their Saturn Returns; if you start paying attention, you may notice this yourself.)

Not to be morbid, but another major life event that can more readily occur during Saturn Return is death. The "27 Club" is a list of famous people who all died at the age of twenty-seven, during their first Saturn Return. For example, Jimi Hendrix, Janis Joplin, Jim Morrison, Kurt Cobain, and Amy Winehouse are all on the list.

Many more die during other years of their first Saturn Return, as well (Heath Ledger, for instance, was twenty-eight).

Every one of these people was living their lives in ways that weren't sustainable enough to take them through the next thirty years, and each of them likely had multiple warning signs and opportunities to course-correct that they didn't heed. This is even more evident by the time someone gets to their second Saturn Return in their late fifties, when the health of their physical body tells the tale of all of their earlier choices in ways that may not be reversible.

Our lives are so intertwined with our parents' lives that people are often born during the first Saturn Return of one or both of their parents, since they came as part of their parents' first round of Saturn lessons. It is also not uncommon to lose a parent to death during the parent's second Saturn Return, which may happen while they themselves are still in their first, because this loss is part of their first Saturn Return. Now, because of this change (either having a child or losing a parent, or both), the person must learn to better stand on their own two feet and take responsibility for their life.

You must grow in maturity and effectiveness in order to build the strong structures that will sustain you and your family into the future. If you lose your parent during your first Saturn Return, for example, you will be called on to find your own deep sense of what is important in your life and how you want to travel your own path, because you will no longer have direct access to the guidance of someone you likely turned to in the past.

Themes of the First Saturn Return

During your first Saturn Return, you are on the threshold of true, mature adulthood, from both an astrological and a psychological perspective. Ideally, you have made it through the compliance of youth and the rebellion of adolescence so that you are on a path of finding your own true self. You are at the beginning of your productive adult years, with a provisional sense of self that is subject to additional modifications based on the tests of the next thirty years.

The influence of a Saturn Return compels you to figure out what *you* want, not what your parents, partner, peers, or colleagues want. (Recall from chapter 2 the discussion about the true self/false self distinction and that depression is a common outcome when we are disconnected from our true selves; no wonder depression is also a frequent experience that accompanies Saturn Return.) You need to be strong and mature enough to set appropriate boundaries with people, including your parents; this is especially true if they themselves lacked the maturity to do a good-enough job of letting you go. You also need to let your parents go on some level, in the sense that you need to let them be separate enough to let you down, just like you ask them to do with you. You need to give each other enough space in the relationship by not expecting things that are not part of reality. This journey of becoming more separate from your parents is an important part of your path of individuation.

Your Saturn Return requires that you live in reality and take stock of your life with clear vision. You are given the opportunity to come out of denial about your circumstances. For example, anyone who has a substance abuse problem will likely face consequences during a Saturn Return. You are also challenged to find a realistic perspective on life as opposed to an overly cynical one, because just like denial, this kind of armor may protect you in the short term but limits your future growth.

Your Saturn Return requires a painful severing of roles and relationships that were based on old, unconscious conditioning so that you can have more conscious, sovereign choice over your life. You are given the opportunity to bring yourself into present time, as Lauren Skye likes to say. Saturn Return requires a grieving, then, of the old roles and relationships that wane during this period in our lives. Ideally, you will engage in this grieving process instead of retreating from it in fear, denial, stubbornness, or arrogance about its existence. For example, if you lose a parent during your first Saturn Return, you will need to do the difficult work of acknowledging that you are now officially in the driver's seat of your own life (or need to be). If you get married, you will have to work on being in a relationship in a more mature way, staying committed and learning how to productively manage conflict because leaving isn't as easy an option as it once was.

Keep in mind that your Saturn Return isn't something to be feared but rather viewed as an important vehicle for your growth. As long as you use it as a time to try to find your true self and path, you will be a better version of yourself for having made your way through it.

Doubling Down on Earlier Commitments During Second (and Third) Returns

If you heed the demands of your first Saturn Return and realign yourself with your path to a good-enough degree, your second Saturn Return will be easier, though it will still involve more pruning of your life. The basic question is, does the structure you built during and after your first Saturn Return allow you to grow and move freely enough to express your whole self and continue to individuate? Again, anything that doesn't pass the test must either be severed or changed so that it can pass. There is a now-or-never quality to the second Saturn Return that wasn't there during the first. Self-awareness becomes increasingly important as we get older as the path in front of us gets shorter.

Self-awareness is also more important as we age because we serve as models for the younger generations. If you navigate your second Saturn Return well and take care of all of your old business, you will gain the wisdom and status of an elder. It is not unusual for people to become grandparents during their second Saturn Return (because of the familial links described earlier) and have a second chance to experience the beauty of being part of the early days of the life of someone they love.

Similarly, one of the themes of the second Saturn Return involves increased separation—or your struggles with it—from your own children if you are a parent. This happens in parallel to your children's journey as they travel further down their paths and take on more of their own commitments. The second Saturn Return also brings up retirement issues, facilitating a different kind of identity crisis than the first. After having a job for your whole adult life, figuring out who you are now that that role is ending requires a great deal of readjustment.

If you turn away from growth during your second Saturn Return, you will only become increasingly dissatisfied and depressed in your later years; earthy Saturn is stubborn like that. If you can't find, love, and accept who you truly are underneath all of your roles and achievements, you will continue to diverge from the path you would have been on had you been more accepting of your true nature. If you continue to face the challenges your Saturn Return presents to you, you will evolve to reach a place of greater spiritual connectedness by the time of your third Saturn Return, to take with you into the last years of your life.

Saturn Return Synchronicities

The following is an interesting example of synchronicity involving Saturn Return. Psychiatrist and author Kay Redfield Jamison, a brilliant and highly intuitive woman who deals with manic depression (also known as bipolar disorder), had an experience during her first Saturn Return when she literally saw Saturn's rings during her first manic episode. Granted, she was in a psychotic state, which involves the blurring of boundaries between internal and external reality; but I think psychosis often results from the psyche being too porous, or too open, to psychic impressions to survive in objective reality. Having access to information or stimuli that others can't see or hear is especially isolating.

In a chapter from her book *An Unquiet Mind* called "Missing Saturn," Jamison recalls her first manic episode, shortly after turning twenty-eight. She describes gliding and flying through space and across fields of ice crystals, sweeping past the rings of Saturn. Based on the fact that Jamison made no mention of astrology in her book, I believe that she had no knowledge she was in her Saturn Return when she had this experience, which means that her description of that experience is a synchronicity.

We discussed in chapter 4 that people with lots of water in their birth chart are more prone to mood disorders due to their increased sensitivity to others' moods and experiences. They pick up all kinds of things that they don't even realize aren't theirs. They have blurry boundaries between their self and other people, and between internal and external reality. Pisces, in particular, is the sign most porous and prone to losing itself because of this blur.

Jamison was born on June 22, 1946; her sun sign is Cancer (water), and her moon sign is on the cusp of Pisces (water) and Aries (fire). (I would need her birth time to know for sure which side of the cusp the moon was in, as the moon changed signs on her birthdate.) My sense is that her incredible intuition, combined with the blurry boundaries inherent in any psychotic experience, enabled her psyche to sense that Saturn was "closer" than usual, in an astrological and psychic sense, at that particular time in her life.

Another interesting synchronicity involving Jamison is that she has the same birthday as one of my dearest girlfriends since childhood, a woman who has also dealt with bipolar disorder. Though they were born in different years and thus have different moon signs, my girlfriend's moon sign is also a water sign: Scorpio. Like Jamison, she also had interesting though terrifying experiences of synchronicity when she was psychotic, though I won't expand on them here.

Jung had a dream during the middle of his first Saturn Return. In it, a giant appeared to bring a large ocean liner to shore. The giant slayed the little horse that had been unsuccessfully trying to pull the ship before the giant appeared. Jung's daughter, an astrologer herself, was sure that this giant Jung saw in his dream represented Saturn.

Speaking of synchronicities, if anything in this chapter resonates or rings true for you in your experience of Saturn Return, that is a synchronicity in itself. The next chapter expands on this notion by explicitly describing how to draw out these synchronicities in your own astrological life. Doing this can help you learn more about your lessons in this life while simultaneously validating astrology for yourself in the process.

PART III
Using Psychstrology for Personal Growth and Relationships

CHAPTER 7

Synchronicity and Resonance—
Seeing the Patterns in Your Life

The most beautiful truth—as history has shown a thousand times—is no use at all unless it has become the innermost experience and possession of the individual.

—Carl Jung

Jung popularized the term *synchronicity*, and he used the phrase "synchronicity on a grand scale" to describe astrology. He used the word to refer to the deeply meaningful and amazing coincidences that astrology reflects back to us, derived in large part from our own remarkably intuitive though largely unconscious selves. If you are open to looking into it, astrology's mirror will reveal your own true self back to you, greatly enriching your life, but to access the room that contains that mirror, you have to walk through the doorway of your own intuition and imagination. This is the only way you will see the synchronicities when they present themselves to you.

Resonance

Resonance is an internal reaction that occurs when something has special meaning or particular importance for us. You will know you are experiencing a synchronicity when you feel some sort of resonance with a particular idea, such as when you are reading a description of one of the signs or about Saturn Return. Does the idea fit for you in a deep way? Does it make your body tingle, or does it blow your mind? Or, if it is a particularly intense moment of synchronicity, does it make you tear up, like it does for me?

When I looked up Jung's birth chart again in a moment of desperate questioning about whether or not I should write this book in the first place (within a few days of having the dream of Jung handing me the baton in a relay race), and I remembered that his sun, moon, and rising signs were the exact same three as my husband's (though in a different configuration), I burst into tears. There was no typical emotion associated with this event—or at least not one that seemed personal to me at that moment. It wasn't sadness or happiness, just a bunch of tears, but I knew what it meant: the synchronicity showed me that writing this book was the next right step on my path of individuation.

In a less extreme form, resonance might inspire you to think, *I'm not totally sure, but something in me tells me that what I'm reading might not be wrong or that there might be something to this. For now, I'm not deciding anything, but I'm bookmarking this thought or feeling for later.* As a jigsaw puzzle person, I think of that interesting piece you occasionally come across, where something about the piece stands out and you set it to the side. Even if you don't know exactly where it fits when you first see it, you know it will end up being important later, so you set it aside for when that time comes.

Why Synchronicity Is Important to Recognize

Recognizing the synchronicities in your life is what helps you know you are on the right path. Synchronicities are like the stepping stones you follow as you make your way through the brush. They can be significant when you are deciding whether something is right for you to incorporate into your life or self-concept. Sometimes seeing a synchronicity can even help you make a decision that has significant real-world consequences for you, as it did for me when I decided to take on the challenge and opportunity of writing this book. The dream in which Jung handed me the baton was the first stepping stone, and remembering that his three major signs matched my husband's was the second. Eventually, the stones line up to reveal an entire path.

Seeing the synchronicities in your life is also calming because it makes you feel—or lets you know, depending on your perspective— that someone, somewhere, is paying attention to what is going on for you. The power of the almost unbelievable connections we encounter when we pay attention to astrology, with all the meaning and significance that those connections bring, are often the only thing that will get us to see ourselves clearly enough to be able to change (or accept change).

Synchronicities Are All Around You

Pattern recognition is how we make sense of things. It helps us in many ways, including when we are trying to figure out what we are doing wrong so we can remedy it. We will address how to use psychstrology for that kind of pattern recognition in the next two chapters. For now, you may still be trying to decide whether you can trust the validity of astrology. In this case, seeing the patterns and synchronicities will help you see that you can trust astrology. It is like learning to trust a person: do they bring your awareness to interesting truths, or are they full of nonsense? Ideally, you will see some of these amazing synchronicities for yourself, because that would help you see that astrology is not nonsense.

Perhaps you have been looking for validation of something you have been trying to deeply understand in your own life. I have been collecting this information for years; my mind has always reminded me to wonder about the sun-moon combination giving rise to whatever I was seeing, hearing, or reading. The birth dates of public figures are usually quite easy to find online, including, in many cases, their birth times and places (so their rising sign is known, as well). I think some part of my psyche has been trying to prove this case for a long time—first to myself, and now to you.

EXAMPLES OF SYNCHRONICITY

Whenever someone unintentionally expresses some aspect of their astrological nature, it is an example of synchronicity. Sometimes this happens when people speak about their own nature, though it also happens when someone's nature is described perfectly by another person; examples of this second type are given later in the chapter.

Many people intuitively know their own true nature. Recently, I was perusing one of the *Us Weekly* magazines I keep in the waiting room at my office. In the February 25, 2019 issue, Michelle Williams, who is a double-Virgo (sun and moon), said, "I'm just not a techy person . . . I guess I don't relate to it, which probably makes me irrelevant." Earth signs such as Virgo tend to not be drawn to technology because they (we; I am triple-earth) don't trust or want to engage with it the way they trust things that exist in the material world. Another synchronicity is that Williams's best friend, Busy Phillips, is a double-Cancer (sun and moon), which is a water sign. Earth and water are known to balance each other out in important ways, so it is no wonder these two are such close friends.

As is often the case with synchronicity, talking about one example, or stepping stone, often leads to another. Speaking of the balance between earth and water, here is another synchronicity involving psychology and astrology: People with a lot of water signs in their chart tend toward mood disorders, one of which is bipolar disorder, or manic depression. One of the most important aspects of treatment for bipolar disorder involves establishing structure in order to promote stable routines and consistent self-care, especially around sleep and hygiene—and structure is the hallmark quality that earth brings to water. Additionally, external structure is known to be helpful to develop internal, emotional self-regulation strategies such as deep breathing and taking a break when upset. The fact that structure is known to help with emotional overload in the worlds of both astrology and psychology is a synchronicity.

Let's return to the synchronicities that can be seen when people speak to their own nature. In music, the expression of the artist's nature is less conscious and instead more felt (including in their lyrics); in other words, they don't consciously intend to express their nature as much as they just naturally do so. My favorite musical artists show me synchronicities all the time because I know their signs. Usually these come via their lyrics, but not always.

For example, when Kurt Cobain designed the cover of Nirvana's album *Nevermind*, he depicted a baby submerged in water eyeing a dollar bill on a fish hook. Cobain was a Pisces, the symbol for which is the twin fish. It is highly doubtful that he was thinking about this aspect of his nature when he chose the cover, so this is an example of synchronicity.

Here is another example, outside the realm of music: Psychologist Doreen Virtue created a deck of oracle cards, and one of the cards is titled "Steady Progress." This card is represented by St. Therese of Lisieux, who, it turns out, was born on January 2, 1873 with the sun in Capricorn. I am sure Virtue didn't know that St. Therese of Lisieux was a Capricorn when she chose her to represent the card of steady progress, but the fact that she did is a synchronicity because, of the twelve signs of the zodiac, Capricorn is the sign that best embodies that description of a nature. (It only added to the degree of synchronicity that I am also a Capricorn, and I was thus especially heartened after looking up St. Therese of Lisieux. I drew the card when I was feeling discouraged about getting this book written, and the additional synchronicity with my own sign helped me feel like I had guidance to keep moving forward with steady progress.)

A Little Math

Understanding a little probability, the chance of something specific happening, helps to understand why synchronicities are so valuable. The chance, or probability, that any two people would have the same sign in the same position is 1 in 12, or 8.3 percent. The chance that any two people would have the same sun and moon signs is 1 in 12 x 1 in 12, or 1 in 144. This translates to 0.69 percent, far below the recommended 5 percent benchmark used to deem something statistically significant in clinical psychology. In other words, there is less than a 1 percent probability that two people will have the same sun and moon combination due to chance.

That said, consider the highly unlikely but very close friendship between Ruth Bader Ginsburg and Antonin Scalia. Justices on the nation's highest court for many years, they couldn't have been more opposed on every issue they were deciding. However, they took international trips together, bonded over their love of opera, and had dinner together every New Year's Eve. People were understandably puzzled by their bond, but I uncovered something very interesting: they both were born with the sun in Pisces and the moon in Scorpio. Again, there is a less than 1 percent probability (0.69 percent, or just over two-thirds of one percent, to be exact) that two people would have the same sun and moon combination due to chance. If there were absolutely nothing to astrology, this is a pretty amazing coincidence, wouldn't you say?

Here is another one: Megan Mullally, who plays Karen Walker on *Will and Grace*, has been married to actor Nick Offerman for nearly twenty years. Nick was born on the exact same day—in the same state, no less—as Sean Hayes, who plays Jack McFarland, Karen's best friend on the show (and a close friend in real life). These men are linked together by their love for and by Mullally. They both have the sun in Cancer and the moon in Aries. Again, there is less than 1 percent likelihood that this fact is due to random chance.

A Tale of Two Fish

I realize that I might be the first person in history to compare Fred Rogers of *Mister Rogers' Neighborhood* fame with Kurt Cobain, the front man for the band *Nirvana*, who committed suicide in 1994. However, both of these men were born with the sun in Pisces, and they both had water moon signs and earth rising signs, so there was more than a small amount of similarity between them. In addition, though they lived and died in different and even opposite ways, they were both Pisces, the sign of the twin fish, which means that they could have gone in one of two directions. They were easily overcome by the human influences that surrounded them, as if they were always swimming in a sort of current. Because Pisces is a dual sign, it is known to be moved by paradoxical, contradictory currents, so it is no wonder that Rogers and Cobain ended up in different rivers.

Rogers was actually a double-Pisces (sun and moon), so he embodied the traits of Pisces in an especially synchronistic way. He was incredibly sensitive and had every imaginable disease as a child. He loved children and animals, and was especially fond of swimming for exercise. He was spiritual, musical (an accomplished pianist who described music as his first language), and thrived in a world of imagination and make-believe. He struggled with the chronic issues of self-trust and self-doubt typical of Pisces; Daniel, one of the puppets he voiced that symbolized his innermost self, once said, "I'm worried I'm a fake."

In true keeping with the healing spirit of Pisces, Rogers used what he experienced as a child to help other children heal their own wounds. "Children have very deep feelings," he said, "just the way parents do." In quotes quite typical of Pisces, he said, "Love is at the root of everything: all learning, all parenting, all relation-ships; love, or the lack of it." He also observed that "love is what keeps us together and afloat." (Note the synchronistic nature of this comment about living in water.)

Cobain was typical of Pisces in many ways, as well, though his moon sign was in the fellow water sign of Cancer, not Pisces like

Rogers's moon sign was. In his book *Serving the Servant: Remembering Kurt Cobain*, Danny Goldberg, Cobain's manager and close friend, writes that "Kurt sometimes came across as a bemused wise man from outer space." He describes Cobain as a "vulnerable victim of physical pain or social rejection. . . . He could be paranoid one minute and preternaturally self-confident the next." These descriptions are highly typical of Pisces.

Goldberg describes Cobain as a "sensitive outsider" and at times "a despairing man-child for whom life often seemed meaningless." Pisces is known to search deeply for meaning in life and to battle depression as a side effect of that trait. Goldberg describes Cobain as "the servant of a muse that only he could see and hear but whose energy he transmuted into a language that millions could identify with." Anyone who tried to describe exactly how it is that a musician with a strong Pisces influence works their magic might have looked for these exact words.

As is typical of Pisces, both Rogers and Cobain strongly identified with being outcasts and wanted to help others who felt like outcasts to feel less alone in their pain. Because Pisces can deeply sense the interconnectedness of all things, both men had a strong focus on inclusivity—typical of the sign that, like the color black, is made up of a little bit of all the other signs and contains them inside itself. Rogers and Cobain showed this focus on inclusivity in different ways, but both of them were adamant about taking a stand against the injustices they saw playing out around them.

In 1969, when black people weren't allowed to share swimming pools with white people, Rogers made a strong statement by inviting his African-American friend Officer Clemmons to share Rogers's swimming pool, and the two soaked their feet together while making sure the camera showcased the moment. Cobain was known for fighting hard for feminist ideals, and he also had a strong public commitment to supporting gay rights. He and the rest of Nirvana performed at a benefit concert to help successfully defeat an Oregon ballot initiative that would have been absolutely atrocious for the rights of gay people in that state.

The biggest similarity between Rogers and Cobain, though, was in their uncanny ability to touch the deepest parts of those who felt connected to them. In *Won't You Be My Neighbor?*, a documentary about Rogers's life, the closing credits involve Rogers asking people to think about someone who made a big difference in their life. As they are listening to Rogers's prompts and thinking about their own most special relationship experiences, every single one of them is teary. Rogers just had that softening, barrier-melting, healing effect on everyone he touched.

Similarly, Goldberg describes Cobain as an artist with the rare gift of helping listeners get in touch with their deepest feelings. He writes about "the misty look I see in people's eyes" when they talk about the effect Cobain had on them. "He made many of his fans feel that there was a force in the universe that accepted them. They felt that they actually knew him and that, somehow, he knew them." Not surprisingly, I am one of those people who can still get emotional when talking about my love for Nirvana and my sadness at the tragic loss of the young Cobain. (I also often get emotional when I see or hear Rogers's messages, as well; again, Pisces just has that effect.) In a lyric in *No Apologies* that is typical of Pisces, Cobain sings, "All in all is all we are."

Both men struggled with addictive tendencies as they figured out how to cope with their strong feelings. Rogers, an overweight child who was cruelly called "Fat Freddie," clearly understood food's power to soothe pain. In his adult life, he maintained an especially rigid control over his weight, swimming a mile and weighing himself every single day, even requiring that the weight stay at the exact same number of 143. Cobain, on the other hand, officially lost his battle with heroin addiction when he committed suicide. Two different men who, with all their pain, went the two different directions so typical of Pisces.

What made their outcomes so different is impossible to know for sure, but my clinical sense is that were it not for heroin, Cobain would have had a better chance of surviving the painful currents of his life. His Cancer moon made him prone to somaticizing (channeling his psychological pain into his body so it manifested in physical symptoms) and stomach problems, which made him susceptible to numbing his pain in order to cope; in the music industry, avoiding drugs is often harder to do than using them. I think Cobain's Virgo rising, which is highly perfectionistic and sensitive to rejection in its own right (besides the double dose of sensitivity from his Pisces sun and Cancer moon), didn't help one bit, either. At least Rogers had Taurus as his rising sign, a more protective earth-based rising sign than Virgo.

Here is one last strange synchronicity I encountered between these two Pisces men: each of them had a man in his life who turned out to be especially important to him and his path, and in both cases, the relationship with this other person was highly synchronistic from an astrological perspective.

For Rogers, the relationship, though brief, was a highly influential one, with a United States senator named John Pastore. Then-president Richard Nixon wanted to cut the proposed funding for PBS, the channel that aired *Mister Rogers' Neighborhood* and a number of other educational programs, from $20 million to $10 million. Pastore chaired a 1969 hearing during which Rogers argued for the full $20 million. Rogers spoke about the need for the social and emotional education that public television provided. "If we in public television can only make it clear that feelings are mentionable, and manageable, we will have done a great service," he said. Typical of Pisces, you could see the deep emotion and tears behind his eyes as he spoke at the hearing, but his Taurus rising acted like a reliable outer crust to keep him contained. It is no wonder that this is exactly what he taught children how to do: to feel but to learn how to contain their strong emotions.

Here is the astrological synchronicity: Pastore, who deeply connected with Rogers's words and awarded him the full $20 million on the spot, was born three days before Rogers, making him a Pisces, as well. Furthermore, Pastore's moon sign was Taurus, the same sign as Rogers's rising sign, so not only did these two men have a connection via their Pisces sun signs, but they also shared a relationship through the Taurus they both possessed. Though these men didn't know the astrological components of their brief, highly synchronistic meeting, they were there nonetheless, powerfully operating in the background.

In Cobain's life, the highly influential and astrologically synchronistic relationship was with Goldberg. Goldberg's sun is in Cancer, like Cobain's moon, and his moon is in Pisces, like Cobain's sun. These two men not only had an ability to understand each other on multiple and extremely deep levels, but given that both Pisces and Cancer are highly psychic and intuitive signs, Goldberg's account that they could often communicate without words is not surprising. He writes, "We had an almost immediate click into a shared attitude, and although Kurt would later articulate a lot of his thinking in interviews, in private a lot was conveyed to me by half-completed sentences, eye rolls, grimaces, or smiles." Not only was their relationship highly synchronistic, but so are many of the ways in which Goldberg describes it and Cobain himself. (The two moon signs Goldberg and Cobain shared are also shared by Jimmy Page and Robert Plant of Led Zeppelin; there is an incredible ability to communicate psychically that comes with this combination.)

It is worth noting one last synchronicity involving Cobain. Eddie Vedder, the front man for the band Pearl Jam, was someone with whom Cobain was notoriously and uncharacteristically competitive. Though the two mended fences before Cobain's death, Pearl Jam was Nirvana's "commercial equal, and they were also politically aware, committed to the same kind of countercultural ethos, and equally well liked in Seattle's indie community," according to Goldberg. Cobain and Vedder both had trauma in their family history and stood for similar things in their lives and music. One main difference between them, however, is that Vedder is double-earth to Cobain's double-water, with his sun in Capricorn and moon in Virgo (Cobain's rising sign).

In fact, Cobain's sun sign of Pisces is polar opposite to Vedder's moon sign of Virgo, and his moon sign of Cancer is polar opposite to Vedder's sun sign of Capricorn, so while both of these men are made up of feminine earth and water signs, they actually represent, on multiple levels, the polar opposite versions of each other. Vedder definitely seems to have the more robust and hearty makeup of someone with his sun and moon in earth signs; though he is still highly sensitive and in touch with his pain, he didn't struggle with staying shored up and upright the way Cobain did. These two men thus personify their different, though somewhat similar, natures.

Seeking Out the Patterns in Your Life

Pattern recognition is how we make sense of things. Right now, you may be trying to decide whether or not you can trust astrology. You may be trying to get a sense of whether you can lean into it, turn to it in times of trouble, and take its advice seriously, and whether it is reliable enough to stand the test of time and repeated consultation.

Here are some questions that might be helpful in your evaluation: In the descriptions of the signs, does astrology get it right often enough to convince you that it could be valid and have an internal cohesion to it? When you look up the signs of people in your life, do you see patterns that are too coincidental to be random? If you used it, did seeing yourself, a partner, or a child through the lens of astrology work? Did it help you? Did the other person feel more seen and understood?

Ernest Hemingway said, "The best way to find out if you can trust somebody is to trust them." Give yourself some time to evaluate the merits of astrology. All of our healthy skepticism comes from a desire to not feel foolish for having trusted someone or something without enough proof. As I said to my skeptical Gemini dad, at some point, when you have observed enough meaningful coincidences to convince a reasonable person, you start to become the fool you are trying not to be if you can't acknowledge that astrology might have some validity. (He agreed that there was logic to this argument.)

My Personal Synchronicities

Seeing the synchronicities in my own life is one of the biggest ways I have come to trust the validity of astrology. Seeing the patterns is absolutely mind-blowing. When you look up your parents and siblings, your past and current romantic partners, your friends, and even the people who have driven you nuts the most, amazingly, you will see that some of the same signs keep showing up in similar roles in your life.

I hope that you will at least look up the sun and moon signs of your immediate family members if not some members of your extended family. (To look up friends and family members, see the moon sign table in appendix A. You can also look up your chart for free on many sites, including my personal favorite, www.cafeastrology.com.) You will likely see some of the same signs repeat themselves again and again, which may seem incredible. *That* is astrology.

Now I want to share with you some synchronicities in my life. I have categorized them so you can better see how they relate to my life.

FAMILY AND FRIENDS

One of the signs that shows up all over my life is Leo. It is my dad's moon sign, so the fact that it has made such a mark, or imprint, on my life makes perfect sense. My dad's mom, my grandmother, had a Leo sun, and I felt very close to her, as well. My grandmother could communicate well with my dad because they both spoke Leo. (Seeing signs in common within a family, such as between parents and kids, is not unusual; it gives them a common language. This is discussed further in chapter 9.)

My dad also has a parent-child connection with both of my brothers, also via Leo; it is the moon sign of one of them and the sun sign of the other. Not surprisingly, my husband has a Leo moon, and my first husband had a Leo sun. It is a sign I understand well and am obviously drawn to (and draw to me) because it was the emotional language of the very first man in my life.

My dad was married twice, both times for more than twenty years. In both cases, he picked women who were born with the sun in Aquarius and the moon in Taurus! (Taurus is also my moon sign, so both of my dad's wives—one of whom is my mom—share my moon sign, and my husband shares my dad's moon sign.) Again, the chance of any two people having the same sun and moon signs, like my mom and stepmom, is 0.69 percent. That is the kind of coincidence I consider mind-blowing.

In a similar vein to my dad and husband sharing the same moon sign, my husband's mom's moon is in Capricorn, which is my sun and rising sign (and hyper-represented in my chart). Just as my dad left an imprint on me in terms of the partners I look for, my mother-in-law left an imprint on my husband.

This pattern, where signs are repeated from our parents to our romantic partners, is another example of a synchronicity between astrology and psychology. Freud coined the term *repetition compulsion* to describe our tendency to keep drawing the same people and situations because they are familiar, and because we (unconsciously) want to finish unfinished business with the person who originally made that mark on us. In these cases, astrology and psychology confirm a common truth: we pick the same people, or at least, they are the same in certain ways.

We don't have to pick *exactly* the same people, of course. Growth means that we should evolve in our choice of partners, eventually picking people who suit us, and can see us, better. My husband, for instance, has a deeply grounded and reality-based Taurus rising, and Taurus is my moon sign, so we share a common language. (When the moon sign of one partner in a relationship is represented in the other's sun, moon, or rising, it is known as a *beneficial conjunction*; this is discussed further in chapter 9.)

Two of the closest women in my life, both of whom I consider soulmates, are my cousin and my best friend since the age of eleven. I have been very close to both of them since I was young, and while neither relationship has been perfect, both relationships have always contained a great deal of ease, understanding, and support. Both of these women have the same sun-moon combination—Virgo sun and Taurus moon, so I share my moon sign with both—and there is a lot of commonality in all that earth. Again, there is a less than 1 percent chance that both of them would have the same sun-moon combination due to chance. To add to the synchronicity factor, their dads' birthdays are two days apart!

All three earth signs, Capricorn, Taurus, and Virgo, show up repeatedly in my friendships. People with earth strongly represented in their chart help me feel safe in the world because I experience them as looking at the same-enough reality as me. They can handle seeing reality on its own terms, tending less toward denial than other signs because they (we) just can't escape reality that easily, being down here on the ground. Of the six people I have kept in touch with since junior high school, every single one of them has at least one of their three major signs in an earth sign—two of them even have the same sun and moon combination as each other; again, 0.69 percent—and that is no coincidence. Earth signs help me feel sane.

Looking at the signs that repeatedly show up in my life helps me to figure out my life lessons, who I need, and who needs me. For instance, in my love relationships, the fixed signs are the ones that have shown up repeatedly, especially Leo, Aquarius, and Scorpio. I have already talked about the Leo and Aquarius marks, the stamps of familiarity, that come from my parents' charts (and up through the lines). Scorpio is my dad's rising sign—it was his mother's moon sign, so they actually shared two of their three major signs—and one of my brothers was born on the cusp of Scorpio and has a son with that sun sign, as well.

I take all of this fixed energy that repeatedly shows up in my romantic relationships to mean that I need my partner to possess a fixed kind of strength in order to be a true counterpart to me, instead of losing themselves due to my strong nature (Capricorn and Taurus can be a bit much at times). Otherwise, I would probably never learn to compromise.

With my friends, though, I can have more ease and flow in the relationships given that I pick people who are other earth signs and thus in a trine relationship to me. (Recall from chapter 4 that signs of the same element are trine, or form a triangle, with each other, and that relationship indicates ease.)

I also have a number of friends with water strongly represented in their charts—much of the time, in addition to earth—which is not surprising given the balancing nature of water and earth to each other. Like earth signs, water signs are feminine and receptive, so they naturally make great friends. In addition to that, my earthy nature must unconsciously realize it needs some serious softening, because I have picked a number of watery people and kept them close. (For them, I am sure I help by providing an anchor to keep them from being swept away by their feelings, or a shoreline when it comes to containment and boundary setting.)

Single people often use astrology to ask which signs they should date, but there are other ways to think about this. Though there is obviously more ease in some astrological relationships than others, I think the more appropriate question is, which signs *do* you date? This is addressed further in chapter 9, but my philosophy is that relationships are in our lives to help us grow, so the signs that show up repeatedly must have something important to teach us.

CLIENTS

Not surprisingly, I have seen a number of patterns and synchronic-ities in my relationships with my clients. (My friend and mentor Lauren Skye calls these *matching pictures*, where we have matching experiences with those we come into contact with so that we can help each other heal in whatever capacity.) I tend toward deeper, long-term work with my clients, so many of them are people with whom I have had close relationships for many years.

As it has in my personal life, the sign of Virgo shows up repeatedly in my clients, especially in their moon placement. As I write this, out of twenty-one people on my caseload, eight of them have Virgo as one of their three major signs, and of these, seven have Virgo as their moon sign. More than a third of my practice has the same sign strongly represented!

The fact that Virgo shows up so much more in the moon than the sun placement makes me think that Virgo sun people, who are used to being and feeling so competent, are not particularly likely to seek out therapy (unless they are in crisis or have other signs in their chart to support deeper psychological exploration). Virgo as the moon sign rules the nighttime self, so in their darkest moments, those with Virgo moon are filled with self-doubt for not being perfect and are thus more open to guidance. Brené Brown, the self-identified "recovering perfectionist" that she is, has her moon sign in Virgo.

As far as the other two earth signs—Capricorn and Taurus—I have seen only one Capricorn sun client and one Taurus sun client for long-term work over many years of having a practice. Generally speaking, people born with their sun in earth signs are more likely to feel they can fix things on their own, and they are not likely to seek therapy unless they are in a state of crisis. However, as with Virgo, I have seen a number of people with either Capricorn or Taurus in their moon placement. (There is a beneficial conjunction with these clients: those with Taurus moon share my same moon sign, and those with their moon in Capricorn have their emotional language represented in my sun and rising signs.)

I have two long-term clients who are double-air—one has sun in Aquarius, the other in Libra, and both have Libra rising—and both have their moon in Capricorn. This means that Capricorn is an important point of connection in our relationships, and it also helps them to be more grounded than other double-air people are. (Again, there is a 0.69 percent chance that these two clients would share two of their three major signs with each other.)

One of my clients is a double-Virgo with a Capricorn rising— the only other person I have ever known well who is triple-earth, like me. (I socially know one other person who is triple-earth, but I don't know her anywhere near as well.) Triple-earth is a heavy combination, and while there are undoubtedly others, I have en-countered only two other people (besides the two I just mentioned, and myself) who have it. One is an astrologer (triple-Capricorn

Jessica Lanyadoo), and the other is Prince Harry, who has a Virgo sun, Taurus moon, and Capricorn rising.

Of my seven clients who have their moon in Virgo, three have their sun in Pisces. If the chances of any two people sharing the same sun and moon combination is less than one percent, the chances that *three* people would share it are infinitesimally smaller. Crazily, one of these Pisces sun-Virgo moon clients has two children, *both* of whom share that same sun-moon combination. I can't make this stuff up.

Speaking of Pisces, it is another sign that shows up a lot in my life, like Virgo. Besides the three clients I just mentioned, I also have another six clients who either have sun in Pisces (or Pisces cusp) or moon in Pisces (or Pisces cusp). That means nine out of twenty-one people, or almost half of my practice, has Pisces as their sun or moon sign. Not surprisingly, I also have a number of friends with Pisces strongly represented in their charts. Again, I anchor them and help them shore up, and they soften me. My mother's sun sign is on the cusp of Pisces, so this must be another one of those marks for me.

Another fascinating set of synchronicities in my practice involves clients who share one or more of their major signs in common with my husband. This has been incredibly helpful in both directions: understanding my husband has helped me better understand these clients, and working with them helps me to better understand my husband. Two of my long-term clients have the same Aquarius sun-Leo moon combination (one of them even married a man with whom I share a birthday), and a past long-term client had the same sun (Aquarius) and rising (Taurus) as my husband. Again, there is a 0.69 percent probability that two people will have two of their three major signs in common, while the chances that would be the case with three people are much smaller than that. In my opinion, this qualifies as mind-blowing. Besides these three Aquarius sun clients, another four have their sun in Aquarius (one on the cusp) or moon in Aquarius, which, in total, is one third of my practice.

Which signs show up in *your* life over and over again? Do they go back through your family lines? Do they balance you out or challenge you, or both? Observing which signs show up repeatedly in your life will help you to more deeply understand the lessons you are here to learn, heal, and teach. This is discussed in further detail in chapters 8 and 9, but figuring out which signs show up most is the first step in the process. Again, look up people you know and the artists and public figures who resonate most with you.

MENTORS AND MUSICIANS

Scorpio is largely represented in my life. Besides showing up in my family, it is polar opposite to my Taurus moon, so I must draw it to me because, on some level, my soul needs to have contact with its shadow side. Scorpios compel and teach me. A number of strong women in my life have acted in maternal roles in some way, and all of them have Scorpio as one of their three major signs. These women include an old boss who is still a dear friend (the one who predicted I would write a book); my graduate school advisor, who is also still near and dear to me; my psychoanalyst, who probably changed my life more than any other person besides my husband; and two other significant female mentors whom I deeply respect and admire.

Scorpio is also strongly represented by two women who speak to me on a professional level: it is Brené Brown's sun sign and psychologist Alice Miller's moon sign (whose birthday is the day before mine; no wonder she resonates with me so much). Both of these women, along with several of the women previously mentioned, have both earth and water strongly represented in their charts; this seems to be an especially important combination for me. Of the women described, three of them have both Scorpio and Virgo represented in their chart.

In addition to Virgo-Scorpio, another earth-water combination that shows up repeatedly in the people who speak to me on a deep level is Capricorn-Pisces. I have one dear client with these two signs, and my first and incredibly influential clinical supervisor,

Dr. Don Weatherley, had a Pisces cusp sun and his moon in Capricorn. Both signs tend toward depression and discontent more than the others, but they express it differently. While Capricorn tends toward anger, Pisces can get us in touch with sadness faster than any other sign, so I think they balance each other out in a particular way.

I say only half-jokingly that I think being a therapist has operated as a defense against my own tendency toward depression; my job is to find and hold hope for others, so I need to keep it going in myself. Pisces is the sign that naturally contains more innate hopefulness than any other; as double-Pisces Fred Rogers said, dying well is "dying with the hopes intact." Thus, people having both Capricorn and Pisces in their chart is great for me because I know they understand the darkness of Capricorn, and yet they still have hope. Michelle Obama is one of those people for me, as is Michael Stipe, the lead singer of the band R.E.M.; when he sings "Everybody Hurts," I believe him more than I believe other people saying those words.

Alan Ball has an earth-water combination (Taurus sun-Scorpio moon), and his series *Six Feet Under* was a super-impactful and defining series for me. I even joked that I want there to be something in my obituary about how much I loved it! My favorite musician, whose name is Blake Schwarzenbach, also has this same combination—Taurus cusp sun, Scorpio moon—and like Alan Ball, he has helped me to get closer to the deep pain and underworld of Scorpio by combining it with the grounding force of Taurus (which is also my moon sign, and thus a beneficial conjunction). Another one of my favorite musicians, Chuck Ragan, has the same two signs but in reverse (Scorpio sun, Taurus moon), so we also have a beneficial conjunction because we share the same moon sign.

Funny enough, Schwarzenbach's birthday is the day before Morrissey's, whose band, The Smiths, was also one of my favorites growing up, and both of these men share the same Scorpio moon placement. While Morrissey's sun sign is technically Gemini (his birthday is May 22; Schwarzenbach's is May 21), there are a lot of lyrical commonalities between them. Both of them write very dark lyrics because of their Scorpio moon, but the Gemini imbues them with the ability to make things light, clever, and funny, as well. It helps the jagged pills of life, death, and heavy lyrics to go down more easily. (Ironically, another of my favorite artists, Alanis Morissette, has this same sun-moon combination, too.) It seems like the moon sign drives the deeper message of the artist's creative expression, while the sun sign provides the packaging the message gets delivered in.

Like the earth-water musicians mentioned earlier, Jimmy Page, guitarist and songwriter for the band Led Zeppelin, also has this combination (Capricorn sun-Cancer moon). Led Zeppelin is my favorite band of all time and always will be. I think the sheer number of amazing and groundbreaking songs they put out has not been paralleled by any other band during my lifetime, at least not yet.

While there has been water in general all over my life, it has been an especially important element for me in the world of music because of the pain those signs (Scorpio, Pisces, and Cancer) are in touch with and help me get in touch with. As discussed before, Kurt Cobain was double-water with an earth rising, and Nirvana might have been the band that eclipsed Led Zeppelin for me had Cobain lived longer. Even though the last feelings I want to get in touch with are sadness, vulnerability, and powerlessness, sometimes I just need a good cry—and water signs, especially when they are combined with some sort of earth anchor that keeps me feeling safe, can take me there like no other ones can.

I have always been drawn to Capricorn musicians, many of whom I have already mentioned: Jimmy Page, Michael Stipe, Eddie Vedder (who is double-earth with a Virgo moon), and Dave Grohl (who is a double-Capricorn, sun and rising, like I am; his birthday is the day after mine, a fact I have always loved and felt honored by).

Finally, the same two signs of Aquarius and Leo show up in this area, too. One of my favorite musical artists for decades, Jason Cruz, has the same sun-moon combination as my husband (Aquarius sun-Leo moon), and these are also two of Jung's three major signs (Leo sun-Aquarius rising). As already mentioned, Jung's moon sign is the same as mine (Taurus), so there are multiple points of connection and balance, and thus resonance, in the mentor-like relationship I have with Jung.

Again, please look up the people who especially impact you, at least your immediate family, partner, and kids. It is easy and informative to use the internet to also look up the birthdays (or birth charts, which are often available) of your favorite musicians, writers, poets, actors, and other celebrities and public figures who have impressed you in some way. Besides the fact that noticing your own patterns and wondering what lessons or dynamics they might represent in your life is interesting and fun, doing this with others close to you will give you a better feel for the signs and what they look like in human form.

In chapter 9, we will continue our discussion of relationships with other people and what we need to learn from them. In the next chapter, we will explore your three signs (sun, moon, and rising), how they relate to each other, and which qualities and elements are underrepresented in your chart. Using psychstrology in this way will help you gain insight and understanding about your life challenges and opportunities for growth. When you use your nature as a starting point, you will be better able to consciously evolve.

CHAPTER 8

Using Your Birth Chart as a Mirror

Only what is really oneself has the power to heal.
—Carl Jung

One of the most useful applications of psychstrology is its ability to support you in knowing yourself, and by extension those in your care, better. You can then bring that self-awareness into the important relationships in your life. Worksheet 3, at the end of this chapter, will help you to synthesize all you have learned about yourself thus far regarding your sun (basic identity), moon (inner self), and rising (outermost layer) signs. Awareness of the self precedes awareness of others. We can't suppose what is going on for them—at least, not as accurately—when we don't deeply understand our own experience.

The reason I started incorporating astrology into my sessions with my clients is that it is highly beneficial to psychological exploration. Besides helping individuals to see themselves more clearly, astrology also contains an inherent wisdom and awareness of our deeper spiritual connectedness to each other—and seeing the synchronicities in your own life can help you feel more connected to that bigger spiritual collective. It can help you to feel aligned with the deeper layers of life, and to be consciously aware of your spiritual connectedness to forces greater than yourself, especially when you are struggling.

An important collateral benefit to the psychstrology approach is that it provides a basis for understanding important concepts such as balance, evolution, and integration by serving as a microcosm of these lessons. Integrating the various parts of yourself is a process of trying to find balance between them so they can work together as harmoniously as possible. When you look to your polar-opposite sign in order to find more balance, or when you look at which elements and qualities you are missing as a way to consciously evolve, those process-oriented concepts—such as the idea that you can foster more balance by taking in what you lack or need—become more deeply integrated into your awareness and way of being in the world. Since these concepts are very important for individuation and a healthy approach to life, those are some powerful additional benefits.

Psychology and astrology share a focus on the balance and integration of the various aspects of yourself, which is why they naturally go together so well. Like peanut butter and jelly, their pairing naturally enhances each of their unique contributions to the mix. Things that are contained in your shadow, which is a psychological concept, are also seen in the astrological signs that are in the polar-opposite position on the zodiac and in the qualities and elements that are missing or underdeveloped in your chart. Everything, to be whole and balanced, needs to integrate what it does not already contain. This principle is also common in eastern traditions, such as Ayurveda (as discussed in chapter 4).

Ideally, as you grow and individuate, you will integrate the healthy contributions of *all* the signs of the zodiac. Just as each sign plays a different and important role in an optimally functioning society, each sign needs to have its own internal representation within you so that you can be a fully and optimally functioning person.

At the very least, you can see astrology as validating your personality in terms of providing reasons why you are the way you are, or, more accurately, *that* you are the way you are. The same goes for your loved ones—if you look up their signs, you can see that they are "that way" just as you are "this way." That alone can help you feel more entitled to express your own true nature, which by extension will naturally help you allow others to feel entitled to express theirs, as well.

When I was in graduate school, I developed sciatica and saw a chiropractor for a period of time. The receptionist in the office was a woman named Annie, and she and I developed a nice relationship and bonded over our mutual love of astrology. When she first asked me what my three major signs were, I told her with embarrassment that I was "all earth." She asked why I wasn't happy with that, and I proceeded to tell her about how serious, practical, and lacking in spontaneity I was. She looked at me closely and said something that forever changed how I view my nature, which I still remember word for word, all these years later: "You must have some very important work to do here, because someone with a lesser chart couldn't get it done." There is validity and importance to every single astrological nature.

While appreciating your nature as valid is important, remembering that your true nature is a starting place, not an ending place, is vital. Accepting your nature is not to say "this is how I am" and leave it at that, nor is using astrology to explain away your shortcomings without working to improve them. Rather, your birth chart points the way to what your challenges are in this life and which traits require tempering. Everything that has happened in your life has been filtered through the lens of your astrological nature, so the flaws of your nature are bound to show up all over your life. (This is another example of that small-to-large projection, where your internal world is projected out into the choices you make in your external life.)

Using Your Chart as a Map for Your Growth Process

Your birth chart is a map, in symbolic language, of your innate resources, strengths, and talents, as well as your challenging tendencies and limitations. What are you here to say and express? What are you here to learn and heal? Your chart reveals all the parts of you and exposes the parts you might try to conceal, not only from others, but from yourself, as well. It tells the whole story of who you are, not just the parts you have edited and curated for public consumption or self-acceptance.

As a psychologist, Jung saw the psyche as structured in terms of opposites and characterized by polarities, and your unconscious is no exception. In a helpful way, your unconscious possesses an innate wisdom as well as a drive toward integration and wholeness. Integration of your parts means that they remain separate and distinct, but they are all allowed to have space to exist and can work together harmoniously. It is similar to a healthy-enough family, where even when people are of different natures they can coexist harmoniously (for the most part) because each of them realizes that the others have their own positive intentions and important roles to play in the group.

Your unconscious can also work against you, however, particularly if you refuse to try to make friends with it. For example, if you see yourself do something that you really don't like, you have one of two choices: you can deny and disavow it, or you can set about trying to understand it better so that you don't have to have a part of yourself doing things you are not happy about. At least, this part of you will be quieter and less intense if it feels seen and understood, like a child who is upset about something but soothed by the attention and care of their mother, even if she can't do anything to fix the problem.

Forcing something to remain unconscious will inevitably thwart the achievement of your conscious objectives, like the left hand undoing what the right hand is doing. In a contest between the conscious and unconscious, the unconscious will always win because it is wiser. For this reason, choosing to make space to see all of your parts is a better choice because their innate and strong desire to be seen will inevitably cause them to rear their heads (or seep out), anyway. As Jung wisely said, "Until you make the unconscious conscious, it will direct your life and you will call it fate."

Sometimes these parts are those you have had to sacrifice, disown, or disavow in order to survive your painful experiences, especially when they started in your childhood. Your parts, both psychological and astrological, may sometimes act out because of the treatment they have received, but none are intrinsically bad; they are just not understood well enough yet. You need to be able to view these parts of yourself through compassionate eyes. If you can do so, then just like a child basking in the warm compassion of their mother's care, your soul will thrive, and its best iteration will emerge over time.

Most of the time, your signs will naturally balance each other to some extent. Through this balancing effect of your multiple signs, you have the astrological ingredients you need to heal your relationship to parts of yourself you have misunderstood, feared, or just never met in a conscious way. Now that you know your three signs, here are four ways you can use them to help you grow.

LOOK TO YOUR POLAR-OPPOSITE SIGNS

In chapter 5, we discussed the idea that each of your signs has a polar-opposite sign on the zodiac wheel. Those polar-opposite signs are made up of characteristics that are needed to bring your signs into greater balance, characteristics that are currently part of your shadow (or unconscious).

There are three pairs of earth-water signs—Taurus-Scorpio, Cancer-Capricorn, and Virgo-Pisces—and three pairs of fire-air signs, Aries-Libra, Gemini-Sagittarius, and Leo-Aquarius. (For the specific ways each sign can incorporate its opposite in order to come into better balance, please review the section "How You Grow" for each sign in chapter 5.)

Think of a see-saw, where the balance point is in the middle. For each of the polar-opposite combinations, or polarities, there is a zone of balance in the middle of the two signs. In other words, whatever your sign, you are most in balance when your nature appreciates the parts it contains that are represented by its opposite, like the principle of yin/yang. Each sign has something beneficial to bring to the mix. Both sides of the polarity are needed, and each sign is enriched by incorporating the other. As Jung said, "Anyone who perceives his shadow and his light simultaneously sees himself from two sides and thus gets in the middle."

While your specific life lessons will depend on your particular combination of signs (because you are integrating a number of different opposites as well as incorporating your missing elements and qualities), here are some general guidelines for the points of growth, or life challenges, of each element. (Please review chapter 4 for detailed descriptions of each of the elements' specific traits and challenges.)

If you have a significant amount of earth in your chart (meaning at least one of your sun, moon, or rising signs is Taurus, Virgo, or Capricorn), you will be working on detachment from things in earth-based reality. This includes attachment to your own experience, and since things tend to get lodged in the earth, you will be working on forgiveness. Your growth will involve trying not to become too hard, rigid, and crusty as a result of life's sometimes harsh lessons. Water (your polarity) will help to keep you softer and more malleable by keeping you connected to your deeper sensitivities.

If you have a lot of water (Cancer, Scorpio, or Pisces) in your chart, you are working on keeping yourself contained. This looks like trying to contain the intensity of your feelings and emotional reactions as well as keeping reasonable boundaries and space between you and other people. Because you are so sensitive and can stew in your emotions, you will be working on forgiveness. (Water and earth are the two receptive elements, so it makes sense that they would internalize pain and then need to work on metabolizing and moving past it.) Earth, your polarity, can provide the structure to help you shore up, set boundaries, and add a dose of reality to the feeling-based world in which you live.

If you have a lot of fire (Aries, Leo, or Sagittarius) in your chart, you are working to calm yourself down (another form of containment). As with water signs, you have overpoweringly intense reactions, but instead of getting emotionally upset in the way that water signs do, you can become hot and explosive. You need to work to contain your enthusiasm and passion at times because it can propel you into acting too intensely or impulsively. The element of air (your polarity) can help you become more detached and objective, adding a needed dose of neutrality and big-picture perspective.

If you have a lot of air (Gemini, Libra, or Aquarius) in your chart, you are working to stay connected enough, on a deeper, internal level, to other people and the world around you. While earth signs are working on detachment, you are working on becoming more attached. (Many of my Aquarius clients have dreams in which they are flying; later in therapy, one had a dream where she was trying to force herself *not* to fly up so high, which indicated growth.) You need to cultivate more passion as well as a deeper, more internal feeling of commitment to aspects of your life.

CULTIVATE THE ELEMENTS AND QUALITIES YOU ARE MISSING

Another part of your shadow, your unconscious and underdeveloped self, lies in the "empty space" in your chart in terms of both the elements and the qualities. Taking your three major signs together, there are certain elements and qualities that you possess, and certain ones you are missing. You will have at least one missing element and no, one, or two missing qualities. As the saying goes, you don't even know what you're missing. (Keep in mind, however, that you have a number of other signs in the deeper layers of your birth chart, so you may possess more of a particular element or quality than meets the eye by looking at your three major signs.)

For this reason, becoming more aware of what you are missing will help you to grow in the direction of balance and wholeness. Jung called this the inferior function, the least developed parts of yourself. It helps to have awareness of and work to cultivate more of whatever you don't naturally possess in large amounts, because all of the parts add up to a whole, balanced, fully functioning person. If you can remain intuitively receptive (mutable) while simultaneously holding your boundaries (fixed) and keeping your goals in mind (cardinal), you will be like a tree that is firmly rooted into the ground yet focused on its growth, and whose leaves rustle in response to the breeze. All three qualities represent different types of strength, and in order for us to function optimally, all three types are necessary to cultivate to some degree.

Just as there are points of growth, or life challenges, for each element, so, too, is the case for each quality. Here is a general description of the challenges associated with each quality. (Please review chapter 4 for a detailed description of each of the qualities' specific traits and challenges.)

The cardinal signs (Aries, Cancer, Libra, and Capricorn) are always working toward the achievement of goals and are therefore looking forward to the future, so if you have strong cardinal representation in your chart, you need to learn how to better stay in the present. This is true in terms of being more present in your relationships instead of always trying to solve problems or improve situations, incorporating some of the loyalty and stability of the fixed signs. Being present also means being more adaptable, flexible, and able to respond to life's *present* demands, incorporating some of the mutable signs' form of strength.

If you have at least one of your three major signs in a fixed sign (Taurus, Leo, Scorpio, or Aquarius), you need to work to let yourself be changed by other people and your experiences. Compromising and letting other people in can feel like losing yourself. Change is hard because you are typically focused on what you are giving up or leaving behind, but you need to look at lost growth opportunities, as well, including those related to intimacy and connection in relationships. You need to incorporate some of the flexibility of the mutable signs and some of the goal-setting of the cardinal signs instead of just opposing whatever is trying to move you.

If you have a strong representation of the mutable signs (Gemini, Virgo, Sagittarius, or Pisces), you are working to learn how to better hold on to yourself. You have a tendency to lose yourself in your roles and relationships and not know who you are deep down, and you need to get clearer on this. Learning how to better tolerate conflict is important; you shy away from conflict because it indicates difference between you and someone else. Incorporating some of the fixed signs' ability to set boundaries against the intrusion of others is helpful, as is incorporating some of the goal-oriented thinking of the cardinal signs so that you can execute what it is that *you* want.

While I have both cardinal and fixed representation in my three signs, I lack mutability, so I like to joke with myself that challenging situations are "mutability training" for me. (This feels especially true when I am sitting in traffic.) Writing this book has definitely been a form of mutability training. The thing that helps is to just keep following the various threads and twists and turns, letting it become what it wants to become so that it can become the best possible version of itself. This is strikingly similar to what is necessary to allow a person to individuate and become their truest self, which is what I do with my clients in my professional life. Intuitively, I have chosen paths that help to bring me into a better state of balance by challenging me to work the muscles that aren't as inherently strong in my nature.

CONSIDER WHICH SIGNS SHOW UP THE MOST

Hopefully, you have looked up your most important people and are noticing some patterns that show up in your life. Looking at the traits of the signs that show up repeatedly is an important way to consider the lessons your soul is here to learn (and teach). It is again worth noting that all of this takes place within the context of a lot of other factors in your birth chart. For example, your lunar nodes are the points at which the moon's orbit and the plane of the ecliptic converge at the time of your birth. The sign that the north node was in represents what you are here to learn or the language you are learning to speak, and the south node sign symbolizes the strengths and challenges you are bringing in from past lifetimes.

It is possible that if you were to have your birth chart read by an astrologer, you would find that the signs that show up in your life show up in your own chart, as well (in places besides your sun, moon, and rising). Regardless, if a sign is frequently showing up in your life, learning about it would be quite helpful.

There is certainly a part of us that is drawn to people who are the same as we are, so when you look at the three signs of the people in your life, you are bound to find some representation of signs within your element, particularly within your friend group. These relationships, known as trine, are typically easy and compatible (though if people are the same sign as you, particularly if your sign is very strong, you may feel like there is too much similarity and not enough balance).

When you look up the people in your life, you may find that your moon sign is represented in their chart (sun, moon, or rising) or that their moon sign is represented in yours. This is known as a *beneficial conjunction* and is a positive dynamic in relationships. Since the moon represents our emotional language, the other person speaking and understanding that language on some level is beneficial.

In addition to seeking ease, though, we also inherently seek growth and wholeness and are drawn to individuals who have what we lack and need for balance. We need both types of relationships in order to grow: those that support us and those that challenge us. Sometimes they are woven together into the same relationship.

Your polar-opposite sign people—and I mean polar opposite to any of your signs, but especially sun and moon—help to balance you in terms of your masculine or feminine role. However, there are also people on the other side of the masculine-feminine equation who balance out your perspective in other ways that are helpful. For example, I have always had a lot of air sign people in my life; my dad has a Gemini sun and my husband an Aquarius sun, and both of these people have helped me very much with their big-picture perspective. While we definitely feel the difference in our natures, there is an element of complementarity and mutual benefit to the difference.

Where water softens me (as a triple-earth person), air lightens me. I need this lightness in two ways: in the way that lightness counters darkness, and how lightness counters heaviness, and both my dad and my husband provide me with that kind of help and perspective. Air sign people help with my perspective in a way that no other element can, because they have the bird's-eye view while I am stuck on the ground. They help me become more detached and objective, both of which are much needed at times. On the other hand, I ground them in reality in a particular way, which is where the mutual benefit comes in. That I have so many clients with air strongly represented in their chart is not surprising; numerous times over the years, I have heard them explicitly confirm this ("I feel more grounded than when I got here").

The quality that is most predominant in my practice is mutable. Given that I am not mutable, these people having shown up in my life and therapy practice is no surprise, because I have things to teach them and to learn from them. I need to soak up their mutability in order to cultivate more of it myself, and they need to learn how to hold on to themselves more. Because I am double-cardinal (sun and rising) and fixed (moon), I can help them find and learn how to better hold on to their true selves by learning to cultivate more of the cardinal and fixed strength that is underdeveloped in them (and highly developed in me). Through our relationship, they can internalize me as I internalized my therapist, who possessed some of the traits that are underdeveloped in me. (Her polar-opposite and softening Scorpio moon to my Taurus moon was balancing, and she also provided balance by teaching me, in an earth-based way that I could understand, how to be more mutable just by being her natural Virgo self.)

ANALYZE THE RELATIONSHIP BETWEEN YOUR PARTS

Besides the fact that your sun, moon, and rising all govern different parts of your life, these three signs have relationships with one another. Depending on the combination, your signs can be harmonious (if they are trine, or the same element), or be different but more complementary than conflicted, or be tense or conflicted (square or polar opposite). Even with your three major signs alone, an analysis can get complicated because there are multiple relationships at play. Because of this, discussing every possible configuration is too difficult, but some general guidelines are below.

Let's start with the more difficult configurations, where two of your signs (especially your sun and moon) are in a relationship to each other that is either square (of the same quality, whether cardinal, fixed, or mutable) or in polar opposition to each other (Aries-Libra, Taurus-Scorpio, Gemini-Sagittarius, Cancer-Capricorn, Leo-Aquarius, Virgo-Pisces).

Square and polar-opposite sign configurations lead to a feeling of inner conflict. If your sun and moon are not in harmony with each other, you can be uncomfortable with your innermost needs and have a hard time integrating them into your sense of self. If this applies to you, chances are you have always had a dynamic in your thought process that sounds like, "I shouldn't feel this way; I'm being too___," indicating a lack of resolution within yourself.

Having signs that are polar opposite to one another (e.g., Pisces sun-Virgo moon, Aquarius sun-Leo moon), can create an interesting internal experience. You have both halves of the polarity inside of you, but they govern different parts of your life. Your moon rules your deepest, most embedded emotional and habitual reactions to things, and your sun represents the adaptations you made as you started to interact more with the outside world. Each sign still needs its polar-opposite influence to balance out the realm it governs.

For example, one of my clients with a Pisces sun and Virgo moon had an eating disorder in her younger years (which is not unusual when Virgo is in someone's chart because of the rigidity and perfectionism it brings to eating and the body, especially if it is the person's moon sign). While she shows up as a Pisces in most aspects of her life—she is compassionate, kind, and can easily make space for other people—she approaches eating and body image with her Virgo moon mindset. This means that her approach to her own body is polar opposite to how she engages with other people. She has had to work hard to become more compassionate with herself, including around food and her body; it has not come naturally to her at all, even though she has compassionate Pisces strongly represented in her chart.

Having two of your major signs either square or in polar opposition to one another can feel internally conflicted or unresolved for you, but the plus side is that this construct also tends to balance you out in important ways. An Aries (fire) with a Cancer (water) moon, for example, is much more compassionate and emotionally intuitive than the typical Aries. I know a number of people with this configuration (as well as the opposite version of Cancer sun-Aries moon), which leads me to believe that this is not an uncommon pairing. Your soul wanted both of these signs together to balance each other out, which makes sense—even if there is a feeling of internal conflict inside of you.

The same is true when your signs are not square or opposite but are not especially harmonious, either (e.g., fire-water, air-earth). In these cases, while your internal experience may not feel particularly resolved, the pairing tends to be beneficial because water and fire really do temper each other, as do air and earth. An Aries (fire) or Leo (fire) can benefit from a pairing with softening Pisces (water), for example, and I know a number of people with this configuration, including two of my clients. I also have two clients who are double-air (sun and rising) with a Capricorn (earth) moon. While their internal experience may feel conflictual, they undoubtedly benefit from the grounding force of their Capricorn moon, which forces them not to float too far from reality in their thinking, as air signs have tendency to do.

Sometimes two of the signs are trine or harmonious, but the third is the odd one out, having a significantly different nature from the other two. If your rising sign is unrelated to or in conflict with your sun-moon dyad, for example, it can look from the outside as though you are in more conflict than you actually are on a deeper, subjective level; however, you still present a conflicted picture of your basic self to the world and struggle with feeling misunderstood. This is because the rising sign restricts the expression of the sun or the moon, or both, so you end up feeling as though people miss an important part of you in the way they respond to you. For example, a Pisces rising may make an Aries sun feel like their strong needs aren't being fully appreciated, because Pisces holds back so much when they first encounter situations.

Or perhaps the moon and rising signs are trine, in which case they can collude to keep the odd sun sign out or mitigate its expression. For example, if someone has their sun in Gemini (air) but their moon in Pisces (water) and their rising in Scorpio (water), they will be much less extroverted than a typical Gemini. Their strong sensitivity and urge to draw inward will thwart Gemini's social nature, but hopefully they are in enough of a state of balance and integration that neither force rules too much of the time.

If your sun and rising are in harmony but in conflict with your moon, your emotional and security needs (moon) will be blocked and repressed to some extent because of the strong identification resulting from the sun and rising signs supporting each other. For example, a double-air person (sun and rising) who has a water moon sign will have a harder time making space for their deeper emotional needs because of their tendency to rationalize and intellectually minimize them.

On the other hand, your three signs may be in a harmonious relationship with one another. This happens when they are either trine (of the same element) or paired with the other feminine (earth and water) or masculine (fire and air) signs (with the exception of the polar-opposite sign, which is a more complicated relationship). Earth and water go well together, as do fire and air. When there is harmony between the sun-moon signs, there is an internal ease to one's functioning. What the moon sign needs for security, the sun sign knows how to create, and there is no significant internal force opposing this manifestation.

Even with trine configurations, however, there is some degree of conflict because of the different qualities. In other words, what sometimes feels like balance can, at other times, feel like conflict. For example, even though my three signs are all earth, I can definitely feel the conflict between my double-cardinal (outer) parts and my fixed (inner) moon. My deep, internal Taurus moon nature wants to relax and keep things simple, but my double-Capricorn sun and rising want to make lots of plans, both inside and outside of my home. There is no real way to be totally harmonious, whether intrapsychically (within oneself) or astrologically. There is always intrapsychic tension, and therefore, growth. Therapists already know this; astrology just gives them a way to illuminate and explain it. This is another example of synchronicity.

Fill out worksheet 3 to help you synthesize this information and understand yourself better. (We will be addressing relationships in the next chapter, where these principles will be helpful to understand the ways in which the signs interact with each other between people.)

WORKSHEET 3.
LOOKING MORE CLOSELY AT YOUR THREE MAJOR SIGNS

My sun sign is _____. This sign is made of _____(quality) _____(element).

The sign that is polar opposite to my sun sign is _____. When I read about that sign with an eye toward becoming more balanced, here are the things that resonate with me and that I want to cultivate more of: _____

My moon sign is _____. This sign is made of _____(quality) _____(element).

The sign that is polar opposite to my moon sign is _____. When I read about that sign with an eye toward becoming more balanced, here are the things that resonate with me and that I want to cultivate more of: _____

My rising sign is _____. This sign is made of _____(quality) _____(element).

The sign that is polar opposite to my rising sign is _____.
When I read about that sign with an eye toward becoming more balanced, here are the things that resonate with me and that I want to cultivate more of: _____

I am missing these elements from my three major signs: _____

_____

When I read the descriptions of these missing elements in chapter 4, here are the things that resonate with me and that I want to cultivate more of:_____

I am missing these qualities from my three major signs: _____

_____

When I read the descriptions of these missing qualities in chapter 4, here are the things that resonate with me and that I want to cultivate more of: _____

Besides those listed above, the signs that many people I know have their sun or moon in are _____. These people are in my life for a reason. When I read about these signs with an eye toward becoming more balanced, here are the things that resonate with me and that I think they are here to help me learn: _____

_____

Here are the things I think I am teaching them, as well: _____

_____

In terms of the relationships between my signs, here are the aspects that are trine (same element) or relatively harmonious: _____

Here are the parts that are different in nature but balance each other out in complementary ways: _____
_____

Here are the things I like about my nature (you can also expand on the previous questions): _____
_____

Here are the parts where there is tension or conflict (squares and polar oppositions): _____
_____

Here are some of the things to keep in mind as I try to integrate the needs of both (square or polar opposite) signs: _____
_____

CHAPTER 9

Understanding Others and Improving Your Relationships

*In insecure relationships, we disguise our vulnerabilities
so our partner never really sees us.*
—Dr. Sue Johnson, *Hold Me Tight*

Psychology is all about relationships. Astrology gives us a code
to understand the raw materials that we and other people
are made of, and it is highly beneficial to use this code to better
understand the dynamics playing out in our relationships. You
don't want to have relationships in which both people hide their
vulnerabilities from each other (and often even themselves) and
never feel truly seen. While understanding and compassion can't
solve every single problem, they can go a long way toward sooth-
ing the unavoidable places of conflict that arise when two people
are doing their best to be their true selves. How helpful, too, that
these principles apply to every type of relationship we have, no
matter the parameters.

Romantic and Other Close Relationships

Couple and other close relationships are one of the most wonderful things available to us in life, yet they are also the source of a significant amount of angst and discord. Unfortunately, astrology can't help you by telling you who to have relationships with; sometimes people claim otherwise—since signs of the same element are trine, that is who you should date—but the reality of it is far from that simple. For one thing, most people are a combination of signs (triple-sign people do exist, though they are rare), including the people you are looking to date.

Besides being overly simplistic, the advice to date people whose sun signs are trine with yours is unrealistic. Are you really going to turn down someone whom you find attractive, even compelling, just because their sun sign isn't one of the two you are trine with? You are much better off, in my opinion, to look at the signs (sun and moon) of the people you actually *do* date and wonder why you are drawn to those particular signs. As discussed in chapter 8, the signs that show up in your life over and over again undoubtedly have things to teach you as well as things to learn from you.

Additionally, psychology tells us that there are reasons you pick who you pick, and it is not necessarily because those signs are easy for you. In fact, it is often to the contrary: that you pick people who are difficult for you in particular ways. This usually mirrors your relationship with one or both of your parents, which is why you can so often see their astrological signs in your choice of partners. In an effort to process and heal unfinished business with your parents, you are drawn to people who have the right nature to potentially play out the scenes with you. (We will address more on family relationships later.)

Emotionally Focused Therapy, or EFT (not to be confused with the Emotional Freedom Technique), is a current, popular, and effective form of couples therapy developed by Dr. Sue Johnson. Based on adult attachment and bonding, EFT focuses on helping couples understanding each other's deeper security and attachment needs. Remember, these needs are contained in your moon sign, your "organ of contact with others." Understanding the language of your own moon, your partner's moon, and how these two signs interact is crucial for a deeper understanding of the emotional patterns that play out in your relationships.

Again, I recommend that you read the sun, moon, and rising sign descriptions of all people with whom you have a close relationship, paying particularly close attention to the moon of your romantic partner or whomever you live with. Once you have more awareness of and compassion for the ways in which you and the other person operate, you will be better able to navigate through the various points of conflict that present themselves in your relationships.

There are many complex dynamics that exist between you and the other person, even when only the three major signs are considered. In addition to your layered astrological nature, your family history (the *nurture* in the equation) comes into play in close relationships more than anywhere else. Using some of the principles from the last chapter, you can at least get a feel for some of the most important dynamics that play out in your relationships.

If you are in a close relationship and really want to better understand what is going on, I recommend consulting a professional astrologer who can cast a synastry chart (overlaying both charts and comparing the aspects) or composite chart (establishing the planetary midpoints between your two charts), and take both of your full astrological natures into account.

Beneficial conjunctions, where the moon of one partner is represented in the other's sun, moon, or rising, are extremely helpful in close relationships. When one person speaks the native moon-sign language of the other person in some capacity, more ease and basis for understanding is built into the fabric of the relationship. This can happen when two people have the same moon sign, but it can also happen when your moon is represented in the other person's sun. For example, *The Office* actor Steve Carell has a Pisces moon, while costar Jenna Fischer has a Pisces sun, and these two actors in particular are known for their very close bond; Steve likely has deep, intuitive understanding of the basic way in which Jenna is organized. A beneficial conjunction can also involve the other person's rising sign being the same as your moon sign, as it is in the unlikely but close relationship between Snoop Dogg (Scorpio moon) and Martha Stewart (Scorpio rising). In this type of beneficial conjunction (moon-rising), one person expresses outwardly (here, Martha) what the other experiences internally (Snoop).

Even beneficial conjunctions can't guarantee relationship success, however. Freud and Jung had a beneficial conjunction in Taurus (earth); it was Freud's sun sign and Jung's moon sign. Freud's moon sign, however, was Gemini (air), and especially in the moon placement, this is very different from Taurus.

There is a complex mathematical concept in astrology called *exaltation*, which involves the degrees of position of the celestial bodies. The sun, the moon, and the planets are each exalted in a particular zodiac sign. The moon is exalted in Taurus, which means that the aspects ruled by the moon are especially strong— including intuition. People with a Taurus moon thus tend to have a strong psychic ability, and this was clearly the case with Jung, who was deeply drawn to cosmic endeavors and psychic phenomena. Freud's Gemini moon, on the other hand, was too logical to make much space for this kind of thing. Furthermore, their Taurus stubbornness about their own ideas undoubtedly contributed to tearing them apart, as did the fact that both of them had other fixed signs, as well—Freud was double-fixed, with a Scorpio rising, and Jung was triple-fixed, with a Leo sun and Aquarius rising. (As I mentioned earlier, my husband is also triple-fixed—or as I like to joke, stubborn about staying stuck.)

Problems arise in relationships because one's comfort zone is another person's point of growth. For example, being double-cardinal earth (Capricorn), my anxiety is soothed by making earth-based plans. My husband, who is triple-fixed with his sun in Aquarius (air), hates making plans, especially on his days off, because it makes him feel fenced in. Realizing this conflict in our natures has made us more able to compromise on how we structure our lives. (On a related but slightly different note, my sense is that in couple relationships where there is a strong cardinal person and a strong fixed person, the cardinal person will play the role of the pursuer/demander while the fixed person will play the role of the distancer/withdrawer. These couple dynamics are commonly observed by researchers and clinicians alike, though none of them reference astrology thus far.)

There is certainly a part of us that is drawn to people who are the same, but we also inherently, not even consciously, seek wholeness and are drawn to individuals who have what we lack and need for balance. Thus, you will often be drawn to people who abound in your missing elements or qualities. (Usually, a combination of both types of experience—ease and challenge—is represented in the charts of those you feel most drawn to.) You need people to mirror what is underdeveloped in yourself to give you an opportunity to internalize and develop it more.

The key is that you must learn and develop your underdeveloped traits inside of yourself instead of having the other person hold all of this unmanifested shadow material for you. Sometimes people do this in order to be able to depend on the other person ("they're strong, I'm not"), and in other cases, people are in a relationship with someone who represents their shadow so that they can (not even consciously) discharge their own anger and shame on the other person. Whatever the reason, relationships where one person holds all of the strength and the other person holds all of the weakness or lack are known as *codependent*. In these cases, both people in the relationship feel constricted, and neither is able to develop into their fullest self. We need to do the excruciatingly hard work of letting people, including ourselves, be uncomfortable; otherwise, no one grows.

Parenting and Family Relationships

How you experience your family members depends on your own chart, because your astrological nature acts as a filter for all of your experiences. This helps to explain how you can have such different experiences of and relationships with your parents than your siblings do. (Also, parents experience you differently based on their own charts, which causes them to show different sides of themselves to you.)

As you may have noticed if you have already looked up the signs of your family members, there are astrological patterns in families in the form of signs that repeat themselves across generations. This corresponds with what can be seen from a psychological vantage point. For example, the signs that tend toward codependence are the ones that tend to show up in enmeshed families (families in which boundaries between people are flimsy or nonexistent).

There are often points of connection between parents and children, and between siblings, as well. In my mother's brother's family, for example, two of the siblings—the youngest and oldest of five, both male—have the same sun and moon combination (0.69 percent chance). In my husband's family, he is the youngest of five, and he shares two of his signs with his oldest brother (in different places—they both have a Taurus rising, but his brother has a Leo sun while my husband has a Leo moon). One of my clients has two siblings with the same sun-moon combination (she is in the middle), and another of my clients has two kids who have the same sun-moon combination as each other, and as does he. (I won't bore you with computing the infinitesimally small mathematical chances of that being due to chance rather than synchronicity; the fact that these probabilities are so slim and yet happen with regularity in families is the mind-blowing part.) All of this lines up with genetics in families, which increases the sense that it is valid, since two things are pointing to the same truth with separate arrows.

Parents have repetition compulsions of their own, so the fact that two of their children grow up looking so similar seems related to that. Again, parents need to work to see their kids clearly, because children are there to teach their parents just as much as parents are there to teach them. It is worth noting that in all four of the cases I just mentioned—my two cousins, my husband, and his brother—Taurus was one of the repetitive signs. It seems especially important for youngest children in large families to have something to focus them on their selfhood so they don't get lost in the fray.

A close girlfriend's family is a lesson in sign repetition. I will first tell you everyone's three signs, and then I will discuss the points of connection between family members. My friend has a Scorpio sun, Capricorn moon, and Libra rising, and her husband has a Scorpio sun, Pisces moon, and Capricorn rising. They have three girls. The oldest has a Libra sun, Taurus moon, and Scorpio rising; the middle child has a Scorpio sun, Capricorn moon, and Cancer rising; and the youngest has a Libra sun, Aries moon, and Gemini rising.

As you can already see, the same signs show up again and again: Scorpio (water), Libra (air), and Capricorn (earth). Everyone in the family has at least one of these signs, which connects them with the other members. My friend and her husband not only share the same sun sign, but they also have a beneficial conjunction in Capricorn (my friend's moon and her husband's rising). The siblings have connections to each other, and the middle child even has the same sun-moon combination as her mom (0.69 percent). There's a really nice balance of all of the elements, however, and having a significant amount of air in the house to balance out all of that water and feminine energy is especially helpful.

The youngest child, with her Libra-Aries polarity, is working on learning how to balance the "me" of her Aries moon with the "we" of her Libra sun. In other words, her life challenges will involve learning how to hold on to herself and still make space for others in the context of her relationships (in a form different from Taurus); again, it doesn't seem like a coincidence that the youngest child in a large family would be working on maintaining a strong sense of herself. One last note: everyone in the family agrees that Dad, with his Pisces (water) moon to everyone else's earth or fire moon, is the mushiest, most sensitive one of the bunch. How fantastic is that?

In terms of the dynamics between parents and children, there is a reason kids are born to their mothers; their mothers naturally have something to teach them. For example, one of my friends has a son who is a double-Pisces (water), and she has a Virgo (earth) moon. Without even thinking about it—intuitively, just by being her natural Virgo moon self—my friend has been able to provide the raw materials to help her son learn how to shore up and develop a day-to-day structure, which helps him contain his emotional experience. She is a therapist, so she has worked hard to attune to what her son needs, which is why he has internalized her so well. Because of this relationship, he has developed a more structured way of being in the world than he would have otherwise, given his own chart.

Here is another example. One of my close girlfriends has a Taurus (fixed) moon. She and her husband have two daughters, one of whom is triple-mutable, and the other is double-cardinal (with a fixed rising). Because of my friend's deeply fixed moon sign (and her husband's fixed moon and rising), both girls have been able to internalize a more fixed sense of themselves—in terms of setting boundaries with other people and finding their own center—than they would have otherwise, because of the natural charts of their parents.

Again, though, it helps when a parent's awareness of their child's chart is accompanied by attuned parenting. I know that this friend has been consciously trying to teach her kids these lessons—what they need to cultivate more of, astrologically speaking—because she and her kids have talks about astrology in her household. She is the girlfriend I mentioned earlier who, along with one of my clients, encouraged me to include the discussion that parents can use the approach of psychstrology with their young children in order to teach the kids about themselves. Speaking of that client, who has also used astrology to help her kids learn about their own natures (and how to deal with the things that need tempering), the illustration in figure 6 shows the picture her seven-year-old son drew in his feelings journal, displaying his pride and self-awareness as he learns more about his own nature.

Another one of my girlfriends asked me if I could consult with her about a parenting issue she was having with her daughter, and

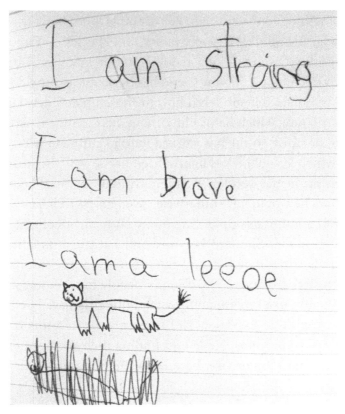

FIGURE 6. YOUNG BOY'S ILLUSTRATION OF HIS PRIDE
IN HIS NATURE (PUN INTENDED)

psychstrology proved to be helpful there, too. The daughter, who
has her sun (and multiple planets) in Pisces, was not responding
well to her mom, who has a Scorpio moon. I suggested that there
are multiple ways to help contain all the mutable, watery Pisces,
one of which is through Scorpio (fixed) control, which the mother
had naturally been trying to do, but another of which is through
the mutable structure of Virgo (the child's moon sign, which is
especially helpful because it is already inside of her). Fixed signs
like Scorpio control with less space than Virgo (the mutable earth
sign), which feels more like structure than control to Pisces.

Some of my clients have been particularly open-minded about
weaving astrology into our psychological analysis of their families,
and they have confirmed that it provides a helpful way to think

about things. (One of my clients, for example, has a son with my moon sign and a husband with my sun sign, so I am often able to help her understand where they are coming from.)

One client has a family who is full of water signs, but she doesn't have any water in her own three major signs. She is double-air (Aquarius sun and Libra rising) with a Capricorn (earth) moon. We have a beneficial conjunction because of my Capricorn sun and rising; I intuitively speak her native language, which has built trust between us. Her husband has his sun in Pisces (water) and moon in Cancer (water); her son is right on the cusp of Pisces (water) and Aries (fire), and has a Cancer (water) moon like his dad; her daughter has a Scorpio (water) sun and Aries (fire) moon. Besides her son's Virgo rising, my client is the only earth force in the family, and thus her role is to anchor and ground her family so they don't float away in a sea of water. For years, I had been working to help my client feel more inclined to speak up about her experience, which was hard for her because of her sun and rising being in air signs. (Air signs have an easier time talking themselves out of their emotions.)

Ironically, while we had long discussed astrology to some degree, this client became more open to weaving it into our sessions when crisis struck her family. Their family home flooded, and they had to move out for many months in order for it to be restored. It was a very hard time, but one that made my client more inclined to value her role as the anchor of her family. She saw the flood as a synchronicity that helped her realize how much water in general was taking over her life, and how much her family needed the anchor that only she could provide. Not surprisingly, her own increased valuing of her role, voice, and viewpoint has benefited her entire family, who are also able to value her role as it gets more integrated into their family system and structure.

Workplace Relationships

As with the MBTI (also known as Meyers-Briggs) and the Enneagram, which group people into types, people have astrological "types" in the sense that their three major signs make up their basic astrological nature. Some natures take better to certain roles than others. Thus, the lens of psychstrology can be used to achieve more clarity and balance in workplace settings. Understanding people better leads to more effective management, teamwork, and job delegation. Using this approach is a great way to better understand the nature of our colleagues, which can improve life tremendously given how much time we spend at work.

Just as with couples and families, even if you look only at the sun, moon, and rising signs, you can see many complex configurations to consider when using psychstrology in the workplace. Again, this is because everyone has not only multiple signs but also family histories that have impacted how their astrological nature has manifested. It is safe to say that all relationships contain areas of strength and ease, and areas of challenge and opportunity for growth. (The relative balance of each is what makes relationships feel so different from one another.) No relationship is good or bad; rather, they are all layered because we are all layered.

My favorite metaphor for relationships is that of a thick rope. If you look closely at a rope, you can see that it is made up of a bunch of smaller strands that are all twisted together. This drives home the point that you can't take relationships apart, keeping the strands you like and leaving out the strands you don't; you have to take them all together, and make decisions about the relationship based on that reality. This metaphor also explains how you can be so hurt and upset by those you love; there are beautiful strands and those twisted in pain.

Since all relationships have some "good" and easy components as well as some "bad" and challenging ones, your best bet is to try to improve your relationships by capitalizing on their strengths and their complementary and beneficial differences while tempering the natural (nature-based) challenges to the extent that this is possible. Worksheet 4 can help you analyze any relationship in your life, no matter the parameters.

WORKSHEET 4. ANALYZING YOUR RELATIONSHIPS

My sun sign is _____. This sign is made of _____(quality) _____(element).

My moon sign is _____. This sign is made of _____(quality) _____(element).

My rising sign is _____. This sign is made of _____(quality) _____(element).

The other person's sun sign is _____. This sign is made of _____(quality) _____(element).

The other person's moon sign is _____. This sign is made of _____(quality) _____(element).

The other person's rising sign is _____. This sign is made of _____(quality) _____(element).

(If applicable) We have a beneficial conjunction in _____ (sign), because it is the moon sign of _____(you/the other person) and the _____(sun, moon, or rising) sign of _____(you/the other person).

(If this is a romantic, family, or otherwise close relationship) After reading the descriptions of our moon signs, here are some of the ways in which I can observe my moon sign (_____) and the other person's moon sign (_____) interact with each other:

_____

Here are the signs we have that are trine (same element) to one another: _____

Here are some of the ways this makes our relationship work more smoothly: _____

_____

Here are some other helpful dynamics in our relationship, where our natures are different but work together in complementary ways that are beneficial for both of us: _____

_____

Here are the signs we have that are in polar opposition to one another: _____

Here are some ways this leads to or shows up as tension or conflict in our relationship:_____

_____

Here are some of the ways in which our polar opposition balances each of us: _____

_____

Here are the signs we have that are square (same quality) to one another: _____

Here are some ways this leads to or shows up as tension or conflict in our relationship:_____

_____

When I read about the other person's signs with an eye toward becoming more balanced, here are the things that resonate with me and that I think this person may be in my life to teach me:

_____

After reading about the other person's signs, here are some things I can keep in mind to help me be more compassionate with the other person: _____

_____

After reading about my own signs, here are some things I can keep in mind to help me be more compassionate with myself as I work to grow and become more balanced through, and in, my relationships:

Hopefully the information you have read here has helped you see that there is value in using astrology in conjunction with psychology to better understand yourself and others. Your astrological nature, the *Cliff's Notes* version of which is the combination of your sun, moon, and rising signs, offers much wisdom for you to incorporate and use as you grow toward balance and wholeness.

When your early psychological (attachment-related) experience—as well as your ongoing, present-day experience, which unfolds in the context of your current relationships—is viewed through this astrological lens, much additional and important insight is available to you. If you already had some degree of trust in and familiarity with astrology before reading this book, weaving it together with psychological principles has hopefully helped to deepen your application of it in your own life and relationships.

The opportunity to connect with ourselves and others on a deeper level can lead to truly extraordinary shifts. This is the case on all levels, projecting out from small (our individual lives) to large (the collective whole). If empathy is our only path out of conflict—within ourselves, our relationships, and as a people—ideally, we will find a way to shine its light into our darkness so that we may travel a purposeful path of growth and evolution.

Hope for the Future

There is no psychological explanation of astrology yet, on account of the fact that the empirical foundation in the sense of a science has not yet been laid. What I miss in astrological literature is chiefly the statistical method by which certain fundamental facts could be scientifically established.

—Carl Jung

There is a need for future research on the validity of astrology. There has been a relative scarcity thus far, but the research has not been nonexistent. Jung himself did some research on moon signs in couples, and in recent years the tide has also started to turn within the field of psychology itself.

For example, a 2018 psychological literature review published in *American Psychologist* looked at multiple studies that have been conducted on parapsychological phenomena such as psychic experiences and synchronicity. The evidence for parapsychological phenomena was examined and found to be comparable to the evidence for established phenomena in psychology and other disciplines. "People in all walks of life have reported events that seem to violate the current common sense view of space and time, ... In various surveys, majorities of respondents have endorsed a belief in such phenomena, . . ." the author, Dr. Etzel Cardeña, found. "In the last few years, parapsychology (psi) research has appeared in major psychology journals, and comprehensive reviews of the evidence for and against psi have been published."

Psychologist Scott Miller conducted a large Consumer Reports-style survey and presented his findings during his address at the 2017 Evolution of Psychotherapy Conference. He found that people rated psychics and other "spiritual advisers" as being more helpful than therapists, physicians, or friends. Dr. Miller argues that people want deeper meaning and a stronger sense of connectedness than standard psychotherapy can offer them. While he noted that he was sure it would cause controversy, he strongly suggested that the field of psychology could benefit from joining forces with a larger community of healers outside the field. This is similar to what I mentioned in the introduction, that psychology could stand to integrate more of the idea that the universe is bigger than we think.

Ideally, more intelligent people are able to make space for ideas that are a little outside the box in an attempt to cultivate more empathy at a time when we desperately need it. Psychology and astrology fit together amazingly well, and my hope is that more people within the field of psychology will expand their minds to make space for this ancient wisdom, evidence of which we can see all around us but never truly understand.

As Jung said, "If one calls it better when consciousness widens out and civilization increases, then I say we are moving towards an improved state of things, for it is very probable that civilization does increase with certain relapses from time to time. There have been cycles when things fall back into relative chaos, but then they picked up again. . . . If one takes the increase of civilization, the widening out of consciousness, for the real goal of mankind, if one says it is bad when things are unconscious and better when they become conscious, then things have become better." Let's prove him right.

Acknowledgments

I am incredibly lucky to have so many smart, capable, and generous people in my life who contributed to my journey. Thank you first to my cousin Stephanie, without whom this book would never have happened because she literally talked me out of my self-doubt and into writing it. We have been connected since we were kids, but the layers keep getting added. Your belief in me has always made me feel like I deserve it because I know you don't give it away.

To the people who made concrete contributions to this book: my editor, Jessica Vineyard, who has the amazing ability to be up in the air and down on the ground at the same time, simultaneously drawing on both realms. You have made me so much clearer as well as more confident in my self-expression, gifts I hope I can hold on to and put to use in other facets of my life. This book is so much better for your influence.

To Martha Bullen, whose willingness to make space for astrology even as a skeptic gave me the drive to push forward at critical times. I am eternally grateful for your belief in me and your excellent intuition, discerning nature, and sense of connection to Jung's ideas (and to your dad for introducing you to them). Thank you for all of your guidance and your tireless work ethic.

To Debby Englander, who made many helpful suggestions thanks to her clever, eagle-eye vision. Thanks also to Geoffrey Berwind, who has a powerful ability to inspire combined with an amazingly psychic intuition. And to my book designer, Christy Collins, who I know I would have been friends with had we grown up together: thank you for your psychic water vision and interest from the get-go.

To my dear friends who were generously willing to read some of the book beforehand, especially Suzanne Farrell, who read the entire first draft from beginning to end. Your friendship, insight, and support is such a gift to me; thank you for always reminding me what friendship should look and feel like.

Thanks also to Denise Detrick Barnes and Todd Barnes, Elizabeth Truglio, Elaine Perea, Trina Woods, Jennifer Grimaldi, and Andrea Scully for reading the earlier pieces and encouraging me to keep going. And a heartfelt thank you to the other numerous friends and family members who supported me, and this effort, along the way.

A special thanks to my friends and family who let me use examples from their own lives in this book, as well as to all the others who were open enough to let me look up their (and their children's) charts. Your openness to this viewpoint has contributed greatly to my ability to understand all of these concepts more deeply. You all contributed to an energetic GoFundMe-like campaign that enabled this book to get off the ground.

Speaking of that energetic campaign, I would like to say a sincere and enormous thank you to my clients. This book would certainly not exist without you and your willingness to share the space with me and these ideas. I value our relationships and your trust and belief in me so highly. I am especially grateful to those who let me use their stories, and in particular to the client whose prior experience with astrology proved to be extraordinarily valuable to me: a huge and heartfelt thank you for all of your amazing insights, whose fruits are all over these pages.

I have been incredibly fortunate for those who have guided, supervised, therapized, or mentored me in some way. I am beyond grateful to the late Dr. Don Weatherley, whose early influence and belief in me laid integral aspects of my professional foundation. To

Dr. Linda Craighead, who has always let me be exactly who I am while still providing powerful guidance; thank you for being the most open-minded person I know.

To Dr. Gary McClelland, who displayed extreme kindness in offering guidance (during his retirement, no less) despite his skepticism of the material. To Cindy Brody, my deep and brilliant psychoanalyst; besides being the first person to tell me I sounded like a Jungian, you also truly helped me heal and understand how to help heal others, and for that, I thank you. I could never have put myself out there like this without all the work we did together.

To the amazing Lauren Skye, founder of the Inner Connection Institute (www.innerconnection.org), for her help in this same vein; I admire you so much and strive to achieve even a tenth of your deep wisdom and insight. Thank you for all of the deep lessons you have helped me to learn. To the late Carolyn Crawford, the most amazing astrologer I ever met in person; I have never had my mind blown quite like that. I wish you were still here to share your gift with others.

I literally wouldn't still be on this earth if it weren't for the amazing musicians, past and present, who kept me feeling connected enough even through the darkest of times. To the earth and water crew who connect me to my feelings but keep me grounded in reality and life: Jimmy Page, Michael Stipe, Blake Schwarzenbach, Chuck Ragan, and Joey Cape. I am so grateful that each of you has found a way to tolerate the intense pain you have felt at times, but not drown in it, so you can continue to turn it into something meaningful that makes other people feel understood and connected (which helps us not lose hope). To the double-earth Capricorns Dave Grohl and Eddie Vedder, who combine their incredible talents with a work ethic that doesn't quit: I am so grateful that both of you continue to make music and touch lives in all the ways that you do. You are serious forces and make me so proud of our shared sign. Thank you also to the incredibly talented Aquarius (air) musicians Jason Cruz—who has the same sun-moon combination as my husband—and Brian Fallon. You both have a way of making me feel way less heavy, even though you are still plenty deep.

To my dad, for being my biggest champion. Your proud tears about my having "shit to say" is truly the coolest thing a parent could ever feel about and say to their child. Thank you for reading every single word and being willing to take in and be moved by the information despite your skepticism. And thank you especially for your willingness to keep growing, even into your later years. It is so admirable, and I am beyond grateful for all of it.

Finally, to my husband, Jeremy, for being the most constant and gentle soul I have ever known. You believed in me from the very beginning, and reminded me of that belief many times when I most needed to hear it. Your love for me has healed me more than anything else in my life. I could not be luckier that you love me so much. For so many reasons, I could never have done this without you.

APPENDIX A
Moon Table

Use this table to find your moon sign. Find your birthday under the year you were born. If it falls between two dates, use the date above it. The following table is in Greenwich Mean Time (GMT), so you will need to adjust your birth time to GMT before you look up your moon sign. Please add the required number of hours to your birth time beforehand; for instance, if you were born at four o'clock a.m. in New York, you would look up nine o'clock a.m. (GMT).

If you were born in Eastern Standard Time, add five hours to your birth time.

If you were born in Central Standard Time, add six hours to your birth time.

If you were born in Mountain Standard Time, add seven hours to your birth time.

If you were born in Pacific Standard Time, add eight hours to your birth time.

If you were born during Daylight Savings Time (DST, which is not observed in Arizona or Hawaii), you will need to make an additional adjustment before looking up your moon sign. If DST was in effect on the day you were born, add one hour less to adjust your birth time to GMT. Besides being in continuous effect from February 9, 1942, to September 9, 1945, DST is observed between the first Sunday in April (the last Sunday in April, if prior to 1986) at two o'clock a.m. and the last Sunday in October at two o'clock a.m. Again, if you were born during DST, add one hour less to adjust your birth time to GMT.

January 1900
2nd 9:26 pm Aquarius
4th 10:09 pm Pisces
6th 11:46 pm Aries
9th 3:26 am Taurus
11th 9:37 am Gemini
13th 6:06 pm Cancer
16th 4:31 am Leo
18th 4:27 pm Virgo
21st 5:07 am Libra
23rd 4:54 pm Scorpio
26th 1:50 am Sagittarius
28th 6:48 am Capricorn
30th 8:14 am Aquarius

February 1900
1st 7:48 am Pisces
3rd 7:39 am Aries
5th 9:42 am Taurus
7th 3:07 pm Gemini
9th 11:50 pm Cancer
12th 10:49 am Leo
14th 11:00 pm Virgo
17th 11:37 am Libra
19th 11:45 pm Scorpio
22nd 9:53 am Sagittarius
24th 4:33 pm Capricorn
26th 7:16 pm Aquarius
28th 7:06 pm Pisces

March 1900
2nd 6:03 pm Aries
4th 6:25 pm Taurus
6th 10:05 pm Gemini
9th 5:46 am Cancer
11th 4:39 pm Leo
14th 5:04 am Virgo
16th 5:39 pm Libra
19th 5:35 am Scorpio
21st 4:03 pm Sagittarius
23rd 11:57 pm Capricorn
26th 4:26 am Aquarius
28th 5:43 am Pisces
30th 5:13 am Aries

April 1900
1st 5:01 am Taurus
3rd 7:14 am Gemini
5th 1:17 pm Cancer
7th 11:11 pm Leo
10th 11:25 am Virgo
13th 12:01 am Libra
15th 11:38 am Scorpio
17th 9:39 pm Sagittarius
20th 5:37 am Capricorn
22nd 11:06 am Aquarius
24th 1:59 pm Pisces
26th 3:01 pm Aries
28th 3:35 pm Taurus
30th 5:30 pm Gemini

May 1900
2nd 10:24 pm Cancer
5th 7:01 am Leo
7th 6:36 pm Virgo
10th 7:10 am Libra
12th 6:41 pm Scorpio
15th 4:08 am Sagittarius
17th 11:20 am Capricorn
19th 4:31 pm Aquarius
21st 8:02 pm Pisces
23rd 10:22 pm Aries
26th 12:21 am Taurus
28th 3:07 am Gemini
30th 7:55 am Cancer

June 1900
1st 3:44 pm Leo
4th 2:34 am Virgo
6th 2:59 pm Libra
9th 2:46 am Scorpio
11th 12:06 pm Sagittarius
13th 6:32 pm Capricorn
15th 10:38 pm Aquarius
18th 1:27 am Pisces
20th 3:57 am Aries
22nd 6:54 am Taurus
24th 10:52 am Gemini
26th 4:28 pm Cancer
29th 12:19 am Leo

July 1900
1st 10:42 am Virgo
3rd 10:59 pm Libra
6th 11:12 am Scorpio
8th 9:05 pm Sagittarius
11th 3:27 am Capricorn
13th 6:42 am Aquarius
15th 8:13 am Pisces
17th 9:38 am Aries
19th 12:17 pm Taurus
21st 4:48 pm Gemini
23rd 11:20 pm Cancer
26th 7:49 am Leo
28th 6:18 pm Virgo
31st 6:30 am Libra

August 1900
2nd 7:08 pm Scorpio
5th 6:01 am Sagittarius
7th 1:14 pm Capricorn
9th 4:32 pm Aquarius
11th 5:11 pm Pisces
13th 5:10 pm Aries
15th 6:25 pm Taurus
17th 10:14 pm Gemini
20th 4:56 am Cancer
22nd 2:03 pm Leo
25th 12:57 am Virgo
27th 1:13 pm Libra
30th 2:03 am Scorpio

September 1900
1st 1:49 pm Sagittarius
3rd 10:27 pm Capricorn
6th 2:53 am Aquarius
8th 3:47 am Pisces
10th 3:00 am Aries
12th 2:45 am Taurus
14th 4:58 am Gemini
16th 10:39 am Cancer
18th 7:38 pm Leo
21st 6:53 am Virgo
23rd 7:19 pm Libra
26th 8:06 am Scorpio
28th 8:10 pm Sagittarius

October 1900
1st 5:57 am Capricorn
3rd 12:04 pm Aquarius
5th 2:23 pm Pisces
7th 2:07 pm Aries
9th 1:17 pm Taurus
11th 2:02 pm Gemini
13th 6:02 pm Cancer
16th 1:53 am Leo
18th 12:52 pm Virgo
21st 1:25 am Libra
23rd 2:04 pm Scorpio
26th 1:50 am Sagittarius
28th 11:47 am Capricorn
30th 7:02 pm Aquarius

November 1900
1st 11:06 pm Pisces
4th 12:27 am Aries
6th 12:25 am Taurus
8th 12:50 am Gemini
10th 3:32 am Cancer
12th 9:49 am Leo
14th 7:47 pm Virgo
17th 8:08 am Libra
19th 8:48 pm Scorpio
22nd 8:09 am Sagittarius
24th 5:26 pm Capricorn
27th 12:30 am Aquarius
29th 5:24 am Pisces

December 1900
1st 8:22 am Aries
3rd 10:02 am Taurus
5th 11:27 am Gemini
7th 2:04 pm Cancer
9th 7:19 pm Leo
12th 4:03 am Virgo
14th 3:48 pm Libra
17th 4:33 am Scorpio
19th 3:54 pm Sagittarius
22nd 12:33 am Capricorn
24th 6:34 am Aquarius
26th 10:47 am Pisces
28th 2:02 pm Aries
30th 4:55 pm Taurus

January 1901
1st 7:54 pm Gemini
3rd 11:36 pm Cancer
6th 4:59 am Leo
8th 1:03 pm Virgo
11th 12:07 am Libra
13th 12:52 pm Scorpio
16th 12:43 am Sagittarius
18th 9:30 am Capricorn
20th 2:48 pm Aquarius
22nd 5:42 pm Pisces
24th 7:45 pm Aries
26th 10:16 pm Taurus
29th 1:54 am Gemini
31st 6:50 am Cancer

February 1901
2nd 1:13 pm Leo
4th 9:33 pm Virgo
7th 8:17 am Libra
9th 8:56 pm Scorpio
12th 9:25 am Sagittarius
14th 7:09 pm Capricorn
17th 12:50 am Aquarius
19th 3:06 am Pisces
21st 3:44 am Aries
23rd 4:41 am Taurus
25th 7:21 am Gemini
27th 12:20 pm Cancer

March 1901
1st 7:30 pm Leo
4th 4:37 am Virgo
6th 3:36 pm Libra
9th 4:11 am Scorpio
11th 5:03 pm Sagittarius
14th 3:56 am Capricorn
16th 10:56 am Aquarius
18th 1:52 pm Pisces
20th 2:07 pm Aries
22nd 1:42 pm Taurus
24th 2:37 pm Gemini
26th 6:14 pm Cancer
29th 1:00 am Leo
31st 10:29 am Virgo

April 1901
2nd 9:57 pm Libra
5th 10:37 am Scorpio
7th 11:31 pm Sagittarius
10th 11:01 am Capricorn
12th 7:27 pm Aquarius
14th 11:56 pm Pisces
17th 1:06 am Aries
19th 12:33 am Taurus
21st 12:18 am Gemini
23rd 2:11 am Cancer
25th 7:28 am Leo
27th 4:19 pm Virgo
30th 3:54 am Libra

May 1901
2nd 4:43 pm Scorpio
5th 5:27 am Sagittarius
7th 4:53 pm Capricorn
10th 1:58 am Aquarius
12th 7:55 am Pisces
14th 10:44 am Aries
16th 11:17 am Taurus
18th 11:07 am Gemini
20th 12:03 pm Cancer
22nd 3:47 pm Leo
24th 11:18 pm Virgo
27th 10:18 am Libra
29th 11:07 pm Scorpio

June 1901
1st 11:44 am Sagittarius
3rd 10:43 pm Capricorn
6th 7:30 am Aquarius
8th 1:55 pm Pisces
10th 6:01 pm Aries
12th 8:10 pm Taurus
14th 9:10 pm Gemini
16th 10:22 pm Cancer
19th 1:23 am Leo
21st 7:40 am Virgo
23rd 5:41 pm Libra
26th 6:14 am Scorpio
28th 6:51 pm Sagittarius

July 1901
1st 5:31 am Capricorn
3rd 1:34 pm Aquarius
5th 7:22 pm Pisces
7th 11:36 pm Aries
10th 2:45 am Taurus
12th 5:10 am Gemini
14th 7:31 am Cancer
16th 10:54 am Leo
18th 4:43 pm Virgo
21st 1:55 am Libra
23rd 1:59 pm Scorpio
26th 2:45 am Sagittarius
28th 1:33 pm Capricorn
30th 9:09 pm Aquarius

August 1901
2nd 1:59 am Pisces
4th 5:16 am Aries
6th 8:07 am Taurus
8th 11:08 am Gemini
10th 2:38 pm Cancer
12th 7:04 pm Leo
15th 1:17 am Virgo
17th 10:14 am Libra
19th 9:58 pm Scorpio
22nd 10:53 am Sagittarius
24th 10:18 pm Capricorn
27th 6:13 am Aquarius
29th 10:36 am Pisces
31st 12:45 pm Aries

September 1901
2nd 2:17 pm Taurus
4th 4:32 pm Gemini
6th 8:11 pm Cancer
9th 1:26 am Leo
11th 8:33 am Virgo
13th 5:52 pm Libra
16th 5:31 am Scorpio
18th 6:33 pm Sagittarius
21st 6:44 am Capricorn
23rd 3:45 pm Aquarius
25th 8:43 pm Pisces
27th 10:29 pm Aries
29th 10:48 pm Taurus

October 1901
1st 11:28 pm Gemini
4th 1:54 am Cancer
6th 6:52 am Leo
8th 2:28 pm Virgo
11th 12:26 am Libra
13th 12:19 pm Scorpio
16th 1:22 am Sagittarius
18th 2:01 pm Capricorn
21st 12:18 am Aquarius
23rd 6:46 am Pisces
25th 9:26 am Aries
27th 9:35 am Taurus
29th 9:02 am Gemini
31st 9:43 am Cancer

November 1901
2nd 1:09 pm Leo
4th 8:06 pm Virgo
7th 6:15 am Libra
9th 6:30 pm Scorpio
12th 7:32 am Sagittarius
14th 8:09 pm Capricorn
17th 7:04 am Aquarius
19th 3:03 pm Pisces
21st 7:32 pm Aries
23rd 8:52 pm Taurus
25th 8:25 pm Gemini
27th 8:03 pm Cancer
29th 9:44 pm Leo

December 1901
2nd 3:02 am Virgo
4th 12:23 pm Libra
7th 12:38 am Scorpio
9th 1:45 pm Sagittarius
12th 2:04 am Capricorn
14th 12:42 pm Aquarius
16th 9:12 pm Pisces
19th 3:09 am Aries
21st 6:23 am Taurus
23rd 7:22 am Gemini
25th 7:23 am Cancer
27th 8:18 am Leo
29th 12:04 pm Virgo
31st 7:56 pm Libra

January 1902
3rd 7:30 am Scorpio
5th 8:36 pm Sagittarius
8th 8:47 am Capricorn
10th 6:48 pm Aquarius
13th 2:40 am Pisces
15th 8:44 am Aries
17th 1:06 pm Taurus
19th 3:49 pm Gemini
21st 5:22 pm Cancer
23rd 6:56 pm Leo
25th 10:16 pm Virgo
28th 4:57 am Libra
30th 3:28 pm Scorpio

February 1902
2nd 4:17 am Sagittarius
4th 4:37 pm Capricorn
7th 2:27 am Aquarius
9th 9:29 am Pisces
11th 2:31 pm Aries
13th 6:26 pm Taurus
15th 9:43 pm Gemini
18th 12:37 am Cancer
20th 3:37 am Leo
22nd 7:45 am Virgo
24th 2:18 pm Libra
27th 12:05 am Scorpio

March 1902
1st 12:26 pm Sagittarius
4th 1:04 am Capricorn
6th 11:21 am Aquarius
8th 6:16 pm Pisces
10th 10:21 pm Aries
13th 12:55 am Taurus
15th 3:13 am Gemini
17th 6:04 am Cancer
19th 9:54 am Leo
21st 3:12 pm Virgo
23rd 10:31 pm Libra
26th 8:20 am Scorpio
28th 8:24 pm Sagittarius
31st 9:11 am Capricorn

April 1902
2nd 8:20 pm Aquarius
5th 4:03 am Pisces
7th 8:11 am Aries
9th 9:51 am Taurus
11th 10:37 am Gemini
13th 12:04 pm Cancer
15th 3:18 pm Leo
17th 8:57 pm Virgo
20th 5:05 am Libra
22nd 3:28 pm Scorpio
25th 3:36 am Sagittarius
27th 4:26 pm Capricorn
30th 4:16 am Aquarius

May 1902
2nd 1:15 pm Pisces
4th 6:30 pm Aries
6th 8:23 pm Taurus
8th 8:21 pm Gemini
10th 8:16 pm Cancer
12th 9:54 pm Leo
15th 2:36 am Virgo
17th 10:42 am Libra
19th 9:33 pm Scorpio
22nd 9:58 am Sagittarius
24th 10:47 pm Capricorn
27th 10:50 am Aquarius
29th 8:49 pm Pisces

June 1902
1st 3:35 am Aries
3rd 6:47 am Taurus
5th 7:11 am Gemini
7th 6:27 am Cancer
9th 6:40 am Leo
11th 9:44 am Virgo
13th 4:45 pm Libra
16th 3:22 am Scorpio
18th 3:57 pm Sagittarius
21st 4:45 am Capricorn
23rd 4:37 pm Aquarius
26th 2:50 am Pisces
28th 10:39 am Aries
30th 3:26 pm Taurus

July 1902
2nd 5:15 pm Gemini
4th 5:08 pm Cancer
6th 4:55 pm Leo
8th 6:44 pm Virgo
11th 12:16 am Libra
13th 9:55 am Scorpio
15th 10:17 pm Sagittarius
18th 11:04 am Capricorn
20th 10:38 pm Aquarius
23rd 8:24 am Pisces
25th 4:15 pm Aries
27th 9:57 pm Taurus
30th 1:16 am Gemini

August 1902
1st 2:34 am Cancer
3rd 3:07 am Leo
5th 4:43 am Virgo
7th 9:14 am Libra
9th 5:42 pm Scorpio
12th 5:26 am Sagittarius
14th 6:09 pm Capricorn
17th 5:38 am Aquarius
19th 2:51 pm Pisces
21st 9:57 pm Aries
24th 3:20 am Taurus
26th 7:13 am Gemini
28th 9:50 am Cancer
30th 11:46 am Leo

September 1902
1st 2:13 pm Virgo
3rd 6:42 pm Libra
6th 2:25 am Scorpio
8th 1:24 pm Sagittarius
11th 2:01 am Capricorn
13th 1:44 pm Aquarius
15th 10:53 pm Pisces
18th 5:14 am Aries
20th 9:31 am Taurus
22nd 12:40 pm Gemini
24th 3:23 pm Cancer
26th 6:16 pm Leo
28th 9:59 pm Virgo

October 1902
1st 3:19 am Libra
3rd 11:07 am Scorpio
5th 9:40 pm Sagittarius
8th 10:05 am Capricorn
10th 10:19 pm Aquarius
13th 8:07 am Pisces
15th 2:30 pm Aries
17th 5:56 pm Taurus
19th 7:41 pm Gemini
21st 9:10 pm Cancer
23rd 11:39 pm Leo
26th 3:53 am Virgo
28th 10:14 am Libra
30th 6:46 pm Scorpio

November 1902
2nd 5:26 am Sagittarius
4th 5:44 pm Capricorn
7th 6:21 am Aquarius
9th 5:15 pm Pisces
12th 12:44 am Aries
14th 4:24 am Taurus
16th 5:19 am Gemini
18th 5:15 am Cancer
20th 6:06 am Leo
22nd 9:24 am Virgo
24th 3:48 pm Libra
27th 1:01 am Scorpio
29th 12:11 pm Sagittarius

December 1902
2nd 12:33 am Capricorn
4th 1:16 pm Aquarius
7th 1:01 am Pisces
9th 10:03 am Aries
11th 3:11 pm Taurus
13th 4:38 pm Gemini
15th 3:56 pm Cancer
17th 3:14 pm Leo
19th 4:40 pm Virgo
21st 9:46 pm Libra
24th 6:39 am Scorpio
26th 6:09 pm Sagittarius
29th 6:44 am Capricorn
31st 7:20 pm Aquarius

January 1903
3rd 7:12 am Pisces
5th 5:14 pm Aries
8th 12:09 am Taurus
10th 3:19 am Gemini
12th 3:29 am Cancer
14th 2:27 am Leo
16th 2:32 am Virgo
18th 5:47 am Libra
20th 1:13 pm Scorpio
23rd 12:15 am Sagittarius
25th 12:54 pm Capricorn
28th 1:27 am Aquarius
30th 12:55 pm Pisces

February 1903
1st 10:52 pm Aries
4th 6:36 am Taurus
6th 11:27 am Gemini
8th 1:26 pm Cancer
10th 1:34 pm Leo
12th 1:42 pm Virgo
14th 3:53 pm Libra
16th 9:43 pm Scorpio
19th 7:29 am Sagittarius
21st 7:46 pm Capricorn
24th 8:20 am Aquarius
26th 7:31 pm Pisces

March 1903
1st 4:45 am Aries
3rd 12:00 pm Taurus
5th 5:16 pm Gemini
7th 8:34 pm Cancer
9th 10:23 pm Leo
11th 11:47 pm Virgo
14th 2:18 am Libra
16th 7:26 am Scorpio
18th 4:01 pm Sagittarius
21st 3:33 am Capricorn
23rd 4:06 pm Aquarius
26th 3:24 am Pisces
28th 12:13 pm Aries
30th 6:29 pm Taurus

April 1903
1st 10:50 pm Gemini
4th 1:59 am Cancer
6th 4:39 am Leo
8th 7:27 am Virgo
10th 11:11 am Libra
12th 4:45 pm Scorpio
15th 12:56 am Sagittarius
17th 11:49 am Capricorn
20th 12:15 am Aquarius
22nd 12:00 pm Pisces
24th 9:07 pm Aries
27th 2:55 am Taurus
29th 6:07 am Gemini

May 1903
1st 8:02 am Cancer
3rd 10:03 am Leo
5th 1:08 pm Virgo
7th 5:52 pm Libra
10th 12:26 am Scorpio
12th 9:02 am Sagittarius
14th 7:45 pm Capricorn
17th 8:04 am Aquarius
19th 8:21 pm Pisces
22nd 6:22 am Aries
24th 12:40 pm Taurus
26th 3:28 pm Gemini
28th 4:11 pm Cancer
30th 4:42 pm Leo

June 1903
1st 6:45 pm Virgo
3rd 11:18 pm Libra
6th 6:28 am Scorpio
8th 3:46 pm Sagittarius
11th 2:47 am Capricorn
13th 3:06 pm Aquarius
16th 3:42 am Pisces
18th 2:43 pm Aries
20th 10:17 pm Taurus
23rd 1:46 am Gemini
25th 2:13 am Cancer
27th 1:36 am Leo
29th 2:04 am Virgo

July 1903
1st 5:19 am Libra
3rd 11:57 am Scorpio
5th 9:31 pm Sagittarius
8th 8:56 am Capricorn
10th 9:21 pm Aquarius
13th 9:59 am Pisces
15th 9:36 pm Aries
18th 6:28 am Taurus
20th 11:26 am Gemini
22nd 12:48 pm Cancer
24th 12:07 pm Leo
26th 11:33 am Virgo
28th 1:13 pm Libra
30th 6:27 pm Scorpio

August 1903
2nd 3:21 am Sagittarius
4th 2:49 pm Capricorn
7th 3:21 am Aquarius
9th 3:50 pm Pisces
12th 3:22 am Aries
14th 12:52 pm Taurus
16th 7:15 pm Gemini
18th 10:12 pm Cancer
20th 10:37 pm Leo
22nd 10:13 pm Virgo
24th 11:01 pm Libra
27th 2:46 am Scorpio
29th 10:21 am Sagittarius
31st 9:14 pm Capricorn

September 1903
3rd 9:45 am Aquarius
5th 10:07 pm Pisces
8th 9:12 am Aries
10th 6:22 pm Taurus
13th 1:11 am Gemini
15th 5:27 am Cancer
17th 7:30 am Leo
19th 8:20 am Virgo
21st 9:28 am Libra
23rd 12:33 pm Scorpio
25th 6:53 pm Sagittarius
28th 4:45 am Capricorn
30th 4:58 pm Aquarius

October 1903
3rd 5:24 am Pisces
5th 4:11 pm Aries
8th 12:34 am Taurus
10th 6:41 am Gemini
12th 11:00 am Cancer
14th 2:03 pm Leo
16th 4:24 pm Virgo
18th 6:50 pm Libra
20th 10:23 pm Scorpio
23rd 4:15 am Sagittarius
25th 1:13 pm Capricorn
28th 12:58 am Aquarius
30th 1:34 pm Pisces

November 1903
2nd 12:36 am Aries
4th 8:36 am Taurus
6th 1:39 pm Gemini
8th 4:50 pm Cancer
10th 7:24 pm Leo
12th 10:16 pm Virgo
15th 1:55 am Libra
17th 6:42 am Scorpio
19th 1:06 pm Sagittarius
21st 9:50 pm Capricorn
24th 9:08 am Aquarius
26th 9:55 pm Pisces
29th 9:41 am Aries

December 1903
1st 6:13 pm Taurus
3rd 10:56 pm Gemini
6th 12:55 am Cancer
8th 1:58 am Leo
10th 3:47 am Virgo
12th 7:21 am Libra
14th 12:55 pm Scorpio
16th 8:19 pm Sagittarius
19th 5:34 am Capricorn
21st 4:48 pm Aquarius
24th 5:35 am Pisces
26th 6:08 pm Aries
29th 3:57 am Taurus
31st 9:33 am Gemini

January 1904
2nd 11:25 am Cancer
4th 11:19 am Leo
6th 11:23 am Virgo
8th 1:25 pm Libra
10th 6:19 pm Scorpio
13th 2:03 am Sagittarius
15th 11:57 am Capricorn
17th 11:32 pm Aquarius
20th 12:18 pm Pisces
23rd 1:10 am Aries
25th 12:09 pm Taurus
27th 7:25 pm Gemini
29th 10:32 pm Cancer
31st 10:38 pm Leo

February 1904
2nd 9:45 pm Virgo
4th 10:02 pm Libra
7th 1:08 am Scorpio
9th 7:49 am Sagittarius
11th 5:40 pm Capricorn
14th 5:36 am Aquarius
16th 6:27 pm Pisces
19th 7:10 am Aries
21st 6:30 pm Taurus
24th 3:04 am Gemini
26th 8:00 am Cancer
28th 9:37 am Leo

March 1904
1st 9:17 am Virgo
3rd 8:53 am Libra
5th 10:24 am Scorpio
7th 3:18 pm Sagittarius
10th 12:03 am Capricorn
12th 11:46 am Aquarius
15th 12:43 am Pisces
17th 1:12 pm Aries
20th 12:09 am Taurus
22nd 8:52 am Gemini
24th 2:55 pm Cancer
26th 6:16 pm Leo
28th 7:31 pm Virgo
30th 7:55 pm Libra

April 1904
1st 9:04 pm Scorpio
4th 12:41 am Sagittarius
6th 7:57 am Capricorn
8th 6:48 pm Aquarius
11th 7:37 am Pisces
13th 8:04 pm Aries
16th 6:31 am Taurus
18th 2:31 pm Gemini
20th 8:22 pm Cancer
23rd 12:27 am Leo
25th 3:11 am Virgo
27th 5:05 am Libra
29th 7:07 am Scorpio

May 1904
1st 10:37 am Sagittarius
3rd 4:58 pm Capricorn
6th 2:50 am Aquarius
8th 3:16 pm Pisces
11th 3:50 am Aries
13th 2:11 pm Taurus
15th 9:30 pm Gemini
18th 2:21 am Cancer
20th 5:50 am Leo
22nd 8:50 am Virgo
24th 11:48 am Libra
26th 3:08 pm Scorpio
28th 7:29 pm Sagittarius
31st 1:53 am Capricorn

June 1904
2nd 11:13 am Aquarius
4th 11:15 pm Pisces
7th 12:01 pm Aries
9th 10:50 pm Taurus
12th 6:06 am Gemini
14th 10:11 am Cancer
16th 12:27 pm Leo
18th 2:26 pm Virgo
20th 5:11 pm Libra
22nd 9:09 pm Scorpio
25th 2:31 am Sagittarius
27th 9:40 am Capricorn
29th 7:07 pm Aquarius

July 1904
2nd 6:57 am Pisces
4th 7:54 pm Aries
7th 7:28 am Taurus
9th 3:31 pm Gemini
11th 7:41 pm Cancer
13th 9:10 pm Leo
15th 9:48 pm Virgo
17th 11:14 pm Libra
20th 2:34 am Scorpio
22nd 8:10 am Sagittarius
24th 4:01 pm Capricorn
27th 2:01 am Aquarius
29th 1:58 pm Pisces

August 1904
1st 2:59 am Aries
3rd 3:13 pm Taurus
6th 12:30 am Gemini
8th 5:44 am Cancer
10th 7:30 am Leo
12th 7:26 am Virgo
14th 7:26 am Libra
16th 9:12 am Scorpio
18th 1:50 pm Sagittarius
20th 9:37 pm Capricorn
23rd 8:02 am Aquarius
25th 8:16 pm Pisces
28th 9:17 am Aries
30th 9:44 pm Taurus

September 1904
2nd 7:59 am Gemini
4th 2:46 pm Cancer
6th 5:53 pm Leo
8th 6:19 pm Virgo
10th 5:45 pm Libra
12th 6:05 pm Scorpio
14th 9:05 pm Sagittarius
17th 3:45 am Capricorn
19th 1:55 pm Aquarius
22nd 2:20 am Pisces
24th 3:20 pm Aries
27th 3:33 am Taurus
29th 1:59 pm Gemini

October 1904
1st 9:50 pm Cancer
4th 2:38 am Leo
6th 4:36 am Virgo
8th 4:45 am Libra
10th 4:43 am Scorpio
12th 6:25 am Sagittarius
14th 11:31 am Capricorn
16th 8:39 pm Aquarius
19th 8:49 am Pisces
21st 9:51 pm Aries
24th 9:44 am Taurus
26th 7:37 pm Gemini
29th 3:24 am Cancer
31st 9:04 am Leo

November 1904
2nd 12:40 pm Virgo
4th 2:27 pm Libra
6th 3:21 pm Scorpio
8th 4:54 pm Sagittarius
10th 8:56 pm Capricorn
13th 4:47 am Aquarius
15th 4:14 pm Pisces
18th 5:14 am Aries
20th 5:06 pm Taurus
23rd 2:25 am Gemini
25th 9:17 am Cancer
27th 2:26 pm Leo
29th 6:27 pm Virgo

December 1904
1st 9:33 pm Virgo
4th 12:01 am Scorpio
6th 2:38 am Sagittarius
8th 6:46 am Capricorn
10th 1:53 pm Aquarius
13th 12:30 am Pisces
15th 1:18 pm Aries
18th 1:33 am Taurus
20th 10:57 pm Gemini
22nd 5:08 pm Cancer
24th 9:04 pm Leo
27th 12:01 am Virgo
29th 2:56 am Libra
31st 6:12 am Scorpio

January 1905
2nd 10:08 am Sagittarius
4th 3:20 pm Capricorn
6th 10:43 pm Aquarius
9th 8:56 am Pisces
11th 9:29 pm Aries
14th 10:10 am Taurus
16th 8:25 pm Gemini
19th 2:56 am Cancer
21st 6:13 am Leo
23rd 7:46 am Virgo
25th 9:10 am Libra
27th 11:35 am Scorpio
29th 3:44 pm Sagittarius
31st 9:51 pm Capricorn

February 1905
3rd 6:08 am Aquarius
5th 4:39 pm Pisces
8th 5:03 am Aries
10th 5:59 pm Taurus
13th 5:17 am Gemini
15th 1:05 pm Cancer
17th 5:01 pm Leo
19th 6:06 pm Virgo
21st 6:04 pm Libra
23rd 6:42 pm Scorpio
25th 9:31 pm Sagittarius
28th 3:18 am Capricorn

March 1905
2nd 12:05 pm Aquarius
4th 11:12 pm Pisces
7th 11:45 am Aries
10th 12:42 am Taurus
12th 12:35 pm Gemini
14th 9:47 pm Cancer
17th 3:19 am Leo
19th 5:19 am Virgo
21st 5:04 am Libra
23rd 4:26 am Scorpio
25th 5:26 am Sagittarius
27th 9:40 am Capricorn
29th 5:47 pm Aquarius

April 1905
1st 5:03 am Pisces
3rd 5:52 pm Aries
6th 6:44 am Taurus
8th 6:34 pm Gemini
11th 4:28 am Cancer
13th 11:30 am Leo
15th 3:13 pm Virgo
17th 4:05 pm Libra
19th 3:31 pm Scorpio
21st 3:29 pm Sagittarius
23rd 6:04 pm Capricorn
26th 12:41 am Aquarius
28th 11:14 pm Pisces

May 1905
1st 12:03 am Aries
3rd 12:52 pm Taurus
6th 12:21 am Gemini
8th 10:01 am Cancer
10th 5:34 pm Leo
12th 10:40 pm Virgo
15th 1:12 am Libra
17th 1:50 am Scorpio
19th 2:05 am Sagittarius
21st 3:56 am Capricorn
23rd 9:11 am Aquarius
25th 6:33 pm Pisces
28th 6:52 am Aries
30th 7:40 pm Taurus

June 1905
2nd 6:55 am Gemini
4th 3:57 pm Cancer
6th 10:59 pm Leo
9th 4:17 am Virgo
11th 7:53 am Libra
13th 10:01 am Scorpio
15th 11:30 am Sagittarius
17th 1:47 pm Capricorn
19th 6:33 pm Aquarius
22nd 2:56 am Pisces
24th 2:32 pm Aries
27th 3:16 am Taurus
29th 2:36 pm Gemini

July 1905
1st 11:17 pm Cancer
4th 5:27 am Leo
6th 9:53 am Virgo
8th 1:16 pm Libra
10th 4:04 pm Scorpio
12th 6:46 pm Sagittarius
14th 10:12 pm Capricorn
17th 3:29 am Aquarius
19th 11:36 am Pisces
21st 10:39 pm Aries
24th 11:15 am Taurus
26th 11:01 pm Gemini
29th 7:59 am Cancer
31st 1:47 pm Leo

August 1905
2nd 5:09 pm Virgo
4th 7:20 pm Libra
6th 9:28 pm Scorpio
9th 12:24 am Sagittarius
11th 4:45 am Capricorn
13th 11:00 am Aquarius
15th 7:34 pm Pisces
18th 6:30 am Aries
20th 7:01 pm Taurus
23rd 7:18 am Gemini
25th 5:11 pm Cancer
27th 11:31 pm Leo
30th 2:32 am Virgo

September 1905
1st 3:33 am Libra
3rd 4:12 am Scorpio
5th 6:04 am Sagittarius
7th 10:13 am Capricorn
9th 5:02 pm Aquarius
12th 2:20 am Pisces
14th 1:34 pm Aries
17th 2:05 am Taurus
19th 2:39 pm Gemini
22nd 1:37 am Cancer
24th 9:17 am Leo
26th 1:07 pm Virgo
28th 1:55 pm Libra
30th 1:23 pm Scorpio

October 1905
2nd 1:35 pm Sagittarius
4th 4:20 pm Capricorn
6th 10:36 pm Aquarius
9th 8:08 am Pisces
11th 7:49 pm Aries
14th 8:25 am Taurus
16th 8:59 pm Gemini
19th 8:29 am Cancer
21st 5:33 pm Leo
23rd 11:02 pm Virgo
26th 12:55 am Libra
28th 12:24 am Scorpio
29th 11:34 pm Sagittarius

November 1905
1st 12:37 am Capricorn
3rd 5:19 am Aquarius
5th 2:05 pm Pisces
8th 1:47 am Aries
10th 2:31 pm Taurus
13th 2:54 am Gemini
15th 2:13 pm Cancer
17th 11:50 pm Leo
20th 6:47 am Virgo
22nd 10:29 am Libra
24th 11:19 am Scorpio
26th 10:48 am Sagittarius
28th 11:03 am Capricorn
30th 2:11 pm Aquarius

December 1905
2nd 9:26 pm Pisces
5th 8:23 am Aries
7th 9:06 pm Taurus
10th 9:24 am Gemini
12th 8:14 pm Cancer
15th 5:19 am Leo
17th 12:29 pm Virgo
19th 5:25 pm Libra
21st 8:01 pm Scorpio
23rd 9:01 pm Sagittarius
25th 9:53 pm Capricorn
28th 12:32 am Aquarius
30th 6:30 am Pisces

January 1906
1st 4:16 pm Aries
4th 4:33 am Taurus
6th 4:58 pm Gemini
9th 3:38 am Cancer
11th 11:57 am Leo
13th 6:11 pm Virgo
15th 10:48 pm Libra
18th 2:08 am Scorpio
20th 4:36 am Sagittarius
22nd 6:59 am Capricorn
24th 10:26 am Aquarius
26th 4:13 pm Pisces
29th 1:06 am Aries
31st 12:44 pm Taurus

February 1906
3rd 1:17 am Gemini
5th 12:21 pm Cancer
7th 8:32 pm Leo
10th 1:50 am Virgo
12th 5:08 am Libra
14th 7:34 am Scorpio
16th 10:08 am Sagittarius
18th 1:32 pm Capricorn
20th 6:17 pm Aquarius
23rd 12:52 am Pisces
25th 9:45 am Aries
27th 8:58 pm Taurus

March 1906
2nd 9:30 am Gemini
4th 9:18 pm Cancer
7th 6:16 am Leo
9th 11:34 am Virgo
11th 1:54 pm Libra
13th 2:48 pm Scorpio
15th 4:01 pm Sagittarius
17th 6:54 pm Capricorn
20th 12:06 am Aquarius
22nd 7:38 am Pisces
24th 5:10 pm Aries
27th 4:27 am Taurus
29th 4:57 pm Gemini

April 1906
1st 5:20 am Cancer
3rd 3:30 pm Leo
5th 9:53 pm Virgo
8th 12:25 am Libra
10th 12:29 am Scorpio
12th 12:08 am Sagittarius
14th 1:23 am Capricorn
16th 5:38 am Aquarius
18th 1:10 pm Pisces
20th 11:15 pm Aries
23rd 10:56 am Taurus
25th 11:28 pm Gemini
28th 12:02 pm Cancer
30th 11:09 pm Leo

May 1906
3rd 7:02 am Virgo
5th 10:53 am Libra
7th 11:24 am Scorpio
9th 10:26 am Sagittarius
11th 10:13 am Capricorn
13th 12:45 pm Aquarius
15th 7:06 pm Pisces
18th 4:54 am Aries
20th 4:48 pm Taurus
23rd 5:27 am Gemini
25th 5:54 pm Cancer
28th 5:14 am Leo
30th 2:10 pm Virgo

June 1906
1st 7:38 pm Libra
3rd 9:35 pm Scorpio
5th 9:16 pm Sagittarius
7th 8:40 pm Capricorn
9th 9:56 pm Aquarius
12th 2:40 am Pisces
14th 11:20 am Aries
16th 10:55 pm Taurus
19th 11:35 am Gemini
21st 11:51 pm Cancer
24th 10:49 am Leo
26th 7:50 pm Virgo
29th 2:13 am Libra

July 1906
1st 5:43 am Scorpio
3rd 6:53 am Sagittarius
5th 7:07 am Capricorn
7th 8:12 am Aquarius
9th 11:52 am Pisces
11th 7:11 pm Aries
14th 5:55 am Taurus
16th 6:25 pm Gemini
19th 6:37 am Cancer
21st 5:09 pm Leo
24th 1:29 am Virgo
26th 7:38 am Libra
28th 11:46 am Scorpio
30th 2:18 pm Sagittarius

August 1906
1st 3:59 pm Capricorn
3rd 5:58 pm Aquarius
5th 9:37 pm Pisces
8th 4:07 am Aries
10th 1:55 pm Taurus
13th 2:03 am Gemini
15th 2:22 pm Cancer
18th 12:50 am Leo
20th 8:31 am Virgo
22nd 1:40 pm Libra
24th 5:11 pm Scorpio
26th 7:55 pm Sagittarius
28th 10:39 pm Capricorn
31st 1:56 am Aquarius

September 1906
2nd 6:29 am Pisces
4th 1:04 pm Aries
6th 10:20 pm Taurus
9th 10:05 am Gemini
11th 10:39 pm Cancer
14th 9:37 am Leo
16th 5:18 pm Virgo
18th 9:40 pm Libra
20th 11:53 pm Scorpio
23rd 1:35 am Sagittarius
25th 4:02 am Capricorn
27th 7:58 am Aquarius
29th 1:34 pm Pisces

October 1906
1st 8:56 pm Aries
4th 6:20 am Taurus
6th 5:52 pm Gemini
9th 6:38 am Cancer
11th 6:27 pm Leo
14th 3:02 am Virgo
16th 7:35 am Libra
18th 9:01 am Scorpio
20th 9:15 am Sagittarius
22nd 10:15 am Capricorn
24th 1:24 pm Aquarius
26th 7:11 pm Pisces
29th 3:18 am Aries
31st 1:18 pm Taurus

November 1906
3rd 12:56 am Gemini
5th 1:43 pm Cancer
8th 2:13 am Leo
10th 12:10 pm Virgo
12th 6:00 pm Libra
14th 7:54 pm Scorpio
16th 7:30 pm Sagittarius
18th 6:59 pm Capricorn
20th 8:23 pm Aquarius
23rd 12:59 am Pisces
25th 8:52 am Aries
27th 7:17 pm Taurus
30th 7:15 am Gemini

December 1906
2nd 8:01 pm Cancer
5th 8:36 am Leo
7th 7:29 pm Virgo
10th 3:00 am Libra
12th 6:32 am Scorpio
14th 6:55 am Sagittarius
16th 6:03 am Capricorn
18th 6:03 am Aquarius
20th 8:48 am Pisces
22nd 3:17 pm Aries
25th 1:15 am Taurus
27th 1:23 pm Gemini
30th 2:11 am Cancer

January 1907
1st 2:29 pm Leo
4th 1:18 am Virgo
6th 9:41 am Libra
8th 2:55 pm Scorpio
10th 5:07 pm Sagittarius
12th 5:22 pm Capricorn
14th 5:20 pm Aquarius
16th 6:55 pm Pisces
18th 11:42 pm Aries
21st 8:21 am Taurus
23rd 8:04 pm Gemini
26th 8:55 am Cancer
28th 8:59 pm Leo
31st 7:12 am Virgo

February 1907
2nd 3:10 pm Libra
4th 8:55 pm Scorpio
7th 12:34 am Sagittarius
9th 2:35 am Capricorn
11th 3:51 am Aquarius
13th 5:41 am Pisces
15th 9:39 am Aries
17th 4:58 pm Taurus
20th 3:46 am Gemini
22nd 4:30 pm Cancer
25th 4:41 am Leo
27th 2:28 pm Virgo

March 1907
1st 9:31 pm Libra
4th 2:26 am Scorpio
6th 6:04 am Sagittarius
8th 9:04 am Capricorn
10th 11:50 am Aquarius
12th 2:57 pm Pisces
14th 7:20 pm Aries
17th 2:10 am Taurus
19th 12:10 pm Gemini
22nd 12:36 am Cancer
24th 1:06 pm Leo
26th 11:10 pm Virgo
29th 5:46 am Libra
31st 9:34 am Scorpio

April 1907
2nd 11:59 am Sagittarius
4th 2:24 pm Capricorn
6th 5:35 pm Aquarius
8th 9:47 pm Pisces
11th 3:16 am Aries
13th 10:36 am Taurus
15th 8:24 pm Gemini
18th 8:33 am Cancer
20th 9:25 pm Leo
23rd 8:17 am Virgo
25th 3:22 pm Libra
27th 6:47 pm Scorpio
29th 8:03 pm Sagittarius

May 1907
1st 8:59 pm Capricorn
3rd 11:07 pm Aquarius
6th 3:12 am Pisces
8th 9:20 am Aries
10th 5:29 pm Taurus
13th 3:41 am Gemini
15th 3:49 pm Cancer
18th 4:52 am Leo
20th 4:37 pm Virgo
23rd 12:54 am Libra
25th 5:03 am Scorpio
27th 6:06 am Sagittarius
29th 5:55 am Capricorn
31st 6:27 am Aquarius

June 1907
2nd 9:10 am Pisces
4th 2:46 pm Aries
6th 11:12 pm Taurus
9th 9:54 am Gemini
11th 10:16 pm Cancer
14th 11:20 am Leo
16th 11:35 pm Virgo
19th 9:05 am Libra
21st 2:43 pm Scorpio
23rd 4:43 pm Sagittarius
25th 4:31 pm Capricorn
27th 4:01 pm Aquarius
29th 5:07 pm Pisces

July 1907
1st 9:14 pm Aries
4th 4:56 am Taurus
6th 3:41 pm Gemini
9th 4:16 am Cancer
11th 5:17 pm Leo
14th 5:29 am Virgo
16th 3:34 pm Libra
18th 10:34 pm Scorpio
21st 2:11 am Sagittarius
23rd 3:07 am Capricorn
25th 2:47 am Aquarius
27th 3:00 am Pisces
29th 5:37 am Aries
31st 11:52 am Taurus

August 1907
2nd 9:55 pm Gemini
5th 10:27 am Cancer
7th 11:26 pm Leo
10th 11:16 am Virgo
12th 9:07 pm Libra
15th 4:35 am Scorpio
17th 9:31 am Sagittarius
19th 12:06 pm Capricorn
21st 1:00 pm Aquarius
23rd 1:34 pm Pisces
25th 3:28 pm Aries
27th 8:26 pm Taurus
30th 5:18 am Gemini

September 1907
1st 5:22 pm Cancer
4th 6:20 am Leo
6th 5:56 pm Virgo
9th 3:07 am Libra
11th 10:01 am Scorpio
13th 3:07 pm Sagittarius
15th 6:46 pm Capricorn
17th 9:12 pm Aquarius
19th 11:02 pm Pisces
22nd 1:25 am Aries
24th 5:55 am Taurus
26th 1:48 pm Gemini
29th 1:09 am Cancer

October 1907
1st 2:04 pm Leo
4th 1:49 am Virgo
6th 10:39 am Libra
8th 4:39 pm Scorpio
10th 8:47 pm Sagittarius
13th 12:07 am Capricorn
15th 3:13 am Aquarius
17th 6:20 am Pisces
19th 9:57 am Aries
21st 3:00 pm Taurus
23rd 10:38 pm Gemini
26th 9:24 am Cancer
28th 10:13 pm Leo
31st 10:27 am Virgo

November 1907
2nd 7:43 pm Libra
5th 1:23 am Scorpio
7th 4:25 am Sagittarius
9th 6:24 am Capricorn
11th 8:38 am Aquarius
13th 11:52 am Pisces
15th 4:24 pm Aries
17th 10:31 pm Gemini
20th 6:43 am Gemini
22nd 5:24 pm Cancer
25th 6:04 am Leo
27th 6:49 pm Virgo
30th 5:09 am Libra

December 1907
2nd 11:35 am Scorpio
4th 2:29 pm Sagittarius
6th 3:19 pm Capricorn
8th 3:54 pm Aquarius
10th 5:44 pm Pisces
12th 9:48 pm Aries
15th 4:24 am Taurus
17th 1:25 pm Gemini
20th 12:31 am Cancer
22nd 1:09 pm Leo
25th 2:06 am Virgo
27th 1:26 pm Libra
29th 9:26 pm Scorpio

January 1908
1st 1:28 am Sagittarius
3rd 2:25 am Capricorn
5th 1:58 am Aquarius
7th 2:03 am Pisces
9th 4:24 am Aries
11th 10:05 am Taurus
13th 7:09 pm Gemini
16th 6:44 am Cancer
18th 7:33 pm Leo
21st 8:23 am Virgo
23rd 8:03 pm Libra
26th 5:17 am Scorpio
28th 11:08 am Sagittarius
30th 1:33 pm Capricorn

February 1908
1st 1:33 pm Aquarius
3rd 12:51 pm Pisces
5th 1:32 pm Aries
7th 5:24 pm Taurus
10th 1:23 am Gemini
12th 12:47 pm Cancer
15th 1:46 am Leo
17th 2:28 pm Virgo
20th 1:48 am Libra
22nd 11:13 am Scorpio
24th 6:15 pm Sagittarius
26th 10:28 pm Capricorn
29th 12:04 am Aquarius

March 1908
2nd 12:05 am Pisces
4th 12:20 am Aries
6th 2:50 am Taurus
8th 9:12 am Gemini
10th 7:39 pm Cancer
13th 8:28 am Leo
15th 9:09 pm Virgo
18th 8:04 am Libra
20th 4:52 pm Scorpio
22nd 11:45 pm Sagittarius
25th 4:48 am Capricorn
27th 7:57 am Aquarius
29th 9:34 am Pisces
31st 10:42 am Aries

April 1908
2nd 1:04 pm Taurus
4th 6:26 pm Gemini
7th 3:42 am Cancer
9th 3:57 pm Leo
12th 4:41 am Virgo
14th 3:33 pm Libra
16th 11:44 pm Scorpio
19th 5:41 am Sagittarius
21st 10:10 am Capricorn
23rd 1:40 pm Aquarius
25th 4:25 pm Pisces
27th 6:57 pm Aries
29th 10:16 pm Taurus

May 1908
2nd 3:44 am Gemini
4th 12:22 pm Cancer
7th 12:01 am Leo
9th 12:45 pm Virgo
12th 12:00 am Libra
14th 8:12 am Scorpio
16th 1:26 pm Sagittarius
18th 4:44 pm Capricorn
20th 7:15 pm Aquarius
22nd 9:49 pm Pisces
25th 1:03 am Aries
27th 5:30 am Taurus
29th 11:48 am Gemini
31st 8:37 pm Cancer

September 1908
3rd 12:52 am Sagittarius
5th 6:40 am Capricorn
7th 9:07 am Aquarius
9th 9:05 am Pisces
11th 8:22 am Aries
13th 9:11 am Taurus
15th 1:27 pm Gemini
17th 9:57 pm Cancer
20th 9:42 am Leo
22nd 10:34 pm Virgo
25th 10:46 am Libra
27th 9:30 pm Scorpio
30th 6:28 am Sagittarius

January 1909
3rd 12:54 am Gemini
5th 8:24 am Cancer
7th 6:01 pm Leo
10th 5:33 am Virgo
12th 6:11 pm Libra
15th 6:02 am Scorpio
17th 3:01 pm Sagittarius
19th 8:09 pm Capricorn
21st 9:59 pm Aquarius
23rd 10:10 pm Pisces
25th 10:36 pm Aries
28th 1:02 am Taurus
30th 6:22 am Gemini

May 1909
1st 8:11 pm Libra
4th 8:04 am Scorpio
6th 6:16 pm Sagittarius
9th 2:26 am Capricorn
11th 8:26 am Aquarius
13th 12:14 pm Pisces
15th 2:14 pm Aries
17th 3:24 pm Taurus
19th 5:14 pm Gemini
21st 9:15 pm Cancer
24th 4:36 am Leo
26th 3:13 pm Virgo
29th 3:38 am Libra
31st 3:37 pm Scorpio

September 1909
1st 5:19 pm Aries
3rd 5:27 pm Taurus
5th 7:55 pm Gemini
8th 1:35 am Cancer
10th 10:11 am Leo
12th 8:54 pm Virgo
15th 8:59 am Libra
17th 9:49 pm Scorpio
20th 10:11 am Sagittarius
22nd 8:13 pm Capricorn
25th 2:22 am Aquarius
27th 4:32 am Pisces
29th 4:07 am Aries

June 1908
3rd 7:59 am Leo
5th 8:42 pm Virgo
8th 8:33 am Libra
10th 5:29 pm Scorpio
12th 10:52 pm Sagittarius
15th 1:25 am Capricorn
17th 2:35 am Aquarius
19th 3:51 am Pisces
21st 6:27 am Aries
23rd 11:09 am Taurus
25th 6:16 pm Gemini
28th 3:44 am Cancer
30th 3:14 pm Leo

October 1908
2nd 1:12 pm Capricorn
4th 5:16 pm Aquarius
6th 6:50 pm Pisces
8th 7:02 pm Aries
10th 7:43 pm Taurus
12th 10:55 pm Gemini
15th 5:59 am Cancer
17th 4:50 pm Leo
20th 5:32 am Virgo
22nd 5:42 pm Libra
25th 3:59 am Scorpio
27th 12:12 pm Sagittarius
29th 6:34 pm Capricorn
31st 11:12 pm Aquarius

February 1909
1st 2:32 am Cancer
4th 12:50 am Leo
6th 12:35 pm Virgo
9th 1:10 am Libra
11th 1:29 pm Scorpio
13th 11:48 pm Sagittarius
16th 6:27 am Capricorn
18th 9:08 am Aquarius
20th 9:01 am Pisces
22nd 8:09 am Aries
24th 8:45 am Taurus
26th 12:33 pm Gemini
28th 8:07 pm Cancer

June 1909
3rd 1:32 am Sagittarius
5th 8:54 am Capricorn
7th 2:04 pm Aquarius
9th 5:40 pm Pisces
11th 8:22 pm Aries
13th 10:50 pm Taurus
16th 1:53 am Gemini
18th 6:28 am Cancer
20th 1:32 pm Leo
22nd 11:29 pm Virgo
25th 11:35 am Libra
27th 11:51 pm Scorpio
30th 10:03 am Sagittarius

October 1909
1st 3:14 am Taurus
3rd 4:04 am Gemini
5th 8:09 am Cancer
7th 3:57 pm Leo
10th 2:42 am Virgo
12th 3:00 pm Libra
15th 3:46 am Scorpio
17th 4:02 pm Sagittarius
20th 2:37 am Capricorn
22nd 10:12 am Aquarius
24th 2:09 pm Pisces
26th 3:02 pm Aries
28th 2:28 pm Taurus
30th 2:27 pm Gemini

July 1908
3rd 3:57 am Virgo
5th 4:19 pm Libra
8th 2:23 am Scorpio
10th 8:49 am Sagittarius
12th 11:40 am Capricorn
14th 12:08 pm Aquarius
16th 11:59 am Pisces
18th 1:02 pm Aries
20th 4:46 pm Taurus
22nd 11:48 pm Gemini
25th 9:44 am Cancer
27th 9:37 pm Leo
30th 10:23 am Virgo

November 1908
3rd 2:10 am Pisces
5th 3:58 am Aries
7th 5:43 am Taurus
9th 9:01 am Gemini
11th 3:18 pm Cancer
14th 1:07 am Leo
16th 1:22 pm Virgo
19th 1:44 am Libra
21st 12:04 pm Scorpio
23rd 7:39 pm Sagittarius
26th 12:55 am Capricorn
28th 4:40 am Aquarius
30th 7:39 am Pisces

March 1909
3rd 6:40 am Leo
5th 6:48 pm Virgo
8th 7:23 am Libra
10th 7:40 pm Scorpio
13th 6:37 am Sagittarius
15th 2:46 pm Capricorn
17th 7:09 pm Aquarius
19th 8:08 pm Pisces
21st 7:18 pm Aries
23rd 6:50 pm Taurus
25th 8:55 pm Gemini
28th 2:55 am Cancer
30th 12:43 pm Leo

July 1909
2nd 5:04 pm Capricorn
4th 9:14 pm Aquarius
6th 11:41 pm Pisces
9th 1:45 am Aries
11th 4:29 am Taurus
13th 8:30 am Gemini
15th 2:07 pm Cancer
17th 9:41 pm Leo
20th 7:31 am Virgo
22nd 7:25 pm Libra
25th 8:01 am Scorpio
27th 6:59 pm Sagittarius
30th 2:32 am Capricorn

November 1909
1st 4:57 pm Cancer
3rd 11:10 pm Leo
6th 9:04 am Virgo
8th 9:19 pm Libra
11th 10:04 am Scorpio
13th 9:57 pm Sagittarius
16th 8:09 am Capricorn
18th 4:04 pm Aquarius
20th 9:20 pm Pisces
23rd 12:02 am Aries
25th 12:57 am Taurus
27th 1:31 am Gemini
29th 3:27 am Cancer

August 1908
1st 10:56 pm Libra
4th 9:52 am Scorpio
6th 5:47 pm Sagittarius
8th 9:57 pm Capricorn
10th 10:53 pm Aquarius
12th 10:10 pm Pisces
14th 9:50 pm Aries
16th 11:55 pm Taurus
19th 5:47 am Gemini
21st 3:26 pm Cancer
24th 3:32 am Leo
26th 4:22 pm Virgo
29th 4:47 am Libra
31st 3:55 pm Scorpio

December 1908
2nd 10:26 am Aries
4th 1:37 pm Taurus
6th 6:01 pm Gemini
9th 12:33 am Cancer
11th 9:52 am Leo
13th 9:38 pm Virgo
16th 10:12 am Libra
18th 9:12 pm Scorpio
21st 5:02 am Sagittarius
23rd 9:38 am Capricorn
25th 12:02 pm Aquarius
27th 1:39 pm Pisces
29th 3:48 pm Aries
31st 7:24 pm Taurus

April 1909
2nd 12:51 am Virgo
4th 1:30 pm Libra
7th 1:33 am Scorpio
9th 12:16 pm Sagittarius
11th 8:57 pm Capricorn
14th 2:44 am Aquarius
16th 5:26 am Pisces
18th 5:52 am Aries
20th 5:43 am Taurus
22nd 7:03 am Gemini
24th 11:34 am Cancer
26th 8:01 pm Leo
29th 7:33 am Virgo

August 1909
1st 6:22 am Aquarius
3rd 7:43 am Pisces
5th 8:23 am Aries
7th 10:05 am Taurus
9th 1:55 pm Gemini
11th 8:08 pm Cancer
14th 4:29 am Leo
16th 2:42 pm Virgo
19th 2:36 am Libra
21st 3:24 pm Scorpio
24th 3:16 am Sagittarius
26th 12:01 pm Capricorn
28th 4:37 pm Aquarius
30th 5:46 pm Pisces

December 1909
1st 8:16 am Leo
3rd 4:50 pm Virgo
6th 4:29 am Libra
8th 5:16 pm Scorpio
11th 5:01 am Sagittarius
13th 2:31 pm Capricorn
15th 9:39 pm Aquarius
18th 2:48 am Pisces
20th 6:25 am Aries
22nd 8:58 am Taurus
24th 11:05 am Gemini
26th 1:46 pm Cancer
28th 6:17 pm Leo
31st 1:49 am Virgo

January 1910
2nd 12:37 pm Libra
5th 1:19 am Scorpio
7th 1:20 pm Sagittarius
9th 10:40 pm Capricorn
12th 4:53 am Aquarius
14th 8:51 am Pisces
16th 11:46 am Aries
18th 2:39 pm Taurus
20th 5:58 pm Gemini
22nd 10:03 pm Cancer
25th 3:24 am Leo
27th 10:52 am Virgo
29th 9:05 pm Libra

February 1910
1st 9:32 am Scorpio
3rd 10:05 pm Sagittarius
6th 8:03 am Capricorn
8th 2:14 pm Aquarius
10th 5:14 pm Pisces
12th 6:41 pm Aries
14th 8:20 pm Taurus
16th 11:19 pm Gemini
19th 4:03 am Cancer
21st 10:28 am Leo
23rd 6:41 pm Virgo
26th 4:58 am Libra
28th 5:15 pm Scorpio

March 1910
3rd 6:09 am Sagittarius
5th 5:11 pm Capricorn
8th 12:23 am Aquarius
10th 3:33 am Pisces
12th 4:10 am Aries
14th 4:15 am Taurus
16th 5:39 am Gemini
18th 9:30 am Cancer
20th 4:03 pm Leo
23rd 12:57 am Virgo
25th 11:46 am Libra
28th 12:07 am Scorpio
30th 1:06 pm Sagittarius

April 1910
2nd 12:56 am Capricorn
4th 9:32 am Aquarius
6th 2:01 pm Pisces
8th 3:06 pm Aries
10th 2:33 pm Taurus
12th 2:27 pm Gemini
14th 4:34 pm Cancer
16th 9:55 pm Leo
19th 6:34 am Virgo
21st 5:44 pm Libra
24th 6:19 am Scorpio
26th 7:13 pm Sagittarius
29th 7:12 am Capricorn

May 1910
1st 4:46 pm Aquarius
3rd 10:50 pm Pisces
6th 1:24 am Aries
8th 1:33 am Taurus
10th 1:03 am Gemini
12th 1:50 am Cancer
14th 5:31 am Leo
16th 12:58 pm Virgo
18th 11:46 pm Libra
21st 12:27 pm Scorpio
24th 1:17 am Sagittarius
26th 12:56 pm Capricorn
28th 10:33 pm Aquarius
31st 5:30 am Pisces

June 1910
2nd 9:38 am Aries
4th 11:19 am Taurus
6th 11:41 am Gemini
8th 12:17 pm Cancer
10th 2:52 pm Leo
12th 8:52 pm Virgo
15th 6:41 am Libra
17th 7:07 pm Scorpio
20th 7:56 am Sagittarius
22nd 7:14 pm Capricorn
25th 4:15 am Aquarius
27th 10:59 am Pisces
29th 3:44 pm Aries

July 1910
1st 6:48 pm Taurus
3rd 8:38 pm Gemini
5th 10:09 pm Cancer
8th 12:44 am Leo
10th 5:54 am Virgo
12th 2:41 pm Libra
15th 2:35 am Scorpio
17th 3:25 pm Sagittarius
20th 2:40 am Capricorn
22nd 11:06 am Aquarius
24th 4:57 pm Pisces
26th 9:08 pm Aries
29th 12:27 am Taurus
31st 3:20 am Gemini

August 1910
2nd 6:11 am Cancer
4th 9:41 am Leo
6th 2:58 pm Virgo
8th 11:13 pm Libra
11th 10:34 am Scorpio
13th 11:26 pm Sagittarius
16th 11:04 am Capricorn
18th 7:31 pm Aquarius
21st 12:40 am Pisces
23rd 3:42 am Aries
25th 6:02 am Taurus
27th 8:44 am Gemini
29th 12:14 pm Cancer
31st 4:49 pm Leo

September 1910
2nd 10:57 pm Virgo
5th 7:22 am Libra
7th 6:28 pm Scorpio
10th 7:21 am Sagittarius
12th 7:38 pm Capricorn
15th 4:53 am Aquarius
17th 10:12 am Pisces
19th 12:31 pm Aries
21st 1:30 pm Taurus
23rd 2:49 pm Gemini
25th 5:37 pm Cancer
27th 10:26 pm Leo
30th 5:22 am Virgo

October 1910
2nd 2:28 pm Libra
5th 1:45 am Scorpio
7th 2:37 pm Sagittarius
10th 3:25 am Capricorn
12th 1:51 pm Aquarius
14th 8:22 pm Pisces
16th 11:06 pm Aries
18th 11:27 pm Taurus
20th 11:18 pm Gemini
23rd 12:26 am Cancer
25th 4:08 am Leo
27th 10:54 am Virgo
29th 8:29 pm Libra

November 1910
1st 8:12 am Scorpio
3rd 9:06 pm Sagittarius
6th 10:00 am Capricorn
8th 9:19 pm Aquarius
11th 5:26 am Pisces
13th 9:43 am Aries
15th 10:48 am Taurus
17th 10:13 am Gemini
19th 9:54 am Cancer
21st 11:45 am Leo
23rd 5:08 pm Virgo
26th 2:17 am Libra
28th 2:12 pm Scorpio

December 1910
1st 3:14 am Sagittarius
3rd 3:57 pm Capricorn
6th 3:16 am Aquarius
8th 12:19 pm Pisces
10th 6:21 pm Aries
12th 9:13 pm Taurus
14th 9:40 pm Gemini
16th 9:12 pm Cancer
18th 9:48 pm Leo
21st 1:25 am Virgo
23rd 9:10 am Libra
25th 8:35 pm Scorpio
28th 9:41 am Sagittarius
30th 10:14 pm Capricorn

January 1911
2nd 9:02 am Aquarius
4th 5:50 pm Pisces
7th 12:33 am Aries
9th 5:01 am Taurus
11th 7:17 am Gemini
13th 8:04 am Cancer
15th 8:50 am Leo
17th 11:31 am Virgo
19th 5:47 pm Libra
22nd 4:05 am Scorpio
24th 4:54 pm Sagittarius
27th 5:30 am Capricorn
29th 3:57 pm Aquarius
31st 11:55 pm Pisces

February 1911
3rd 5:57 am Aries
5th 10:36 am Taurus
7th 2:03 pm Gemini
9th 4:28 pm Cancer
11th 6:34 pm Leo
13th 9:39 pm Virgo
16th 3:22 am Libra
18th 12:39 pm Scorpio
21st 12:53 am Sagittarius
23rd 1:37 pm Capricorn
26th 12:17 am Aquarius
28th 7:51 am Pisces

March 1911
2nd 12:50 pm Aries
4th 4:22 pm Taurus
6th 7:23 pm Gemini
8th 10:24 pm Cancer
11th 1:45 am Leo
13th 6:05 am Virgo
15th 12:19 pm Libra
17th 9:20 pm Scorpio
20th 9:04 am Sagittarius
22nd 9:53 pm Capricorn
25th 9:12 am Aquarius
27th 5:14 pm Pisces
29th 9:52 pm Aries

April 1911
1st 12:14 am Taurus
3rd 1:49 am Gemini
5th 3:53 am Cancer
7th 7:15 am Leo
9th 12:23 pm Virgo
11th 7:36 pm Libra
14th 5:06 am Scorpio
16th 4:46 pm Sagittarius
19th 5:34 am Capricorn
21st 5:33 pm Aquarius
24th 2:41 am Pisces
26th 8:03 am Aries
28th 10:13 am Taurus
30th 10:40 am Gemini

May 1911
2nd 11:07 am Cancer
4th 1:09 pm Leo
6th 5:49 pm Virgo
9th 1:26 am Libra
11th 11:35 am Scorpio
13th 11:33 pm Sagittarius
16th 12:20 pm Capricorn
19th 12:40 am Aquarius
21st 10:53 am Pisces
23rd 5:40 pm Aries
25th 8:48 pm Taurus
27th 9:13 pm Gemini
29th 8:38 pm Cancer
31st 9:03 pm Leo

June 1911
3rd 12:14 am Virgo
5th 7:06 am Libra
7th 5:21 pm Scorpio
10th 5:37 am Sagittarius
12th 6:27 pm Capricorn
15th 6:44 am Aquarius
17th 5:26 pm Pisces
20th 1:32 am Aries
22nd 6:14 am Taurus
24th 7:46 am Gemini
26th 7:21 am Cancer
28th 6:55 am Leo
30th 8:35 am Virgo

July 1911
2nd 1:59 pm Libra
4th 11:27 pm Scorpio
7th 11:39 am Sagittarius
10th 12:32 am Capricorn
12th 12:33 pm Aquarius
14th 11:04 pm Pisces
17th 7:35 am Aries
19th 1:33 pm Taurus
21st 4:42 pm Gemini
23rd 5:30 pm Cancer
25th 5:25 pm Leo
27th 6:27 pm Virgo
29th 10:32 pm Libra

August 1911
1st 6:44 am Scorpio
3rd 6:20 pm Sagittarius
6th 7:09 am Capricorn
8th 7:02 pm Aquarius
11th 5:00 am Pisces
13th 1:02 pm Aries
15th 7:12 pm Taurus
17th 11:23 pm Gemini
20th 1:42 am Cancer
22nd 2:54 am Leo
24th 4:26 am Virgo
26th 8:06 am Libra
28th 3:16 pm Scorpio
31st 2:01 am Sagittarius

September 1911
2nd 2:36 pm Capricorn
5th 2:35 am Aquarius
7th 12:17 pm Pisces
9th 7:31 am Aries
12th 12:49 am Taurus
14th 4:47 am Gemini
16th 7:48 am Cancer
18th 10:18 am Leo
20th 1:06 pm Virgo
22nd 5:22 pm Libra
25th 12:17 am Scorpio
27th 10:20 am Sagittarius
29th 10:39 pm Capricorn

October 1911
2nd 10:55 am Aquarius
4th 8:59 pm Pisces
7th 3:56 am Aries
9th 8:13 am Taurus
11th 10:56 am Gemini
13th 1:12 pm Cancer
15th 3:55 pm Leo
17th 7:41 pm Virgo
20th 1:05 am Libra
22nd 8:36 am Scorpio
24th 6:34 pm Sagittarius
27th 6:36 am Capricorn
29th 7:13 pm Aquarius

November 1911
1st 6:11 am Pisces
3rd 1:49 pm Aries
5th 5:54 pm Taurus
7th 7:29 pm Gemini
9th 8:11 pm Cancer
11th 9:39 pm Leo
14th 1:05 am Virgo
16th 7:04 am Libra
18th 3:28 pm Scorpio
21st 1:54 am Sagittarius
23rd 1:55 pm Capricorn
26th 2:40 am Aquarius
28th 2:31 pm Pisces
30th 11:35 pm Aries

December 1911
3rd 4:43 am Taurus
5th 6:19 am Gemini
7th 5:56 am Cancer
9th 5:39 am Leo
11th 7:27 am Virgo
13th 12:35 pm Libra
15th 9:08 pm Scorpio
18th 8:08 am Sagittarius
20th 8:24 pm Capricorn
23rd 9:05 am Aquarius
25th 9:17 pm Pisces
28th 7:36 am Aries
30th 2:30 pm Taurus

January 1912
1st 5:29 pm Gemini
3rd 5:26 pm Cancer
5th 4:18 pm Leo
7th 4:24 pm Virgo
9th 7:42 pm Libra
12th 3:07 am Scorpio
14th 1:57 pm Sagittarius
17th 2:28 am Capricorn
19th 3:07 pm Aquarius
22nd 3:05 am Pisces
24th 1:41 pm Aries
26th 9:51 pm Taurus
29th 2:42 am Gemini
31st 4:15 am Cancer

February 1912
2nd 3:48 am Leo
4th 3:23 am Virgo
6th 5:13 am Libra
8th 10:52 am Scorpio
10th 8:35 pm Sagittarius
13th 8:51 am Capricorn
15th 9:33 pm Aquarius
18th 9:13 am Pisces
20th 7:17 pm Aries
23rd 3:26 am Taurus
25th 9:14 am Gemini
27th 12:30 pm Cancer
29th 1:43 pm Leo

March 1912
2nd 2:15 pm Virgo
4th 3:54 pm Libra
6th 8:25 pm Scorpio
9th 4:43 am Sagittarius
11th 4:11 pm Capricorn
14th 4:50 am Aquarius
16th 4:28 pm Pisces
19th 1:59 am Aries
21st 9:16 am Taurus
23rd 2:37 pm Gemini
25th 6:22 pm Cancer
27th 8:54 pm Leo
29th 10:58 pm Virgo

April 1912
1st 1:40 am Libra
3rd 6:15 am Scorpio
5th 1:47 pm Sagittarius
8th 12:24 am Capricorn
10th 12:47 pm Aquarius
13th 12:42 am Pisces
15th 10:15 am Aries
17th 4:51 pm Taurus
19th 9:03 pm Gemini
21st 11:53 pm Cancer
24th 2:22 am Leo
26th 5:18 am Virgo
28th 9:15 am Libra
30th 2:48 pm Scorpio

May 1912
2nd 10:30 pm Sagittarius
5th 8:42 am Capricorn
7th 8:50 pm Aquarius
10th 9:08 am Pisces
12th 7:20 pm Aries
15th 2:04 am Taurus
17th 5:33 am Gemini
19th 7:05 am Cancer
21st 8:18 am Leo
23rd 10:40 am Virgo
25th 2:59 pm Libra
27th 9:27 pm Scorpio
30th 5:54 am Sagittarius

June 1912
1st 4:17 pm Capricorn
4th 4:19 am Aquarius
6th 4:54 pm Pisces
9th 4:03 am Aries
11th 11:46 am Taurus
13th 3:33 pm Gemini
15th 4:25 pm Cancer
17th 4:17 pm Leo
19th 5:10 pm Virgo
21st 8:33 pm Libra
24th 2:57 am Scorpio
26th 11:58 am Sagittarius
28th 10:49 pm Capricorn

July 1912
1st 10:57 am Aquarius
3rd 11:40 pm Pisces
6th 11:30 am Aries
8th 8:33 pm Taurus
11th 1:34 am Gemini
13th 2:55 am Cancer
15th 2:16 am Leo
17th 1:49 am Virgo
19th 3:37 am Libra
21st 8:52 am Scorpio
23rd 5:34 pm Sagittarius
26th 4:41 am Capricorn
28th 5:01 pm Aquarius
31st 5:40 am Pisces

August 1912
2nd 5:39 pm Aries
5th 3:37 am Taurus
7th 10:09 am Gemini
9th 12:57 pm Cancer
11th 1:01 pm Leo
13th 12:15 pm Virgo
15th 12:48 pm Libra
17th 4:28 pm Scorpio
19th 11:59 pm Sagittarius
22nd 10:42 am Capricorn
24th 11:07 pm Aquarius
27th 11:40 am Pisces
29th 11:21 pm Aries

September 1912
1st 9:19 am Taurus
3rd 4:45 pm Gemini
5th 9:06 pm Cancer
7th 10:43 pm Leo
9th 10:51 pm Virgo
11th 11:18 pm Libra
14th 1:54 am Scorpio
16th 7:58 am Sagittarius
18th 5:42 pm Capricorn
21st 5:51 am Aquarius
23rd 6:24 pm Pisces
26th 5:44 am Aries
28th 3:04 pm Taurus
30th 10:12 pm Gemini

October 1912
3rd 3:09 am Cancer
5th 6:11 am Leo
7th 7:55 am Virgo
9th 9:25 am Libra
11th 12:05 pm Scorpio
13th 5:18 pm Sagittarius
16th 1:56 am Capricorn
18th 1:30 pm Aquarius
21st 2:08 am Pisces
23rd 1:29 pm Aries
25th 10:15 pm Taurus
28th 4:22 am Gemini
30th 8:36 am Cancer

November 1912
1st 11:46 am Leo
3rd 2:34 pm Virgo
5th 5:32 pm Libra
7th 9:17 pm Scorpio
10th 2:44 am Sagittarius
12th 10:47 am Capricorn
14th 9:45 pm Aquarius
17th 10:23 am Pisces
19th 10:17 pm Aries
22nd 7:13 am Taurus
24th 12:41 pm Gemini
26th 3:37 pm Cancer
28th 5:34 pm Leo
30th 7:55 pm Virgo

December 1912
2nd 11:26 pm Libra
5th 4:22 am Scorpio
7th 10:48 am Sagittarius
9th 7:10 pm Capricorn
12th 5:51 am Aquarius
14th 6:25 pm Pisces
17th 6:59 am Aries
19th 4:56 pm Taurus
21st 10:51 pm Gemini
24th 1:11 am Cancer
26th 1:43 am Leo
28th 2:27 am Virgo
30th 4:55 am Libra

January 1913
1st 9:49 am Scorpio
3rd 5:01 pm Sagittarius
6th 2:10 am Capricorn
8th 1:07 pm Aquarius
11th 1:38 am Pisces
13th 2:35 pm Aries
16th 1:46 am Taurus
18th 9:07 am Gemini
20th 12:14 pm Cancer
22nd 12:27 pm Leo
24th 11:49 am Virgo
26th 12:26 pm Libra
28th 3:49 pm Scorpio
30th 10:30 pm Sagittarius

February 1913
2nd 7:59 am Capricorn
4th 7:25 pm Aquarius
7th 8:03 am Pisces
9th 8:59 pm Aries
12th 8:47 am Taurus
14th 5:37 pm Gemini
16th 10:29 pm Cancer
18th 11:47 pm Leo
20th 11:08 pm Virgo
22nd 10:37 pm Libra
25th 12:11 am Scorpio
27th 5:11 am Sagittarius

March 1913
1st 1:52 pm Capricorn
4th 1:21 am Aquarius
6th 2:10 pm Pisces
9th 2:57 am Aries
11th 2:34 pm Taurus
13th 11:59 pm Gemini
16th 6:21 am Cancer
18th 9:28 am Leo
20th 10:09 am Virgo
22nd 9:55 am Libra
24th 10:37 am Scorpio
26th 1:59 pm Sagittarius
28th 9:08 pm Capricorn
31st 7:53 am Aquarius

April 1913
2nd 8:39 pm Pisces
5th 9:21 am Aries
7th 8:32 pm Taurus
10th 5:31 am Gemini
12th 12:09 pm Cancer
14th 4:30 pm Leo
16th 6:53 pm Virgo
18th 8:03 pm Libra
20th 9:15 pm Scorpio
23rd 12:03 am Sagittarius
25th 5:56 am Capricorn
27th 3:32 pm Aquarius
30th 3:54 am Pisces

May 1913
2nd 4:38 pm Aries
5th 3:34 am Taurus
7th 11:50 am Gemini
9th 5:43 pm Cancer
11th 9:57 pm Leo
14th 1:10 am Virgo
16th 3:44 am Libra
18th 6:15 am Scorpio
20th 9:39 am Sagittarius
22nd 3:13 pm Capricorn
24th 11:59 pm Aquarius
27th 11:46 am Pisces
30th 12:36 am Aries

June 1913
1st 11:45 am Taurus
3rd 7:42 pm Gemini
6th 12:40 am Cancer
8th 3:52 am Leo
10th 6:31 am Virgo
12th 9:27 am Libra
14th 1:00 pm Scorpio
16th 5:31 pm Sagittarius
18th 11:41 pm Capricorn
21st 8:21 am Aquarius
23rd 7:45 pm Pisces
26th 8:37 am Aries
28th 8:22 pm Taurus

July 1913
1st 4:47 am Gemini
3rd 9:30 am Cancer
5th 11:40 am Leo
7th 1:01 pm Virgo
9th 2:59 pm Libra
11th 6:26 pm Scorpio
13th 11:37 pm Sagittarius
16th 6:39 am Capricorn
18th 3:48 pm Aquarius
21st 3:12 am Pisces
23rd 4:06 pm Aries
26th 4:29 am Taurus
28th 1:57 pm Gemini
30th 7:23 pm Cancer

August 1913
1st 9:25 pm Leo
3rd 9:44 pm Virgo
5th 10:13 pm Libra
8th 12:22 am Scorpio
10th 5:03 am Sagittarius
12th 12:24 pm Capricorn
14th 10:09 pm Aquarius
17th 9:52 am Pisces
19th 10:47 pm Aries
22nd 11:30 am Taurus
24th 10:03 pm Gemini
27th 4:54 am Cancer
29th 7:55 am Leo
31st 8:17 am Virgo

September 1913
2nd 7:47 am Libra
4th 8:21 am Virgo
6th 11:32 am Sagittarius
8th 6:07 pm Capricorn
11th 3:56 am Aquarius
13th 3:57 pm Pisces
16th 4:55 am Aries
18th 5:33 pm Taurus
21st 4:34 am Gemini
23rd 12:44 pm Cancer
25th 5:26 pm Leo
27th 7:02 pm Virgo
29th 6:48 pm Libra

October 1913
1st 6:32 pm Scorpio
3rd 8:08 pm Sagittarius
6th 1:10 am Capricorn
8th 10:08 am Aquarius
10th 10:06 pm Pisces
13th 11:08 am Aries
15th 11:30 pm Taurus
18th 10:13 am Gemini
20th 6:45 pm Cancer
23rd 12:45 am Leo
25th 4:07 am Virgo
27th 5:18 am Libra
29th 5:30 am Scorpio
31st 6:30 am Sagittarius

November 1913
2nd 10:08 am Capricorn
4th 5:43 pm Aquarius
7th 5:01 am Pisces
9th 6:01 pm Aries
12th 6:17 am Taurus
14th 4:24 pm Gemini
17th 12:17 am Cancer
19th 6:18 am Leo
21st 10:40 am Virgo
23rd 1:30 pm Libra
25th 3:13 pm Scorpio
27th 4:55 pm Sagittarius
29th 8:12 pm Capricorn

December 1913
2nd 2:42 am Aquarius
4th 12:59 pm Pisces
7th 1:45 am Aries
9th 2:11 pm Taurus
12th 12:09 am Gemini
14th 7:12 am Cancer
16th 12:09 pm Leo
18th 4:00 pm Virgo
20th 7:19 pm Libra
22nd 10:21 pm Scorpio
25th 1:28 am Sagittarius
27th 5:36 am Capricorn
29th 12:01 pm Aquarius
31st 9:38 pm Pisces

January 1914
3rd 9:57 am Aries
5th 10:43 pm Taurus
8th 9:13 am Gemini
10th 4:12 pm Cancer
12th 8:13 pm Leo
14th 10:40 pm Virgo
17th 12:53 am Libra
19th 3:44 am Scorpio
21st 7:40 am Sagittarius
23rd 12:59 pm Capricorn
25th 8:13 pm Aquarius
28th 5:54 am Pisces
30th 5:56 pm Aries

February 1914
2nd 6:54 am Taurus
4th 6:19 pm Gemini
7th 4:16 am Cancer
9th 6:27 am Leo
11th 8:00 am Virgo
13th 8:38 am Libra
15th 9:55 am Scorpio
17th 1:03 pm Sagittarius
19th 6:37 pm Capricorn
22nd 2:41 am Aquarius
24th 1:00 pm Pisces
27th 1:09 am Aries

March 1914
1st 2:07 pm Taurus
4th 2:14 am Gemini
6th 11:34 am Cancer
8th 5:03 pm Leo
10th 7:03 pm Virgo
12th 6:58 pm Libra
14th 6:40 pm Scorpio
16th 8:01 pm Sagittarius
19th 12:23 am Capricorn
21st 8:15 am Aquarius
23rd 7:01 pm Pisces
26th 7:29 am Aries
28th 8:26 pm Taurus
31st 8:42 am Gemini

April 1914
2nd 6:58 pm Cancer
5th 2:06 am Leo
7th 5:37 am Virgo
9th 6:13 am Libra
11th 5:27 am Scorpio
13th 5:23 am Sagittarius
15th 7:58 am Capricorn
17th 2:31 pm Aquarius
20th 12:52 am Pisces
22nd 1:29 pm Aries
25th 2:28 am Taurus
27th 2:29 pm Gemini
30th 12:50 am Cancer

May 1914
2nd 8:53 am Leo
4th 2:02 pm Virgo
6th 4:14 pm Libra
8th 4:21 pm Scorpio
10th 4:05 pm Sagittarius
12th 5:31 pm Capricorn
14th 10:29 pm Aquarius
17th 7:39 am Pisces
19th 7:54 pm Aries
22nd 8:51 am Taurus
24th 8:37 pm Gemini
27th 6:28 am Cancer
29th 2:22 pm Leo
31st 8:13 pm Virgo

June 1914
2nd 11:51 pm Libra
5th 1:30 am Scorpio
7th 2:12 am Sagittarius
9th 3:40 am Capricorn
11th 7:46 am Aquarius
13th 3:44 pm Pisces
16th 3:11 am Aries
18th 4:00 pm Taurus
21st 3:44 am Gemini
23rd 1:07 pm Cancer
25th 8:14 pm Leo
28th 1:35 am Virgo
30th 5:32 am Libra

July 1914
2nd 8:20 am Scorpio
4th 10:26 am Sagittarius
6th 12:54 pm Capricorn
8th 5:11 pm Aquarius
11th 12:33 am Pisces
13th 11:14 am Aries
15th 11:49 pm Taurus
18th 11:46 am Gemini
20th 9:12 pm Cancer
23rd 3:42 am Leo
25th 8:00 am Virgo
27th 11:05 am Libra
29th 1:45 pm Scorpio
31st 4:36 pm Sagittarius

August 1914
2nd 8:14 pm Capricorn
5th 1:27 am Aquarius
7th 9:03 am Pisces
9th 7:25 pm Aries
12th 7:45 am Taurus
14th 8:06 pm Gemini
17th 6:11 am Cancer
19th 12:52 pm Leo
21st 4:31 pm Virgo
23rd 6:19 pm Libra
25th 7:44 pm Scorpio
27th 9:59 pm Sagittarius
30th 1:57 am Capricorn

September 1914
1st 8:03 am Aquarius
3rd 4:26 pm Pisces
6th 2:59 am Aries
8th 3:15 pm Taurus
11th 3:53 am Gemini
13th 2:56 pm Cancer
15th 10:41 pm Leo
18th 2:42 am Virgo
20th 3:52 am Libra
22nd 3:53 am Scorpio
24th 4:36 am Sagittarius
26th 7:34 am Capricorn
28th 1:36 pm Aquarius
30th 10:33 pm Pisces

October 1914
3rd 9:37 am Aries
5th 9:58 pm Taurus
8th 10:40 am Gemini
10th 10:26 pm Cancer
13th 7:36 am Leo
15th 1:02 pm Virgo
17th 2:50 pm Libra
19th 2:22 pm Scorpio
21st 1:41 pm Sagittarius
23rd 2:55 pm Capricorn
25th 7:39 pm Aquarius
28th 4:13 am Pisces
30th 3:34 pm Aries

November 1914
2nd 4:08 am Taurus
4th 4:43 pm Gemini
7th 4:33 am Cancer
9th 2:36 pm Leo
11th 9:42 pm Virgo
14th 1:10 am Libra
16th 1:36 am Scorpio
18th 12:42 am Sagittarius
20th 12:42 am Capricorn
22nd 3:42 am Aquarius
24th 10:52 am Pisces
26th 9:43 pm Aries
29th 10:21 am Taurus

December 1914
1st 10:53 pm Gemini
4th 10:19 am Cancer
6th 8:13 pm Leo
9th 4:03 am Virgo
11th 9:09 am Libra
13th 11:23 am Scorpio
15th 11:41 am Sagittarius
17th 11:47 am Capricorn
19th 1:48 pm Aquarius
21st 7:24 pm Pisces
24th 5:02 am Aries
26th 5:18 pm Taurus
29th 5:53 am Gemini
31st 5:01 pm Cancer

January 1915
3rd 2:12 am Leo
5th 9:28 am Virgo
7th 2:53 pm Libra
9th 6:25 pm Scorpio
11th 8:25 pm Sagittarius
13th 9:52 pm Capricorn
16th 12:17 am Aquarius
18th 5:14 am Pisces
20th 1:42 pm Aries
23rd 1:12 am Taurus
25th 1:47 pm Gemini
28th 1:08 am Cancer
30th 9:55 am Leo

February 1915
1st 4:10 pm Virgo
3rd 8:33 pm Libra
5th 11:48 pm Scorpio
8th 2:33 am Sagittarius
10th 5:25 am Capricorn
12th 9:09 am Aquarius
14th 2:40 pm Pisces
16th 10:46 pm Aries
19th 9:36 am Taurus
21st 10:05 pm Gemini
24th 9:57 am Cancer
26th 7:10 pm Leo

March 1915
1st 1:03 am Virgo
3rd 4:15 am Libra
5th 6:05 am Scorpio
7th 7:59 am Sagittarius
9th 10:59 am Capricorn
11th 3:40 pm Aquarius
13th 10:16 pm Pisces
16th 6:55 am Aries
18th 5:38 pm Taurus
21st 5:57 am Gemini
23rd 6:21 pm Cancer
26th 4:37 am Leo
28th 11:13 am Virgo
30th 2:10 pm Libra

April 1915
1st 2:50 pm Scorpio
3rd 3:06 pm Sagittarius
5th 4:47 pm Capricorn
7th 9:03 pm Aquarius
10th 4:08 am Pisces
12th 1:31 pm Aries
15th 12:38 am Taurus
17th 12:57 pm Gemini
20th 1:36 am Cancer
22nd 12:53 pm Leo
24th 8:53 pm Virgo
27th 12:47 am Libra
29th 1:24 am Scorpio

May 1915
1st 12:37 am Sagittarius
3rd 12:39 am Capricorn
5th 3:23 am Aquarius
7th 9:40 am Pisces
9th 7:09 pm Aries
12th 6:40 am Taurus
14th 7:09 pm Gemini
17th 7:47 am Cancer
19th 7:31 pm Leo
22nd 4:46 am Virgo
24th 10:16 am Libra
26th 12:02 pm Scorpio
28th 11:28 am Sagittarius
30th 10:40 am Capricorn

June 1915
1st 11:49 am Aquarius
3rd 4:31 pm Pisces
6th 1:06 am Aries
8th 12:30 pm Taurus
11th 1:06 am Gemini
13th 1:37 pm Cancer
16th 1:12 am Leo
18th 10:53 am Virgo
20th 5:39 pm Libra
22nd 9:03 pm Scorpio
24th 9:45 pm Sagittarius
26th 9:22 pm Capricorn
28th 9:55 pm Aquarius

July 1915
1st 1:14 am Pisces
3rd 8:23 am Aries
5th 7:01 pm Taurus
8th 7:30 am Gemini
10th 7:56 pm Cancer
13th 7:06 am Leo
15th 4:22 pm Virgo
17th 11:21 pm Libra
20th 3:50 am Scorpio
22nd 6:06 am Sagittarius
24th 7:04 am Capricorn
26th 8:10 am Aquarius
28th 11:04 am Pisces
30th 5:06 pm Aries

August 1915
2nd 2:39 am Taurus
4th 2:42 pm Gemini
7th 3:11 am Cancer
9th 2:08 pm Leo
11th 10:42 pm Virgo
14th 4:55 am Libra
16th 9:17 am Scorpio
18th 12:18 pm Sagittarius
20th 2:38 pm Capricorn
22nd 5:03 pm Aquarius
24th 8:35 pm Pisces
27th 2:21 am Aries
29th 11:07 am Taurus
31st 10:38 pm Gemini

September 1915
3rd 11:11 am Cancer
5th 10:24 pm Leo
8th 6:42 am Virgo
10th 12:00 pm Libra
12th 3:15 pm Scorpio
14th 5:41 pm Sagittarius
16th 8:20 pm Capricorn
18th 11:49 pm Aquarius
21st 4:32 am Pisces
23rd 10:55 am Aries
25th 7:35 pm Taurus
28th 6:42 am Gemini
30th 7:20 pm Cancer

October 1915
3rd 7:13 am Leo
5th 4:04 pm Virgo
7th 9:09 pm Libra
9th 11:20 pm Scorpio
12th 12:21 am Sagittarius
14th 1:56 am Capricorn
16th 5:15 am Aquarius
18th 10:38 am Pisces
20th 5:57 pm Aries
23rd 3:08 am Taurus
25th 2:15 pm Gemini
28th 2:53 am Cancer
30th 3:26 pm Leo

November 1915
2nd 1:30 am Virgo
4th 7:29 am Libra
6th 9:38 am Scorpio
8th 9:37 am Sagittarius
10th 9:34 am Capricorn
12th 11:22 am Aquarius
14th 4:04 pm Pisces
16th 11:40 pm Aries
19th 9:29 am Taurus
21st 8:56 pm Gemini
24th 9:33 am Cancer
26th 10:23 pm Leo
29th 9:32 am Virgo

December 1915
1st 5:09 pm Libra
3rd 8:33 pm Scorpio
5th 8:48 pm Sagittarius
7th 7:53 pm Capricorn
9th 8:01 pm Aquarius
11th 10:57 pm Pisces
14th 5:29 am Aries
16th 3:14 pm Taurus
19th 3:02 am Gemini
21st 3:44 pm Cancer
24th 4:23 am Leo
26th 3:50 pm Virgo
29th 12:41 am Libra
31st 5:55 am Scorpio

January 1916
2nd 7:44 am Sagittarius
4th 7:26 am Capricorn
6th 6:59 am Aquarius
8th 8:21 am Pisces
10th 1:06 pm Aries
12th 9:43 pm Taurus
15th 9:18 am Gemini
17th 10:07 pm Cancer
20th 10:32 am Leo
22nd 9:32 pm Virgo
25th 6:26 am Libra
27th 12:43 pm Scorpio
29th 4:18 pm Sagittarius
31st 5:43 pm Capricorn

February 1916
2nd 6:10 pm Aquarius
4th 7:16 pm Pisces
6th 10:45 pm Aries
9th 5:50 am Taurus
11th 4:30 pm Gemini
14th 5:12 am Cancer
16th 5:38 pm Leo
19th 4:08 am Virgo
21st 12:13 pm Libra
23rd 6:09 pm Scorpio
25th 10:20 pm Sagittarius
28th 1:13 am Capricorn

March 1916
1st 3:18 am Aquarius
3rd 5:27 am Pisces
5th 8:56 am Aries
7th 3:08 pm Taurus
10th 12:45 am Gemini
12th 1:03 pm Cancer
15th 1:41 am Leo
17th 12:12 pm Virgo
19th 7:37 pm Libra
22nd 12:26 am Scorpio
24th 3:48 am Sagittarius
26th 6:43 am Capricorn
28th 9:47 am Aquarius
30th 1:18 pm Pisces

April 1916
1st 5:49 pm Aries
4th 12:11 am Taurus
6th 9:19 am Gemini
8th 9:10 pm Cancer
11th 10:00 am Leo
13th 9:07 pm Virgo
16th 4:40 am Libra
18th 8:48 am Scorpio
20th 10:53 am Sagittarius
22nd 12:34 pm Capricorn
24th 3:07 pm Aquarius
26th 7:05 pm Pisces
29th 12:35 am Aries

May 1916
1st 7:49 am Taurus
3rd 5:12 pm Gemini
6th 4:53 am Cancer
8th 5:51 pm Leo
11th 5:44 am Virgo
13th 2:15 pm Libra
15th 6:42 pm Scorpio
17th 8:10 pm Sagittarius
19th 8:31 pm Capricorn
21st 9:34 pm Aquarius
24th 12:35 am Pisces
26th 6:03 am Aries
28th 1:54 pm Taurus
30th 11:53 pm Gemini

June 1916
2nd 11:45 am Cancer
5th 12:47 am Leo
7th 1:14 pm Virgo
9th 10:59 pm Libra
12th 4:40 am Scorpio
14th 6:41 am Sagittarius
16th 6:33 am Capricorn
18th 6:17 am Aquarius
20th 7:39 am Pisces
22nd 11:55 am Aries
24th 7:25 pm Taurus
27th 5:43 am Gemini
29th 5:54 pm Cancer

July 1916
2nd 6:57 am Leo
4th 7:32 pm Virgo
7th 6:05 am Libra
9th 1:16 pm Scorpio
11th 4:44 pm Sagittarius
13th 5:21 pm Capricorn
15th 4:47 pm Aquarius
17th 4:56 pm Pisces
19th 7:32 pm Aries
22nd 1:46 am Taurus
24th 11:35 am Gemini
26th 11:53 pm Cancer
29th 12:56 pm Leo

August 1916
1st 1:18 am Virgo
3rd 11:54 am Libra
5th 7:56 pm Scorpio
8th 12:56 am Sagittarius
10th 3:08 am Capricorn
12th 3:28 am Aquarius
14th 3:30 am Pisces
16th 5:02 am Aries
18th 9:45 am Taurus
20th 6:26 pm Gemini
23rd 6:21 am Cancer
25th 7:23 pm Leo
28th 7:29 am Virgo
30th 5:34 pm Libra

September 1916
2nd 1:24 am Scorpio
4th 7:05 am Sagittarius
6th 10:44 am Capricorn
8th 12:39 pm Aquarius
10th 1:42 pm Pisces
12th 3:18 pm Aries
14th 7:09 pm Taurus
17th 2:38 am Gemini
19th 1:44 pm Cancer
22nd 2:41 am Leo
24th 2:46 pm Virgo
27th 12:22 am Libra
29th 7:21 am Scorpio

January 1917
2nd 1:04 am Taurus
4th 9:39 am Gemini
6th 8:35 pm Cancer
9th 9:03 am Leo
11th 10:01 pm Virgo
14th 10:04 am Libra
16th 7:31 pm Scorpio
19th 1:17 am Sagittarius
21st 3:28 am Capricorn
23rd 3:19 am Aquarius
25th 2:41 am Pisces
27th 3:33 am Aries
29th 7:34 am Taurus
31st 3:25 pm Gemini

May 1917
1st 1:19 am Virgo
3rd 12:52 pm Libra
5th 9:39 pm Scorpio
8th 3:44 am Sagittarius
10th 7:59 am Capricorn
12th 11:18 am Aquarius
14th 2:11 pm Pisces
16th 5:04 pm Aries
18th 8:38 pm Taurus
21st 1:53 am Gemini
23rd 9:49 am Cancer
25th 8:42 pm Leo
28th 9:20 am Virgo
30th 9:20 pm Libra

September 1917
2nd 10:21 pm Aries
4th 11:06 pm Taurus
7th 3:19 am Gemini
9th 11:39 am Cancer
11th 11:13 pm Leo
14th 12:02 pm Virgo
17th 12:33 am Libra
19th 11:55 am Scorpio
21st 9:32 pm Sagittarius
24th 4:37 am Capricorn
26th 8:34 am Aquarius
28th 9:40 am Pisces
30th 9:16 am Aries

January 1918
1st 6:23 pm Virgo
4th 6:56 am Libra
6th 6:49 pm Scorpio
9th 3:57 am Sagittarius
11th 9:27 am Capricorn
13th 11:56 am Aquarius
15th 12:54 pm Pisces
17th 2:04 pm Aries
19th 4:48 pm Taurus
21st 9:52 pm Gemini
24th 5:17 am Cancer
26th 2:45 pm Leo
29th 1:59 am Virgo
31st 2:26 pm Libra

October 1916
1st 12:28 pm Sagittarius
3rd 4:23 pm Capricorn
5th 7:28 pm Aquarius
7th 9:59 pm Pisces
10th 12:40 am Aries
12th 4:45 am Taurus
14th 11:38 am Gemini
16th 9:58 pm Cancer
19th 10:39 am Leo
21st 11:03 pm Virgo
24th 8:45 am Libra
26th 3:09 pm Scorpio
28th 7:07 pm Sagittarius
30th 10:00 pm Capricorn

February 1917
3rd 2:30 am Cancer
5th 3:15 pm Leo
8th 4:09 am Virgo
10th 4:04 pm Libra
13th 2:06 am Scorpio
15th 9:22 am Sagittarius
17th 1:24 pm Capricorn
19th 2:33 pm Aquarius
21st 2:07 pm Pisces
23rd 2:01 pm Aries
25th 4:19 pm Taurus
27th 10:34 pm Gemini

June 1917
2nd 6:34 am Scorpio
4th 12:28 pm Sagittarius
6th 3:46 pm Capricorn
8th 5:46 pm Aquarius
10th 7:42 pm Pisces
12th 10:31 pm Aries
15th 2:48 am Taurus
17th 9:02 am Gemini
19th 5:33 pm Cancer
22nd 4:27 am Leo
24th 4:59 pm Virgo
27th 5:26 am Libra
29th 3:37 pm Scorpio

October 1917
2nd 9:25 am Taurus
4th 12:14 pm Gemini
6th 7:06 pm Cancer
9th 5:49 am Leo
11th 6:32 pm Virgo
14th 6:58 am Libra
16th 5:53 pm Scorpio
19th 3:00 am Sagittarius
21st 10:13 am Capricorn
23rd 3:16 pm Aquarius
25th 6:03 pm Pisces
27th 7:09 pm Aries
29th 7:59 pm Taurus
31st 10:26 pm Gemini

February 1918
3rd 2:51 am Scorpio
5th 1:14 pm Sagittarius
7th 7:57 pm Capricorn
9th 10:46 pm Aquarius
11th 10:57 pm Pisces
13th 10:31 pm Aries
15th 11:31 pm Taurus
18th 3:29 am Gemini
20th 10:50 am Cancer
22nd 8:52 pm Leo
25th 8:32 am Virgo
27th 9:01 pm Libra

November 1916
2nd 12:50 am Aquarius
4th 4:04 am Pisces
6th 7:59 am Aries
8th 1:07 pm Taurus
10th 8:19 pm Gemini
13th 6:19 am Cancer
15th 6:44 pm Leo
18th 7:32 am Virgo
20th 6:03 pm Libra
23rd 12:48 am Scorpio
25th 4:12 am Sagittarius
27th 5:45 am Capricorn
29th 7:06 am Aquarius

March 1917
2nd 8:51 am Cancer
4th 9:35 pm Leo
7th 10:29 am Virgo
9th 10:01 pm Libra
12th 7:40 am Scorpio
14th 3:18 pm Sagittarius
16th 8:38 pm Capricorn
18th 11:33 pm Aquarius
21st 12:31 am Pisces
23rd 12:53 am Aries
25th 2:35 am Taurus
27th 7:28 am Gemini
29th 4:27 pm Cancer

July 1917
1st 10:14 pm Sagittarius
4th 1:25 am Capricorn
6th 2:25 am Aquarius
8th 2:53 am Pisces
10th 4:25 am Aries
12th 8:13 am Taurus
14th 2:47 pm Gemini
16th 11:59 pm Cancer
19th 11:17 am Leo
21st 11:51 pm Virgo
24th 12:32 pm Libra
26th 11:40 pm Scorpio
29th 7:38 am Sagittarius
31st 11:48 am Capricorn

November 1917
3rd 4:09 am Cancer
5th 1:42 pm Leo
8th 1:56 am Virgo
10th 2:26 pm Libra
13th 1:13 am Scorpio
15th 9:36 am Sagittarius
17th 3:55 pm Capricorn
19th 8:38 pm Aquarius
22nd 12:04 am Pisces
24th 2:36 am Aries
26th 4:56 am Taurus
28th 8:13 am Gemini
30th 1:48 pm Cancer

March 1918
2nd 9:32 am Scorpio
4th 8:47 pm Sagittarius
7th 5:04 am Capricorn
9th 9:23 am Aquarius
11th 10:13 am Pisces
13th 9:16 am Aries
15th 8:49 am Taurus
17th 10:57 am Gemini
19th 4:57 pm Cancer
22nd 2:37 am Leo
24th 2:30 pm Virgo
27th 3:07 am Libra
29th 3:28 pm Scorpio

December 1916
1st 9:29 am Pisces
3rd 1:34 pm Aries
5th 7:35 pm Taurus
8th 3:40 am Gemini
10th 1:59 pm Cancer
13th 2:17 am Leo
15th 3:18 pm Virgo
18th 2:49 am Libra
20th 10:52 am Scorpio
22nd 2:58 pm Sagittarius
24th 4:07 pm Capricorn
26th 4:05 pm Aquarius
28th 4:42 pm Pisces
30th 7:25 pm Aries

April 1917
1st 4:38 am Leo
3rd 5:32 pm Virgo
6th 4:54 am Libra
8th 1:54 pm Scorpio
10th 8:50 pm Sagittarius
13th 2:08 am Capricorn
15th 5:56 am Aquarius
17th 8:25 am Pisces
19th 10:11 am Aries
21st 12:31 pm Taurus
23rd 5:05 pm Gemini
26th 1:07 am Cancer
28th 12:31 pm Leo

August 1917
2nd 12:50 pm Aquarius
4th 12:21 pm Pisces
6th 12:19 pm Aries
8th 2:36 pm Taurus
10th 8:23 pm Gemini
13th 5:39 am Cancer
15th 5:19 pm Leo
18th 6:02 am Virgo
20th 6:41 pm Libra
23rd 6:15 am Scorpio
25th 3:28 pm Sagittarius
27th 9:14 pm Capricorn
29th 11:27 pm Aquarius
31st 11:11 pm Pisces

December 1917
2nd 10:32 pm Leo
5th 10:06 am Virgo
7th 10:41 pm Libra
10th 9:52 am Scorpio
12th 6:10 pm Sagittarius
14th 11:35 pm Capricorn
17th 2:59 am Aquarius
19th 5:31 am Pisces
21st 8:06 am Aries
23rd 11:26 am Taurus
25th 4:03 pm Gemini
27th 10:29 pm Cancer
30th 7:15 am Leo

April 1918
1st 2:47 am Sagittarius
3rd 11:58 am Capricorn
5th 5:56 pm Aquarius
7th 8:22 pm Pisces
9th 8:19 pm Aries
11th 7:41 pm Taurus
13th 8:37 pm Gemini
16th 12:57 am Cancer
18th 9:18 am Leo
20th 8:46 pm Virgo
23rd 9:25 am Libra
25th 9:37 pm Scorpio
28th 8:30 am Sagittarius
30th 5:33 pm Capricorn

May 1918
3rd 12:12 am Aquarius
5th 4:07 am Pisces
7th 5:41 am Aries
9th 6:05 am Taurus
11th 7:06 am Gemini
13th 10:31 am Cancer
15th 5:31 pm Leo
18th 4:00 am Virgo
20th 4:25 pm Libra
23rd 4:38 am Scorpio
25th 3:08 pm Sagittarius
27th 11:27 pm Capricorn
30th 5:38 am Aquarius

June 1918
1st 9:54 am Pisces
3rd 12:37 pm Aries
5th 2:30 pm Taurus
7th 4:36 pm Gemini
9th 8:14 pm Cancer
12th 2:35 am Leo
14th 12:10 pm Virgo
17th 12:10 am Libra
19th 12:30 pm Scorpio
21st 11:04 pm Sagittarius
24th 6:51 am Capricorn
26th 12:01 pm Aquarius
28th 3:27 pm Pisces
30th 6:05 pm Aries

July 1918
2nd 8:44 pm Taurus
5th 12:04 am Gemini
7th 4:42 am Cancer
9th 11:20 am Leo
11th 8:33 pm Virgo
14th 8:09 am Libra
16th 8:41 pm Scorpio
19th 7:49 am Sagittarius
21st 3:46 pm Capricorn
23rd 8:19 pm Aquarius
25th 10:32 pm Pisces
27th 11:59 pm Aries
30th 2:06 am Taurus

August 1918
1st 5:48 am Gemini
3rd 11:21 am Cancer
5th 6:49 pm Leo
8th 4:17 am Virgo
10th 3:45 pm Libra
13th 4:26 am Scorpio
15th 4:22 pm Sagittarius
18th 1:17 am Capricorn
20th 6:11 am Aquarius
22nd 7:49 am Pisces
24th 7:57 am Aries
26th 8:35 am Taurus
28th 11:19 am Gemini
30th 4:49 pm Cancer

September 1918
2nd 12:53 am Leo
4th 10:56 am Virgo
6th 10:35 pm Libra
9th 11:19 am Scorpio
11th 11:50 pm Sagittarius
14th 10:02 am Capricorn
16th 4:15 pm Aquarius
18th 6:27 pm Pisces
20th 6:08 pm Aries
22nd 5:27 pm Taurus
24th 6:31 pm Gemini
26th 10:45 pm Cancer
29th 6:25 am Leo

October 1918
1st 4:45 pm Virgo
4th 4:43 am Libra
6th 5:27 pm Scorpio
9th 6:04 am Sagittarius
11th 5:06 pm Capricorn
14th 12:54 am Aquarius
16th 4:42 am Pisces
18th 5:15 am Aries
20th 4:21 am Taurus
22nd 4:10 am Gemini
24th 6:40 am Cancer
26th 12:54 pm Leo
28th 10:42 pm Virgo
31st 10:45 am Libra

November 1918
2nd 11:31 pm Scorpio
5th 11:51 am Sagittarius
7th 10:50 pm Capricorn
10th 7:25 am Aquarius
12th 12:52 pm Pisces
14th 3:12 pm Aries
16th 3:27 pm Taurus
18th 3:21 pm Gemini
20th 4:47 pm Cancer
22nd 9:23 pm Leo
25th 5:50 am Virgo
27th 5:24 pm Libra
30th 6:13 am Scorpio

December 1918
2nd 6:20 pm Sagittarius
5th 4:41 am Capricorn
7th 12:52 pm Aquarius
9th 6:47 pm Pisces
11th 10:33 pm Aries
14th 12:35 am Taurus
16th 1:49 am Gemini
18th 3:35 am Cancer
20th 7:25 am Leo
22nd 2:33 pm Virgo
25th 1:10 am Libra
27th 1:48 pm Scorpio
30th 2:03 am Sagittarius

January 1919
1st 12:01 pm Capricorn
3rd 7:16 pm Aquarius
6th 12:18 am Pisces
8th 4:01 am Aries
10th 7:01 am Taurus
12th 9:49 am Gemini
14th 12:56 pm Cancer
16th 5:16 pm Leo
18th 11:57 pm Virgo
21st 9:42 am Libra
23rd 9:59 pm Scorpio
26th 10:34 am Sagittarius
28th 8:53 pm Capricorn
31st 3:44 am Aquarius

February 1919
2nd 7:38 am Pisces
4th 10:03 am Aries
6th 12:22 pm Taurus
8th 3:31 pm Gemini
10th 7:46 pm Cancer
13th 1:17 am Leo
15th 8:32 am Virgo
17th 6:06 pm Libra
20th 6:03 am Scorpio
22nd 6:56 pm Sagittarius
25th 6:08 am Capricorn
27th 1:36 pm Aquarius

March 1919
1st 5:15 pm Pisces
3rd 6:29 pm Aries
5th 7:14 pm Taurus
7th 9:10 pm Gemini
10th 1:09 am Cancer
12th 7:18 am Leo
14th 3:26 pm Virgo
17th 1:29 am Libra
19th 1:24 pm Scorpio
22nd 2:23 am Sagittarius
24th 2:24 pm Capricorn
26th 11:11 pm Aquarius
29th 3:46 am Pisces
31st 4:58 am Aries

April 1919
2nd 4:40 am Taurus
4th 4:56 am Gemini
6th 7:22 am Cancer
8th 12:48 pm Leo
10th 9:07 pm Virgo
13th 7:42 am Libra
15th 7:54 pm Scorpio
18th 8:51 am Sagittarius
20th 9:13 pm Capricorn
23rd 7:09 am Aquarius
25th 1:17 pm Pisces
27th 3:40 pm Aries
29th 3:37 pm Taurus

May 1919
1st 3:01 pm Gemini
3rd 3:51 pm Cancer
5th 7:38 pm Leo
8th 3:00 am Virgo
10th 1:31 pm Libra
13th 1:57 am Scorpio
15th 2:54 pm Sagittarius
18th 3:06 am Capricorn
20th 1:23 pm Aquarius
22nd 8:45 pm Pisces
25th 12:47 am Aries
27th 2:02 am Taurus
29th 1:53 am Gemini
31st 2:05 am Cancer

June 1919
2nd 4:26 am Leo
4th 10:18 am Virgo
6th 7:57 pm Libra
9th 8:15 am Scorpio
11th 9:11 pm Sagittarius
14th 9:04 am Capricorn
16th 6:58 pm Aquarius
19th 2:31 am Pisces
21st 7:38 am Aries
23rd 10:29 am Taurus
25th 11:42 am Gemini
27th 12:29 pm Cancer
29th 2:24 pm Leo

July 1919
1st 7:06 pm Virgo
4th 3:34 am Libra
6th 3:18 pm Scorpio
9th 4:13 am Sagittarius
11th 3:56 pm Capricorn
14th 1:14 am Aquarius
16th 8:06 am Pisces
18th 1:06 pm Aries
20th 4:43 pm Taurus
22nd 7:19 pm Gemini
24th 9:25 pm Cancer
26th 11:59 pm Leo
29th 4:28 am Virgo
31st 12:06 pm Libra

August 1919
2nd 11:08 pm Scorpio
5th 11:57 am Sagittarius
7th 11:52 pm Capricorn
10th 8:56 am Aquarius
12th 2:59 pm Pisces
14th 6:59 pm Aries
16th 10:05 pm Taurus
19th 1:03 am Gemini
21st 4:14 am Cancer
23rd 7:59 am Leo
25th 1:08 pm Virgo
27th 8:41 pm Libra
30th 7:15 am Scorpio

September 1919
1st 7:57 pm Sagittarius
4th 8:20 am Capricorn
6th 5:53 pm Aquarius
8th 11:45 pm Pisces
11th 2:48 am Aries
13th 4:36 am Taurus
15th 6:35 am Gemini
17th 9:39 am Cancer
19th 2:08 pm Leo
21st 8:15 pm Virgo
24th 4:24 am Libra
26th 2:59 pm Scorpio
29th 3:36 am Sagittarius

October 1919
1st 4:28 pm Capricorn
4th 3:03 am Aquarius
6th 9:44 am Pisces
8th 12:45 pm Aries
10th 1:33 pm Taurus
12th 1:59 pm Gemini
14th 3:39 pm Cancer
16th 7:32 pm Leo
19th 1:58 am Virgo
21st 10:51 am Libra
23rd 9:52 pm Scorpio
26th 10:30 am Sagittarius
28th 11:34 pm Capricorn
31st 11:07 am Aquarius

November 1919
2nd 7:19 pm Pisces
4th 11:30 pm Aries
7th 12:31 am Taurus
9th 12:03 am Gemini
11th 12:03 am Cancer
13th 2:14 am Leo
15th 7:40 am Virgo
17th 4:31 pm Libra
20th 3:58 am Scorpio
22nd 4:47 pm Sagittarius
25th 5:45 am Capricorn
27th 5:37 pm Aquarius
30th 3:03 am Pisces

December 1919
2nd 9:02 am Aries
4th 11:34 am Taurus
6th 11:37 am Gemini
8th 10:55 am Cancer
10th 11:29 am Leo
12th 3:06 pm Virgo
14th 10:47 pm Libra
17th 10:00 am Scorpio
19th 10:59 pm Sagittarius
22nd 11:49 am Capricorn
24th 11:20 pm Aquarius
27th 8:55 am Pisces
29th 4:05 pm Aries
31st 8:28 pm Taurus

January 1920
2nd 10:13 pm Gemini
4th 10:19 pm Cancer
6th 10:30 pm Leo
9th 12:46 am Virgo
11th 6:47 am Libra
13th 4:57 pm Scorpio
16th 5:43 am Sagittarius
18th 6:33 pm Capricorn
21st 5:39 am Aquarius
23rd 2:34 pm Pisces
25th 9:32 pm Aries
28th 2:43 am Taurus
30th 6:05 am Gemini

May 1920
2nd 1:37 am Scorpio
4th 12:59 pm Sagittarius
7th 1:39 am Capricorn
9th 2:08 pm Aquarius
12th 12:32 am Pisces
14th 7:23 am Aries
16th 10:36 am Taurus
18th 11:14 am Gemini
20th 11:01 am Cancer
22nd 11:50 am Leo
24th 3:10 pm Virgo
26th 9:50 pm Libra
29th 7:32 am Scorpio
31st 7:20 pm Sagittarius

September 1920
2nd 4:19 pm Taurus
4th 8:58 pm Gemini
7th 12:04 am Cancer
9th 2:02 am Leo
11th 3:55 am Virgo
13th 7:11 am Libra
15th 1:19 pm Scorpio
17th 10:57 pm Sagittarius
20th 11:08 am Capricorn
22nd 11:33 pm Aquarius
25th 9:57 am Pisces
27th 5:35 pm Aries
29th 10:49 pm Taurus

January 1921
2nd 5:26 pm Scorpio
5th 3:57 am Sagittarius
7th 4:09 pm Capricorn
10th 4:49 am Aquarius
12th 5:10 pm Pisces
15th 4:14 am Aries
17th 12:40 pm Taurus
19th 5:23 pm Gemini
21st 6:36 pm Cancer
23rd 5:46 pm Leo
25th 5:05 pm Virgo
27th 6:46 pm Libra
30th 12:25 am Scorpio

May 1921
1st 9:46 pm Pisces
4th 8:13 am Aries
6th 3:32 pm Taurus
8th 7:51 pm Gemini
10th 10:19 pm Cancer
13th 12:16 am Leo
15th 2:51 am Virgo
17th 6:46 am Libra
19th 12:21 pm Scorpio
21st 7:53 pm Sagittarius
24th 5:34 am Capricorn
26th 5:17 pm Aquarius
29th 5:50 am Pisces
31st 5:04 pm Aries

February 1920
1st 7:54 am Cancer
3rd 9:06 am Leo
5th 11:19 am Virgo
7th 4:19 pm Libra
10th 1:13 am Scorpio
12th 1:20 pm Sagittarius
15th 2:14 am Capricorn
17th 1:20 pm Aquarius
19th 9:39 pm Pisces
22nd 3:36 am Aries
24th 8:06 am Taurus
26th 11:42 am Gemini
28th 2:41 pm Cancer

June 1920
3rd 8:04 am Capricorn
5th 8:38 pm Aquarius
8th 7:42 am Pisces
10th 3:57 pm Aries
12th 8:35 pm Taurus
14th 9:57 pm Gemini
16th 9:27 pm Cancer
18th 9:02 pm Leo
20th 10:45 pm Virgo
23rd 4:05 am Libra
25th 1:18 pm Scorpio
28th 1:15 am Sagittarius
30th 2:06 pm Capricorn

October 1920
2nd 2:32 am Gemini
4th 5:29 am Cancer
6th 8:14 am Leo
8th 11:23 am Virgo
10th 3:44 pm Libra
12th 10:14 pm Scorpio
15th 7:30 am Sagittarius
17th 7:16 pm Capricorn
20th 7:52 am Aquarius
22nd 6:56 pm Pisces
25th 2:52 am Aries
27th 7:34 am Taurus
29th 9:59 am Gemini
31st 11:35 am Cancer

February 1921
1st 10:03 am Sagittarius
3rd 10:14 pm Capricorn
6th 10:59 am Aquarius
8th 11:03 pm Pisces
11th 9:51 am Aries
13th 6:44 pm Taurus
16th 12:54 am Gemini
18th 3:58 am Leo
20th 4:34 am Leo
22nd 4:21 am Virgo
24th 5:21 am Libra
26th 9:28 am Scorpio
28th 5:36 pm Sagittarius

June 1921
3rd 1:03 am Taurus
5th 5:17 am Gemini
7th 6:47 am Cancer
9th 7:19 am Leo
11th 8:41 am Virgo
13th 12:10 pm Libra
15th 6:10 pm Scorpio
18th 2:28 am Sagittarius
20th 12:39 pm Capricorn
23rd 12:24 am Aquarius
25th 1:03 pm Pisces
28th 1:02 am Aries
30th 10:13 am Taurus

March 1920
1st 5:23 pm Leo
3rd 8:41 pm Virgo
6th 1:53 am Libra
8th 10:10 am Scorpio
10th 9:35 pm Sagittarius
13th 10:24 am Capricorn
15th 9:58 pm Aquarius
18th 6:25 am Pisces
20th 11:43 am Aries
22nd 2:58 pm Taurus
24th 5:26 pm Gemini
26th 8:02 pm Cancer
28th 11:20 pm Leo
31st 3:48 am Virgo

July 1920
3rd 2:30 am Aquarius
5th 1:37 pm Pisces
7th 10:38 pm Aries
10th 4:45 am Taurus
12th 7:40 am Gemini
14th 8:04 am Cancer
16th 7:32 am Leo
18th 8:12 am Virgo
20th 12:02 pm Libra
22nd 8:02 pm Scorpio
25th 7:30 am Sagittarius
27th 8:22 pm Capricorn
30th 8:37 am Aquarius

November 1920
2nd 1:37 pm Leo
4th 5:03 pm Virgo
6th 10:23 pm Libra
9th 5:49 am Scorpio
11th 3:26 pm Sagittarius
14th 3:03 am Capricorn
16th 3:44 pm Aquarius
19th 3:39 am Pisces
21st 12:45 pm Aries
23rd 6:02 pm Taurus
25th 8:00 pm Gemini
27th 8:12 pm Cancer
29th 8:33 pm Leo

March 1921
3rd 5:03 am Capricorn
5th 5:45 pm Aquarius
8th 5:44 am Pisces
10th 3:58 pm Aries
13th 12:14 am Taurus
15th 6:29 am Gemini
17th 10:36 am Cancer
19th 12:52 pm Leo
21st 2:08 pm Virgo
23rd 3:50 pm Libra
25th 7:34 pm Scorpio
28th 2:34 am Sagittarius
30th 12:57 pm Capricorn

July 1921
2nd 3:23 pm Gemini
4th 4:56 pm Cancer
6th 4:34 pm Leo
8th 4:27 pm Virgo
10th 6:28 pm Libra
12th 11:43 pm Scorpio
15th 8:05 am Sagittarius
17th 6:43 pm Capricorn
20th 6:43 am Aquarius
22nd 7:23 pm Pisces
25th 7:41 am Aries
27th 5:57 pm Taurus
30th 12:37 am Gemini

April 1920
2nd 9:59 am Libra
4th 6:33 pm Scorpio
7th 5:41 am Sagittarius
9th 6:24 pm Capricorn
12th 6:31 am Aquarius
14th 3:50 pm Pisces
16th 9:29 pm Aries
19th 12:08 am Taurus
21st 1:14 am Gemini
23rd 2:22 am Cancer
25th 4:49 am Leo
27th 9:21 am Virgo
29th 4:18 pm Libra

August 1920
1st 7:18 pm Pisces
4th 4:10 am Aries
6th 10:56 am Taurus
8th 3:15 pm Gemini
10th 5:11 pm Cancer
12th 5:42 pm Leo
14th 6:28 pm Virgo
16th 9:28 pm Libra
19th 4:12 am Scorpio
21st 2:44 pm Sagittarius
24th 3:22 am Capricorn
26th 3:36 pm Aquarius
29th 1:55 am Pisces
31st 10:03 am Aries

December 1920
1st 10:45 pm Virgo
4th 3:50 am Libra
6th 11:51 am Scorpio
8th 10:09 pm Sagittarius
11th 9:59 am Capricorn
13th 10:39 pm Aquarius
16th 11:03 am Pisces
18th 9:29 pm Aries
21st 4:22 am Taurus
23rd 7:15 am Gemini
25th 7:14 am Cancer
27th 6:17 am Leo
29th 6:37 am Virgo
31st 10:06 am Libra

April 1921
2nd 1:22 am Aquarius
4th 1:27 pm Pisces
6th 11:31 pm Aries
9th 6:59 am Taurus
11th 12:16 pm Gemini
13th 3:59 pm Cancer
15th 6:48 pm Leo
17th 9:21 pm Virgo
20th 12:24 am Libra
22nd 4:54 am Scorpio
24th 11:45 am Sagittarius
26th 9:27 pm Capricorn
29th 9:25 am Aquarius

August 1921
1st 3:18 am Cancer
3rd 3:11 am Leo
5th 2:18 am Virgo
7th 2:51 am Libra
9th 6:33 am Scorpio
11th 1:59 pm Sagittarius
14th 12:30 am Capricorn
16th 12:41 pm Aquarius
19th 1:20 am Pisces
21st 1:29 pm Aries
24th 12:07 am Taurus
26th 7:57 am Gemini
28th 12:17 pm Cancer
30th 1:31 pm Leo

September 1921
1st 1:07 pm Virgo
3rd 1:06 pm Libra
5th 3:24 pm Scorpio
7th 9:20 pm Sagittarius
10th 6:58 am Capricorn
12th 7:00 pm Aquarius
15th 7:39 am Pisces
17th 7:29 pm Aries
20th 5:41 am Taurus
22nd 1:41 pm Gemini
24th 7:06 pm Cancer
26th 9:58 pm Leo
28th 11:02 pm Virgo
30th 11:41 pm Libra

January 1922
2nd 2:44 pm Pisces
5th 3:41 am Aries
7th 2:58 pm Taurus
9th 10:27 pm Gemini
12th 1:47 am Cancer
14th 2:21 am Leo
16th 2:13 am Virgo
18th 3:21 am Libra
20th 7:02 am Scorpio
22nd 1:33 pm Sagittarius
24th 10:28 pm Capricorn
27th 9:16 am Aquarius
29th 9:33 pm Pisces

May 1922
1st 9:12 am Cancer
3rd 2:05 pm Leo
5th 5:19 pm Virgo
7th 7:22 pm Libra
9th 9:01 pm Scorpio
11th 11:32 pm Sagittarius
14th 4:25 am Capricorn
16th 12:45 pm Aquarius
19th 12:20 am Pisces
21st 1:12 pm Aries
24th 12:46 am Taurus
26th 9:29 am Gemini
28th 3:27 pm Cancer
30th 7:34 pm Leo

September 1922
2nd 6:12 pm Aquarius
5th 5:41 am Pisces
7th 6:29 pm Aries
10th 7:24 am Taurus
12th 6:50 pm Gemini
15th 3:13 am Cancer
17th 7:48 am Leo
19th 9:09 am Virgo
21st 8:44 am Libra
23rd 8:28 am Scorpio
25th 10:11 am Sagittarius
27th 3:15 pm Capricorn
30th 12:02 am Aquarius

January 1923
2nd 5:39 am Cancer
4th 10:34 am Leo
6th 1:59 pm Virgo
8th 4:59 pm Libra
10th 8:04 pm Scorpio
12th 11:34 pm Sagittarius
15th 3:56 am Capricorn
17th 10:06 am Aquarius
19th 6:57 pm Pisces
22nd 6:37 am Aries
24th 7:33 pm Taurus
27th 7:07 am Gemini
29th 3:19 pm Cancer
31st 7:57 pm Leo

October 1921
3rd 1:37 am Scorpio
5th 6:22 am Sagittarius
7th 2:45 pm Capricorn
10th 2:12 am Aquarius
12th 2:50 pm Pisces
15th 2:34 am Aries
17th 12:08 pm Taurus
19th 7:21 pm Gemini
22nd 12:32 am Cancer
24th 4:08 am Leo
26th 6:40 am Virgo
28th 8:49 am Libra
30th 11:34 am Scorpio

February 1922
1st 10:35 am Aries
3rd 10:40 pm Taurus
6th 7:41 am Gemini
8th 12:30 pm Cancer
10th 1:40 pm Leo
12th 12:59 pm Virgo
14th 12:35 pm Libra
16th 2:23 pm Scorpio
18th 7:31 pm Sagittarius
21st 4:05 am Capricorn
23rd 3:12 pm Aquarius
26th 3:45 am Pisces
28th 4:41 pm Aries

June 1922
1st 10:48 pm Virgo
4th 1:43 am Libra
6th 4:42 am Scorpio
8th 8:18 am Sagittarius
10th 1:30 pm Capricorn
12th 9:25 pm Aquarius
15th 8:24 am Pisces
17th 9:12 pm Aries
20th 9:08 am Taurus
22nd 6:02 pm Gemini
24th 11:27 pm Cancer
27th 2:28 am Leo
29th 4:37 am Virgo

October 1922
2nd 11:40 am Pisces
5th 12:36 am Aries
7th 1:20 pm Taurus
10th 12:44 am Gemini
12th 9:52 am Cancer
14th 4:01 pm Leo
16th 7:04 pm Virgo
18th 7:44 pm Libra
20th 7:27 pm Scorpio
22nd 8:06 pm Sagittarius
24th 11:33 pm Capricorn
27th 6:59 am Aquarius
29th 6:06 pm Pisces

February 1923
2nd 10:12 pm Virgo
4th 11:38 pm Libra
7th 1:37 am Scorpio
9th 4:59 am Sagittarius
11th 10:08 am Capricorn
13th 5:18 pm Aquarius
16th 2:43 am Pisces
18th 2:20 pm Aries
21st 3:15 am Taurus
23rd 3:30 pm Gemini
26th 12:57 am Cancer
28th 6:30 am Leo

November 1921
1st 4:08 pm Sagittarius
3rd 11:38 pm Capricorn
6th 10:17 am Aquarius
8th 10:51 pm Pisces
11th 10:52 am Aries
13th 8:19 pm Taurus
16th 2:41 am Gemini
18th 6:41 am Cancer
20th 9:32 am Leo
22nd 12:17 pm Virgo
24th 3:32 pm Libra
26th 7:37 pm Scorpio
29th 1:03 am Sagittarius

March 1922
3rd 4:51 am Taurus
5th 2:48 pm Gemini
7th 9:18 pm Cancer
10th 12:09 am Leo
12th 12:22 am Virgo
13th 11:44 pm Libra
16th 12:13 am Scorpio
18th 3:33 am Sagittarius
20th 10:41 am Capricorn
22nd 9:17 pm Aquarius
25th 9:55 am Pisces
27th 10:49 pm Aries
30th 10:38 am Taurus

July 1922
1st 7:05 am Libra
3rd 10:29 am Scorpio
5th 3:05 pm Sagittarius
7th 9:12 pm Capricorn
10th 5:27 am Aquarius
12th 4:16 pm Pisces
15th 4:59 am Aries
17th 5:27 pm Taurus
20th 3:10 am Gemini
22nd 8:56 am Cancer
24th 11:27 am Leo
26th 12:22 pm Virgo
28th 1:27 pm Libra
30th 3:59 pm Scorpio

November 1922
1st 7:04 am Aries
3rd 7:39 pm Taurus
6th 6:33 am Gemini
8th 3:23 pm Cancer
10th 10:05 pm Leo
13th 2:36 am Virgo
15th 5:01 am Libra
17th 5:59 am Scorpio
19th 6:53 am Sagittarius
21st 9:32 am Capricorn
23rd 3:35 pm Aquarius
26th 1:39 am Pisces
28th 2:20 pm Aries

March 1923
2nd 8:42 am Virgo
4th 9:01 am Libra
6th 9:16 am Scorpio
8th 11:05 am Sagittarius
10th 3:34 pm Capricorn
12th 11:02 pm Aquarius
15th 9:07 am Pisces
17th 9:06 pm Aries
20th 9:59 am Taurus
22nd 10:33 pm Gemini
25th 9:05 am Cancer
27th 4:13 pm Leo
29th 7:36 pm Virgo
31st 8:07 pm Libra

December 1921
1st 8:32 am Capricorn
3rd 6:41 pm Aquarius
6th 7:03 am Pisces
8th 7:36 pm Aries
11th 5:45 am Taurus
13th 12:08 pm Gemini
15th 3:12 pm Cancer
17th 4:35 pm Leo
19th 6:03 pm Virgo
21st 8:52 pm Libra
24th 1:33 am Scorpio
26th 8:01 am Sagittarius
28th 4:16 pm Capricorn
31st 2:31 am Aquarius

April 1922
1st 8:29 pm Gemini
4th 3:46 am Cancer
6th 8:13 am Leo
8th 10:09 am Virgo
10th 10:37 am Libra
12th 11:07 am Scorpio
14th 1:25 pm Sagittarius
16th 7:01 pm Capricorn
19th 4:11 am Aquarius
21st 4:43 pm Pisces
24th 5:37 am Aries
26th 5:07 pm Taurus
29th 2:19 am Gemini

August 1922
1st 8:35 pm Sagittarius
4th 3:22 am Capricorn
6th 12:18 pm Aquarius
8th 11:23 pm Pisces
11th 12:05 pm Aries
14th 12:57 am Taurus
16th 11:42 am Gemini
18th 6:40 pm Cancer
20th 9:45 pm Leo
22nd 10:16 pm Virgo
24th 10:05 pm Libra
26th 11:02 pm Scorpio
29th 2:26 am Sagittarius
31st 8:53 am Capricorn

December 1922
1st 2:59 am Taurus
3rd 1:34 pm Gemini
5th 9:34 pm Cancer
8th 3:33 am Leo
10th 8:09 am Virgo
12th 11:39 am Libra
14th 2:14 pm Scorpio
16th 4:28 pm Sagittarius
18th 7:35 pm Capricorn
21st 1:08 am Aquarius
23rd 10:13 am Pisces
25th 10:22 pm Aries
28th 11:12 am Taurus
30th 10:02 pm Gemini

April 1923
2nd 7:26 pm Scorpio
4th 7:34 pm Sagittarius
6th 10:19 pm Capricorn
9th 4:48 am Aquarius
11th 2:50 pm Pisces
14th 3:08 am Aries
16th 4:07 pm Taurus
19th 4:33 am Gemini
21st 3:27 pm Cancer
23rd 11:50 pm Leo
26th 4:56 am Virgo
28th 6:49 am Libra
30th 6:33 am Scorpio

May 1923
2nd 5:59 am Sagittarius
4th 7:14 am Capricorn
6th 12:04 pm Aquarius
8th 9:06 pm Pisces
11th 9:12 am Aries
13th 10:14 pm Taurus
16th 10:27 am Gemini
18th 9:03 pm Cancer
21st 5:40 am Leo
23rd 11:54 am Virgo
25th 3:25 pm Libra
27th 4:35 pm Scorpio
29th 4:38 pm Sagittarius
31st 5:28 pm Capricorn

June 1923
2nd 9:04 pm Aquarius
5th 4:43 am Pisces
7th 4:02 pm Aries
10th 4:56 am Taurus
12th 5:03 pm Gemini
15th 3:10 am Cancer
17th 11:12 am Leo
19th 5:22 pm Virgo
21st 9:44 pm Libra
24th 12:20 am Scorpio
26th 1:46 am Sagittarius
28th 3:20 am Capricorn
30th 6:44 am Aquarius

July 1923
2nd 1:27 pm Pisces
4th 11:51 pm Aries
7th 12:24 pm Taurus
10th 12:37 am Gemini
12th 10:34 am Cancer
14th 5:53 pm Leo
16th 11:10 pm Virgo
19th 3:05 am Libra
21st 6:08 am Scorpio
23rd 8:43 am Sagittarius
25th 11:33 am Capricorn
27th 3:42 pm Aquarius
29th 10:23 pm Pisces

August 1923
1st 8:11 am Aries
3rd 8:22 pm Taurus
6th 8:47 am Gemini
8th 7:07 pm Cancer
11th 2:19 am Leo
13th 6:44 am Virgo
15th 9:27 am Libra
17th 11:38 am Scorpio
19th 2:12 pm Sagittarius
21st 5:49 pm Capricorn
23rd 11:03 pm Aquarius
26th 6:25 am Pisces
28th 4:14 pm Aries
31st 4:11 am Taurus

September 1923
2nd 4:50 pm Gemini
5th 3:59 am Cancer
7th 11:54 am Leo
9th 4:17 pm Virgo
11th 6:03 pm Libra
13th 6:47 pm Scorpio
15th 8:05 pm Sagittarius
17th 11:14 pm Capricorn
20th 4:52 am Aquarius
22nd 1:03 pm Pisces
24th 11:23 pm Aries
27th 11:22 am Taurus
30th 12:06 am Gemini

October 1923
2nd 11:59 am Cancer
4th 9:14 pm Leo
7th 2:41 am Virgo
9th 4:36 am Libra
11th 4:25 am Scorpio
13th 4:09 am Sagittarius
15th 5:43 am Capricorn
17th 10:29 am Aquarius
19th 6:42 pm Pisces
22nd 5:33 am Aries
24th 5:48 pm Taurus
27th 6:28 am Gemini
29th 6:39 pm Cancer

November 1923
1st 4:59 am Leo
3rd 12:06 pm Virgo
5th 3:24 pm Libra
7th 3:38 pm Scorpio
9th 2:38 pm Sagittarius
11th 2:38 pm Capricorn
13th 5:39 pm Aquarius
16th 12:46 am Pisces
18th 11:25 am Aries
20th 11:53 pm Taurus
23rd 12:32 pm Gemini
26th 12:48 am Cancer
28th 11:01 am Leo
30th 7:18 pm Virgo

December 1923
3rd 12:24 am Libra
5th 2:15 am Scorpio
7th 1:57 am Sagittarius
9th 1:31 am Capricorn
11th 3:10 am Aquarius
13th 8:35 am Pisces
15th 6:07 pm Aries
18th 6:21 am Taurus
20th 7:03 pm Gemini
23rd 6:40 am Cancer
25th 4:40 pm Leo
28th 12:51 am Virgo
30th 6:51 am Libra

January 1924
1st 10:23 am Scorpio
3rd 11:48 am Sagittarius
5th 12:22 pm Capricorn
7th 1:54 pm Aquarius
9th 6:13 pm Pisces
12th 2:22 am Aries
14th 1:48 pm Taurus
17th 2:27 am Gemini
19th 2:05 pm Cancer
21st 11:33 pm Leo
24th 6:49 am Virgo
26th 12:14 pm Libra
28th 4:09 pm Scorpio
30th 6:53 pm Sagittarius

February 1924
1st 9:03 pm Capricorn
3rd 11:43 pm Aquarius
6th 4:12 am Pisces
8th 11:36 am Aries
10th 10:09 pm Taurus
13th 10:34 am Gemini
15th 10:33 pm Cancer
18th 8:09 am Leo
20th 2:46 pm Virgo
22nd 6:57 pm Libra
24th 9:47 pm Scorpio
27th 12:16 am Sagittarius
29th 3:12 am Capricorn

March 1924
2nd 7:11 am Aquarius
4th 12:45 pm Pisces
6th 8:26 pm Aries
9th 6:35 am Taurus
11th 6:43 pm Gemini
14th 7:07 am Cancer
16th 5:31 pm Leo
19th 12:27 am Virgo
21st 4:00 am Libra
23rd 5:28 am Scorpio
25th 6:29 am Sagittarius
27th 8:37 am Capricorn
29th 12:47 pm Aquarius
31st 7:13 pm Pisces

April 1924
3rd 3:45 am Aries
5th 2:11 pm Taurus
8th 2:13 am Gemini
10th 2:52 pm Cancer
13th 2:15 am Leo
15th 10:21 am Virgo
17th 2:27 pm Libra
19th 3:25 pm Scorpio
21st 3:05 pm Sagittarius
23rd 3:33 pm Capricorn
25th 6:30 pm Aquarius
28th 12:39 am Pisces
30th 9:39 am Aries

May 1924
2nd 8:37 pm Taurus
5th 8:48 am Gemini
7th 9:30 pm Cancer
10th 9:29 am Leo
12th 6:56 pm Virgo
15th 12:28 am Libra
17th 2:11 am Scorpio
19th 1:34 am Sagittarius
21st 12:49 am Capricorn
23rd 2:04 am Aquarius
25th 6:49 am Pisces
27th 3:15 pm Aries
30th 2:23 am Taurus

June 1924
1st 2:47 pm Gemini
4th 3:27 am Cancer
6th 3:29 pm Leo
9th 1:41 am Virgo
11th 8:41 am Libra
13th 11:57 am Scorpio
15th 12:18 pm Sagittarius
17th 11:29 am Capricorn
19th 11:43 am Aquarius
21st 2:52 pm Pisces
23rd 9:56 pm Aries
26th 8:27 am Taurus
28th 8:51 pm Gemini

July 1924
1st 9:28 am Cancer
3rd 9:11 pm Leo
6th 7:15 am Virgo
8th 2:54 pm Libra
10th 7:36 pm Scorpio
12th 9:32 pm Sagittarius
14th 9:49 pm Capricorn
16th 10:11 pm Aquarius
19th 12:30 am Pisces
21st 6:12 am Aries
23rd 3:36 pm Taurus
26th 3:36 am Gemini
28th 4:11 pm Cancer
31st 3:38 am Leo

August 1924
2nd 1:05 pm Virgo
4th 8:20 pm Libra
7th 1:24 am Scorpio
9th 4:32 am Sagittarius
11th 6:21 am Capricorn
13th 7:52 am Aquarius
15th 10:29 am Pisces
17th 3:32 pm Aries
19th 11:54 pm Taurus
22nd 11:14 am Gemini
24th 11:48 pm Cancer
27th 11:18 am Leo
29th 8:19 pm Virgo

September 1924
1st 2:38 am Libra
3rd 6:54 am Scorpio
5th 10:00 am Sagittarius
7th 12:41 pm Capricorn
9th 3:33 pm Aquarius
11th 7:17 pm Pisces
14th 12:42 am Aries
16th 8:39 am Taurus
18th 7:24 pm Gemini
21st 7:54 am Cancer
23rd 7:52 pm Leo
26th 5:06 am Virgo
28th 10:54 am Libra
30th 2:00 pm Scorpio

October 1924
2nd 3:55 pm Sagittarius
4th 6:03 pm Capricorn
6th 9:20 pm Aquarius
9th 2:06 am Pisces
11th 8:31 am Aries
13th 4:50 pm Taurus
16th 3:23 am Gemini
18th 3:47 pm Cancer
21st 4:21 am Leo
23rd 2:33 pm Virgo
25th 8:49 pm Libra
27th 11:27 pm Scorpio
30th 12:03 am Sagittarius

November 1924
1st 12:39 am Capricorn
3rd 2:53 am Aquarius
5th 7:34 am Pisces
7th 2:39 pm Aries
9th 11:44 pm Taurus
12th 10:34 am Gemini
14th 10:57 pm Cancer
17th 11:50 am Leo
19th 11:11 pm Virgo
22nd 6:51 am Libra
24th 10:18 am Scorpio
26th 10:39 am Sagittarius
28th 9:58 am Capricorn
30th 10:26 am Aquarius

December 1924
2nd 1:38 pm Pisces
4th 8:10 pm Aries
7th 5:33 am Taurus
9th 4:52 pm Gemini
12th 5:21 am Cancer
14th 6:12 pm Leo
17th 6:06 am Virgo
19th 3:15 pm Libra
21st 8:26 pm Scorpio
23rd 9:56 pm Sagittarius
25th 9:19 pm Capricorn
27th 8:41 pm Aquarius
29th 10:06 pm Pisces

January 1925
1st 2:57 am Aries
3rd 11:31 am Taurus
5th 10:52 pm Gemini
8th 11:32 am Cancer
11th 12:14 am Leo
13th 11:54 am Virgo
15th 9:32 pm Libra
18th 4:11 am Scorpio
20th 7:34 am Sagittarius
22nd 8:23 am Capricorn
24th 8:10 am Aquarius
26th 8:46 am Pisces
28th 11:59 am Aries
30th 6:58 pm Taurus

February 1925
2nd 5:32 am Gemini
4th 6:10 pm Cancer
7th 6:49 am Leo
9th 6:01 pm Virgo
12th 3:06 am Libra
14th 9:54 am Scorpio
16th 2:28 pm Sagittarius
18th 5:02 pm Capricorn
20th 6:21 pm Aquarius
22nd 7:37 pm Pisces
24th 10:21 pm Aries
27th 4:04 am Taurus

March 1925
1st 1:25 pm Gemini
4th 1:38 am Cancer
6th 2:22 pm Leo
9th 1:24 am Virgo
11th 9:44 am Libra
13th 3:38 pm Scorpio
15th 7:52 pm Sagittarius
17th 11:07 pm Capricorn
20th 1:51 am Aquarius
22nd 4:33 am Pisces
24th 8:04 am Aries
26th 1:34 pm Taurus
28th 10:08 pm Gemini
31st 9:42 am Cancer

April 1925
2nd 10:32 pm Leo
5th 9:54 am Virgo
7th 6:04 pm Libra
9th 11:04 pm Scorpio
12th 2:05 am Sagittarius
14th 4:32 am Capricorn
16th 7:23 am Aquarius
18th 11:02 am Pisces
20th 3:45 pm Aries
22nd 9:59 pm Taurus
25th 6:33 am Gemini
27th 5:45 pm Cancer
30th 6:36 am Leo

May 1925
2nd 6:37 pm Virgo
5th 3:26 am Libra
7th 8:22 am Scorpio
9th 10:28 am Sagittarius
11th 11:31 am Capricorn
13th 1:09 pm Aquarius
15th 4:23 pm Pisces
17th 9:34 pm Aries
20th 4:41 am Taurus
22nd 1:50 pm Gemini
25th 1:07 am Cancer
27th 1:58 pm Leo
30th 2:35 am Virgo

June 1925
1st 12:30 pm Libra
3rd 6:21 pm Scorpio
5th 8:34 pm Sagittarius
7th 8:45 pm Capricorn
9th 8:54 pm Aquarius
11th 10:40 pm Pisces
14th 3:03 am Aries
16th 10:15 am Taurus
18th 7:57 pm Gemini
21st 7:36 am Cancer
23rd 8:30 pm Leo
26th 9:21 am Virgo
28th 8:14 pm Libra

July 1925
1st 3:32 am Scorpio
3rd 6:55 am Sagittarius
5th 7:25 am Capricorn
7th 6:50 am Aquarius
9th 7:06 am Pisces
11th 9:53 am Aries
13th 4:05 pm Taurus
16th 1:37 am Gemini
18th 1:32 pm Cancer
21st 2:32 am Leo
23rd 3:17 pm Virgo
26th 2:30 am Libra
28th 10:56 am Scorpio
30th 3:56 pm Sagittarius

August 1925
1st 5:47 pm Capricorn
3rd 5:41 pm Aquarius
5th 5:24 pm Pisces
7th 6:46 pm Aries
9th 11:24 pm Taurus
12th 7:56 am Gemini
14th 7:38 pm Cancer
17th 8:41 am Leo
19th 9:13 pm Virgo
22nd 8:05 am Libra
24th 4:44 pm Scorpio
26th 10:50 pm Sagittarius
29th 2:19 am Capricorn
31st 3:41 am Aquarius

September 1925
2nd 4:03 am Pisces
4th 5:02 am Aries
6th 8:27 am Taurus
8th 3:38 pm Gemini
11th 2:35 am Cancer
13th 3:29 pm Leo
16th 3:56 am Virgo
18th 2:18 pm Libra
20th 10:18 pm Scorpio
23rd 4:17 am Sagittarius
25th 8:37 am Capricorn
27th 11:29 am Aquarius
29th 1:19 pm Pisces

October 1925
1st 3:06 pm Aries
3rd 6:20 pm Taurus
6th 12:35 am Gemini
8th 10:32 am Cancer
10th 11:09 pm Leo
13th 11:43 am Virgo
15th 9:57 pm Libra
18th 5:13 am Scorpio
20th 10:12 am Sagittarius
22nd 1:57 pm Capricorn
24th 5:12 pm Aquarius
26th 8:14 pm Pisces
28th 11:24 pm Aries
31st 3:29 am Taurus

November 1925
2nd 9:44 am Gemini
4th 7:05 pm Cancer
7th 7:15 am Leo
9th 8:06 pm Virgo
12th 6:52 am Libra
14th 2:06 pm Scorpio
16th 6:13 pm Sagittarius
18th 8:38 pm Capricorn
20th 10:48 pm Aquarius
23rd 1:37 am Pisces
25th 5:31 am Aries
27th 10:46 am Taurus
29th 5:50 pm Gemini

December 1925
2nd 3:19 am Cancer
4th 3:12 pm Leo
7th 4:13 am Virgo
9th 3:52 pm Libra
12th 12:03 am Scorpio
14th 4:23 am Sagittarius
16th 5:59 am Capricorn
18th 6:36 am Aquarius
20th 7:52 am Pisces
22nd 10:57 am Aries
24th 4:25 pm Taurus
27th 12:18 am Gemini
29th 10:26 am Cancer
31st 10:26 pm Leo

January 1926
3rd 11:26 am Virgo
5th 11:44 pm Libra
8th 9:19 am Scorpio
10th 3:02 pm Sagittarius
12th 5:09 pm Capricorn
14th 5:07 pm Aquarius
16th 4:48 pm Pisces
18th 6:03 pm Aries
20th 10:15 pm Taurus
23rd 5:55 am Gemini
25th 4:30 pm Cancer
28th 4:52 am Leo
30th 5:49 pm Virgo

February 1926
2nd 6:10 am Libra
4th 4:39 pm Scorpio
7th 12:02 am Sagittarius
9th 3:49 am Capricorn
11th 4:38 am Aquarius
13th 3:57 am Pisces
15th 3:48 am Aries
17th 6:08 am Taurus
19th 12:21 pm Gemini
21st 10:28 pm Cancer
24th 10:59 am Leo
26th 11:59 pm Virgo

March 1926
1st 12:03 pm Libra
3rd 10:28 pm Scorpio
6th 6:40 am Sagittarius
8th 12:06 pm Capricorn
10th 2:40 pm Aquarius
12th 3:04 pm Pisces
14th 2:53 pm Aries
16th 4:07 pm Taurus
18th 8:42 pm Gemini
21st 5:30 am Cancer
23rd 5:35 pm Leo
26th 6:36 am Virgo
28th 6:27 pm Libra
31st 4:17 am Scorpio

April 1926
2nd 12:08 pm Sagittarius
4th 6:04 pm Capricorn
6th 10:01 pm Aquarius
9th 12:03 am Pisces
11th 1:03 am Aries
13th 2:31 am Taurus
15th 6:20 am Gemini
17th 1:54 pm Cancer
20th 1:07 am Leo
22nd 1:58 pm Virgo
25th 1:52 am Libra
27th 11:19 am Scorpio
29th 6:19 pm Sagittarius

May 1926
1st 11:32 pm Capricorn
4th 3:31 am Aquarius
6th 6:32 am Pisces
8th 8:55 am Aries
10th 11:34 am Taurus
12th 3:46 pm Gemini
14th 10:53 pm Cancer
17th 9:20 am Leo
19th 9:54 pm Virgo
22nd 10:03 am Libra
24th 7:41 pm Scorpio
27th 2:14 am Sagittarius
29th 6:24 am Capricorn
31st 9:19 am Aquarius

June 1926
2nd 11:53 am Pisces
4th 2:46 pm Aries
6th 6:28 pm Taurus
8th 11:43 pm Gemini
11th 7:14 am Cancer
13th 5:28 pm Leo
16th 5:48 am Virgo
18th 6:18 pm Libra
21st 4:40 am Scorpio
23rd 11:35 am Sagittarius
25th 3:18 pm Capricorn
27th 5:01 pm Aquarius
29th 6:14 pm Pisces

July 1926
1st 8:14 pm Aries
3rd 11:59 pm Taurus
6th 5:57 am Gemini
8th 2:16 pm Cancer
11th 12:50 am Leo
13th 1:07 pm Virgo
16th 1:52 am Libra
18th 1:07 pm Scorpio
20th 9:10 pm Sagittarius
23rd 1:28 am Capricorn
25th 2:48 am Aquarius
27th 2:46 am Pisces
29th 3:13 am Aries
31st 5:46 am Taurus

August 1926
2nd 11:24 am Gemini
4th 8:08 pm Cancer
7th 7:12 am Leo
9th 7:39 pm Virgo
12th 8:26 am Libra
14th 8:17 pm Scorpio
17th 5:39 am Sagittarius
19th 11:23 am Capricorn
21st 1:31 pm Aquarius
23rd 1:15 pm Pisces
25th 12:31 pm Aries
27th 1:25 pm Taurus
29th 5:39 pm Gemini

September 1926
1st 1:48 am Cancer
3rd 1:01 pm Leo
6th 1:40 am Virgo
8th 2:23 pm Libra
11th 2:15 am Scorpio
13th 12:21 pm Sagittarius
15th 7:37 pm Capricorn
17th 11:23 pm Aquarius
20th 12:06 am Pisces
21st 11:20 am Aries
23rd 11:12 pm Taurus
26th 1:50 am Gemini
28th 8:34 am Cancer
30th 7:10 pm Leo

October 1926
3rd 7:49 am Virgo
5th 8:28 pm Libra
8th 7:59 am Scorpio
10th 5:53 pm Sagittarius
13th 1:47 am Capricorn
15th 7:02 am Aquarius
17th 9:30 am Pisces
19th 9:56 am Aries
21st 10:02 am Taurus
23rd 11:50 am Gemini
25th 5:08 pm Cancer
28th 2:30 am Leo
30th 2:42 pm Virgo

November 1926
2nd 3:22 am Libra
4th 2:37 pm Scorpio
6th 11:51 pm Sagittarius
9th 7:11 am Capricorn
11th 12:41 pm Aquarius
13th 4:22 pm Pisces
15th 6:28 pm Aries
17th 7:54 pm Taurus
19th 10:10 pm Gemini
22nd 2:54 am Cancer
24th 11:10 am Leo
26th 10:36 pm Virgo
29th 11:13 am Libra

December 1926
1st 10:39 pm Scorpio
4th 7:32 am Sagittarius
6th 1:53 pm Capricorn
8th 6:22 pm Aquarius
10th 9:44 pm Pisces
13th 12:33 am Aries
15th 3:23 am Taurus
17th 6:59 am Gemini
19th 12:20 pm Cancer
21st 8:16 pm Leo
24th 7:02 am Virgo
26th 7:30 pm Libra
29th 7:28 am Scorpio
31st 4:50 pm Sagittarius

January 1927
2nd 10:51 pm Capricorn
5th 2:10 am Aquarius
7th 4:06 am Pisces
9th 5:59 am Aries
11th 8:56 am Taurus
13th 1:30 pm Gemini
15th 7:59 pm Cancer
18th 4:31 am Leo
20th 3:09 pm Virgo
23rd 3:27 am Libra
25th 3:53 pm Scorpio
28th 2:21 am Sagittarius
30th 9:12 am Capricorn

February 1927
1st 12:22 pm Aquarius
3rd 1:07 pm Pisces
5th 1:20 pm Aries
7th 2:50 pm Taurus
9th 6:54 pm Gemini
12th 1:51 am Cancer
14th 11:11 am Leo
16th 10:15 pm Virgo
19th 10:31 am Libra
21st 11:08 pm Scorpio
24th 10:34 am Sagittarius
26th 6:55 pm Capricorn
28th 11:14 pm Aquarius

March 1927
3rd 12:05 am Pisces
4th 11:19 pm Aries
6th 11:07 pm Taurus
9th 1:29 am Gemini
11th 7:29 am Cancer
13th 4:51 pm Leo
16th 4:22 am Virgo
18th 4:48 pm Libra
21st 5:21 am Scorpio
23rd 5:06 pm Sagittarius
26th 2:39 am Capricorn
28th 8:39 am Aquarius
30th 10:53 am Pisces

April 1927
1st 10:31 am Aries
3rd 9:37 am Taurus
5th 10:25 am Gemini
7th 2:42 pm Cancer
9th 10:59 pm Leo
12th 10:18 am Virgo
14th 10:53 pm Libra
17th 11:20 am Scorpio
19th 10:49 pm Sagittarius
22nd 8:35 am Capricorn
24th 3:43 pm Aquarius
26th 7:37 pm Pisces
28th 8:44 pm Aries
30th 8:29 pm Taurus

May 1927
2nd 8:53 pm Gemini
4th 11:51 pm Cancer
7th 6:38 am Leo
9th 5:02 pm Virgo
12th 5:27 am Libra
14th 5:52 pm Scorpio
17th 4:57 am Sagittarius
19th 2:11 pm Capricorn
21st 9:16 pm Aquarius
24th 2:01 am Pisces
26th 4:37 am Aries
28th 5:51 am Taurus
30th 7:03 am Gemini

June 1927
1st 9:50 am Cancer
3rd 3:37 pm Leo
6th 12:55 am Virgo
8th 12:49 pm Libra
11th 1:16 am Scorpio
13th 12:16 pm Sagittarius
15th 8:51 pm Capricorn
18th 3:05 am Aquarius
20th 7:25 am Pisces
22nd 10:29 am Aries
24th 12:54 pm Taurus
26th 3:26 pm Gemini
28th 7:04 pm Cancer

July 1927
1st 12:48 am Leo
3rd 9:26 am Virgo
5th 8:47 pm Libra
8th 9:17 am Scorpio
10th 8:36 pm Sagittarius
13th 5:06 am Capricorn
15th 10:31 am Aquarius
17th 1:43 pm Pisces
19th 3:58 pm Aries
21st 6:24 pm Taurus
23rd 9:46 pm Gemini
26th 2:31 am Cancer
28th 9:00 am Leo
30th 5:42 pm Virgo

August 1927
2nd 4:44 am Libra
4th 5:16 pm Scorpio
7th 5:14 am Sagittarius
9th 2:23 pm Capricorn
11th 7:46 pm Aquarius
13th 10:04 pm Pisces
15th 10:57 pm Aries
18th 12:12 am Taurus
20th 3:08 am Gemini
22nd 8:19 am Cancer
24th 3:39 pm Leo
27th 12:55 am Virgo
29th 12:02 pm Libra

September 1927
1st 12:36 am Scorpio
3rd 1:09 pm Sagittarius
5th 11:28 pm Capricorn
8th 5:50 am Aquarius
10th 8:16 am Pisces
12th 8:18 am Aries
14th 8:03 am Taurus
16th 9:29 am Gemini
18th 1:49 pm Cancer
20th 9:13 pm Leo
23rd 7:01 am Virgo
25th 6:30 pm Libra
28th 7:05 am Scorpio
30th 7:53 pm Sagittarius

October 1927
3rd 7:12 am Capricorn
5th 3:07 pm Aquarius
7th 6:50 pm Pisces
9th 7:15 pm Aries
11th 6:18 pm Taurus
13th 6:12 pm Gemini
15th 8:50 pm Cancer
18th 3:07 am Leo
20th 12:43 pm Virgo
23rd 12:28 am Libra
25th 1:08 pm Scorpio
28th 1:48 am Sagittarius
30th 1:22 pm Capricorn

November 1927
1st 10:26 pm Aquarius
4th 3:56 am Pisces
6th 5:54 am Aries
8th 5:37 am Taurus
10th 5:04 am Gemini
12th 6:16 am Cancer
14th 10:48 am Leo
16th 7:13 pm Virgo
19th 6:40 am Libra
21st 7:26 pm Scorpio
24th 7:53 am Sagittarius
26th 7:00 pm Capricorn
29th 4:06 am Aquarius

December 1927
1st 10:37 am Pisces
3rd 2:20 pm Aries
5th 3:47 pm Taurus
7th 4:11 pm Gemini
9th 5:12 pm Cancer
11th 8:31 pm Leo
14th 3:25 am Virgo
16th 1:54 pm Libra
19th 2:31 am Scorpio
21st 2:59 pm Sagittarius
24th 1:38 am Capricorn
26th 9:54 am Aquarius
28th 4:00 pm Pisces
30th 8:19 pm Aries

January 1928
1st 11:15 pm Taurus
4th 1:20 am Gemini
6th 3:28 am Cancer
8th 6:52 am Leo
10th 12:53 pm Virgo
12th 10:18 pm Libra
15th 10:26 am Scorpio
17th 11:06 pm Sagittarius
20th 9:49 am Capricorn
22nd 5:27 pm Aquarius
24th 10:24 pm Pisces
27th 1:48 am Aries
29th 4:42 am Taurus
31st 7:47 am Gemini

February 1928
2nd 11:22 am Cancer
4th 3:53 pm Leo
6th 10:09 pm Virgo
9th 7:03 am Libra
11th 6:41 pm Scorpio
14th 7:31 am Sagittarius
16th 6:53 pm Capricorn
19th 2:47 am Aquarius
21st 7:06 am Pisces
23rd 9:10 am Aries
25th 10:42 am Taurus
27th 1:08 pm Gemini
29th 5:04 pm Cancer

March 1928
2nd 10:38 pm Leo
5th 5:51 am Virgo
7th 3:04 pm Libra
10th 2:31 am Scorpio
12th 3:24 pm Sagittarius
15th 3:33 am Capricorn
17th 12:31 pm Aquarius
19th 5:20 pm Pisces
21st 6:54 pm Aries
23rd 7:07 pm Taurus
25th 7:54 pm Gemini
27th 10:42 pm Cancer
30th 4:04 am Leo

April 1928
1st 11:53 am Virgo
3rd 9:47 pm Libra
6th 9:27 am Scorpio
8th 10:20 pm Sagittarius
11th 10:56 am Capricorn
13th 9:06 pm Aquarius
16th 3:19 am Pisces
18th 5:40 am Aries
20th 5:36 am Taurus
22nd 5:09 am Gemini
24th 6:14 am Cancer
26th 10:11 am Leo
28th 5:28 pm Virgo

May 1928
1st 3:36 am Libra
3rd 3:38 pm Scorpio
6th 4:32 am Sagittarius
8th 5:08 pm Capricorn
11th 3:57 am Aquarius
13th 11:35 am Pisces
15th 3:30 pm Aries
17th 4:26 pm Taurus
19th 3:57 pm Gemini
21st 3:58 pm Cancer
23rd 6:17 pm Leo
26th 12:07 am Virgo
28th 9:36 am Libra
30th 9:40 pm Scorpio

June 1928
2nd 10:38 am Sagittarius
4th 10:59 pm Capricorn
7th 9:41 am Aquarius
9th 5:54 pm Pisces
11th 11:13 pm Aries
14th 1:46 am Taurus
16th 2:24 am Gemini
18th 2:34 am Cancer
20th 4:02 am Leo
22nd 8:27 am Virgo
24th 4:42 pm Libra
27th 4:16 am Scorpio
29th 5:13 pm Sagittarius

July 1928
2nd 5:23 am Capricorn
4th 3:32 pm Aquarius
6th 11:23 pm Pisces
9th 5:04 am Aries
11th 8:49 am Taurus
13th 10:59 am Gemini
15th 12:20 pm Cancer
17th 2:06 pm Leo
19th 5:53 pm Virgo
22nd 1:02 am Libra
24th 11:47 am Scorpio
27th 12:34 am Sagittarius
29th 12:47 pm Capricorn
31st 10:33 pm Aquarius

August 1928
3rd 5:35 am Pisces
5th 10:33 am Aries
7th 2:19 pm Taurus
9th 5:22 pm Gemini
11th 8:03 pm Cancer
13th 10:57 pm Leo
16th 3:08 am Virgo
18th 9:53 am Libra
20th 7:57 pm Scorpio
23rd 8:28 am Sagittarius
25th 8:59 pm Capricorn
28th 6:57 am Aquarius
30th 1:31 pm Pisces

September 1928
1st 5:27 pm Aries
3rd 8:07 pm Taurus
5th 10:43 pm Gemini
8th 1:51 am Cancer
10th 5:50 am Leo
12th 11:01 am Virgo
14th 6:12 pm Libra
17th 4:04 am Scorpio
19th 4:23 pm Sagittarius
22nd 5:16 am Capricorn
24th 4:01 pm Aquarius
26th 11:01 pm Pisces
29th 2:31 am Aries

October 1928
1st 3:59 am Taurus
3rd 5:10 am Gemini
5th 7:21 am Cancer
7th 11:18 am Leo
9th 5:13 pm Virgo
12th 1:14 am Libra
14th 11:28 am Scorpio
16th 11:44 pm Sagittarius
19th 12:50 pm Capricorn
22nd 12:33 am Aquarius
24th 8:50 am Pisces
26th 1:05 pm Aries
28th 2:17 pm Taurus
30th 2:12 pm Gemini

November 1928
1st 2:41 pm Cancer
3rd 5:14 pm Leo
5th 10:41 pm Virgo
8th 7:05 am Libra
10th 5:53 pm Scorpio
13th 6:20 am Sagittarius
15th 7:25 pm Capricorn
18th 7:39 am Aquarius
20th 5:19 pm Pisces
22nd 11:14 pm Aries
25th 1:30 am Taurus
27th 1:23 am Gemini
29th 12:43 am Cancer

December 1928
1st 1:29 am Leo
3rd 5:16 am Virgo
5th 12:52 pm Libra
7th 11:46 pm Scorpio
10th 12:29 pm Sagittarius
13th 1:29 am Capricorn
15th 1:35 pm Aquarius
17th 11:49 pm Pisces
20th 7:15 am Aries
22nd 11:25 am Taurus
24th 12:41 pm Gemini
26th 12:18 pm Cancer
28th 12:07 pm Leo
30th 2:13 pm Virgo

January 1929
1st 8:08 pm Libra
4th 6:10 am Scorpio
6th 6:49 pm Sagittarius
9th 7:50 am Capricorn
11th 7:33 pm Aquarius
14th 5:21 am Pisces
16th 1:07 pm Aries
18th 6:37 pm Taurus
20th 9:44 pm Gemini
22nd 10:52 pm Cancer
24th 11:17 pm Leo
27th 12:47 am Virgo
29th 5:19 am Libra
31st 1:56 pm Scorpio

February 1929
3rd 1:59 am Sagittarius
5th 2:59 pm Capricorn
8th 2:34 am Aquarius
10th 11:43 am Pisces
12th 6:41 pm Aries
15th 12:02 am Taurus
17th 4:01 am Gemini
19th 6:45 am Cancer
21st 8:41 am Leo
23rd 10:59 am Virgo
25th 3:15 pm Libra
27th 10:54 pm Scorpio

March 1929
2nd 10:02 am Sagittarius
4th 10:55 pm Capricorn
7th 10:44 am Aquarius
9th 7:44 pm Pisces
12th 1:51 am Aries
14th 6:05 am Taurus
16th 9:23 am Gemini
18th 12:24 pm Cancer
20th 3:27 pm Leo
22nd 7:05 pm Virgo
25th 12:11 am Libra
27th 7:49 am Scorpio
29th 6:26 pm Sagittarius

April 1929
1st 7:02 am Capricorn
3rd 7:17 pm Aquarius
6th 4:52 am Pisces
8th 10:58 am Aries
10th 2:17 pm Taurus
12th 4:13 pm Gemini
14th 6:05 pm Cancer
16th 8:50 pm Leo
19th 1:05 am Virgo
21st 7:13 am Libra
23rd 3:34 pm Scorpio
26th 2:16 am Sagittarius
28th 2:43 pm Capricorn

May 1929
1st 3:18 am Aquarius
3rd 1:51 pm Pisces
5th 8:51 pm Aries
8th 12:18 am Taurus
10th 1:22 am Gemini
12th 1:44 am Cancer
14th 3:03 am Leo
16th 6:33 am Virgo
18th 12:52 pm Libra
20th 9:53 pm Scorpio
23rd 9:03 am Sagittarius
25th 9:34 pm Capricorn
28th 10:17 am Aquarius
30th 9:37 pm Pisces

June 1929
2nd 5:58 am Aries
4th 10:35 am Taurus
6th 11:58 am Gemini
8th 11:36 am Cancer
10th 11:26 am Leo
12th 1:20 pm Virgo
14th 6:38 pm Libra
17th 3:32 am Scorpio
19th 3:03 pm Sagittarius
22nd 3:45 am Capricorn
24th 4:24 pm Aquarius
27th 3:59 am Pisces
29th 1:21 pm Aries

July 1929
1st 7:31 pm Taurus
3rd 10:14 pm Gemini
5th 10:21 pm Cancer
7th 9:37 pm Leo
9th 10:10 pm Virgo
12th 1:54 am Libra
14th 9:44 am Scorpio
16th 8:59 pm Sagittarius
19th 9:47 am Capricorn
21st 10:20 pm Aquarius
24th 9:39 am Pisces
26th 7:13 pm Aries
29th 2:25 am Taurus
31st 6:43 am Gemini

August 1929
2nd 8:16 am Cancer
4th 8:12 am Leo
6th 8:23 am Virgo
8th 10:56 am Libra
10th 5:21 pm Scorpio
13th 3:44 am Sagittarius
15th 4:20 pm Capricorn
18th 4:50 am Aquarius
20th 3:46 pm Pisces
23rd 12:47 am Aries
25th 7:55 am Taurus
27th 1:03 pm Gemini
29th 4:04 pm Cancer
31st 5:27 pm Leo

September 1929
2nd 6:27 pm Virgo
4th 8:51 pm Libra
7th 2:20 am Scorpio
9th 11:38 am Sagittarius
11th 11:45 pm Capricorn
14th 12:16 pm Aquarius
16th 11:07 pm Pisces
19th 7:30 am Aries
21st 1:45 pm Taurus
23rd 6:25 pm Gemini
25th 9:52 pm Cancer
28th 12:28 am Leo
30th 2:52 am Virgo

October 1929
2nd 6:10 am Libra
4th 11:40 am Scorpio
6th 8:25 pm Sagittarius
9th 7:49 am Capricorn
11th 8:25 pm Aquarius
14th 7:40 am Pisces
16th 4:02 pm Aries
18th 9:29 pm Taurus
21st 12:54 am Gemini
23rd 3:24 am Cancer
25th 5:55 am Leo
27th 9:09 am Virgo
29th 1:39 pm Libra
31st 8:02 pm Scorpio

November 1929
3rd 4:47 am Sagittarius
5th 3:57 pm Capricorn
8th 4:33 am Aquarius
10th 4:30 pm Pisces
13th 1:43 am Aries
15th 7:19 am Taurus
17th 9:54 am Gemini
19th 10:54 am Cancer
21st 11:58 am Leo
23rd 2:32 pm Virgo
25th 7:23 pm Libra
28th 2:40 am Scorpio
30th 12:08 pm Sagittarius

December 1929
2nd 11:25 pm Capricorn
5th 11:57 am Aquarius
8th 12:27 am Pisces
10th 10:57 am Aries
12th 5:49 pm Taurus
14th 8:49 pm Gemini
16th 9:05 pm Cancer
18th 8:35 pm Leo
20th 9:22 pm Virgo
23rd 1:03 am Libra
25th 8:11 am Scorpio
27th 6:11 pm Sagittarius
30th 5:56 am Capricorn

January 1930
1st 6:29 am Aquarius
4th 7:04 am Pisces
6th 6:27 pm Aries
9th 2:59 am Taurus
11th 7:35 am Gemini
13th 8:35 am Cancer
15th 7:38 am Leo
17th 6:57 am Virgo
19th 8:44 am Libra
21st 2:24 pm Scorpio
23rd 11:56 pm Sagittarius
26th 11:53 am Capricorn
29th 12:35 am Aquarius
31st 12:59 pm Pisces

February 1930
3rd 12:23 am Aries
5th 9:48 am Taurus
7th 4:08 pm Gemini
9th 6:55 pm Cancer
11th 7:01 pm Leo
13th 6:15 pm Virgo
15th 6:51 pm Libra
17th 10:45 pm Scorpio
20th 6:48 am Sagittarius
22nd 6:12 pm Capricorn
25th 6:57 am Aquarius
27th 7:13 pm Pisces

March 1930
2nd 6:08 am Aries
4th 3:18 pm Taurus
6th 10:16 pm Gemini
9th 2:34 am Cancer
11th 4:26 am Leo
13th 4:54 am Virgo
15th 5:44 am Libra
17th 8:46 am Scorpio
19th 3:23 pm Sagittarius
22nd 1:40 am Capricorn
24th 2:04 pm Aquarius
27th 2:24 am Pisces
29th 12:59 pm Aries
31st 9:24 pm Taurus

April 1930
3rd 3:42 am Gemini
5th 8:11 am Cancer
7th 11:09 am Leo
9th 1:11 pm Virgo
11th 3:17 pm Libra
13th 6:45 pm Scorpio
16th 12:49 am Sagittarius
18th 10:07 am Capricorn
20th 9:58 pm Aquarius
23rd 10:23 am Pisces
25th 9:10 pm Aries
28th 5:08 am Taurus
30th 10:26 am Gemini

May 1930
2nd 1:54 pm Cancer
4th 4:32 pm Leo
6th 7:11 pm Virgo
8th 10:30 pm Libra
11th 3:06 am Scorpio
13th 9:39 am Sagittarius
15th 6:39 pm Capricorn
18th 6:03 am Aquarius
20th 6:33 pm Pisces
23rd 5:55 am Aries
25th 2:15 pm Taurus
27th 7:07 pm Gemini
29th 9:26 pm Cancer
31st 10:45 pm Leo

June 1930
3rd 12:37 am Virgo
5th 4:04 am Libra
7th 9:30 am Scorpio
9th 4:56 pm Sagittarius
12th 2:20 am Capricorn
14th 1:39 pm Aquarius
17th 2:12 am Pisces
19th 2:14 pm Aries
21st 11:35 pm Taurus
24th 5:00 am Gemini
26th 6:58 am Cancer
28th 7:07 am Leo
30th 7:29 am Virgo

July 1930
2nd 9:47 am Libra
4th 2:56 pm Scorpio
6th 10:49 pm Sagittarius
9th 8:49 am Capricorn
11th 8:23 pm Aquarius
14th 8:57 am Pisces
16th 9:26 pm Aries
19th 7:54 am Taurus
21st 2:39 pm Gemini
23rd 5:23 pm Cancer
25th 5:20 pm Leo
27th 4:35 pm Virgo
29th 5:18 pm Libra
31st 9:05 pm Scorpio

August 1930
3rd 4:24 am Sagittarius
5th 2:34 pm Capricorn
8th 2:26 am Aquarius
10th 3:02 pm Pisces
13th 3:32 am Aries
15th 2:37 pm Taurus
17th 10:46 pm Gemini
20th 3:02 am Cancer
22nd 3:58 am Leo
24th 3:14 am Virgo
26th 2:58 am Libra
28th 5:11 am Scorpio
30th 11:04 am Sagittarius

September 1930
1st 8:35 pm Capricorn
4th 8:27 am Aquarius
6th 9:06 pm Pisces
9th 9:21 am Aries
11th 8:18 pm Taurus
14th 5:01 am Gemini
16th 10:42 am Cancer
18th 1:19 pm Leo
20th 1:46 pm Virgo
22nd 1:44 pm Libra
24th 3:08 pm Scorpio
26th 7:34 pm Sagittarius
29th 3:48 am Capricorn

October 1930
1st 3:09 pm Aquarius
4th 3:48 am Pisces
6th 3:52 pm Aries
9th 2:14 am Taurus
11th 10:29 am Gemini
13th 4:29 pm Cancer
15th 8:19 pm Leo
17th 10:26 pm Virgo
19th 11:43 pm Libra
22nd 1:33 am Scorpio
24th 5:23 am Sagittarius
26th 12:26 pm Capricorn
28th 10:54 pm Aquarius
31st 11:22 am Pisces

November 1930
2nd 11:34 pm Aries
5th 9:37 am Taurus
7th 4:59 pm Gemini
9th 10:05 pm Cancer
12th 1:45 am Leo
14th 4:42 am Virgo
16th 7:27 am Libra
18th 10:36 am Scorpio
20th 3:01 pm Sagittarius
22nd 9:42 pm Capricorn
25th 7:22 am Aquarius
27th 7:32 pm Pisces
30th 8:06 am Aries

December 1930
2nd 6:32 pm Taurus
5th 1:32 am Gemini
7th 5:32 am Cancer
9th 7:53 am Leo
11th 10:04 am Virgo
13th 1:05 pm Libra
15th 5:19 pm Scorpio
17th 10:54 pm Sagittarius
20th 6:11 am Capricorn
22nd 3:43 pm Aquarius
25th 3:35 am Pisces
27th 4:29 pm Aries
30th 3:51 am Taurus

January 1931
1st 11:34 am Gemini
3rd 3:21 pm Cancer
5th 4:33 pm Leo
7th 5:07 pm Virgo
9th 6:49 pm Libra
11th 10:40 pm Scorpio
14th 4:50 am Sagittarius
16th 1:01 pm Capricorn
18th 11:04 pm Aquarius
21st 10:55 am Pisces
23rd 11:55 pm Aries
26th 12:09 pm Taurus
28th 9:18 pm Gemini
31st 2:09 am Cancer

February 1931
2nd 3:25 am Leo
4th 2:57 am Virgo
6th 2:55 am Libra
8th 5:04 am Scorpio
10th 10:21 am Sagittarius
12th 6:39 pm Capricorn
15th 5:14 am Aquarius
17th 5:23 pm Pisces
20th 6:20 am Aries
22nd 6:53 pm Taurus
25th 5:13 am Gemini
27th 11:47 am Cancer

March 1931
1st 2:26 pm Leo
3rd 2:22 pm Virgo
5th 1:33 pm Libra
7th 2:03 pm Scorpio
9th 5:30 pm Sagittarius
12th 12:39 am Capricorn
14th 11:03 am Aquarius
16th 11:26 pm Pisces
19th 12:24 pm Aries
22nd 12:44 am Taurus
24th 11:19 am Gemini
26th 7:04 pm Cancer
28th 11:29 pm Leo
31st 12:58 am Virgo

April 1931
2nd 12:49 am Libra
4th 12:50 am Scorpio
6th 2:52 am Sagittarius
8th 8:20 am Capricorn
10th 5:39 pm Aquarius
13th 5:48 am Pisces
15th 6:48 pm Aries
18th 6:50 am Taurus
20th 4:56 pm Gemini
23rd 12:42 am Cancer
25th 6:04 am Leo
27th 9:10 am Virgo
29th 10:36 am Libra

May 1931
1st 11:27 am Scorpio
3rd 1:14 pm Sagittarius
5th 5:35 pm Capricorn
8th 1:36 am Aquarius
10th 1:01 pm Pisces
13th 1:56 am Aries
15th 1:54 pm Taurus
17th 11:26 pm Gemini
20th 6:26 am Cancer
22nd 11:27 am Leo
24th 3:07 pm Virgo
26th 5:51 pm Libra
28th 8:08 pm Scorpio
30th 10:48 pm Sagittarius

June 1931
2nd 3:07 am Capricorn
4th 10:23 am Aquarius
6th 9:01 pm Pisces
9th 9:43 am Aries
11th 9:54 pm Taurus
14th 7:22 am Gemini
16th 1:38 pm Cancer
18th 5:37 pm Leo
20th 8:33 pm Virgo
22nd 11:23 pm Libra
25th 2:34 am Scorpio
27th 6:26 am Sagittarius
29th 11:35 am Capricorn

July 1931
1st 6:56 pm Aquarius
4th 5:09 am Pisces
6th 5:39 pm Aries
9th 6:13 am Taurus
11th 4:14 pm Gemini
13th 10:30 pm Cancer
16th 1:41 am Leo
18th 3:22 am Virgo
20th 5:06 am Libra
22nd 7:56 am Scorpio
24th 12:18 pm Sagittarius
26th 6:22 pm Capricorn
29th 2:24 am Aquarius
31st 12:45 pm Pisces

August 1931
3rd 1:10 am Aries
5th 2:04 pm Taurus
8th 1:01 am Gemini
10th 8:10 am Cancer
12th 11:31 am Leo
14th 12:26 pm Virgo
16th 12:46 pm Libra
18th 2:11 pm Scorpio
20th 5:47 pm Sagittarius
22nd 11:58 pm Capricorn
25th 8:38 am Aquarius
27th 7:27 pm Pisces
30th 7:56 am Aries

September 1931
1st 8:59 pm Taurus
4th 8:43 am Gemini
6th 5:14 pm Cancer
8th 9:47 pm Leo
10th 11:04 pm Virgo
12th 10:43 pm Libra
14th 10:40 pm Scorpio
17th 12:39 am Sagittarius
19th 5:47 am Capricorn
21st 2:17 pm Aquarius
24th 1:28 am Pisces
26th 2:09 pm Aries
29th 3:07 am Taurus

October 1931
1st 3:03 pm Gemini
4th 12:38 am Cancer
6th 6:49 am Leo
8th 9:35 am Virgo
10th 9:51 am Libra
12th 9:18 am Scorpio
14th 9:51 am Sagittarius
16th 1:18 pm Capricorn
18th 8:39 pm Aquarius
21st 7:32 am Pisces
23rd 8:21 pm Aries
26th 9:12 am Taurus
28th 8:47 pm Gemini
31st 6:26 am Cancer

November 1931
2nd 1:39 pm Leo
4th 6:08 pm Virgo
6th 8:03 pm Libra
8th 8:21 pm Scorpio
10th 8:39 pm Sagittarius
12th 10:52 pm Capricorn
15th 4:40 am Aquarius
17th 2:32 pm Pisces
20th 3:08 am Aries
22nd 3:59 pm Taurus
25th 3:12 am Gemini
27th 12:09 pm Cancer
29th 7:06 pm Leo

December 1931
2nd 12:16 am Virgo
4th 3:44 am Libra
6th 5:43 am Scorpio
8th 7:04 am Sagittarius
10th 9:18 am Capricorn
12th 2:10 pm Aquarius
14th 10:50 pm Pisces
17th 10:49 am Aries
19th 11:45 pm Taurus
22nd 10:59 am Gemini
24th 7:22 pm Cancer
27th 1:16 am Leo
29th 5:41 am Virgo
31st 9:17 am Libra

January 1932
2nd 12:24 pm Scorpio
4th 3:16 pm Sagittarius
6th 6:37 pm Capricorn
8th 11:44 pm Aquarius
11th 7:49 am Pisces
13th 7:07 pm Aries
16th 8:02 am Taurus
18th 7:47 pm Gemini
21st 4:22 am Cancer
23rd 9:40 am Leo
25th 12:47 pm Virgo
27th 3:08 pm Libra
29th 5:43 pm Scorpio
31st 9:07 pm Sagittarius

February 1932
3rd 1:39 am Capricorn
5th 7:48 am Aquarius
7th 4:15 pm Pisces
10th 3:17 am Aries
12th 4:04 pm Taurus
15th 4:27 am Gemini
17th 2:02 pm Cancer
19th 7:49 pm Leo
21st 10:25 pm Virgo
23rd 11:22 pm Libra
26th 12:20 am Scorpio
28th 2:39 am Sagittarius

March 1932
1st 7:06 am Capricorn
3rd 1:59 pm Aquarius
5th 11:15 pm Pisces
8th 10:35 am Aries
10th 11:19 pm Taurus
13th 12:02 pm Gemini
15th 10:46 pm Cancer
18th 5:56 am Leo
20th 9:19 am Virgo
22nd 9:57 am Libra
24th 9:36 am Scorpio
26th 10:07 am Sagittarius
28th 1:08 pm Capricorn
30th 7:30 pm Aquarius

April 1932
2nd 5:04 am Pisces
4th 4:53 pm Aries
7th 5:43 am Taurus
9th 6:27 pm Gemini
12th 5:47 am Cancer
14th 2:21 pm Leo
16th 7:21 pm Virgo
18th 9:00 pm Libra
20th 8:34 pm Scorpio
22nd 7:58 pm Sagittarius
24th 9:15 pm Capricorn
27th 2:04 am Aquarius
29th 10:55 am Pisces

May 1932
1st 10:46 pm Aries
4th 11:45 am Taurus
7th 12:20 am Gemini
9th 11:34 am Cancer
11th 8:46 pm Leo
14th 3:13 am Virgo
16th 6:32 am Libra
18th 7:15 am Scorpio
20th 6:48 am Sagittarius
22nd 7:13 am Capricorn
24th 10:31 am Aquarius
26th 5:57 pm Pisces
29th 5:08 am Aries
31st 6:04 pm Taurus

June 1932
3rd 6:32 am Gemini
5th 5:21 pm Cancer
8th 2:14 am Leo
10th 9:06 am Virgo
12th 1:41 pm Libra
14th 4:00 pm Scorpio
16th 4:46 pm Sagittarius
18th 5:32 pm Capricorn
20th 8:12 pm Aquarius
23rd 2:25 am Pisces
25th 12:33 pm Aries
28th 1:08 am Taurus
30th 1:35 pm Gemini

July 1932
3rd 12:07 am Cancer
5th 8:18 am Leo
7th 2:33 pm Virgo
9th 7:12 pm Libra
11th 10:27 pm Scorpio
14th 12:38 am Sagittarius
16th 2:36 am Capricorn
18th 5:45 am Aquarius
20th 11:34 am Pisces
22nd 8:52 pm Aries
25th 8:54 am Taurus
27th 9:26 pm Gemini
30th 8:07 am Cancer

August 1932
1st 3:57 pm Leo
3rd 9:15 pm Virgo
6th 12:56 am Libra
8th 3:49 am Scorpio
10th 6:32 am Sagittarius
12th 9:38 am Capricorn
14th 1:54 pm Aquarius
16th 8:13 pm Pisces
19th 5:18 am Aries
21st 4:55 pm Taurus
24th 5:33 am Gemini
26th 4:50 pm Cancer
29th 1:03 am Leo
31st 5:58 am Virgo

September 1932
2nd 8:32 am Libra
4th 10:06 am Scorpio
6th 11:59 am Sagittarius
8th 3:11 pm Capricorn
10th 8:16 pm Aquarius
13th 3:31 am Pisces
15th 1:01 pm Aries
18th 12:34 am Taurus
20th 1:13 pm Gemini
23rd 1:13 am Cancer
25th 10:31 am Leo
27th 4:07 pm Virgo
29th 6:22 pm Libra

October 1932
1st 6:44 pm Scorpio
3rd 7:03 pm Sagittarius
5th 9:00 pm Capricorn
8th 1:44 am Aquarius
10th 9:26 am Pisces
12th 7:35 pm Aries
15th 7:24 am Taurus
17th 8:02 pm Gemini
20th 8:26 am Cancer
22nd 6:57 pm Leo
25th 2:03 am Virgo
27th 5:16 am Libra
29th 5:31 am Scorpio
31st 4:40 am Sagittarius

November 1932
2nd 4:55 am Capricorn
4th 8:05 am Aquarius
6th 3:06 pm Pisces
9th 1:24 am Aries
11th 1:33 pm Taurus
14th 2:13 am Gemini
16th 2:32 pm Cancer
19th 1:35 am Leo
21st 10:08 am Virgo
23rd 3:08 pm Libra
25th 4:39 pm Scorpio
27th 3:59 pm Sagittarius
29th 3:17 pm Capricorn

December 1932
1st 4:46 pm Aquarius
3rd 10:08 pm Pisces
6th 7:34 am Aries
8th 7:41 pm Taurus
11th 8:26 am Gemini
13th 8:28 pm Cancer
16th 7:12 am Leo
18th 4:08 pm Virgo
20th 10:32 pm Libra
23rd 1:53 am Scorpio
25th 2:42 am Sagittarius
27th 2:31 am Capricorn
29th 3:23 am Aquarius
31st 7:16 am Pisces

January 1933
2nd 3:13 pm Aries
5th 2:36 am Taurus
7th 3:19 pm Gemini
10th 3:16 am Cancer
12th 1:26 pm Leo
14th 9:42 pm Virgo
17th 4:03 am Libra
19th 8:25 am Scorpio
21st 10:55 am Sagittarius
23rd 12:18 pm Capricorn
25th 1:57 pm Aquarius
27th 5:31 pm Pisces
30th 12:21 am Aries

February 1933
1st 10:40 am Taurus
3rd 11:05 pm Gemini
6th 11:13 am Cancer
8th 9:16 pm Leo
11th 4:43 am Virgo
13th 9:59 am Libra
15th 1:46 pm Scorpio
17th 4:43 pm Sagittarius
19th 7:23 pm Capricorn
21st 10:29 pm Aquarius
24th 2:56 am Pisces
26th 9:42 am Aries
28th 7:20 pm Taurus

March 1933
3rd 7:17 am Gemini
5th 7:43 pm Cancer
8th 6:18 am Leo
10th 1:42 pm Virgo
12th 6:03 pm Libra
14th 8:28 pm Scorpio
16th 10:18 pm Sagittarius
19th 12:47 am Capricorn
21st 4:39 am Aquarius
23rd 10:16 am Pisces
25th 5:49 pm Aries
28th 3:32 am Taurus
30th 3:13 pm Gemini

April 1933
2nd 3:50 am Cancer
4th 3:16 pm Leo
6th 11:33 pm Virgo
9th 4:01 am Libra
11th 5:32 am Scorpio
13th 5:52 am Sagittarius
15th 6:54 am Capricorn
17th 10:02 am Aquarius
19th 3:34 pm Pisces
22nd 12:14 am Aries
24th 10:31 am Taurus
26th 10:18 pm Gemini
29th 10:58 am Cancer

May 1933
1st 11:06 pm Leo
4th 8:40 am Virgo
6th 2:17 pm Libra
8th 4:07 pm Scorpio
10th 3:44 pm Sagittarius
12th 3:16 pm Capricorn
14th 4:46 pm Aquarius
16th 9:33 pm Pisces
19th 5:45 am Aries
21st 4:26 pm Taurus
24th 4:31 am Gemini
26th 5:12 pm Cancer
29th 5:33 am Leo
31st 4:05 pm Virgo

June 1933
2nd 11:15 pm Libra
5th 2:25 am Scorpio
7th 2:32 am Sagittarius
9th 1:33 am Capricorn
11th 1:41 am Aquarius
13th 4:49 am Pisces
15th 11:50 am Aries
17th 10:12 pm Taurus
20th 10:25 am Gemini
22nd 11:06 pm Cancer
25th 11:17 am Leo
27th 10:01 pm Virgo
30th 6:11 am Libra

July 1933
2nd 10:57 am Scorpio
4th 12:32 pm Sagittarius
6th 12:16 pm Capricorn
8th 12:06 pm Aquarius
10th 2:02 pm Pisces
12th 7:31 pm Aries
15th 4:48 am Taurus
17th 4:44 pm Gemini
20th 5:24 am Cancer
22nd 5:18 pm Leo
25th 3:35 am Virgo
27th 11:44 am Libra
29th 5:21 pm Scorpio
31st 8:27 pm Sagittarius

August 1933
2nd 9:41 pm Capricorn
4th 10:22 pm Aquarius
7th 12:10 am Pisces
9th 4:40 am Aries
11th 12:44 pm Taurus
13th 11:57 pm Gemini
16th 12:32 pm Cancer
19th 12:22 am Leo
21st 10:07 am Virgo
23rd 5:29 pm Libra
25th 10:45 pm Scorpio
28th 2:21 am Sagittarius
30th 4:52 am Capricorn

September 1933
1st 6:59 am Aquarius
3rd 9:44 am Pisces
5th 2:15 pm Aries
7th 9:35 pm Taurus
10th 8:00 am Gemini
12th 8:25 pm Cancer
15th 8:30 am Leo
17th 6:13 pm Virgo
20th 12:51 am Libra
22nd 5:00 am Scorpio
24th 7:49 am Sagittarius
26th 10:23 am Capricorn
28th 1:27 pm Aquarius
30th 5:27 pm Pisces

October 1933
2nd 10:51 pm Aries
5th 6:18 am Taurus
7th 4:18 pm Gemini
10th 4:29 am Cancer
12th 5:01 pm Leo
15th 3:24 am Virgo
17th 10:08 am Libra
19th 1:28 pm Scorpio
21st 2:55 pm Sagittarius
23rd 4:14 pm Capricorn
25th 6:48 pm Aquarius
27th 11:17 pm Pisces
30th 5:40 am Aries

November 1933
1st 1:53 pm Taurus
4th 12:02 am Gemini
6th 12:05 pm Cancer
9th 12:58 am Leo
11th 12:39 pm Virgo
13th 8:12 pm Libra
15th 11:52 pm Scorpio
18th 12:35 am Sagittarius
20th 12:24 am Capricorn
22nd 1:21 am Aquarius
24th 4:49 am Pisces
26th 11:12 am Aries
28th 8:03 pm Taurus

December 1933
1st 6:44 am Gemini
3rd 6:53 pm Cancer
6th 7:48 am Leo
8th 7:59 pm Virgo
11th 5:18 am Libra
13th 10:27 am Scorpio
15th 11:49 am Sagittarius
17th 11:09 am Capricorn
19th 10:38 am Aquarius
21st 12:15 pm Pisces
23rd 5:15 pm Aries
26th 1:42 am Taurus
28th 12:42 pm Gemini
31st 1:07 am Cancer

January 1934
2nd 1:56 pm Leo
5th 2:09 am Virgo
7th 12:20 pm Libra
9th 7:10 pm Scorpio
11th 10:18 pm Sagittarius
13th 10:37 pm Capricorn
15th 9:56 pm Aquarius
17th 10:17 pm Pisces
20th 1:28 am Aries
22nd 8:26 am Taurus
24th 6:54 pm Gemini
27th 7:24 am Cancer
29th 8:11 pm Leo

February 1934
1st 8:00 am Virgo
3rd 5:59 pm Libra
6th 1:31 am Scorpio
8th 6:14 am Sagittarius
10th 8:24 am Capricorn
12th 8:58 am Aquarius
14th 9:28 am Pisces
16th 11:39 am Aries
18th 5:03 pm Taurus
21st 2:16 am Gemini
23rd 2:22 pm Cancer
26th 3:13 am Leo
28th 2:46 pm Virgo

March 1934
3rd 12:02 am Libra
5th 6:59 am Scorpio
7th 11:58 am Sagittarius
9th 3:22 pm Capricorn
11th 5:36 pm Aquarius
13th 7:26 pm Pisces
15th 10:00 pm Aries
18th 2:46 am Taurus
20th 10:51 am Gemini
22nd 10:12 pm Cancer
25th 11:02 am Leo
27th 10:44 pm Virgo
30th 7:37 am Libra

April 1934
1st 1:36 pm Scorpio
3rd 5:37 pm Sagittarius
5th 8:45 pm Capricorn
7th 11:43 pm Aquarius
10th 2:52 am Pisces
12th 6:40 am Aries
14th 11:56 am Taurus
16th 7:41 pm Gemini
19th 6:26 am Cancer
21st 7:09 pm Leo
24th 7:19 am Virgo
26th 4:32 pm Libra
28th 10:07 pm Scorpio

May 1934
1st 1:02 am Sagittarius
3rd 2:54 am Capricorn
5th 5:06 am Aquarius
7th 8:26 am Pisces
9th 1:09 pm Aries
11th 7:24 pm Taurus
14th 3:38 am Gemini
16th 2:17 pm Cancer
19th 2:55 am Leo
21st 3:35 pm Virgo
24th 1:43 am Libra
26th 7:52 am Scorpio
28th 10:29 am Sagittarius
30th 11:13 am Capricorn

June 1934
1st 11:56 am Aquarius
3rd 2:06 pm Pisces
5th 6:31 pm Aries
8th 1:17 am Taurus
10th 10:13 am Gemini
12th 9:14 pm Cancer
15th 9:52 am Leo
17th 10:51 pm Virgo
20th 9:58 am Libra
22nd 5:24 pm Scorpio
24th 8:50 pm Sagittarius
26th 9:25 pm Capricorn
28th 9:03 pm Aquarius
30th 9:38 pm Pisces

July 1934
3rd 12:39 am Aries
5th 6:47 am Taurus
7th 3:55 pm Gemini
10th 3:20 am Cancer
12th 4:07 pm Leo
15th 5:07 am Virgo
17th 4:47 pm Libra
20th 1:31 am Scorpio
22nd 6:28 am Sagittarius
24th 8:04 am Capricorn
26th 7:44 am Aquarius
28th 7:21 am Pisces
30th 8:46 am Aries

August 1934
1st 1:25 pm Taurus
3rd 9:48 pm Gemini
6th 9:13 am Cancer
8th 10:08 pm Leo
11th 10:59 am Virgo
13th 10:33 pm Libra
16th 7:51 am Scorpio
18th 2:11 pm Sagittarius
20th 5:27 pm Capricorn
22nd 6:19 pm Aquarius
24th 6:09 pm Pisces
26th 6:44 pm Aries
28th 9:55 pm Taurus
31st 4:55 am Gemini

September 1934
2nd 3:40 pm Cancer
5th 4:32 am Leo
7th 5:16 pm Virgo
10th 4:23 am Libra
12th 1:19 pm Scorpio
14th 8:03 pm Sagittarius
17th 12:36 am Capricorn
19th 3:06 am Aquarius
21st 4:14 am Pisces
23rd 5:13 am Aries
25th 7:47 am Taurus
27th 1:33 pm Gemini
29th 11:14 pm Cancer

October 1934
2nd 11:44 am Leo
5th 12:31 am Virgo
7th 11:20 am Libra
9th 7:32 pm Scorpio
12th 1:32 am Sagittarius
14th 6:04 am Capricorn
16th 9:32 am Aquarius
18th 12:10 pm Pisces
20th 2:29 pm Aries
22nd 5:35 pm Taurus
24th 10:58 pm Gemini
27th 7:46 am Cancer
29th 7:42 pm Leo

November 1934
1st 8:36 am Virgo
3rd 7:41 pm Libra
6th 3:33 am Scorpio
8th 8:33 am Sagittarius
10th 11:57 am Capricorn
12th 2:52 pm Aquarius
14th 5:56 pm Pisces
16th 9:26 pm Aries
19th 1:46 am Taurus
21st 7:47 am Gemini
23rd 4:25 pm Cancer
26th 3:54 am Leo
28th 4:51 pm Virgo

December 1934
1st 4:39 am Libra
3rd 1:06 pm Scorpio
5th 5:53 pm Sagittarius
7th 8:09 pm Capricorn
9th 9:34 pm Aquarius
11th 11:31 pm Pisces
14th 2:51 am Aries
16th 7:56 am Taurus
18th 2:58 pm Gemini
21st 12:11 am Cancer
23rd 11:37 am Leo
26th 12:32 am Virgo
28th 12:59 pm Libra
30th 10:41 pm Scorpio

January 1935
2nd 4:27 am Sagittarius
4th 6:44 am Capricorn
6th 7:04 am Aquarius
8th 7:18 am Pisces
10th 9:03 am Aries
12th 1:24 pm Taurus
14th 8:43 pm Gemini
17th 6:37 am Cancer
19th 6:27 pm Leo
22nd 7:19 am Virgo
24th 7:59 pm Libra
27th 6:46 am Scorpio
29th 2:10 pm Sagittarius
31st 5:47 pm Capricorn

May 1935
2nd 2:09 am Taurus
4th 5:26 am Gemini
6th 11:50 am Cancer
8th 9:55 pm Leo
11th 10:25 am Virgo
13th 10:48 pm Libra
16th 8:54 am Scorpio
18th 4:13 pm Sagittarius
20th 9:20 pm Capricorn
23rd 1:08 am Aquarius
25th 4:13 am Pisces
27th 6:59 am Aries
29th 9:59 am Taurus
31st 2:11 pm Gemini

September 1935
2nd 4:22 pm Scorpio
5th 2:48 am Sagittarius
7th 10:07 am Capricorn
9th 1:44 pm Aquarius
11th 2:16 pm Pisces
13th 1:22 pm Aries
15th 1:11 pm Taurus
17th 3:48 pm Gemini
19th 10:27 pm Cancer
22nd 8:49 am Leo
24th 9:18 pm Virgo
27th 10:05 am Libra
29th 10:06 pm Scorpio

January 1936
3rd 1:11 am Taurus
5th 5:04 am Gemini
7th 10:29 am Cancer
9th 6:02 pm Leo
12th 4:05 am Virgo
14th 4:10 pm Libra
17th 4:38 am Scorpio
19th 3:11 pm Sagittarius
21st 10:18 pm Capricorn
24th 2:02 am Aquarius
26th 3:35 am Pisces
28th 4:36 am Aries
30th 6:37 am Taurus

May 1936
2nd 6:42 am Libra
5th 7:16 am Scorpio
7th 6:54 pm Sagittarius
10th 4:57 am Capricorn
12th 12:47 pm Aquarius
14th 5:52 pm Pisces
16th 8:14 pm Aries
18th 8:48 pm Taurus
20th 9:12 pm Gemini
22nd 11:19 pm Cancer
25th 4:41 am Leo
27th 1:47 pm Virgo
30th 1:38 am Libra

February 1935
2nd 6:26 am Aquarius
4th 5:48 pm Pisces
6th 5:49 pm Aries
8th 8:22 pm Taurus
11th 2:35 am Gemini
13th 12:24 pm Cancer
16th 12:35 am Leo
18th 1:33 pm Virgo
21st 2:02 am Libra
23rd 1:04 pm Scorpio
25th 9:40 pm Sagittarius
28th 3:05 am Capricorn

June 1935
2nd 8:44 am Cancer
5th 6:19 am Leo
7th 6:25 pm Virgo
10th 6:59 am Libra
12th 5:35 pm Scorpio
15th 12:57 am Sagittarius
17th 5:21 am Capricorn
19th 7:56 am Aquarius
21st 9:56 am Pisces
23rd 12:21 pm Aries
25th 3:54 pm Taurus
27th 9:06 pm Gemini
30th 4:26 am Cancer

October 1935
2nd 8:41 am Sagittarius
4th 5:02 pm Capricorn
6th 10:20 pm Aquarius
9th 12:27 am Pisces
11th 12:20 am Aries
12th 11:53 pm Taurus
15th 1:17 am Gemini
17th 6:21 am Cancer
19th 3:35 pm Leo
22nd 3:44 am Virgo
24th 4:31 pm Libra
27th 4:15 am Scorpio
29th 2:17 pm Sagittarius
31st 10:31 pm Capricorn

February 1936
1st 10:38 am Gemini
3rd 4:58 pm Cancer
6th 1:26 am Leo
8th 11:48 am Virgo
10th 11:45 pm Libra
13th 12:24 pm Scorpio
15th 11:56 pm Sagittarius
18th 8:21 am Capricorn
20th 12:47 pm Aquarius
22nd 1:56 pm Pisces
24th 1:36 pm Aries
26th 1:51 pm Taurus
28th 4:30 pm Gemini

June 1936
1st 2:11 pm Scorpio
4th 1:37 am Sagittarius
6th 11:03 am Capricorn
8th 6:17 pm Aquarius
10th 11:27 pm Pisces
13th 2:47 am Aries
15th 4:48 am Taurus
17th 6:30 am Gemini
19th 9:09 am Cancer
21st 2:06 pm Leo
23rd 10:15 pm Virgo
26th 9:23 am Libra
28th 9:52 pm Scorpio

March 1935
2nd 5:16 am Aquarius
4th 5:14 am Pisces
6th 4:41 am Aries
8th 5:43 am Taurus
10th 10:11 am Gemini
12th 6:51 pm Cancer
15th 6:48 am Leo
17th 7:51 pm Virgo
20th 8:08 am Libra
22nd 6:44 pm Scorpio
25th 3:24 am Sagittarius
27th 9:48 am Capricorn
29th 1:41 pm Aquarius
31st 3:15 pm Pisces

July 1935
2nd 2:13 pm Leo
5th 2:08 am Virgo
7th 2:52 pm Libra
10th 2:15 am Scorpio
12th 10:27 am Sagittarius
14th 3:03 pm Capricorn
16th 4:54 pm Aquarius
18th 5:31 pm Pisces
20th 6:33 pm Aries
22nd 9:21 pm Taurus
25th 2:42 am Gemini
27th 10:43 am Cancer
29th 9:04 pm Leo

November 1935
3rd 4:38 am Aquarius
5th 8:20 am Pisces
7th 9:54 am Aries
9th 10:29 am Taurus
11th 11:53 am Gemini
13th 3:56 pm Cancer
15th 11:51 pm Leo
18th 11:09 am Virgo
20th 11:52 pm Libra
23rd 11:36 am Scorpio
25th 9:08 pm Sagittarius
28th 4:28 am Capricorn
30th 9:59 am Aquarius

March 1936
1st 10:25 pm Cancer
4th 7:20 am Leo
6th 6:18 pm Virgo
9th 6:26 am Libra
11th 7:03 pm Scorpio
14th 7:05 am Sagittarius
16th 4:51 pm Capricorn
18th 10:52 pm Aquarius
21st 12:59 am Pisces
23rd 12:31 am Aries
24th 11:37 pm Taurus
27th 12:31 am Gemini
29th 4:52 am Cancer
31st 1:03 pm Leo

July 1936
1st 9:27 am Sagittarius
3rd 6:34 pm Capricorn
6th 12:56 am Aquarius
8th 5:10 am Pisces
10th 8:10 am Aries
12th 10:46 am Taurus
14th 1:39 pm Gemini
16th 5:28 pm Cancer
18th 10:58 pm Leo
21st 6:53 am Virgo
23rd 5:30 pm Libra
26th 5:54 am Scorpio
28th 5:55 pm Sagittarius
31st 3:24 am Capricorn

April 1935
2nd 3:32 pm Aries
4th 4:19 pm Taurus
6th 7:35 pm Gemini
9th 2:49 am Cancer
11th 1:51 pm Leo
14th 2:46 am Virgo
16th 3:01 pm Libra
19th 1:09 am Scorpio
21st 9:06 am Sagittarius
23rd 3:13 pm Capricorn
25th 7:43 pm Aquarius
27th 10:40 pm Pisces
30th 12:26 am Aries

August 1935
1st 9:06 am Virgo
3rd 9:55 pm Libra
6th 9:56 am Scorpio
8th 7:24 pm Sagittarius
11th 1:10 am Capricorn
13th 3:22 am Aquarius
15th 3:19 am Pisces
17th 2:55 am Aries
19th 4:07 am Taurus
21st 8:25 am Gemini
23rd 4:16 pm Cancer
26th 3:00 am Leo
28th 3:20 pm Virgo
31st 4:08 am Libra

December 1935
2nd 2:03 pm Pisces
4th 4:53 pm Aries
6th 7:04 pm Taurus
8th 9:37 pm Gemini
11th 1:54 am Cancer
13th 9:06 am Leo
15th 7:32 pm Virgo
18th 7:58 am Libra
20th 8:02 pm Scorpio
23rd 5:45 am Sagittarius
25th 12:28 pm Capricorn
27th 4:46 pm Aquarius
29th 7:42 pm Pisces
31st 10:15 pm Aries

April 1936
3rd 12:07 am Virgo
5th 12:31 pm Libra
8th 1:05 am Scorpio
10th 1:02 pm Sagittarius
12th 11:23 pm Capricorn
15th 6:49 am Aquarius
17th 10:38 am Pisces
19th 11:21 am Aries
21st 10:38 am Taurus
23rd 10:38 am Gemini
25th 1:22 pm Cancer
27th 8:03 pm Leo
30th 6:22 am Virgo

August 1936
2nd 9:25 am Aquarius
4th 12:36 pm Pisces
6th 2:22 pm Aries
8th 4:12 pm Taurus
10th 7:12 pm Gemini
12th 11:52 pm Cancer
15th 6:20 am Leo
17th 2:44 pm Virgo
20th 1:17 am Libra
22nd 1:35 pm Scorpio
25th 2:09 am Sagittarius
27th 12:34 pm Capricorn
29th 7:12 pm Aquarius
31st 10:06 pm Pisces

September 1936
2nd 10:43 pm Aries
4th 11:04 pm Taurus
7th 12:54 am Gemini
9th 5:16 am Cancer
11th 12:13 pm Leo
13th 9:20 pm Virgo
16th 8:12 am Libra
18th 8:32 pm Scorpio
21st 9:24 am Sagittarius
23rd 8:53 pm Capricorn
26th 4:53 am Aquarius
28th 8:39 am Pisces
30th 9:11 am Aries

October 1936
2nd 8:26 am Taurus
4th 8:37 am Gemini
6th 11:28 am Cancer
8th 5:44 pm Leo
11th 3:01 am Virgo
13th 2:19 pm Libra
16th 2:47 am Scorpio
18th 3:37 pm Sagittarius
21st 3:37 am Capricorn
23rd 12:59 pm Aquarius
25th 6:28 pm Pisces
27th 8:10 pm Aries
29th 7:35 pm Taurus
31st 6:50 pm Gemini

November 1936
2nd 8:00 pm Cancer
5th 12:37 am Leo
7th 8:59 am Virgo
9th 8:14 pm Libra
12th 8:52 am Scorpio
14th 9:33 pm Sagittarius
17th 9:20 am Capricorn
19th 7:10 pm Aquarius
22nd 2:04 am Pisces
24th 5:37 am Aries
26th 6:29 am Taurus
28th 6:12 am Gemini
30th 6:40 am Cancer

December 1936
2nd 9:43 am Leo
4th 4:30 pm Virgo
7th 2:55 am Libra
9th 3:27 pm Scorpio
12th 4:07 am Sagittarius
14th 3:25 pm Capricorn
17th 12:42 am Aquarius
19th 7:43 am Pisces
21st 12:26 pm Aries
23rd 3:06 pm Taurus
25th 4:25 pm Gemini
27th 5:37 pm Cancer
29th 8:14 pm Leo

January 1937
1st 1:45 am Virgo
3rd 10:55 am Libra
5th 10:58 pm Scorpio
8th 11:42 am Sagittarius
10th 10:53 pm Capricorn
13th 7:25 am Aquarius
15th 1:28 pm Pisces
17th 5:48 pm Aries
19th 9:07 pm Taurus
21st 11:54 pm Gemini
24th 2:38 am Cancer
26th 6:08 am Leo
28th 11:30 am Virgo
30th 7:49 pm Libra

February 1937
2nd 7:10 am Scorpio
4th 7:58 pm Sagittarius
7th 7:34 am Capricorn
9th 4:00 pm Aquarius
11th 9:10 pm Pisces
14th 12:12 am Aries
16th 2:35 am Taurus
18th 5:22 am Gemini
20th 9:04 am Cancer
22nd 1:51 pm Leo
24th 8:04 pm Virgo
27th 4:26 am Libra

March 1937
1st 3:22 pm Scorpio
4th 4:08 am Sagittarius
6th 4:22 pm Capricorn
9th 1:35 am Aquarius
11th 6:50 am Pisces
13th 9:00 am Aries
15th 9:54 am Taurus
17th 11:19 am Gemini
19th 2:25 pm Cancer
21st 7:35 pm Leo
24th 2:44 am Virgo
26th 11:47 am Libra
28th 10:51 pm Scorpio
31st 11:32 am Sagittarius

April 1937
3rd 12:16 am Capricorn
5th 10:38 am Aquarius
7th 4:59 pm Pisces
9th 7:29 pm Aries
11th 7:40 pm Taurus
13th 7:35 pm Gemini
15th 9:03 pm Cancer
18th 1:11 am Leo
20th 8:16 am Virgo
22nd 5:51 pm Libra
25th 5:20 am Scorpio
27th 6:05 pm Sagittarius
30th 6:56 am Capricorn

May 1937
2nd 6:08 pm Aquarius
5th 1:57 am Pisces
7th 5:48 am Aries
9th 6:32 am Taurus
11th 5:57 am Gemini
13th 6:00 am Cancer
15th 8:27 am Leo
17th 2:18 pm Virgo
19th 11:34 pm Libra
22nd 11:18 am Scorpio
25th 12:10 am Sagittarius
27th 12:53 pm Capricorn
30th 12:13 am Aquarius

June 1937
1st 8:57 am Pisces
3rd 2:22 pm Aries
5th 4:36 pm Taurus
7th 4:46 pm Gemini
9th 4:32 pm Cancer
11th 5:45 pm Leo
13th 10:01 pm Virgo
16th 6:08 am Libra
18th 5:30 pm Scorpio
21st 6:25 am Sagittarius
23rd 6:58 pm Capricorn
26th 5:54 am Aquarius
28th 2:36 pm Pisces
30th 8:50 pm Aries

July 1937
3rd 12:34 am Taurus
5th 2:15 am Gemini
7th 2:53 am Cancer
9th 3:59 am Leo
11th 7:15 am Virgo
13th 2:04 pm Libra
16th 12:36 am Scorpio
18th 1:20 pm Sagittarius
21st 1:50 am Capricorn
23rd 12:20 pm Aquarius
25th 8:21 pm Pisces
28th 2:15 am Aries
30th 6:31 am Taurus

August 1937
1st 9:29 am Gemini
3rd 11:34 am Cancer
5th 1:36 pm Leo
7th 4:54 pm Virgo
9th 10:58 pm Libra
12th 8:36 am Scorpio
14th 8:59 pm Sagittarius
17th 9:37 am Capricorn
19th 8:05 pm Aquarius
22nd 3:28 am Pisces
24th 8:23 am Aries
26th 11:57 am Taurus
28th 3:01 pm Gemini
30th 6:03 pm Cancer

September 1937
1st 9:21 pm Leo
4th 1:34 am Virgo
6th 7:48 am Libra
8th 4:59 pm Scorpio
11th 4:59 am Sagittarius
13th 5:51 pm Capricorn
16th 4:51 am Aquarius
18th 12:19 pm Pisces
20th 4:31 pm Aries
22nd 6:50 pm Taurus
24th 8:46 pm Gemini
26th 11:24 pm Cancer
29th 3:14 am Leo

October 1937
1st 8:29 am Virgo
3rd 3:32 pm Libra
6th 12:55 am Scorpio
8th 12:43 pm Sagittarius
11th 1:46 am Capricorn
13th 1:37 pm Aquarius
15th 10:03 pm Pisces
18th 2:33 am Aries
20th 4:10 am Taurus
22nd 4:40 am Gemini
24th 5:47 am Cancer
26th 8:42 am Leo
28th 2:01 pm Virgo
30th 9:47 pm Libra

November 1937
2nd 7:48 am Scorpio
4th 7:46 pm Sagittarius
7th 8:50 am Capricorn
9th 9:19 pm Aquarius
12th 7:07 am Pisces
14th 12:59 pm Aries
16th 3:12 pm Taurus
18th 3:11 pm Gemini
20th 2:48 pm Cancer
22nd 3:55 pm Leo
24th 7:55 pm Virgo
27th 3:21 am Libra
29th 1:46 pm Scorpio

December 1937
2nd 2:05 am Sagittarius
4th 3:07 pm Capricorn
7th 3:40 am Aquarius
9th 2:21 pm Pisces
11th 9:55 pm Aries
14th 1:50 am Taurus
16th 2:42 am Gemini
18th 2:03 am Cancer
20th 1:48 am Leo
22nd 3:57 am Virgo
24th 9:53 am Libra
26th 7:44 pm Scorpio
29th 8:11 am Sagittarius
31st 9:17 pm Capricorn

January 1938
3rd 9:31 am Aquarius
5th 8:06 pm Pisces
8th 4:29 am Aries
10th 10:06 am Taurus
12th 12:50 pm Gemini
14th 1:22 pm Cancer
16th 1:10 pm Leo
18th 2:13 pm Virgo
20th 6:27 pm Libra
23rd 2:55 am Scorpio
25th 2:51 pm Sagittarius
28th 3:58 am Capricorn
30th 3:59 pm Aquarius

February 1938
2nd 1:58 am Pisces
4th 9:54 am Aries
6th 3:58 pm Taurus
8th 8:08 pm Gemini
10th 10:26 pm Cancer
12th 11:33 pm Leo
15th 12:57 am Virgo
17th 4:28 am Libra
19th 11:36 am Scorpio
21st 10:33 pm Sagittarius
24th 11:27 am Capricorn
26th 11:36 pm Aquarius

March 1938
1st 9:13 am Pisces
3rd 4:16 pm Aries
5th 9:29 pm Taurus
8th 1:33 am Gemini
10th 4:46 am Cancer
12th 7:23 am Leo
14th 10:06 am Virgo
16th 2:08 pm Libra
18th 8:53 pm Scorpio
21st 7:00 am Sagittarius
23rd 7:31 pm Capricorn
26th 7:56 am Aquarius
28th 5:52 pm Pisces
31st 12:33 am Aries

April 1938
2nd 4:43 am Taurus
4th 7:34 am Gemini
6th 10:08 am Cancer
8th 1:04 pm Leo
10th 4:51 pm Virgo
12th 10:02 pm Libra
15th 5:21 am Scorpio
17th 3:19 pm Sagittarius
20th 3:31 am Capricorn
22nd 4:10 pm Aquarius
25th 2:53 am Pisces
27th 10:08 am Aries
29th 2:02 pm Taurus

May 1938
1st 3:45 pm Gemini
3rd 4:51 pm Cancer
5th 6:42 pm Leo
7th 10:17 pm Virgo
10th 4:05 am Libra
12th 12:16 pm Scorpio
14th 10:40 pm Sagittarius
17th 10:51 am Capricorn
19th 11:37 pm Aquarius
22nd 11:08 am Pisces
24th 7:35 pm Aries
27th 12:17 am Taurus
29th 1:52 am Gemini
31st 1:53 am Cancer

September 1938
1st 12:28 am Sagittarius
3rd 12:29 pm Capricorn
6th 1:10 am Aquarius
8th 12:28 pm Pisces
10th 9:40 pm Aries
13th 4:54 am Taurus
15th 10:23 am Gemini
17th 2:09 pm Cancer
19th 4:26 pm Leo
21st 6:02 pm Virgo
23rd 8:19 pm Libra
26th 12:57 am Scorpio
28th 9:02 am Sagittarius
30th 8:20 pm Capricorn

January 1939
2nd 9:19 pm Gemini
4th 10:20 am Cancer
6th 9:33 pm Leo
8th 9:08 pm Virgo
10th 11:11 pm Libra
13th 4:54 am Scorpio
15th 2:09 pm Sagittarius
18th 1:43 am Capricorn
20th 2:15 pm Aquarius
23rd 2:51 am Pisces
25th 2:41 pm Aries
28th 12:29 am Taurus
30th 6:50 am Gemini

May 1939
2nd 5:36 pm Scorpio
4th 11:11 pm Sagittarius
7th 7:33 am Capricorn
9th 6:41 pm Aquarius
12th 7:09 am Pisces
14th 6:40 pm Aries
17th 3:28 am Taurus
19th 9:07 am Gemini
21st 12:23 pm Cancer
23rd 2:34 pm Leo
25th 4:51 pm Virgo
27th 8:06 pm Libra
30th 12:47 am Scorpio

September 1939
3rd 10:47 am Taurus
5th 8:02 pm Gemini
8th 1:52 am Cancer
10th 4:12 am Leo
12th 4:10 am Virgo
14th 3:39 am Libra
16th 4:43 am Scorpio
18th 9:01 am Sagittarius
20th 5:10 pm Capricorn
23rd 4:24 am Aquarius
25th 4:59 pm Pisces
28th 5:22 am Aries
30th 4:28 pm Taurus

June 1938
2nd 2:09 am Leo
4th 4:21 am Virgo
6th 9:35 am Libra
8th 6:01 pm Scorpio
11th 4:57 am Sagittarius
13th 5:21 pm Capricorn
16th 6:07 am Aquarius
18th 6:02 pm Pisces
21st 3:39 am Aries
23rd 9:49 am Taurus
25th 12:25 pm Gemini
27th 12:28 pm Cancer
29th 11:46 am Leo

October 1938
3rd 8:57 am Aquarius
5th 8:27 pm Pisces
8th 5:22 am Aries
10th 11:43 am Taurus
12th 4:10 pm Gemini
14th 7:31 pm Cancer
16th 10:20 pm Leo
19th 1:09 am Virgo
21st 4:43 am Libra
23rd 10:00 am Scorpio
25th 5:54 pm Sagittarius
28th 4:38 am Capricorn
30th 5:08 pm Aquarius

February 1939
1st 9:22 am Cancer
3rd 9:07 am Leo
5th 8:03 am Virgo
7th 8:30 am Libra
9th 12:21 pm Scorpio
11th 8:23 pm Sagittarius
14th 7:41 am Capricorn
16th 8:22 pm Aquarius
19th 8:52 am Pisces
21st 8:23 pm Aries
24th 6:19 am Taurus
26th 1:47 pm Gemini
28th 6:06 pm Cancer

June 1939
1st 7:15 am Sagittarius
3rd 3:50 pm Capricorn
6th 2:40 am Aquarius
8th 3:04 pm Pisces
11th 3:10 am Aries
13th 12:42 pm Taurus
15th 6:32 pm Gemini
17th 9:07 pm Cancer
19th 9:58 pm Leo
21st 10:56 pm Virgo
24th 1:30 am Libra
26th 6:25 am Scorpio
28th 1:39 pm Sagittarius
30th 10:53 pm Capricorn

October 1939
3rd 1:38 am Gemini
5th 8:16 am Cancer
7th 12:10 pm Leo
9th 1:46 pm Virgo
11th 2:16 pm Libra
13th 3:19 pm Scorpio
15th 6:36 pm Sagittarius
18th 1:22 am Capricorn
20th 11:39 am Aquarius
23rd 12:05 am Pisces
25th 12:28 pm Aries
27th 11:09 pm Taurus
30th 7:31 am Gemini

July 1938
1st 12:24 pm Virgo
3rd 4:09 pm Libra
5th 11:49 pm Scorpio
8th 10:45 am Sagittarius
10th 11:22 pm Capricorn
13th 12:05 pm Aquarius
15th 11:55 pm Pisces
18th 10:02 am Aries
20th 5:31 pm Taurus
22nd 9:43 pm Gemini
24th 10:55 pm Cancer
26th 10:26 pm Leo
28th 10:17 pm Virgo
31st 12:35 am Libra

November 1938
2nd 5:09 am Pisces
4th 2:35 pm Aries
6th 8:41 pm Taurus
9th 12:03 am Gemini
11th 1:59 am Cancer
13th 3:50 am Leo
15th 6:38 am Virgo
17th 11:03 am Libra
19th 5:26 pm Scorpio
22nd 1:56 am Sagittarius
24th 12:37 pm Capricorn
27th 12:58 am Aquarius
29th 1:29 pm Pisces

March 1939
2nd 7:30 am Leo
4th 7:17 am Virgo
6th 7:26 pm Libra
8th 9:59 pm Scorpio
11th 4:23 am Sagittarius
13th 2:35 pm Capricorn
16th 3:01 am Aquarius
18th 3:31 pm Pisces
21st 2:41 am Aries
23rd 11:58 am Taurus
25th 7:14 pm Gemini
28th 12:19 am Cancer
30th 3:15 am Leo

July 1939
3rd 9:54 am Aquarius
5th 10:17 pm Pisces
8th 10:49 am Aries
10th 9:26 pm Taurus
13th 4:20 am Gemini
15th 7:16 am Cancer
17th 7:31 am Leo
19th 7:08 am Virgo
21st 8:10 am Libra
23rd 12:04 pm Scorpio
25th 7:09 pm Sagittarius
28th 4:50 am Capricorn
30th 4:14 pm Aquarius

November 1939
1st 1:41 am Cancer
3rd 6:01 pm Leo
5th 8:57 pm Virgo
7th 11:03 pm Libra
10th 1:14 am Scorpio
12th 4:41 am Sagittarius
14th 10:42 am Capricorn
16th 7:59 pm Aquarius
19th 7:59 am Pisces
21st 8:35 pm Aries
24th 7:22 am Taurus
26th 3:09 pm Gemini
28th 8:12 pm Cancer
30th 11:34 pm Leo

August 1938
2nd 6:49 am Scorpio
4th 5:01 pm Sagittarius
7th 5:33 am Capricorn
9th 6:15 pm Aquarius
12th 5:45 am Pisces
14th 3:34 pm Aries
16th 11:25 pm Taurus
19th 4:51 am Gemini
21st 7:40 am Cancer
23rd 8:27 am Leo
25th 8:43 am Virgo
27th 10:26 am Libra
29th 3:26 pm Scorpio

December 1938
2nd 12:02 am Aries
4th 7:01 am Taurus
6th 10:19 am Gemini
8th 11:08 am Cancer
10th 11:18 am Leo
12th 12:38 pm Virgo
14th 4:27 pm Libra
16th 11:13 pm Scorpio
19th 8:31 am Sagittarius
21st 7:39 pm Capricorn
24th 7:59 am Aquarius
26th 8:41 pm Pisces
29th 8:14 am Aries
31st 4:47 pm Taurus

April 1939
1st 4:39 am Virgo
3rd 5:49 am Libra
5th 8:22 am Scorpio
7th 1:47 pm Sagittarius
9th 10:47 pm Capricorn
12th 10:33 am Aquarius
14th 11:04 pm Pisces
17th 10:13 am Aries
19th 6:57 pm Taurus
22nd 1:16 am Gemini
24th 5:43 am Cancer
26th 8:55 am Leo
28th 11:27 am Virgo
30th 2:02 pm Libra

August 1939
2nd 4:41 am Pisces
4th 5:22 pm Aries
7th 4:47 am Taurus
9th 1:06 pm Gemini
11th 5:21 pm Cancer
13th 6:10 pm Leo
15th 5:20 pm Virgo
17th 5:04 pm Libra
19th 7:20 pm Scorpio
22nd 1:14 am Sagittarius
24th 10:33 am Capricorn
26th 10:09 pm Aquarius
29th 10:42 am Pisces
31st 11:15 pm Aries

December 1939
3rd 2:23 am Virgo
5th 5:22 am Libra
7th 8:57 am Scorpio
9th 1:32 pm Sagittarius
11th 7:51 pm Capricorn
14th 4:42 am Aquarius
16th 4:14 pm Pisces
19th 5:02 am Aries
21st 4:31 pm Taurus
24th 12:37 am Gemini
26th 5:03 am Cancer
28th 7:05 am Leo
30th 8:29 am Virgo

January 1940
1st 10:44 am Libra
3rd 2:36 pm Scorpio
5th 8:12 pm Sagittarius
8th 3:30 am Capricorn
10th 12:42 pm Aquarius
13th 12:03 am Pisces
15th 12:55 pm Aries
18th 1:15 am Taurus
20th 10:31 am Gemini
22nd 3:35 pm Cancer
24th 5:11 pm Leo
26th 5:13 pm Virgo
28th 5:43 pm Libra
30th 8:17 pm Scorpio

May 1940
1st 1:56 am Pisces
3rd 2:51 pm Aries
6th 3:12 am Taurus
8th 1:33 pm Gemini
10th 9:33 pm Cancer
13th 3:22 am Leo
15th 7:18 am Virgo
17th 9:41 am Libra
19th 11:12 am Scorpio
21st 1:01 pm Sagittarius
23rd 4:35 pm Capricorn
25th 11:19 pm Aquarius
28th 9:39 am Pisces
30th 10:18 pm Aries

September 1940
1st 12:57 pm Virgo
3rd 12:55 pm Libra
5th 1:17 pm Scorpio
7th 3:36 pm Sagittarius
9th 8:45 pm Capricorn
12th 4:51 am Aquarius
14th 3:25 pm Pisces
17th 3:43 am Aries
19th 4:45 pm Taurus
22nd 5:05 am Gemini
24th 2:57 pm Cancer
26th 9:09 pm Leo
28th 11:41 pm Virgo
30th 11:46 pm Libra

January 1941
1st 8:35 pm Pisces
4th 7:34 am Aries
6th 8:28 pm Taurus
9th 8:27 am Gemini
11th 5:33 pm Cancer
13th 11:39 pm Leo
16th 3:46 am Virgo
18th 6:59 am Libra
20th 10:04 am Scorpio
22nd 1:17 pm Sagittarius
24th 5:01 pm Capricorn
26th 10:06 pm Aquarius
29th 5:34 am Pisces
31st 4:02 pm Aries

May 1941
1st 1:56 am Cancer
3rd 11:33 am Leo
5th 6:05 pm Virgo
7th 9:11 pm Libra
9th 9:34 pm Scorpio
11th 8:50 pm Sagittarius
13th 9:04 pm Capricorn
16th 12:15 am Aquarius
18th 7:33 am Pisces
20th 6:34 pm Aries
23rd 7:26 am Taurus
25th 8:10 pm Gemini
28th 7:36 am Cancer
30th 5:15 pm Leo

February 1940
2nd 1:36 am Sagittarius
4th 9:27 am Capricorn
6th 7:21 pm Aquarius
9th 6:58 am Pisces
11th 7:49 pm Aries
14th 8:35 am Taurus
16th 7:09 pm Gemini
19th 1:46 am Cancer
21st 4:19 am Leo
23rd 4:12 am Virgo
25th 3:29 am Libra
27th 4:13 am Scorpio
29th 7:54 am Sagittarius

June 1940
2nd 10:43 am Taurus
4th 8:49 pm Gemini
7th 4:02 am Cancer
9th 9:01 am Leo
11th 12:41 pm Virgo
13th 3:44 pm Libra
15th 6:32 pm Scorpio
17th 9:34 pm Sagittarius
20th 1:44 am Capricorn
22nd 8:15 am Aquarius
24th 5:55 pm Pisces
27th 6:13 am Aries
29th 6:52 pm Taurus

October 1940
2nd 11:12 pm Scorpio
4th 11:54 pm Sagittarius
7th 3:28 am Capricorn
9th 10:43 am Aquarius
11th 9:17 pm Pisces
14th 9:50 am Aries
16th 10:49 pm Taurus
19th 10:59 am Gemini
21st 9:18 pm Cancer
24th 4:50 am Leo
26th 9:10 am Virgo
28th 10:37 am Libra
30th 10:25 am Scorpio

February 1941
3rd 4:41 am Taurus
5th 5:09 pm Gemini
8th 2:57 am Cancer
10th 9:07 am Leo
12th 12:22 pm Virgo
14th 2:08 pm Libra
16th 3:53 pm Scorpio
18th 6:37 pm Sagittarius
20th 10:54 pm Capricorn
23rd 5:02 am Aquarius
25th 1:18 pm Pisces
27th 11:54 pm Aries

June 1941
2nd 12:38 am Virgo
4th 5:17 am Libra
6th 7:14 am Scorpio
8th 7:24 am Sagittarius
10th 7:32 am Capricorn
12th 9:41 am Aquarius
14th 3:33 pm Pisces
17th 1:30 am Aries
19th 2:02 pm Taurus
22nd 2:44 am Gemini
24th 1:51 pm Cancer
26th 10:55 pm Leo
29th 6:03 am Virgo

March 1940
2nd 3:02 pm Capricorn
5th 1:07 am Aquarius
7th 1:07 pm Pisces
10th 2:01 am Aries
12th 2:44 pm Taurus
15th 1:53 am Gemini
17th 9:57 am Cancer
19th 2:15 pm Leo
21st 3:21 pm Virgo
23rd 2:48 pm Libra
25th 2:34 pm Scorpio
27th 4:31 pm Sagittarius
29th 9:59 pm Capricorn

July 1940
2nd 5:15 am Gemini
4th 12:11 pm Cancer
6th 4:13 pm Leo
8th 6:45 pm Virgo
10th 9:07 pm Libra
13th 12:07 am Scorpio
15th 4:05 am Sagittarius
17th 9:18 am Capricorn
19th 4:22 pm Aquarius
22nd 1:58 am Pisces
24th 2:01 pm Aries
27th 2:56 am Taurus
29th 2:03 pm Gemini
31st 9:32 pm Cancer

November 1940
1st 10:21 am Sagittarius
3rd 12:23 pm Capricorn
5th 6:03 pm Aquarius
8th 3:45 am Pisces
10th 4:12 pm Aries
13th 5:13 am Taurus
15th 5:00 pm Gemini
18th 2:52 am Cancer
20th 10:38 am Leo
22nd 4:10 pm Virgo
24th 7:25 pm Libra
26th 8:45 pm Scorpio
28th 9:19 pm Sagittarius
30th 10:50 pm Capricorn

March 1941
2nd 12:23 pm Taurus
5th 1:12 am Gemini
7th 12:03 pm Cancer
9th 7:19 pm Leo
11th 10:51 pm Virgo
13th 11:51 pm Libra
16th 12:03 am Scorpio
18th 1:08 am Sagittarius
20th 4:25 am Capricorn
22nd 10:34 am Aquarius
24th 7:30 pm Pisces
27th 6:39 am Aries
29th 7:13 pm Taurus

July 1941
1st 11:17 am Libra
3rd 2:34 pm Scorpio
5th 4:14 pm Sagittarius
7th 5:21 pm Capricorn
9th 7:36 pm Aquarius
12th 12:42 am Pisces
14th 9:34 am Aries
16th 9:29 pm Taurus
19th 10:09 am Gemini
21st 9:15 pm Cancer
24th 5:48 am Leo
26th 12:03 pm Virgo
28th 4:41 pm Libra
30th 8:09 pm Scorpio

April 1940
1st 7:13 am Aquarius
3rd 7:11 pm Pisces
6th 8:10 am Aries
8th 8:38 pm Taurus
11th 7:32 am Gemini
13th 4:04 pm Cancer
15th 9:44 pm Leo
18th 12:35 am Virgo
20th 1:23 am Libra
22nd 1:33 am Scorpio
24th 2:48 am Sagittarius
26th 6:49 am Capricorn
28th 2:38 pm Aquarius

August 1940
3rd 1:20 am Leo
5th 2:51 am Virgo
7th 3:50 am Libra
9th 5:46 am Scorpio
11th 9:29 am Sagittarius
13th 3:15 pm Capricorn
15th 11:07 pm Aquarius
18th 9:10 am Pisces
20th 9:14 pm Aries
23rd 10:16 am Taurus
25th 10:13 pm Gemini
28th 6:53 am Cancer
30th 11:31 am Leo

December 1940
3rd 3:12 am Aquarius
5th 11:35 am Pisces
7th 11:26 pm Aries
10th 12:27 pm Taurus
13th 12:08 am Gemini
15th 9:20 am Cancer
17th 4:16 pm Leo
19th 9:35 pm Virgo
22nd 1:37 am Libra
24th 4:30 am Scorpio
26th 8:37 am Sagittarius
28th 8:59 am Capricorn
30th 1:09 pm Aquarius

April 1941
1st 8:06 am Gemini
3rd 7:43 pm Cancer
6th 4:26 am Leo
8th 9:21 am Virgo
10th 10:55 am Libra
12th 10:32 am Scorpio
14th 10:08 am Sagittarius
16th 11:39 am Capricorn
18th 4:31 pm Aquarius
21st 1:07 am Pisces
23rd 12:34 pm Aries
26th 1:22 am Taurus
28th 2:11 pm Gemini

August 1941
1st 10:50 pm Sagittarius
4th 1:17 am Capricorn
6th 4:32 am Aquarius
8th 9:51 am Pisces
10th 6:12 pm Aries
13th 5:32 am Taurus
15th 6:09 pm Gemini
18th 5:37 am Cancer
20th 2:15 pm Leo
22nd 7:53 pm Virgo
24th 11:21 pm Libra
27th 1:49 am Scorpio
29th 4:13 am Sagittarius
31st 7:18 am Capricorn

September 1941
2nd 11:39 am Aquarius
4th 5:52 pm Pisces
7th 2:28 am Aries
9th 1:31 pm Taurus
12th 2:05 am Gemini
14th 2:08 pm Cancer
16th 11:36 pm Leo
19th 5:29 am Virgo
21st 8:18 am Libra
23rd 9:24 am Scorpio
25th 10:25 am Sagittarius
27th 12:44 pm Capricorn
29th 5:17 pm Aquarius

October 1941
2nd 12:18 am Pisces
4th 9:37 am Aries
6th 8:52 pm Taurus
9th 9:22 am Gemini
11th 9:52 pm Cancer
14th 8:29 am Leo
16th 3:36 pm Virgo
18th 6:54 pm Libra
20th 7:26 pm Scorpio
22nd 7:01 pm Sagittarius
24th 7:40 pm Capricorn
26th 11:02 pm Aquarius
29th 5:50 am Pisces
31st 3:38 pm Aries

November 1941
3rd 3:19 am Taurus
5th 3:52 pm Gemini
8th 4:25 am Cancer
10th 3:48 pm Leo
13th 12:29 am Virgo
15th 5:22 am Libra
17th 6:40 am Scorpio
19th 5:54 am Sagittarius
21st 5:12 am Capricorn
23rd 6:46 am Aquarius
25th 12:08 pm Pisces
27th 9:26 pm Aries
30th 9:18 am Taurus

December 1941
2nd 9:59 pm Gemini
5th 10:21 am Cancer
7th 9:43 pm Leo
10th 7:12 am Virgo
12th 1:45 pm Libra
14th 4:52 pm Scorpio
16th 5:11 pm Sagittarius
18th 4:27 pm Capricorn
20th 4:54 pm Aquarius
22nd 8:33 pm Pisces
25th 4:24 am Aries
27th 3:42 pm Taurus
30th 4:27 am Gemini

January 1942
1st 4:41 pm Cancer
4th 3:32 am Leo
6th 12:42 pm Virgo
8th 7:48 pm Libra
11th 12:24 am Scorpio
13th 2:32 am Sagittarius
15th 3:07 am Capricorn
17th 3:52 am Aquarius
19th 6:43 am Pisces
21st 1:08 pm Aries
23rd 11:18 pm Taurus
26th 11:43 am Gemini
29th 12:03 am Cancer
31st 10:37 am Leo

February 1942
2nd 6:57 pm Virgo
5th 1:18 am Libra
7th 5:56 am Scorpio
9th 9:07 am Sagittarius
11th 11:19 am Capricorn
13th 1:28 am Aquarius
15th 4:51 pm Pisces
17th 10:46 pm Aries
20th 7:57 am Taurus
22nd 7:47 pm Gemini
25th 8:15 am Cancer
27th 7:06 pm Leo

March 1942
2nd 3:06 am Virgo
4th 8:23 am Libra
6th 11:50 am Scorpio
8th 2:28 pm Sagittarius
10th 5:09 pm Capricorn
12th 8:30 pm Aquarius
15th 1:09 am Pisces
17th 7:41 am Aries
19th 4:38 pm Taurus
22nd 3:59 am Gemini
24th 4:32 pm Cancer
27th 4:04 am Leo
29th 12:36 pm Virgo
31st 5:37 pm Libra

April 1942
2nd 7:55 pm Scorpio
4th 9:05 pm Sagittarius
6th 10:42 pm Capricorn
9th 1:56 am Aquarius
11th 7:19 am Pisces
13th 2:49 pm Aries
16th 12:18 am Taurus
18th 11:36 am Gemini
21st 12:10 am Cancer
23rd 12:21 pm Leo
25th 10:02 pm Virgo
28th 3:50 am Libra
30th 5:59 am Scorpio

May 1942
2nd 6:04 am Sagittarius
4th 6:05 am Capricorn
6th 7:56 am Aquarius
8th 12:43 pm Pisces
10th 8:31 pm Aries
13th 6:37 am Taurus
15th 6:15 pm Gemini
18th 6:49 am Cancer
20th 7:21 pm Leo
23rd 6:07 am Virgo
25th 1:22 pm Libra
27th 4:32 pm Scorpio
29th 4:40 pm Sagittarius
31st 3:44 pm Capricorn

June 1942
2nd 3:59 pm Aquarius
4th 7:14 pm Pisces
7th 2:11 am Aries
9th 12:15 pm Taurus
12th 12:11 am Gemini
14th 12:50 pm Cancer
17th 1:19 am Leo
19th 12:33 pm Virgo
21st 9:04 pm Libra
24th 1:50 am Scorpio
26th 3:09 am Sagittarius
28th 2:30 am Capricorn
30th 2:01 am Aquarius

July 1942
2nd 3:46 am Pisces
4th 9:10 am Aries
6th 6:22 pm Taurus
9th 6:10 am Gemini
11th 6:51 pm Cancer
14th 7:08 am Leo
16th 6:08 pm Virgo
19th 3:02 am Libra
21st 9:02 am Scorpio
23rd 11:58 am Sagittarius
25th 12:39 pm Capricorn
27th 12:38 pm Aquarius
29th 1:49 pm Pisces
31st 5:55 pm Aries

August 1942
3rd 1:47 am Taurus
5th 12:54 pm Gemini
8th 1:30 am Cancer
10th 1:39 pm Leo
13th 12:09 am Virgo
15th 8:31 am Libra
17th 2:38 pm Scorpio
19th 6:35 pm Sagittarius
21st 8:47 pm Capricorn
23rd 10:07 pm Aquarius
25th 11:55 pm Pisces
28th 3:39 am Aries
30th 10:29 am Taurus

September 1942
1st 8:40 pm Gemini
4th 8:59 am Cancer
6th 9:15 pm Leo
9th 7:31 am Virgo
11th 3:05 pm Libra
13th 8:19 pm Scorpio
15th 11:58 pm Sagittarius
18th 2:48 am Capricorn
20th 5:27 am Aquarius
22nd 8:34 am Pisces
24th 12:57 pm Aries
26th 7:34 pm Taurus
29th 5:05 am Gemini

October 1942
1st 5:03 pm Cancer
4th 5:35 am Leo
6th 4:13 pm Virgo
8th 11:33 pm Libra
11th 3:46 am Scorpio
13th 6:11 am Sagittarius
15th 8:14 am Capricorn
17th 11:01 am Aquarius
19th 3:05 pm Pisces
21st 8:37 pm Aries
24th 3:52 am Taurus
26th 1:18 pm Gemini
29th 12:59 am Cancer
31st 1:47 pm Leo

November 1942
3rd 1:19 am Virgo
5th 9:21 am Libra
7th 1:27 pm Scorpio
9th 2:48 pm Sagittarius
11th 3:18 pm Capricorn
13th 4:49 pm Aquarius
15th 8:28 pm Pisces
18th 2:30 am Aries
20th 10:37 am Taurus
22nd 8:35 pm Gemini
25th 8:16 am Cancer
27th 9:09 pm Leo
30th 9:29 am Virgo

December 1942
2nd 6:55 pm Libra
5th 12:06 am Scorpio
7th 1:34 am Sagittarius
9th 1:07 am Capricorn
11th 12:57 am Aquarius
13th 2:56 am Pisces
15th 8:04 am Aries
17th 4:16 pm Taurus
20th 2:46 am Gemini
22nd 2:46 pm Cancer
25th 3:35 am Leo
27th 4:10 pm Virgo
30th 2:44 am Libra

January 1943
1st 9:39 am Scorpio
3rd 12:34 pm Sagittarius
5th 12:36 pm Capricorn
7th 11:43 am Aquarius
9th 12:03 pm Pisces
11th 3:20 pm Aries
13th 10:21 pm Taurus
16th 8:38 am Gemini
18th 8:53 pm Cancer
21st 9:43 am Leo
23rd 10:03 pm Virgo
26th 8:47 am Libra
28th 4:50 pm Scorpio
30th 9:34 pm Sagittarius

February 1943
1st 11:15 pm Capricorn
3rd 11:10 pm Aquarius
5th 11:08 pm Pisces
8th 1:00 am Aries
10th 6:17 am Taurus
12th 3:24 pm Gemini
15th 3:24 am Cancer
17th 4:18 pm Leo
20th 4:20 am Virgo
22nd 2:30 pm Libra
24th 10:25 pm Scorpio
27th 3:59 am Sagittarius

March 1943
1st 7:19 am Capricorn
3rd 8:57 am Aquarius
5th 9:55 am Pisces
7th 11:42 am Aries
9th 3:53 pm Taurus
11th 11:39 pm Gemini
14th 10:50 am Cancer
16th 11:41 pm Leo
19th 11:43 am Virgo
21st 9:21 pm Libra
24th 4:23 am Scorpio
26th 9:23 am Sagittarius
28th 1:05 pm Capricorn
30th 3:57 pm Aquarius

April 1943
1st 6:27 pm Pisces
3rd 9:18 pm Aries
6th 1:37 am Taurus
8th 8:41 am Gemini
10th 7:03 pm Cancer
13th 7:39 am Leo
15th 7:59 pm Virgo
18th 5:41 am Libra
20th 12:04 pm Scorpio
22nd 3:57 pm Capricorn
24th 6:40 pm Capricorn
26th 9:21 pm Aquarius
29th 12:36 am Pisces

May 1943
1st 4:39 am Aries
3rd 9:57 am Taurus
5th 5:16 pm Gemini
8th 3:16 am Cancer
10th 3:38 pm Leo
13th 4:21 am Virgo
15th 2:44 pm Libra
17th 9:19 pm Scorpio
20th 12:33 am Sagittarius
22nd 1:59 am Capricorn
24th 3:23 am Aquarius
26th 5:58 am Pisces
28th 10:16 am Aries
30th 4:25 pm Taurus

June 1943
2nd 12:29 am Gemini
4th 10:45 am Cancer
6th 11:03 pm Leo
9th 12:02 pm Virgo
11th 11:22 pm Libra
14th 6:59 am Scorpio
16th 10:37 am Sagittarius
18th 11:30 am Capricorn
20th 11:34 am Aquarius
22nd 12:36 pm Pisces
24th 3:52 pm Aries
26th 9:52 pm Taurus
29th 6:27 am Gemini

July 1943
1st 5:13 pm Cancer
4th 5:39 am Leo
6th 6:44 pm Virgo
9th 6:44 am Libra
11th 3:40 pm Scorpio
13th 8:37 pm Sagittarius
15th 10:07 pm Capricorn
17th 9:46 pm Aquarius
19th 9:31 pm Pisces
21st 11:08 pm Aries
24th 3:52 am Taurus
26th 12:03 pm Gemini
28th 11:04 pm Cancer
31st 11:43 am Leo

August 1943
3rd 12:45 am Virgo
5th 12:51 pm Libra
7th 10:40 pm Scorpio
10th 5:08 am Sagittarius
12th 8:09 am Capricorn
14th 8:37 am Aquarius
16th 8:07 am Pisces
18th 8:33 am Aries
20th 11:39 am Taurus
22nd 6:34 pm Gemini
25th 5:06 am Cancer
27th 5:49 pm Leo
30th 6:47 am Virgo

September 1943
1st 6:33 pm Libra
4th 4:20 am Scorpio
6th 11:38 am Sagittarius
8th 4:13 pm Capricorn
10th 6:18 pm Aquarius
12th 6:47 pm Pisces
14th 7:09 pm Aries
16th 9:14 pm Taurus
19th 2:42 am Gemini
21st 12:10 pm Cancer
24th 12:34 am Leo
26th 1:30 pm Virgo
29th 12:56 am Libra

October 1943
1st 10:04 am Scorpio
3rd 5:03 pm Sagittarius
5th 10:11 pm Capricorn
8th 1:39 am Aquarius
10th 3:44 am Pisces
12th 5:12 am Aries
14th 7:26 am Taurus
16th 12:07 pm Gemini
18th 8:28 pm Cancer
21st 8:12 am Leo
23rd 9:09 pm Virgo
26th 8:38 am Libra
28th 5:14 pm Scorpio
30th 11:14 pm Sagittarius

November 1943
2nd 3:37 am Capricorn
4th 7:10 am Aquarius
6th 10:16 am Pisces
8th 1:11 pm Aries
10th 4:33 pm Taurus
12th 9:32 pm Gemini
15th 5:22 am Cancer
17th 4:27 pm Leo
20th 5:21 am Virgo
22nd 5:18 pm Libra
25th 2:09 am Scorpio
27th 7:35 am Sagittarius
29th 10:43 am Capricorn

December 1943
1st 1:01 pm Aquarius
3rd 3:36 pm Pisces
5th 6:59 pm Aries
7th 11:30 pm Taurus
10th 5:32 am Gemini
12th 1:46 pm Cancer
15th 12:37 am Leo
17th 1:22 pm Virgo
20th 1:55 am Libra
22nd 11:45 am Scorpio
24th 5:44 pm Sagittarius
26th 8:24 pm Capricorn
28th 9:21 pm Aquarius
30th 10:17 pm Pisces

January 1944
2nd 12:34 am Aries
4th 4:58 am Taurus
6th 11:44 am Gemini
8th 8:48 pm Cancer
11th 7:57 am Leo
13th 8:38 pm Virgo
16th 9:28 am Libra
18th 8:27 pm Scorpio
21st 3:53 am Sagittarius
23rd 7:27 am Capricorn
25th 8:10 am Aquarius
27th 7:48 am Pisces
29th 8:15 am Aries
31st 11:07 am Taurus

February 1944
2nd 5:17 pm Gemini
5th 2:40 am Cancer
7th 2:20 pm Leo
10th 3:08 am Virgo
12th 3:54 pm Libra
15th 3:24 am Scorpio
17th 12:14 pm Sagittarius
19th 5:33 pm Capricorn
21st 7:27 pm Aquarius
23rd 7:09 pm Pisces
25th 6:32 pm Aries
27th 7:36 pm Taurus

March 1944
1st 12:06 am Gemini
3rd 8:38 am Cancer
5th 8:19 pm Leo
8th 9:18 am Virgo
10th 9:55 pm Libra
13th 9:12 am Scorpio
15th 6:31 pm Sagittarius
18th 1:13 am Capricorn
20th 4:55 am Aquarius
22nd 5:59 am Pisces
24th 5:42 am Aries
26th 6:01 am Taurus
28th 8:58 am Gemini
30th 3:59 pm Cancer

April 1944
2nd 2:54 am Leo
4th 3:48 pm Virgo
7th 4:22 am Libra
9th 3:12 pm Scorpio
12th 12:02 am Sagittarius
14th 6:56 am Capricorn
16th 11:46 am Aquarius
18th 2:28 pm Pisces
20th 3:36 pm Aries
22nd 4:29 pm Taurus
24th 6:59 pm Gemini
27th 12:49 am Cancer
29th 10:35 am Leo

May 1944
1st 11:04 pm Virgo
4th 11:39 am Libra
6th 10:18 pm Scorpio
9th 6:27 am Sagittarius
11th 12:33 pm Capricorn
13th 5:10 pm Aquarius
15th 8:35 pm Pisces
17th 11:03 pm Aries
20th 1:16 am Taurus
22nd 4:26 am Gemini
24th 10:04 am Cancer
26th 7:04 pm Leo
29th 6:58 am Virgo
31st 7:37 pm Libra

June 1944
3rd 6:31 am Scorpio
5th 2:27 pm Sagittarius
7th 7:41 pm Capricorn
9th 11:12 pm Aquarius
12th 1:58 am Pisces
14th 4:41 am Aries
16th 7:52 am Taurus
18th 12:11 pm Gemini
20th 6:28 pm Cancer
23rd 3:25 am Leo
25th 2:57 pm Virgo
28th 3:39 am Libra
30th 3:10 pm Scorpio

July 1944
2nd 11:38 pm Sagittarius
5th 4:42 am Capricorn
7th 7:14 am Aquarius
9th 8:39 am Pisces
11th 10:19 am Aries
13th 1:16 pm Taurus
15th 6:11 pm Gemini
18th 1:21 am Cancer
20th 10:51 am Leo
22nd 10:24 pm Virgo
25th 11:07 am Libra
27th 11:16 pm Scorpio
30th 8:50 am Sagittarius

August 1944
1st 2:42 pm Capricorn
3rd 5:11 pm Aquarius
5th 5:36 pm Pisces
7th 5:44 pm Aries
9th 7:20 pm Taurus
11th 11:38 pm Gemini
14th 7:03 am Cancer
16th 5:08 pm Leo
19th 5:00 am Virgo
21st 5:45 pm Libra
24th 6:13 am Scorpio
26th 4:51 pm Sagittarius
29th 12:12 am Capricorn
31st 3:44 am Aquarius

September 1944
2nd 4:15 am Pisces
4th 3:27 am Aries
6th 3:29 am Taurus
8th 6:13 am Gemini
10th 12:46 pm Cancer
12th 10:50 pm Leo
15th 11:00 am Virgo
17th 11:48 pm Libra
20th 12:11 pm Scorpio
22nd 11:16 pm Sagittarius
25th 7:55 am Capricorn
27th 1:10 pm Aquarius
29th 2:58 pm Pisces

October 1944
1st 2:31 pm Aries
3rd 1:47 pm Taurus
5th 2:59 pm Gemini
7th 7:56 pm Cancer
10th 5:03 am Leo
12th 5:04 pm Virgo
15th 5:55 am Libra
17th 6:03 pm Scorpio
20th 4:50 am Sagittarius
22nd 1:48 pm Capricorn
24th 8:19 pm Aquarius
26th 11:53 pm Pisces
29th 12:54 am Aries
31st 12:45 am Taurus

November 1944
2nd 1:28 am Gemini
4th 5:04 am Cancer
6th 12:44 pm Leo
8th 11:59 pm Virgo
11th 12:44 pm Libra
14th 12:48 am Scorpio
16th 11:02 am Sagittarius
18th 7:20 pm Capricorn
21st 1:47 am Aquarius
23rd 6:18 am Pisces
25th 8:57 am Aries
27th 10:23 am Taurus
29th 11:55 am Gemini

December 1944
1st 3:17 pm Cancer
3rd 9:53 pm Leo
6th 8:03 am Virgo
8th 8:28 pm Libra
11th 8:42 am Scorpio
13th 6:50 pm Sagittarius
16th 2:22 am Capricorn
18th 7:44 am Aquarius
20th 11:39 am Pisces
22nd 2:42 pm Aries
24th 5:24 pm Taurus
26th 8:26 pm Gemini
29th 12:44 am Cancer
31st 7:19 am Leo

January 1945
2nd 4:49 pm Virgo
5th 4:44 am Libra
7th 5:12 pm Scorpio
10th 3:55 am Sagittarius
12th 11:28 am Capricorn
14th 3:57 pm Aquarius
16th 6:28 pm Pisces
18th 8:21 pm Aries
20th 10:48 pm Taurus
23rd 2:35 am Gemini
25th 8:05 am Cancer
27th 3:33 pm Leo
30th 1:09 am Virgo

February 1945
1st 12:45 pm Libra
4th 1:22 am Scorpio
6th 12:57 pm Sagittarius
8th 9:29 pm Capricorn
11th 2:12 am Aquarius
13th 3:53 am Pisces
15th 4:13 am Aries
17th 5:05 am Taurus
19th 8:01 am Gemini
21st 1:42 pm Cancer
23rd 9:58 pm Leo
26th 8:13 am Virgo
28th 7:57 pm Libra

March 1945
3rd 8:32 am Scorpio
5th 8:44 pm Sagittarius
8th 6:37 am Capricorn
10th 12:40 pm Aquarius
12th 2:50 pm Pisces
14th 2:33 pm Aries
16th 1:55 pm Taurus
18th 3:05 pm Gemini
20th 7:31 pm Cancer
23rd 3:31 am Leo
25th 2:11 pm Virgo
28th 2:15 am Libra
30th 2:50 pm Scorpio

April 1945
2nd 3:07 am Sagittarius
4th 1:51 pm Capricorn
6th 9:28 pm Aquarius
9th 1:10 am Pisces
11th 1:38 am Aries
13th 12:40 am Taurus
15th 12:31 am Gemini
17th 3:13 am Cancer
19th 9:52 am Leo
21st 8:03 pm Virgo
24th 8:14 am Libra
26th 8:52 pm Scorpio
29th 8:56 am Sagittarius

May 1945
1st 7:40 pm Capricorn
4th 4:05 am Aquarius
6th 9:21 am Pisces
8th 11:25 am Aries
10th 11:25 am Taurus
12th 11:13 am Gemini
14th 12:51 pm Cancer
16th 5:57 pm Leo
19th 2:56 am Virgo
21st 2:42 pm Libra
24th 3:20 am Scorpio
26th 3:11 pm Sagittarius
29th 1:24 am Capricorn
31st 9:35 am Aquarius

June 1945
2nd 3:25 pm Pisces
4th 6:51 pm Aries
6th 8:23 pm Taurus
8th 9:15 pm Gemini
10th 11:02 pm Cancer
13th 3:20 am Leo
15th 11:07 am Virgo
17th 10:06 pm Libra
20th 10:36 am Scorpio
22nd 10:27 pm Sagittarius
25th 8:14 am Capricorn
27th 3:36 pm Aquarius
29th 8:51 pm Pisces

July 1945
2nd 12:29 am Aries
4th 3:05 am Taurus
6th 5:20 am Gemini
8th 8:11 am Cancer
10th 12:43 pm Leo
12th 7:58 pm Virgo
15th 6:12 am Libra
17th 6:28 pm Scorpio
20th 6:36 am Sagittarius
22nd 4:28 pm Capricorn
24th 11:16 pm Aquarius
27th 3:27 am Pisces
29th 6:07 am Aries
31st 8:29 am Taurus

August 1945
2nd 11:23 am Gemini
4th 3:23 pm Cancer
6th 8:53 pm Leo
9th 4:24 am Virgo
11th 2:21 pm Libra
14th 2:24 am Scorpio
16th 2:55 pm Sagittarius
19th 1:31 am Capricorn
21st 8:32 am Aquarius
23rd 12:06 pm Pisces
25th 1:31 pm Aries
27th 2:34 pm Taurus
29th 4:47 pm Gemini
31st 8:59 pm Cancer

September 1945
3rd 3:19 am Leo
5th 11:36 am Virgo
7th 9:48 pm Libra
10th 9:47 am Scorpio
12th 10:37 pm Sagittarius
15th 10:11 am Capricorn
17th 6:19 pm Aquarius
19th 10:19 pm Pisces
21st 11:11 pm Aries
23rd 10:53 pm Taurus
25th 11:32 pm Gemini
28th 2:38 am Cancer
30th 8:47 am Leo

October 1945
2nd 5:34 pm Virgo
5th 4:16 am Libra
7th 4:24 pm Scorpio
10th 5:17 am Sagittarius
12th 5:32 pm Capricorn
15th 3:06 am Aquarius
17th 8:34 am Pisces
19th 10:10 am Aries
21st 9:31 am Taurus
23rd 8:50 am Gemini
25th 10:11 am Cancer
27th 2:55 pm Leo
29th 11:12 pm Virgo

November 1945
1st 10:07 am Libra
3rd 10:29 pm Scorpio
6th 11:18 am Sagittarius
8th 11:35 pm Capricorn
11th 9:58 am Aquarius
13th 5:05 pm Pisces
15th 8:24 pm Aries
17th 8:48 pm Taurus
19th 8:03 pm Gemini
21st 8:14 pm Cancer
23rd 11:12 pm Leo
26th 5:59 am Virgo
28th 4:18 pm Libra

December 1945
1st 4:43 am Scorpio
3rd 5:30 pm Sagittarius
6th 5:23 am Capricorn
8th 3:34 pm Aquarius
10th 11:20 pm Pisces
13th 4:15 am Aries
15th 6:30 am Taurus
17th 7:03 am Gemini
19th 7:28 am Cancer
21st 9:31 am Leo
23rd 2:43 pm Virgo
25th 11:45 pm Libra
28th 11:42 am Scorpio
31st 12:32 am Sagittarius

January 1946
2nd 12:11 pm Capricorn
4th 9:38 pm Aquarius
7th 4:47 am Pisces
9th 9:56 am Aries
11th 1:25 pm Taurus
13th 3:43 pm Gemini
15th 5:33 pm Cancer
17th 8:04 pm Leo
20th 12:40 am Virgo
22nd 8:31 am Libra
24th 7:39 pm Scorpio
27th 8:27 am Sagittarius
29th 8:18 pm Capricorn

February 1946
1st 5:23 am Aquarius
3rd 11:33 am Pisces
5th 3:38 pm Aries
7th 6:47 pm Taurus
9th 9:45 pm Gemini
12th 12:59 am Cancer
14th 4:50 am Leo
16th 10:03 am Virgo
18th 5:36 pm Libra
21st 4:04 am Scorpio
23rd 4:40 pm Sagittarius
26th 5:01 am Capricorn
28th 2:34 pm Aquarius

March 1946
2nd 8:25 pm Pisces
4th 11:23 pm Aries
7th 1:08 am Taurus
9th 3:12 am Gemini
11th 6:28 am Cancer
13th 11:14 am Leo
15th 5:32 pm Virgo
18th 1:40 am Libra
20th 12:04 pm Scorpio
23rd 12:30 am Sagittarius
25th 1:17 pm Capricorn
27th 11:51 pm Aquarius
30th 6:26 am Pisces

April 1946
1st 9:17 am Aries
3rd 9:57 am Taurus
5th 10:25 am Gemini
7th 12:21 pm Cancer
9th 4:37 pm Leo
11th 11:20 pm Virgo
14th 8:13 am Libra
16th 7:03 pm Scorpio
19th 7:29 am Sagittarius
21st 8:28 pm Capricorn
24th 7:56 am Aquarius
26th 3:54 pm Pisces
28th 7:46 pm Aries
30th 8:31 pm Taurus

May 1946
2nd 8:04 pm Gemini
4th 8:23 pm Cancer
6th 11:04 pm Leo
9th 4:57 am Virgo
11th 1:53 pm Libra
14th 1:08 am Scorpio
16th 1:46 pm Sagittarius
19th 2:42 am Capricorn
21st 2:31 pm Aquarius
23rd 11:39 pm Pisces
26th 5:05 am Aries
28th 7:04 am Taurus
30th 6:55 am Gemini

June 1946
1st 6:29 am Cancer
3rd 7:40 am Leo
5th 11:56 am Virgo
7th 7:57 pm Libra
10th 7:04 am Scorpio
12th 7:50 pm Sagittarius
15th 8:39 am Capricorn
17th 8:16 pm Aquarius
20th 5:43 am Pisces
22nd 12:19 pm Aries
24th 3:56 pm Taurus
26th 5:08 pm Gemini
28th 5:11 pm Cancer
30th 5:48 pm Leo

July 1946
2nd 8:45 pm Virgo
5th 3:21 am Libra
7th 1:41 pm Scorpio
10th 2:20 am Sagittarius
12th 3:05 pm Capricorn
15th 2:17 am Aquarius
17th 11:15 am Pisces
19th 5:59 pm Aries
21st 10:35 pm Taurus
24th 1:18 am Gemini
26th 2:44 am Cancer
28th 3:57 am Leo
30th 6:33 am Virgo

August 1946
1st 12:04 pm Libra
3rd 9:22 pm Scorpio
6th 9:36 am Sagittarius
8th 10:23 pm Capricorn
11th 9:23 am Aquarius
13th 5:41 pm Pisces
15th 11:37 pm Aries
18th 3:59 am Taurus
20th 7:22 am Gemini
22nd 10:06 am Cancer
24th 12:38 pm Leo
26th 3:54 pm Virgo
28th 9:15 pm Libra
31st 5:49 am Scorpio

September 1946
2nd 5:30 pm Sagittarius
5th 6:23 am Capricorn
7th 5:41 am Aquarius
10th 1:46 am Pisces
12th 6:49 am Aries
14th 10:04 am Taurus
16th 12:46 pm Gemini
18th 3:42 pm Cancer
20th 7:13 pm Leo
22nd 11:38 pm Virgo
25th 5:40 am Libra
27th 2:12 pm Scorpio
30th 1:32 am Sagittarius

October 1946
2nd 2:28 pm Capricorn
5th 2:27 am Aquarius
7th 11:09 am Pisces
9th 4:05 pm Aries
11th 6:21 pm Taurus
13th 7:37 pm Gemini
15th 9:23 pm Cancer
18th 12:35 am Leo
20th 5:35 am Virgo
22nd 12:33 pm Libra
24th 9:41 pm Scorpio
27th 9:03 am Sagittarius
29th 9:59 pm Capricorn

November 1946
1st 10:36 am Aquarius
3rd 8:32 pm Pisces
6th 2:28 am Aries
8th 4:49 am Taurus
10th 5:08 am Gemini
12th 5:16 am Cancer
14th 6:53 am Leo
16th 11:04 am Virgo
18th 6:12 pm Libra
21st 3:58 am Scorpio
23rd 3:43 pm Sagittarius
26th 4:39 am Capricorn
28th 5:29 pm Aquarius

December 1946
1st 4:29 am Pisces
3rd 12:05 pm Aries
5th 3:49 pm Taurus
7th 4:30 pm Gemini
9th 3:51 pm Cancer
11th 3:47 pm Leo
13th 6:09 pm Virgo
16th 12:07 am Libra
18th 9:43 am Scorpio
20th 9:48 pm Sagittarius
23rd 10:50 am Capricorn
25th 11:29 pm Aquarius
28th 10:43 am Pisces
30th 7:31 pm Aries

January 1947
2nd 1:06 am Taurus
4th 3:26 am Gemini
6th 3:28 am Cancer
8th 2:53 am Leo
10th 3:45 am Virgo
12th 7:54 am Libra
14th 4:15 pm Scorpio
17th 4:03 am Sagittarius
19th 5:10 pm Capricorn
22nd 5:37 am Aquarius
24th 4:23 pm Pisces
27th 1:10 am Aries
29th 7:45 am Taurus
31st 11:52 am Gemini

February 1947
2nd 1:39 pm Cancer
4th 2:02 pm Leo
6th 2:43 pm Virgo
8th 5:40 pm Libra
11th 12:28 am Scorpio
13th 11:15 am Sagittarius
16th 12:12 am Capricorn
18th 12:38 pm Aquarius
20th 10:57 pm Pisces
23rd 6:58 am Aries
25th 1:08 pm Taurus
27th 5:47 pm Gemini

March 1947
1st 8:59 pm Cancer
3rd 10:59 pm Leo
6th 12:46 am Virgo
8th 3:51 am Libra
10th 9:51 am Scorpio
12th 7:33 pm Sagittarius
15th 7:59 am Capricorn
17th 8:35 pm Aquarius
20th 6:57 am Pisces
22nd 2:23 pm Aries
24th 7:29 pm Taurus
26th 11:16 pm Gemini
29th 2:26 am Cancer
31st 5:22 am Leo

April 1947
2nd 8:30 am Virgo
4th 12:40 pm Libra
6th 6:57 pm Scorpio
9th 4:12 am Sagittarius
11th 4:08 pm Capricorn
14th 4:51 am Aquarius
16th 3:47 pm Pisces
18th 11:25 pm Aries
21st 3:56 am Taurus
23rd 6:28 am Gemini
25th 8:22 am Cancer
27th 10:44 am Leo
29th 2:15 pm Virgo

May 1947
1st 7:24 pm Libra
4th 2:35 am Scorpio
6th 12:09 pm Sagittarius
8th 11:55 pm Capricorn
11th 12:40 pm Aquarius
14th 12:20 am Pisces
16th 8:56 am Aries
18th 1:52 pm Taurus
20th 3:52 pm Gemini
22nd 4:27 pm Cancer
24th 5:18 pm Leo
26th 7:50 pm Virgo
29th 12:54 am Libra
31st 8:42 am Scorpio

June 1947
2nd 6:54 pm Sagittarius
5th 6:51 am Capricorn
7th 7:38 pm Aquarius
10th 7:47 am Pisces
12th 5:33 pm Aries
14th 11:45 pm Taurus
17th 2:22 am Gemini
19th 2:32 am Cancer
21st 2:07 am Leo
23rd 3:01 am Virgo
25th 6:51 am Libra
27th 2:16 pm Scorpio
30th 12:46 am Sagittarius

July 1947
2nd 1:02 pm Capricorn
5th 1:50 am Aquarius
7th 2:03 pm Pisces
10th 12:34 am Aries
12th 8:12 am Taurus
14th 12:17 pm Gemini
16th 1:15 pm Cancer
18th 12:35 pm Leo
20th 12:20 pm Virgo
22nd 2:33 pm Libra
24th 8:41 pm Scorpio
27th 6:40 am Sagittarius
29th 7:01 pm Capricorn

August 1947
1st 7:49 am Aquarius
3rd 7:49 pm Pisces
6th 6:19 am Aries
8th 2:43 pm Taurus
10th 8:17 pm Gemini
12th 10:50 pm Cancer
14th 11:06 pm Leo
16th 10:49 pm Virgo
19th 12:04 am Libra
21st 4:44 am Scorpio
23rd 1:34 pm Sagittarius
26th 1:31 am Capricorn
28th 2:18 pm Aquarius
31st 2:03 am Pisces

September 1947
2nd 12:02 pm Aries
4th 8:10 pm Taurus
7th 2:18 am Gemini
9th 6:12 am Cancer
11th 8:03 am Leo
13th 8:51 am Virgo
15th 10:17 am Libra
17th 2:11 pm Scorpio
19th 9:49 pm Sagittarius
22nd 8:57 am Capricorn
24th 9:37 pm Aquarius
27th 9:24 am Pisces
29th 6:58 pm Aries

October 1947
2nd 2:15 am Taurus
4th 7:44 am Gemini
6th 11:47 am Cancer
8th 2:42 pm Leo
10th 4:57 pm Virgo
12th 7:32 pm Libra
14th 11:45 pm Scorpio
17th 6:52 am Sagittarius
19th 5:13 pm Capricorn
22nd 5:38 am Aquarius
24th 5:45 pm Pisces
27th 3:31 am Aries
29th 10:16 am Taurus
31st 2:36 pm Gemini

November 1947
2nd 5:32 pm Cancer
4th 8:03 pm Leo
6th 10:55 pm Virgo
9th 2:42 am Libra
11th 8:03 am Scorpio
13th 3:33 pm Sagittarius
16th 1:37 am Capricorn
18th 1:44 pm Aquarius
21st 2:16 am Pisces
23rd 12:53 pm Aries
25th 8:06 pm Taurus
27th 11:55 pm Gemini
30th 1:31 am Cancer

December 1947
2nd 2:30 am Leo
4th 4:24 am Virgo
6th 8:14 am Libra
8th 2:24 pm Scorpio
10th 10:49 pm Sagittarius
13th 9:14 am Capricorn
15th 9:15 pm Aquarius
18th 9:58 am Pisces
20th 9:37 pm Aries
23rd 6:11 am Taurus
25th 10:47 am Gemini
27th 12:04 pm Cancer
29th 11:42 am Leo
31st 11:47 am Virgo

January 1948
2nd 2:10 pm Libra
4th 7:51 pm Scorpio
7th 4:40 am Sagittarius
9th 3:41 pm Capricorn
12th 3:54 am Aquarius
14th 4:35 pm Pisces
17th 4:43 am Aries
19th 2:42 pm Taurus
21st 9:01 pm Gemini
23rd 11:23 pm Cancer
25th 10:59 pm Leo
27th 9:56 pm Virgo
29th 10:29 pm Libra

February 1948
1st 2:27 am Scorpio
3rd 10:25 am Sagittarius
5th 9:29 pm Capricorn
8th 9:59 am Aquarius
10th 10:37 pm Pisces
13th 10:37 am Aries
15th 9:08 pm Taurus
18th 4:56 am Gemini
20th 9:09 am Cancer
22nd 10:08 am Leo
24th 9:23 am Virgo
26th 9:06 am Libra
28th 11:24 am Scorpio

March 1948
1st 5:41 pm Sagittarius
4th 3:50 am Capricorn
6th 4:14 pm Aquarius
9th 4:53 am Pisces
11th 4:33 pm Aries
14th 2:40 am Taurus
16th 10:45 am Gemini
18th 4:14 pm Cancer
20th 6:58 pm Leo
22nd 7:43 pm Virgo
24th 8:02 pm Libra
26th 9:50 pm Scorpio
29th 2:46 am Sagittarius
31st 11:33 am Capricorn

April 1948
2nd 11:18 pm Aquarius
5th 11:56 am Pisces
7th 11:28 pm Aries
10th 8:58 am Taurus
12th 4:20 pm Gemini
14th 9:41 pm Cancer
17th 1:16 am Leo
19th 3:30 am Virgo
21st 5:16 am Libra
23rd 7:49 am Scorpio
25th 12:31 pm Sagittarius
27th 8:21 pm Capricorn
30th 7:15 am Aquarius

May 1948
2nd 7:43 pm Pisces
5th 7:28 am Aries
7th 4:48 pm Taurus
9th 11:20 pm Gemini
12th 3:38 am Cancer
14th 6:39 am Leo
16th 9:14 am Virgo
18th 12:07 pm Libra
20th 3:56 pm Scorpio
22nd 9:22 pm Sagittarius
25th 5:08 am Capricorn
27th 3:30 pm Aquarius
30th 3:46 am Pisces

June 1948
1st 3:54 pm Aries
4th 1:43 am Taurus
6th 8:06 am Gemini
8th 11:29 am Cancer
10th 1:12 pm Leo
12th 2:49 pm Virgo
14th 5:33 pm Libra
16th 10:03 pm Scorpio
19th 4:28 am Sagittarius
21st 12:51 pm Capricorn
23rd 11:15 pm Aquarius
26th 11:23 am Pisces
28th 11:56 pm Aries

July 1948
1st 10:39 am Taurus
3rd 5:48 pm Gemini
5th 9:07 pm Cancer
7th 9:53 pm Leo
9th 10:04 pm Virgo
11th 11:31 pm Libra
14th 3:28 am Scorpio
16th 10:11 am Sagittarius
18th 7:13 pm Capricorn
21st 6:02 am Aquarius
23rd 6:13 pm Pisces
26th 6:57 am Aries
28th 6:33 pm Taurus
31st 3:01 am Gemini

August 1948
2nd 7:20 am Cancer
4th 8:14 am Leo
6th 7:33 am Virgo
8th 7:30 am Libra
10th 9:56 am Scorpio
12th 3:49 pm Sagittarius
15th 12:51 am Capricorn
17th 12:02 pm Aquarius
20th 12:23 am Pisces
22nd 1:05 pm Aries
25th 1:03 am Taurus
27th 10:39 am Gemini
29th 4:34 pm Cancer
31st 6:41 pm Leo

September 1948
2nd 6:21 pm Virgo
4th 5:36 pm Libra
6th 6:34 pm Scorpio
8th 10:51 pm Sagittarius
11th 6:56 am Capricorn
13th 5:58 pm Aquarius
16th 6:27 am Pisces
18th 7:02 pm Aries
21st 6:45 am Taurus
23rd 4:40 pm Gemini
25th 11:46 pm Cancer
28th 3:35 am Leo
30th 4:41 am Virgo

October 1948
2nd 4:30 am Libra
4th 4:59 am Scorpio
6th 7:55 am Sagittarius
8th 2:30 pm Capricorn
11th 12:42 am Aquarius
13th 1:03 pm Pisces
16th 1:36 am Aries
18th 12:54 pm Taurus
20th 10:14 pm Gemini
23rd 5:21 am Cancer
25th 10:10 am Leo
27th 12:54 pm Virgo
29th 2:16 pm Libra
31st 3:32 pm Scorpio

November 1948
2nd 6:11 pm Sagittarius
4th 11:39 pm Capricorn
7th 8:41 am Aquarius
9th 8:33 pm Pisces
12th 9:12 am Aries
14th 8:24 pm Taurus
17th 5:02 am Gemini
19th 11:11 am Cancer
21st 3:32 pm Leo
23rd 6:48 pm Virgo
25th 9:33 pm Libra
28th 12:19 am Scorpio
30th 3:52 am Sagittarius

December 1948
2nd 9:16 am Capricorn
4th 5:32 pm Aquarius
7th 4:45 am Pisces
9th 5:29 pm Aries
12th 5:08 am Taurus
14th 1:44 pm Gemini
16th 7:01 pm Cancer
18th 10:03 pm Leo
21st 12:19 am Virgo
23rd 2:59 am Libra
25th 6:39 am Scorpio
27th 11:29 am Sagittarius
29th 5:47 pm Capricorn

January 1949
1st 2:07 am Aquarius
3rd 12:58 pm Pisces
6th 1:40 am Aries
8th 2:02 pm Taurus
10th 11:31 pm Gemini
13th 4:57 am Cancer
15th 7:08 am Leo
17th 7:53 am Virgo
19th 9:03 am Libra
21st 11:59 am Scorpio
23rd 5:09 pm Sagittarius
26th 12:22 am Capricorn
28th 9:26 am Aquarius
30th 8:26 pm Pisces

February 1949
2nd 9:04 am Aries
4th 9:57 pm Taurus
7th 8:40 am Gemini
9th 3:22 pm Cancer
11th 6:01 pm Leo
13th 6:06 pm Virgo
15th 5:44 pm Libra
17th 6:53 pm Scorpio
19th 10:49 pm Sagittarius
22nd 5:50 am Capricorn
24th 3:26 pm Aquarius
27th 2:54 am Pisces

March 1949
1st 3:35 pm Aries
4th 4:33 am Taurus
6th 4:05 pm Gemini
9th 12:21 am Cancer
11th 4:33 am Leo
13th 5:25 am Virgo
15th 4:40 am Libra
17th 4:25 am Scorpio
19th 6:30 am Sagittarius
21st 12:04 pm Capricorn
23rd 9:10 pm Aquarius
26th 8:49 am Pisces
28th 9:41 pm Aries
31st 10:29 am Taurus

April 1949
2nd 10:03 pm Gemini
5th 7:10 am Cancer
7th 12:59 pm Leo
9th 3:32 pm Virgo
11th 3:48 pm Libra
13th 3:28 pm Scorpio
15th 4:24 pm Sagittarius
17th 8:16 pm Capricorn
20th 3:59 am Aquarius
22nd 3:07 pm Pisces
25th 4:01 am Aries
27th 4:41 pm Taurus
30th 3:48 am Gemini

May 1949
2nd 12:43 pm Cancer
4th 7:11 pm Leo
6th 11:11 pm Virgo
9th 1:07 am Libra
11th 1:54 am Scorpio
13th 2:57 am Sagittarius
15th 5:57 am Capricorn
17th 12:19 pm Aquarius
19th 10:26 pm Pisces
22nd 11:01 am Aries
24th 11:42 pm Taurus
27th 10:27 am Gemini
29th 6:39 pm Cancer

June 1949
1st 12:36 am Leo
3rd 4:53 am Virgo
5th 7:58 am Libra
7th 10:14 am Scorpio
9th 12:24 pm Sagittarius
11th 3:40 pm Capricorn
13th 9:26 pm Aquarius
16th 6:38 am Pisces
18th 6:44 pm Aries
21st 7:30 am Taurus
23rd 6:19 pm Gemini
26th 2:01 am Cancer
28th 7:01 am Leo
30th 10:27 am Virgo

July 1949
2nd 1:22 pm Libra
4th 4:22 pm Scorpio
6th 7:45 pm Sagittarius
9th 12:02 am Capricorn
11th 6:09 am Aquarius
13th 3:01 pm Pisces
16th 2:43 am Aries
18th 3:35 pm Taurus
21st 2:57 am Gemini
23rd 10:52 am Cancer
25th 3:19 pm Leo
27th 5:36 pm Virgo
29th 7:20 pm Libra
31st 9:44 pm Scorpio

August 1949
3rd 1:25 am Sagittarius
5th 6:36 am Capricorn
7th 1:34 pm Aquarius
9th 10:45 pm Pisces
12th 10:19 am Aries
14th 11:18 pm Taurus
17th 11:22 am Gemini
19th 8:15 pm Cancer
22nd 1:08 am Leo
24th 2:56 am Virgo
26th 3:24 am Libra
28th 4:20 am Scorpio
30th 7:00 am Sagittarius

September 1949
1st 12:05 pm Capricorn
3rd 7:37 pm Aquarius
6th 5:26 am Pisces
8th 5:13 pm Aries
11th 6:12 am Taurus
13th 6:46 pm Gemini
16th 4:51 am Cancer
18th 11:04 am Leo
20th 1:34 pm Virgo
22nd 1:42 pm Libra
24th 1:21 pm Scorpio
26th 2:21 pm Sagittarius
28th 6:07 pm Capricorn

October 1949
1st 1:13 am Aquarius
3rd 11:19 am Pisces
5th 11:27 pm Aries
8th 12:26 pm Taurus
11th 1:02 am Gemini
13th 11:50 am Cancer
15th 7:35 pm Leo
17th 11:42 pm Virgo
20th 12:48 am Libra
22nd 12:18 am Scorpio
24th 12:08 am Sagittarius
26th 2:10 am Capricorn
28th 7:50 am Aquarius
30th 5:21 pm Pisces

November 1949
2nd 5:34 am Aries
4th 6:36 pm Taurus
7th 6:55 am Gemini
9th 5:35 pm Cancer
12th 2:00 am Leo
14th 7:42 am Virgo
16th 10:36 am Libra
18th 11:19 am Scorpio
20th 11:16 am Sagittarius
22nd 12:20 pm Capricorn
24th 4:24 pm Aquarius
27th 12:35 am Pisces
29th 12:17 pm Aries

December 1949
2nd 1:22 am Taurus
4th 1:28 pm Gemini
6th 11:31 pm Cancer
9th 7:27 am Leo
11th 1:31 pm Virgo
13th 5:45 pm Libra
15th 8:14 pm Scorpio
17th 9:32 pm Sagittarius
19th 10:59 pm Capricorn
22nd 2:24 am Aquarius
24th 9:19 am Pisces
26th 8:04 pm Aries
29th 8:57 am Taurus
31st 9:13 pm Gemini

January 1950
3rd 6:56 am Cancer
5th 1:58 pm Leo
7th 7:06 pm Virgo
9th 11:08 pm Libra
12th 2:28 am Scorpio
14th 5:16 am Sagittarius
16th 8:07 am Capricorn
18th 12:07 pm Aquarius
20th 6:41 pm Pisces
23rd 4:37 am Aries
25th 5:07 pm Taurus
28th 5:43 am Gemini
30th 3:50 pm Cancer

May 1950
1st 11:38 am Scorpio
3rd 10:51 am Sagittarius
5th 11:08 am Capricorn
7th 2:22 pm Aquarius
9th 9:33 pm Pisces
12th 8:18 am Aries
14th 8:58 pm Taurus
17th 9:52 am Gemini
19th 9:50 pm Cancer
22nd 8:06 am Leo
24th 3:50 pm Virgo
26th 8:26 pm Libra
28th 10:01 pm Scorpio
30th 9:44 pm Sagittarius

September 1950
1st 2:18 am Taurus
3rd 2:45 pm Gemini
6th 2:53 am Cancer
8th 12:34 pm Leo
10th 6:55 pm Virgo
12th 10:28 pm Libra
15th 12:27 am Scorpio
17th 2:12 am Sagittarius
19th 4:49 am Capricorn
21st 8:59 am Aquarius
23rd 3:09 pm Pisces
25th 11:32 pm Aries
28th 10:08 am Taurus
30th 10:26 pm Gemini

January 1951
2nd 3:58 pm Scorpio
4th 5:39 pm Sagittarius
6th 5:33 pm Capricorn
8th 5:36 pm Aquarius
10th 7:56 pm Pisces
13th 2:05 am Aries
15th 12:10 pm Taurus
18th 12:36 am Gemini
20th 1:06 pm Cancer
23rd 12:12 am Leo
25th 9:26 am Virgo
27th 4:46 pm Libra
29th 10:04 pm Scorpio
February 1951

May 1951
2nd 11:26 am Aries
4th 8:46 pm Taurus
7th 7:51 am Gemini
9th 8:13 pm Cancer
12th 8:49 am Leo
14th 7:43 pm Virgo
17th 3:05 am Libra
19th 6:23 am Scorpio
21st 6:44 am Sagittarius
23rd 6:08 am Capricorn
25th 6:42 am Aquarius
27th 10:05 am Pisces
29th 4:53 pm Aries

February 1950
1st 10:34 pm Leo
4th 2:37 am Virgo
6th 5:19 am Libra
8th 7:50 am Scorpio
10th 10:51 am Sagittarius
12th 2:45 pm Capricorn
14th 7:58 pm Aquarius
17th 3:11 am Pisces
19th 1:00 pm Aries
22nd 1:12 am Taurus
24th 2:02 pm Gemini
27th 1:04 am Cancer

June 1950
1st 9:27 pm Capricorn
3rd 11:18 pm Aquarius
6th 4:57 am Pisces
8th 2:43 pm Aries
11th 3:12 am Taurus
13th 4:05 pm Gemini
16th 3:45 am Cancer
18th 1:37 pm Leo
20th 9:31 pm Virgo
23rd 3:09 am Libra
25th 6:19 am Scorpio
27th 7:26 am Sagittarius
29th 7:49 am Capricorn

October 1950
3rd 10:59 am Cancer
5th 9:40 pm Leo
8th 4:54 am Virgo
10th 8:29 am Libra
12th 9:32 am Scorpio
14th 9:45 am Sagittarius
16th 10:55 am Capricorn
18th 2:26 pm Aquarius
20th 8:53 pm Pisces
23rd 5:58 am Aries
25th 5:02 pm Taurus
28th 5:22 am Gemini
30th 6:04 pm Cancer

1st 1:16 am Sagittarius
3rd 2:53 am Capricorn
5th 4:04 am Aquarius
7th 6:29 am Pisces
9th 11:42 am Aries
11th 8:33 pm Taurus
14th 8:18 am Gemini
16th 8:51 pm Cancer
19th 8:01 am Leo
21st 4:43 pm Virgo
23rd 11:01 pm Libra
26th 3:31 am Scorpio
28th 6:49 am Sagittarius

June 1951
1st 2:33 am Taurus
3rd 2:02 pm Gemini
6th 2:31 am Cancer
8th 3:11 pm Leo
11th 2:46 am Virgo
13th 11:30 am Libra
15th 4:17 pm Scorpio
17th 5:27 pm Sagittarius
19th 4:39 pm Capricorn
21st 4:04 pm Aquarius
23rd 5:49 pm Pisces
25th 11:13 pm Aries
28th 8:17 am Taurus
30th 7:51 pm Gemini

March 1950
1st 8:30 am Leo
3rd 12:25 pm Virgo
5th 2:01 pm Libra
7th 2:56 pm Scorpio
9th 4:38 pm Sagittarius
11th 8:07 pm Capricorn
14th 1:52 am Aquarius
16th 9:59 am Pisces
18th 8:21 pm Aries
21st 8:32 am Taurus
23rd 9:28 pm Gemini
26th 9:16 am Cancer
28th 6:04 pm Leo
30th 11:01 pm Virgo

July 1950
1st 9:20 am Aquarius
3rd 1:51 pm Pisces
5th 10:24 pm Aries
8th 10:13 am Taurus
10th 11:01 pm Gemini
13th 10:33 am Cancer
15th 7:52 pm Leo
18th 3:05 am Virgo
20th 8:34 am Libra
22nd 12:27 pm Scorpio
24th 2:56 pm Sagittarius
26th 4:40 pm Capricorn
28th 6:56 pm Aquarius
30th 11:19 pm Pisces

November 1950
2nd 5:38 am Leo
4th 2:20 pm Virgo
6th 7:10 pm Libra
8th 8:29 pm Scorpio
10th 7:52 pm Sagittarius
12th 7:26 pm Capricorn
14th 9:14 pm Aquarius
17th 2:38 am Pisces
19th 11:39 am Aries
21st 11:08 pm Taurus
24th 11:38 am Gemini
27th 12:13 am Cancer
29th 12:02 pm Leo

March 1951
2nd 9:30 am Capricorn
4th 12:11 pm Aquarius
6th 3:46 pm Pisces
8th 9:16 pm Aries
11th 5:32 am Taurus
13th 4:36 pm Gemini
16th 5:06 am Cancer
18th 4:44 pm Leo
21st 1:39 am Virgo
23rd 7:21 am Libra
25th 10:36 am Scorpio
27th 12:41 pm Sagittarius
29th 2:51 pm Capricorn
31th 6:02 pm Aquarius

July 1951
3rd 8:27 am Cancer
5th 9:00 pm Leo
8th 8:35 am Virgo
10th 6:04 pm Libra
13th 12:19 am Scorpio
15th 3:04 am Sagittarius
17th 3:15 am Capricorn
19th 2:41 am Aquarius
21st 3:29 am Pisces
23rd 7:21 am Aries
25th 3:06 pm Taurus
28th 2:07 am Gemini
30th 2:42 pm Cancer

April 1950
2nd 12:41 am Libra
4th 12:35 am Scorpio
6th 12:37 am Sagittarius
8th 2:29 am Capricorn
10th 7:24 am Aquarius
12th 3:38 pm Pisces
15th 2:31 am Aries
17th 2:59 pm Taurus
20th 3:54 am Gemini
22nd 4:01 pm Cancer
25th 1:57 am Leo
27th 8:30 am Virgo
29th 11:25 am Libra

August 1950
2nd 7:02 am Aries
4th 6:05 pm Taurus
7th 6:44 am Gemini
9th 6:27 pm Cancer
12th 3:36 am Leo
14th 10:04 am Virgo
16th 2:31 pm Libra
18th 5:49 pm Scorpio
20th 8:36 pm Sagittarius
22nd 11:23 pm Capricorn
25th 2:53 am Aquarius
27th 8:02 am Pisces
29th 3:44 pm Aries

December 1950
1st 9:53 pm Virgo
4th 4:29 am Libra
6th 7:20 am Scorpio
8th 7:18 am Sagittarius
10th 6:17 am Capricorn
12th 6:34 am Aquarius
14th 10:10 am Pisces
16th 5:58 pm Aries
19th 5:09 am Taurus
21st 5:49 pm Gemini
24th 6:18 am Cancer
26th 5:45 pm Leo
29th 3:41 am Virgo
31th 11:20 am Libra

April 1951
2nd 10:45 pm Pisces
5th 5:16 am Aries
7th 1:52 pm Taurus
10th 12:41 am Gemini
12th 1:04 pm Cancer
15th 1:18 am Leo
17th 11:07 am Virgo
19th 5:13 pm Libra
21st 7:55 pm Scorpio
23rd 8:40 pm Sagittarius
25th 9:20 pm Capricorn
27th 11:32 pm Aquarius
30th 4:13 am Pisces

August 1951
2nd 3:07 am Leo
4th 2:18 pm Virgo
6th 11:34 pm Libra
9th 6:24 am Scorpio
11th 10:31 am Sagittarius
13th 12:19 pm Capricorn
15th 12:54 pm Aquarius
17th 1:53 pm Pisces
19th 4:58 pm Aries
21st 11:26 pm Taurus
24th 9:27 am Gemini
26th 9:44 pm Cancer
29th 10:09 am Leo
31th 8:59 pm Virgo

September 1951
3rd 5:32 am Libra
5th 11:49 am Scorpio
7th 4:11 pm Sagittarius
9th 7:06 pm Capricorn
11th 9:12 pm Aquarius
13th 11:22 pm Pisces
16th 2:47 am Aries
18th 8:41 am Taurus
20th 5:46 pm Gemini
23rd 5:34 am Cancer
25th 6:07 pm Leo
28th 5:05 am Virgo
30th 1:08 pm Libra

January 1952
1st 2:10 am Pisces
3rd 5:41 am Aries
5th 12:43 pm Taurus
7th 10:42 pm Gemini
10th 10:34 am Cancer
12th 11:19 pm Leo
15th 11:59 am Virgo
17th 11:19 pm Libra
20th 7:44 am Scorpio
22nd 12:22 pm Sagittarius
24th 1:40 pm Capricorn
26th 1:07 pm Aquarius
28th 12:46 pm Pisces
30th 2:33 pm Aries

May 1952
1st 4:12 am Leo
3rd 4:57 pm Virgo
6th 3:39 am Libra
8th 10:49 am Scorpio
10th 2:51 pm Sagittarius
12th 5:09 pm Capricorn
14th 7:14 pm Aquarius
16th 10:05 pm Pisces
19th 2:07 am Aries
21st 7:29 am Taurus
23rd 2:37 pm Gemini
26th 12:06 am Cancer
28th 11:59 am Leo
31st 12:57 am Virgo

September 1952
1st 9:04 am Aquarius
3rd 9:01 am Pisces
5th 8:58 am Aries
7th 10:48 am Taurus
9th 4:06 pm Gemini
12th 1:24 am Cancer
14th 1:38 pm Leo
17th 2:41 am Virgo
19th 2:41 pm Libra
22nd 12:43 am Scorpio
24th 8:33 am Sagittarius
26th 2:06 pm Capricorn
28th 5:24 pm Aquarius
30th 6:53 pm Pisces

January 1953
1st 9:17 pm Leo
4th 9:40 am Virgo
6th 10:36 pm Libra
9th 9:43 am Scorpio
11th 5:14 pm Sagittarius
13th 8:55 pm Capricorn
15th 9:57 pm Aquarius
17th 10:07 pm Pisces
19th 11:08 pm Aries
22nd 2:20 am Taurus
24th 8:21 am Gemini
26th 5:06 pm Cancer
29th 4:06 am Leo
31th 4:35 pm Virgo

October 1951
2nd 6:23 pm Scorpio
4th 9:48 pm Sagittarius
7th 12:30 am Capricorn
9th 3:19 am Aquarius
11th 6:46 am Pisces
13th 11:20 am Aries
15th 5:37 pm Taurus
18th 2:22 am Gemini
20th 1:42 pm Cancer
23rd 2:25 am Leo
25th 2:01 pm Virgo
27th 10:25 pm Libra
30th 3:09 am Scorpio

February 1952
1st 7:50 pm Taurus
4th 4:55 am Gemini
6th 4:44 pm Cancer
9th 5:36 am Leo
11th 6:01 pm Virgo
14th 4:59 am Libra
16th 1:45 pm Scorpio
18th 7:42 pm Sagittarius
20th 10:49 pm Capricorn
22nd 11:48 pm Aquarius
25th 12:01 am Pisces
27th 1:12 am Aries
29th 5:02 am Taurus

June 1952
2nd 12:25 pm Libra
4th 8:19 pm Scorpio
7th 12:21 am Sagittarius
9th 1:46 am Capricorn
11th 2:27 am Aquarius
13th 4:01 am Pisces
15th 7:29 am Aries
17th 1:10 pm Taurus
19th 9:04 pm Gemini
22nd 7:04 am Cancer
24th 7:02 pm Leo
27th 8:06 am Virgo
29th 8:18 pm Libra

October 1952
2nd 7:34 am Aries
4th 9:06 pm Taurus
7th 1:15 am Gemini
9th 9:15 am Cancer
11th 8:50 pm Leo
14th 9:50 am Virgo
16th 9:44 pm Libra
19th 7:10 am Scorpio
21st 2:12 pm Sagittarius
23rd 7:28 pm Capricorn
25th 11:28 pm Aquarius
28th 2:23 am Pisces
30th 4:35 am Aries

February 1953
3rd 5:31 am Libra
5th 5:20 pm Scorpio
8th 2:20 am Sagittarius
10th 7:32 am Capricorn
12th 9:17 am Aquarius
14th 8:59 am Pisces
16th 8:31 am Aries
18th 9:51 am Taurus
20th 2:27 pm Gemini
22nd 10:47 pm Cancer
25th 10:05 am Leo
27th 10:51 pm Virgo

November 1951
1st 5:20 am Sagittarius
3rd 6:40 am Capricorn
5th 8:43 am Aquarius
7th 12:23 pm Pisces
9th 5:52 pm Aries
12th 1:07 am Taurus
14th 10:15 am Gemini
16th 9:27 pm Cancer
19th 10:11 am Leo
21st 10:35 pm Virgo
24th 8:08 am Libra
26th 1:32 pm Scorpio
28th 3:21 pm Sagittarius
30th 3:23 pm Capricorn

March 1952
2nd 12:36 pm Gemini
4th 11:40 pm Cancer
7th 12:30 pm Leo
10th 12:51 am Virgo
12th 11:16 am Libra
14th 7:20 pm Scorpio
17th 1:15 am Sagittarius
19th 5:19 am Capricorn
21st 7:55 am Aquarius
23rd 9:39 am Pisces
25th 11:34 am Aries
27th 3:06 pm Taurus
29th 9:36 pm Gemini

July 1952
2nd 5:25 am Scorpio
4th 10:27 am Sagittarius
6th 12:04 pm Capricorn
8th 11:55 am Aquarius
10th 11:59 am Pisces
12th 1:56 pm Aries
14th 6:45 pm Taurus
17th 2:37 am Gemini
19th 1:04 pm Cancer
22nd 1:20 am Leo
24th 2:24 pm Virgo
27th 2:54 am Libra
29th 1:04 pm Scorpio
31th 7:37 pm Sagittarius

November 1952
1st 6:59 am Taurus
3rd 11:02 am Gemini
5th 6:12 pm Cancer
8th 4:56 am Leo
10th 5:46 pm Virgo
13th 5:57 am Libra
15th 3:18 pm Scorpio
17th 9:33 pm Sagittarius
20th 1:40 am Capricorn
22nd 4:52 am Aquarius
24th 7:55 am Pisces
26th 11:09 am Aries
28th 2:54 pm Taurus
30th 7:53 pm Gemini

March 1953
2nd 11:41 am Libra
4th 11:31 pm Scorpio
7th 9:20 am Sagittarius
9th 4:10 pm Capricorn
11th 7:37 pm Aquarius
13th 8:17 pm Pisces
15th 7:39 pm Aries
17th 7:45 pm Taurus
19th 10:35 pm Gemini
22nd 5:29 am Cancer
24th 4:13 pm Leo
27th 5:04 am Virgo
29th 5:51 pm Libra

December 1951
2nd 3:45 pm Aquarius
4th 6:08 pm Pisces
6th 11:18 pm Aries
9th 7:04 am Taurus
11th 4:54 pm Gemini
14th 4:22 am Cancer
16th 5:04 pm Leo
19th 5:52 am Virgo
21st 4:40 pm Libra
23rd 11:38 pm Scorpio
26th 2:27 am Sagittarius
28th 2:24 am Capricorn
30th 1:36 am Aquarius

April 1952
1st 7:38 am Cancer
3rd 8:09 pm Leo
6th 8:40 am Virgo
8th 6:56 pm Libra
11th 2:13 am Scorpio
13th 7:08 am Sagittarius
15th 10:42 am Capricorn
17th 1:43 pm Aquarius
19th 4:40 pm Pisces
21st 7:56 pm Aries
24th 12:15 am Taurus
26th 6:40 am Gemini
28th 4:05 pm Cancer

August 1952
2nd 10:27 pm Capricorn
4th 10:41 pm Aquarius
6th 10:05 pm Pisces
8th 10:33 pm Aries
11th 1:46 am Taurus
13th 8:36 am Gemini
15th 6:52 pm Cancer
18th 7:18 am Leo
20th 8:22 pm Virgo
23rd 8:41 am Libra
25th 7:10 pm Scorpio
28th 2:53 am Sagittarius
30th 7:24 am Capricorn

December 1952
3rd 3:09 am Cancer
5th 1:22 pm Leo
8th 1:57 am Virgo
10th 2:34 pm Libra
13th 12:39 am Scorpio
15th 6:59 am Sagittarius
17th 10:18 am Capricorn
19th 12:04 pm Aquarius
21st 1:46 pm Pisces
23rd 4:30 pm Aries
25th 8:46 pm Taurus
28th 2:48 am Gemini
30th 10:53 am Cancer

April 1953
1st 5:19 am Scorpio
3rd 2:58 pm Sagittarius
5th 10:29 pm Capricorn
8th 3:27 am Aquarius
10th 5:49 am Pisces
12th 6:20 am Aries
14th 6:32 am Taurus
16th 8:27 am Gemini
18th 1:22 pm Cancer
20th 11:27 pm Leo
23rd 11:52 am Virgo
26th 12:40 am Libra
28th 11:52 am Scorpio
30th 8:52 pm Sagittarius

May 1953
3rd 3:55 am Capricorn
5th 9:12 am Aquarius
7th 12:46 pm Pisces
9th 2:49 pm Aries
11th 4:13 pm Taurus
13th 6:27 pm Gemini
15th 11:16 pm Cancer
18th 7:47 am Leo
20th 7:30 pm Virgo
23rd 8:15 am Libra
25th 7:32 pm Scorpio
28th 4:08 am Sagittarius
30th 10:17 am Capricorn

June 1953
1st 2:45 pm Aquarius
3rd 6:12 pm Pisces
5th 9:01 pm Aries
7th 11:41 pm Taurus
10th 3:04 am Gemini
12th 8:17 am Cancer
14th 4:27 pm Leo
17th 3:36 am Virgo
19th 4:16 pm Libra
22nd 3:57 am Scorpio
24th 12:47 pm Sagittarius
26th 6:29 pm Capricorn
28th 9:52 pm Aquarius

July 1953
1st 12:08 am Pisces
3rd 2:24 am Aries
5th 5:23 am Taurus
7th 9:42 am Gemini
9th 3:54 pm Cancer
12th 12:28 am Leo
14th 11:28 am Virgo
17th 12:04 am Libra
19th 12:16 pm Scorpio
21st 9:59 pm Sagittarius
24th 4:07 am Capricorn
26th 7:04 am Aquarius
28th 8:07 am Pisces
30th 8:56 am Aries

August 1953
1st 10:57 am Taurus
3rd 3:10 pm Gemini
5th 9:59 pm Cancer
8th 7:16 am Leo
10th 6:33 pm Virgo
13th 7:08 am Libra
15th 7:43 pm Scorpio
18th 6:29 am Sagittarius
20th 1:53 pm Capricorn
22nd 5:29 pm Aquarius
24th 6:12 pm Pisces
26th 5:47 pm Aries
28th 6:10 pm Taurus
30th 9:07 pm Gemini

September 1953
2nd 3:30 am Cancer
4th 1:04 pm Leo
7th 12:47 am Virgo
9th 1:27 pm Libra
12th 2:05 am Scorpio
14th 1:31 pm Sagittarius
16th 10:21 pm Capricorn
19th 3:30 am Aquarius
21st 5:07 am Pisces
23rd 4:31 am Aries
25th 3:45 am Taurus
27th 5:01 am Gemini
29th 9:56 am Cancer

October 1953
1st 6:53 pm Leo
4th 6:40 am Virgo
6th 7:28 pm Libra
9th 7:56 am Scorpio
11th 7:19 pm Sagittarius
14th 4:51 am Capricorn
16th 11:34 am Aquarius
18th 2:55 pm Pisces
20th 3:28 pm Aries
22nd 2:48 pm Taurus
24th 3:05 pm Gemini
26th 6:24 pm Cancer
29th 1:55 am Leo
31st 1:04 pm Virgo

November 1953
3rd 1:51 am Libra
5th 2:12 pm Scorpio
8th 1:06 am Sagittarius
10th 10:18 am Capricorn
12th 5:30 pm Aquarius
14th 10:17 pm Pisces
17th 12:35 am Aries
19th 1:15 am Taurus
21st 1:55 am Gemini
23rd 4:32 am Cancer
25th 10:40 am Leo
27th 8:40 pm Virgo
30th 9:05 am Libra

December 1953
2nd 9:30 pm Scorpio
5th 8:09 am Sagittarius
7th 4:33 pm Capricorn
9th 10:59 pm Aquarius
12th 3:46 am Pisces
14th 7:06 am Aries
16th 9:23 am Taurus
18th 11:28 am Gemini
20th 2:40 pm Cancer
22nd 8:23 pm Leo
25th 5:24 am Virgo
27th 5:10 pm Libra
30th 5:43 am Scorpio

January 1954
1st 4:39 pm Sagittarius
4th 12:45 am Capricorn
6th 6:09 am Aquarius
8th 9:43 am Pisces
10th 12:27 pm Aries
12th 3:10 pm Taurus
14th 6:29 pm Gemini
16th 11:01 pm Cancer
19th 5:24 am Leo
21st 2:14 pm Virgo
24th 1:30 am Libra
26th 2:04 pm Scorpio
29th 1:42 am Sagittarius
31st 10:26 am Capricorn

February 1954
2nd 3:38 pm Aquarius
4th 6:04 pm Pisces
6th 7:15 pm Aries
8th 8:47 pm Taurus
10th 11:54 pm Gemini
13th 5:10 am Cancer
15th 12:35 pm Leo
17th 10:00 pm Virgo
20th 9:14 am Libra
22nd 9:43 pm Scorpio
25th 9:59 am Sagittarius
27th 7:57 pm Capricorn

March 1954
2nd 2:07 am Aquarius
4th 4:33 am Pisces
6th 4:40 am Aries
8th 4:33 am Taurus
10th 6:06 am Gemini
12th 10:37 am Cancer
14th 6:16 pm Leo
17th 4:21 am Virgo
19th 3:57 pm Libra
22nd 4:26 am Scorpio
24th 4:56 pm Sagittarius
27th 3:55 am Capricorn
29th 11:37 am Aquarius
31st 3:17 pm Pisces

April 1954
2nd 3:41 pm Aries
4th 2:44 pm Taurus
6th 2:40 pm Gemini
8th 5:28 pm Cancer
11th 12:05 am Leo
13th 10:02 am Virgo
15th 9:57 pm Libra
18th 10:32 am Scorpio
20th 10:55 pm Sagittarius
23rd 10:11 am Capricorn
25th 7:02 pm Aquarius
28th 12:21 am Pisces
30th 2:09 am Aries

May 1954
2nd 1:43 am Taurus
4th 1:06 am Gemini
6th 2:30 am Cancer
8th 7:28 am Leo
10th 4:22 pm Virgo
13th 4:04 am Libra
15th 4:42 pm Scorpio
18th 4:53 am Sagittarius
20th 3:49 pm Capricorn
23rd 12:48 am Aquarius
25th 7:08 am Pisces
27th 10:32 am Aries
29th 11:34 am Taurus
31st 11:41 am Gemini

June 1954
2nd 12:46 pm Cancer
4th 4:34 pm Leo
7th 12:06 am Virgo
9th 10:58 am Libra
11th 11:29 pm Scorpio
14th 11:37 am Sagittarius
16th 10:05 pm Capricorn
19th 6:26 am Aquarius
21st 12:37 pm Pisces
23rd 4:44 pm Aries
25th 7:09 pm Taurus
27th 8:42 pm Gemini
29th 10:36 pm Cancer

July 1954
2nd 2:16 am Leo
4th 8:56 am Virgo
6th 6:53 pm Libra
9th 7:04 am Scorpio
11th 7:18 pm Sagittarius
14th 5:40 am Capricorn
16th 1:19 pm Aquarius
18th 6:33 pm Pisces
20th 10:07 pm Aries
23rd 12:52 am Taurus
25th 3:30 am Gemini
27th 6:41 am Cancer
29th 11:11 am Leo
31st 5:50 pm Virgo

August 1954
3rd 3:14 am Libra
5th 3:02 pm Scorpio
8th 3:32 am Sagittarius
10th 2:20 pm Capricorn
12th 9:54 pm Aquarius
15th 2:17 am Pisces
17th 4:38 am Aries
19th 6:26 am Taurus
21st 8:56 am Gemini
23rd 12:50 pm Cancer
25th 6:22 pm Leo
28th 1:44 am Virgo
30th 11:12 am Libra

September 1954
1st 10:48 pm Scorpio
4th 11:32 am Sagittarius
6th 11:10 pm Capricorn
9th 7:31 am Aquarius
11th 11:55 pm Pisces
13th 1:23 pm Aries
15th 1:45 pm Taurus
17th 2:55 pm Gemini
19th 6:13 pm Cancer
22nd 12:04 am Leo
24th 8:10 am Virgo
26th 6:11 pm Libra
29th 5:52 am Scorpio

October 1954
1st 6:41 pm Sagittarius
4th 7:04 am Capricorn
6th 4:45 pm Aquarius
8th 10:17 pm Pisces
10th 11:58 pm Aries
12th 11:32 pm Taurus
14th 11:10 pm Gemini
17th 12:50 am Cancer
19th 5:41 am Leo
21st 1:44 pm Virgo
24th 12:12 am Libra
26th 12:10 pm Scorpio
29th 12:59 am Sagittarius
31st 1:36 pm Capricorn

November 1954
3rd 12:22 am Aquarius
5th 7:34 am Pisces
7th 10:43 am Aries
9th 10:49 am Taurus
11th 9:51 am Gemini
13th 9:59 am Cancer
15th 1:04 pm Leo
17th 7:52 pm Virgo
20th 6:02 am Libra
22nd 6:13 pm Scorpio
25th 7:01 am Sagittarius
27th 7:24 pm Capricorn
30th 6:19 am Aquarius

December 1954
2nd 2:38 pm Pisces
4th 7:35 pm Aries
6th 9:23 pm Taurus
8th 9:17 pm Gemini
10th 9:07 pm Cancer
12th 10:48 pm Leo
15th 3:54 am Virgo
17th 12:51 pm Libra
20th 12:43 am Scorpio
22nd 1:34 pm Sagittarius
25th 1:40 am Capricorn
27th 12:00 pm Aquarius
29th 8:09 pm Pisces

January 1955
1st 1:56 am Aries
3rd 5:24 am Taurus
5th 7:05 am Gemini
7th 8:01 am Cancer
9th 9:42 am Leo
11th 1:43 pm Virgo
13th 9:15 pm Libra
16th 8:14 am Scorpio
18th 9:01 pm Sagittarius
21st 9:09 am Capricorn
23rd 6:58 pm Aquarius
26th 2:11 am Pisces
28th 7:20 am Aries
30th 11:06 am Taurus

February 1955
1st 2:04 pm Gemini
3rd 4:36 pm Cancer
5th 7:29 pm Leo
7th 11:43 pm Virgo
10th 6:33 am Libra
12th 4:38 pm Scorpio
15th 5:07 am Sagittarius
17th 5:34 pm Capricorn
20th 3:33 am Aquarius
22nd 10:10 am Pisces
24th 2:07 pm Aries
26th 4:47 pm Taurus
28th 7:24 pm Gemini

March 1955
2nd 10:40 pm Cancer
5th 2:49 am Leo
7th 8:09 am Virgo
9th 3:20 pm Libra
12th 1:04 am Scorpio
14th 1:12 pm Sagittarius
17th 2:01 am Capricorn
19th 12:46 pm Aquarius
21st 7:45 pm Pisces
23rd 11:09 pm Aries
26th 12:31 am Taurus
28th 1:42 am Gemini
30th 4:05 am Cancer

April 1955
1st 8:20 am Leo
3rd 2:31 pm Virgo
5th 10:34 pm Libra
8th 8:38 am Scorpio
10th 8:41 pm Sagittarius
13th 9:40 am Capricorn
15th 9:19 pm Aquarius
18th 5:28 am Pisces
20th 9:30 am Aries
22nd 10:30 am Taurus
24th 10:24 am Gemini
26th 11:09 am Cancer
28th 2:08 pm Leo
30th 7:57 pm Virgo

May 1955
3rd 4:26 am Libra
5th 3:04 pm Scorpio
8th 3:18 am Sagittarius
10th 4:18 pm Capricorn
13th 4:29 am Aquarius
15th 1:53 pm Pisces
17th 7:21 pm Aries
19th 9:12 pm Taurus
21st 8:57 pm Gemini
23rd 8:33 pm Cancer
25th 9:53 pm Leo
28th 2:16 am Virgo
30th 10:07 am Libra

June 1955
1st 8:53 pm Scorpio
4th 9:23 am Sagittarius
6th 10:21 pm Capricorn
9th 10:29 am Aquarius
11th 8:32 pm Pisces
14th 3:24 am Aries
16th 6:50 am Taurus
18th 7:37 am Gemini
20th 7:16 am Cancer
22nd 7:37 am Leo
24th 10:26 am Virgo
26th 4:55 pm Libra
29th 3:04 am Scorpio

July 1955
1st 3:34 pm Sagittarius
4th 4:29 am Capricorn
6th 4:18 pm Aquarius
9th 2:08 am Pisces
11th 9:33 am Aries
13th 2:20 pm Taurus
15th 4:43 pm Gemini
17th 5:30 pm Cancer
19th 6:04 pm Leo
21st 8:06 pm Virgo
24th 1:16 am Libra
26th 10:18 am Scorpio
28th 10:24 pm Sagittarius
31th 11:18 am Capricorn

August 1955
2nd 10:52 pm Aquarius
5th 8:04 am Pisces
7th 2:59 pm Aries
9th 8:04 pm Taurus
11th 11:33 pm Gemini
14th 1:50 am Cancer
16th 3:34 am Leo
18th 5:58 am Virgo
20th 10:34 am Libra
22nd 6:37 pm Scorpio
25th 6:04 am Sagittarius
27th 6:56 pm Capricorn
30th 6:35 am Aquarius

September 1955
1st 3:23 pm Pisces
3rd 9:24 pm Aries
6th 1:36 am Taurus
8th 4:58 am Gemini
10th 8:01 am Cancer
12th 11:02 am Leo
14th 2:33 pm Virgo
16th 7:35 pm Libra
19th 3:18 am Scorpio
21st 2:11 pm Sagittarius
24th 3:01 am Capricorn
26th 3:07 pm Aquarius
29th 12:12 am Pisces

October 1955
1st 5:47 am Aries
3rd 8:52 am Taurus
5th 10:59 am Gemini
7th 1:23 pm Cancer
9th 4:41 pm Leo
11th 9:11 pm Virgo
14th 3:13 am Libra
16th 11:23 am Scorpio
18th 10:07 pm Sagittarius
21st 10:51 am Capricorn
23rd 11:33 pm Aquarius
26th 9:37 am Pisces
28th 3:46 pm Aries
30th 6:30 pm Taurus

November 1955
1st 7:23 pm Gemini
3rd 8:11 pm Cancer
5th 10:20 pm Leo
8th 2:36 am Virgo
10th 9:15 am Libra
12th 6:12 pm Scorpio
15th 5:17 am Sagittarius
17th 5:59 pm Capricorn
20th 6:58 am Aquarius
22nd 6:10 pm Pisces
25th 1:47 am Aries
27th 5:27 am Taurus
29th 6:11 am Gemini

December 1955
1st 5:47 am Cancer
3rd 6:07 am Leo
5th 8:50 am Virgo
7th 2:48 pm Libra
9th 11:59 pm Scorpio
12th 11:33 am Sagittarius
15th 12:23 am Capricorn
17th 1:19 pm Aquarius
20th 1:02 am Pisces
22nd 10:05 am Aries
24th 3:33 pm Taurus
26th 5:33 pm Gemini
28th 5:18 pm Cancer
30th 4:37 pm Leo

January 1956
1st 5:31 pm Virgo
3rd 9:44 pm Libra
6th 5:59 am Scorpio
8th 5:32 pm Sagittarius
11th 6:33 am Capricorn
13th 7:19 pm Aquarius
16th 6:47 am Pisces
18th 4:17 pm Aries
20th 11:11 pm Taurus
23rd 3:06 am Gemini
25th 4:20 am Cancer
27th 4:07 am Leo
29th 4:18 am Virgo
31th 6:56 am Libra

February 1956
2nd 1:32 pm Scorpio
5th 12:13 am Sagittarius
7th 1:08 pm Capricorn
10th 1:52 am Aquarius
12th 12:52 pm Pisces
14th 9:48 pm Aries
17th 4:48 am Taurus
19th 9:50 am Gemini
21st 12:50 pm Cancer
23rd 2:11 pm Leo
25th 3:06 pm Virgo
27th 5:21 pm Libra
29th 10:45 pm Scorpio

March 1956
3rd 8:09 am Sagittarius
5th 8:32 pm Capricorn
8th 9:19 am Aquarius
10th 8:11 pm Pisces
13th 4:26 am Aries
15th 10:32 am Taurus
17th 3:12 pm Gemini
19th 6:47 pm Cancer
21st 9:31 pm Leo
23rd 11:53 pm Virgo
26th 2:59 am Libra
28th 8:19 am Scorpio
30th 4:55 pm Sagittarius

April 1956
2nd 4:37 am Capricorn
4th 5:24 pm Aquarius
7th 4:37 am Pisces
9th 12:47 pm Aries
11th 6:04 pm Taurus
13th 9:31 pm Gemini
16th 12:15 am Cancer
18th 3:00 am Leo
20th 6:17 am Virgo
22nd 10:36 am Libra
24th 4:44 pm Scorpio
27th 1:25 am Sagittarius
29th 12:44 pm Capricorn

May 1956
2nd 1:27 am Aquarius
4th 1:15 pm Pisces
6th 10:05 pm Aries
9th 3:24 am Taurus
11th 6:01 am Gemini
13th 7:21 am Cancer
15th 8:52 am Leo
17th 11:40 am Virgo
19th 4:25 pm Libra
21st 11:26 pm Scorpio
24th 8:46 am Sagittarius
26th 8:11 pm Capricorn
29th 8:51 am Aquarius
31th 9:09 pm Pisces

June 1956
3rd 7:04 am Aries
5th 1:22 pm Taurus
7th 4:10 pm Gemini
9th 4:43 pm Cancer
11th 4:45 pm Leo
13th 6:04 pm Virgo
15th 9:58 pm Libra
18th 5:04 am Scorpio
20th 2:55 pm Sagittarius
23rd 2:43 am Capricorn
25th 3:25 pm Aquarius
28th 3:54 am Pisces
30th 2:42 pm Aries

July 1956
2nd 10:25 pm Taurus
5th 2:26 am Gemini
7th 3:20 am Cancer
9th 2:42 am Leo
11th 2:34 am Virgo
13th 4:54 am Libra
15th 10:56 am Scorpio
17th 8:37 pm Sagittarius
20th 8:40 am Capricorn
22nd 9:28 pm Aquarius
25th 9:50 am Pisces
27th 8:53 pm Aries
30th 5:40 am Taurus

August 1956
1st 11:16 am Gemini
3rd 1:33 pm Cancer
5th 1:28 pm Leo
7th 12:51 pm Virgo
9th 1:51 pm Libra
11th 6:20 pm Scorpio
14th 2:59 am Sagittarius
16th 2:47 pm Capricorn
19th 3:37 am Aquarius
21st 3:47 pm Pisces
24th 2:29 am Aries
26th 11:23 am Taurus
28th 5:59 pm Gemini
30th 9:51 pm Cancer

September 1956
1st 11:14 pm Leo
3rd 11:20 pm Virgo
6th 12:04 am Libra
8th 3:26 am Scorpio
10th 10:45 am Sagittarius
12th 9:45 pm Capricorn
15th 10:27 am Aquarius
17th 10:33 pm Pisces
20th 8:47 am Aries
22nd 5:01 pm Taurus
24th 11:25 pm Gemini
27th 3:59 am Cancer
29th 6:49 am Leo

October 1956
1st 8:25 am Virgo
3rd 10:02 am Libra
5th 1:19 pm Scorpio
7th 7:46 pm Sagittarius
10th 5:47 am Capricorn
12th 6:09 pm Aquarius
15th 6:24 am Pisces
17th 4:35 pm Aries
20th 12:07 am Taurus
22nd 5:29 am Gemini
24th 9:23 am Cancer
26th 12:27 pm Leo
28th 3:10 pm Virgo
30th 6:10 pm Libra

November 1956
1st 10:24 pm Scorpio
4th 4:56 am Sagittarius
6th 2:24 pm Capricorn
9th 2:19 am Aquarius
11th 2:50 pm Pisces
14th 1:36 am Aries
16th 9:12 am Taurus
18th 1:45 pm Gemini
20th 4:18 pm Cancer
22nd 6:10 pm Leo
24th 8:32 pm Virgo
27th 12:11 am Libra
29th 5:34 am Scorpio

December 1956
1st 12:59 pm Sagittarius
3rd 10:36 pm Capricorn
6th 10:16 am Aquarius
8th 10:57 pm Pisces
11th 10:36 am Aries
13th 7:15 pm Taurus
16th 12:06 am Gemini
18th 1:52 am Cancer
20th 2:11 am Leo
22nd 2:56 am Virgo
24th 5:39 am Libra
26th 11:08 am Scorpio
28th 7:20 pm Sagittarius
31st 5:37 am Capricorn

January 1957
2nd 5:24 pm Aquarius
5th 6:04 am Pisces
7th 6:22 pm Aries
10th 4:26 am Taurus
12th 10:44 am Gemini
14th 1:06 pm Cancer
16th 12:51 pm Leo
18th 12:04 pm Virgo
20th 12:55 pm Libra
22nd 5:02 pm Scorpio
25th 12:52 am Sagittarius
27th 11:32 am Capricorn
29th 11:42 pm Aquarius

February 1957
1st 12:20 pm Pisces
4th 12:42 am Aries
6th 11:37 am Taurus
8th 7:34 pm Gemini
10th 11:39 pm Cancer
13th 12:19 am Leo
14th 11:17 pm Virgo
16th 10:50 pm Libra
19th 1:06 am Scorpio
21st 7:22 am Sagittarius
23rd 5:26 pm Capricorn
26th 5:42 am Aquarius
28th 6:25 pm Pisces

March 1957
3rd 6:31 am Aries
5th 5:20 pm Taurus
8th 2:04 am Gemini
10th 7:45 am Cancer
12th 10:12 am Leo
14th 10:21 am Virgo
16th 9:59 am Libra
18th 11:15 am Scorpio
20th 3:53 pm Sagittarius
23rd 12:34 am Capricorn
25th 12:17 pm Aquarius
28th 12:59 am Pisces
30th 12:54 pm Aries

April 1957
1st 11:11 pm Taurus
4th 7:30 am Gemini
6th 1:37 pm Cancer
8th 5:24 pm Leo
10th 7:13 pm Virgo
12th 8:09 pm Libra
14th 9:45 pm Scorpio
17th 1:43 am Sagittarius
19th 9:08 am Capricorn
21st 7:53 pm Aquarius
24th 8:22 am Pisces
26th 8:22 pm Aries
29th 6:18 am Taurus

May 1957
1st 1:47 pm Gemini
3rd 7:08 pm Cancer
5th 10:54 pm Leo
8th 1:37 am Virgo
10th 3:57 am Libra
12th 6:48 am Scorpio
14th 11:14 am Sagittarius
16th 6:13 pm Capricorn
19th 4:12 am Aquarius
21st 4:20 pm Pisces
24th 4:34 am Aries
26th 2:43 pm Taurus
28th 9:47 pm Gemini
31st 2:06 am Cancer

June 1957
2nd 4:45 am Leo
4th 6:59 am Virgo
6th 9:46 am Libra
8th 1:41 pm Scorpio
10th 7:09 pm Sagittarius
13th 2:36 am Capricorn
15th 12:23 pm Aquarius
18th 12:15 am Pisces
20th 12:45 pm Aries
22nd 11:38 pm Taurus
25th 7:07 am Gemini
27th 11:01 am Cancer
29th 12:32 pm Leo

July 1957
1st 1:24 pm Virgo
3rd 3:16 pm Libra
5th 7:10 pm Scorpio
8th 1:20 am Sagittarius
10th 9:35 am Capricorn
12th 7:43 pm Aquarius
15th 7:32 am Pisces
17th 8:14 pm Aries
20th 7:57 am Taurus
22nd 4:33 pm Gemini
24th 9:05 pm Cancer
26th 10:17 pm Leo
28th 9:59 pm Virgo
30th 10:20 pm Libra

August 1957
2nd 1:00 am Scorpio
4th 6:47 am Sagittarius
6th 3:23 pm Capricorn
9th 2:01 am Aquarius
11th 2:02 pm Pisces
14th 2:46 am Aries
16th 2:59 pm Taurus
19th 12:51 am Gemini
21st 6:48 am Cancer
23rd 8:52 am Leo
25th 8:27 am Virgo
27th 7:42 am Libra
29th 8:46 am Scorpio
31st 1:07 pm Sagittarius

September 1957
2nd 9:05 pm Capricorn
5th 7:50 am Aquarius
7th 8:04 pm Pisces
10th 8:45 am Aries
12th 8:57 pm Taurus
15th 7:26 am Gemini
17th 2:49 pm Cancer
19th 6:31 pm Leo
21st 7:12 pm Virgo
23rd 6:33 pm Libra
25th 6:41 pm Scorpio
27th 9:27 pm Sagittarius
30th 3:59 am Capricorn

October 1957
2nd 2:04 pm Aquarius
5th 2:17 am Pisces
7th 2:57 pm Aries
10th 2:48 am Taurus
12th 1:00 pm Gemini
14th 8:54 pm Cancer
17th 1:59 am Leo
19th 4:24 am Virgo
21st 5:04 am Libra
23rd 5:31 am Scorpio
25th 7:33 am Sagittarius
27th 12:41 pm Capricorn
29th 9:32 pm Aquarius

November 1957
1st 9:18 am Pisces
3rd 9:59 pm Aries
6th 9:38 am Taurus
8th 7:09 pm Gemini
11th 2:24 am Cancer
13th 7:36 am Leo
15th 11:07 am Virgo
17th 1:26 pm Libra
19th 3:18 pm Scorpio
21st 5:52 pm Sagittarius
23rd 10:29 pm Capricorn
26th 6:16 am Aquarius
28th 5:15 pm Pisces

December 1957
1st 5:56 am Aries
3rd 5:47 pm Taurus
6th 3:00 am Gemini
8th 9:16 am Cancer
10th 1:24 pm Leo
12th 4:29 pm Virgo
14th 7:23 pm Libra
16th 10:35 pm Scorpio
19th 2:31 am Sagittarius
21st 7:47 am Capricorn
23rd 3:19 pm Aquarius
26th 1:41 am Pisces
28th 2:12 pm Aries
31st 2:37 am Taurus

January 1958
2nd 12:21 pm Gemini
4th 6:22 pm Cancer
6th 9:22 pm Leo
8th 10:59 pm Virgo
11th 12:52 am Libra
13th 4:02 am Scorpio
15th 8:49 am Sagittarius
17th 3:13 pm Capricorn
19th 11:22 pm Aquarius
22nd 9:41 am Pisces
24th 10:04 pm Aries
27th 10:56 am Taurus
29th 9:47 pm Gemini

February 1958
1st 4:41 am Cancer
3rd 7:38 am Leo
5th 8:11 am Virgo
7th 8:24 am Libra
9th 10:04 am Scorpio
11th 2:11 pm Sagittarius
13th 8:55 pm Capricorn
16th 5:51 am Aquarius
18th 4:39 pm Pisces
21st 5:02 am Aries
23rd 6:04 pm Taurus
26th 5:52 am Gemini
28th 2:16 pm Cancer

March 1958
2nd 6:27 pm Leo
4th 7:16 pm Virgo
6th 6:36 pm Libra
8th 6:35 pm Scorpio
10th 8:56 pm Sagittarius
13th 2:36 am Capricorn
15th 11:28 am Aquarius
17th 10:41 pm Pisces
20th 11:17 am Aries
23rd 12:16 am Taurus
25th 12:19 pm Gemini
27th 9:53 pm Cancer
30th 3:45 am Leo

April 1958
1st 6:01 am Virgo
3rd 5:54 am Libra
5th 5:17 am Scorpio
7th 6:07 am Sagittarius
9th 10:00 am Capricorn
11th 5:41 pm Aquarius
14th 4:38 am Pisces
16th 5:22 pm Aries
19th 6:16 am Taurus
21st 6:04 pm Gemini
24th 3:46 am Cancer
26th 10:43 am Leo
28th 2:41 pm Virgo
30th 4:07 pm Libra

May 1958	June 1958	July 1958	August 1958
2nd 4:15 pm Scorpio	1st 2:54 am Sagittarius	2nd 7:45 pm Aquarius	1st 12:11 pm Pisces
4th 4:44 pm Sagittarius	3rd 5:23 am Capricorn	5th 3:57 am Pisces	3rd 11:14 pm Aries
6th 7:21 pm Capricorn	5th 10:34 am Aquarius	7th 3:17 am Aries	6th 12:04 pm Taurus
9th 1:29 am Aquarius	7th 7:23 pm Pisces	10th 4:09 am Taurus	9th 12:16 am Gemini
11th 11:26 am Pisces	10th 7:20 am Aries	12th 3:46 pm Gemini	11th 9:25 am Cancer
13th 11:58 pm Aries	12th 8:12 pm Taurus	15th 12:15 am Cancer	13th 2:44 pm Leo
16th 12:49 pm Taurus	15th 7:31 am Gemini	17th 5:31 am Leo	15th 5:07 pm Virgo
19th 12:14 am Gemini	17th 4:04 pm Cancer	19th 8:42 am Virgo	17th 6:17 pm Libra
21st 9:23 am Cancer	19th 10:04 pm Leo	21st 11:12 am Libra	19th 7:50 pm Scorpio
23rd 4:14 pm Leo	22nd 2:22 am Virgo	23rd 1:57 pm Scorpio	21st 10:48 pm Sagittarius
25th 8:59 pm Virgo	24th 5:42 am Libra	25th 5:26 pm Sagittarius	24th 3:38 am Capricorn
27th 11:55 pm Libra	26th 8:31 am Scorpio	27th 9:53 pm Capricorn	26th 10:28 am Aquarius
30th 1:33 am Scorpio	28th 11:12 am Sagittarius	30th 3:52 am Aquarius	28th 7:25 pm Pisces
	30th 2:33 pm Capricorn		31st 6:35 am Aries

September 1958	October 1958	November 1958	December 1958
2nd 7:23 pm Taurus	2nd 2:50 pm Gemini	1st 8:08 am Cancer	3rd 5:18 am Virgo
5th 8:06 am Gemini	5th 1:59 am Cancer	3rd 5:02 pm Leo	5th 9:31 am Libra
7th 6:22 pm Cancer	7th 9:50 am Leo	5th 10:45 pm Virgo	7th 11:28 am Scorpio
10th 12:42 am Leo	9th 1:50 pm Virgo	8th 1:16 am Libra	9th 12:02 pm Sagittarius
12th 3:20 am Virgo	11th 2:44 pm Libra	10th 1:30 am Scorpio	11th 12:47 pm Capricorn
14th 3:45 am Libra	13th 2:12 pm Scorpio	12th 1:04 am Sagittarius	13th 3:38 pm Aquarius
16th 3:50 am Scorpio	15th 2:09 pm Sagittarius	14th 1:54 am Capricorn	15th 10:12 pm Pisces
18th 5:16 am Sagittarius	17th 4:23 pm Capricorn	16th 5:53 am Aquarius	18th 8:45 am Aries
20th 9:12 am Capricorn	19th 10:04 pm Aquarius	18th 1:56 pm Pisces	20th 9:37 pm Taurus
22nd 4:04 pm Aquarius	22nd 7:19 am Pisces	21st 1:28 am Aries	23rd 10:09 am Gemini
25th 1:33 am Pisces	24th 7:10 pm Aries	23rd 2:30 pm Taurus	25th 8:33 pm Cancer
27th 1:07 pm Aries	27th 8:07 am Taurus	26th 3:00 am Gemini	28th 4:33 am Leo
30th 1:58 am Taurus	29th 8:49 pm Gemini	28th 1:51 pm Cancer	30th 10:41 am Virgo
		30th 10:41 pm Leo	

January 1959	February 1959	March 1959	April 1959
1st 3:21 pm Libra	2nd 3:11 am Sagittarius	1st 8:33 am Sagittarius	1st 10:41 pm Aquarius
3rd 6:42 pm Scorpio	4th 6:29 am Capricorn	3rd 12:06 pm Capricorn	4th 6:23 am Pisces
5th 8:56 pm Sagittarius	6th 10:41 am Aquarius	5th 5:16 pm Aquarius	6th 4:32 pm Aries
7th 10:50 pm Capricorn	8th 4:50 pm Pisces	8th 12:25 am Pisces	9th 4:32 am Taurus
10th 1:52 am Aquarius	11th 1:54 am Aries	10th 9:53 am Aries	11th 5:24 pm Gemini
12th 7:39 am Pisces	13th 1:46 pm Taurus	12th 9:36 pm Taurus	14th 5:47 am Cancer
14th 5:09 pm Aries	16th 2:39 am Gemini	15th 10:30 am Gemini	16th 3:54 pm Leo
17th 5:32 am Taurus	18th 1:50 pm Cancer	17th 10:28 pm Cancer	18th 10:27 pm Virgo
19th 6:15 pm Gemini	20th 9:38 pm Leo	20th 7:22 am Leo	21st 1:19 am Libra
22nd 4:47 am Cancer	23rd 2:06 am Virgo	22nd 12:28 pm Virgo	23rd 1:34 am Scorpio
24th 12:13 pm Leo	25th 4:29 am Libra	24th 2:28 pm Libra	25th 12:59 am Sagittarius
26th 5:14 pm Virgo	27th 6:15 am Scorpio	26th 2:54 pm Scorpio	27th 1:32 am Capricorn
28th 8:54 pm Libra		28th 3:32 pm Sagittarius	29th 4:55 am Aquarius
31st 12:05 am Scorpio		30th 5:49 pm Capricorn	

May 1959	June 1959	July 1959	August 1959
1st 11:58 am Pisces	2nd 4:36 pm Taurus	2nd 12:05 pm Gemini	1st 7:23 am Cancer
3rd 10:19 pm Aries	5th 5:35 am Gemini	5th 12:04 am Cancer	3rd 5:09 pm Leo
6th 10:39 am Taurus	7th 5:43 pm Cancer	7th 10:08 am Leo	6th 12:29 am Virgo
8th 11:34 pm Gemini	10th 4:19 am Leo	9th 6:15 pm Virgo	8th 5:56 am Libra
11th 11:56 am Cancer	12th 12:50 pm Virgo	12th 12:26 am Libra	10th 9:59 am Scorpio
13th 10:40 pm Leo	14th 6:42 pm Libra	14th 4:33 am Scorpio	12th 12:58 pm Sagittarius
16th 6:37 am Virgo	16th 9:38 pm Scorpio	16th 6:42 am Sagittarius	14th 3:19 pm Capricorn
18th 11:06 am Libra	18th 10:15 pm Sagittarius	18th 7:42 am Capricorn	16th 5:54 pm Aquarius
20th 12:25 pm Scorpio	20th 10:02 pm Capricorn	20th 9:05 am Aquarius	18th 9:59 pm Pisces
22nd 11:52 am Sagittarius	22nd 11:01 pm Aquarius	22nd 12:41 pm Pisces	21st 4:51 am Aries
24th 11:25 am Capricorn	25th 3:09 am Pisces	24th 7:53 pm Aries	23rd 2:58 pm Taurus
26th 1:09 pm Aquarius	27th 11:27 am Aries	27th 6:43 am Taurus	26th 3:18 am Gemini
28th 6:42 pm Pisces	29th 11:11 pm Taurus	29th 7:23 pm Gemini	28th 3:33 pm Cancer
31st 4:18 am Aries			31st 1:33 am Leo

September 1959	October 1959	November 1959	December 1959
2nd 8:31 am Virgo	1st 10:08 pm Libra	2nd 10:04 am Sagittarius	1st 8:11 pm Capricorn
4th 12:57 pm Libra	3rd 11:54 pm Scorpio	4th 10:05 am Capricorn	3rd 8:35 pm Aquarius
6th 3:53 pm Scorpio	6th 12:54 am Sagittarius	6th 12:14 pm Aquarius	6th 12:16 am Pisces
8th 6:20 pm Sagittarius	8th 2:38 am Capricorn	8th 5:35 pm Pisces	8th 7:59 am Aries
10th 9:05 pm Capricorn	10th 6:12 am Aquarius	11th 2:10 am Aries	10th 6:55 pm Taurus
13th 12:43 am Aquarius	12th 12:06 pm Pisces	13th 1:04 pm Taurus	13th 7:24 am Gemini
15th 5:54 am Pisces	14th 8:20 pm Aries	16th 1:16 am Gemini	15th 8:00 pm Cancer
17th 1:16 pm Aries	17th 6:40 am Taurus	18th 1:56 pm Cancer	18th 7:57 am Leo
19th 11:12 pm Taurus	19th 6:40 pm Gemini	21st 2:04 am Leo	20th 6:29 pm Virgo
22nd 11:15 am Gemini	22nd 7:22 am Cancer	23rd 12:07 pm Virgo	23rd 2:28 am Libra
24th 11:49 pm Cancer	24th 7:04 pm Leo	25th 6:41 pm Libra	25th 7:01 am Scorpio
27th 10:36 am Leo	27th 3:48 am Virgo	27th 9:22 pm Scorpio	27th 8:16 am Sagittarius
29th 6:04 pm Virgo	29th 8:42 am Libra	29th 9:12 pm Sagittarius	29th 7:39 am Capricorn
	31th 10:15 am Scorpio		31st 7:15 am Aquarius

January 1960
2nd 9:19 am Pisces
4th 3:21 pm Aries
7th 1:22 am Taurus
9th 1:45 am Gemini
12th 2:23 am Cancer
14th 1:59 am Leo
17th 12:04 am Virgo
19th 8:14 am Libra
21st 1:59 pm Scorpio
23rd 5:04 pm Sagittarius
25th 6:00 pm Capricorn
27th 6:20 pm Aquarius
29th 7:57 pm Pisces

February 1960
1st 12:39 am Aries
3rd 9:15 am Taurus
5th 8:58 pm Gemini
8th 9:37 am Cancer
10th 9:08 pm Leo
13th 6:35 am Virgo
15th 1:55 pm Libra
17th 7:24 pm Scorpio
19th 11:12 pm Sagittarius
22nd 1:39 am Capricorn
24th 3:33 am Aquarius
26th 6:04 am Pisces
28th 10:38 am Aries

March 1960
1st 6:18 pm Taurus
4th 5:07 am Gemini
6th 5:36 pm Cancer
9th 5:25 am Leo
11th 2:47 pm Virgo
13th 9:20 pm Libra
16th 1:37 am Scorpio
18th 4:37 am Sagittarius
20th 7:14 am Capricorn
22nd 10:10 am Aquarius
24th 2:02 pm Pisces
26th 7:30 pm Aries
29th 3:13 am Taurus
31th 1:31 pm Gemini

April 1960
3rd 1:46 am Cancer
5th 2:00 pm Leo
8th 12:02 am Virgo
10th 6:36 am Libra
12th 10:02 am Scorpio
14th 11:38 am Sagittarius
16th 1:01 pm Capricorn
18th 3:32 pm Aquarius
20th 7:55 pm Pisces
23rd 2:23 am Aries
25th 10:50 am Taurus
27th 9:16 pm Gemini
30th 9:22 am Cancer

May 1960
2nd 9:58 pm Leo
5th 8:58 am Virgo
7th 4:30 pm Libra
9th 8:07 pm Scorpio
11th 8:55 pm Sagittarius
13th 8:51 pm Capricorn
15th 9:51 pm Aquarius
18th 1:23 am Pisces
20th 7:55 am Aries
22nd 4:59 pm Taurus
25th 3:55 am Gemini
27th 4:06 pm Cancer
30th 4:50 am Leo

June 1960
1st 4:37 pm Virgo
4th 1:31 am Libra
6th 6:20 am Scorpio
8th 7:32 am Sagittarius
10th 6:48 am Capricorn
12th 6:23 am Aquarius
14th 8:17 am Pisces
16th 1:42 pm Aries
18th 10:33 pm Taurus
21st 9:46 am Gemini
23rd 10:10 pm Cancer
26th 10:51 am Leo
28th 10:53 pm Virgo

July 1960
1st 8:46 am Libra
3rd 3:08 pm Scorpio
5th 5:43 pm Sagittarius
7th 5:35 pm Capricorn
9th 4:44 pm Aquarius
11th 5:19 pm Pisces
13th 9:07 pm Aries
16th 4:48 am Taurus
18th 3:40 pm Gemini
21st 4:09 am Cancer
23rd 4:45 pm Leo
26th 4:31 am Virgo
28th 2:33 pm Libra
30th 9:55 pm Scorpio

August 1960
2nd 2:04 am Sagittarius
4th 3:26 am Capricorn
6th 3:21 am Aquarius
8th 3:42 am Pisces
10th 6:21 am Aries
12th 12:35 pm Taurus
14th 10:29 pm Gemini
17th 10:42 am Cancer
19th 11:17 pm Leo
22nd 10:41 am Virgo
24th 8:09 pm Libra
27th 3:23 am Scorpio
29th 8:19 am Sagittarius
31th 11:09 am Capricorn

September 1960
2nd 12:36 pm Aquarius
4th 1:51 pm Pisces
6th 4:26 pm Aries
8th 9:44 pm Taurus
11th 6:31 am Gemini
13th 6:10 pm Cancer
16th 6:46 am Leo
18th 6:07 pm Virgo
21st 2:58 am Libra
23rd 9:18 am Scorpio
25th 1:42 pm Sagittarius
27th 4:54 pm Capricorn
29th 7:32 pm Aquarius

October 1960
1st 10:14 pm Pisces
4th 1:46 am Aries
6th 7:09 am Taurus
8th 3:16 pm Gemini
11th 2:18 am Cancer
13th 2:54 pm Leo
16th 3:40 am Virgo
18th 11:32 am Libra
20th 5:06 pm Scorpio
22nd 8:16 pm Sagittarius
24th 10:28 pm Capricorn
27th 12:57 am Aquarius
29th 4:26 am Pisces
31th 9:11 am Aries

November 1960
2nd 3:27 pm Taurus
4th 11:44 pm Gemini
7th 10:26 am Cancer
9th 10:59 pm Leo
12th 11:23 am Virgo
14th 9:07 pm Libra
17th 2:53 am Scorpio
19th 5:17 am Sagittarius
21st 6:02 am Capricorn
23rd 7:05 am Aquarius
25th 9:49 am Pisces
27th 2:50 pm Aries
29th 9:59 pm Taurus

December 1960
2nd 7:01 am Gemini
4th 5:52 pm Cancer
7th 6:21 am Leo
9th 7:13 pm Virgo
12th 6:10 am Libra
14th 1:13 pm Scorpio
16th 4:07 pm Sagittarius
18th 4:17 pm Capricorn
20th 3:49 pm Aquarius
22nd 4:47 pm Pisces
24th 8:34 pm Aries
27th 3:30 am Taurus
29th 1:01 pm Gemini

January 1961
1st 12:22 am Cancer
3rd 12:53 pm Leo
6th 1:48 am Virgo
8th 1:30 pm Libra
10th 10:08 pm Scorpio
13th 2:40 am Sagittarius
15th 3:41 am Capricorn
17th 2:56 am Aquarius
19th 2:32 am Pisces
21st 4:26 am Aries
23rd 9:51 am Taurus
25th 6:49 pm Gemini
28th 6:22 am Cancer
30th 7:05 pm Leo

February 1961
2nd 7:48 am Virgo
4th 7:27 pm Libra
7th 4:50 am Scorpio
9th 11:01 am Sagittarius
11th 1:51 pm Capricorn
13th 2:15 pm Aquarius
15th 1:54 pm Pisces
17th 2:41 pm Aries
19th 6:21 pm Taurus
22nd 1:51 am Gemini
24th 12:48 pm Cancer
27th 1:34 am Leo

March 1961
1st 2:12 pm Virgo
4th 1:21 am Libra
6th 10:23 am Scorpio
8th 5:04 pm Sagittarius
10th 9:19 pm Capricorn
12th 11:29 pm Aquarius
15th 12:26 am Pisces
17th 1:32 am Aries
19th 4:25 am Taurus
21st 10:32 am Gemini
23rd 8:22 pm Cancer
26th 8:48 am Leo
28th 9:29 pm Virgo
31th 8:21 am Libra

April 1961
2nd 4:37 pm Scorpio
4th 10:34 pm Sagittarius
7th 2:52 am Capricorn
9th 6:21 am Aquarius
11th 8:32 am Pisces
13th 10:56 am Aries
15th 2:17 pm Taurus
17th 7:55 pm Gemini
20th 4:50 am Cancer
22nd 4:42 pm Leo
25th 5:31 am Virgo
27th 4:34 pm Libra
30th 12:27 am Scorpio

May 1961
2nd 5:25 am Sagittarius
4th 8:40 am Capricorn
6th 11:24 am Aquarius
8th 2:23 pm Pisces
10th 5:56 pm Aries
12th 10:25 pm Taurus
15th 4:34 am Gemini
17th 1:16 pm Cancer
20th 12:45 am Leo
22nd 1:37 pm Virgo
25th 1:18 am Libra
27th 9:34 am Scorpio
29th 2:11 pm Sagittarius
31th 4:21 pm Capricorn

June 1961
2nd 5:45 am Aquarius
4th 7:50 pm Pisces
6th 11:23 pm Aries
9th 4:38 am Taurus
11th 11:40 am Gemini
13th 8:50 pm Cancer
16th 8:15 am Leo
18th 9:12 pm Virgo
21st 9:31 am Libra
23rd 6:50 pm Scorpio
26th 12:05 am Sagittarius
28th 1:59 am Capricorn
30th 2:18 am Aquarius

July 1961
2nd 2:53 am Pisces
4th 5:12 am Aries
6th 10:01 am Taurus
8th 5:27 pm Gemini
11th 3:13 am Cancer
13th 2:56 pm Leo
16th 3:54 am Virgo
18th 4:38 pm Libra
21st 3:04 am Scorpio
23rd 9:42 am Sagittarius
25th 12:29 pm Capricorn
27th 12:42 pm Aquarius
29th 12:13 pm Pisces
31th 12:56 pm Aries

August 1961
2nd 4:19 pm Taurus
4th 11:04 pm Gemini
7th 8:56 am Cancer
9th 8:59 pm Leo
12th 9:59 am Virgo
14th 10:43 pm Libra
17th 9:44 am Scorpio
19th 5:43 pm Sagittarius
21st 10:07 pm Capricorn
23rd 11:25 pm Aquarius
25th 11:04 pm Pisces
27th 10:49 pm Aries
30th 12:37 am Taurus

September 1961
1st 5:52 am Gemini
3rd 2:59 pm Cancer
6th 3:01 am Leo
8th 4:05 pm Virgo
11th 4:33 am Libra
13th 3:23 pm Scorpio
15th 11:54 pm Sagittarius
18th 5:42 am Capricorn
20th 8:43 am Aquarius
22nd 9:37 am Pisces
24th 9:41 am Aries
26th 10:42 am Taurus
28th 2:31 pm Gemini
30th 10:19 pm Cancer

January 1962
3rd 6:23 am Sagittarius
5th 10:24 am Capricorn
7th 12:01 pm Aquarius
9th 12:54 pm Pisces
11th 2:34 pm Aries
13th 6:01 pm Taurus
15th 11:42 pm Gemini
18th 7:39 am Cancer
20th 5:50 pm Leo
23rd 5:53 am Virgo
25th 6:52 pm Libra
28th 6:54 am Scorpio
30th 3:59 pm Sagittarius

May 1962
1st 6:12 am Aries
3rd 6:50 am Taurus
5th 8:17 am Gemini
7th 12:28 pm Cancer
9th 8:35 pm Leo
12th 8:11 am Virgo
14th 9:02 pm Libra
17th 8:43 am Scorpio
19th 6:02 pm Sagittarius
22nd 1:08 am Capricorn
24th 6:31 am Aquarius
26th 10:29 am Pisces
28th 1:15 pm Aries
30th 3:17 pm Taurus

September 1962
1st 3:01 am Libra
3rd 3:46 pm Scorpio
6th 3:26 am Sagittarius
8th 12:19 pm Capricorn
10th 5:26 pm Aquarius
12th 7:02 pm Pisces
14th 6:33 pm Aries
16th 6:01 pm Taurus
18th 7:29 pm Gemini
21st 12:26 am Cancer
23rd 9:06 am Leo
25th 8:30 pm Virgo
28th 9:08 am Libra
30th 9:49 pm Scorpio

January 1963
2nd 4:48 am Aries
4th 7:34 am Taurus
6th 10:14 am Gemini
8th 1:42 pm Cancer
10th 7:01 pm Leo
13th 3:07 am Virgo
15th 2:04 pm Libra
18th 2:35 am Scorpio
20th 2:20 pm Sagittarius
22nd 11:23 pm Capricorn
25th 5:14 am Aquarius
27th 8:35 am Pisces
29th 10:44 am Aries
31th 12:55 pm Taurus

October 1961
3rd 9:43 am Leo
5th 10:45 pm Virgo
8th 11:04 am Libra
10th 9:19 pm Scorpio
13th 5:21 am Sagittarius
15th 11:24 am Capricorn
17th 3:37 pm Aquarius
19th 6:10 pm Pisces
21st 7:36 pm Aries
23rd 9:07 pm Taurus
26th 12:24 am Gemini
28th 7:02 am Cancer
30th 5:29 pm Leo

February 1962
1st 9:10 pm Capricorn
3rd 10:57 pm Aquarius
5th 10:53 pm Pisces
7th 10:51 pm Aries
10th 12:35 am Taurus
12th 5:18 am Gemini
14th 1:19 pm Cancer
17th 12:04 am Leo
19th 12:26 pm Virgo
22nd 1:21 am Libra
24th 1:36 pm Scorpio
26th 11:46 pm Sagittarius

June 1962
1st 5:41 pm Gemini
3rd 9:56 pm Cancer
6th 5:23 am Leo
8th 4:11 pm Virgo
11th 4:50 am Libra
13th 4:44 pm Scorpio
16th 2:04 am Sagittarius
18th 8:30 am Capricorn
20th 12:49 pm Aquarius
22nd 3:59 pm Pisces
24th 6:43 pm Aries
26th 9:34 pm Taurus
29th 1:09 am Gemini

October 1962
3rd 9:39 am Sagittarius
5th 7:35 pm Capricorn
8th 2:21 am Aquarius
10th 5:29 am Pisces
12th 5:41 am Aries
14th 4:44 am Taurus
16th 4:50 am Gemini
18th 8:04 am Cancer
20th 3:30 pm Leo
23rd 2:31 am Virgo
25th 3:13 pm Libra
28th 3:48 am Scorpio
30th 3:19 pm Sagittarius

February 1963
2nd 4:04 pm Gemini
4th 8:40 pm Cancer
7th 3:06 am Leo
9th 11:36 am Virgo
11th 10:18 pm Libra
14th 10:38 am Scorpio
16th 10:57 pm Sagittarius
19th 8:59 am Capricorn
21st 3:23 pm Aquarius
23rd 6:18 pm Pisces
25th 7:06 pm Aries
27th 7:39 pm Taurus

November 1961
2nd 6:17 am Virgo
4th 6:42 pm Libra
7th 4:40 am Scorpio
9th 11:51 am Sagittarius
11th 4:59 pm Capricorn
13th 8:59 pm Aquarius
16th 12:18 am Pisces
18th 3:10 am Aries
20th 6:04 am Taurus
22nd 9:59 am Gemini
24th 4:20 pm Cancer
27th 2:01 am Leo
29th 2:24 pm Virgo

March 1962
1st 6:38 am Capricorn
3rd 9:52 am Aquarius
5th 10:17 am Pisces
7th 9:33 am Aries
9th 9:40 am Taurus
11th 12:35 pm Gemini
13th 7:25 pm Cancer
16th 5:55 am Leo
18th 6:32 pm Virgo
21st 7:28 am Libra
23rd 7:28 pm Scorpio
26th 5:48 am Sagittarius
28th 1:45 pm Capricorn
30th 6:43 pm Aquarius

July 1962
1st 6:19 am Cancer
3rd 1:55 pm Leo
6th 12:22 am Virgo
8th 12:47 pm Libra
11th 1:05 am Scorpio
13th 10:59 am Sagittarius
15th 5:32 pm Capricorn
17th 9:07 pm Aquarius
19th 11:00 pm Pisces
22nd 12:34 am Aries
24th 2:57 am Taurus
26th 6:57 am Gemini
28th 1:00 pm Cancer
30th 9:21 pm Leo

November 1962
2nd 1:17 am Capricorn
4th 9:02 am Aquarius
6th 1:52 pm Pisces
8th 3:46 pm Aries
10th 3:46 pm Taurus
12th 3:44 pm Gemini
14th 5:09 pm Cancer
16th 11:40 pm Leo
19th 9:33 am Virgo
21st 9:58 pm Libra
24th 10:33 am Scorpio
26th 9:43 pm Sagittarius
29th 7:00 am Capricorn

March 1963
1st 9:39 pm Gemini
4th 2:08 am Cancer
6th 9:15 am Leo
8th 6:34 pm Virgo
11th 5:35 am Libra
13th 5:51 pm Scorpio
16th 6:26 am Sagittarius
18th 5:34 pm Capricorn
21st 1:21 am Aquarius
23rd 5:04 am Pisces
25th 5:38 am Aries
27th 4:57 am Taurus
29th 5:13 am Gemini
31th 8:13 am Cancer

December 1961
2nd 3:08 am Libra
4th 1:30 pm Scorpio
6th 8:25 pm Sagittarius
9th 12:31 am Capricorn
11th 3:11 am Aquarius
13th 5:41 am Pisces
15th 8:44 am Aries
17th 12:39 pm Taurus
19th 5:47 pm Gemini
22nd 12:50 am Cancer
24th 10:25 am Leo
26th 10:29 pm Virgo
29th 11:26 am Libra
31th 10:42 pm Scorpio

April 1962
1st 8:42 pm Pisces
3rd 8:42 pm Aries
5th 8:26 pm Taurus
7th 9:59 pm Gemini
10th 3:12 am Cancer
12th 12:35 pm Leo
15th 12:57 am Virgo
17th 1:53 pm Libra
20th 1:37 am Scorpio
22nd 11:27 am Sagittarius
24th 7:20 pm Capricorn
27th 1:08 am Aquarius
29th 4:40 am Pisces

August 1962
2nd 7:57 am Virgo
4th 8:17 pm Libra
7th 8:55 am Scorpio
9th 7:48 pm Sagittarius
12th 3:18 am Capricorn
14th 7:08 am Aquarius
16th 8:17 am Pisces
18th 8:26 am Aries
20th 9:20 am Taurus
22nd 12:28 pm Gemini
24th 6:33 pm Cancer
27th 3:30 am Leo
29th 2:35 pm Virgo

December 1962
1st 2:25 pm Aquarius
3rd 7:53 pm Pisces
5th 11:17 pm Aries
8th 12:59 am Taurus
10th 2:07 am Gemini
12th 4:21 am Cancer
14th 9:20 am Leo
16th 5:59 pm Virgo
19th 5:41 am Libra
21st 6:17 pm Scorpio
24th 5:32 am Sagittarius
26th 2:19 pm Capricorn
28th 8:42 pm Aquarius
31th 1:20 am Pisces

April 1963
2nd 2:45 pm Leo
5th 12:20 am Virgo
7th 11:49 am Libra
10th 12:14 am Scorpio
12th 12:48 pm Sagittarius
15th 12:27 am Capricorn
17th 9:34 am Aquarius
19th 2:53 pm Pisces
21st 4:30 pm Aries
23rd 3:52 pm Taurus
25th 3:07 pm Gemini
27th 4:27 pm Cancer
29th 9:25 pm Leo

May 1963
2nd 6:13 am Virgo
4th 5:42 pm Libra
7th 6:16 am Scorpio
9th 6:42 pm Sagittarius
12th 6:13 am Capricorn
14th 3:51 pm Aquarius
16th 10:32 pm Pisces
19th 1:48 am Aries
21st 2:21 am Taurus
23rd 1:54 am Gemini
25th 2:29 am Cancer
27th 5:58 am Leo
29th 1:21 pm Virgo

June 1963
1st 12:09 am Libra
3rd 12:38 pm Scorpio
6th 1:01 am Sagittarius
8th 12:06 pm Capricorn
10th 9:22 pm Aquarius
13th 4:20 am Pisces
15th 8:46 am Aries
17th 10:55 am Taurus
19th 11:44 am Gemini
21st 12:47 pm Cancer
23rd 3:44 pm Leo
25th 9:56 pm Virgo
28th 7:40 am Libra
30th 7:47 pm Scorpio

July 1963
3rd 8:11 am Sagittarius
5th 7:04 pm Capricorn
8th 3:36 am Aquarius
10th 9:53 am Pisces
12th 2:16 pm Aries
14th 5:15 pm Taurus
16th 7:27 pm Gemini
18th 9:45 pm Cancer
21st 1:15 am Leo
23rd 7:06 am Virgo
25th 4:02 pm Libra
28th 3:38 am Scorpio
30th 4:07 pm Sagittarius

August 1963
2nd 3:12 am Capricorn
4th 11:25 am Aquarius
6th 4:46 pm Pisces
8th 8:07 pm Aries
10th 10:38 pm Taurus
13th 1:16 am Gemini
15th 4:39 am Cancer
17th 9:17 am Leo
19th 3:40 pm Virgo
22nd 12:25 am Libra
24th 11:38 am Scorpio
27th 12:15 am Sagittarius
29th 11:57 am Capricorn
31th 8:37 pm Aquarius

September 1963
3rd 1:37 am Pisces
5th 3:52 am Aries
7th 5:02 am Taurus
9th 6:46 am Gemini
11th 10:08 am Cancer
13th 3:30 pm Leo
15th 10:47 pm Virgo
18th 7:59 am Libra
20th 7:10 pm Scorpio
23rd 7:49 am Sagittarius
25th 8:15 pm Capricorn
28th 6:04 am Aquarius
30th 11:47 am Pisces

October 1963
2nd 1:49 pm Aries
4th 1:51 pm Taurus
6th 1:59 pm Gemini
8th 4:01 pm Cancer
10th 8:54 pm Leo
13th 4:34 am Virgo
15th 2:24 pm Libra
18th 1:52 am Scorpio
20th 2:32 pm Sagittarius
23rd 3:20 am Capricorn
25th 2:19 pm Aquarius
27th 9:36 pm Pisces
30th 12:40 am Aries

November 1963
1st 12:42 am Taurus
2nd 11:48 pm Gemini
5th 12:08 am Cancer
7th 3:24 am Leo
9th 10:13 am Virgo
11th 8:07 pm Libra
14th 7:56 am Scorpio
16th 8:40 pm Sagittarius
19th 9:22 am Capricorn
21st 8:51 pm Aquarius
24th 5:32 am Pisces
26th 10:25 am Aries
28th 11:50 am Taurus
30th 11:16 am Gemini

December 1963
2nd 10:45 am Cancer
4th 12:20 pm Leo
6th 5:26 pm Virgo
9th 2:21 am Libra
11th 2:04 pm Scorpio
14th 2:53 am Sagittarius
16th 3:21 pm Capricorn
19th 2:29 am Aquarius
21st 11:28 am Pisces
23rd 5:41 pm Aries
25th 8:57 pm Taurus
27th 9:58 pm Gemini
29th 10:07 pm Cancer
31th 11:09 pm Leo

January 1964
3rd 2:48 am Virgo
5th 10:09 am Libra
7th 9:04 pm Scorpio
10th 9:49 am Sagittarius
12th 10:14 pm Capricorn
15th 8:48 am Aquarius
17th 5:04 pm Pisces
19th 11:10 pm Aries
22nd 3:23 am Taurus
24th 6:05 am Gemini
26th 7:52 am Cancer
28th 9:45 am Leo
30th 1:09 pm Virgo

February 1964
1st 7:25 pm Libra
4th 5:12 am Scorpio
6th 5:35 pm Sagittarius
9th 6:10 am Capricorn
11th 4:39 pm Aquarius
14th 12:09 am Pisces
16th 5:10 am Aries
18th 8:45 am Taurus
20th 11:48 am Gemini
22nd 2:49 pm Cancer
24th 6:11 pm Leo
26th 10:30 pm Virgo
29th 4:46 am Libra

March 1964
2nd 1:54 pm Scorpio
5th 1:47 am Sagittarius
7th 2:35 pm Capricorn
10th 1:35 am Aquarius
12th 9:05 am Pisces
14th 1:16 pm Aries
16th 3:31 pm Taurus
18th 5:26 pm Gemini
20th 8:11 pm Cancer
23rd 12:15 am Leo
25th 5:42 am Virgo
27th 12:48 pm Libra
29th 10:04 pm Scorpio

April 1964
1st 9:40 am Sagittarius
3rd 10:36 pm Capricorn
6th 10:24 am Aquarius
8th 6:47 pm Pisces
10th 11:08 pm Aries
13th 12:37 am Taurus
15th 1:06 am Gemini
17th 2:23 am Cancer
19th 5:40 am Leo
21st 11:17 am Virgo
23rd 7:08 pm Libra
26th 5:01 am Scorpio
28th 4:46 pm Sagittarius

May 1964
1st 5:42 am Capricorn
3rd 6:06 pm Aquarius
6th 3:43 am Pisces
8th 9:16 am Aries
10th 11:10 am Taurus
12th 11:02 am Gemini
14th 10:54 am Cancer
16th 12:31 pm Leo
18th 5:02 pm Virgo
21st 12:41 am Libra
23rd 10:58 am Scorpio
25th 11:04 pm Sagittarius
28th 11:59 am Capricorn
31th 12:32 am Aquarius

June 1964
2nd 11:01 am Pisces
4th 6:04 pm Aries
6th 9:20 pm Taurus
8th 9:50 pm Gemini
10th 9:17 pm Cancer
12th 9:35 pm Leo
15th 12:27 am Virgo
17th 6:54 am Libra
19th 4:49 pm Scorpio
22nd 5:04 am Sagittarius
24th 6:02 pm Capricorn
27th 6:21 am Aquarius
29th 4:56 pm Pisces

July 1964
2nd 12:52 am Aries
4th 5:42 am Taurus
6th 7:43 am Gemini
8th 7:58 am Cancer
10th 8:01 am Leo
12th 9:44 am Virgo
14th 2:41 pm Libra
16th 11:32 pm Scorpio
19th 11:27 am Sagittarius
22nd 12:27 am Capricorn
24th 12:30 pm Aquarius
26th 10:36 pm Pisces
29th 6:25 am Aries
31th 12:00 pm Taurus

August 1964
2nd 3:28 pm Gemini
4th 5:13 pm Cancer
6th 6:12 pm Leo
8th 7:50 pm Virgo
10th 11:51 pm Libra
13th 7:31 am Scorpio
15th 6:44 pm Sagittarius
18th 7:38 am Capricorn
20th 7:39 pm Aquarius
23rd 5:13 am Pisces
25th 12:15 pm Aries
27th 5:24 pm Taurus
29th 9:16 pm Gemini

September 1964
1st 12:13 am Cancer
3rd 2:36 am Leo
5th 5:13 am Virgo
7th 9:19 am Libra
9th 4:19 pm Scorpio
12th 2:47 am Sagittarius
14th 3:29 pm Capricorn
17th 3:47 am Aquarius
19th 1:22 pm Pisces
21st 7:44 pm Aries
23rd 11:46 pm Taurus
26th 2:46 am Gemini
28th 5:39 am Cancer
30th 8:53 am Leo

October 1964
2nd 12:42 pm Virgo
4th 5:45 pm Libra
7th 12:57 am Scorpio
9th 11:02 am Sagittarius
11th 11:32 pm Capricorn
14th 12:15 pm Aquarius
16th 10:33 pm Pisces
19th 5:05 am Aries
21st 8:25 am Taurus
23rd 10:04 am Gemini
25th 11:38 am Cancer
27th 2:14 pm Leo
29th 6:25 pm Virgo

November 1964
1st 12:24 am Libra
3rd 8:25 am Scorpio
5th 6:43 pm Sagittarius
8th 7:05 am Capricorn
10th 8:08 pm Aquarius
13th 7:28 am Pisces
15th 3:10 pm Aries
17th 6:57 pm Taurus
19th 7:59 pm Gemini
21st 8:04 pm Cancer
23rd 8:59 pm Leo
26th 12:02 am Virgo
28th 5:54 am Libra
30th 2:30 pm Scorpio

December 1964
3rd 1:24 am Sagittarius
5th 1:53 pm Capricorn
8th 2:57 am Aquarius
10th 2:59 pm Pisces
13th 12:12 am Aries
15th 5:33 am Taurus
17th 7:22 am Gemini
19th 7:04 am Cancer
21st 6:31 am Leo
23rd 7:42 am Virgo
25th 12:04 pm Libra
27th 8:11 pm Scorpio
30th 7:20 am Sagittarius

January 1965
1st 8:06 pm Capricorn
4th 9:04 am Aquarius
6th 9:06 pm Pisces
9th 7:08 am Aries
11th 2:10 pm Taurus
13th 5:48 pm Gemini
15th 6:35 pm Cancer
17th 5:58 pm Leo
19th 5:55 pm Virgo
21st 8:28 pm Libra
24th 3:01 am Scorpio
26th 1:31 pm Sagittarius
29th 2:21 am Capricorn
31th 3:17 pm Aquarius

February 1965
3rd 2:56 am Pisces
5th 12:43 pm Aries
7th 8:24 pm Taurus
10th 1:36 am Gemini
12th 4:14 am Cancer
14th 4:55 am Leo
16th 5:06 am Virgo
18th 6:45 am Libra
20th 11:45 am Scorpio
22nd 8:57 pm Sagittarius
25th 9:16 am Capricorn
27th 10:14 pm Aquarius

March 1965
2nd 9:38 am Pisces
4th 6:45 pm Aries
7th 1:49 am Taurus
9th 7:14 am Gemini
11th 11:04 am Cancer
13th 1:23 pm Leo
15th 2:56 pm Virgo
17th 5:04 pm Libra
19th 9:32 pm Scorpio
22nd 5:36 am Sagittarius
24th 5:06 pm Capricorn
27th 5:58 am Aquarius
29th 5:32 pm Pisces

April 1965
1st 2:19 am Aries
3rd 8:29 am Taurus
5th 12:55 pm Gemini
7th 4:24 pm Cancer
9th 7:24 pm Leo
11th 10:14 pm Virgo
14th 1:38 am Libra
16th 6:42 am Scorpio
18th 2:31 pm Sagittarius
21st 1:24 am Capricorn
23rd 2:04 pm Aquarius
26th 2:02 am Pisces
28th 11:12 am Aries
30th 5:04 pm Taurus

May 1965
2nd 8:27 pm Gemini
4th 10:39 pm Cancer
7th 12:50 am Leo
9th 3:47 am Virgo
11th 8:04 am Libra
13th 2:10 pm Scorpio
15th 10:32 pm Sagittarius
18th 9:19 am Capricorn
20th 9:50 pm Aquarius
23rd 10:14 am Pisces
25th 8:18 pm Aries
28th 2:48 am Taurus
30th 5:59 am Gemini

June 1965
1st 7:06 am Cancer
3rd 7:47 am Leo
5th 9:33 am Virgo
7th 1:29 pm Libra
9th 8:04 pm Scorpio
12th 5:10 am Sagittarius
14th 4:20 pm Capricorn
17th 4:51 am Aquarius
19th 5:28 pm Pisces
22nd 4:29 am Aries
24th 12:16 pm Taurus
26th 4:18 pm Gemini
28th 5:21 pm Cancer
30th 4:59 pm Leo

July 1965
2nd 5:12 pm Virgo
4th 7:43 pm Libra
7th 1:38 am Scorpio
9th 10:53 am Sagittarius
11th 10:29 pm Capricorn
14th 11:08 am Aquarius
16th 11:45 pm Pisces
19th 11:12 am Aries
21st 8:14 pm Taurus
24th 1:48 am Gemini
26th 3:53 am Cancer
28th 3:38 am Leo
30th 2:55 am Virgo

August 1965
1st 3:54 am Libra
3rd 8:20 am Scorpio
5th 4:48 pm Sagittarius
8th 4:22 am Capricorn
10th 5:09 pm Aquarius
13th 5:37 am Pisces
15th 4:57 pm Aries
18th 2:27 am Taurus
20th 9:20 am Gemini
22nd 1:04 pm Cancer
24th 2:02 pm Leo
26th 1:37 pm Virgo
28th 1:53 pm Libra
30th 4:54 pm Scorpio

September 1965
1st 11:59 pm Sagittarius
4th 10:51 am Capricorn
6th 11:33 pm Aquarius
9th 11:56 am Pisces
11th 10:50 pm Aries
14th 7:56 am Taurus
16th 3:06 pm Gemini
18th 8:01 pm Cancer
20th 10:35 pm Leo
22nd 11:30 pm Virgo
25th 12:15 am Libra
27th 2:47 am Scorpio
29th 8:42 am Sagittarius

October 1965
1st 6:28 pm Capricorn
4th 6:48 am Aquarius
6th 7:14 pm Pisces
9th 5:54 am Aries
11th 2:16 pm Taurus
13th 8:40 pm Gemini
16th 1:27 am Cancer
18th 4:51 am Leo
20th 7:13 am Virgo
22nd 9:21 am Libra
24th 12:32 pm Scorpio
26th 6:09 pm Sagittarius
29th 3:05 am Capricorn
31th 2:49 pm Aquarius

November 1965
3rd 3:22 am Pisces
5th 2:21 pm Aries
7th 10:29 pm Taurus
10th 3:55 am Gemini
12th 7:30 am Cancer
14th 10:14 am Leo
16th 12:55 pm Virgo
18th 4:10 pm Libra
20th 8:37 pm Scorpio
23rd 2:57 am Sagittarius
25th 11:45 am Capricorn
27th 11:04 pm Aquarius
30th 11:39 am Pisces

December 1965
2nd 11:22 pm Aries
5th 8:11 am Taurus
7th 1:28 pm Gemini
9th 3:57 pm Cancer
11th 5:09 pm Leo
13th 6:36 pm Virgo
15th 9:33 pm Libra
18th 2:40 am Scorpio
20th 10:01 am Sagittarius
22nd 7:27 pm Capricorn
25th 6:44 am Aquarius
27th 7:17 pm Pisces
30th 7:39 am Aries

January 1966
1st 5:46 pm Taurus
4th 12:06 am Gemini
6th 2:40 am Cancer
8th 2:50 am Leo
10th 2:34 am Virgo
12th 3:53 am Libra
14th 8:08 am Scorpio
16th 3:39 pm Sagittarius
19th 1:45 am Capricorn
21st 1:26 pm Aquarius
24th 1:58 am Pisces
26th 2:32 pm Aries
29th 1:43 am Taurus
31th 9:43 am Gemini

February 1966
2nd 1:41 pm Cancer
4th 2:15 pm Leo
6th 1:12 pm Virgo
8th 12:51 pm Libra
10th 3:15 pm Scorpio
12th 9:33 pm Sagittarius
15th 7:25 am Capricorn
17th 7:25 pm Aquarius
20th 8:05 am Pisces
22nd 8:30 pm Aries
25th 7:53 am Taurus
27th 5:02 pm Gemini

March 1966
1st 10:48 pm Cancer
4th 12:57 am Leo
6th 12:37 am Virgo
7th 11:49 pm Libra
10th 12:47 am Scorpio
12th 5:18 am Sagittarius
14th 1:55 pm Capricorn
17th 1:35 am Aquarius
19th 2:18 pm Pisces
22nd 2:33 am Aries
24th 1:31 pm Taurus
26th 10:41 pm Gemini
29th 5:23 am Cancer
31th 9:12 am Leo

April 1966
2nd 10:32 am Virgo
4th 10:40 am Libra
6th 11:30 am Scorpio
8th 2:54 pm Sagittarius
10th 10:01 pm Capricorn
13th 8:41 am Aquarius
15th 9:13 pm Pisces
18th 9:27 am Aries
20th 8:00 pm Taurus
23rd 4:27 am Gemini
25th 10:48 am Cancer
27th 3:09 pm Leo
29th 5:50 pm Virgo

May 1966
1st 7:31 pm Libra
3rd 9:24 pm Scorpio
6th 12:52 am Sagittarius
8th 7:12 am Capricorn
10th 4:51 pm Aquarius
13th 4:54 am Pisces
15th 5:15 pm Aries
18th 3:49 am Taurus
20th 11:40 am Gemini
22nd 5:00 pm Cancer
24th 8:37 pm Leo
26th 11:22 pm Virgo
29th 1:59 am Libra
31th 5:11 am Scorpio

June 1966
2nd 9:39 am Sagittarius
4th 4:10 pm Capricorn
7th 1:21 am Aquarius
9th 12:56 pm Pisces
12th 1:26 am Aries
14th 12:29 pm Taurus
16th 8:26 pm Gemini
19th 1:05 am Cancer
21st 3:29 am Leo
23rd 5:08 am Virgo
25th 7:23 am Libra
27th 11:04 am Scorpio
29th 4:31 pm Sagittarius

July 1966
1st 11:51 pm Capricorn
4th 9:14 am Aquarius
6th 8:39 pm Pisces
9th 9:15 am Aries
11th 9:04 pm Taurus
14th 5:51 am Gemini
16th 10:44 am Cancer
18th 12:28 pm Leo
20th 12:47 pm Virgo
22nd 1:39 pm Libra
24th 4:32 pm Scorpio
26th 10:04 pm Sagittarius
29th 6:04 am Capricorn
31th 4:02 pm Aquarius

August 1966
3rd 3:35 am Pisces
5th 4:14 pm Aries
8th 4:37 am Taurus
10th 2:38 pm Gemini
12th 8:41 pm Cancer
14th 10:50 pm Leo
16th 10:35 pm Virgo
18th 10:05 pm Libra
20th 11:24 pm Scorpio
23rd 3:51 am Sagittarius
25th 11:36 am Capricorn
27th 9:56 pm Aquarius
30th 9:48 am Pisces

September 1966
1st 10:27 pm Aries
4th 10:59 am Taurus
6th 9:52 pm Gemini
9th 5:26 am Cancer
11th 9:01 am Leo
13th 9:26 am Virgo
15th 8:34 am Libra
17th 8:34 am Scorpio
19th 11:21 am Sagittarius
21st 5:52 pm Capricorn
24th 3:48 am Aquarius
26th 3:48 pm Pisces
29th 4:29 am Aries

October 1966
1st 4:47 pm Taurus
4th 3:43 am Gemini
6th 12:12 pm Cancer
8th 5:25 pm Leo
10th 7:27 pm Virgo
12th 7:30 pm Libra
14th 7:22 pm Scorpio
16th 8:59 pm Sagittarius
19th 1:55 am Capricorn
21st 10:40 am Aquarius
23rd 10:20 pm Pisces
26th 11:04 am Aries
28th 11:05 pm Taurus
31th 9:28 am Gemini

November 1966
2nd 5:42 pm Cancer
4th 11:36 pm Leo
7th 3:10 am Virgo
9th 4:54 am Libra
11th 5:54 am Scorpio
13th 7:36 am Sagittarius
15th 11:37 am Capricorn
17th 7:04 pm Aquarius
20th 5:52 am Pisces
22nd 6:30 pm Aries
25th 6:37 am Taurus
27th 4:31 pm Gemini
29th 11:50 pm Cancer

December 1966
2nd 5:02 am Leo
4th 8:48 am Virgo
6th 11:43 am Libra
8th 2:18 pm Scorpio
10th 5:13 pm Sagittarius
12th 9:30 pm Capricorn
15th 4:19 am Aquarius
17th 2:17 pm Pisces
20th 2:39 am Aries
22nd 3:07 pm Taurus
25th 1:14 am Gemini
27th 7:58 am Cancer
29th 11:58 am Leo
31th 2:33 pm Virgo

January 1967
2nd 5:04 pm Libra
4th 8:16 pm Scorpio
7th 12:28 am Sagittarius
9th 5:53 am Capricorn
11th 1:05 pm Aquarius
13th 10:44 pm Pisces
16th 10:47 am Aries
18th 11:39 pm Taurus
21st 10:38 am Gemini
23rd 5:51 pm Cancer
25th 9:21 pm Leo
27th 10:36 pm Virgo
29th 11:33 pm Libra

February 1967
1st 1:44 am Scorpio
3rd 5:55 am Sagittarius
5th 12:10 pm Capricorn
7th 8:17 pm Aquarius
10th 6:19 am Pisces
12th 6:16 pm Aries
15th 7:18 am Taurus
17th 7:15 pm Gemini
20th 3:48 am Cancer
22nd 8:04 am Leo
24th 9:05 am Virgo
26th 8:45 am Libra
28th 9:10 am Scorpio

March 1967
2nd 11:53 am Sagittarius
4th 5:35 pm Capricorn
7th 2:04 am Aquarius
9th 12:41 pm Pisces
12th 12:53 am Aries
14th 1:53 pm Taurus
17th 2:19 am Gemini
19th 12:09 pm Cancer
21st 6:04 pm Leo
23rd 8:08 pm Virgo
25th 7:51 pm Libra
27th 7:11 pm Scorpio
29th 8:08 pm Sagittarius

April 1967
1st 12:11 am Capricorn
3rd 7:48 am Aquarius
5th 6:28 pm Pisces
8th 6:56 am Aries
10th 7:56 pm Taurus
13th 8:14 am Gemini
15th 6:36 pm Cancer
18th 1:54 am Leo
20th 5:43 am Virgo
22nd 6:42 am Libra
24th 6:19 am Scorpio
26th 6:27 am Sagittarius
28th 8:54 am Capricorn
30th 2:57 pm Aquarius

May 1967
3rd 12:47 am Pisces
5th 1:09 pm Aries
8th 2:09 am Taurus
10th 2:08 pm Gemini
13th 12:11 am Cancer
15th 7:49 am Leo
17th 12:52 pm Virgo
19th 3:31 pm Libra
21st 4:30 pm Scorpio
23rd 5:06 pm Sagittarius
25th 6:58 pm Capricorn
27th 11:44 pm Aquarius
30th 8:18 am Pisces

June 1967
1st 8:06 pm Aries
4th 9:04 am Taurus
6th 8:52 pm Gemini
9th 6:18 am Cancer
11th 1:19 pm Leo
13th 6:24 pm Virgo
15th 9:58 pm Libra
18th 12:25 am Scorpio
20th 2:20 am Sagittarius
22nd 4:47 am Capricorn
24th 9:11 am Aquarius
26th 4:49 pm Pisces
29th 3:52 am Aries

July 1967
1st 4:42 pm Taurus
4th 4:38 am Gemini
6th 1:47 pm Cancer
8th 7:59 pm Leo
11th 12:07 am Virgo
13th 3:20 am Libra
15th 6:17 am Scorpio
17th 9:22 am Sagittarius
19th 12:59 pm Capricorn
21st 5:59 pm Aquarius
24th 1:28 am Pisces
26th 11:59 am Aries
29th 12:40 am Taurus
31th 12:59 pm Gemini

August 1967
2nd 10:32 pm Cancer
5th 4:26 am Leo
7th 7:36 am Virgo
9th 9:35 am Libra
11th 11:44 am Scorpio
13th 2:52 pm Sagittarius
15th 7:18 pm Capricorn
18th 1:17 am Aquarius
20th 9:18 am Pisces
22nd 7:47 pm Aries
25th 8:21 am Taurus
27th 9:08 pm Gemini
30th 7:34 am Cancer

September 1967
1st 2:08 pm Leo
3rd 5:08 pm Virgo
5th 6:04 pm Libra
7th 6:44 pm Scorpio
9th 8:40 pm Sagittarius
12th 12:43 am Capricorn
14th 7:08 am Aquarius
16th 3:53 pm Pisces
19th 2:46 am Aries
21st 3:20 pm Taurus
24th 4:21 am Gemini
26th 3:45 pm Cancer
28th 11:41 pm Leo

October 1967
1st 3:39 am Virgo
3rd 4:35 am Libra
5th 4:14 am Scorpio
7th 4:32 am Sagittarius
9th 7:04 am Capricorn
11th 12:45 pm Aquarius
13th 9:37 pm Pisces
16th 8:57 am Aries
18th 9:41 pm Taurus
21st 10:38 am Gemini
23rd 10:27 pm Cancer
26th 7:40 am Leo
28th 1:19 pm Virgo
30th 3:32 pm Libra

November 1967
1st 3:27 pm Scorpio
3rd 2:52 pm Sagittarius
5th 3:44 pm Capricorn
7th 7:45 pm Aquarius
10th 3:42 am Pisces
12th 2:58 pm Aries
15th 3:52 am Taurus
17th 4:40 pm Gemini
20th 4:13 am Cancer
22nd 1:47 pm Leo
24th 8:45 pm Virgo
27th 12:48 am Libra
29th 2:13 am Scorpio

December 1967
1st 2:10 am Sagittarius
3rd 2:25 am Capricorn
5th 4:57 am Aquarius
7th 11:19 am Pisces
9th 9:43 pm Aries
12th 10:31 am Taurus
14th 11:18 pm Gemini
17th 10:23 am Cancer
19th 7:21 pm Leo
22nd 2:21 am Virgo
24th 7:27 am Libra
26th 10:36 am Scorpio
28th 12:10 pm Sagittarius
30th 1:12 pm Capricorn

January 1968
1st 3:24 pm Aquarius
3rd 8:35 pm Pisces
6th 5:45 am Aries
8th 6:02 pm Taurus
11th 6:54 am Gemini
13th 5:53 pm Cancer
16th 2:09 am Leo
18th 8:11 am Virgo
20th 12:47 pm Libra
22nd 4:28 pm Scorpio
24th 7:24 pm Sagittarius
26th 9:57 pm Capricorn
29th 1:06 am Aquarius
31th 6:16 am Pisces

February 1968
2nd 2:39 pm Aries
5th 2:15 am Taurus
7th 3:08 pm Gemini
10th 2:34 am Cancer
12th 10:50 am Leo
14th 4:04 pm Virgo
16th 7:21 pm Libra
18th 9:59 pm Scorpio
21st 12:48 am Sagittarius
23rd 4:12 am Capricorn
25th 8:37 am Aquarius
27th 2:42 pm Pisces
29th 11:14 pm Aries

March 1968
3rd 10:27 am Taurus
5th 11:17 pm Gemini
8th 11:21 am Cancer
10th 8:27 pm Leo
13th 1:51 am Virgo
15th 4:23 am Libra
17th 5:33 am Scorpio
19th 6:54 am Sagittarius
21st 9:35 am Capricorn
23rd 2:16 pm Aquarius
25th 9:15 pm Pisces
28th 6:32 am Aries
30th 5:55 pm Taurus

April 1968
2nd 6:40 am Gemini
4th 7:12 pm Cancer
7th 5:28 am Leo
9th 12:04 pm Virgo
11th 3:01 pm Libra
13th 3:33 pm Scorpio
15th 3:24 pm Sagittarius
17th 4:23 pm Capricorn
19th 7:57 pm Aquarius
22nd 2:45 am Pisces
24th 12:32 pm Aries
27th 12:22 am Taurus
29th 1:11 pm Gemini

May 1968
2nd 1:50 am Cancer
4th 12:53 pm Leo
6th 8:58 pm Virgo
9th 1:21 am Libra
11th 2:30 am Scorpio
13th 1:53 am Sagittarius
15th 1:31 am Capricorn
17th 3:22 am Aquarius
19th 8:52 am Pisces
21st 6:14 pm Aries
24th 6:15 am Taurus
26th 7:12 pm Gemini
29th 7:42 am Cancer
31st 6:53 pm Leo

June 1968
3rd 3:52 am Virgo
5th 9:49 am Libra
7th 12:31 pm Scorpio
9th 12:43 pm Sagittarius
11th 12:06 pm Capricorn
13th 12:47 pm Aquarius
15th 4:42 pm Pisces
18th 12:50 am Aries
20th 12:24 pm Taurus
23rd 1:22 am Gemini
25th 1:43 pm Cancer
28th 12:30 am Leo
30th 9:26 am Virgo

July 1968
2nd 4:10 pm Libra
4th 8:20 pm Scorpio
6th 10:05 pm Sagittarius
8th 10:24 pm Capricorn
10th 11:04 pm Aquarius
13th 2:04 am Pisces
15th 8:51 am Aries
17th 7:30 pm Taurus
20th 8:12 am Gemini
22nd 8:31 pm Cancer
25th 6:55 am Leo
27th 3:10 pm Virgo
29th 9:32 pm Libra

August 1968
1st 2:11 am Scorpio
3rd 5:11 am Sagittarius
5th 6:58 am Capricorn
7th 8:38 am Aquarius
9th 11:46 am Pisces
11th 5:53 pm Aries
14th 3:36 am Taurus
16th 3:50 pm Gemini
19th 4:15 am Cancer
21st 2:40 pm Leo
23rd 10:21 pm Virgo
26th 3:45 am Libra
28th 7:38 am Scorpio
30th 10:41 am Sagittarius

September 1968
1st 1:22 pm Capricorn
3rd 4:19 pm Aquarius
5th 8:27 pm Pisces
8th 2:49 am Aries
10th 12:05 pm Taurus
12th 11:54 pm Gemini
15th 12:28 pm Cancer
17th 11:25 pm Leo
20th 7:15 am Virgo
22nd 12:00 pm Libra
24th 2:39 pm Scorpio
26th 4:31 pm Sagittarius
28th 6:44 pm Capricorn
30th 10:11 pm Aquarius

October 1968
3rd 3:21 am Pisces
5th 10:35 am Aries
7th 8:06 pm Taurus
10th 7:43 am Gemini
12th 8:23 pm Cancer
15th 8:08 am Leo
17th 4:58 pm Virgo
19th 10:05 pm Libra
22nd 12:05 am Scorpio
24th 12:32 am Sagittarius
26th 1:13 am Capricorn
28th 3:43 am Aquarius
30th 8:54 am Pisces

November 1968
1st 4:50 pm Aries
4th 3:01 am Taurus
6th 2:47 pm Gemini
9th 3:26 am Cancer
11th 3:44 pm Leo
14th 1:55 am Virgo
16th 8:26 am Libra
18th 11:06 am Scorpio
20th 11:05 am Sagittarius
22nd 10:20 am Capricorn
24th 11:02 am Aquarius
26th 2:52 pm Pisces
28th 10:26 pm Aries

December 1968
1st 8:57 am Taurus
3rd 9:06 pm Gemini
6th 9:43 am Cancer
8th 10:02 pm Leo
11th 8:59 am Virgo
13th 5:08 pm Libra
15th 9:31 pm Scorpio
17th 10:28 pm Sagittarius
19th 9:33 pm Capricorn
21st 8:59 pm Aquarius
23rd 11:01 pm Pisces
26th 5:02 am Aries
28th 2:56 pm Taurus
31st 3:11 am Gemini

January 1969
2nd 3:52 pm Cancer
5th 3:54 am Leo
7th 2:42 pm Virgo
9th 11:32 pm Libra
12th 5:32 am Scorpio
14th 8:19 am Sagittarius
16th 8:40 am Capricorn
18th 8:17 am Aquarius
20th 9:21 am Pisces
22nd 1:43 pm Aries
24th 10:12 pm Taurus
27th 9:53 am Gemini
29th 10:36 pm Cancer

February 1969
1st 10:29 am Leo
3rd 8:40 pm Virgo
6th 5:00 am Libra
8th 11:18 am Scorpio
10th 3:23 pm Sagittarius
12th 5:29 pm Capricorn
14th 6:31 pm Aquarius
16th 8:04 pm Pisces
18th 11:48 pm Aries
21st 7:01 am Taurus
23rd 5:41 pm Gemini
26th 6:11 am Cancer
28th 6:11 pm Leo

March 1969
3rd 4:07 am Virgo
5th 11:34 am Libra
7th 4:56 pm Scorpio
9th 8:48 pm Sagittarius
11th 11:40 pm Capricorn
14th 2:09 am Aquarius
16th 5:04 am Pisces
18th 9:27 am Aries
20th 4:20 pm Taurus
23rd 2:12 am Gemini
25th 2:18 pm Cancer
28th 2:37 am Leo
30th 12:53 pm Virgo

April 1969
1st 8:04 pm Libra
4th 12:22 am Scorpio
6th 2:57 am Sagittarius
8th 5:05 am Capricorn
10th 7:46 am Aquarius
12th 11:41 am Pisces
14th 5:13 pm Aries
17th 12:43 am Taurus
19th 10:28 am Gemini
21st 10:17 pm Cancer
24th 10:50 am Leo
26th 9:57 pm Virgo
29th 5:43 am Libra

May 1969
1st 9:50 am Scorpio
3rd 11:20 am Sagittarius
5th 11:57 am Capricorn
7th 1:28 pm Aquarius
9th 5:04 pm Pisces
11th 11:09 pm Aries
14th 7:28 am Taurus
16th 5:41 pm Gemini
19th 5:30 am Cancer
21st 6:12 pm Leo
24th 6:06 am Virgo
26th 3:07 pm Libra
28th 8:05 pm Scorpio
30th 9:30 pm Sagittarius

June 1969
1st 9:07 pm Capricorn
3rd 9:04 pm Aquarius
5th 11:13 pm Pisces
8th 4:36 am Aries
10th 1:05 pm Taurus
12th 11:48 pm Gemini
15th 11:52 am Cancer
18th 12:35 am Leo
20th 12:53 pm Virgo
22nd 11:04 pm Libra
25th 5:31 am Scorpio
27th 8:00 am Sagittarius
29th 7:45 am Capricorn

July 1969
1st 6:50 am Aquarius
3rd 7:26 am Pisces
5th 11:16 am Aries
7th 6:52 pm Taurus
10th 5:31 am Gemini
12th 5:47 pm Cancer
15th 6:29 am Leo
17th 6:42 pm Virgo
20th 5:19 am Libra
22nd 1:04 pm Scorpio
24th 5:10 pm Sagittarius
26th 6:10 pm Capricorn
28th 5:35 pm Aquarius
30th 5:31 pm Pisces

August 1969
1st 7:55 pm Aries
4th 2:01 am Taurus
6th 11:49 am Gemini
8th 11:57 pm Cancer
11th 12:38 pm Leo
14th 12:32 am Virgo
16th 10:51 am Libra
18th 6:54 pm Scorpio
21st 12:12 am Sagittarius
23rd 2:49 am Capricorn
25th 3:36 am Aquarius
27th 4:04 am Pisces
29th 5:57 am Aries
31st 10:50 am Taurus

September 1969
2nd 7:23 pm Gemini
5th 6:56 am Cancer
7th 7:36 pm Leo
10th 7:20 am Virgo
12th 5:01 pm Libra
15th 12:25 am Scorpio
17th 5:42 am Sagittarius
19th 9:14 am Capricorn
21st 11:31 am Aquarius
23rd 1:23 pm Pisces
25th 3:56 am Aries
27th 8:29 pm Taurus
30th 4:05 am Gemini

October 1969
2nd 2:51 pm Cancer
5th 3:25 am Leo
7th 3:21 pm Virgo
10th 12:48 am Libra
12th 7:19 am Scorpio
14th 11:33 am Sagittarius
16th 2:36 pm Capricorn
18th 5:21 pm Aquarius
20th 8:26 pm Pisces
23rd 12:17 am Aries
25th 5:33 am Taurus
27th 1:00 pm Gemini
29th 11:13 pm Cancer

November 1969
1st 11:34 am Leo
4th 12:00 am Virgo
6th 9:58 am Libra
8th 4:18 pm Scorpio
10th 7:30 pm Sagittarius
12th 9:09 pm Capricorn
14th 10:53 pm Aquarius
17th 1:52 am Pisces
19th 6:32 am Aries
21st 12:52 pm Taurus
23rd 8:59 pm Gemini
26th 7:10 am Cancer
28th 7:22 pm Leo

December 1969
1st 8:13 am Virgo
3rd 7:16 pm Libra
6th 2:30 am Scorpio
8th 5:43 am Sagittarius
10th 6:21 am Capricorn
12th 6:28 am Aquarius
14th 7:56 am Pisces
16th 11:55 am Aries
18th 6:35 pm Taurus
21st 3:28 am Gemini
23rd 2:08 pm Cancer
26th 2:21 am Leo
28th 3:20 pm Virgo
31th 3:18 am Libra

January 1970
2nd 12:04 pm Scorpio
4th 4:33 pm Sagittarius
6th 5:31 pm Capricorn
8th 4:48 pm Aquarius
10th 4:37 pm Pisces
12th 6:48 pm Aries
15th 12:20 am Taurus
17th 9:07 am Gemini
19th 8:13 pm Cancer
22nd 8:40 am Leo
24th 9:33 pm Virgo
27th 9:42 am Libra
29th 7:34 pm Scorpio

February 1970
1st 1:50 am Sagittarius
3rd 4:22 am Capricorn
5th 4:20 am Aquarius
7th 3:38 am Pisces
9th 4:17 am Aries
11th 7:59 am Taurus
13th 3:28 pm Gemini
16th 2:17 am Cancer
18th 2:53 pm Leo
21st 3:41 am Virgo
23rd 3:29 pm Libra
26th 1:23 am Scorpio
28th 8:38 am Sagittarius

March 1970
2nd 12:54 pm Capricorn
4th 2:35 pm Aquarius
6th 2:50 pm Pisces
8th 3:17 pm Aries
10th 5:44 pm Taurus
12th 11:37 pm Gemini
15th 9:18 am Cancer
17th 9:39 pm Leo
20th 10:29 am Virgo
22nd 9:56 pm Libra
25th 7:10 am Scorpio
27th 2:07 pm Sagittarius
29th 7:00 pm Capricorn
31th 10:08 pm Aquarius

April 1970
3rd 12:01 am Pisces
5th 1:32 am Aries
7th 4:02 am Taurus
9th 9:02 am Gemini
11th 5:33 pm Cancer
14th 5:15 am Leo
16th 6:06 pm Virgo
19th 5:35 am Libra
21st 2:15 pm Scorpio
23rd 8:15 pm Sagittarius
26th 12:26 am Capricorn
28th 3:43 am Aquarius
30th 6:38 am Pisces

May 1970
2nd 9:33 am Aries
4th 1:05 pm Taurus
6th 6:18 pm Gemini
9th 2:17 am Cancer
11th 1:21 pm Leo
14th 2:10 am Virgo
16th 2:02 pm Libra
18th 10:49 pm Scorpio
21st 4:11 am Sagittarius
23rd 7:13 am Capricorn
25th 9:26 am Aquarius
27th 11:59 am Pisces
29th 3:27 pm Aries
31th 8:04 pm Taurus

June 1970
3rd 2:10 am Gemini
5th 10:25 am Cancer
7th 9:16 pm Leo
10th 10:01 am Virgo
12th 10:27 pm Libra
15th 8:01 am Scorpio
17th 1:39 pm Sagittarius
19th 4:05 pm Capricorn
21st 5:01 pm Aquarius
23rd 6:12 pm Pisces
25th 8:52 pm Aries
28th 1:35 am Taurus
30th 8:24 am Gemini

July 1970
2nd 5:21 pm Cancer
5th 4:26 am Leo
7th 5:10 pm Virgo
10th 6:02 am Libra
12th 4:40 pm Scorpio
14th 11:26 pm Sagittarius
17th 2:19 am Capricorn
19th 2:45 am Aquarius
21st 2:37 am Pisces
23rd 3:42 am Aries
25th 7:18 am Taurus
27th 1:52 pm Gemini
29th 11:14 pm Cancer

August 1970
1st 10:44 am Leo
3rd 11:34 pm Virgo
6th 12:32 pm Libra
8th 11:57 pm Scorpio
11th 8:07 am Sagittarius
13th 12:25 pm Capricorn
15th 1:32 pm Aquarius
17th 1:02 pm Pisces
19th 12:51 pm Aries
21st 2:46 pm Taurus
23rd 8:04 pm Gemini
26th 4:58 am Cancer
28th 4:38 pm Leo
31th 5:36 am Virgo

September 1970
2nd 6:25 pm Libra
5th 5:54 am Scorpio
7th 2:58 pm Sagittarius
9th 8:51 pm Capricorn
11th 11:34 pm Aquarius
13th 11:57 pm Pisces
15th 11:35 pm Aries
18th 12:21 am Taurus
20th 4:02 am Gemini
22nd 11:40 am Cancer
24th 10:54 pm Leo
27th 11:53 am Virgo
30th 12:33 am Libra

October 1970
2nd 11:35 am Scorpio
4th 8:31 pm Sagittarius
7th 3:10 am Capricorn
9th 7:26 am Aquarius
11th 9:30 am Pisces
13th 10:13 am Aries
15th 11:00 am Taurus
17th 1:43 pm Gemini
19th 7:58 pm Cancer
22nd 6:12 am Leo
24th 6:56 pm Virgo
27th 7:37 am Libra
29th 6:15 pm Scorpio

November 1970
1st 2:24 am Sagittarius
3rd 8:32 am Capricorn
5th 1:11 pm Aquarius
7th 4:33 pm Pisces
9th 6:52 pm Aries
11th 8:50 pm Taurus
13th 11:48 pm Gemini
16th 5:23 am Cancer
18th 2:35 pm Leo
21st 2:50 am Virgo
23rd 3:38 pm Libra
26th 2:25 am Scorpio
28th 10:02 am Sagittarius
30th 3:06 pm Capricorn

December 1970
2nd 6:45 pm Aquarius
4th 9:55 pm Pisces
7th 1:04 am Aries
9th 4:24 am Taurus
11th 8:33 am Gemini
13th 2:32 pm Cancer
15th 11:21 pm Leo
18th 11:04 am Virgo
21st 12:01 am Libra
23rd 11:26 am Scorpio
25th 7:27 pm Sagittarius
28th 12:01 am Capricorn
30th 2:24 am Aquarius

January 1971
1st 4:08 am Pisces
3rd 6:26 am Aries
5th 10:00 am Taurus
7th 3:08 pm Gemini
9th 10:09 pm Cancer
12th 7:24 am Leo
14th 6:57 pm Virgo
17th 7:53 am Libra
19th 8:04 pm Scorpio
22nd 5:15 am Sagittarius
24th 10:33 am Capricorn
26th 12:37 pm Aquarius
28th 1:02 pm Pisces
30th 1:36 pm Aries

February 1971
1st 3:49 pm Taurus
3rd 8:34 pm Gemini
6th 4:07 am Cancer
8th 2:06 pm Leo
11th 1:58 am Virgo
13th 2:50 pm Libra
16th 3:21 am Scorpio
18th 1:45 pm Sagittarius
20th 8:37 pm Capricorn
22nd 11:43 pm Aquarius
25th 12:05 am Pisces
26th 11:30 pm Aries
28th 11:54 pm Taurus

March 1971
3rd 3:01 am Gemini
5th 9:47 am Cancer
7th 7:55 pm Leo
10th 8:10 am Virgo
12th 9:05 pm Libra
15th 9:31 am Scorpio
17th 8:23 pm Sagittarius
20th 4:37 am Capricorn
22nd 9:29 am Aquarius
24th 11:08 am Pisces
26th 10:46 am Aries
28th 10:16 am Taurus
30th 11:44 am Gemini

April 1971
1st 4:50 pm Cancer
4th 2:05 am Leo
6th 2:16 pm Virgo
9th 3:17 am Libra
11th 3:28 pm Scorpio
14th 2:04 am Sagittarius
16th 10:38 am Capricorn
18th 4:45 pm Aquarius
20th 8:08 pm Pisces
22nd 9:09 pm Aries
24th 9:07 pm Taurus
26th 9:59 pm Gemini
29th 1:43 am Cancer

May 1971
1st 9:34 am Leo
3rd 9:02 pm Virgo
6th 9:59 am Libra
8th 10:04 pm Scorpio
11th 8:08 am Sagittarius
13th 4:09 pm Capricorn
15th 10:19 pm Aquarius
18th 2:39 am Pisces
20th 5:11 am Aries
22nd 6:32 am Taurus
24th 8:01 am Gemini
26th 11:26 am Cancer
28th 6:16 pm Leo
31th 4:48 am Virgo

June 1971
2nd 5:26 pm Libra
5th 5:36 am Scorpio
7th 3:28 pm Sagittarius
9th 10:45 pm Capricorn
12th 4:04 am Aquarius
14th 8:01 am Pisces
16th 11:06 am Aries
18th 1:39 pm Taurus
20th 4:24 pm Gemini
22nd 8:30 pm Cancer
25th 3:12 am Leo
27th 1:06 pm Virgo
30th 1:22 am Libra

July 1971
2nd 1:45 pm Scorpio
4th 11:59 pm Sagittarius
7th 7:04 am Capricorn
9th 11:27 am Aquarius
11th 2:15 pm Pisces
13th 4:32 pm Aries
15th 7:10 pm Taurus
17th 10:47 pm Gemini
20th 3:57 am Cancer
22nd 11:16 am Leo
24th 9:09 pm Virgo
27th 9:11 am Libra
29th 9:50 pm Scorpio

August 1971
1st 8:49 am Sagittarius
3rd 4:32 pm Capricorn
5th 8:47 pm Aquarius
7th 10:34 pm Pisces
9th 11:27 pm Aries
12th 12:55 am Taurus
14th 4:10 am Gemini
16th 9:49 am Cancer
18th 5:57 pm Leo
21st 4:18 am Virgo
23rd 4:22 pm Libra
26th 5:09 am Scorpio
28th 4:56 pm Sagittarius
31th 1:54 am Capricorn

September 1971
2nd 7:04 am Aquarius
4th 8:51 am Pisces
6th 8:44 am Aries
8th 8:38 am Taurus
10th 10:25 am Gemini
12th 3:20 pm Cancer
14th 11:38 pm Leo
17th 10:28 am Virgo
19th 10:47 pm Libra
22nd 11:33 am Scorpio
24th 11:43 pm Sagittarius
27th 9:52 am Capricorn
29th 4:38 pm Aquarius

January 1972
2nd 8:22 am Leo
4th 3:50 pm Virgo
7th 2:33 am Libra
9th 3:04 pm Scorpio
12th 2:57 am Sagittarius
14th 12:26 pm Capricorn
16th 7:04 pm Aquarius
18th 11:28 pm Pisces
21st 2:35 am Aries
23rd 5:17 am Taurus
25th 8:14 am Gemini
27th 12:02 pm Cancer
29th 5:21 pm Leo

May 1972
2nd 8:28 pm Capricorn
5th 6:35 am Aquarius
7th 1:27 pm Pisces
9th 4:35 pm Aries
11th 4:48 pm Taurus
13th 3:58 pm Gemini
15th 4:16 pm Cancer
17th 7:37 pm Leo
20th 2:56 am Virgo
22nd 1:36 pm Libra
25th 2:01 am Scorpio
27th 2:33 am Sagittarius
30th 2:13 am Capricorn

September 1972
2nd 2:11 am Cancer
4th 6:54 am Leo
6th 1:15 pm Virgo
8th 9:36 pm Libra
11th 8:15 am Scorpio
13th 8:42 pm Sagittarius
16th 9:07 am Capricorn
18th 7:04 pm Aquarius
21st 1:09 am Pisces
23rd 3:45 am Aries
25th 4:28 am Taurus
27th 5:15 am Gemini
29th 7:39 am Cancer

January 1973
3rd 11:30 am Capricorn
5th 10:47 pm Aquarius
8th 8:02 am Pisces
10th 2:57 pm Aries
12th 7:24 pm Taurus
14th 9:41 pm Gemini
16th 10:39 pm Cancer
18th 11:40 pm Leo
21st 2:24 am Virgo
23rd 8:16 am Libra
25th 5:51 pm Scorpio
28th 6:10 am Sagittarius
30th 6:54 pm Capricorn

October 1971
1st 7:37 pm Pisces
3rd 7:41 pm Aries
5th 6:43 pm Taurus
7th 6:53 pm Gemini
9th 10:10 pm Cancer
12th 5:30 am Leo
14th 4:16 pm Virgo
17th 4:47 am Libra
19th 5:31 pm Scorpio
22nd 5:31 am Sagittarius
24th 4:05 pm Capricorn
27th 12:11 am Aquarius
29th 4:57 am Pisces
31st 6:26 am Aries

February 1972
1st 12:56 am Virgo
3rd 11:06 am Libra
5th 11:18 pm Scorpio
8th 11:37 am Sagittarius
10th 9:50 pm Capricorn
13th 4:36 am Aquarius
15th 8:11 am Pisces
17th 9:51 am Aries
19th 11:12 am Taurus
21st 1:36 pm Gemini
23rd 5:52 pm Cancer
26th 12:15 am Leo
28th 8:39 am Virgo

June 1972
1st 12:15 am Aquarius
3rd 7:52 am Pisces
6th 12:27 am Aries
8th 2:15 am Taurus
10th 2:24 am Gemini
12th 2:45 am Cancer
14th 5:10 am Leo
16th 11:04 am Virgo
18th 8:38 pm Libra
21st 8:42 am Scorpio
23rd 9:14 pm Sagittarius
26th 8:36 am Capricorn
28th 6:02 pm Aquarius

October 1972
1st 12:25 pm Leo
3rd 7:31 pm Virgo
6th 4:35 am Libra
8th 3:27 pm Scorpio
11th 3:52 am Sagittarius
13th 4:43 pm Capricorn
16th 3:51 am Aquarius
18th 11:12 am Pisces
20th 2:23 pm Aries
22nd 2:38 pm Taurus
24th 2:04 pm Gemini
26th 2:45 pm Cancer
28th 6:14 pm Leo
31st 12:59 am Virgo

February 1973
2nd 5:55 am Aquarius
4th 2:22 pm Pisces
6th 8:29 pm Aries
9th 12:53 am Taurus
11th 4:10 am Gemini
13th 6:44 am Cancer
15th 9:12 am Leo
17th 12:31 pm Virgo
19th 5:58 pm Libra
22nd 2:35 am Scorpio
24th 2:14 pm Sagittarius
27th 3:04 am Capricorn

November 1971
2nd 5:56 am Taurus
4th 5:28 am Gemini
6th 7:15 am Cancer
8th 12:56 pm Leo
10th 10:44 pm Virgo
13th 11:05 am Libra
15th 11:49 pm Scorpio
18th 11:30 am Sagittarius
20th 9:36 pm Capricorn
23rd 5:52 am Aquarius
25th 11:47 am Pisces
27th 3:04 pm Aries
29th 4:09 pm Taurus

March 1972
1st 6:59 pm Libra
4th 6:59 am Scorpio
6th 7:36 pm Sagittarius
9th 6:49 am Capricorn
11th 2:42 pm Aquarius
13th 6:39 pm Pisces
15th 7:38 pm Aries
17th 7:28 pm Taurus
19th 8:13 pm Gemini
21st 11:26 pm Cancer
24th 5:46 am Leo
26th 2:47 pm Virgo
29th 1:42 am Libra
31st 1:48 pm Scorpio

July 1972
1st 1:18 am Pisces
3rd 6:22 am Aries
5th 9:25 am Taurus
7th 11:05 am Gemini
9th 12:30 pm Cancer
11th 3:06 pm Leo
13th 8:16 pm Virgo
16th 4:48 am Libra
18th 4:15 pm Scorpio
21st 4:46 am Sagittarius
23rd 4:10 pm Capricorn
26th 1:07 am Aquarius
28th 7:29 am Pisces
30th 11:50 am Aries

November 1972
2nd 10:27 am Libra
4th 9:46 pm Scorpio
7th 10:16 am Sagittarius
9th 11:11 pm Capricorn
12th 11:02 am Aquarius
14th 7:56 pm Pisces
17th 12:44 am Aries
19th 1:53 am Taurus
21st 1:05 am Gemini
23rd 12:31 am Cancer
25th 2:12 am Leo
27th 7:24 am Virgo
29th 4:14 pm Libra

March 1973
1st 2:22 pm Aquarius
3rd 10:31 pm Pisces
6th 3:37 am Aries
8th 6:51 am Taurus
10th 9:31 am Gemini
12th 12:29 pm Cancer
14th 4:07 pm Leo
16th 8:42 pm Virgo
19th 2:48 am Libra
21st 11:15 am Scorpio
23rd 10:26 pm Sagittarius
26th 11:15 am Capricorn
28th 11:12 pm Aquarius
31th 7:55 am Pisces

December 1971
1st 4:26 pm Gemini
3rd 5:51 pm Cancer
5th 10:17 pm Leo
8th 6:40 am Virgo
10th 6:18 pm Libra
13th 7:01 am Scorpio
15th 6:37 pm Sagittarius
18th 4:07 am Capricorn
20th 11:32 am Aquarius
22nd 5:10 pm Pisces
24th 9:09 pm Aries
26th 11:45 pm Taurus
29th 1:38 am Gemini
31th 4:01 am Cancer

April 1972
3rd 2:27 am Sagittarius
5th 2:20 pm Capricorn
7th 11:37 pm Aquarius
10th 4:58 am Pisces
12th 6:33 am Aries
14th 5:55 am Taurus
16th 5:17 am Gemini
18th 6:46 am Cancer
20th 11:46 am Leo
22nd 8:24 pm Virgo
25th 7:34 am Libra
27th 7:55 pm Scorpio
30th 8:30 am Sagittarius

August 1972
1st 2:58 pm Taurus
3rd 5:33 pm Gemini
5th 8:18 pm Cancer
7th 11:56 pm Leo
10th 5:23 am Virgo
12th 1:27 pm Libra
15th 12:19 am Scorpio
17th 12:48 pm Sagittarius
20th 12:38 am Capricorn
22nd 9:43 am Aquarius
24th 3:29 pm Pisces
26th 6:41 pm Aries
28th 8:43 pm Taurus
30th 10:56 pm Gemini

December 1972
2nd 3:42 am Scorpio
4th 4:22 pm Sagittarius
7th 5:06 am Capricorn
9th 4:53 pm Aquarius
12th 2:32 am Pisces
14th 8:59 am Aries
16th 11:59 am Taurus
18th 12:25 pm Gemini
20th 11:57 am Cancer
22nd 12:35 pm Leo
24th 4:02 pm Virgo
26th 11:21 pm Libra
29th 10:09 am Scorpio
31th 10:51 pm Sagittarius

April 1973
2nd 12:48 pm Aries
4th 2:59 pm Taurus
6th 4:12 pm Gemini
8th 6:04 pm Cancer
10th 9:31 pm Leo
13th 2:47 am Virgo
15th 9:50 am Libra
17th 6:51 pm Scorpio
20th 6:01 am Sagittarius
22nd 6:48 pm Capricorn
25th 7:20 am Aquarius
27th 5:09 pm Pisces
29th 10:53 pm Aries

May 1973
2nd 1:01 am Taurus
4th 1:16 am Gemini
6th 1:35 am Cancer
8th 3:36 am Leo
10th 8:13 am Virgo
12th 3:30 pm Libra
15th 1:09 am Scorpio
17th 12:41 pm Sagittarius
20th 1:30 am Capricorn
22nd 2:17 pm Aquarius
25th 1:05 am Pisces
27th 8:14 am Aries
29th 11:28 am Taurus
31st 11:53 am Gemini

June 1973
2nd 11:22 am Cancer
4th 11:49 am Leo
6th 2:51 pm Virgo
8th 9:15 pm Libra
11th 6:51 am Scorpio
13th 6:42 pm Sagittarius
16th 7:36 am Capricorn
18th 8:19 pm Aquarius
21st 7:28 am Pisces
23rd 3:48 pm Aries
25th 8:37 pm Taurus
27th 10:18 pm Gemini
29th 10:08 pm Cancer

July 1973
1st 9:56 pm Leo
3rd 11:31 pm Virgo
6th 4:23 am Libra
8th 1:05 pm Scorpio
11th 12:48 am Sagittarius
13th 1:45 pm Capricorn
16th 2:15 am Aquarius
18th 1:07 pm Pisces
20th 9:43 pm Aries
23rd 3:41 am Taurus
25th 6:58 am Gemini
27th 8:11 am Cancer
29th 8:30 am Leo
31st 9:35 am Virgo

August 1973
2nd 1:12 pm Libra
4th 8:35 pm Scorpio
7th 7:36 am Sagittarius
9th 8:29 pm Capricorn
12th 8:52 am Aquarius
14th 7:14 pm Pisces
17th 3:16 am Aries
19th 9:14 am Taurus
21st 1:26 pm Gemini
23rd 4:08 pm Cancer
25th 5:49 pm Leo
27th 7:34 pm Virgo
29th 10:52 pm Libra

September 1973
1st 5:17 am Scorpio
3rd 3:24 pm Sagittarius
6th 4:01 am Capricorn
8th 4:30 pm Aquarius
11th 2:40 am Pisces
13th 9:56 am Aries
15th 2:59 pm Taurus
17th 6:48 pm Gemini
19th 10:01 pm Cancer
22nd 12:56 am Leo
24th 3:58 am Virgo
26th 8:01 am Libra
28th 2:18 pm Scorpio
30th 11:47 pm Sagittarius

October 1973
3rd 12:01 pm Capricorn
6th 12:48 am Aquarius
8th 11:23 am Pisces
10th 6:29 pm Aries
12th 10:36 pm Taurus
15th 1:09 am Gemini
17th 3:28 am Cancer
19th 6:25 am Leo
21st 10:19 am Virgo
23rd 3:28 pm Libra
25th 10:28 pm Scorpio
28th 7:57 am Sagittarius
30th 7:57 pm Capricorn

November 1973
2nd 8:58 am Aquarius
4th 8:25 pm Pisces
7th 4:19 am Aries
9th 8:26 am Taurus
11th 10:00 am Gemini
13th 10:47 am Cancer
15th 12:20 pm Leo
17th 3:41 pm Virgo
19th 9:15 pm Libra
22nd 5:06 am Scorpio
24th 3:10 pm Sagittarius
27th 3:12 am Capricorn
29th 4:17 pm Aquarius

December 1973
2nd 4:32 am Pisces
4th 1:50 pm Aries
6th 7:08 pm Taurus
8th 8:58 pm Gemini
10th 8:52 pm Cancer
12th 8:45 pm Leo
14th 10:21 pm Virgo
17th 2:53 am Libra
19th 10:43 am Scorpio
21st 9:19 pm Sagittarius
24th 9:41 am Capricorn
26th 10:43 pm Aquarius
29th 11:09 am Pisces
31th 9:34 pm Aries

January 1974
3rd 4:38 am Taurus
5th 7:59 am Gemini
7th 8:29 am Cancer
9th 7:43 am Leo
11th 7:42 am Virgo
13th 10:21 am Libra
15th 4:53 pm Scorpio
18th 3:12 am Sagittarius
20th 3:47 pm Capricorn
23rd 4:50 am Aquarius
25th 5:00 pm Pisces
28th 3:32 am Aries
30th 11:41 am Taurus

February 1974
1st 4:53 pm Gemini
3rd 7:06 pm Cancer
5th 7:12 pm Leo
7th 6:52 pm Virgo
9th 8:10 pm Libra
12th 12:58 am Scorpio
14th 10:00 am Sagittarius
16th 10:15 pm Capricorn
19th 11:20 am Aquarius
21st 11:15 pm Pisces
24th 9:12 am Aries
26th 5:11 pm Taurus
28th 11:10 pm Gemini

March 1974
3rd 2:59 am Cancer
5th 4:49 am Leo
7th 5:34 am Virgo
9th 6:52 am Libra
11th 10:40 am Scorpio
13th 6:19 pm Sagittarius
16th 5:41 am Capricorn
18th 6:38 pm Aquarius
21st 6:33 am Pisces
23rd 4:02 pm Aries
25th 11:09 pm Taurus
28th 4:33 am Gemini
30th 8:40 am Cancer

April 1974
1st 11:41 am Leo
3rd 1:57 pm Virgo
5th 4:23 pm Libra
7th 8:25 pm Scorpio
10th 3:27 am Sagittarius
12th 1:56 pm Capricorn
15th 2:34 am Aquarius
17th 2:44 pm Pisces
20th 12:20 am Aries
22nd 6:54 am Taurus
24th 11:11 am Gemini
26th 2:18 pm Cancer
28th 5:04 pm Leo
30th 8:00 pm Virgo

May 1974
2nd 11:39 pm Libra
5th 4:43 am Scorpio
7th 12:05 pm Sagittarius
9th 10:15 pm Capricorn
12th 10:34 am Aquarius
14th 11:04 pm Pisces
17th 9:19 am Aries
19th 4:10 pm Taurus
21st 7:54 pm Gemini
23rd 9:46 pm Cancer
25th 11:12 pm Leo
28th 1:25 am Virgo
30th 5:16 am Libra

June 1974
1st 11:10 am Scorpio
3rd 7:21 pm Sagittarius
6th 5:48 am Capricorn
8th 6:02 pm Aquarius
11th 6:43 am Pisces
13th 5:52 pm Aries
16th 1:46 am Taurus
18th 5:59 am Gemini
20th 7:22 am Cancer
22nd 7:30 am Leo
24th 8:11 am Virgo
26th 10:57 am Libra
28th 4:40 pm Scorpio

July 1974
1st 1:20 am Sagittarius
3rd 12:19 pm Capricorn
6th 12:41 am Aquarius
8th 1:25 pm Pisces
11th 1:10 am Aries
13th 10:21 am Taurus
15th 3:54 pm Gemini
17th 5:56 pm Cancer
19th 5:44 pm Leo
21st 5:10 pm Virgo
23rd 6:19 pm Libra
25th 10:45 pm Scorpio
28th 6:59 am Sagittarius
30th 6:10 pm Capricorn

August 1974
2nd 6:46 am Aquarius
4th 7:26 pm Pisces
7th 7:15 am Aries
9th 5:12 pm Taurus
12th 12:15 am Gemini
14th 3:49 am Cancer
16th 4:27 am Leo
18th 3:43 am Virgo
20th 3:45 am Libra
22nd 6:37 am Scorpio
24th 1:33 pm Sagittarius
27th 12:15 am Capricorn
29th 12:52 pm Aquarius

September 1974
1st 1:29 am Pisces
3rd 12:58 pm Aries
5th 10:50 pm Taurus
8th 6:36 am Gemini
10th 11:39 am Cancer
12th 1:54 pm Leo
14th 2:13 pm Virgo
16th 2:18 pm Libra
18th 4:14 pm Scorpio
20th 9:46 pm Sagittarius
23rd 7:21 am Capricorn
25th 7:38 pm Aquarius
28th 8:14 am Pisces
30th 7:25 pm Aries

October 1974
3rd 4:39 am Taurus
5th 12:00 pm Gemini
7th 5:30 pm Cancer
9th 9:04 pm Leo
11th 10:56 pm Virgo
14th 12:11 am Libra
16th 2:23 am Scorpio
18th 7:14 am Sagittarius
20th 3:43 pm Capricorn
23rd 3:20 am Aquarius
25th 3:56 pm Pisces
28th 3:13 am Aries
30th 11:59 am Taurus

November 1974
1st 6:23 pm Gemini
3rd 11:01 pm Cancer
6th 2:30 am Leo
8th 5:18 am Virgo
10th 7:59 am Libra
12th 11:24 am Scorpio
14th 4:39 pm Sagittarius
17th 12:42 am Capricorn
19th 11:38 am Aquarius
22nd 12:11 am Pisces
24th 11:58 am Aries
26th 9:05 pm Taurus
29th 2:58 am Gemini

December 1974
1st 6:22 am Cancer
3rd 8:32 am Leo
5th 10:40 am Virgo
7th 1:43 pm Libra
9th 6:13 pm Scorpio
12th 12:34 am Sagittarius
14th 9:04 am Capricorn
16th 7:48 pm Aquarius
19th 8:11 am Pisces
21st 8:35 pm Aries
24th 6:44 am Taurus
26th 1:15 pm Gemini
28th 4:16 pm Cancer
30th 5:05 pm Leo

January 1975
1st 5:33 pm Virgo
3rd 7:22 pm Libra
5th 11:39 pm Scorpio
8th 6:39 am Sagittarius
10th 3:58 pm Capricorn
13th 3:04 am Aquarius
15th 3:23 pm Pisces
18th 4:04 am Aries
20th 3:20 pm Taurus
22nd 11:23 pm Gemini
25th 3:20 am Cancer
27th 4:00 am Leo
29th 3:14 am Virgo
31th 3:13 am Libra

May 1975
2nd 5:33 am Aquarius
4th 5:34 pm Pisces
7th 6:02 am Aries
9th 5:04 pm Taurus
12th 1:44 am Gemini
14th 8:08 am Cancer
16th 12:38 pm Leo
18th 3:46 pm Virgo
20th 6:05 pm Libra
22nd 8:26 pm Scorpio
24th 11:51 pm Sagittarius
27th 5:31 am Capricorn
29th 2:09 pm Aquarius

September 1975
2nd 11:08 pm Leo
4th 11:29 pm Virgo
6th 10:38 pm Libra
8th 10:46 pm Scorpio
11th 1:41 am Sagittarius
13th 8:11 am Capricorn
15th 5:51 pm Aquarius
18th 5:32 am Pisces
20th 6:07 pm Aries
23rd 6:43 am Taurus
25th 6:12 pm Gemini
28th 3:07 am Cancer
30th 8:20 am Leo

January 1976
3rd 2:33 am Aquarius
5th 11:35 am Pisces
7th 11:21 pm Aries
10th 12:09 pm Taurus
12th 11:19 pm Gemini
15th 7:00 am Cancer
17th 11:16 am Leo
19th 1:26 pm Virgo
21st 3:11 pm Libra
23rd 5:48 pm Scorpio
25th 9:51 pm Sagittarius
28th 3:24 am Capricorn
30th 10:34 am Aquarius

May 1976
1st 4:05 am Gemini
3rd 2:53 pm Cancer
5th 11:09 pm Leo
8th 4:21 am Virgo
10th 6:40 am Libra
12th 7:04 am Scorpio
14th 7:05 am Sagittarius
16th 8:32 am Capricorn
18th 1:02 pm Aquarius
20th 9:26 pm Pisces
23rd 9:06 am Aries
25th 10:07 pm Taurus
28th 10:22 am Gemini
30th 8:39 pm Cancer

February 1975
2nd 5:53 am Scorpio
4th 12:10 pm Sagittarius
6th 9:42 pm Capricorn
9th 9:16 am Aquarius
11th 9:45 pm Pisces
14th 10:22 am Aries
16th 10:09 pm Taurus
19th 7:34 am Gemini
21st 1:18 pm Cancer
23rd 3:14 pm Leo
25th 2:38 pm Virgo
27th 1:39 pm Libra

June 1975
1st 1:32 am Pisces
3rd 2:01 pm Aries
6th 1:19 am Taurus
8th 9:49 am Gemini
10th 3:22 pm Cancer
12th 6:45 pm Leo
14th 9:11 pm Virgo
16th 11:41 pm Libra
19th 2:59 am Scorpio
21st 7:34 am Sagittarius
23rd 1:56 pm Capricorn
25th 10:33 pm Aquarius
28th 9:33 am Pisces
30th 10:02 pm Aries

October 1975
2nd 10:04 am Virgo
4th 9:40 am Libra
6th 9:09 am Scorpio
8th 10:36 am Sagittarius
10th 3:28 pm Capricorn
13th 12:10 am Aquarius
15th 11:40 am Pisces
18th 12:20 am Aries
20th 12:43 pm Taurus
22nd 11:51 pm Gemini
25th 8:57 am Cancer
27th 3:20 pm Leo
29th 6:47 pm Virgo
31th 7:55 pm Libra

February 1976
1st 7:46 pm Pisces
4th 7:17 am Aries
6th 8:13 pm Taurus
9th 8:15 am Gemini
11th 4:58 pm Cancer
13th 9:33 pm Leo
15th 10:59 pm Virgo
17th 11:14 pm Libra
20th 12:14 am Scorpio
22nd 3:18 am Sagittarius
24th 8:54 am Capricorn
26th 4:48 pm Aquarius
29th 2:41 pm Pisces

June 1976
2nd 4:37 am Leo
4th 10:21 am Virgo
6th 1:59 pm Libra
8th 3:58 pm Scorpio
10th 5:07 pm Sagittarius
12th 6:46 pm Capricorn
14th 10:31 pm Aquarius
17th 5:43 am Pisces
19th 4:32 pm Aries
22nd 5:21 am Taurus
24th 5:36 pm Gemini
27th 3:29 am Cancer
29th 10:40 am Leo

March 1975
1st 2:34 pm Scorpio
3rd 7:05 pm Sagittarius
6th 3:39 am Capricorn
8th 3:09 pm Aquarius
11th 3:49 am Pisces
13th 4:18 pm Aries
16th 3:52 am Taurus
18th 1:43 pm Gemini
20th 8:48 pm Cancer
23rd 12:31 am Leo
25th 1:21 am Virgo
27th 12:51 am Libra
29th 1:08 am Scorpio
31th 4:09 am Sagittarius

July 1975
3rd 9:53 am Taurus
5th 6:58 pm Gemini
8th 12:23 am Cancer
10th 2:50 am Leo
12th 3:56 am Virgo
14th 5:21 am Libra
16th 8:23 am Scorpio
18th 1:32 pm Sagittarius
20th 8:46 pm Capricorn
23rd 5:56 am Aquarius
25th 4:58 pm Pisces
28th 5:27 am Aries
30th 5:53 pm Taurus

November 1975
2nd 8:08 pm Scorpio
4th 9:10 pm Sagittarius
7th 12:45 am Capricorn
9th 7:59 am Aquarius
11th 6:41 pm Pisces
14th 7:17 am Aries
16th 7:37 pm Taurus
19th 6:14 am Gemini
21st 2:36 pm Cancer
23rd 8:48 pm Leo
26th 1:04 am Virgo
28th 3:48 am Libra
30th 5:37 am Scorpio

March 1976
2nd 2:22 pm Aries
5th 3:18 am Taurus
7th 3:55 pm Gemini
10th 1:59 am Cancer
12th 7:55 am Leo
14th 9:59 am Virgo
16th 9:45 am Libra
18th 9:18 am Scorpio
20th 10:34 am Sagittarius
22nd 2:48 pm Capricorn
24th 10:19 pm Aquarius
27th 8:33 am Pisces
29th 8:37 pm Aries

July 1976
1st 3:46 pm Virgo
3rd 7:34 pm Libra
5th 10:33 pm Scorpio
8th 1:05 am Sagittarius
10th 3:49 am Capricorn
12th 7:53 am Aquarius
14th 2:36 pm Pisces
17th 12:40 am Aries
19th 1:10 pm Taurus
22nd 1:40 am Gemini
24th 11:39 am Cancer
26th 6:19 pm Leo
28th 10:23 pm Virgo
31th 1:13 am Libra

April 1975
2nd 11:08 am Capricorn
4th 9:45 pm Aquarius
7th 10:16 am Pisces
9th 10:44 pm Aries
12th 9:53 am Taurus
14th 7:14 pm Gemini
17th 2:27 am Cancer
19th 7:14 am Leo
21st 9:43 am Virgo
23rd 10:42 am Libra
25th 11:40 am Scorpio
27th 2:20 pm Sagittarius
29th 8:08 pm Capricorn

August 1975
2nd 4:02 am Gemini
4th 10:17 am Cancer
6th 12:44 pm Leo
8th 12:54 pm Virgo
10th 12:52 pm Libra
12th 2:30 pm Scorpio
14th 6:59 pm Sagittarius
17th 2:25 am Capricorn
19th 12:09 pm Aquarius
21st 11:32 pm Pisces
24th 12:02 pm Aries
27th 12:45 am Taurus
29th 11:53 am Gemini
31th 7:35 pm Cancer

December 1975
2nd 7:33 am Sagittarius
4th 10:59 am Capricorn
6th 5:12 pm Aquarius
9th 2:51 am Pisces
11th 3:05 pm Aries
14th 3:39 am Taurus
16th 2:12 pm Gemini
18th 9:49 pm Cancer
21st 2:54 am Leo
23rd 6:28 am Virgo
25th 9:27 am Libra
27th 12:28 pm Scorpio
29th 3:53 pm Sagittarius
31th 8:16 pm Capricorn

April 1976
1st 9:34 am Taurus
3rd 10:15 pm Gemini
6th 9:06 am Cancer
8th 4:36 pm Leo
10th 8:16 pm Virgo
12th 8:55 pm Libra
14th 8:15 pm Scorpio
16th 8:15 pm Sagittarius
18th 10:43 pm Capricorn
21st 4:47 am Aquarius
23rd 2:27 pm Pisces
26th 2:36 am Aries
28th 3:37 pm Taurus

August 1976
2nd 3:55 am Scorpio
4th 7:04 am Sagittarius
6th 10:55 am Capricorn
8th 3:57 pm Aquarius
10th 11:00 pm Pisces
13th 8:49 am Aries
15th 9:05 pm Taurus
18th 9:53 am Gemini
20th 8:33 pm Cancer
23rd 3:31 am Leo
25th 7:04 am Virgo
27th 8:42 am Libra
29th 10:05 am Scorpio
31th 12:28 pm Sagittarius

September 1976
2nd 4:29 pm Capricorn
4th 10:20 pm Aquarius
7th 6:11 am Pisces
9th 4:18 pm Aries
12th 4:30 am Taurus
14th 5:32 pm Gemini
17th 5:06 am Cancer
19th 1:10 pm Leo
21st 5:16 pm Virgo
23rd 6:28 pm Libra
25th 6:34 pm Scorpio
27th 7:22 pm Sagittarius
29th 10:13 pm Capricorn

October 1976
2nd 3:49 am Aquarius
4th 12:09 pm Pisces
6th 10:50 pm Aries
9th 11:11 am Taurus
12th 12:14 am Gemini
14th 12:23 pm Cancer
16th 9:49 pm Leo
19th 3:25 am Virgo
21st 5:27 am Libra
23rd 5:17 am Scorpio
25th 4:49 am Sagittarius
27th 5:55 am Capricorn
29th 10:05 am Aquarius
31th 5:53 pm Pisces

November 1976
3rd 4:45 am Aries
5th 5:23 pm Taurus
8th 6:21 am Gemini
10th 6:27 pm Cancer
13th 4:36 am Leo
15th 11:46 am Virgo
17th 3:34 pm Libra
19th 4:32 pm Scorpio
21st 4:04 pm Sagittarius
23rd 4:04 pm Capricorn
25th 6:30 pm Aquarius
28th 12:47 am Pisces
30th 11:01 am Aries

December 1976
2nd 11:41 pm Taurus
5th 12:38 pm Gemini
8th 12:21 am Cancer
10th 10:12 am Leo
12th 5:55 pm Virgo
14th 11:13 pm Libra
17th 2:01 am Scorpio
19th 2:54 am Sagittarius
21st 3:12 am Capricorn
23rd 4:48 am Aquarius
25th 9:36 am Pisces
27th 6:31 pm Aries
30th 6:43 am Taurus

January 1977
1st 7:42 pm Gemini
4th 7:12 am Cancer
6th 4:21 pm Leo
8th 11:23 pm Virgo
11th 4:48 am Libra
13th 8:44 am Scorpio
15th 11:18 am Sagittarius
17th 1:02 pm Capricorn
19th 3:12 pm Aquarius
21st 7:30 pm Pisces
24th 3:19 am Aries
26th 2:40 pm Taurus
29th 3:37 am Gemini
31th 3:19 pm Cancer

February 1977
3rd 12:11 am Leo
5th 6:17 am Virgo
7th 10:36 am Libra
9th 2:04 pm Scorpio
11th 5:11 pm Sagittarius
13th 8:14 pm Capricorn
15th 11:45 pm Aquarius
18th 4:45 am Pisces
20th 12:22 pm Aries
22nd 11:06 pm Taurus
25th 11:49 am Gemini
28th 12:02 am Cancer

March 1977
2nd 9:25 am Leo
4th 3:19 pm Virgo
6th 6:35 pm Libra
8th 8:37 pm Scorpio
10th 10:42 pm Sagittarius
13th 1:40 am Capricorn
15th 5:59 am Aquarius
17th 12:06 pm Pisces
19th 8:23 pm Aries
22nd 7:05 am Taurus
24th 7:38 pm Gemini
27th 8:16 am Cancer
29th 6:40 pm Leo

April 1977
1st 1:25 am Virgo
3rd 4:39 am Libra
5th 5:40 am Scorpio
7th 6:09 am Sagittarius
9th 7:40 am Capricorn
11th 11:24 am Aquarius
13th 5:49 pm Pisces
16th 2:52 am Aries
18th 2:02 pm Taurus
21st 2:37 am Gemini
23rd 3:25 pm Cancer
26th 2:43 am Leo
28th 10:52 am Virgo
30th 3:13 pm Libra

May 1977
2nd 4:24 pm Scorpio
4th 3:59 pm Sagittarius
6th 3:55 pm Capricorn
8th 5:59 pm Aquarius
10th 11:29 pm Pisces
13th 8:29 am Aries
15th 8:04 pm Taurus
18th 8:50 am Gemini
20th 9:35 pm Cancer
23rd 9:13 am Leo
25th 6:31 pm Virgo
28th 12:28 am Libra
30th 2:57 am Scorpio

June 1977
1st 2:54 am Sagittarius
3rd 2:07 am Capricorn
5th 2:44 am Aquarius
7th 6:35 am Pisces
9th 2:34 pm Aries
12th 1:56 am Taurus
14th 2:49 pm Gemini
17th 3:28 am Cancer
19th 2:53 pm Leo
22nd 12:29 am Virgo
24th 7:35 am Libra
26th 11:42 am Scorpio
28th 1:02 pm Sagittarius
30th 12:49 pm Capricorn

July 1977
2nd 12:57 pm Aquarius
4th 3:31 pm Pisces
6th 10:04 pm Aries
9th 8:32 am Taurus
11th 9:15 pm Gemini
14th 9:49 am Cancer
16th 8:51 pm Leo
19th 5:58 am Virgo
21st 1:09 pm Libra
23rd 6:13 pm Scorpio
25th 9:05 pm Sagittarius
27th 10:15 pm Capricorn
29th 11:04 pm Aquarius

August 1977
1st 1:23 am Pisces
3rd 6:54 am Aries
5th 4:17 pm Taurus
8th 4:29 am Gemini
10th 5:04 pm Cancer
13th 3:57 am Leo
15th 12:26 pm Virgo
17th 6:49 pm Libra
19th 11:35 pm Scorpio
22nd 3:04 am Sagittarius
24th 5:30 am Capricorn
26th 7:41 am Aquarius
28th 10:47 am Pisces
30th 4:11 pm Aries

September 1977
2nd 12:52 am Taurus
4th 12:26 pm Gemini
7th 1:04 am Cancer
9th 12:13 pm Leo
11th 8:34 pm Virgo
14th 2:08 am Libra
16th 5:46 am Scorpio
18th 8:28 am Sagittarius
20th 11:04 am Capricorn
22nd 2:12 pm Aquarius
24th 6:30 pm Pisces
27th 12:40 am Aries
29th 9:21 am Taurus

October 1977
1st 8:33 pm Gemini
4th 9:08 am Cancer
6th 8:57 pm Leo
9th 5:58 am Virgo
11th 11:30 am Libra
13th 2:11 pm Scorpio
15th 3:28 pm Sagittarius
17th 4:51 pm Capricorn
19th 7:36 pm Aquarius
22nd 12:26 am Pisces
24th 7:34 am Aries
26th 4:53 pm Taurus
29th 4:08 am Gemini
31th 4:39 pm Cancer

November 1977
3rd 5:04 am Leo
5th 3:16 pm Virgo
7th 9:51 pm Libra
10th 12:42 am Scorpio
12th 1:04 am Sagittarius
14th 12:50 am Capricorn
16th 1:59 am Aquarius
18th 5:58 am Pisces
20th 1:13 pm Aries
22nd 11:09 pm Taurus
25th 10:48 am Gemini
27th 11:20 pm Cancer
30th 11:52 am Leo

December 1977
2nd 11:05 pm Virgo
5th 7:17 am Libra
7th 11:33 am Scorpio
9th 12:23 pm Sagittarius
11th 11:27 am Capricorn
13th 11:00 am Aquarius
15th 1:09 pm Pisces
17th 7:11 pm Aries
20th 4:54 am Taurus
22nd 4:51 pm Gemini
25th 5:30 am Cancer
27th 5:51 pm Leo
30th 5:13 am Virgo

January 1978
1st 2:31 pm Libra
3rd 8:35 pm Scorpio
5th 11:04 pm Sagittarius
7th 10:55 pm Capricorn
9th 10:05 pm Aquarius
11th 10:50 pm Pisces
14th 3:05 am Aries
16th 11:30 am Taurus
18th 11:06 pm Gemini
21st 11:50 am Cancer
24th 12:02 am Leo
26th 10:56 am Virgo
28th 8:07 pm Libra
31th 3:04 am Scorpio

February 1978
2nd 7:13 am Sagittarius
4th 8:50 am Capricorn
6th 9:05 am Aquarius
8th 9:48 am Pisces
10th 12:56 pm Aries
12th 7:50 pm Taurus
15th 6:24 am Gemini
17th 6:55 pm Cancer
20th 7:09 am Leo
22nd 5:39 pm Virgo
25th 2:04 am Libra
27th 8:28 am Scorpio

March 1978
1st 1:02 pm Sagittarius
3rd 3:58 pm Capricorn
5th 5:51 pm Aquarius
7th 7:46 pm Pisces
9th 11:08 pm Aries
12th 5:18 am Taurus
14th 2:48 pm Gemini
17th 2:49 am Cancer
19th 3:12 pm Leo
22nd 1:49 am Virgo
24th 9:41 am Libra
26th 3:01 pm Scorpio
28th 6:37 pm Sagittarius
30th 9:24 pm Capricorn

April 1978
2nd 12:05 am Aquarius
4th 3:20 am Pisces
6th 7:51 am Aries
8th 2:22 pm Taurus
10th 11:27 pm Gemini
13th 10:58 am Cancer
15th 11:30 pm Leo
18th 10:43 am Virgo
20th 6:53 pm Libra
22nd 11:39 pm Scorpio
25th 2:00 am Sagittarius
27th 3:28 am Capricorn
29th 5:28 am Aquarius

May 1978
1st 8:59 am Pisces
3rd 2:27 pm Aries
5th 9:52 pm Taurus
8th 7:18 am Gemini
10th 6:41 pm Cancer
13th 7:16 am Leo
15th 7:14 pm Virgo
18th 4:24 am Libra
20th 9:39 am Scorpio
22nd 11:32 am Sagittarius
24th 11:42 am Capricorn
26th 12:10 pm Aquarius
28th 2:36 pm Pisces
30th 7:52 pm Aries

June 1978
2nd 3:50 am Taurus
4th 1:53 pm Gemini
7th 1:30 am Cancer
9th 2:07 pm Leo
12th 2:34 am Virgo
14th 12:55 pm Libra
16th 7:28 pm Scorpio
18th 10:01 pm Sagittarius
20th 9:52 pm Capricorn
22nd 9:08 pm Aquarius
24th 9:57 pm Pisces
27th 1:53 am Aries
29th 9:21 am Taurus

July 1978
1st 7:37 pm Gemini
4th 7:33 am Cancer
6th 8:13 pm Leo
9th 8:44 am Virgo
11th 7:48 pm Libra
14th 3:47 am Scorpio
16th 7:50 am Sagittarius
18th 8:34 am Capricorn
20th 7:42 am Aquarius
22nd 7:26 am Pisces
24th 9:46 am Aries
26th 3:50 pm Taurus
29th 1:31 am Gemini
31st 1:28 pm Cancer

August 1978
3rd 2:10 am Leo
5th 2:29 pm Virgo
8th 1:30 am Libra
10th 10:11 am Scorpio
12th 3:43 pm Sagittarius
14th 6:04 pm Capricorn
16th 6:16 pm Aquarius
18th 6:05 pm Pisces
20th 7:30 pm Aries
23rd 12:06 am Taurus
25th 8:31 am Gemini
27th 7:59 pm Cancer
30th 8:39 am Leo

September 1978
1st 8:46 pm Virgo
4th 7:15 am Libra
6th 3:38 pm Scorpio
8th 9:39 pm Sagittarius
11th 1:20 am Capricorn
13th 3:09 am Aquarius
15th 4:10 am Pisces
17th 5:50 am Aries
19th 9:43 am Taurus
21st 4:56 pm Gemini
24th 3:31 am Cancer
26th 4:01 pm Leo
29th 4:11 am Virgo

October 1978
1st 2:16 pm Libra
3rd 9:48 pm Scorpio
6th 3:07 am Sagittarius
8th 6:52 am Capricorn
10th 9:43 am Aquarius
12th 12:13 pm Pisces
14th 3:06 pm Aries
16th 7:22 pm Taurus
19th 2:05 am Gemini
21st 11:52 am Cancer
24th 12:04 am Leo
26th 12:31 pm Virgo
28th 10:51 pm Libra
31st 5:53 am Scorpio

November 1978
2nd 10:04 am Sagittarius
4th 12:41 pm Capricorn
6th 3:04 pm Aquarius
8th 6:06 pm Pisces
10th 10:11 pm Aries
13th 3:35 am Taurus
15th 10:45 am Gemini
17th 8:16 pm Cancer
20th 8:08 am Leo
22nd 8:57 pm Virgo
25th 8:06 am Libra
27th 3:38 pm Scorpio
29th 7:24 pm Sagittarius

December 1978
1st 8:44 pm Capricorn
3rd 9:36 pm Aquarius
5th 11:36 pm Pisces
8th 3:39 am Aries
10th 9:50 am Taurus
12th 5:54 pm Gemini
15th 3:50 am Cancer
17th 3:37 pm Leo
20th 4:34 am Virgo
22nd 4:39 pm Libra
25th 1:32 am Scorpio
27th 6:08 am Sagittarius
29th 7:16 am Capricorn
31st 6:53 am Aquarius

January 1979
2nd 7:08 am Pisces
4th 9:41 am Aries
6th 3:17 pm Taurus
8th 11:42 pm Gemini
11th 10:14 am Cancer
13th 10:16 pm Leo
16th 11:10 am Virgo
18th 11:40 pm Libra
21st 9:50 am Scorpio
23rd 4:08 pm Sagittarius
25th 6:28 pm Capricorn
27th 6:13 pm Aquarius
29th 5:26 pm Pisces
31st 6:12 pm Aries

February 1979
2nd 10:04 pm Taurus
5th 5:33 am Gemini
7th 4:05 pm Cancer
10th 4:25 am Leo
12th 5:17 pm Virgo
15th 5:37 am Libra
17th 4:11 pm Scorpio
19th 11:51 pm Sagittarius
22nd 4:01 am Capricorn
24th 5:12 am Aquarius
26th 4:53 am Pisces
28th 4:54 am Aries

March 1979
2nd 7:09 am Taurus
4th 12:58 pm Gemini
6th 10:34 pm Cancer
9th 10:47 am Leo
11th 11:42 pm Virgo
14th 11:41 am Libra
16th 9:49 pm Scorpio
19th 5:38 am Sagittarius
21st 10:56 am Capricorn
23rd 1:52 pm Aquarius
25th 3:05 pm Pisces
27th 3:48 pm Aries
29th 5:37 pm Taurus
31st 10:08 pm Gemini

April 1979
3rd 6:23 am Cancer
5th 5:57 pm Leo
8th 6:51 am Virgo
10th 6:45 pm Libra
13th 4:16 am Scorpio
15th 11:18 am Sagittarius
17th 4:23 pm Capricorn
19th 8:02 pm Aquarius
21st 10:41 pm Pisces
24th 12:51 am Aries
26th 3:27 am Taurus
28th 7:49 am Gemini
30th 3:11 pm Cancer

May 1979
3rd 1:56 am Leo
5th 2:41 pm Virgo
8th 2:47 am Libra
10th 12:10 pm Scorpio
12th 6:25 pm Sagittarius
14th 10:26 pm Capricorn
17th 1:26 am Aquarius
19th 4:18 am Pisces
21st 7:30 am Aries
23rd 11:21 am Taurus
25th 4:28 pm Gemini
27th 11:51 pm Cancer
30th 10:07 am Leo

June 1979
1st 10:40 pm Virgo
4th 11:11 am Libra
6th 9:05 pm Scorpio
9th 3:15 am Sagittarius
11th 6:24 am Capricorn
13th 8:07 am Aquarius
15th 9:56 am Pisces
17th 12:52 pm Aries
19th 5:18 pm Taurus
21st 11:23 pm Gemini
24th 7:24 am Cancer
26th 5:47 pm Leo
29th 6:13 am Virgo

July 1979
1st 7:07 pm Libra
4th 5:57 am Scorpio
6th 12:56 pm Sagittarius
8th 4:08 pm Capricorn
10th 4:59 pm Aquarius
12th 5:23 pm Pisces
14th 6:57 pm Aries
16th 10:43 pm Taurus
19th 4:59 am Gemini
21st 1:40 pm Cancer
24th 12:30 am Leo
26th 1:01 pm Virgo
29th 2:06 am Libra
31st 1:46 pm Scorpio

August 1979
2nd 10:05 pm Sagittarius
5th 2:23 am Capricorn
7th 3:28 am Aquarius
9th 3:06 am Pisces
11th 3:10 am Aries
13th 5:21 am Taurus
15th 10:41 am Gemini
17th 7:17 pm Cancer
20th 6:28 am Leo
22nd 7:11 pm Virgo
25th 8:13 am Libra
27th 8:12 pm Scorpio
30th 5:39 am Sagittarius

September 1979
1st 11:33 am Capricorn
3rd 1:59 pm Aquarius
5th 2:04 pm Pisces
7th 1:30 pm Aries
9th 2:13 pm Taurus
11th 5:54 pm Gemini
14th 1:27 am Cancer
16th 12:25 pm Leo
19th 1:15 am Virgo
21st 2:10 pm Libra
24th 1:54 am Scorpio
26th 11:35 am Sagittarius
28th 6:40 pm Capricorn
30th 10:49 pm Aquarius

October 1979
3rd 12:23 am Pisces
5th 12:28 am Aries
7th 12:45 am Taurus
9th 3:07 am Gemini
11th 9:09 am Cancer
13th 7:11 pm Leo
16th 7:51 am Virgo
18th 8:44 pm Libra
21st 8:02 am Scorpio
23rd 5:09 pm Sagittarius
26th 12:11 am Capricorn
28th 5:16 am Aquarius
30th 8:29 am Pisces

November 1979
1st 10:09 am Aries
3rd 11:16 am Taurus
5th 1:26 pm Gemini
7th 6:24 pm Cancer
10th 3:14 am Leo
12th 3:20 pm Virgo
15th 4:16 am Libra
17th 3:29 pm Scorpio
19th 11:56 pm Sagittarius
22nd 6:02 am Capricorn
24th 10:37 am Aquarius
26th 2:17 pm Pisces
28th 5:17 pm Aries
30th 7:55 pm Taurus

December 1979
2nd 11:02 pm Gemini
5th 4:01 am Cancer
7th 12:08 pm Leo
9th 11:33 pm Virgo
12th 12:28 pm Libra
15th 12:08 am Scorpio
17th 8:37 am Sagittarius
19th 1:55 pm Capricorn
21st 5:13 pm Aquarius
23rd 7:50 pm Pisces
25th 10:40 pm Aries
28th 2:08 am Taurus
30th 6:32 am Gemini

January 1980
1st 12:29 pm Cancer
3rd 8:47 pm Leo
6th 7:48 am Virgo
8th 8:37 pm Libra
11th 8:55 am Scorpio
13th 6:17 pm Sagittarius
15th 11:51 pm Capricorn
18th 2:25 am Aquarius
20th 3:33 am Pisces
22nd 4:52 am Aries
24th 7:31 am Taurus
26th 12:11 pm Gemini
28th 7:02 pm Cancer
31th 4:08 am Leo

February 1980
2nd 3:21 pm Virgo
5th 4:04 am Libra
7th 4:45 pm Scorpio
10th 3:19 am Sagittarius
12th 10:12 am Capricorn
14th 1:20 pm Aquarius
16th 1:55 pm Pisces
18th 1:43 pm Aries
20th 2:35 pm Taurus
22nd 5:58 pm Gemini
25th 12:34 am Cancer
27th 10:10 am Leo
29th 9:53 pm Virgo

March 1980
3rd 10:40 am Libra
5th 11:22 pm Scorpio
8th 10:38 am Sagittarius
10th 7:01 pm Capricorn
12th 11:45 pm Aquarius
15th 1:11 am Pisces
17th 12:41 am Aries
19th 12:13 am Taurus
21st 1:47 am Gemini
23rd 6:55 am Cancer
25th 3:58 pm Leo
28th 3:52 am Virgo
30th 4:48 pm Libra

April 1980
2nd 5:21 am Scorpio
4th 4:34 pm Sagittarius
7th 1:43 am Capricorn
9th 7:59 am Aquarius
11th 11:07 am Pisces
13th 11:41 am Aries
15th 11:12 am Taurus
17th 11:42 am Gemini
19th 3:11 pm Cancer
21st 10:52 pm Leo
24th 10:11 am Virgo
26th 11:09 pm Libra
29th 11:35 am Scorpio

May 1980
1st 10:22 pm Sagittarius
4th 7:14 am Capricorn
6th 2:04 pm Aquarius
8th 6:33 pm Pisces
10th 8:45 pm Aries
12th 9:24 pm Taurus
14th 10:08 pm Gemini
17th 12:52 am Cancer
19th 7:14 am Leo
21st 5:32 pm Virgo
24th 6:10 am Libra
26th 6:36 pm Scorpio
29th 5:05 am Sagittarius
31th 1:15 pm Capricorn

June 1980
2nd 7:29 pm Aquarius
5th 12:10 am Pisces
7th 3:23 am Aries
9th 5:30 am Taurus
11th 7:23 am Gemini
13th 10:30 am Cancer
15th 4:22 pm Leo
18th 1:47 am Virgo
20th 1:54 pm Libra
23rd 2:26 am Scorpio
25th 1:01 pm Sagittarius
27th 8:46 pm Capricorn
30th 2:04 am Aquarius

July 1980
2nd 5:48 am Pisces
4th 8:46 am Aries
6th 11:30 am Taurus
8th 2:34 pm Gemini
10th 6:45 pm Cancer
13th 1:04 am Leo
15th 10:11 am Virgo
17th 9:55 pm Libra
20th 10:32 am Scorpio
22nd 9:42 pm Sagittarius
25th 5:45 am Capricorn
27th 10:35 am Aquarius
29th 1:11 pm Pisces
31th 2:54 pm Aries

August 1980
2nd 4:55 pm Taurus
4th 8:10 pm Gemini
7th 1:12 am Cancer
9th 8:23 am Leo
11th 5:54 pm Virgo
14th 5:32 am Libra
16th 6:14 pm Scorpio
19th 6:07 am Sagittarius
21st 3:11 pm Capricorn
23rd 8:33 pm Aquarius
25th 10:43 pm Pisces
27th 11:11 pm Aries
29th 11:41 pm Taurus

September 1980
1st 1:50 am Gemini
3rd 6:39 am Cancer
5th 2:22 pm Leo
8th 12:31 am Virgo
10th 12:22 pm Libra
13th 1:06 am Scorpio
15th 1:27 am Sagittarius
17th 11:45 pm Capricorn
20th 6:30 am Aquarius
22nd 9:27 am Pisces
24th 9:38 am Aries
26th 8:54 am Taurus
28th 9:21 am Gemini
30th 12:46 pm Cancer

October 1980
2nd 7:56 pm Leo
5th 6:19 am Virgo
7th 6:30 pm Libra
10th 7:15 am Scorpio
12th 7:37 pm Sagittarius
15th 6:36 am Capricorn
17th 2:53 pm Aquarius
19th 7:31 pm Pisces
21st 8:43 pm Aries
23rd 7:56 pm Taurus
25th 7:17 pm Gemini
27th 9:00 pm Cancer
30th 2:38 am Leo

November 1980
1st 12:18 pm Virgo
4th 12:31 am Libra
6th 1:19 pm Scorpio
9th 1:25 am Sagittarius
11th 12:15 pm Capricorn
13th 9:10 pm Aquarius
16th 3:21 am Pisces
18th 6:22 am Aries
20th 6:51 am Taurus
22nd 6:28 am Gemini
24th 7:19 am Cancer
26th 11:23 am Leo
28th 7:37 pm Virgo

December 1980
1st 7:13 am Libra
3rd 7:59 pm Scorpio
6th 7:57 am Sagittarius
8th 6:12 pm Capricorn
11th 2:36 am Aquarius
13th 9:04 am Pisces
15th 1:21 pm Aries
17th 3:37 pm Taurus
19th 4:40 pm Gemini
21st 6:04 pm Cancer
23rd 9:34 pm Leo
26th 4:32 am Virgo
28th 3:04 pm Libra
31th 3:36 am Scorpio

January 1981
2nd 3:41 pm Sagittarius
5th 1:41 am Capricorn
7th 9:13 am Aquarius
9th 2:42 pm Pisces
11th 6:44 pm Aries
13th 9:45 pm Taurus
16th 12:17 am Gemini
18th 3:08 am Cancer
20th 7:21 am Leo
22nd 2:02 pm Virgo
24th 11:45 pm Libra
27th 11:48 am Scorpio
30th 12:12 am Sagittarius

February 1981
1st 10:37 am Capricorn
3rd 5:55 pm Aquarius
5th 10:21 pm Pisces
8th 1:01 am Aries
10th 3:11 am Taurus
12th 5:51 am Gemini
14th 9:43 am Cancer
16th 3:10 pm Leo
18th 10:34 pm Virgo
21st 8:12 am Libra
23rd 7:54 pm Scorpio
26th 8:28 am Sagittarius
28th 7:46 pm Capricorn

March 1981
3rd 3:51 am Aquarius
5th 8:12 am Pisces
7th 9:49 am Aries
9th 10:23 am Taurus
11th 11:42 am Gemini
13th 3:05 pm Cancer
15th 9:02 pm Leo
18th 5:20 am Virgo
20th 3:31 pm Libra
23rd 3:14 am Scorpio
25th 3:50 pm Sagittarius
28th 3:52 am Capricorn
30th 1:15 pm Aquarius

April 1981
1st 6:41 pm Pisces
3rd 8:25 pm Aries
5th 8:05 pm Taurus
7th 7:48 pm Gemini
9th 9:34 pm Cancer
12th 2:36 am Leo
14th 10:56 am Virgo
16th 9:38 pm Libra
19th 9:39 am Scorpio
21st 10:15 pm Sagittarius
24th 10:31 am Capricorn
26th 8:57 pm Aquarius
29th 3:56 am Pisces

May 1981
1st 6:58 am Aries
3rd 6:59 am Taurus
5th 6:02 am Gemini
7th 6:18 am Cancer
9th 9:40 am Leo
11th 4:55 pm Virgo
14th 3:24 am Libra
16th 3:37 pm Scorpio
19th 4:14 am Sagittarius
21st 4:20 pm Capricorn
24th 3:00 am Aquarius
26th 11:05 am Pisces
28th 3:44 pm Aries
30th 5:11 pm Taurus

June 1981
1st 4:49 pm Gemini
3rd 4:39 pm Cancer
5th 6:43 pm Leo
8th 12:25 am Virgo
10th 9:54 am Libra
12th 9:54 pm Scorpio
15th 10:31 am Sagittarius
17th 10:21 pm Capricorn
20th 8:36 am Aquarius
22nd 4:44 pm Pisces
24th 10:18 pm Aries
27th 1:16 am Taurus
29th 2:21 am Gemini

July 1981
1st 2:57 am Cancer
3rd 4:47 am Leo
5th 9:26 am Virgo
7th 5:42 pm Libra
10th 5:01 am Scorpio
12th 5:34 pm Sagittarius
15th 5:19 am Capricorn
17th 3:02 pm Aquarius
19th 10:26 pm Pisces
22nd 3:44 am Aries
24th 7:18 am Taurus
26th 9:42 am Gemini
28th 11:41 am Cancer
30th 2:21 pm Leo

August 1981
1st 6:54 pm Virgo
4th 2:24 am Libra
6th 12:58 pm Scorpio
9th 1:22 am Sagittarius
11th 1:20 pm Capricorn
13th 10:56 pm Aquarius
16th 5:35 am Pisces
18th 9:49 am Aries
20th 12:44 pm Taurus
22nd 3:18 pm Gemini
24th 6:17 pm Cancer
26th 10:10 pm Leo
29th 3:32 am Virgo
31th 11:02 am Libra

September 1981
2nd 9:10 pm Scorpio
5th 9:23 am Sagittarius
7th 9:48 pm Capricorn
10th 7:58 am Aquarius
12th 2:34 pm Pisces
14th 5:56 pm Aries
16th 7:31 pm Taurus
18th 8:59 pm Gemini
20th 11:39 pm Cancer
23rd 4:08 am Leo
25th 10:29 am Virgo
27th 6:40 pm Libra
30th 4:53 am Scorpio

October 1981
2nd 4:59 pm Sagittarius
5th 5:48 am Capricorn
7th 5:00 pm Aquarius
10th 12:32 am Pisces
12th 4:01 am Aries
14th 4:44 am Taurus
16th 4:41 am Gemini
18th 5:53 am Cancer
20th 9:34 am Leo
22nd 4:04 pm Virgo
25th 12:56 am Libra
27th 11:38 am Scorpio
29th 11:48 pm Sagittarius

November 1981
1st 12:45 pm Capricorn
4th 12:51 am Aquarius
6th 9:52 am Pisces
8th 2:39 pm Aries
10th 3:45 pm Taurus
12th 3:00 pm Gemini
14th 2:37 pm Cancer
16th 4:33 pm Leo
18th 9:53 pm Virgo
21st 6:33 am Libra
23rd 5:36 pm Scorpio
26th 6:00 am Sagittarius
28th 6:52 pm Capricorn

December 1981
1st 7:09 am Aquarius
3rd 5:15 pm Pisces
5th 11:49 pm Aries
8th 2:31 am Taurus
10th 2:30 am Gemini
12th 1:41 am Cancer
14th 2:08 am Leo
16th 5:38 am Virgo
18th 12:57 pm Libra
20th 11:39 pm Scorpio
23rd 12:11 pm Sagittarius
26th 12:59 am Capricorn
28th 12:53 am Aquarius
30th 11:01 pm Pisces

January 1982
2nd 6:33 am Aries
4th 11:02 am Taurus
6th 12:49 pm Gemini
8th 1:02 pm Cancer
10th 1:22 pm Leo
12th 3:37 pm Virgo
14th 9:17 pm Libra
17th 6:46 am Scorpio
19th 6:59 pm Sagittarius
22nd 7:50 am Capricorn
24th 7:25 pm Aquarius
27th 4:49 am Pisces
29th 11:58 am Aries
31th 5:04 pm Taurus

February 1982
2nd 8:20 pm Gemini
4th 10:18 pm Cancer
6th 11:50 pm Leo
9th 2:15 am Virgo
11th 7:02 am Libra
13th 3:15 pm Scorpio
16th 2:45 am Sagittarius
18th 3:35 pm Capricorn
21st 3:15 am Aquarius
23rd 12:09 pm Pisces
25th 6:17 pm Aries
27th 10:32 pm Taurus

March 1982
2nd 1:50 am Gemini
4th 4:48 am Cancer
6th 7:50 am Leo
8th 11:27 am Virgo
10th 4:34 pm Libra
13th 12:17 am Scorpio
15th 11:04 am Sagittarius
17th 11:47 pm Capricorn
20th 11:52 am Aquarius
22nd 9:01 pm Pisces
25th 2:37 am Aries
27th 5:40 am Taurus
29th 7:44 am Gemini
31th 10:09 am Cancer

April 1982
2nd 1:36 pm Leo
4th 6:18 pm Virgo
7th 12:26 am Libra
9th 8:33 am Scorpio
11th 7:06 pm Sagittarius
14th 7:41 am Capricorn
16th 8:17 pm Aquarius
19th 6:19 am Pisces
21st 12:23 pm Aries
23rd 2:59 pm Taurus
25th 3:49 pm Gemini
27th 4:44 pm Cancer
29th 7:09 pm Leo

May 1982
1st 11:45 pm Virgo
4th 6:32 am Libra
6th 3:24 pm Scorpio
9th 2:17 am Sagittarius
11th 2:49 pm Capricorn
14th 3:44 am Aquarius
16th 2:46 pm Pisces
18th 10:04 pm Aries
21st 1:22 am Taurus
23rd 1:55 am Gemini
25th 1:38 am Cancer
27th 2:27 am Leo
29th 5:43 am Virgo
31th 12:02 pm Libra

June 1982
2nd 9:12 pm Scorpio
5th 8:31 am Sagittarius
7th 9:12 pm Capricorn
10th 10:07 am Aquarius
12th 9:44 pm Pisces
15th 6:20 am Aries
17th 11:07 am Taurus
19th 12:35 pm Gemini
21st 12:14 pm Cancer
23rd 11:57 am Leo
25th 1:36 pm Virgo
27th 6:30 pm Libra
30th 3:01 am Scorpio

July 1982
2nd 2:25 pm Sagittarius
5th 3:15 am Capricorn
7th 4:04 pm Aquarius
10th 3:35 am Pisces
12th 12:49 pm Aries
14th 6:59 pm Taurus
16th 10:04 pm Gemini
18th 10:46 pm Cancer
20th 10:36 pm Leo
22nd 11:20 pm Virgo
25th 2:45 am Libra
27th 9:58 am Scorpio
29th 8:47 pm Sagittarius

August 1982
1st 9:36 am Capricorn
3rd 10:17 pm Aquarius
6th 9:23 am Pisces
8th 6:20 pm Aries
11th 1:00 am Taurus
13th 5:22 am Gemini
15th 7:41 am Cancer
17th 8:41 am Leo
19th 9:40 am Virgo
21st 12:22 pm Libra
23rd 6:21 pm Scorpio
26th 4:11 am Sagittarius
28th 4:41 pm Capricorn
31th 5:23 am Aquarius

September 1982
2nd 4:11 pm Pisces
5th 12:24 am Aries
7th 6:27 am Taurus
9th 10:57 am Gemini
11th 2:18 pm Cancer
13th 4:46 pm Leo
15th 6:58 pm Virgo
17th 10:04 pm Libra
20th 3:32 am Scorpio
22nd 12:30 pm Sagittarius
25th 12:31 am Capricorn
27th 1:21 pm Aquarius
30th 12:18 am Pisces

October 1982
2nd 8:06 am Aries
4th 1:09 pm Taurus
6th 4:39 pm Gemini
8th 7:40 pm Cancer
10th 10:44 pm Leo
13th 2:09 am Virgo
15th 6:23 am Libra
17th 12:21 pm Scorpio
19th 9:02 pm Sagittarius
22nd 8:37 am Capricorn
24th 9:35 pm Aquarius
27th 9:12 am Pisces
29th 5:25 pm Aries
31th 10:04 pm Taurus

November 1982
3rd 12:23 am Gemini
5th 1:59 am Cancer
7th 4:10 am Leo
9th 7:40 am Virgo
11th 12:46 pm Libra
13th 7:42 pm Scorpio
16th 4:52 am Sagittarius
18th 4:21 pm Capricorn
21st 5:20 am Aquarius
23rd 5:42 pm Pisces
26th 3:07 am Aries
28th 8:32 am Taurus
30th 10:36 am Gemini

December 1982
2nd 10:58 am Cancer
4th 11:27 am Leo
6th 1:32 pm Virgo
8th 6:10 pm Libra
11th 1:34 am Scorpio
13th 11:26 am Sagittarius
15th 11:15 pm Capricorn
18th 12:12 pm Aquarius
21st 12:56 am Pisces
23rd 11:34 am Aries
25th 6:36 pm Taurus
27th 9:49 pm Gemini
29th 10:12 pm Cancer
31th 9:33 pm Leo

January 1983
2nd 9:50 pm Virgo
5th 12:44 am Libra
7th 7:16 am Scorpio
9th 5:13 pm Sagittarius
12th 5:26 am Capricorn
14th 6:26 pm Aquarius
17th 7:02 am Pisces
19th 6:08 pm Aries
22nd 2:36 am Taurus
24th 7:40 am Gemini
26th 9:29 am Cancer
28th 9:11 am Leo
30th 8:35 am Virgo

February 1983
1st 9:47 am Libra
3rd 2:32 pm Scorpio
5th 11:28 pm Sagittarius
8th 11:33 am Capricorn
11th 12:40 am Aquarius
13th 1:01 pm Pisces
15th 11:46 pm Aries
18th 8:30 am Taurus
20th 2:52 pm Gemini
22nd 6:31 pm Cancer
24th 7:47 pm Leo
26th 7:50 pm Virgo
28th 8:30 pm Libra

March 1983
2nd 11:51 pm Scorpio
5th 7:14 am Sagittarius
7th 6:28 pm Capricorn
10th 7:29 am Aquarius
12th 7:47 pm Pisces
15th 6:00 am Aries
17th 2:04 pm Taurus
19th 8:20 pm Gemini
22nd 12:52 am Cancer
24th 3:43 am Leo
26th 5:18 am Virgo
28th 6:49 am Libra
30th 9:57 am Scorpio

April 1983
1st 4:19 pm Sagittarius
4th 2:29 am Capricorn
6th 3:05 pm Aquarius
9th 3:30 am Pisces
11th 1:37 pm Aries
13th 8:59 pm Taurus
16th 2:15 am Gemini
18th 6:14 am Cancer
20th 9:26 am Leo
22nd 12:12 pm Virgo
24th 3:04 pm Libra
26th 7:05 pm Scorpio
29th 1:28 am Sagittarius

May 1983
1st 11:01 am Capricorn
3rd 11:09 pm Aquarius
6th 11:43 am Pisces
8th 10:16 pm Aries
11th 5:36 am Taurus
13th 10:04 am Gemini
15th 12:48 pm Cancer
17th 3:01 pm Leo
19th 5:37 pm Virgo
21st 9:11 pm Libra
24th 2:17 am Scorpio
26th 9:27 am Sagittarius
28th 7:06 pm Capricorn
31st 6:59 am Aquarius

September 1983
2nd 2:53 am Cancer
4th 4:47 am Leo
6th 4:36 am Virgo
8th 4:14 am Libra
10th 5:49 am Scorpio
12th 11:07 am Sagittarius
14th 8:33 pm Capricorn
17th 8:45 am Aquarius
19th 9:30 pm Pisces
22nd 9:10 am Aries
24th 7:12 pm Taurus
27th 3:24 am Gemini
29th 9:24 am Cancer

January 1984
2nd 6:07 am Capricorn
4th 4:30 pm Aquarius
7th 4:34 am Pisces
9th 5:15 pm Aries
12th 4:36 am Taurus
14th 12:40 pm Gemini
16th 4:48 pm Cancer
18th 5:50 pm Leo
20th 5:36 pm Virgo
22nd 6:07 pm Libra
24th 9:04 pm Scorpio
27th 3:12 am Sagittarius
29th 12:12 pm Capricorn
31th 11:11 pm Aquarius

May 1984
2nd 4:02 pm Gemini
4th 11:26 pm Cancer
7th 4:43 am Leo
9th 8:02 am Virgo
11th 9:55 am Libra
13th 11:22 am Scorpio
15th 1:50 pm Sagittarius
17th 6:43 pm Capricorn
20th 2:55 am Aquarius
22nd 2:08 pm Pisces
25th 2:39 am Aries
27th 2:13 am Taurus
29th 11:23 pm Gemini

September 1984
1st 4:29 pm Sagittarius
3rd 10:55 pm Capricorn
6th 8:11 am Aquarius
8th 7:24 pm Pisces
11th 7:46 am Aries
13th 8:33 pm Taurus
16th 8:25 am Gemini
18th 5:35 pm Cancer
20th 10:49 pm Leo
23rd 12:19 am Virgo
24th 11:41 pm Libra
26th 11:04 pm Scorpio
29th 12:32 am Sagittarius

June 1983
2nd 7:41 pm Pisces
5th 6:59 am Aries
7th 3:05 pm Taurus
9th 7:37 pm Gemini
11th 9:33 pm Cancer
13th 10:21 pm Leo
15th 11:38 pm Virgo
18th 2:36 am Libra
20th 7:59 am Scorpio
22nd 3:55 pm Sagittarius
25th 2:08 am Capricorn
27th 2:06 pm Aquarius
30th 2:51 am Pisces

October 1983
1st 12:55 pm Leo
3rd 2:16 pm Virgo
5th 2:43 pm Libra
7th 4:06 pm Scorpio
9th 8:21 pm Sagittarius
12th 4:30 am Capricorn
14th 3:59 pm Aquarius
17th 4:41 am Pisces
19th 4:18 pm Aries
22nd 1:47 am Taurus
24th 9:10 am Gemini
26th 2:47 pm Cancer
28th 6:50 pm Leo
30th 9:33 pm Virgo

February 1984
3rd 11:22 am Pisces
6th 12:04 am Aries
8th 12:05 pm Taurus
10th 9:39 pm Gemini
13th 3:20 am Cancer
15th 5:10 am Leo
17th 4:32 am Virgo
19th 3:40 am Libra
21st 4:44 am Scorpio
23rd 9:22 am Sagittarius
25th 5:49 pm Capricorn
28th 5:02 am Aquarius

June 1984
1st 5:54 am Cancer
3rd 10:19 am Leo
5th 1:27 pm Virgo
7th 4:04 pm Libra
9th 6:48 pm Scorpio
11th 10:26 pm Sagittarius
14th 3:48 am Capricorn
16th 11:41 am Aquarius
18th 10:18 pm Pisces
21st 10:40 am Aries
23rd 10:38 pm Taurus
26th 8:04 am Gemini
28th 2:09 pm Cancer
30th 5:30 pm Leo

October 1984
1st 5:28 am Capricorn
3rd 2:04 pm Aquarius
6th 1:19 am Pisces
8th 1:50 pm Aries
11th 2:28 am Taurus
13th 2:13 pm Gemini
16th 12:00 am Cancer
18th 6:41 am Leo
20th 9:56 am Virgo
22nd 10:32 am Libra
24th 10:08 am Scorpio
26th 10:43 am Sagittarius
28th 2:05 pm Capricorn
30th 9:13 pm Aquarius

July 1983
2nd 2:47 pm Aries
5th 12:05 am Taurus
7th 5:41 am Gemini
9th 7:51 am Cancer
11th 7:54 am Leo
13th 7:43 am Virgo
15th 9:10 am Libra
17th 1:38 pm Scorpio
19th 9:31 pm Sagittarius
22nd 8:11 am Capricorn
24th 8:26 pm Aquarius
27th 9:11 am Pisces
29th 9:20 pm Aries

November 1983
1st 11:31 pm Libra
4th 1:53 am Scorpio
6th 6:09 am Sagittarius
8th 1:31 pm Capricorn
11th 12:10 am Aquarius
13th 12:40 pm Pisces
16th 12:36 am Aries
18th 10:06 am Taurus
20th 4:45 pm Gemini
22nd 9:11 pm Cancer
25th 12:19 am Leo
27th 3:02 am Virgo
29th 5:57 am Libra

March 1984
1st 5:29 pm Pisces
4th 6:07 am Aries
6th 6:08 pm Taurus
9th 4:29 am Gemini
11th 11:47 am Cancer
13th 3:21 pm Leo
15th 3:48 pm Virgo
17th 2:53 pm Libra
19th 2:49 pm Scorpio
21st 5:41 pm Sagittarius
24th 12:36 am Capricorn
26th 11:08 am Aquarius
28th 11:37 pm Pisces
31th 12:14 pm Aries

July 1984
2nd 7:28 pm Virgo
4th 9:27 pm Libra
7th 12:28 am Scorpio
9th 5:04 am Sagittarius
11th 11:23 am Capricorn
13th 7:41 pm Aquarius
16th 6:10 am Pisces
18th 6:25 am Aries
21st 6:52 am Taurus
23rd 5:10 pm Gemini
25th 11:44 pm Cancer
28th 2:41 am Leo
30th 3:29 am Virgo

November 1984
2nd 7:49 am Pisces
4th 8:20 pm Aries
7th 8:53 am Taurus
9th 8:10 pm Gemini
12th 5:31 am Cancer
14th 12:33 pm Leo
16th 5:08 pm Virgo
18th 7:30 pm Libra
20th 8:31 pm Scorpio
22nd 9:34 pm Sagittarius
25th 12:17 am Capricorn
27th 6:06 am Aquarius
29th 3:33 pm Pisces

August 1983
1st 7:36 am Taurus
3rd 2:43 pm Gemini
5th 6:09 pm Cancer
7th 6:38 pm Leo
9th 5:50 pm Virgo
11th 5:52 pm Libra
13th 8:44 pm Scorpio
16th 3:33 am Sagittarius
18th 1:59 pm Capricorn
21st 2:25 am Aquarius
23rd 3:09 pm Pisces
26th 3:08 am Aries
28th 1:38 pm Taurus
30th 9:48 pm Gemini

December 1983
1st 9:41 am Scorpio
3rd 2:56 pm Sagittarius
5th 10:28 pm Capricorn
8th 8:39 am Aquarius
10th 8:53 pm Pisces
13th 9:16 am Aries
15th 7:32 pm Taurus
18th 2:24 am Gemini
20th 6:04 am Cancer
22nd 7:44 am Leo
24th 9:02 am Virgo
26th 11:18 am Libra
28th 3:26 pm Scorpio
30th 9:44 pm Sagittarius

April 1984
2nd 11:55 pm Taurus
5th 10:04 am Gemini
7th 5:59 pm Cancer
9th 11:01 pm Leo
12th 1:11 am Virgo
14th 1:29 am Libra
16th 1:41 am Scorpio
18th 3:44 am Sagittarius
20th 9:10 am Capricorn
22nd 6:27 pm Aquarius
25th 6:26 am Pisces
27th 7:02 pm Aries
30th 6:30 am Taurus

August 1984
1st 4:04 am Libra
3rd 6:04 am Scorpio
5th 10:29 am Sagittarius
7th 5:24 pm Capricorn
10th 2:25 am Aquarius
12th 1:13 pm Pisces
15th 1:28 am Aries
17th 2:13 pm Taurus
20th 1:31 am Gemini
22nd 9:20 am Cancer
24th 1:00 pm Leo
26th 1:33 pm Virgo
28th 12:58 pm Libra
30th 1:23 pm Scorpio

December 1984
2nd 3:42 am Aries
4th 4:20 pm Taurus
7th 3:24 am Gemini
9th 11:56 am Cancer
11th 6:08 pm Leo
13th 10:35 pm Virgo
16th 1:52 am Libra
18th 4:27 am Scorpio
20th 6:58 am Sagittarius
22nd 10:21 am Capricorn
24th 3:47 pm Aquarius
27th 12:18 am Pisces
29th 11:49 am Aries

January 1985
1st 12:36 am Taurus
3rd 11:59 am Gemini
5th 8:18 pm Cancer
8th 1:28 am Leo
10th 4:40 am Virgo
12th 7:14 am Libra
14th 10:08 am Scorpio
16th 1:48 pm Sagittarius
18th 6:29 pm Capricorn
21st 12:38 am Aquarius
23rd 9:02 am Pisces
25th 8:05 am Aries
28th 8:53 am Taurus
30th 9:00 pm Gemini

May 1985
1st 9:22 pm Libra
3rd 9:17 pm Scorpio
5th 8:56 pm Sagittarius
7th 10:12 pm Capricorn
10th 2:38 am Aquarius
12th 10:55 am Pisces
14th 10:25 pm Aries
17th 11:23 am Taurus
20th 12:01 am Gemini
22nd 11:04 am Cancer
24th 7:54 pm Leo
27th 2:06 am Virgo
29th 5:41 am Libra
31th 7:08 am Scorpio

September 1985
1st 5:42 am Aries
3rd 5:27 pm Taurus
6th 6:27 am Gemini
8th 6:10 pm Cancer
11th 2:27 am Leo
13th 6:53 am Virgo
15th 8:34 am Libra
17th 9:18 am Scorpio
19th 10:41 am Sagittarius
21st 1:49 pm Capricorn
23rd 7:11 pm Aquarius
26th 2:50 am Pisces
28th 12:42 pm Aries

January 1986
2nd 8:45 pm Libra
5th 12:44 am Scorpio
7th 2:47 am Sagittarius
9th 3:42 am Capricorn
11th 5:02 am Aquarius
13th 8:39 am Pisces
15th 4:04 pm Aries
18th 3:13 am Taurus
20th 4:11 pm Gemini
23rd 4:14 am Cancer
25th 1:47 pm Leo
27th 8:51 pm Virgo
30th 2:10 am Libra

May 1986
2nd 2:30 pm Pisces
4th 11:01 pm Aries
7th 9:58 am Taurus
9th 10:26 pm Gemini
12th 11:17 am Cancer
14th 11:15 pm Leo
17th 8:45 am Virgo
19th 2:41 pm Libra
21st 5:04 pm Scorpio
23rd 4:57 pm Sagittarius
25th 4:16 pm Capricorn
27th 5:00 pm Aquarius
29th 8:54 pm Pisces

February 1985
2nd 5:59 am Cancer
4th 11:02 am Leo
6th 1:10 pm Virgo
8th 2:11 pm Libra
10th 3:49 pm Scorpio
12th 7:09 pm Sagittarius
15th 12:27 am Capricorn
17th 7:36 am Aquarius
19th 4:38 pm Pisces
22nd 3:42 am Aries
24th 4:27 pm Taurus
27th 5:11 am Gemini

June 1985
2nd 7:34 am Sagittarius
4th 8:34 am Capricorn
6th 11:52 am Aquarius
8th 6:46 pm Pisces
11th 5:24 am Aries
13th 6:11 pm Taurus
16th 6:45 am Gemini
18th 5:22 pm Cancer
21st 1:32 am Leo
23rd 7:33 am Virgo
25th 11:48 am Libra
27th 2:37 pm Scorpio
29th 4:31 pm Sagittarius

October 1985
1st 12:35 am Taurus
3rd 1:36 pm Gemini
6th 1:59 am Cancer
8th 11:33 am Leo
10th 5:09 pm Virgo
12th 7:12 pm Libra
14th 7:13 pm Scorpio
16th 7:06 pm Sagittarius
18th 8:35 pm Capricorn
21st 12:54 am Aquarius
23rd 8:27 am Pisces
25th 6:47 pm Aries
28th 6:59 am Taurus
30th 7:59 pm Gemini

February 1986
1st 6:19 am Scorpio
3rd 9:32 am Sagittarius
5th 12:02 pm Capricorn
7th 2:35 pm Aquarius
9th 6:32 pm Pisces
12th 1:21 am Aries
14th 11:37 am Taurus
17th 12:17 am Gemini
19th 12:38 pm Cancer
21st 10:25 pm Leo
24th 4:58 am Virgo
26th 9:07 am Libra
28th 12:06 pm Scorpio

June 1986
1st 4:42 am Aries
3rd 3:45 pm Taurus
6th 4:26 am Gemini
8th 5:16 pm Cancer
11th 5:11 am Leo
13th 3:17 pm Virgo
15th 10:38 pm Libra
18th 2:36 am Scorpio
20th 3:36 am Sagittarius
22nd 3:00 am Capricorn
24th 2:50 am Aquarius
26th 5:12 am Pisces
28th 11:34 am Aries
30th 9:54 pm Taurus

March 1985
1st 3:23 pm Cancer
3rd 9:28 pm Leo
5th 11:43 pm Virgo
7th 11:47 pm Libra
9th 11:47 pm Scorpio
12th 1:29 am Sagittarius
14th 5:54 am Capricorn
16th 1:11 pm Aquarius
18th 10:50 pm Pisces
21st 10:20 am Aries
23rd 11:06 pm Taurus
26th 12:01 pm Gemini
28th 11:13 pm Cancer
31th 6:51 am Leo

July 1985
1st 6:23 pm Capricorn
3rd 9:36 pm Aquarius
6th 3:40 am Pisces
8th 1:20 pm Aries
11th 1:44 am Taurus
13th 2:23 pm Gemini
16th 12:54 am Cancer
18th 8:25 am Leo
20th 1:30 pm Virgo
22nd 5:10 pm Libra
24th 8:16 pm Scorpio
26th 11:12 pm Sagittarius
29th 2:21 am Capricorn
31th 6:26 am Aquarius

November 1985
2nd 8:30 am Cancer
4th 7:04 pm Leo
7th 2:18 am Virgo
9th 5:52 am Libra
11th 6:31 am Scorpio
13th 5:53 am Sagittarius
15th 5:53 am Capricorn
17th 8:25 am Aquarius
19th 2:42 pm Pisces
22nd 12:42 am Aries
24th 1:06 pm Taurus
27th 2:08 am Gemini
29th 2:23 pm Cancer

March 1986
2nd 2:52 pm Sagittarius
4th 5:56 pm Capricorn
6th 9:43 pm Aquarius
9th 2:48 am Pisces
11th 10:04 am Aries
13th 8:04 pm Taurus
16th 8:22 am Gemini
18th 9:04 pm Cancer
21st 7:38 am Leo
23rd 2:40 pm Virgo
25th 6:23 pm Libra
27th 8:06 pm Scorpio
29th 9:20 pm Sagittarius
31th 11:25 pm Capricorn

July 1986
3rd 10:31 am Gemini
5th 11:19 pm Cancer
8th 10:55 am Leo
10th 8:50 pm Virgo
13th 4:40 am Libra
15th 9:58 am Scorpio
17th 12:35 pm Sagittarius
19th 1:11 pm Capricorn
21st 1:18 pm Aquarius
23rd 2:59 pm Pisces
25th 8:02 pm Aries
28th 5:11 am Taurus
30th 5:18 pm Gemini

April 1985
2nd 10:25 am Virgo
4th 10:54 am Libra
6th 10:11 am Scorpio
8th 10:18 am Sagittarius
10th 12:57 pm Capricorn
12th 7:04 pm Aquarius
15th 4:30 am Pisces
17th 4:18 pm Aries
20th 5:12 am Taurus
22nd 6:00 pm Gemini
25th 5:26 am Cancer
27th 2:10 pm Leo
29th 7:24 pm Virgo

August 1985
2nd 12:33 pm Pisces
4th 9:42 pm Aries
7th 9:41 am Taurus
9th 10:31 pm Gemini
12th 9:28 am Cancer
14th 4:57 pm Leo
16th 9:15 pm Virgo
18th 11:44 pm Libra
21st 1:51 am Scorpio
23rd 4:36 am Sagittarius
25th 8:24 am Capricorn
27th 1:31 pm Aquarius
29th 8:25 pm Pisces

December 1985
2nd 12:59 am Leo
4th 9:14 am Virgo
6th 2:33 pm Libra
8th 4:57 pm Scorpio
10th 5:14 pm Sagittarius
12th 5:00 pm Capricorn
14th 6:15 pm Aquarius
16th 10:50 pm Pisces
19th 7:36 am Aries
21st 7:40 pm Taurus
24th 8:45 am Gemini
26th 8:44 pm Cancer
29th 6:44 am Leo
31th 2:43 pm Virgo

April 1986
3rd 3:11 am Aquarius
5th 9:04 am Pisces
7th 5:12 pm Aries
10th 3:36 am Taurus
12th 3:50 pm Gemini
15th 4:42 am Cancer
17th 4:09 pm Leo
20th 12:24 am Virgo
22nd 4:50 am Libra
24th 6:16 am Scorpio
26th 6:17 am Sagittarius
28th 6:41 am Capricorn
30th 9:06 am Aquarius

August 1986
2nd 6:04 am Cancer
4th 5:26 pm Leo
7th 2:44 am Virgo
9th 10:05 am Libra
11th 3:36 pm Scorpio
13th 7:17 pm Sagittarius
15th 9:23 pm Capricorn
17th 10:44 pm Aquarius
20th 12:52 am Pisces
22nd 5:27 am Aries
24th 1:36 pm Taurus
27th 1:00 am Gemini
29th 1:39 pm Cancer

September 1986
1st 1:08 am Leo
3rd 10:06 am Virgo
5th 4:33 pm Libra
7th 9:12 pm Scorpio
10th 12:40 am Sagittarius
12th 3:28 am Capricorn
14th 6:07 am Aquarius
16th 9:27 am Pisces
18th 2:34 pm Aries
20th 10:25 pm Taurus
23rd 9:13 am Gemini
25th 9:44 pm Cancer
28th 9:39 am Leo
30th 6:57 pm Virgo

October 1986
3rd 1:04 am Libra
5th 4:35 am Scorpio
7th 6:48 am Sagittarius
9th 8:53 am Capricorn
11th 11:45 am Aquarius
13th 4:04 pm Pisces
15th 10:13 pm Aries
18th 6:35 am Taurus
20th 5:15 pm Gemini
23rd 5:37 am Cancer
25th 6:02 pm Leo
28th 4:20 am Virgo
30th 11:04 am Libra

November 1986
1st 2:20 pm Scorpio
3rd 3:20 pm Sagittarius
5th 3:49 pm Capricorn
7th 5:29 pm Aquarius
9th 9:29 pm Pisces
12th 4:14 am Aries
14th 1:24 pm Taurus
17th 12:26 am Gemini
19th 12:45 pm Cancer
22nd 1:25 am Leo
24th 12:45 pm Virgo
26th 8:59 pm Libra
29th 1:13 am Scorpio

December 1986
1st 2:08 am Sagittarius
3rd 1:28 am Capricorn
5th 1:23 am Aquarius
7th 3:48 am Pisces
9th 9:48 am Aries
11th 7:10 pm Taurus
14th 6:41 am Gemini
16th 7:09 pm Cancer
19th 7:44 am Leo
21st 7:30 pm Virgo
24th 5:04 am Libra
26th 11:06 am Scorpio
28th 1:20 pm Sagittarius
30th 12:55 pm Capricorn

January 1987
1st 11:54 am Aquarius
3rd 12:36 pm Pisces
5th 4:50 pm Aries
8th 1:13 am Taurus
10th 12:39 pm Gemini
13th 1:18 am Cancer
15th 1:45 pm Leo
18th 1:15 am Virgo
20th 11:09 am Libra
22nd 6:30 pm Scorpio
24th 10:35 pm Sagittarius
26th 11:42 pm Capricorn
28th 11:17 pm Aquarius
30th 11:24 pm Pisces

February 1987
2nd 2:09 am Aries
4th 8:52 am Taurus
6th 7:23 pm Gemini
9th 7:55 am Cancer
11th 8:21 pm Leo
14th 7:26 am Virgo
16th 4:44 pm Libra
19th 12:04 am Scorpio
21st 5:09 am Sagittarius
23rd 7:57 am Capricorn
25th 9:09 am Aquarius
27th 10:07 am Pisces

March 1987
1st 12:37 pm Aries
3rd 6:11 pm Taurus
6th 3:26 am Gemini
8th 3:24 pm Cancer
11th 3:54 am Leo
13th 2:55 pm Virgo
15th 11:34 pm Libra
18th 5:57 am Scorpio
20th 10:32 am Sagittarius
22nd 1:49 pm Capricorn
24th 4:18 pm Aquarius
26th 6:46 pm Pisces
28th 10:12 pm Aries
31th 3:46 am Taurus

April 1987
2nd 12:16 pm Gemini
4th 11:33 pm Cancer
7th 12:04 pm Leo
9th 11:28 pm Virgo
12th 8:06 am Libra
14th 1:41 pm Scorpio
16th 5:02 pm Sagittarius
18th 7:21 pm Capricorn
20th 9:45 pm Aquarius
23rd 1:02 am Pisces
25th 5:41 am Aries
27th 12:06 pm Taurus
29th 8:43 pm Gemini

May 1987
2nd 7:39 am Cancer
4th 8:06 pm Leo
7th 8:07 am Virgo
9th 5:29 pm Libra
11th 11:09 pm Scorpio
14th 1:41 am Sagittarius
16th 2:37 am Capricorn
18th 3:43 am Aquarius
20th 6:24 am Pisces
22nd 11:23 am Aries
24th 6:39 pm Taurus
27th 3:55 am Gemini
29th 2:59 pm Cancer

June 1987
1st 3:25 am Leo
3rd 3:56 pm Virgo
6th 2:24 am Libra
8th 9:06 am Scorpio
10th 11:54 am Sagittarius
12th 12:06 pm Capricorn
14th 11:45 am Aquarius
16th 12:55 pm Pisces
18th 4:56 pm Aries
21st 12:09 am Taurus
23rd 9:54 am Gemini
25th 9:22 pm Cancer
28th 9:52 am Leo
30th 10:34 pm Virgo

July 1987
3rd 9:54 am Libra
5th 6:04 pm Scorpio
7th 10:05 pm Sagittarius
9th 10:44 pm Capricorn
11th 9:50 pm Aquarius
13th 9:36 pm Pisces
16th 12:00 am Aries
18th 6:04 am Taurus
20th 3:32 pm Gemini
23rd 3:13 am Cancer
25th 3:49 pm Leo
28th 4:25 am Virgo
30th 3:59 pm Libra

August 1987
2nd 1:09 am Scorpio
4th 6:47 am Sagittarius
6th 8:52 am Capricorn
8th 8:38 am Aquarius
10th 8:02 am Pisces
12th 9:09 am Aries
14th 1:38 pm Taurus
16th 9:58 pm Gemini
19th 9:19 am Cancer
21st 9:58 pm Leo
24th 10:23 am Virgo
26th 9:35 pm Libra
29th 6:49 am Scorpio
31th 1:24 pm Sagittarius

September 1987
2nd 5:04 pm Capricorn
4th 6:22 pm Aquarius
6th 6:37 pm Pisces
8th 7:34 pm Aries
10th 10:57 pm Taurus
13th 5:54 am Gemini
15th 4:21 pm Cancer
18th 4:50 am Leo
20th 5:13 pm Virgo
23rd 3:58 am Libra
25th 12:30 pm Scorpio
27th 6:49 pm Sagittarius
29th 11:08 pm Capricorn

October 1987
2nd 1:51 am Aquarius
4th 3:39 am Pisces
6th 5:35 am Aries
8th 8:58 am Taurus
10th 3:04 pm Gemini
13th 12:31 am Cancer
15th 12:33 pm Leo
18th 1:06 am Virgo
20th 11:50 am Libra
22nd 7:42 pm Scorpio
25th 12:57 am Sagittarius
27th 4:33 am Capricorn
29th 7:27 am Aquarius
31th 10:20 am Pisces

November 1987
2nd 1:40 pm Aries
4th 6:02 pm Taurus
7th 12:16 am Gemini
9th 9:10 am Cancer
11th 8:45 pm Leo
14th 9:29 am Virgo
16th 8:48 pm Libra
19th 4:47 am Scorpio
21st 9:17 am Sagittarius
23rd 11:32 am Capricorn
25th 1:13 pm Aquarius
27th 3:41 pm Pisces
29th 7:36 pm Aries

December 1987
2nd 1:06 am Taurus
4th 8:14 am Gemini
6th 5:20 pm Cancer
9th 4:40 am Leo
11th 5:29 pm Virgo
14th 5:40 am Libra
16th 2:41 pm Scorpio
18th 7:33 pm Sagittarius
20th 9:08 pm Capricorn
22nd 9:20 pm Aquarius
24th 10:10 pm Pisces
27th 1:05 am Aries
29th 6:36 am Taurus
31th 2:28 pm Gemini

January 1988
3rd 12:17 am Cancer
5th 11:47 am Leo
8th 12:35 am Virgo
10th 1:17 pm Libra
12th 11:39 pm Scorpio
15th 5:58 am Sagittarius
17th 8:16 am Capricorn
19th 8:04 am Aquarius
21st 7:27 am Pisces
23rd 8:31 am Aries
25th 12:36 pm Taurus
27th 8:02 pm Gemini
30th 6:11 am Cancer

February 1988
1st 6:06 pm Leo
4th 6:54 am Virgo
6th 7:36 pm Libra
9th 6:41 am Scorpio
11th 2:35 pm Sagittarius
13th 6:36 pm Capricorn
15th 7:26 pm Aquarius
17th 6:45 pm Pisces
19th 6:35 pm Aries
21st 8:51 pm Taurus
24th 2:42 am Gemini
26th 12:11 pm Cancer
29th 12:12 am Leo

March 1988
2nd 1:06 pm Virgo
5th 1:32 am Libra
7th 12:27 pm Scorpio
9th 8:59 pm Sagittarius
12th 2:31 am Capricorn
14th 5:08 am Aquarius
16th 5:42 am Pisces
18th 5:46 am Aries
20th 7:05 am Taurus
22nd 11:21 am Gemini
24th 7:27 pm Cancer
27th 6:53 am Leo
29th 7:48 pm Virgo

April 1988
1st 8:05 am Libra
3rd 6:26 pm Scorpio
6th 2:29 am Sagittarius
8th 8:19 am Capricorn
10th 12:10 pm Aquarius
12th 2:25 pm Pisces
14th 3:47 pm Aries
16th 5:32 pm Taurus
18th 9:10 pm Gemini
21st 4:04 am Cancer
23rd 2:33 pm Leo
26th 3:16 am Virgo
28th 3:37 pm Libra

May 1988
1st 1:39 am Scorpio
3rd 8:52 am Sagittarius
5th 1:54 pm Capricorn
7th 5:37 pm Aquarius
9th 8:39 pm Pisces
11th 11:23 pm Aries
14th 2:22 am Taurus
16th 6:32 am Gemini
18th 1:05 pm Cancer
20th 10:51 pm Leo
23rd 11:12 am Virgo
25th 11:49 pm Libra
28th 10:06 am Scorpio
30th 4:57 pm Sagittarius

September 1988
2nd 8:11 am Gemini
4th 3:36 pm Cancer
7th 2:14 am Leo
9th 2:47 pm Virgo
12th 3:51 am Libra
14th 4:07 pm Scorpio
17th 2:25 am Sagittarius
19th 9:45 am Capricorn
21st 1:43 pm Aquarius
23rd 2:51 pm Pisces
25th 2:30 pm Aries
27th 2:29 pm Taurus
29th 4:43 pm Gemini

January 1989
1st 9:33 pm Scorpio
4th 7:11 am Sagittarius
6th 1:14 pm Capricorn
8th 4:31 pm Aquarius
10th 6:31 pm Pisces
12th 8:36 pm Aries
14th 11:36 pm Taurus
17th 3:57 am Gemini
19th 9:57 am Cancer
21st 6:02 pm Leo
24th 4:32 am Virgo
26th 5:01 pm Libra
29th 5:48 am Scorpio
31th 4:30 pm Sagittarius

May 1989
2nd 11:51 am Aries
4th 11:56 am Taurus
6th 12:04 pm Gemini
8th 2:20 pm Cancer
10th 8:22 pm Leo
13th 6:30 am Virgo
15th 7:07 pm Libra
18th 7:47 am Scorpio
20th 6:52 pm Sagittarius
23rd 3:54 am Capricorn
25th 11:01 am Aquarius
27th 4:13 pm Pisces
29th 7:25 pm Aries
31th 8:59 pm Taurus

September 1989
2nd 1:47 am Libra
4th 2:23 pm Scorpio
7th 2:50 am Sagittarius
9th 1:13 pm Capricorn
11th 8:02 pm Aquarius
13th 11:08 pm Pisces
15th 11:38 pm Aries
17th 11:22 pm Taurus
20th 12:16 am Gemini
22nd 3:50 am Cancer
24th 10:44 am Leo
26th 8:32 pm Virgo
29th 8:15 am Libra

June 1988
1st 8:59 pm Capricorn
3rd 11:34 pm Aquarius
6th 2:00 am Pisces
8th 5:04 am Aries
10th 9:02 am Taurus
12th 2:15 pm Gemini
14th 9:19 pm Cancer
17th 6:57 am Leo
19th 7:04 pm Virgo
22nd 7:57 am Libra
24th 6:58 pm Scorpio
27th 2:18 am Sagittarius
29th 6:00 am Capricorn

October 1988
1st 10:38 pm Cancer
4th 8:30 am Leo
6th 9:01 pm Virgo
9th 10:04 am Libra
11th 9:58 pm Scorpio
14th 7:58 am Sagittarius
16th 3:44 pm Capricorn
18th 9:05 pm Aquarius
20th 11:58 pm Pisces
23rd 12:59 am Aries
25th 1:22 am Taurus
27th 2:56 am Gemini
29th 7:28 am Cancer
31th 4:04 pm Leo

February 1989
2nd 11:30 pm Capricorn
5th 2:51 am Aquarius
7th 3:52 am Pisces
9th 4:18 am Aries
11th 5:45 am Taurus
13th 9:22 am Gemini
15th 3:40 pm Cancer
18th 12:33 am Leo
20th 11:34 am Virgo
23rd 12:05 am Libra
25th 12:56 pm Scorpio
28th 12:29 am Sagittarius

June 1989
2nd 10:04 pm Gemini
5th 12:17 am Cancer
7th 5:28 am Leo
9th 2:29 pm Virgo
12th 2:31 am Libra
14th 3:11 pm Scorpio
17th 2:12 am Sagittarius
19th 10:41 am Capricorn
21st 4:57 pm Aquarius
23rd 9:36 pm Pisces
26th 1:06 am Aries
28th 3:45 am Taurus
30th 6:08 am Gemini

October 1989
1st 8:53 pm Scorpio
4th 9:29 am Sagittarius
6th 8:45 pm Capricorn
9th 5:06 am Aquarius
11th 9:38 am Pisces
13th 10:42 am Aries
15th 9:53 am Taurus
17th 9:20 am Gemini
19th 11:09 am Cancer
21st 4:47 pm Leo
24th 2:15 am Virgo
26th 2:11 pm Libra
29th 2:56 am Scorpio
31th 3:22 pm Sagittarius

July 1988
1st 7:30 am Aquarius
3rd 8:34 am Pisces
5th 10:37 am Aries
7th 2:27 pm Taurus
9th 8:16 pm Gemini
12th 4:08 am Cancer
14th 2:11 pm Leo
17th 2:17 am Virgo
19th 3:21 pm Libra
22nd 3:13 am Scorpio
24th 11:42 am Sagittarius
26th 4:07 pm Capricorn
28th 5:25 pm Aquarius
30th 5:23 pm Pisces

November 1988
3rd 4:01 am Virgo
5th 5:04 pm Libra
8th 4:46 am Scorpio
10th 2:06 pm Sagittarius
12th 9:12 pm Capricorn
15th 2:36 am Aquarius
17th 6:34 am Pisces
19th 9:13 am Aries
21st 11:02 am Taurus
23rd 1:12 pm Gemini
25th 5:20 pm Cancer
28th 12:52 am Leo
30th 11:59 am Virgo

March 1989
2nd 8:58 am Capricorn
4th 1:37 pm Aquarius
6th 2:59 pm Pisces
8th 2:37 pm Aries
10th 2:26 pm Taurus
12th 4:16 pm Gemini
14th 9:27 pm Cancer
17th 6:12 am Leo
19th 5:39 pm Virgo
22nd 6:24 am Libra
24th 7:10 pm Scorpio
27th 6:54 am Sagittarius
29th 4:25 pm Capricorn
31th 10:45 pm Aquarius

July 1989
2nd 9:19 am Cancer
4th 2:37 pm Leo
6th 11:04 pm Virgo
9th 10:30 am Libra
11th 11:09 pm Scorpio
14th 10:31 am Sagittarius
16th 7:01 pm Capricorn
19th 12:35 am Aquarius
21st 4:07 am Pisces
23rd 6:41 am Aries
25th 9:10 am Taurus
27th 12:15 pm Gemini
29th 4:32 pm Cancer
31th 10:41 pm Leo

November 1989
3rd 2:46 am Capricorn
5th 12:09 pm Aquarius
7th 6:24 pm Pisces
9th 9:08 pm Aries
11th 9:10 pm Taurus
13th 8:19 pm Gemini
15th 8:51 pm Cancer
18th 12:45 am Leo
20th 8:54 am Virgo
22nd 8:25 pm Libra
25th 9:13 am Scorpio
27th 9:30 pm Sagittarius
30th 8:26 am Capricorn

August 1988
1st 5:53 pm Aries
3rd 8:24 pm Taurus
6th 1:43 am Gemini
8th 9:52 am Cancer
10th 8:26 pm Leo
13th 8:45 am Virgo
15th 9:52 pm Libra
18th 10:11 am Scorpio
20th 7:54 pm Sagittarius
23rd 1:49 am Capricorn
25th 4:05 am Aquarius
27th 4:01 am Pisces
29th 3:29 am Aries
31th 4:22 am Taurus

December 1988
3rd 12:56 am Libra
5th 12:51 pm Scorpio
7th 9:55 pm Sagittarius
10th 4:07 am Capricorn
12th 8:26 am Aquarius
14th 11:53 am Pisces
16th 3:04 pm Aries
18th 6:11 pm Taurus
20th 9:43 pm Gemini
23rd 2:35 am Cancer
25th 9:57 am Leo
27th 8:27 pm Virgo
30th 9:09 am Libra

April 1989
3rd 1:37 am Pisces
5th 1:51 am Aries
7th 1:07 am Taurus
9th 1:31 am Gemini
11th 4:58 am Cancer
13th 12:30 pm Leo
15th 11:39 pm Virgo
18th 12:31 pm Libra
21st 1:13 am Scorpio
23rd 12:38 pm Sagittarius
25th 10:15 pm Capricorn
28th 5:33 am Aquarius
30th 10:04 am Pisces

August 1989
3rd 7:19 am Virgo
5th 6:28 pm Libra
8th 7:04 am Scorpio
10th 7:02 pm Sagittarius
13th 4:16 am Capricorn
15th 9:59 am Aquarius
17th 12:46 pm Pisces
19th 1:59 pm Aries
21st 3:11 pm Taurus
23rd 5:39 pm Gemini
25th 10:13 pm Cancer
28th 5:11 am Leo
30th 2:29 pm Virgo

December 1989
2nd 5:42 pm Aquarius
5th 12:48 am Pisces
7th 5:11 am Aries
9th 6:59 am Taurus
11th 7:16 am Gemini
13th 7:49 am Cancer
15th 10:41 am Leo
17th 5:19 pm Virgo
20th 3:45 am Libra
22nd 4:18 pm Scorpio
25th 4:37 am Sagittarius
27th 3:10 pm Capricorn
29th 11:38 pm Aquarius

January 1990
1st 6:10 am Pisces
3rd 10:56 am Aries
5th 2:04 pm Taurus
7th 4:02 pm Gemini
9th 5:52 pm Cancer
11th 9:02 pm Leo
14th 2:57 am Virgo
16th 12:17 pm Libra
19th 12:16 am Scorpio
21st 12:43 pm Sagittarius
23rd 11:27 pm Capricorn
26th 7:25 am Aquarius
28th 12:51 pm Pisces
30th 4:34 pm Aries

May 1990
1st 12:08 am Leo
3rd 7:18 am Virgo
5th 5:28 pm Libra
8th 5:22 am Scorpio
10th 5:56 pm Sagittarius
13th 6:21 am Capricorn
15th 5:30 pm Aquarius
18th 1:54 am Pisces
20th 6:31 am Aries
22nd 7:43 am Taurus
24th 7:01 am Gemini
26th 6:34 am Cancer
28th 8:29 am Leo
30th 2:07 pm Virgo

September 1990
1st 8:51 pm Aquarius
4th 4:06 am Pisces
6th 8:23 am Aries
8th 10:56 am Taurus
10th 1:05 pm Gemini
12th 3:53 pm Cancer
14th 7:52 pm Leo
17th 1:19 am Virgo
19th 8:34 am Libra
21st 6:05 pm Scorpio
24th 5:52 am Sagittarius
26th 6:36 pm Capricorn
29th 5:53 am Aquarius

January 1991
2nd 2:54 am Leo
4th 4:57 am Virgo
6th 10:33 am Libra
8th 7:59 pm Scorpio
11th 8:06 am Sagittarius
13th 9:00 pm Capricorn
16th 9:04 am Aquarius
18th 7:23 pm Pisces
21st 3:27 am Aries
23rd 9:01 am Taurus
25th 12:07 pm Gemini
27th 1:24 pm Cancer
29th 2:04 pm Leo
31th 3:44 pm Virgo

May 1991
3rd 3:54 am Capricorn
5th 4:50 pm Aquarius
8th 4:04 am Pisces
10th 11:34 am Aries
12th 3:08 pm Taurus
14th 4:04 pm Gemini
16th 4:14 pm Cancer
18th 5:30 pm Leo
20th 9:00 pm Virgo
23rd 3:08 am Libra
25th 11:41 am Scorpio
27th 10:21 pm Sagittarius
30th 10:40 am Capricorn

February 1990
1st 7:27 pm Taurus
3rd 10:12 pm Gemini
6th 1:27 am Cancer
8th 5:51 am Leo
10th 12:13 pm Virgo
12th 9:09 pm Libra
15th 8:34 am Scorpio
17th 9:07 pm Sagittarius
20th 8:30 am Capricorn
22nd 4:52 pm Aquarius
24th 9:50 pm Pisces
27th 12:16 am Aries

June 1990
1st 11:31 pm Libra
4th 11:21 am Scorpio
6th 11:59 pm Sagittarius
9th 12:11 pm Capricorn
11th 11:09 pm Aquarius
14th 7:59 am Pisces
16th 1:55 pm Aries
18th 4:43 pm Taurus
20th 5:15 pm Gemini
22nd 5:10 pm Cancer
24th 6:25 pm Leo
26th 10:42 pm Virgo
29th 6:47 am Libra

October 1990
1st 1:42 pm Pisces
3rd 5:42 pm Aries
5th 7:07 pm Taurus
7th 7:48 pm Gemini
9th 9:29 pm Cancer
12th 1:16 am Leo
14th 7:20 am Virgo
16th 3:26 pm Libra
19th 1:24 am Scorpio
21st 1:09 pm Sagittarius
24th 2:04 am Capricorn
26th 2:13 pm Aquarius
28th 11:22 pm Pisces
31th 4:14 am Aries

February 1991
2nd 8:02 pm Libra
5th 4:01 am Scorpio
7th 3:22 pm Sagittarius
10th 4:15 am Capricorn
12th 4:16 pm Aquarius
15th 1:59 am Pisces
17th 9:12 am Aries
19th 2:24 pm Taurus
21st 6:10 pm Gemini
23rd 8:56 pm Cancer
25th 11:13 pm Leo
28th 1:50 am Virgo

June 1991
1st 11:41 pm Aquarius
4th 11:36 am Pisces
6th 8:25 pm Aries
9th 1:13 am Taurus
11th 2:37 am Gemini
13th 2:17 am Cancer
15th 2:11 am Leo
17th 4:04 am Virgo
19th 9:01 am Libra
21st 5:18 pm Scorpio
24th 4:16 am Sagittarius
26th 4:49 pm Capricorn
29th 5:47 am Aquarius

March 1990
1st 1:43 am Taurus
3rd 3:38 am Gemini
5th 7:02 am Cancer
7th 12:24 pm Leo
9th 7:47 pm Virgo
12th 5:09 am Libra
14th 4:25 pm Scorpio
17th 4:56 am Sagittarius
19th 5:01 pm Capricorn
22nd 2:31 am Aquarius
24th 8:09 am Pisces
26th 10:16 am Aries
28th 10:27 am Taurus
30th 10:43 am Gemini

July 1990
1st 6:00 pm Scorpio
4th 6:35 am Sagittarius
6th 6:39 pm Capricorn
9th 5:06 am Aquarius
11th 1:29 pm Pisces
13th 7:36 pm Aries
15th 11:29 pm Taurus
18th 1:32 am Gemini
20th 2:44 am Cancer
22nd 4:29 am Leo
24th 8:17 am Virgo
26th 3:18 pm Libra
29th 1:39 am Scorpio
31th 1:59 pm Sagittarius

November 1990
2nd 5:32 am Taurus
4th 5:06 am Gemini
6th 5:08 am Cancer
8th 7:24 am Leo
10th 12:48 pm Virgo
12th 9:08 pm Libra
15th 7:39 am Scorpio
17th 7:39 pm Sagittarius
20th 8:31 am Capricorn
22nd 9:07 pm Aquarius
25th 7:31 am Pisces
27th 2:06 pm Aries
29th 4:38 pm Taurus

March 1991
2nd 6:04 am Libra
4th 1:08 pm Scorpio
6th 11:35 pm Sagittarius
9th 12:13 pm Capricorn
12th 12:31 am Aquarius
14th 10:11 am Pisces
16th 4:38 pm Aries
18th 8:41 pm Taurus
20th 11:37 pm Gemini
23rd 2:27 am Cancer
25th 5:43 am Leo
27th 9:41 am Virgo
29th 2:50 pm Libra
31th 10:01 pm Scorpio

July 1991
1st 5:50 pm Pisces
4th 3:33 am Aries
6th 9:52 am Taurus
8th 12:42 pm Gemini
10th 1:04 pm Cancer
12th 12:36 pm Leo
14th 1:12 pm Virgo
16th 4:34 pm Libra
18th 11:41 pm Scorpio
21st 10:16 am Sagittarius
23rd 10:55 pm Capricorn
26th 11:49 am Aquarius
28th 11:35 pm Pisces
31th 9:20 am Aries

April 1990
1st 12:50 pm Cancer
3rd 5:50 pm Leo
6th 1:42 am Virgo
8th 11:44 am Libra
10th 11:18 pm Scorpio
13th 11:47 am Sagittarius
16th 12:15 am Capricorn
18th 10:52 am Aquarius
20th 5:56 pm Pisces
22nd 8:58 pm Aries
24th 9:04 pm Taurus
26th 8:13 pm Gemini
28th 8:39 pm Cancer

August 1990
3rd 2:08 am Capricorn
5th 12:19 pm Aquarius
7th 7:54 pm Pisces
10th 1:13 am Aries
12th 4:55 am Taurus
14th 7:42 am Gemini
16th 10:12 am Cancer
18th 1:11 pm Leo
20th 5:33 pm Virgo
23rd 12:17 am Libra
25th 9:56 am Scorpio
27th 9:57 pm Sagittarius
30th 10:22 am Capricorn

December 1990
1st 4:24 pm Gemini
3rd 3:28 pm Cancer
5th 4:00 pm Leo
7th 7:39 pm Virgo
10th 2:59 am Libra
12th 1:27 pm Scorpio
15th 1:44 am Sagittarius
17th 2:34 pm Capricorn
20th 2:59 am Aquarius
22nd 1:47 pm Pisces
24th 9:45 pm Aries
27th 2:09 am Taurus
29th 3:26 am Gemini
31th 3:04 am Cancer

April 1991
3rd 7:58 am Sagittarius
5th 8:19 pm Capricorn
8th 8:59 am Aquarius
10th 7:17 pm Pisces
13th 1:50 am Aries
15th 5:06 am Taurus
17th 6:41 am Gemini
19th 8:18 am Cancer
21st 11:04 am Leo
23rd 3:29 pm Virgo
25th 9:36 pm Libra
28th 5:34 am Scorpio
30th 3:42 pm Sagittarius

August 1991
2nd 4:31 pm Taurus
4th 8:54 pm Gemini
6th 10:47 pm Cancer
8th 11:09 pm Leo
10th 11:35 pm Virgo
13th 1:52 am Libra
15th 7:33 am Scorpio
17th 5:10 pm Sagittarius
20th 5:34 am Capricorn
22nd 6:26 pm Aquarius
25th 5:51 am Pisces
27th 3:01 pm Aries
29th 9:59 pm Taurus

September 1991
1st 3:02 am Gemini
3rd 6:20 am Cancer
5th 8:13 am Leo
7th 9:36 am Virgo
9th 11:52 am Libra
11th 4:42 pm Scorpio
14th 1:14 am Sagittarius
16th 1:04 pm Capricorn
19th 1:57 am Aquarius
21st 1:20 pm Pisces
23rd 9:56 pm Aries
26th 3:59 am Taurus
28th 8:26 am Gemini
30th 11:58 am Cancer

January 1992
1st 7:30 am Sagittarius
3rd 7:09 pm Capricorn
6th 7:59 am Aquarius
8th 8:52 pm Pisces
11th 8:22 am Aries
13th 4:59 pm Taurus
15th 9:55 pm Gemini
17th 11:26 pm Cancer
19th 10:57 pm Leo
21st 10:22 pm Virgo
23rd 11:42 pm Libra
26th 4:32 am Scorpio
28th 1:19 pm Sagittarius
31th 1:07 am Capricorn

May 1992
1st 7:09 pm Taurus
4th 12:28 am Gemini
6th 4:10 am Cancer
8th 7:07 am Leo
10th 9:56 am Virgo
12th 1:05 pm Libra
14th 5:15 pm Scorpio
16th 11:22 pm Sagittarius
19th 8:12 am Capricorn
21st 7:43 pm Aquarius
24th 8:25 am Pisces
26th 7:52 am Aries
29th 4:16 am Taurus
31th 9:19 am Gemini

September 1992
3rd 12:50 am Sagittarius
5th 10:05 am Capricorn
7th 10:08 pm Aquarius
10th 10:56 am Pisces
12th 11:02 pm Aries
15th 9:47 am Taurus
17th 6:39 pm Gemini
20th 12:59 am Cancer
22nd 4:19 am Leo
24th 5:08 am Virgo
26th 4:56 am Libra
28th 5:44 am Scorpio
30th 9:33 am Sagittarius

January 1993
2nd 5:29 pm Taurus
5th 1:42 am Gemini
7th 6:10 am Cancer
9th 7:50 am Leo
11th 8:21 am Virgo
13th 9:31 am Libra
15th 12:42 pm Scorpio
17th 6:30 pm Sagittarius
20th 2:46 am Capricorn
22nd 1:00 pm Aquarius
25th 12:47 am Pisces
27th 1:27 pm Aries
30th 1:37 am Taurus

October 1991
2nd 2:59 pm Leo
4th 5:45 pm Virgo
6th 9:01 pm Libra
9th 1:59 am Scorpio
11th 9:57 am Sagittarius
13th 9:10 pm Capricorn
16th 10:04 am Aquarius
18th 9:53 pm Pisces
21st 6:33 am Aries
23rd 11:56 am Taurus
25th 3:09 pm Gemini
27th 5:37 pm Cancer
29th 8:20 pm Leo
31th 11:47 pm Virgo

February 1992
2nd 2:08 pm Aquarius
5th 2:51 am Pisces
7th 2:15 pm Aries
9th 11:36 pm Taurus
12th 6:08 am Gemini
14th 9:31 am Cancer
16th 10:16 am Leo
18th 9:48 am Virgo
20th 10:05 am Libra
22nd 1:11 pm Scorpio
24th 8:26 pm Sagittarius
27th 7:33 am Capricorn
29th 8:34 pm Aquarius

June 1992
2nd 11:58 am Cancer
4th 1:35 pm Leo
6th 3:28 pm Virgo
8th 6:33 pm Libra
10th 11:27 pm Scorpio
13th 6:29 am Sagittarius
15th 3:50 pm Capricorn
18th 3:19 am Aquarius
20th 3:59 pm Pisces
23rd 4:04 am Aries
25th 1:28 pm Taurus
27th 7:14 pm Gemini
29th 9:42 pm Cancer

October 1992
2nd 5:28 pm Capricorn
5th 4:52 am Aquarius
7th 5:37 pm Pisces
10th 5:36 am Aries
12th 3:48 pm Taurus
15th 12:08 am Gemini
17th 6:36 am Cancer
19th 11:01 am Leo
21st 1:28 pm Virgo
23rd 2:40 pm Libra
25th 4:05 pm Scorpio
27th 7:29 pm Sagittarius
30th 2:18 am Capricorn

February 1993
1st 11:14 am Gemini
3rd 4:56 pm Cancer
5th 6:52 pm Leo
7th 6:30 pm Virgo
9th 5:59 pm Libra
11th 7:24 pm Scorpio
14th 12:08 am Sagittarius
16th 8:20 am Capricorn
18th 7:05 pm Aquarius
21st 7:12 am Pisces
23rd 7:50 pm Aries
26th 8:11 am Taurus
28th 6:52 pm Gemini

November 1991
3rd 4:13 am Libra
5th 10:09 am Scorpio
7th 6:21 pm Sagittarius
10th 5:16 am Capricorn
12th 6:06 pm Aquarius
15th 6:33 am Pisces
17th 4:07 pm Aries
19th 9:49 pm Taurus
22nd 12:22 am Gemini
24th 1:25 am Cancer
26th 2:37 am Leo
28th 5:12 am Virgo
30th 9:47 am Libra

March 1992
3rd 9:11 am Pisces
5th 8:07 pm Aries
8th 5:05 am Taurus
10th 12:04 pm Gemini
12th 4:49 pm Cancer
14th 7:21 pm Leo
16th 8:14 pm Virgo
18th 8:55 pm Libra
20th 11:20 pm Scorpio
23rd 5:13 am Sagittarius
25th 3:08 pm Capricorn
28th 3:44 am Aquarius
30th 4:23 pm Pisces

July 1992
1st 10:15 pm Leo
3rd 10:37 pm Virgo
6th 12:27 am Libra
8th 4:53 am Scorpio
10th 12:17 pm Sagittarius
12th 10:15 pm Capricorn
15th 10:02 am Aquarius
17th 10:44 pm Pisces
20th 11:07 am Aries
22nd 9:36 pm Taurus
25th 4:44 am Gemini
27th 8:08 am Cancer
29th 8:40 am Leo
31th 8:02 am Virgo

November 1992
1st 12:42 pm Aquarius
4th 1:12 am Pisces
6th 1:19 pm Aries
8th 11:19 pm Taurus
11th 6:50 am Gemini
13th 12:19 pm Cancer
15th 4:23 pm Leo
17th 7:28 pm Virgo
19th 10:04 pm Libra
22nd 12:52 am Scorpio
24th 5:01 am Sagittarius
26th 11:38 am Capricorn
28th 9:19 pm Aquarius

March 1993
3rd 2:16 am Cancer
5th 5:41 am Leo
7th 5:53 am Virgo
9th 4:47 am Libra
11th 4:40 am Scorpio
13th 7:33 am Sagittarius
15th 2:27 pm Capricorn
18th 12:52 am Aquarius
20th 1:10 pm Pisces
23rd 1:51 am Aries
25th 1:59 pm Taurus
28th 12:48 am Gemini
30th 9:14 am Cancer

December 1991
2nd 4:33 pm Scorpio
5th 1:32 am Sagittarius
7th 12:41 pm Capricorn
10th 1:26 am Aquarius
12th 2:18 pm Pisces
15th 1:06 am Aries
17th 8:10 am Taurus
19th 11:22 am Gemini
21st 11:55 am Cancer
23rd 11:39 am Leo
25th 12:24 pm Virgo
27th 3:37 pm Libra
29th 10:04 pm Scorpio

April 1992
2nd 3:04 am Aries
4th 11:18 am Taurus
6th 5:33 pm Gemini
8th 10:18 pm Cancer
11th 1:46 am Leo
13th 4:09 am Virgo
15th 6:11 am Libra
17th 9:10 am Scorpio
19th 2:40 pm Sagittarius
21st 11:40 pm Capricorn
24th 11:38 am Aquarius
27th 12:20 am Pisces
29th 11:13 am Aries

August 1992
2nd 8:17 am Libra
4th 11:16 am Scorpio
6th 5:57 pm Sagittarius
9th 4:00 am Capricorn
11th 4:06 pm Aquarius
14th 4:51 am Pisces
16th 5:11 pm Aries
19th 4:09 am Taurus
21st 12:36 pm Gemini
23rd 5:36 pm Cancer
25th 7:15 pm Leo
27th 6:47 pm Virgo
29th 6:11 pm Libra
31th 7:39 pm Scorpio

December 1992
1st 9:23 am Pisces
3rd 9:48 pm Aries
6th 8:16 am Taurus
8th 3:37 pm Gemini
10th 8:06 pm Cancer
12th 10:47 pm Leo
15th 12:56 am Virgo
17th 3:33 am Libra
19th 7:20 am Scorpio
21st 12:42 pm Sagittarius
23rd 8:04 pm Capricorn
26th 5:43 am Aquarius
28th 5:28 pm Pisces
31th 6:06 am Aries

April 1993
1st 2:21 pm Leo
3rd 4:11 pm Virgo
5th 3:55 pm Libra
7th 3:33 pm Scorpio
9th 5:10 pm Sagittarius
11th 10:24 pm Capricorn
14th 7:35 am Aquarius
16th 7:32 pm Pisces
19th 8:14 am Aries
21st 8:08 pm Taurus
24th 6:27 am Gemini
26th 2:45 pm Cancer
28th 8:39 pm Leo
30th 11:59 pm Virgo

May 1993	June 1993	July 1993	August 1993
3rd 1:20 am Libra	1st 10:23 am Scorpio	3rd 1:49 am Capricorn	1st 4:36 pm Aquarius
5th 1:57 am Scorpio	3rd 1:01 pm Sagittarius	5th 9:14 am Aquarius	4th 2:43 am Pisces
7th 3:35 am Sagittarius	5th 5:26 pm Capricorn	7th 7:09 pm Pisces	6th 2:39 pm Aries
9th 7:51 am Capricorn	8th 12:39 am Aquarius	10th 7:11 am Aries	9th 3:22 am Taurus
11th 3:43 pm Aquarius	10th 10:56 am Pisces	12th 7:37 pm Taurus	11th 2:46 pm Gemini
14th 2:50 am Pisces	12th 11:14 pm Aries	15th 6:06 am Gemini	13th 10:46 pm Cancer
16th 3:24 pm Aries	15th 11:19 am Taurus	17th 1:08 pm Cancer	16th 2:44 am Leo
19th 3:16 am Taurus	17th 9:12 pm Gemini	19th 4:48 pm Leo	18th 3:41 am Virgo
21st 1:07 pm Gemini	20th 4:05 am Cancer	21st 6:24 pm Virgo	20th 3:35 am Libra
23rd 8:38 pm Cancer	22nd 8:26 am Leo	23rd 7:40 pm Libra	22nd 4:28 am Scorpio
26th 2:04 am Leo	24th 11:19 am Virgo	25th 10:00 pm Scorpio	24th 7:45 am Sagittarius
28th 5:46 am Virgo	26th 1:46 pm Libra	28th 2:13 am Sagittarius	26th 1:57 pm Capricorn
30th 8:18 am Libra	28th 4:37 pm Scorpio	30th 8:26 am Capricorn	28th 10:41 pm Aquarius
	30th 8:28 pm Sagittarius		31st 9:18 am Pisces

September 1993	October 1993	November 1993	December 1993
2nd 9:21 pm Aries	2nd 4:13 pm Taurus	1st 10:12 am Gemini	1st 2:17 am Cancer
5th 10:09 am Taurus	5th 4:27 am Gemini	3rd 8:24 pm Cancer	3rd 9:33 am Leo
7th 10:16 pm Gemini	7th 2:42 pm Cancer	6th 4:06 am Leo	5th 2:43 pm Virgo
10th 7:36 am Cancer	9th 9:33 pm Leo	8th 8:47 am Virgo	7th 6:04 pm Libra
12th 12:51 pm Leo	12th 12:36 am Virgo	10th 10:43 am Libra	9th 8:04 pm Scorpio
14th 2:21 pm Virgo	14th 12:47 am Libra	12th 11:00 am Scorpio	11th 9:39 pm Sagittarius
16th 1:45 pm Libra	16th 12:01 am Scorpio	14th 11:21 am Sagittarius	14th 12:06 am Capricorn
18th 1:15 pm Scorpio	18th 12:23 am Sagittarius	16th 1:34 pm Capricorn	16th 4:51 am Aquarius
20th 2:53 pm Sagittarius	20th 3:42 am Capricorn	18th 7:08 pm Aquarius	18th 12:58 pm Pisces
22nd 7:53 pm Capricorn	22nd 10:48 am Aquarius	21st 4:27 am Pisces	21st 12:19 am Aries
25th 4:19 am Aquarius	24th 9:17 pm Pisces	23rd 4:30 pm Aries	23rd 1:04 pm Taurus
27th 3:12 pm Pisces	27th 9:39 am Aries	26th 5:14 am Taurus	26th 12:46 am Gemini
30th 3:29 am Aries	29th 10:20 pm Taurus	28th 4:47 pm Gemini	28th 9:46 am Cancer
			30th 3:59 pm Leo

January 1994	February 1994	March 1994	April 1994
1st 8:15 pm Virgo	2nd 7:49 am Scorpio	1st 2:44 pm Scorpio	2nd 3:37 am Capricorn
3rd 11:31 pm Libra	4th 11:14 am Sagittarius	3rd 4:54 pm Sagittarius	4th 9:45 am Aquarius
6th 2:29 am Scorpio	6th 4:02 pm Capricorn	5th 9:24 pm Capricorn	6th 6:51 pm Pisces
8th 5:34 am Sagittarius	8th 10:16 pm Aquarius	8th 4:15 am Aquarius	9th 6:08 am Aries
10th 9:16 am Capricorn	11th 6:23 am Pisces	10th 1:09 pm Pisces	11th 6:47 pm Taurus
12th 2:25 pm Aquarius	13th 4:49 pm Aries	12th 11:59 pm Aries	14th 7:47 am Gemini
14th 10:04 pm Pisces	16th 5:19 am Taurus	15th 12:27 pm Taurus	16th 7:41 pm Cancer
17th 8:41 am Aries	18th 6:05 pm Gemini	18th 1:29 am Gemini	19th 4:45 am Leo
19th 9:21 pm Taurus	21st 4:27 am Cancer	20th 12:53 pm Cancer	21st 9:58 am Virgo
22nd 9:34 am Gemini	23rd 10:48 am Leo	22nd 8:39 pm Leo	23rd 11:41 am Libra
24th 6:55 pm Cancer	25th 1:28 pm Virgo	25th 12:14 am Virgo	25th 11:19 am Scorpio
27th 12:38 am Leo	27th 2:07 pm Libra	27th 12:46 am Libra	27th 10:49 am Sagittarius
29th 3:39 am Virgo		29th 12:15 am Scorpio	29th 12:05 pm Capricorn
31st 5:34 am Libra		31st 12:41 am Sagittarius	

May 1994	June 1994	July 1994	August 1994
1st 4:34 pm Aquarius	2nd 6:31 pm Aries	2nd 2:22 pm Taurus	1st 11:04 am Gemini
4th 12:47 am Pisces	5th 7:14 am Taurus	5th 3:12 am Gemini	3rd 10:22 pm Cancer
6th 12:01 pm Aries	7th 8:04 pm Gemini	7th 2:17 pm Cancer	6th 6:31 am Leo
9th 12:50 am Taurus	10th 7:22 am Cancer	9th 10:43 pm Leo	8th 11:42 am Virgo
11th 1:43 pm Gemini	12th 4:29 pm Leo	12th 4:48 am Virgo	10th 3:07 pm Libra
14th 1:27 am Cancer	14th 11:16 pm Virgo	14th 9:15 am Libra	12th 5:56 pm Scorpio
16th 10:58 am Leo	17th 3:48 am Libra	16th 12:35 pm Scorpio	14th 8:53 pm Sagittarius
18th 5:31 pm Virgo	19th 6:20 am Scorpio	18th 3:09 pm Sagittarius	17th 12:18 am Capricorn
20th 8:55 pm Libra	21st 7:33 am Sagittarius	20th 5:31 pm Capricorn	19th 4:34 am Aquarius
22nd 9:51 pm Scorpio	23rd 8:37 am Capricorn	22nd 8:39 pm Aquarius	21st 10:27 am Pisces
24th 9:43 pm Sagittarius	25th 11:10 am Aquarius	25th 1:56 am Pisces	23rd 6:54 pm Aries
26th 10:17 pm Capricorn	27th 4:44 pm Pisces	27th 10:30 am Aries	26th 6:13 am Taurus
29th 1:19 am Aquarius	30th 2:06 am Aries	29th 10:13 pm Taurus	28th 7:07 pm Gemini
31st 8:04 am Pisces			31st 6:59 am Cancer

September 1994	October 1994	November 1994	December 1994
2nd 3:37 pm Leo	2nd 6:39 am Virgo	2nd 8:20 pm Scorpio	2nd 7:13 am Sagittarius
4th 8:34 pm Virgo	4th 8:57 am Libra	4th 7:46 pm Sagittarius	4th 6:43 am Capricorn
6th 10:57 pm Libra	6th 9:22 am Scorpio	6th 8:02 pm Capricorn	6th 7:52 am Aquarius
9th 12:26 am Scorpio	8th 9:47 am Sagittarius	8th 10:48 pm Aquarius	8th 12:24 pm Pisces
11th 2:25 am Sagittarius	10th 11:44 am Capricorn	11th 5:04 am Pisces	10th 9:04 pm Aries
13th 5:44 am Capricorn	12th 4:09 pm Aquarius	13th 2:43 pm Aries	13th 8:55 am Taurus
15th 10:42 am Aquarius	14th 11:18 pm Pisces	16th 2:44 am Taurus	15th 9:59 pm Gemini
17th 5:31 pm Pisces	17th 8:56 am Aries	18th 3:41 pm Gemini	18th 10:24 am Cancer
20th 2:30 am Aries	19th 8:34 pm Taurus	21st 4:21 am Cancer	20th 9:13 pm Leo
22nd 1:47 pm Taurus	22nd 9:27 am Gemini	23rd 3:33 pm Leo	23rd 6:01 am Virgo
25th 2:41 am Gemini	24th 10:15 pm Cancer	26th 12:09 am Virgo	25th 12:27 pm Libra
27th 3:11 pm Cancer	27th 9:04 am Leo	28th 5:22 am Libra	27th 4:17 pm Scorpio
30th 12:55 am Leo	29th 4:21 pm Virgo	30th 7:22 am Scorpio	29th 5:46 pm Sagittarius
	31st 7:46 pm Libra		31st 5:58 pm Capricorn

January 1995	February 1995	March 1995	April 1995
2nd 6:39 pm Aquarius	1st 8:05 am Pisces	2nd 11:30 am Aries	1st 4:58 pm Taurus
4th 9:49 pm Pisces	3rd 2:12 pm Aries	5th 8:50 am Taurus	4th 4:49 am Gemini
7th 4:56 am Aries	6th 12:08 am Taurus	7th 8:55 pm Gemini	6th 5:39 pm Cancer
9th 3:57 pm Taurus	8th 12:43 pm Gemini	10th 9:40 am Cancer	9th 5:15 am Leo
12th 4:57 am Gemini	11th 1:17 am Cancer	12th 8:28 pm Leo	11th 1:39 pm Virgo
14th 5:20 pm Cancer	13th 11:31 am Leo	15th 3:54 am Virgo	13th 6:20 pm Libra
17th 3:36 am Leo	15th 6:52 pm Virgo	17th 8:18 am Libra	15th 8:13 pm Scorpio
19th 11:39 am Virgo	18th 12:00 am Libra	19th 10:53 am Scorpio	17th 8:52 pm Sagittarius
21st 5:53 pm Libra	20th 3:55 am Scorpio	21st 12:58 pm Sagittarius	19th 9:54 pm Capricorn
23rd 10:32 pm Scorpio	22nd 7:13 am Sagittarius	23rd 3:32 pm Capricorn	22nd 12:38 am Aquarius
26th 1:37 am Sagittarius	24th 10:11 am Capricorn	25th 7:10 pm Aquarius	24th 5:50 am Pisces
28th 3:26 am Capricorn	26th 1:14 pm Aquarius	28th 12:18 am Pisces	26th 1:41 pm Aries
30th 5:04 am Aquarius	28th 5:16 pm Pisces	30th 7:26 am Aries	28th 11:53 pm Taurus

May 1995	June 1995	July 1995	August 1995
1st 11:53 am Gemini	2nd 7:17 pm Leo	2nd 11:35 am Virgo	1st 1:23 am Libra
4th 12:45 am Cancer	5th 5:46 am Virgo	4th 7:55 pm Libra	3rd 7:29 am Scorpio
6th 12:54 pm Leo	7th 1:13 pm Libra	7th 1:19 am Scorpio	5th 11:14 am Sagittarius
8th 10:33 pm Virgo	9th 5:04 pm Scorpio	9th 3:38 am Sagittarius	7th 12:52 pm Capricorn
11th 4:30 am Libra	11th 5:50 pm Sagittarius	11th 3:44 am Capricorn	9th 1:28 pm Aquarius
13th 6:54 am Scorpio	13th 5:06 pm Capricorn	13th 3:21 am Aquarius	11th 2:47 pm Pisces
15th 6:59 am Sagittarius	15th 4:53 pm Aquarius	15th 4:37 am Pisces	13th 6:41 pm Aries
17th 6:36 am Capricorn	17th 7:13 pm Pisces	17th 9:23 am Aries	16th 2:25 am Taurus
19th 7:40 am Aquarius	20th 1:29 am Aries	19th 6:20 pm Taurus	18th 1:39 pm Gemini
21st 11:40 am Pisces	22nd 11:35 am Taurus	22nd 6:23 am Gemini	21st 2:24 am Cancer
23rd 7:13 pm Aries	25th 12:20 am Gemini	24th 7:16 pm Cancer	23rd 2:12 pm Leo
26th 5:46 am Taurus	27th 12:56 pm Cancer	27th 7:07 am Leo	25th 11:50 pm Virgo
28th 6:07 pm Gemini	30th 1:02 am Leo	29th 5:12 pm Virgo	28th 7:15 am Libra
31st 6:59 am Cancer			30th 12:51 pm Scorpio

September 1995	October 1995	November 1995	December 1995
1st 4:57 pm Sagittarius	1st 1:10 am Capricorn	1st 1:17 pm Pisces	1st 12:51 am Aries
3rd 7:45 pm Capricorn	3rd 3:59 am Aquarius	3rd 7:20 pm Aries	3rd 9:40 am Taurus
5th 9:47 pm Aquarius	5th 7:35 am Pisces	6th 3:35 am Taurus	5th 8:34 pm Gemini
8th 12:08 am Pisces	7th 12:42 pm Aries	8th 1:54 pm Gemini	8th 8:44 am Cancer
10th 4:14 am Aries	9th 8:05 pm Taurus	11th 1:56 am Cancer	10th 9:24 pm Leo
12th 11:21 am Taurus	12th 6:09 am Gemini	13th 2:36 pm Leo	13th 9:26 am Virgo
14th 9:48 pm Gemini	14th 6:19 pm Cancer	16th 2:02 am Virgo	15th 7:09 pm Libra
17th 10:15 am Cancer	17th 6:46 am Leo	18th 10:17 am Libra	18th 1:07 am Scorpio
19th 10:19 pm Leo	19th 5:11 pm Virgo	20th 2:41 pm Scorpio	20th 3:13 am Sagittarius
22nd 8:01 am Virgo	22nd 12:15 am Libra	22nd 3:57 pm Sagittarius	22nd 2:46 am Capricorn
24th 2:50 pm Libra	24th 4:07 am Scorpio	24th 3:49 pm Capricorn	24th 1:52 am Aquarius
26th 7:20 pm Scorpio	26th 5:57 am Sagittarius	26th 4:16 pm Aquarius	26th 2:45 am Pisces
28th 10:30 pm Sagittarius	28th 7:15 am Capricorn	28th 6:59 pm Pisces	28th 7:06 am Aries
	30th 9:24 am Aquarius		30th 3:20 am Taurus

January 1996	February 1996	March 1996	April 1996
2nd 2:29 am Gemini	3rd 9:45 am Leo	1st 4:47 pm Leo	2nd 9:26 pm Libra
4th 2:55 pm Cancer	5th 9:22 pm Virgo	4th 4:13 am Virgo	5th 3:57 am Scorpio
7th 3:30 am Leo	8th 7:30 am Libra	6th 1:40 pm Libra	7th 8:22 am Sagittarius
9th 3:29 pm Virgo	10th 3:35 pm Scorpio	8th 9:05 pm Scorpio	9th 11:30 am Capricorn
12th 1:55 am Libra	12th 8:58 pm Sagittarius	11th 2:32 am Sagittarius	11th 2:10 pm Aquarius
14th 9:30 am Scorpio	14th 11:29 pm Capricorn	13th 6:08 am Capricorn	13th 5:00 pm Pisces
16th 1:25 pm Sagittarius	16th 11:59 pm Aquarius	15th 8:15 am Aquarius	15th 8:43 pm Aries
18th 2:08 pm Capricorn	19th 12:09 am Pisces	17th 9:51 am Pisces	18th 2:05 am Taurus
20th 1:16 pm Aquarius	21st 1:58 am Aries	19th 12:16 pm Aries	20th 9:54 am Gemini
22nd 1:02 pm Pisces	23rd 7:08 am Taurus	21st 4:59 pm Taurus	22nd 8:24 pm Cancer
24th 3:37 pm Aries	25th 4:13 pm Gemini	24th 12:59 am Gemini	25th 8:44 am Leo
26th 10:16 pm Taurus	28th 4:10 am Cancer	26th 12:05 pm Cancer	27th 8:48 pm Virgo
29th 8:42 am Gemini		29th 12:37 am Leo	30th 6:27 am Libra
31st 9:10 pm Cancer		31st 12:14 pm Virgo	

May 1996	June 1996	July 1996	August 1996
2nd 12:43 pm Scorpio	1st 1:43 am Sagittarius	2nd 12:06 am Aquarius	2nd 11:05 pm Aries
4th 4:05 pm Sagittarius	3rd 2:29 am Capricorn	4th 12:07 pm Pisces	5th 3:33 am Taurus
6th 5:54 pm Capricorn	5th 2:45 am Aquarius	6th 2:42 pm Aries	7th 11:48 am Gemini
8th 7:39 pm Aquarius	7th 4:19 am Pisces	8th 8:43 pm Taurus	9th 10:57 pm Cancer
10th 10:29 pm Pisces	9th 8:23 am Aries	11th 5:52 am Gemini	12th 11:29 am Leo
13th 3:00 am Aries	11th 3:10 pm Taurus	13th 5:07 pm Cancer	15th 12:07 am Virgo
15th 9:25 am Taurus	14th 12:16 am Gemini	16th 5:31 am Leo	17th 11:55 am Libra
17th 5:48 pm Gemini	16th 11:08 am Cancer	18th 6:16 pm Virgo	19th 9:50 pm Scorpio
20th 4:16 am Cancer	18th 11:22 pm Leo	21st 6:13 am Libra	22nd 4:48 am Sagittarius
22nd 4:27 pm Leo	21st 12:06 pm Virgo	23rd 3:42 pm Scorpio	24th 8:22 am Capricorn
25th 4:58 am Virgo	23rd 11:37 pm Libra	25th 9:24 pm Sagittarius	26th 9:11 am Aquarius
27th 3:33 pm Libra	26th 7:53 am Scorpio	27th 11:17 pm Capricorn	28th 8:49 pm Pisces
29th 10:30 pm Scorpio	28th 12:01 pm Sagittarius	29th 10:48 pm Aquarius	30th 9:15 am Aries
	30th 12:48 pm Capricorn	31st 10:01 pm Pisces	

September 1996
1st 12:19 pm Taurus
3rd 7:08 pm Gemini
6th 5:29 am Cancer
8th 5:53 pm Leo
11th 6:28 am Virgo
13th 5:51 pm Libra
16th 3:20 am Scorpio
18th 10:30 am Sagittarius
20th 3:12 pm Capricorn
22nd 5:40 pm Aquarius
24th 6:43 pm Pisces
26th 7:46 pm Aries
28th 10:24 pm Taurus

October 1996
1st 4:01 am Gemini
3rd 1:14 pm Cancer
6th 1:12 am Leo
8th 1:48 pm Virgo
11th 1:00 am Libra
13th 9:46 am Scorpio
15th 4:07 pm Sagittarius
17th 8:37 pm Capricorn
19th 11:51 pm Aquarius
22nd 2:22 am Pisces
24th 4:50 am Aries
26th 8:12 am Taurus
28th 1:35 pm Gemini
30th 9:56 pm Cancer

November 1996
2nd 9:15 am Leo
4th 9:57 pm Virgo
7th 9:28 am Libra
9th 6:02 pm Scorpio
11th 11:26 pm Sagittarius
14th 2:44 am Capricorn
16th 5:14 am Aquarius
18th 7:59 am Pisces
20th 11:34 am Aries
22nd 4:12 pm Taurus
24th 10:20 pm Gemini
27th 6:37 am Cancer
29th 5:29 pm Leo

December 1996
2nd 6:10 am Virgo
4th 6:23 pm Libra
7th 3:38 am Scorpio
9th 8:59 am Sagittarius
11th 11:15 am Capricorn
13th 12:15 pm Aquarius
15th 1:44 pm Pisces
17th 4:55 pm Aries
19th 10:09 pm Taurus
22nd 5:17 am Gemini
24th 2:14 pm Cancer
27th 1:09 am Leo
29th 1:44 pm Virgo

January 1997
1st 2:32 am Libra
3rd 1:01 pm Scorpio
5th 7:27 pm Sagittarius
7th 9:55 pm Capricorn
9th 10:00 pm Aquarius
11th 9:51 pm Pisces
13th 11:22 pm Aries
16th 3:40 am Taurus
18th 10:53 am Gemini
20th 8:28 pm Cancer
23rd 7:50 am Leo
25th 8:26 pm Virgo
28th 9:21 am Libra
30th 8:48 pm Scorpio

February 1997
2nd 4:50 am Sagittarius
4th 8:45 am Capricorn
6th 9:22 am Aquarius
8th 8:34 am Pisces
10th 8:30 am Aries
12th 10:56 am Taurus
14th 4:53 pm Gemini
17th 2:12 am Cancer
19th 1:52 pm Leo
22nd 2:38 am Virgo
24th 3:23 pm Libra
27th 2:56 am Scorpio

March 1997
1st 12:00 pm Sagittarius
3rd 5:38 pm Capricorn
5th 7:55 pm Aquarius
7th 7:57 pm Pisces
9th 7:33 pm Aries
11th 8:38 pm Taurus
14th 12:48 am Gemini
16th 8:50 am Cancer
18th 8:08 pm Leo
21st 8:59 am Virgo
23rd 9:35 pm Libra
26th 8:42 am Scorpio
28th 5:40 pm Sagittarius
31th 12:07 am Capricorn

April 1997
2nd 3:59 am Aquarius
4th 5:42 am Pisces
6th 6:19 am Aries
8th 7:21 am Taurus
10th 10:28 am Gemini
12th 5:04 pm Cancer
15th 3:22 am Leo
17th 3:59 pm Virgo
20th 4:36 am Libra
22nd 3:19 pm Scorpio
24th 11:32 pm Sagittarius
27th 5:32 am Capricorn
29th 9:50 am Aquarius

May 1997
1st 12:50 pm Pisces
3rd 2:59 pm Aries
5th 5:05 pm Taurus
7th 8:21 pm Gemini
10th 2:13 am Cancer
12th 11:32 am Leo
14th 11:43 pm Virgo
17th 12:26 pm Libra
19th 11:11 pm Scorpio
22nd 6:51 am Sagittarius
24th 11:51 am Capricorn
26th 3:20 pm Aquarius
28th 6:18 pm Pisces
30th 9:18 pm Aries

June 1997
2nd 12:39 am Taurus
4th 4:55 am Gemini
6th 11:02 am Cancer
8th 7:58 pm Leo
11th 7:42 am Virgo
13th 8:35 pm Libra
16th 7:50 am Scorpio
18th 3:39 pm Sagittarius
20th 8:04 pm Capricorn
22nd 10:21 pm Aquarius
25th 12:09 am Pisces
27th 2:38 am Aries
29th 6:23 am Taurus

July 1997
1st 11:35 am Gemini
3rd 6:33 pm Cancer
6th 3:45 am Leo
8th 3:21 pm Virgo
11th 4:20 am Libra
13th 4:20 pm Scorpio
16th 1:02 am Sagittarius
18th 5:45 am Capricorn
20th 7:29 am Aquarius
22nd 8:00 am Pisces
24th 9:04 am Aries
26th 11:53 am Taurus
28th 5:04 pm Gemini
31th 12:38 am Cancer

August 1997
2nd 10:27 am Leo
4th 10:15 pm Virgo
7th 11:16 am Libra
9th 11:50 pm Scorpio
12th 9:45 am Sagittarius
14th 3:42 pm Capricorn
16th 5:59 pm Aquarius
18th 6:01 pm Pisces
20th 5:45 pm Aries
22nd 6:57 pm Taurus
24th 10:56 pm Gemini
27th 6:10 am Cancer
29th 4:18 pm Leo

September 1997
1st 4:27 am Virgo
3rd 5:29 pm Libra
6th 6:09 am Scorpio
8th 4:54 pm Sagittarius
11th 12:23 am Capricorn
13th 4:10 am Aquarius
15th 4:59 am Pisces
17th 4:25 am Aries
19th 4:21 am Taurus
21st 6:38 am Gemini
23rd 12:33 pm Cancer
25th 10:12 pm Leo
28th 10:27 am Virgo
30th 11:32 pm Libra

October 1997
3rd 11:57 am Scorpio
5th 10:43 pm Sagittarius
8th 7:04 am Capricorn
10th 12:29 pm Aquarius
12th 2:59 pm Pisces
14th 3:26 pm Aries
16th 3:17 pm Taurus
18th 4:27 pm Gemini
20th 8:45 pm Cancer
23rd 5:09 am Leo
25th 4:59 pm Virgo
28th 6:05 am Libra
30th 6:15 pm Scorpio

November 1997
2nd 4:27 am Sagittarius
4th 12:31 pm Capricorn
6th 6:33 pm Aquarius
8th 10:34 pm Pisces
11th 12:44 am Aries
13th 1:45 am Taurus
15th 3:05 am Gemini
17th 6:32 am Cancer
19th 1:37 pm Leo
22nd 12:33 am Virgo
24th 1:29 pm Libra
27th 1:43 am Scorpio
29th 11:28 am Sagittarius

December 1997
1st 6:38 pm Capricorn
3rd 11:58 pm Aquarius
6th 4:07 am Pisces
8th 7:24 am Aries
10th 10:00 am Taurus
12th 12:35 pm Gemini
14th 4:25 pm Cancer
16th 10:58 pm Leo
19th 8:59 am Virgo
21st 9:34 pm Libra
24th 10:07 am Scorpio
26th 8:07 pm Sagittarius
29th 2:48 am Capricorn
31th 6:59 am Aquarius

January 1998
2nd 9:56 am Pisces
4th 12:43 pm Aries
6th 3:52 pm Taurus
8th 7:42 pm Gemini
11th 12:43 am Cancer
13th 7:45 am Leo
15th 5:31 pm Virgo
18th 5:44 am Libra
20th 6:34 pm Scorpio
23rd 5:25 am Sagittarius
25th 12:39 pm Capricorn
27th 4:27 pm Aquarius
29th 6:09 pm Pisces
31th 7:21 pm Aries

February 1998
2nd 9:25 am Taurus
5th 1:09 am Gemini
7th 6:57 am Cancer
9th 2:57 pm Leo
12th 1:09 am Virgo
14th 1:17 pm Libra
17th 2:13 am Scorpio
19th 1:55 pm Sagittarius
21st 10:29 pm Capricorn
24th 3:10 am Aquarius
26th 4:42 am Pisces
28th 4:42 am Aries

March 1998
2nd 5:01 am Taurus
4th 7:15 am Gemini
6th 12:26 pm Cancer
8th 8:45 pm Leo
11th 7:35 am Virgo
13th 7:58 pm Libra
16th 8:50 am Scorpio
18th 8:56 pm Sagittarius
21st 6:43 am Capricorn
23rd 1:01 pm Aquarius
25th 3:43 pm Pisces
27th 3:49 pm Aries
29th 3:07 pm Taurus
31th 3:38 pm Gemini

April 1998
2nd 7:09 pm Cancer
5th 2:35 am Leo
7th 1:25 pm Virgo
10th 2:04 am Libra
12th 2:55 pm Scorpio
15th 2:52 am Sagittarius
17th 1:05 pm Capricorn
19th 8:41 pm Aquarius
22nd 1:06 am Pisces
24th 2:31 am Aries
26th 2:09 am Taurus
28th 1:55 am Gemini
30th 3:57 am Cancer

May 1998
2nd 9:49 am Leo
4th 7:46 pm Virgo
7th 8:18 am Libra
9th 9:10 pm Scorpio
12th 8:48 am Sagittarius
14th 6:39 pm Capricorn
17th 2:30 am Aquarius
19th 8:04 am Pisces
21st 11:06 am Aries
23rd 12:07 pm Taurus
25th 12:26 pm Gemini
27th 1:59 pm Cancer
29th 6:38 pm Leo

June 1998
1st 3:20 am Virgo
3rd 3:16 pm Libra
6th 4:05 am Scorpio
8th 3:34 pm Sagittarius
11th 12:50 am Capricorn
13th 8:04 am Aquarius
15th 1:31 pm Pisces
17th 5:23 pm Aries
19th 7:48 pm Taurus
21st 9:26 pm Gemini
23rd 11:39 pm Cancer
26th 4:04 am Leo
28th 11:54 am Virgo
30th 11:05 pm Libra

July 1998
3rd 11:45 am Scorpio
5th 11:24 pm Sagittarius
8th 8:27 am Capricorn
10th 2:52 pm Aquarius
12th 7:22 pm Pisces
14th 10:45 pm Aries
17th 1:33 am Taurus
19th 4:18 am Gemini
21st 7:43 am Cancer
23rd 12:49 pm Leo
25th 8:33 pm Virgo
28th 7:14 am Libra
30th 7:44 pm Scorpio

August 1998
2nd 7:47 am Sagittarius
4th 5:18 pm Capricorn
6th 11:31 pm Aquarius
9th 3:04 am Pisces
11th 5:11 am Aries
13th 7:05 am Taurus
15th 9:46 am Gemini
17th 1:55 pm Cancer
19th 8:00 pm Leo
22nd 4:21 am Virgo
24th 3:01 pm Libra
27th 3:25 am Scorpio
29th 3:55 pm Sagittarius

September 1998
1st 2:23 am Capricorn
3rd 9:21 am Aquarius
5th 12:48 pm Pisces
7th 1:53 pm Aries
9th 2:17 pm Taurus
11th 3:40 pm Gemini
13th 7:20 pm Cancer
16th 1:48 am Leo
18th 10:52 am Virgo
20th 9:57 pm Libra
23rd 10:21 am Scorpio
25th 11:05 pm Sagittarius
28th 10:30 am Capricorn
30th 6:53 pm Aquarius

October 1998
2nd 11:23 pm Pisces
5th 12:32 am Aries
6th 11:57 pm Taurus
8th 11:44 pm Gemini
11th 1:48 am Cancer
13th 7:25 am Leo
15th 4:31 pm Virgo
18th 4:02 am Libra
20th 4:36 pm Scorpio
23rd 5:16 am Sagittarius
25th 5:04 pm Capricorn
28th 2:44 am Aquarius
30th 8:58 am Pisces

November 1998
1st 11:27 am Aries
3rd 11:13 am Taurus
5th 10:12 am Gemini
7th 10:40 am Cancer
9th 2:33 pm Leo
11th 10:37 pm Virgo
14th 9:57 am Libra
16th 10:41 pm Scorpio
19th 11:12 am Sagittarius
21st 10:45 pm Capricorn
24th 8:43 am Aquarius
26th 4:14 pm Pisces
28th 8:34 pm Aries
30th 9:53 pm Taurus

December 1998
2nd 9:30 pm Gemini
4th 9:28 pm Cancer
6th 11:55 pm Leo
9th 6:21 am Virgo
11th 4:42 pm Libra
14th 5:16 am Scorpio
16th 5:47 pm Sagittarius
19th 4:55 am Capricorn
21st 2:16 pm Aquarius
23rd 9:45 pm Pisces
26th 3:04 am Aries
28th 6:05 am Taurus
30th 7:22 am Gemini

January 1999
1st 8:15 am Cancer
3rd 10:31 am Leo
5th 3:49 pm Virgo
8th 12:53 am Libra
10th 12:48 pm Scorpio
13th 1:23 am Sagittarius
15th 12:28 pm Capricorn
17th 9:11 pm Aquarius
20th 3:40 am Pisces
22nd 8:25 am Aries
24th 11:52 am Taurus
26th 2:30 pm Gemini
28th 4:57 pm Cancer
30th 8:16 pm Leo

February 1999
2nd 1:37 am Virgo
4th 9:55 am Libra
6th 9:06 pm Scorpio
9th 9:37 am Sagittarius
11th 9:10 pm Capricorn
14th 5:57 am Aquarius
16th 11:40 am Pisces
18th 3:07 pm Aries
20th 5:29 pm Taurus
22nd 7:54 pm Gemini
24th 11:09 pm Cancer
27th 3:44 am Leo

March 1999
1st 10:05 am Virgo
3rd 6:34 pm Libra
6th 5:22 am Scorpio
8th 5:45 pm Sagittarius
11th 5:53 am Capricorn
13th 3:31 pm Aquarius
15th 9:30 pm Pisces
18th 12:13 am Aries
20th 1:09 am Taurus
22nd 2:05 am Gemini
24th 4:33 am Cancer
26th 9:22 am Leo
28th 4:34 pm Virgo
31st 1:49 am Libra

April 1999
2nd 12:48 pm Scorpio
5th 1:07 am Sagittarius
7th 1:38 pm Capricorn
10th 12:24 am Aquarius
12th 7:35 am Pisces
14th 10:46 am Aries
16th 11:08 am Taurus
18th 10:40 am Gemini
20th 11:27 am Cancer
22nd 3:05 pm Leo
24th 10:04 pm Virgo
27th 7:46 am Libra
29th 7:12 pm Scorpio

May 1999
2nd 7:36 am Sagittarius
4th 8:12 pm Capricorn
7th 7:40 am Aquarius
9th 4:16 pm Pisces
11th 8:53 pm Aries
13th 9:57 pm Taurus
15th 9:08 pm Gemini
17th 8:40 pm Cancer
19th 10:37 pm Leo
22nd 4:15 am Virgo
24th 1:28 pm Libra
27th 1:05 am Scorpio
29th 1:37 pm Sagittarius

June 1999
1st 2:05 am Capricorn
3rd 1:36 pm Aquarius
5th 11:00 pm Pisces
8th 5:08 am Aries
10th 7:44 am Taurus
12th 7:49 am Gemini
14th 7:15 am Cancer
16th 8:07 am Leo
18th 12:12 pm Virgo
20th 8:10 pm Libra
23rd 7:18 am Scorpio
25th 7:51 pm Sagittarius
28th 8:12 am Capricorn
30th 7:19 pm Aquarius

July 1999
3rd 4:34 am Pisces
5th 11:21 am Aries
7th 3:22 pm Taurus
9th 5:00 pm Gemini
11th 5:28 pm Cancer
13th 6:26 pm Leo
15th 9:39 pm Virgo
18th 4:19 am Libra
20th 2:29 pm Scorpio
23rd 2:48 am Sagittarius
25th 3:08 pm Capricorn
28th 1:54 am Aquarius
30th 10:27 am Pisces

August 1999
1st 4:47 pm Aries
3rd 9:09 pm Taurus
5th 11:57 pm Gemini
8th 1:53 am Cancer
10th 3:56 am Leo
12th 7:22 am Virgo
14th 1:24 pm Libra
16th 10:40 pm Scorpio
19th 10:31 am Sagittarius
21st 10:59 pm Capricorn
24th 9:49 am Aquarius
26th 5:50 pm Pisces
28th 11:09 pm Aries
31st 2:41 am Taurus

September 1999
2nd 5:25 am Gemini
4th 8:10 am Cancer
6th 11:29 am Leo
8th 3:57 pm Virgo
10th 10:16 pm Libra
13th 7:08 am Scorpio
15th 6:34 pm Sagittarius
18th 7:13 am Capricorn
20th 6:38 pm Aquarius
23rd 2:51 am Pisces
25th 7:34 am Aries
27th 9:51 am Taurus
29th 11:21 am Gemini

October 1999
1st 1:32 pm Cancer
3rd 5:13 pm Leo
5th 10:40 pm Virgo
8th 5:52 am Libra
10th 3:01 pm Scorpio
13th 2:18 am Sagittarius
15th 3:04 pm Capricorn
18th 3:17 am Aquarius
20th 12:32 pm Pisces
22nd 5:42 pm Aries
24th 7:26 pm Taurus
26th 7:34 pm Gemini
28th 8:09 pm Cancer
30th 10:47 pm Leo

November 1999
2nd 4:07 am Virgo
4th 11:56 am Libra
6th 9:46 pm Scorpio
9th 9:15 am Sagittarius
11th 9:59 pm Capricorn
14th 10:45 am Aquarius
16th 9:20 pm Pisces
19th 3:57 am Aries
21st 6:27 am Taurus
23rd 6:14 am Gemini
25th 5:29 am Cancer
27th 6:19 am Leo
29th 10:11 am Virgo

December 1999
1st 5:29 pm Libra
4th 3:35 am Scorpio
6th 3:27 pm Sagittarius
9th 4:13 am Capricorn
11th 4:58 pm Aquarius
14th 4:17 am Pisces
16th 12:30 pm Aries
18th 4:45 pm Taurus
20th 5:39 pm Gemini
22nd 4:53 pm Cancer
24th 4:32 pm Leo
26th 6:34 pm Virgo
29th 12:14 am Libra
31th 9:36 am Scorpio

January 2000
2nd 9:32 am Sagittarius
5th 10:24 am Capricorn
7th 10:53 am Aquarius
10th 9:59 am Pisces
12th 6:48 pm Aries
15th 12:38 am Taurus
17th 3:25 am Gemini
19th 4:01 am Cancer
21st 3:59 am Leo
23rd 5:08 am Virgo
25th 9:09 am Libra
27th 5:01 pm Scorpio
30th 4:17 am Sagittarius

May 2000
1st 12:55 am Aries
3rd 4:54 am Taurus
5th 6:24 am Gemini
7th 7:14 am Cancer
9th 9:01 am Leo
11th 12:41 pm Virgo
13th 6:27 pm Libra
16th 2:16 am Scorpio
18th 12:09 pm Sagittarius
21st 12:01 am Capricorn
23rd 12:59 pm Aquarius
26th 1:07 am Pisces
28th 10:07 am Aries
30th 3:02 pm Taurus

September 2000
2nd 5:55 am Scorpio
4th 2:08 pm Sagittarius
7th 1:47 am Capricorn
9th 2:44 pm Aquarius
12th 2:34 am Pisces
14th 12:00 pm Aries
16th 7:05 pm Taurus
19th 12:22 am Gemini
21st 4:16 am Cancer
23rd 7:00 am Leo
25th 9:02 am Virgo
27th 11:22 am Libra
29th 3:30 pm Scorpio

January 2001
1st 10:14 pm Aries
4th 6:56 am Taurus
6th 11:44 am Gemini
8th 1:09 pm Cancer
10th 12:45 pm Leo
12th 12:26 pm Virgo
14th 2:05 pm Libra
16th 7:02 pm Scorpio
19th 3:35 am Sagittarius
21st 2:56 pm Capricorn
24th 3:43 am Aquarius
26th 4:38 pm Pisces
29th 4:35 am Aries
31st 2:21 pm Taurus

May 2001
2nd 2:16 am Virgo
4th 4:50 am Libra
6th 8:01 am Scorpio
8th 1:05 pm Sagittarius
10th 9:10 pm Capricorn
13th 8:19 am Aquarius
15th 9:01 pm Pisces
18th 8:41 am Aries
20th 5:29 pm Taurus
22nd 11:12 pm Gemini
25th 2:43 am Cancer
27th 5:12 am Leo
29th 7:38 am Virgo
31st 10:42 am Libra

February 2000
1st 5:09 pm Capricorn
4th 5:31 am Aquarius
6th 4:02 pm Pisces
9th 12:17 am Aries
11th 6:21 am Taurus
13th 10:23 am Gemini
15th 12:45 pm Cancer
17th 2:12 pm Leo
19th 3:54 pm Virgo
21st 7:22 pm Libra
240 1:58 am Scorpio
26th 12:09 pm Sagittarius
29th 12:45 am Capricorn

June 2000
1st 4:35 pm Gemini
3rd 4:31 pm Cancer
5th 4:46 pm Leo
7th 6:57 pm Virgo
9th 11:59 pm Libra
12th 7:55 am Scorpio
14th 6:18 pm Sagittarius
17th 6:26 am Capricorn
19th 7:26 pm Aquarius
22nd 7:51 am Pisces
24th 5:55 pm Aries
27th 12:19 am Taurus
29th 2:59 am Gemini

October 2000
1st 10:50 pm Sagittarius
4th 9:42 am Capricorn
6th 10:33 pm Aquarius
9th 10:36 am Pisces
11th 7:51 pm Aries
14th 2:06 am Taurus
16th 6:19 am Gemini
18th 9:37 am Cancer
20th 12:42 pm Leo
22nd 3:53 pm Virgo
24th 7:30 pm Libra
27th 12:23 am Scorpio
29th 7:40 am Sagittarius
31st 6:01 pm Capricorn

February 2001
2nd 8:55 pm Gemini
5th 12:00 am Cancer
7th 12:21 am Leo
8th 11:35 pm Virgo
10th 11:46 pm Libra
13th 2:51 am Scorpio
15th 10:02 am Sagittarius
17th 8:58 pm Capricorn
20th 9:53 am Aquarius
22nd 10:45 pm Pisces
25th 10:20 am Aries
27th 8:05 pm Taurus

June 2001
2nd 2:56 pm Scorpio
4th 8:58 pm Sagittarius
7th 5:23 am Capricorn
9th 4:19 pm Aquarius
12th 4:53 am Pisces
14th 5:02 pm Aries
17th 2:39 am Taurus
19th 8:42 am Gemini
21st 11:41 am Cancer
23rd 12:55 pm Leo
25th 1:58 pm Virgo
27th 4:11 pm Libra
29th 8:28 pm Scorpio

March 2000
2nd 1:14 pm Aquarius
4th 11:30 pm Pisces
7th 6:54 am Aries
9th 12:01 pm Taurus
11th 3:46 pm Gemini
13th 6:51 pm Cancer
15th 9:43 pm Leo
18th 12:48 am Virgo
20th 4:57 am Libra
22nd 11:17 am Scorpio
24th 8:43 pm Sagittarius
27th 8:50 am Capricorn
29th 9:34 am Aquarius

July 2000
1st 3:10 am Cancer
3rd 2:38 am Leo
5th 3:19 am Virgo
7th 6:47 am Libra
9th 1:48 pm Scorpio
12th 12:06 am Sagittarius
14th 12:27 pm Capricorn
17th 1:27 am Aquarius
19th 1:44 pm Pisces
22nd 12:09 am Aries
24th 7:43 am Taurus
26th 12:02 pm Gemini
28th 1:30 pm Cancer
30th 1:24 pm Leo

November 2000
3rd 6:40 am Aquarius
5th 7:12 pm Pisces
8th 5:02 am Aries
10th 11:12 am Taurus
12th 2:28 pm Gemini
14th 4:22 pm Cancer
16th 6:19 pm Leo
18th 9:15 pm Virgo
21st 1:35 am Libra
23rd 7:33 am Scorpio
25th 3:33 pm Sagittarius
28th 1:57 am Capricorn
30th 2:26 pm Aquarius

March 2001
2nd 3:36 am Gemini
4th 8:24 am Cancer
6th 10:30 am Leo
8th 10:45 am Virgo
10th 10:48 am Libra
12th 12:43 pm Scorpio
14th 6:16 pm Sagittarius
17th 4:02 am Capricorn
19th 4:35 pm Aquarius
22nd 5:28 am Pisces
24th 4:43 pm Aries
27th 1:51 am Taurus
29th 9:01 am Gemini
31st 2:23 pm Cancer

July 2001
2nd 3:13 am Sagittarius
4th 12:21 pm Capricorn
6th 11:33 pm Aquarius
9th 12:05 pm Pisces
12th 12:36 am Aries
14th 11:12 am Taurus
16th 6:25 pm Gemini
18th 9:56 pm Cancer
20th 10:43 pm Leo
22nd 10:29 pm Virgo
24th 11:08 pm Libra
27th 2:17 am Scorpio
29th 8:44 am Sagittarius
31st 6:16 pm Capricorn

April 2000
1st 8:12 am Pisces
3rd 3:22 pm Aries
5th 7:29 pm Taurus
7th 9:58 pm Gemini
10th 12:16 am Cancer
12th 3:16 am Leo
14th 7:19 am Virgo
16th 12:36 pm Libra
18th 7:35 pm Scorpio
21st 4:57 am Sagittarius
23rd 4:47 pm Capricorn
26th 5:41 am Aquarius
28th 5:05 pm Pisces

August 2000
1st 1:28 pm Virgo
3rd 3:32 pm Libra
5th 9:04 pm Scorpio
8th 6:30 am Sagittarius
10th 6:43 pm Capricorn
13th 7:42 am Aquarius
15th 7:41 pm Pisces
18th 5:44 am Aries
20th 1:31 pm Taurus
22nd 6:55 pm Gemini
24th 9:59 pm Cancer
26th 11:17 pm Leo
28th 11:55 pm Virgo
31st 1:33 am Libra

December 2000
3rd 3:22 am Pisces
5th 2:17 pm Aries
7th 9:26 pm Taurus
10th 12:50 am Gemini
12th 1:49 am Cancer
14th 2:09 am Leo
16th 3:30 am Virgo
18th 7:01 am Libra
20th 1:12 pm Scorpio
22nd 9:57 pm Sagittarius
25th 8:53 am Capricorn
27th 9:25 pm Aquarius
30th 10:27 am Pisces

April 2001
2nd 5:54 pm Leo
4th 7:47 pm Virgo
6th 8:57 pm Libra
8th 11:01 pm Scorpio
11th 3:47 am Sagittarius
13th 12:20 pm Capricorn
16th 12:11 am Aquarius
18th 12:59 pm Pisces
21st 12:18 am Aries
23rd 8:56 am Taurus
25th 3:11 pm Gemini
27th 7:49 pm Cancer
29th 11:25 pm Leo

August 2001
3rd 5:53 am Aquarius
5th 6:30 pm Pisces
8th 7:05 am Aries
10th 6:23 pm Taurus
13th 2:59 am Gemini
15th 7:55 am Cancer
17th 9:26 am Leo
19th 8:54 am Virgo
21st 8:19 am Libra
23rd 9:50 am Scorpio
25th 2:59 pm Sagittarius
28th 12:02 am Capricorn
30th 11:47 am Aquarius

September 2001
2nd 12:32 am Pisces
4th 12:58 pm Aries
7th 12:18 am Taurus
9th 9:41 am Gemini
11th 4:09 pm Cancer
13th 7:16 pm Leo
15th 7:40 pm Virgo
17th 7:01 pm Libra
19th 7:28 pm Scorpio
21st 11:02 pm Sagittarius
24th 6:48 am Capricorn
26th 6:04 am Aquarius
29th 6:50 am Pisces

October 2001
1st 7:07 pm Aries
4th 6:01 am Taurus
6th 3:12 pm Gemini
8th 10:19 pm Cancer
11th 2:54 am Leo
13th 4:58 am Virgo
15th 5:27 am Libra
17th 6:03 am Scorpio
19th 8:47 am Sagittarius
21st 3:11 pm Capricorn
24th 1:26 am Aquarius
26th 1:55 pm Pisces
29th 2:15 am Aries
31st 12:48 pm Taurus

November 2001
2nd 9:13 pm Gemini
5th 3:44 am Cancer
7th 8:34 am Leo
9th 11:49 am Virgo
11th 1:53 pm Libra
13th 3:45 pm Scorpio
15th 6:51 pm Sagittarius
18th 12:40 am Capricorn
20th 9:54 am Aquarius
22nd 9:52 pm Pisces
25th 10:21 am Aries
27th 9:06 pm Taurus
30th 5:04 am Gemini

December 2001
2nd 10:30 am Cancer
4th 2:16 pm Leo
6th 5:11 pm Virgo
8th 7:57 pm Libra
10th 11:09 pm Scorpio
13th 3:30 am Sagittarius
15th 9:48 am Capricorn
17th 6:43 pm Aquarius
20th 6:09 am Pisces
22nd 6:45 pm Aries
25th 6:12 am Taurus
27th 2:39 pm Gemini
29th 7:40 pm Cancer
31st 10:09 pm Leo

January 2002
2nd 11:34 pm Virgo
5th 1:24 am Libra
7th 4:41 am Scorpio
9th 9:57 am Sagittarius
11th 5:18 pm Capricorn
14th 2:41 am Aquarius
16th 1:59 pm Pisces
19th 2:35 am Aries
21st 2:46 pm Taurus
24th 12:28 am Gemini
26th 6:17 am Cancer
28th 8:31 am Leo
30th 8:41 am Virgo

February 2002
1st 8:45 am Libra
3rd 10:35 am Scorpio
5th 3:21 pm Sagittarius
7th 11:08 pm Capricorn
10th 9:15 am Aquarius
12th 8:53 pm Pisces
15th 9:25 am Aries
17th 9:58 pm Taurus
20th 8:50 am Gemini
22nd 4:16 pm Cancer
24th 7:36 pm Leo
26th 7:48 pm Virgo
28th 6:48 pm Libra

March 2002
2nd 6:52 pm Scorpio
4th 9:55 pm Sagittarius
7th 4:47 am Capricorn
9th 2:56 pm Aquarius
12th 2:56 am Pisces
14th 3:34 pm Aries
17th 4:01 am Taurus
19th 3:19 pm Gemini
22nd 12:06 am Cancer
24th 5:13 am Leo
26th 6:44 am Virgo
28th 6:04 am Libra
30th 5:22 am Scorpio

April 2002
1st 6:48 am Sagittarius
3rd 11:58 am Capricorn
5th 9:06 pm Aquarius
8th 8:57 am Pisces
10th 9:40 pm Aries
13th 9:55 am Taurus
15th 8:56 pm Gemini
18th 6:01 am Cancer
20th 12:20 pm Leo
22nd 3:35 pm Virgo
24th 4:23 pm Libra
26th 4:16 pm Scorpio
28th 5:13 pm Sagittarius
30th 9:03 pm Capricorn

May 2002
3rd 4:43 am Aquarius
5th 3:46 pm Pisces
8th 4:22 am Aries
10th 4:32 pm Taurus
13th 3:04 am Gemini
15th 11:33 am Cancer
17th 5:52 pm Leo
19th 10:01 pm Virgo
22nd 12:19 am Libra
24th 1:38 am Scorpio
26th 3:20 am Sagittarius
28th 6:54 am Capricorn
30th 1:35 pm Aquarius

June 2002
1st 11:37 pm Pisces
4th 11:51 am Aries
7th 12:07 am Taurus
9th 10:29 am Gemini
11th 6:15 pm Cancer
13th 11:39 pm Leo
16th 3:24 am Virgo
18th 6:11 am Libra
20th 8:43 am Scorpio
22nd 11:42 am Sagittarius
24th 4:02 pm Capricorn
26th 10:36 pm Aquarius
29th 8:00 am Pisces

July 2002
1st 7:49 pm Aries
4th 8:16 am Taurus
6th 7:00 pm Gemini
9th 2:36 am Cancer
11th 7:08 am Leo
13th 9:41 am Virgo
15th 11:40 am Libra
17th 2:13 pm Scorpio
19th 6:02 pm Sagittarius
21st 11:26 pm Capricorn
24th 6:40 am Aquarius
26th 4:04 pm Pisces
29th 3:38 am Aries
31st 4:16 pm Taurus

August 2002
3rd 3:46 am Gemini
5th 12:02 pm Cancer
7th 4:27 pm Leo
9th 6:04 pm Virgo
11th 6:39 pm Libra
13th 8:01 pm Scorpio
15th 11:25 pm Sagittarius
18th 5:15 am Capricorn
20th 1:16 pm Aquarius
22nd 11:11 pm Pisces
25th 10:47 am Aries
27th 11:31 pm Taurus
30th 11:45 am Gemini

September 2002
1st 9:14 pm Cancer
4th 2:37 am Leo
6th 4:17 am Virgo
8th 3:57 am Libra
10th 3:49 am Scorpio
12th 5:44 am Sagittarius
14th 10:47 am Capricorn
16th 6:54 pm Aquarius
19th 5:18 am Pisces
21st 5:11 pm Aries
24th 5:54 am Taurus
26th 6:26 pm Gemini
29th 5:01 am Cancer

October 2002
1st 11:58 am Leo
3rd 2:53 pm Virgo
5th 2:52 pm Libra
7th 1:58 pm Scorpio
9th 2:21 pm Sagittarius
11th 5:45 pm Capricorn
14th 12:51 am Aquarius
16th 11:06 am Pisces
18th 11:13 pm Aries
21st 11:56 am Taurus
24th 12:17 am Gemini
26th 11:10 am Cancer
28th 7:20 pm Leo
30th 11:59 pm Virgo

November 2002
2nd 1:28 am Libra
4th 1:10 am Scorpio
6th 1:01 am Sagittarius
8th 2:59 am Capricorn
10th 8:26 am Aquarius
12th 5:41 pm Pisces
15th 5:37 am Aries
17th 6:23 pm Taurus
20th 6:25 am Gemini
22nd 4:47 pm Cancer
25th 12:59 am Leo
27th 6:42 am Virgo
29th 9:55 am Libra

December 2002
1st 11:16 am Scorpio
3rd 11:59 am Sagittarius
5th 1:39 pm Capricorn
7th 5:54 pm Aquarius
10th 1:46 am Pisces
12th 12:58 pm Aries
15th 1:43 am Taurus
17th 1:43 pm Gemini
19th 11:30 pm Cancer
22nd 6:49 am Leo
24th 12:05 pm Virgo
26th 3:53 pm Libra
28th 6:41 pm Scorpio
30th 9:01 pm Sagittarius

January 2003
1st 11:42 pm Capricorn
4th 3:57 am Aquarius
6th 10:57 am Pisces
8th 9:14 pm Aries
11th 9:47 am Taurus
13th 10:07 pm Gemini
16th 7:56 am Cancer
18th 2:29 pm Leo
20th 6:32 pm Virgo
22nd 9:23 pm Libra
25th 12:09 am Scorpio
27th 3:26 am Sagittarius
29th 7:30 am Capricorn
31st 12:44 pm Aquarius

February 2003
2nd 7:55 pm Pisces
5th 5:44 am Aries
7th 5:59 pm Taurus
10th 6:45 am Gemini
12th 5:19 pm Cancer
15th 12:04 am Leo
17th 3:23 am Virgo
19th 4:48 am Libra
21st 6:09 am Scorpio
23rd 8:46 am Sagittarius
25th 1:11 pm Capricorn
27th 7:24 pm Aquarius

March 2003
2nd 3:26 am Pisces
4th 1:30 pm Aries
7th 1:36 am Taurus
9th 2:37 pm Gemini
12th 2:11 am Cancer
14th 10:06 am Leo
16th 1:53 pm Virgo
18th 2:44 pm Libra
20th 2:39 pm Scorpio
22nd 3:33 pm Sagittarius
24th 6:48 pm Capricorn
27th 12:51 am Aquarius
29th 9:25 am Pisces
31st 8:04 pm Aries

April 2003
3rd 8:20 am Taurus
5th 9:24 pm Gemini
8th 9:36 am Cancer
10th 6:53 pm Leo
13th 12:07 am Virgo
15th 1:42 am Libra
17th 1:16 am Scorpio
19th 12:52 am Sagittarius
21st 2:20 am Capricorn
23rd 6:58 am Aquarius
25th 3:02 pm Pisces
28th 1:54 am Aries
30th 2:26 pm Taurus

May 2003
3rd 3:27 am Gemini
5th 3:42 am Cancer
8th 1:46 am Leo
10th 8:31 am Virgo
12th 11:43 am Libra
14th 12:14 pm Scorpio
16th 11:44 am Sagittarius
18th 12:04 pm Capricorn
20th 3:01 pm Aquarius
22nd 9:41 pm Pisces
25th 7:58 am Aries
27th 8:32 pm Taurus
30th 9:31 am Gemini

June 2003
1st 9:27 pm Cancer
4th 7:25 am Leo
6th 2:51 pm Virgo
8th 7:30 pm Libra
10th 9:39 pm Scorpio
12th 10:13 pm Sagittarius
14th 10:39 pm Capricorn
17th 12:41 am Aquarius
19th 5:57 am Pisces
21st 3:05 pm Aries
24th 3:15 am Taurus
26th 4:12 pm Gemini
29th 3:52 am Cancer

July 2003
1st 1:13 pm Leo
3rd 8:16 pm Virgo
6th 1:20 am Libra
8th 4:44 am Scorpio
10th 6:49 am Sagittarius
12th 8:21 am Capricorn
14th 10:38 am Aquarius
16th 3:14 pm Pisces
18th 11:20 pm Aries
21st 10:47 am Taurus
23rd 11:42 pm Gemini
26th 11:23 am Cancer
28th 8:17 pm Leo
31st 2:27 am Virgo

August 2003
2nd 6:48 am Libra
4th 10:12 am Scorpio
6th 1:11 pm Sagittarius
8th 4:03 pm Capricorn
10th 7:24 pm Aquarius
13th 12:19 am Pisces
15th 7:59 am Aries
17th 6:52 pm Taurus
20th 7:40 am Gemini
22nd 7:44 pm Cancer
25th 4:48 am Leo
27th 10:27 am Virgo
29th 1:42 pm Libra
31st 4:00 pm Scorpio

September 2003
2nd 6:32 pm Sagittarius
4th 9:51 pm Capricorn
7th 2:15 am Aquarius
9th 8:07 am Pisces
11th 4:09 pm Aries
14th 2:50 am Taurus
16th 3:31 pm Gemini
19th 4:07 am Cancer
21st 2:02 pm Leo
23rd 8:05 pm Virgo
25th 10:49 pm Scorpio
27th 11:52 pm Scorpio
30th 12:57 am Sagittarius

October 2003
2nd 3:21 am Capricorn
4th 7:45 am Aquarius
6th 2:20 pm Pisces
8th 11:08 pm Aries
11th 10:05 am Taurus
13th 10:45 pm Gemini
16th 11:40 am Cancer
18th 10:41 pm Leo
21st 6:01 am Virgo
23rd 9:27 am Libra
25th 10:09 am Scorpio
27th 9:56 am Sagittarius
29th 10:37 am Capricorn
31st 1:41 pm Aquarius

November 2003
2nd 7:52 pm Pisces
5th 5:02 am Aries
7th 4:29 pm Taurus
10th 5:14 am Gemini
12th 6:10 pm Cancer
15th 5:48 am Leo
17th 2:36 pm Virgo
19th 7:42 pm Libra
21st 9:24 pm Scorpio
23rd 9:03 pm Sagittarius
25th 8:32 pm Capricorn
27th 9:48 pm Aquarius
30th 2:25 am Pisces

December 2003
2nd 10:55 am Aries
4th 10:30 pm Taurus
7th 11:26 am Gemini
10th 12:11 am Cancer
12th 11:40 am Leo
14th 9:07 pm Virgo
17th 3:46 am Libra
19th 7:20 am Scorpio
21st 8:16 am Sagittarius
23rd 7:56 am Capricorn
25th 8:14 am Aquarius
27th 11:10 am Pisces
29th 6:08 pm Aries

January 2004
1st 5:01 am Taurus
3rd 5:58 pm Gemini
6th 6:38 am Cancer
8th 5:38 pm Leo
11th 2:37 am Virgo
13th 9:38 am Libra
15th 2:32 pm Scorpio
17th 5:18 pm Sagittarius
19th 6:25 pm Capricorn
21st 7:11 pm Aquarius
23rd 9:29 pm Pisces
26th 3:06 am Aries
28th 12:45 pm Taurus
31st 1:18 am Gemini

February 2004
2nd 2:03 pm Cancer
5th 12:50 am Leo
7th 9:03 am Virgo
9th 3:13 pm Libra
11th 7:58 pm Scorpio
13th 11:35 pm Sagittarius
16th 2:14 am Capricorn
18th 4:27 am Aquarius
20th 7:27 am Pisces
22nd 12:45 pm Aries
24th 9:30 pm Taurus
27th 9:22 am Gemini
29th 10:12 pm Cancer

March 2004
3rd 9:18 am Leo
5th 5:18 pm Virgo
7th 10:31 pm Libra
10th 2:03 am Scorpio
12th 4:57 am Sagittarius
14th 7:52 am Capricorn
16th 11:11 am Aquarius
18th 3:26 pm Pisces
20th 9:29 pm Aries
23rd 6:09 am Taurus
25th 5:34 pm Gemini
28th 6:23 am Cancer
30th 6:07 pm Leo

April 2004
2nd 2:45 am Virgo
4th 7:52 am Libra
6th 10:25 am Scorpio
8th 11:51 am Sagittarius
10th 1:33 pm Capricorn
12th 4:33 pm Aquarius
14th 9:24 pm Pisces
17th 4:24 am Aries
19th 1:42 pm Taurus
22nd 1:10 am Gemini
24th 1:55 pm Cancer
27th 2:14 am Leo
29th 11:59 am Virgo

May 2004
1st 6:03 pm Libra
3rd 8:39 pm Scorpio
5th 9:08 pm Sagittarius
7th 9:17 pm Capricorn
9th 10:46 pm Aquarius
12th 2:52 am Pisces
14th 10:02 am Aries
16th 7:57 pm Taurus
19th 7:47 am Gemini
21st 8:35 pm Cancer
24th 9:07 am Leo
26th 7:52 pm Virgo
29th 3:22 am Libra
31st 7:08 am Scorpio

June 2004
2nd 7:53 am Sagittarius
4th 7:13 am Capricorn
6th 7:10 am Aquarius
8th 9:38 am Pisces
10th 3:49 pm Aries
13th 1:37 am Taurus
15th 1:44 pm Gemini
18th 2:37 am Cancer
20th 3:05 pm Leo
23rd 2:10 am Virgo
25th 10:50 am Libra
27th 4:13 pm Scorpio
29th 6:16 pm Sagittarius

July 2004
1st 6:02 pm Capricorn
3rd 5:23 pm Aquarius
5th 6:27 pm Pisces
7th 11:03 pm Aries
10th 7:50 am Taurus
12th 7:44 pm Gemini
15th 8:40 am Cancer
17th 8:56 pm Leo
20th 7:44 am Virgo
22nd 4:38 pm Libra
24th 11:08 pm Scorpio
27th 2:48 am Sagittarius
29th 3:58 am Capricorn
31st 3:54 am Aquarius

August 2004
2nd 4:35 am Pisces
4th 7:59 am Aries
6th 3:25 pm Taurus
9th 2:33 am Gemini
11th 3:20 pm Cancer
14th 3:30 am Leo
16th 1:49 pm Virgo
18th 10:09 pm Libra
21st 4:37 am Scorpio
23rd 9:08 am Sagittarius
25th 11:47 am Capricorn
27th 1:09 pm Aquarius
29th 2:34 pm Pisces
31st 5:46 pm Aries

September 2004
3rd 12:16 am Taurus
5th 10:24 am Gemini
7th 10:50 pm Cancer
10th 11:05 am Leo
12th 9:16 pm Virgo
15th 4:54 am Libra
17th 10:25 am Scorpio
19th 2:30 pm Sagittarius
21st 5:36 pm Capricorn
23rd 8:10 pm Aquarius
25th 10:55 pm Pisces
28th 2:57 am Aries
30th 9:24 am Taurus

October 2004
2nd 6:54 pm Gemini
5th 6:54 am Cancer
7th 7:22 pm Leo
10th 6:00 am Virgo
12th 1:32 pm Libra
14th 6:11 pm Scorpio
16th 8:58 pm Sagittarius
18th 11:07 pm Capricorn
21st 1:38 am Aquarius
23rd 5:13 am Pisces
25th 10:24 am Aries
27th 5:37 pm Taurus
30th 3:11 am Gemini

November 2004
1st 2:53 pm Cancer
4th 3:32 am Leo
6th 2:59 pm Virgo
8th 11:23 pm Libra
11th 4:05 am Scorpio
13th 5:57 am Sagittarius
15th 6:33 am Capricorn
17th 7:39 am Aquarius
19th 10:38 am Pisces
21st 4:11 pm Aries
24th 12:16 am Taurus
26th 10:25 am Gemini
28th 10:10 pm Cancer

December 2004
1st 10:49 am Leo
3rd 11:00 pm Virgo
6th 8:46 am Libra
8th 2:43 pm Scorpio
10th 4:55 pm Sagittarius
12th 4:43 pm Capricorn
14th 4:11 pm Aquarius
16th 5:24 pm Pisces
18th 9:52 pm Aries
21st 5:52 am Taurus
23rd 4:32 pm Gemini
26th 4:38 am Cancer
28th 5:14 pm Leo
31st 5:33 am Virgo

January 2005
2nd 4:19 pm Libra
4th 11:59 pm Scorpio
7th 3:44 am Sagittarius
9th 4:11 am Capricorn
11th 3:07 am Aquarius
13th 2:50 am Pisces
15th 5:27 am Aries
17th 12:06 pm Taurus
19th 10:24 pm Gemini
22nd 10:42 am Cancer
24th 11:21 pm Leo
27th 11:24 am Virgo
29th 10:13 pm Libra

February 2005
1st 6:51 am Scorpio
3rd 12:21 pm Sagittarius
5th 2:33 pm Capricorn
7th 2:27 pm Aquarius
9th 2:00 pm Pisces
11th 3:22 pm Aries
13th 8:17 pm Taurus
16th 5:18 am Gemini
18th 5:12 pm Cancer
21st 5:54 am Leo
23rd 5:44 pm Virgo
26th 3:59 am Libra
28th 12:20 pm Scorpio

March 2005
2nd 6:29 pm Sagittarius
4th 10:12 pm Capricorn
6th 11:49 pm Aquarius
9th 12:32 am Pisces
11th 2:03 am Aries
13th 6:05 am Taurus
15th 1:44 pm Gemini
18th 12:44 am Cancer
20th 1:17 pm Leo
23rd 1:10 am Virgo
25th 10:59 am Libra
27th 6:29 pm Scorpio
29th 11:56 pm Sagittarius

April 2005
1st 3:48 am Capricorn
3rd 6:31 am Aquarius
5th 8:46 am Pisces
7th 11:28 am Aries
9th 3:50 pm Taurus
11th 10:55 pm Gemini
14th 9:03 am Cancer
16th 9:17 pm Leo
19th 9:27 am Virgo
21st 7:27 pm Libra
24th 2:25 am Scorpio
26th 6:46 am Sagittarius
28th 9:33 am Capricorn
30th 11:54 am Aquarius

May 2005
2nd 2:43 pm Pisces
4th 6:36 pm Aries
7th 12:01 am Taurus
9th 7:29 am Gemini
11th 5:20 pm Cancer
14th 5:17 am Leo
16th 5:46 pm Virgo
19th 4:30 am Libra
21st 11:49 am Scorpio
23rd 3:38 pm Sagittarius
25th 5:11 pm Capricorn
27th 6:10 pm Aquarius
29th 8:09 pm Pisces

June 2005
1st 12:08 am Aries
3rd 6:20 am Taurus
5th 2:36 pm Gemini
8th 12:46 am Cancer
10th 12:39 pm Leo
13th 1:22 am Virgo
15th 12:58 pm Libra
17th 9:23 pm Scorpio
20th 1:45 am Sagittarius
22nd 2:52 am Capricorn
24th 2:36 am Aquarius
26th 3:03 am Pisces
28th 5:51 am Aries
30th 11:44 am Taurus

July 2005
2nd 8:25 pm Gemini
5th 7:07 am Cancer
7th 7:11 pm Leo
10th 7:57 am Virgo
12th 8:09 pm Libra
15th 5:50 am Scorpio
17th 11:35 am Sagittarius
19th 1:27 pm Capricorn
21st 12:56 pm Aquarius
23rd 12:12 pm Pisces
25th 1:23 pm Aries
27th 5:54 pm Taurus
30th 2:02 am Gemini

August 2005
1st 12:52 pm Cancer
4th 1:10 am Leo
6th 1:54 pm Virgo
9th 2:08 am Libra
11th 12:34 pm Scorpio
13th 7:47 pm Sagittarius
15th 11:13 pm Capricorn
17th 11:39 pm Aquarius
19th 10:52 pm Pisces
21st 11:01 pm Aries
24th 1:58 am Taurus
26th 8:42 am Gemini
28th 6:57 pm Cancer
31st 7:14 am Leo

September 2005
2nd 7:56 pm Virgo
5th 7:52 am Libra
7th 6:10 pm Scorpio
10th 2:03 am Sagittarius
12th 6:57 am Capricorn
14th 9:03 am Aquarius
16th 9:25 am Pisces
18th 9:44 am Aries
20th 11:48 am Taurus
22nd 5:06 pm Gemini
25th 2:10 am Cancer
27th 2:02 pm Leo
30th 2:44 am Virgo

October 2005
2nd 2:24 pm Libra
5th 12:03 am Scorpio
7th 7:28 am Sagittarius
9th 12:44 pm Capricorn
11th 4:05 pm Aquarius
13th 6:06 pm Pisces
15th 7:40 pm Aries
17th 10:04 pm Taurus
20th 2:44 am Gemini
22nd 10:41 am Cancer
24th 9:48 pm Leo
27th 10:28 am Virgo
29th 10:15 pm Libra

November 2005
1st 7:29 am Scorpio
3rd 1:55 pm Sagittarius
5th 6:17 pm Capricorn
7th 9:31 pm Aquarius
10th 12:22 am Pisces
12th 3:22 am Aries
14th 7:03 am Taurus
16th 12:10 pm Gemini
18th 7:42 pm Cancer
21st 6:09 am Leo
23rd 6:41 pm Virgo
26th 6:57 am Libra
28th 4:33 pm Scorpio
30th 10:32 pm Sagittarius

December 2005
3rd 1:42 am Capricorn
5th 3:36 am Aquarius
7th 5:44 am Pisces
9th 9:02 am Aries
11th 1:46 pm Taurus
13th 7:59 pm Gemini
16th 4:01 am Cancer
18th 2:18 pm Leo
21st 2:39 am Virgo
23rd 3:26 pm Libra
26th 2:04 am Scorpio
28th 8:44 am Sagittarius
30th 11:36 am Capricorn

January 2006
1st 12:15 pm Aquarius
3rd 12:44 pm Pisces
5th 2:44 pm Aries
7th 7:09 pm Taurus
10th 1:58 am Gemini
12th 10:50 am Cancer
14th 9:31 pm Leo
17th 9:49 am Virgo
19th 10:49 pm Libra
22nd 10:28 am Scorpio
24th 6:37 pm Sagittarius
26th 10:31 pm Capricorn
28th 11:10 pm Aquarius
30th 10:32 pm Pisces

February 2006
1st 10:46 pm Aries
4th 1:31 am Taurus
6th 7:32 am Gemini
8th 4:33 pm Cancer
11th 3:44 am Leo
13th 4:13 pm Virgo
16th 5:09 am Libra
18th 5:11 pm Scorpio
21st 2:38 am Sagittarius
23rd 8:16 am Capricorn
25th 10:15 am Aquarius
27th 9:57 am Pisces

March 2006
1st 9:19 am Aries
3rd 10:22 am Taurus
5th 2:37 pm Gemini
7th 10:38 pm Cancer
10th 9:42 am Leo
12th 10:23 pm Virgo
15th 11:12 am Libra
17th 10:59 pm Scorpio
20th 8:43 am Sagittarius
22nd 3:36 pm Capricorn
24th 7:21 pm Aquarius
26th 8:33 pm Pisces
28th 8:31 pm Aries
30th 9:01 pm Taurus

April 2006
1st 11:49 pm Gemini
4th 6:14 am Cancer
6th 4:24 pm Leo
9th 4:58 am Virgo
11th 5:46 pm Libra
14th 5:08 am Scorpio
16th 2:19 pm Sagittarius
18th 9:13 pm Capricorn
21st 1:56 am Aquarius
23rd 4:43 am Pisces
25th 6:12 am Aries
27th 7:27 am Taurus
29th 9:58 am Gemini

May 2006
1st 3:17 pm Cancer
4th 12:18 am Leo
6th 12:19 pm Virgo
9th 1:10 am Libra
11th 12:24 pm Scorpio
13th 8:56 pm Sagittarius
16th 2:59 am Capricorn
18th 7:19 am Aquarius
20th 10:39 am Pisces
22nd 1:24 pm Aries
24th 4:01 pm Taurus
26th 7:19 pm Gemini
29th 12:34 am Cancer
31st 8:51 am Leo

June 2006
2nd 8:17 pm Virgo
5th 9:08 am Libra
7th 8:41 pm Scorpio
10th 5:05 am Sagittarius
12th 10:19 am Capricorn
14th 1:33 pm Aquarius
16th 4:06 pm Pisces
18th 6:54 pm Aries
20th 10:23 pm Taurus
23rd 2:49 am Gemini
25th 8:48 am Cancer
27th 5:09 pm Leo
30th 4:15 am Virgo

July 2006
2nd 5:05 pm Libra
5th 5:13 am Scorpio
7th 2:13 pm Sagittarius
9th 7:25 pm Capricorn
11th 9:46 pm Aquarius
13th 10:59 pm Pisces
16th 12:39 am Aries
18th 3:44 am Taurus
20th 8:38 am Gemini
22nd 3:20 pm Cancer
25th 12:24 am Leo
27th 11:36 am Virgo
30th 12:27 am Libra

August 2006
1st 1:07 pm Scorpio
3rd 11:13 pm Sagittarius
6th 5:20 am Capricorn
8th 7:48 am Aquarius
10th 8:11 am Pisces
12th 8:22 am Aries
14th 9:59 am Taurus
16th 2:07 pm Gemini
18th 9:03 pm Cancer
21st 6:33 am Leo
23rd 6:08 pm Virgo
26th 7:01 am Libra
28th 7:56 pm Scorpio
31st 6:59 am Sagittarius

September 2006
2nd 2:34 pm Capricorn
4th 6:15 pm Aquarius
6th 6:57 pm Pisces
8th 6:24 pm Aries
10th 6:30 pm Taurus
12th 8:59 pm Gemini
15th 2:53 am Cancer
17th 12:15 pm Leo
20th 12:07 am Virgo
22nd 1:06 pm Libra
25th 1:54 am Scorpio
27th 1:16 pm Sagittarius
29th 10:01 pm Capricorn

October 2006
2nd 3:24 am Aquarius
4th 5:33 am Pisces
6th 5:33 am Aries
8th 5:05 am Taurus
10th 6:06 am Gemini
12th 10:21 am Cancer
14th 6:38 pm Leo
17th 6:15 am Virgo
19th 7:19 pm Libra
22nd 7:54 am Scorpio
24th 6:53 pm Sagittarius
27th 3:47 am Capricorn
29th 10:17 am Aquarius
31st 2:11 pm Pisces

November 2006
2nd 3:47 pm Aries
4th 4:06 pm Taurus
6th 4:47 pm Gemini
8th 7:46 pm Cancer
11th 2:34 am Leo
13th 1:18 pm Virgo
16th 2:14 am Libra
18th 2:46 pm Scorpio
21st 1:15 am Sagittarius
23rd 9:25 am Capricorn
25th 3:41 pm Aquarius
27th 8:21 pm Pisces
29th 11:30 pm Aries

December 2006
2nd 1:26 am Taurus
4th 3:06 am Gemini
6th 6:01 am Cancer
8th 11:52 am Leo
10th 9:31 pm Virgo
13th 9:59 am Libra
15th 10:42 pm Scorpio
18th 9:10 am Sagittarius
20th 4:39 pm Capricorn
22nd 9:49 pm Aquarius
25th 1:43 am Pisces
27th 5:04 am Aries
29th 8:09 am Taurus
31st 11:16 am Gemini

January 2007
2nd 3:14 pm Cancer
4th 9:14 pm Leo
7th 6:18 am Virgo
9th 6:15 pm Libra
12th 7:07 am Scorpio
14th 6:11 pm Sagittarius
17th 1:49 am Capricorn
19th 6:16 am Aquarius
21st 8:49 am Pisces
23rd 10:52 am Aries
25th 1:29 pm Taurus
27th 5:10 pm Gemini
29th 10:16 pm Cancer

February 2007
1st 5:15 am Leo
3rd 2:34 pm Virgo
6th 2:15 am Libra
8th 3:09 pm Scorpio
11th 3:01 am Sagittarius
13th 11:42 am Capricorn
15th 4:35 pm Aquarius
17th 6:30 pm Pisces
19th 7:06 pm Aries
21st 8:04 pm Taurus
23rd 10:42 pm Gemini
26th 3:48 am Cancer
28th 11:29 am Leo

March 2007
2nd 9:32 pm Virgo
5th 9:25 am Libra
7th 10:16 pm Scorpio
10th 10:37 am Sagittarius
12th 8:34 pm Capricorn
15th 2:52 am Aquarius
17th 5:30 am Pisces
19th 5:42 am Aries
21st 5:16 am Taurus
23rd 6:07 am Gemini
25th 9:49 am Cancer
27th 5:04 pm Leo
30th 3:27 am Virgo

April 2007
1st 3:43 pm Libra
4th 4:35 am Scorpio
6th 4:56 pm Sagittarius
9th 3:36 am Capricorn
11th 11:23 am Aquarius
13th 3:39 pm Pisces
15th 4:47 pm Aries
17th 4:12 pm Taurus
19th 3:52 pm Gemini
21st 5:50 pm Cancer
23rd 11:38 pm Leo
26th 9:23 am Virgo
28th 9:44 pm Libra

May 2007
1st 10:41 am Scorpio
3rd 10:48 pm Sagittarius
6th 9:21 am Capricorn
8th 5:48 pm Aquarius
10th 11:32 pm Pisces
13th 2:19 am Aries
15th 2:49 am Taurus
17th 2:34 am Gemini
19th 3:38 am Cancer
21st 7:56 am Leo
23rd 4:26 pm Virgo
26th 4:16 am Libra
28th 5:11 pm Scorpio
31st 5:07 am Sagittarius

June 2007
2nd 3:09 pm Capricorn
4th 11:15 pm Aquarius
7th 5:24 am Pisces
9th 9:26 am Aries
11th 11:29 am Taurus
13th 12:24 pm Gemini
15th 1:46 pm Cancer
17th 5:25 pm Leo
20th 12:46 am Virgo
22nd 11:43 am Libra
25th 12:26 am Scorpio
27th 12:23 pm Sagittarius
29th 10:05 pm Capricorn

July 2007
2nd 5:24 am Aquarius
4th 10:52 am Pisces
6th 2:57 pm Aries
8th 5:54 pm Taurus
10th 8:10 pm Gemini
12th 10:40 pm Cancer
15th 2:43 am Leo
17th 9:39 am Virgo
19th 7:53 pm Libra
22nd 8:17 am Scorpio
24th 8:29 pm Sagittarius
27th 6:21 am Capricorn
29th 1:14 pm Aquarius
31st 5:41 pm Pisces

August 2007
2nd 8:43 pm Aries
4th 11:16 pm Taurus
7th 2:01 am Gemini
9th 5:36 am Cancer
11th 10:42 am Leo
13th 6:03 pm Virgo
16th 4:04 am Libra
18th 4:13 pm Scorpio
21st 4:44 am Sagittarius
23rd 3:19 pm Capricorn
25th 10:35 pm Aquarius
28th 2:34 am Pisces
30th 4:25 am Aries

September 2007
1st 5:36 am Taurus
3rd 7:30 am Gemini
5th 11:08 am Cancer
7th 4:59 pm Leo
10th 1:10 am Virgo
12th 11:31 am Libra
14th 11:37 pm Scorpio
17th 12:20 pm Sagittarius
19th 11:52 pm Capricorn
22nd 8:18 am Aquarius
24th 12:55 pm Pisces
26th 2:23 pm Aries
28th 2:18 pm Taurus
30th 2:34 pm Gemini

October 2007
2nd 4:57 pm Cancer
4th 10:27 pm Leo
7th 7:03 am Virgo
9th 5:57 pm Libra
12th 6:13 am Scorpio
14th 6:58 pm Sagittarius
17th 7:03 am Capricorn
19th 4:51 pm Aquarius
21st 11:02 pm Pisces
24th 1:24 am Aries
26th 1:07 am Taurus
28th 12:11 am Gemini
30th 12:49 am Cancer

November 2007
1st 4:48 am Leo
3rd 12:44 pm Virgo
5th 11:47 pm Libra
8th 12:18 pm Scorpio
11th 12:59 am Sagittarius
13th 1:00 pm Capricorn
15th 11:30 pm Aquarius
18th 7:14 am Pisces
20th 11:24 am Aries
22nd 12:19 pm Taurus
24th 11:30 am Gemini
26th 11:08 am Cancer
28th 1:23 pm Leo
30th 7:44 pm Virgo

December 2007
3rd 6:01 am Libra
5th 6:30 pm Scorpio
8th 7:11 am Sagittarius
10th 6:50 pm Capricorn
13th 5:01 am Aquarius
15th 1:15 pm Pisces
17th 6:52 pm Aries
19th 9:38 pm Taurus
21st 10:14 pm Gemini
23rd 10:18 pm Cancer
25th 11:52 pm Leo
28th 4:44 am Virgo
30th 1:37 pm Libra

January 2008
2nd 1:32 am Scorpio
4th 2:13 pm Sagittarius
7th 1:43 am Capricorn
9th 11:13 am Aquarius
11th 6:44 pm Pisces
14th 12:23 am Aries
16th 4:13 am Taurus
18th 6:30 am Gemini
20th 8:05 am Cancer
22nd 10:21 am Leo
24th 2:48 pm Virgo
26th 10:35 pm Libra
29th 9:34 am Scorpio
31st 10:08 pm Sagittarius

February 2008
3rd 9:52 am Capricorn
5th 7:10 pm Aquarius
8th 1:46 am Pisces
10th 6:17 am Aries
12th 9:34 am Taurus
14th 12:20 pm Gemini
16th 3:12 pm Cancer
18th 6:52 pm Leo
21st 12:06 am Virgo
23rd 7:45 am Libra
25th 6:05 pm Scorpio
28th 6:22 am Sagittarius

March 2008
1st 6:33 pm Capricorn
4th 4:24 am Aquarius
6th 10:53 am Pisces
8th 2:24 pm Aries
10th 4:14 pm Taurus
12th 5:55 pm Gemini
14th 8:38 pm Cancer
17th 1:04 am Leo
19th 7:25 am Virgo
21st 3:45 pm Libra
24th 2:06 am Scorpio
26th 2:10 pm Sagittarius
29th 2:43 am Capricorn
31st 1:33 pm Aquarius

April 2008
2nd 8:55 pm Pisces
5th 12:27 am Aries
7th 1:20 am Taurus
9th 1:27 am Gemini
11th 2:43 am Cancer
13th 6:29 am Leo
15th 1:06 pm Virgo
17th 10:10 pm Libra
20th 9:00 am Scorpio
22nd 9:07 pm Sagittarius
25th 9:46 am Capricorn
27th 9:27 pm Aquarius
30th 6:11 am Pisces

May 2008
2nd 10:51 am Aries
4th 11:59 am Taurus
6th 11:18 am Gemini
8th 11:02 am Cancer
10th 1:10 pm Leo
12th 6:48 pm Virgo
15th 3:46 am Libra
17th 2:59 pm Scorpio
20th 3:18 am Sagittarius
22nd 3:55 pm Capricorn
25th 3:51 am Aquarius
27th 1:38 pm Pisces
29th 7:52 pm Aries
31st 10:19 pm Taurus

June 2008
2nd 10:06 pm Gemini
4th 9:16 pm Cancer
6th 10:00 pm Leo
9th 2:01 am Virgo
11th 9:54 am Libra
13th 8:53 pm Scorpio
16th 9:19 am Sagittarius
18th 9:51 pm Capricorn
21st 9:33 am Aquarius
23rd 7:32 pm Pisces
26th 2:49 am Aries
28th 6:50 am Taurus
30th 8:04 am Gemini

July 2008
2nd 7:54 am Cancer
4th 8:16 am Leo
6th 11:04 am Virgo
8th 5:31 pm Libra
11th 3:35 am Scorpio
13th 3:49 pm Sagittarius
16th 4:20 am Capricorn
18th 3:40 pm Aquarius
21st 1:08 am Pisces
23rd 8:22 am Aries
25th 1:14 pm Taurus
27th 3:55 pm Gemini
29th 5:12 pm Cancer
31st 6:22 pm Leo

August 2008
2nd 8:59 pm Virgo
5th 2:28 am Libra
7th 11:26 am Scorpio
9th 11:10 pm Sagittarius
12th 11:41 am Capricorn
14th 10:56 pm Aquarius
17th 7:46 am Pisces
19th 2:10 pm Aries
21st 6:38 pm Taurus
23rd 9:48 pm Gemini
26th 12:19 am Cancer
28th 2:51 am Leo
30th 6:18 am Virgo

September 2008
1st 11:45 am Libra
3rd 8:02 pm Scorpio
6th 7:10 am Sagittarius
8th 7:44 pm Capricorn
11th 7:19 am Aquarius
13th 4:04 pm Pisces
15th 9:39 pm Aries
18th 12:57 am Taurus
20th 3:17 am Gemini
22nd 5:49 am Cancer
24th 9:14 am Leo
26th 1:52 pm Virgo
28th 8:06 pm Libra

October 2008
1st 4:26 am Scorpio
3rd 3:14 pm Sagittarius
6th 3:48 am Capricorn
8th 4:02 pm Aquarius
11th 1:31 am Pisces
13th 7:07 am Aries
15th 9:32 am Taurus
17th 10:26 am Gemini
19th 11:41 am Cancer
21st 2:35 pm Leo
23rd 7:40 pm Virgo
26th 2:48 am Libra
28th 11:47 am Scorpio
30th 10:41 pm Sagittarius

November 2008
2nd 11:13 am Capricorn
5th 12:01 am Aquarius
7th 10:43 am Pisces
9th 5:26 pm Aries
11th 8:06 pm Taurus
13th 8:12 pm Gemini
15th 7:53 pm Cancer
17th 9:08 pm Leo
20th 1:13 am Virgo
22nd 8:20 am Libra
24th 5:54 pm Scorpio
27th 5:14 am Sagittarius
29th 5:47 pm Capricorn

December 2008
2nd 6:44 am Aquarius
4th 6:23 pm Pisces
7th 2:44 am Aries
9th 6:52 am Taurus
11th 7:34 am Gemini
13th 6:40 am Cancer
15th 6:23 am Leo
17th 8:36 am Virgo
19th 2:22 pm Libra
21st 11:36 pm Scorpio
24th 11:13 am Sagittarius
26th 11:56 pm Capricorn
29th 12:42 pm Aquarius

January 2009
1st 12:27 am Pisces
3rd 9:49 am Aries
5th 3:46 pm Taurus
7th 6:12 pm Gemini
9th 6:14 pm Cancer
11th 5:42 pm Leo
13th 6:33 pm Virgo
15th 10:30 pm Libra
18th 6:20 am Scorpio
20th 5:30 pm Sagittarius
23rd 6:18 am Capricorn
25th 6:56 pm Aquarius
28th 6:12 am Pisces
30th 3:25 pm Aries

February 2009
1st 10:08 pm Taurus
4th 2:15 am Gemini
6th 4:06 am Cancer
8th 4:44 am Leo
10th 5:39 am Virgo
12th 8:33 am Libra
14th 2:50 pm Scorpio
17th 12:53 am Sagittarius
19th 1:25 pm Capricorn
22nd 2:06 am Aquarius
24th 12:59 pm Pisces
26th 9:24 am Aries

March 2009
1st 3:33 am Taurus
3rd 7:59 am Gemini
5th 11:07 am Cancer
7th 1:25 pm Leo
9th 3:35 pm Virgo
11th 6:46 pm Libra
14th 12:22 am Scorpio
16th 9:21 am Sagittarius
18th 9:18 pm Capricorn
21st 10:06 am Aquarius
23rd 9:08 pm Pisces
26th 5:03 am Aries
28th 10:09 am Taurus
30th 1:36 pm Gemini

April 2009
1st 4:30 pm Cancer
3rd 7:33 pm Leo
5th 11:01 pm Virgo
8th 3:22 am Libra
10th 9:23 am Scorpio
12th 6:00 pm Sagittarius
15th 5:27 am Capricorn
17th 6:18 pm Aquarius
20th 5:55 am Pisces
22nd 2:09 pm Aries
24th 6:46 pm Taurus
26th 9:02 pm Gemini
28th 10:38 pm Cancer

May 2009
1st 12:56 am Leo
3rd 4:37 am Virgo
5th 9:51 am Libra
7th 4:48 pm Scorpio
10th 1:49 am Sagittarius
12th 1:09 pm Capricorn
15th 2:01 am Aquarius
17th 2:16 pm Pisces
19th 11:30 pm Aries
22nd 4:40 am Taurus
24th 6:34 am Gemini
26th 6:58 am Cancer
28th 7:45 am Leo
30th 10:17 am Virgo

June 2009
1st 3:17 pm Libra
3rd 10:43 pm Scorpio
6th 8:23 am Sagittarius
8th 7:59 pm Capricorn
11th 8:52 am Aquarius
13th 9:32 pm Pisces
16th 7:51 am Aries
18th 2:20 pm Taurus
20th 5:01 pm Gemini
22nd 5:13 pm Cancer
24th 4:51 pm Leo
26th 5:47 pm Virgo
28th 9:24 pm Libra

July 2009
1st 4:18 am Scorpio
3rd 2:10 pm Sagittarius
6th 2:07 am Capricorn
8th 3:03 pm Aquarius
11th 3:44 am Pisces
13th 2:39 pm Aries
15th 10:30 pm Taurus
18th 2:41 am Gemini
20th 3:51 am Cancer
22nd 3:28 am Leo
24th 3:23 am Virgo
26th 5:26 am Libra
28th 10:55 am Scorpio
30th 8:10 pm Sagittarius

August 2009
2nd 8:08 am Capricorn
4th 9:08 pm Aquarius
7th 9:34 am Pisces
9th 8:23 pm Aries
12th 4:49 am Taurus
14th 10:25 am Gemini
16th 1:13 pm Cancer
18th 1:57 pm Leo
20th 2:01 pm Virgo
22nd 3:12 pm Libra
24th 7:16 pm Scorpio
27th 3:16 am Sagittarius
29th 2:44 pm Capricorn

September 2009
1st 3:43 am Aquarius
3rd 3:58 pm Pisces
6th 2:14 am Aries
8th 10:18 am Taurus
10th 4:17 pm Gemini
12th 8:20 pm Cancer
14th 10:39 pm Leo
16th 11:56 pm Virgo
19th 1:26 am Libra
21st 4:52 am Scorpio
23rd 11:43 am Sagittarius
25th 10:18 pm Capricorn
28th 11:06 am Aquarius
30th 11:26 pm Pisces

October 2009
3rd 9:20 am Aries
5th 4:33 pm Taurus
7th 9:47 pm Gemini
10th 1:48 am Cancer
12th 5:03 am Leo
14th 7:45 am Virgo
16th 10:30 am Libra
18th 2:23 pm Scorpio
20th 8:49 pm Sagittarius
23rd 6:39 am Capricorn
25th 7:07 pm Aquarius
28th 7:45 am Pisces
30th 5:56 pm Aries

November 2009
2nd 12:45 am Taurus
4th 4:53 am Gemini
6th 7:43 am Cancer
8th 10:23 am Leo
10th 1:30 pm Virgo
12th 5:22 pm Libra
14th 10:24 pm Scorpio
17th 5:22 am Sagittarius
19th 3:00 pm Capricorn
22nd 3:11 am Aquarius
24th 4:07 pm Pisces
27th 3:10 am Aries
29th 10:34 am Taurus

December 2009
1st 2:24 pm Gemini
3rd 4:01 pm Cancer
5th 5:07 pm Leo
7th 7:06 pm Virgo
9th 10:47 pm Libra
12th 4:31 am Scorpio
14th 12:25 pm Sagittarius
16th 10:32 pm Capricorn
19th 10:38 am Aquarius
21st 11:42 pm Pisces
24th 11:39 am Aries
26th 8:26 pm Taurus
29th 1:13 am Gemini
31st 2:46 am Cancer

January 2010
2nd 2:41 am Leo
4th 2:53 am Virgo
6th 4:58 am Libra
8th 9:59 am Scorpio
10th 6:10 pm Sagittarius
13th 4:54 am Capricorn
15th 5:17 pm Aquarius
18th 6:17 am Pisces
20th 6:36 pm Aries
23rd 4:39 am Taurus
25th 11:11 am Gemini
27th 2:02 pm Cancer
29th 2:11 pm Leo
31st 1:24 pm Virgo

February 2010
2nd 1:42 pm Libra
4th 4:55 pm Scorpio
7th 12:04 am Sagittarius
9th 10:43 am Capricorn
11th 11:24 pm Aquarius
14th 12:23 pm Pisces
17th 12:30 am Aries
19th 10:55 am Taurus
21st 6:47 pm Gemini
23rd 11:29 pm Cancer
26th 1:08 am Leo
28th 12:52 am Virgo

March 2010
2nd 12:31 am Libra
4th 2:11 am Scorpio
6th 7:36 am Sagittarius
8th 5:12 pm Capricorn
11th 5:42 am Aquarius
13th 6:43 pm Pisces
16th 6:32 am Aries
18th 4:29 pm Taurus
21st 12:28 am Gemini
23rd 6:16 am Cancer
25th 9:39 am Leo
27th 10:58 am Virgo
29th 11:22 am Libra
31st 12:42 pm Scorpio

April 2010
2nd 4:52 pm Sagittarius
5th 1:07 am Capricorn
7th 12:50 pm Aquarius
10th 1:48 am Pisces
12th 1:31 pm Aries
14th 10:55 pm Taurus
17th 6:08 am Gemini
19th 11:39 am Cancer
21st 3:42 pm Leo
23rd 6:24 pm Virgo
25th 8:17 pm Libra
27th 10:29 pm Scorpio
30th 2:36 am Sagittarius

May 2010
2nd 9:59 am Capricorn
4th 8:51 pm Aquarius
7th 9:33 am Pisces
9th 9:29 pm Aries
12th 6:48 am Taurus
14th 1:18 pm Gemini
16th 5:46 pm Cancer
18th 9:06 pm Leo
20th 11:58 pm Virgo
23rd 2:50 am Libra
25th 6:17 am Scorpio
27th 11:16 am Sagittarius
29th 6:44 pm Capricorn

June 2010
1st 5:08 am Aquarius
3rd 5:33 pm Pisces
6th 5:49 am Aries
8th 3:40 pm Taurus
10th 10:11 pm Gemini
13th 1:50 am Cancer
15th 3:54 am Leo
17th 5:41 am Virgo
19th 8:13 am Libra
21st 12:14 pm Scorpio
23rd 6:10 pm Sagittarius
26th 2:21 am Capricorn
28th 12:52 pm Aquarius

July 2010
1st 1:09 am Pisces
3rd 1:43 pm Aries
6th 12:29 am Taurus
8th 7:51 am Gemini
10th 11:38 am Cancer
12th 12:54 pm Leo
14th 1:16 pm Virgo
16th 2:25 pm Libra
18th 5:42 pm Scorpio
20th 11:48 pm Sagittarius
23rd 8:38 am Capricorn
25th 7:38 pm Aquarius
28th 7:59 am Pisces
30th 8:41 pm Aries

August 2010
2nd 8:13 am Taurus
4th 4:54 pm Gemini
6th 9:50 pm Cancer
8th 11:23 pm Leo
10th 11:01 pm Virgo
12th 10:43 pm Libra
15th 12:26 am Scorpio
17th 5:34 am Sagittarius
19th 2:17 pm Capricorn
22nd 1:37 am Aquarius
24th 2:11 pm Pisces
27th 2:49 am Aries
29th 2:35 pm Taurus

September 2010
1st 12:19 am Gemini
3rd 6:50 am Cancer
5th 9:45 am Leo
7th 9:54 am Virgo
9th 9:02 am Libra
11th 9:21 am Scorpio
13th 12:52 pm Sagittarius
15th 8:29 pm Capricorn
18th 7:34 am Aquarius
20th 8:15 pm Pisces
23rd 8:47 am Aries
25th 8:16 pm Taurus
28th 6:10 am Gemini
30th 1:45 pm Cancer

October 2010
2nd 6:21 pm Leo
4th 8:00 pm Virgo
6th 7:52 pm Libra
8th 7:52 pm Scorpio
10th 10:09 pm Sagittarius
13th 4:17 am Capricorn
15th 2:23 pm Aquarius
18th 2:51 am Pisces
20th 3:23 pm Aries
23rd 2:30 am Taurus
25th 11:47 am Gemini
27th 7:14 pm Cancer
30th 12:39 am Leo

November 2010
1st 3:51 am Virgo
3rd 5:19 am Libra
5th 6:16 am Scorpio
7th 8:28 am Sagittarius
9th 1:36 pm Capricorn
11th 10:32 pm Aquarius
14th 10:23 am Pisces
16th 10:58 pm Aries
19th 10:04 am Taurus
21st 6:46 pm Gemini
24th 1:14 am Cancer
26th 6:01 am Leo
28th 9:34 am Virgo
30th 12:16 pm Libra

December 2010
2nd 2:44 pm Scorpio
4th 5:59 pm Sagittarius
6th 11:16 pm Capricorn
9th 7:30 am Aquarius
11th 6:40 pm Pisces
14th 7:14 am Aries
16th 6:48 pm Taurus
19th 3:37 am Gemini
21st 9:22 am Cancer
23rd 12:51 pm Leo
25th 3:14 pm Virgo
27th 5:38 pm Libra
29th 8:50 pm Scorpio

January 2011
1st 1:21 am Sagittarius
3rd 7:39 am Capricorn
5th 4:08 pm Aquarius
8th 2:57 am Pisces
10th 3:23 pm Aries
13th 3:37 am Taurus
15th 1:22 pm Gemini
17th 7:29 pm Cancer
19th 10:16 pm Leo
21st 11:10 pm Virgo
23rd 11:59 pm Libra
26th 2:15 am Scorpio
28th 6:55 am Sagittarius
30th 2:04 pm Capricorn

February 2011
1st 11:21 pm Aquarius
4th 10:24 am Pisces
6th 10:45 pm Aries
9th 11:22 am Taurus
11th 10:20 pm Gemini
14th 5:48 am Cancer
16th 9:14 am Leo
18th 9:40 am Virgo
20th 9:01 am Libra
22nd 9:29 am Scorpio
24th 12:45 pm Sagittarius
26th 7:31 pm Capricorn

March 2011
1st 5:14 am Aquarius
3rd 4:46 pm Pisces
6th 5:14 am Aries
8th 5:52 pm Taurus
11th 5:31 am Gemini
13th 2:29 pm Cancer
15th 7:33 pm Leo
17th 8:53 pm Virgo
19th 8:04 pm Libra
21st 7:17 pm Scorpio
23rd 8:45 pm Sagittarius
26th 1:57 am Capricorn
28th 10:59 am Aquarius
30th 10:38 pm Pisces

April 2011
2nd 11:16 am Aries
4th 11:46 pm Taurus
7th 11:21 am Gemini
9th 9:01 pm Cancer
12th 3:37 am Leo
14th 6:41 am Virgo
16th 6:59 am Libra
18th 6:20 am Scorpio
20th 6:50 am Sagittarius
22nd 10:24 am Capricorn
24th 5:58 pm Aquarius
27th 4:57 am Pisces
29th 5:33 pm Aries

May 2011
2nd 5:58 am Taurus
4th 5:09 pm Gemini
7th 2:31 am Cancer
9th 9:35 am Leo
11th 1:59 pm Virgo
13th 3:57 pm Libra
15th 4:32 pm Scorpio
17th 5:23 pm Sagittarius
19th 8:16 pm Capricorn
22nd 2:31 am Aquarius
24th 12:23 pm Pisces
27th 12:36 am Aries
29th 1:01 pm Taurus
31st 11:56 pm Gemini

June 2011
3rd 8:36 am Cancer
5th 3:03 pm Leo
7th 7:33 pm Virgo
9th 10:31 pm Libra
12th 12:33 am Scorpio
14th 2:38 am Sagittarius
16th 5:59 am Capricorn
18th 11:47 am Aquarius
20th 8:45 pm Pisces
23rd 8:23 am Aries
25th 8:52 pm Taurus
28th 7:56 am Gemini
30th 4:13 pm Cancer

July 2011
2nd 9:43 pm Leo
5th 1:15 am Virgo
7th 3:54 am Libra
9th 6:31 am Scorpio
11th 9:47 am Sagittarius
13th 2:14 pm Capricorn
15th 8:30 pm Aquarius
18th 5:13 am Pisces
20th 4:25 pm Aries
23rd 4:58 am Taurus
25th 4:34 pm Gemini
28th 1:11 am Cancer
30th 6:16 am Leo

August 2011
1st 8:42 am Virgo
3rd 10:05 am Libra
5th 11:57 am Scorpio
7th 3:21 pm Sagittarius
9th 8:37 pm Capricorn
12th 3:47 am Aquarius
14th 12:54 pm Pisces
17th 12:01 am Aries
19th 12:36 pm Taurus
22nd 12:53 am Gemini
24th 10:30 am Cancer
26th 4:09 pm Leo
28th 6:14 pm Virgo
30th 6:26 pm Libra

September 2011
1st 6:48 pm Scorpio
3rd 9:04 pm Sagittarius
6th 2:03 am Capricorn
8th 9:42 am Aquarius
10th 7:26 pm Pisces
13th 6:49 am Aries
15th 7:25 pm Taurus
18th 8:06 am Gemini
20th 6:53 pm Cancer
23rd 1:55 am Leo
25th 4:50 am Virgo
27th 4:51 am Libra
29th 4:05 am Scorpio

January 2012
2nd 10:16 pm Taurus
5th 10:44 am Gemini
7th 9:05 pm Cancer
10th 4:35 am Leo
12th 9:44 am Virgo
14th 1:28 pm Libra
16th 4:34 pm Scorpio
18th 7:29 pm Sagittarius
20th 10:40 pm Capricorn
23rd 2:53 am Aquarius
25th 9:11 am Pisces
27th 6:28 pm Aries
30th 6:28 am Taurus

May 2012
3rd 2:04 am Libra
5th 2:20 am Scorpio
7th 1:39 am Sagittarius
9th 2:00 am Capricorn
11th 5:03 am Aquarius
13th 11:41 am Pisces
15th 9:45 pm Aries
18th 10:03 am Taurus
20th 11:05 pm Gemini
23rd 11:31 am Cancer
25th 10:11 pm Leo
28th 6:06 am Virgo
30th 10:46 am Libra

September 2012
2nd 5:37 am Aries
4th 3:41 pm Taurus
7th 4:09 am Gemini
9th 4:49 pm Cancer
12th 3:00 am Leo
14th 9:31 am Virgo
16th 12:56 pm Libra
18th 2:46 pm Scorpio
20th 4:34 pm Sagittarius
22nd 7:20 pm Capricorn
24th 11:32 pm Aquarius
27th 5:24 am Pisces
29th 1:14 pm Aries

January 2013
1st 5:35 pm Virgo
4th 1:11 am Libra
6th 6:09 am Scorpio
8th 8:28 am Sagittarius
10th 8:55 am Capricorn
12th 9:02 am Aquarius
14th 10:50 am Pisces
16th 4:07 pm Aries
19th 1:36 am Taurus
21st 2:04 pm Gemini
24th 2:59 am Cancer
26th 2:20 pm Leo
28th 11:27 pm Virgo
31st 6:36 am Libra

October 2011
1st 4:42 am Sagittarius
3rd 8:15 am Capricorn
5th 3:18 pm Aquarius
8th 1:13 am Pisces
10th 12:57 pm Aries
13th 1:35 am Taurus
15th 2:14 pm Gemini
18th 1:38 am Cancer
20th 10:05 am Leo
22nd 2:41 pm Virgo
24th 3:50 pm Libra
26th 3:09 pm Scorpio
28th 2:46 pm Sagittarius
30th 4:39 pm Capricorn

February 2012
1st 7:14 pm Gemini
4th 6:04 am Cancer
6th 1:24 pm Leo
8th 5:33 pm Virgo
10th 7:55 pm Libra
12th 10:01 pm Scorpio
15th 12:56 am Sagittarius
17th 5:03 am Capricorn
19th 10:28 am Aquarius
21st 5:31 pm Pisces
24th 2:48 am Aries
26th 2:29 pm Taurus
29th 3:27 am Gemini

June 2012
1st 12:32 pm Scorpio
3rd 12:33 pm Sagittarius
5th 12:32 pm Capricorn
7th 2:17 pm Aquarius
9th 7:22 pm Pisces
12th 4:21 am Aries
14th 4:21 pm Taurus
17th 5:24 am Gemini
19th 5:33 pm Cancer
22nd 3:47 am Leo
24th 11:42 am Virgo
26th 5:15 pm Libra
28th 8:32 pm Scorpio
30th 10:04 pm Sagittarius

October 2012
1st 11:26 pm Taurus
4th 11:46 am Gemini
7th 12:45 am Cancer
9th 11:54 am Leo
11th 7:23 pm Virgo
13th 11:02 pm Libra
16th 12:06 am Scorpio
18th 12:26 am Sagittarius
20th 1:41 am Capricorn
22nd 5:02 am Aquarius
24th 10:59 am Pisces
26th 7:31 pm Aries
29th 6:15 am Taurus
31st 6:40 pm Gemini

February 2013
2nd 12:01 pm Scorpio
4th 3:45 pm Sagittarius
6th 5:55 pm Capricorn
8th 7:17 pm Aquarius
10th 9:20 pm Pisces
13th 1:51 am Aries
15th 10:07 am Taurus
17th 9:50 pm Gemini
20th 10:44 am Cancer
22nd 10:12 pm Leo
25th 6:53 am Virgo
27th 1:02 pm Libra

November 2011
1st 10:08 pm Aquarius
4th 7:17 am Pisces
6th 7:02 pm Aries
9th 7:45 am Taurus
11th 8:10 pm Gemini
14th 7:18 am Cancer
16th 4:17 pm Leo
18th 10:19 pm Virgo
21st 1:16 am Libra
23rd 1:58 am Scorpio
25th 1:57 am Sagittarius
27th 3:05 am Capricorn
29th 7:01 am Aquarius

March 2012
2nd 3:08 pm Cancer
4th 11:17 pm Leo
7th 3:27 am Virgo
9th 4:51 am Libra
11th 5:24 am Scorpio
13th 6:54 am Sagittarius
15th 10:24 am Capricorn
17th 4:11 pm Aquarius
20th 12:05 am Pisces
22nd 9:57 am Aries
24th 9:43 pm Taurus
27th 10:43 am Gemini
29th 11:07 pm Cancer

July 2012
2nd 10:51 pm Capricorn
5th 12:26 am Aquarius
7th 4:29 am Pisces
9th 12:13 pm Aries
11th 11:30 pm Taurus
14th 12:26 pm Gemini
17th 12:31 am Cancer
19th 10:13 am Leo
21st 5:24 pm Virgo
23rd 10:38 pm Libra
26th 2:29 am Scorpio
28th 5:18 am Sagittarius
30th 7:30 am Capricorn

November 2012
3rd 7:43 am Cancer
5th 7:39 pm Leo
8th 4:35 am Virgo
10th 9:35 am Libra
12th 11:11 am Scorpio
14th 10:53 am Sagittarius
16th 10:36 am Capricorn
18th 12:10 pm Aquarius
20th 4:55 pm Pisces
23rd 1:11 am Aries
25th 12:18 pm Taurus
28th 12:58 am Gemini
30th 1:55 pm Cancer

March 2013
1st 5:34 pm Scorpio
3rd 9:11 pm Sagittarius
6th 12:14 am Capricorn
8th 3:02 am Aquarius
10th 6:19 am Pisces
12th 11:17 am Aries
14th 7:08 pm Taurus
17th 6:09 am Gemini
19th 6:55 pm Cancer
22nd 6:49 am Leo
24th 3:49 pm Virgo
26th 9:32 pm Libra
29th 12:54 am Scorpio
31st 3:13 am Sagittarius

December 2011
1st 2:45 pm Pisces
4th 1:51 am Aries
6th 2:34 pm Taurus
9th 2:52 am Gemini
11th 1:26 pm Cancer
13th 9:48 pm Leo
16th 3:58 am Virgo
18th 8:06 am Libra
20th 10:33 am Scorpio
22nd 12:03 pm Sagittarius
24th 1:48 pm Capricorn
26th 5:15 pm Aquarius
28th 11:45 pm Pisces
31st 9:48 am Aries

April 2012
1st 8:35 am Leo
3rd 1:53 pm Virgo
5th 3:33 pm Libra
7th 3:18 pm Scorpio
9th 3:13 pm Sagittarius
11th 5:02 pm Capricorn
13th 9:48 pm Aquarius
16th 5:38 am Pisces
18th 3:59 am Aries
21st 4:05 am Taurus
23rd 5:05 pm Gemini
26th 5:42 am Cancer
28th 4:10 pm Leo
30th 11:02 pm Virgo

August 2012
1st 9:56 am Aquarius
3rd 1:58 pm Pisces
5th 8:58 pm Aries
8th 7:27 am Taurus
10th 8:10 pm Gemini
13th 8:27 am Cancer
15th 6:04 pm Leo
18th 12:33 am Virgo
20th 4:46 am Libra
22nd 7:54 am Scorpio
24th 10:50 am Sagittarius
26th 1:59 pm Capricorn
28th 5:39 pm Aquarius
30th 10:31 pm Pisces

December 2012
3rd 1:57 am Leo
5th 11:51 am Virgo
7th 6:35 pm Libra
9th 9:51 pm Scorpio
11th 10:22 pm Sagittarius
13th 9:43 pm Capricorn
15th 9:53 pm Aquarius
18th 12:48 am Pisces
20th 7:43 am Aries
22nd 6:25 pm Taurus
25th 7:13 am Gemini
27th 8:06 pm Cancer
30th 7:45 am Leo

April 2013
2nd 5:35 am Capricorn
4th 8:42 am Aquarius
6th 1:00 pm Pisces
8th 7:02 pm Aries
11th 3:22 am Taurus
13th 2:12 pm Gemini
16th 2:49 am Cancer
18th 3:13 pm Leo
21st 1:08 am Virgo
23rd 7:25 am Libra
25th 10:26 am Scorpio
27th 11:32 am Sagittarius
29th 12:22 pm Capricorn

May 2013
1st 2:20 pm Aquarius
3rd 6:25 pm Pisces
6th 1:03 am Aries
8th 10:09 am Taurus
10th 9:21 pm Gemini
13th 9:56 am Cancer
15th 10:37 pm Leo
18th 9:32 am Virgo
20th 5:07 pm Libra
22nd 8:55 pm Scorpio
24th 9:49 pm Sagittarius
26th 9:29 pm Capricorn
28th 9:48 pm Aquarius
31st 12:30 am Pisces

June 2013
2nd 6:33 am Aries
4th 3:53 pm Taurus
7th 3:32 am Gemini
9th 4:15 pm Cancer
12th 4:58 am Leo
14th 4:25 pm Virgo
17th 1:18 am Libra
19th 6:38 am Scorpio
21st 8:31 am Sagittarius
23rd 8:09 am Capricorn
25th 7:27 am Aquarius
27th 8:32 am Pisces
29th 1:06 pm Aries

July 2013
1st 9:42 pm Taurus
4th 9:21 am Gemini
6th 10:13 pm Cancer
9th 10:48 am Leo
11th 10:12 pm Virgo
14th 7:40 am Libra
16th 2:24 pm Scorpio
18th 5:54 pm Sagittarius
20th 6:39 pm Capricorn
22nd 6:08 pm Aquarius
24th 6:23 pm Pisces
26th 9:29 pm Aries
29th 4:43 am Taurus
31st 3:41 pm Gemini

August 2013
3rd 4:29 am Cancer
5th 4:57 pm Leo
8th 3:57 am Virgo
10th 1:08 pm Libra
12th 8:17 pm Scorpio
15th 1:04 am Sagittarius
17th 3:25 am Capricorn
19th 4:07 am Aquarius
21st 4:44 am Pisces
23rd 7:13 am Aries
25th 1:13 pm Taurus
27th 11:08 pm Gemini
30th 11:32 am Cancer

September 2013
2nd 12:01 am Leo
4th 10:43 am Virgo
6th 7:12 pm Libra
9th 1:44 am Scorpio
11th 6:36 am Sagittarius
13th 9:56 am Capricorn
15th 12:06 pm Aquarius
17th 1:59 pm Pisces
19th 4:58 pm Aries
21st 10:33 pm Taurus
24th 7:34 am Gemini
26th 7:24 pm Cancer
29th 7:57 am Leo

October 2013
1st 6:51 pm Virgo
4th 2:59 am Libra
6th 8:33 am Scorpio
8th 12:22 pm Sagittarius
10th 3:17 pm Capricorn
12th 6:00 pm Aquarius
14th 9:06 pm Pisces
17th 1:18 am Aries
19th 7:27 am Taurus
21st 4:14 pm Gemini
24th 3:36 am Cancer
26th 4:11 pm Leo
29th 3:44 am Virgo
31st 12:21 pm Libra

November 2013
2nd 5:35 pm Scorpio
4th 8:14 pm Sagittarius
6th 9:44 pm Capricorn
8th 11:30 pm Aquarius
11th 2:36 am Pisces
13th 7:39 am Aries
15th 2:49 pm Taurus
18th 12:07 am Gemini
20th 11:23 am Cancer
22nd 11:56 pm Leo
25th 12:10 pm Virgo
27th 9:59 pm Libra
30th 4:03 am Scorpio

December 2013
2nd 6:32 am Sagittarius
4th 6:50 am Capricorn
6th 6:54 am Aquarius
8th 8:34 am Pisces
10th 1:05 pm Aries
12th 8:40 pm Taurus
15th 6:40 am Gemini
17th 6:17 pm Cancer
20th 6:47 am Leo
22nd 7:19 pm Virgo
25th 6:17 am Libra
27th 1:57 pm Scorpio
29th 5:37 pm Sagittarius
31st 6:02 pm Capricorn

January 2014
2nd 5:04 pm Aquarius
4th 4:59 pm Pisces
6th 7:45 pm Aries
9th 2:24 am Taurus
11th 12:25 pm Gemini
14th 12:25 am Cancer
16th 1:00 pm Leo
19th 1:23 am Virgo
21st 12:43 pm Libra
23rd 9:43 pm Scorpio
26th 3:13 am Sagittarius
28th 5:05 am Capricorn
30th 4:34 am Aquarius

February 2014
1st 3:45 am Pisces
3rd 4:55 am Aries
5th 9:46 am Taurus
7th 6:43 pm Gemini
10th 6:32 am Cancer
12th 7:15 pm Leo
15th 7:25 am Virgo
17th 6:22 pm Libra
20th 3:33 am Scorpio
22nd 10:11 am Sagittarius
24th 1:50 pm Capricorn
26th 2:49 pm Aquarius
28th 2:54 pm Pisces

March 2014
2nd 3:40 pm Aries
4th 7:12 pm Taurus
7th 2:37 am Gemini
9th 1:32 pm Cancer
12th 2:08 am Leo
14th 2:17 pm Virgo
17th 12:46 am Libra
19th 9:13 am Scorpio
21st 3:39 pm Sagittarius
23rd 8:03 pm Capricorn
25th 10:39 pm Aquarius
28th 12:10 am Pisces
30th 1:54 am Aries

April 2014
1st 5:20 am Taurus
3rd 11:48 am Gemini
5th 9:39 pm Cancer
8th 9:50 am Leo
10th 10:07 pm Virgo
13th 8:33 am Libra
15th 4:20 pm Scorpio
17th 9:44 pm Sagittarius
20th 1:28 am Capricorn
22nd 4:18 am Aquarius
24th 6:55 am Pisces
26th 10:01 am Aries
28th 2:24 pm Taurus
30th 8:56 pm Gemini

May 2014
3rd 6:13 am Cancer
5th 5:55 pm Leo
8th 6:24 am Virgo
10th 5:19 pm Libra
13th 1:07 am Scorpio
15th 5:44 am Sagittarius
17th 8:12 am Capricorn
19th 9:58 am Aquarius
21st 12:19 pm Pisces
23rd 4:01 pm Aries
25th 9:28 pm Taurus
28th 4:47 am Gemini
30th 2:13 pm Cancer

June 2014
2nd 1:43 am Leo
4th 2:19 pm Virgo
7th 2:01 am Libra
9th 10:38 am Scorpio
11th 3:23 pm Sagittarius
13th 5:05 pm Capricorn
15th 5:28 pm Aquarius
17th 6:26 pm Pisces
19th 9:26 pm Aries
22nd 3:03 am Taurus
24th 11:05 am Gemini
26th 9:05 pm Cancer
29th 8:42 am Leo

July 2014
1st 9:23 pm Virgo
4th 9:42 am Libra
6th 7:33 pm Scorpio
9th 1:24 am Sagittarius
11th 3:25 am Capricorn
13th 3:07 am Aquarius
15th 2:40 am Pisces
17th 4:07 am Aries
19th 8:42 am Taurus
21st 4:36 pm Gemini
24th 2:59 am Cancer
26th 2:54 pm Leo
29th 3:37 am Virgo
31st 4:09 pm Libra

August 2014
3rd 2:57 am Scorpio
5th 10:18 am Sagittarius
7th 1:39 pm Capricorn
9th 1:53 pm Aquarius
11th 12:56 pm Pisces
13th 1:01 pm Aries
15th 3:58 pm Taurus
17th 10:41 pm Gemini
20th 8:44 am Cancer
22nd 8:49 pm Leo
25th 9:32 am Virgo
27th 9:54 pm Libra
30th 8:52 am Scorpio

September 2014
1st 5:16 pm Sagittarius
3rd 10:15 pm Capricorn
5th 11:59 pm Aquarius
7th 11:47 pm Pisces
9th 11:33 pm Aries
12th 1:17 am Taurus
14th 6:26 am Gemini
16th 3:24 pm Cancer
19th 3:10 am Leo
21st 3:54 pm Virgo
24th 3:59 am Libra
26th 2:29 pm Scorpio
28th 10:50 pm Sagittarius

October 2014
1st 4:41 am Capricorn
3rd 8:00 am Aquarius
5th 9:25 am Pisces
7th 10:07 am Aries
9th 11:44 am Taurus
11th 3:51 pm Gemini
13th 11:30 pm Cancer
16th 10:29 am Leo
18th 11:08 pm Virgo
21st 11:11 am Libra
23rd 9:10 pm Scorpio
26th 4:40 am Sagittarius
28th 10:03 am Capricorn
30th 1:52 pm Aquarius

November 2014
1st 4:37 pm Pisces
3rd 6:54 pm Aries
5th 9:33 pm Taurus
8th 1:45 am Gemini
10th 8:38 am Cancer
12th 6:44 pm Leo
15th 7:08 am Virgo
17th 7:29 pm Libra
20th 5:31 am Scorpio
22nd 12:19 pm Sagittarius
24th 4:32 pm Capricorn
26th 7:23 pm Aquarius
28th 10:03 pm Pisces

December 2014
1st 1:14 am Aries
3rd 5:15 am Taurus
5th 10:28 am Gemini
7th 5:34 pm Cancer
10th 3:14 am Leo
12th 3:18 pm Virgo
15th 4:04 am Libra
17th 2:51 pm Scorpio
19th 9:55 pm Sagittarius
22nd 1:25 am Capricorn
24th 2:52 am Aquarius
26th 4:07 am Pisces
28th 6:35 am Aries
30th 10:56 am Taurus

January 2015
1st 5:09 pm Gemini
4th 1:08 am Cancer
6th 11:03 am Leo
8th 10:58 pm Virgo
11th 11:56 am Libra
13th 11:44 pm Scorpio
16th 8:01 am Sagittarius
18th 12:04 pm Capricorn
20th 1:00 pm Aquarius
22nd 12:49 pm Pisces
24th 1:32 pm Aries
26th 4:37 pm Taurus
28th 10:36 pm Gemini
31st 7:08 am Cancer

February 2015
2nd 5:41 pm Leo
5th 5:46 am Virgo
7th 6:43 pm Libra
10th 7:05 am Scorpio
12th 4:46 pm Sagittarius
14th 10:24 pm Capricorn
17th 12:13 am Aquarius
18th 11:47 pm Pisces
20th 11:13 pm Aries
23rd 12:28 am Taurus
25th 4:54 am Gemini
27th 12:49 pm Cancer

March 2015
1st 11:34 pm Leo
4th 11:57 am Virgo
7th 12:52 am Libra
9th 1:09 pm Scorpio
11th 11:30 pm Sagittarius
14th 6:40 am Capricorn
16th 10:14 am Aquarius
18th 10:59 am Pisces
20th 10:29 am Aries
22nd 10:41 am Taurus
24th 1:22 pm Gemini
26th 7:45 pm Cancer
29th 5:48 am Leo
31st 6:12 pm Virgo

April 2015
3rd 7:07 am Libra
5th 7:04 pm Scorpio
8th 5:08 am Sagittarius
10th 12:47 pm Capricorn
12th 5:44 pm Aquarius
14th 8:12 pm Pisces
16th 9:00 pm Aries
18th 9:32 pm Taurus
20th 11:28 pm Gemini
23rd 4:25 am Cancer
25th 1:12 pm Leo
28th 1:07 am Virgo
30th 2:02 pm Libra

May 2015
3rd 1:47 am Scorpio
5th 11:13 am Sagittarius
7th 6:16 pm Capricorn
9th 11:22 pm Aquarius
12th 2:53 am Pisces
14th 5:14 am Aries
16th 7:03 am Taurus
18th 9:28 am Gemini
20th 1:56 pm Cancer
22nd 9:42 pm Leo
25th 8:51 am Virgo
27th 9:42 pm Libra
30th 9:33 am Scorpio

June 2015
1st 6:39 pm Sagittarius
4th 12:50 am Capricorn
6th 5:02 am Aquarius
8th 8:16 am Pisces
10th 11:14 am Aries
12th 2:16 pm Taurus
14th 5:51 pm Gemini
16th 10:51 pm Cancer
19th 6:22 am Leo
21st 4:58 pm Virgo
24th 5:40 am Libra
26th 5:56 pm Scorpio
29th 3:21 am Sagittarius

July 2015
1st 9:11 am Capricorn
3rd 12:21 pm Aquarius
5th 2:23 pm Pisces
7th 4:38 pm Aries
9th 7:49 pm Taurus
12th 12:16 am Gemini
14th 6:14 am Cancer
16th 2:15 pm Leo
19th 12:47 am Virgo
21st 1:22 pm Libra
24th 2:07 am Scorpio
26th 12:24 pm Sagittarius
28th 6:47 pm Capricorn
30th 9:40 pm Aquarius

August 2015
1st 10:36 pm Pisces
3rd 11:24 pm Aries
6th 1:29 am Taurus
8th 5:40 am Gemini
10th 12:08 pm Cancer
12th 8:52 pm Leo
15th 7:45 am Virgo
17th 8:22 pm Libra
20th 9:24 am Scorpio
22nd 8:41 pm Sagittarius
25th 4:22 am Capricorn
27th 8:04 am Aquarius
29th 8:52 am Pisces
31st 8:34 am Aries

September 2015
2nd 9:02 am Taurus
4th 11:48 am Gemini
6th 5:39 pm Cancer
9th 2:36 am Leo
11th 1:55 pm Virgo
14th 2:41 am Libra
16th 3:42 pm Scorpio
19th 3:31 am Sagittarius
21st 12:32 pm Capricorn
23rd 5:51 pm Aquarius
25th 7:44 pm Pisces
27th 7:29 pm Aries
29th 6:58 pm Taurus

October 2015
1st 8:04 pm Gemini
4th 12:22 am Cancer
6th 8:30 am Leo
8th 7:50 pm Virgo
11th 8:45 am Libra
13th 9:38 pm Scorpio
16th 9:18 am Sagittarius
18th 6:52 pm Capricorn
21st 1:38 am Aquarius
23rd 5:18 am Pisces
25th 6:22 am Aries
27th 6:08 am Taurus
29th 6:25 am Gemini
31st 9:09 am Cancer

November 2015
2nd 3:47 pm Leo
5th 2:22 am Virgo
7th 3:14 pm Libra
10th 4:02 am Scorpio
12th 3:14 pm Sagittarius
15th 12:21 am Capricorn
17th 7:24 am Aquarius
19th 12:21 pm Pisces
21st 3:13 pm Aries
23rd 4:27 pm Taurus
25th 5:16 pm Gemini
27th 7:27 pm Cancer
30th 12:47 am Leo

December 2015
2nd 10:09 am Virgo
4th 10:33 pm Libra
7th 11:25 am Scorpio
9th 10:25 pm Sagittarius
12th 6:47 am Capricorn
14th 12:59 pm Aquarius
16th 5:45 pm Pisces
18th 9:26 pm Aries
21st 12:13 am Taurus
23rd 2:31 am Gemini
25th 5:27 am Cancer
27th 10:31 am Leo
29th 6:58 pm Virgo

January 2016
1st 6:40 am Libra
3rd 7:35 pm Scorpio
6th 6:56 am Sagittarius
8th 3:07 pm Capricorn
10th 8:23 pm Aquarius
12th 11:53 pm Pisces
15th 2:48 am Aries
17th 5:48 am Taurus
19th 9:13 am Gemini
21st 1:28 pm Cancer
23rd 7:21 pm Leo
26th 3:46 am Virgo
28th 2:59 pm Libra
31st 3:50 am Scorpio

February 2016
2nd 3:49 pm Sagittarius
5th 12:44 am Capricorn
7th 5:59 am Aquarius
9th 8:32 am Pisces
11th 9:55 am Aries
13th 11:36 am Taurus
15th 2:35 pm Gemini
17th 7:24 pm Cancer
20th 2:17 am Leo
22nd 11:24 am Virgo
24th 10:41 pm Libra
27th 11:26 am Scorpio
29th 11:56 pm Sagittarius

March 2016
3rd 10:01 am Capricorn
5th 4:22 pm Aquarius
7th 7:09 pm Pisces
9th 7:40 pm Aries
11th 7:44 pm Taurus
13th 9:04 pm Gemini
16th 12:57 am Cancer
18th 7:54 am Leo
20th 5:39 pm Virgo
23rd 5:23 am Libra
25th 6:09 pm Scorpio
28th 6:46 am Sagittarius
30th 5:44 pm Capricorn

April 2016
2nd 1:37 am Aquarius
4th 5:46 am Pisces
6th 6:46 am Aries
8th 6:11 am Taurus
10th 5:59 am Gemini
12th 8:07 am Cancer
14th 1:53 pm Leo
16th 11:23 pm Virgo
19th 11:23 am Libra
22nd 12:17 am Scorpio
24th 12:46 pm Sagittarius
26th 11:54 pm Capricorn
29th 8:46 am Aquarius

May 2016
1st 2:33 pm Pisces
3rd 5:04 pm Aries
5th 5:11 pm Taurus
7th 4:35 pm Gemini
9th 5:24 pm Cancer
11th 9:32 pm Leo
14th 5:51 am Virgo
16th 5:32 pm Libra
19th 6:29 am Scorpio
21st 6:48 pm Sagittarius
24th 5:34 am Capricorn
26th 2:27 pm Aquarius
28th 9:06 pm Pisces
31st 1:09 am Aries

June 2016
2nd 2:47 am Taurus
4th 3:02 am Gemini
6th 3:42 am Cancer
8th 6:47 am Leo
10th 1:45 pm Virgo
13th 12:33 am Libra
15th 1:18 pm Scorpio
18th 1:34 am Sagittarius
20th 11:55 am Capricorn
22nd 8:08 pm Aquarius
25th 2:30 am Pisces
27th 7:08 am Aries
29th 10:03 am Taurus

July 2016
1st 11:45 am Gemini
3rd 1:21 pm Cancer
5th 4:28 pm Leo
7th 10:41 pm Virgo
10th 8:32 am Libra
12th 8:52 pm Scorpio
15th 9:14 am Sagittarius
17th 7:33 pm Capricorn
20th 3:10 am Aquarius
22nd 8:35 am Pisces
24th 12:33 pm Aries
26th 3:38 pm Taurus
28th 6:17 pm Gemini
30th 9:09 pm Cancer

August 2016
2nd 1:12 am Leo
4th 7:34 am Virgo
6th 4:56 pm Libra
9th 4:51 am Scorpio
11th 5:23 pm Sagittarius
14th 4:11 am Capricorn
16th 11:52 am Aquarius
18th 4:34 pm Pisces
20th 7:19 pm Aries
22nd 9:19 pm Taurus
24th 11:40 pm Gemini
27th 3:06 am Cancer
29th 8:11 am Leo
31st 3:22 pm Virgo

September 2016
3rd 12:55 am Libra
5th 12:38 pm Scorpio
8th 1:20 am Sagittarius
10th 12:54 pm Capricorn
12th 9:28 pm Aquarius
15th 2:23 am Pisces
17th 4:23 am Aries
19th 4:58 am Taurus
21st 5:53 am Gemini
23rd 8:33 am Cancer
25th 1:48 pm Leo
27th 9:43 pm Virgo
30th 7:52 am Libra

October 2016
2nd 7:43 pm Scorpio
5th 8:26 am Sagittarius
7th 8:40 pm Capricorn
10th 6:33 am Aquarius
12th 12:43 pm Pisces
14th 3:09 pm Aries
16th 3:05 pm Taurus
18th 2:31 pm Gemini
20th 3:29 pm Cancer
22nd 7:34 pm Leo
25th 3:16 am Virgo
27th 1:50 pm Libra
30th 2:01 am Scorpio

November 2016
1st 2:43 pm Sagittarius
4th 3:05 am Capricorn
6th 1:55 pm Aquarius
8th 9:45 pm Pisces
11th 1:45 am Aries
13th 2:24 am Taurus
15th 1:23 am Gemini
17th 12:57 am Cancer
19th 3:14 am Leo
21st 9:34 am Virgo
23rd 7:42 pm Libra
26th 8:01 am Scorpio
28th 8:46 pm Sagittarius

December 2016
1st 8:52 am Capricorn
3rd 7:44 pm Aquarius
6th 4:31 am Pisces
8th 10:15 am Aries
10th 12:41 pm Taurus
12th 12:42 pm Gemini
14th 12:10 pm Cancer
16th 1:15 pm Leo
18th 5:52 pm Virgo
21st 2:39 am Libra
23rd 2:32 pm Scorpio
26th 3:19 am Sagittarius
28th 3:12 pm Capricorn
31st 1:29 am Aquarius

January 2017
2nd 9:57 am Pisces
4th 4:19 pm Aries
6th 8:18 pm Taurus
8th 10:06 pm Gemini
10th 10:49 pm Cancer
13th 12:08 am Leo
15th 3:52 am Virgo
17th 11:16 am Libra
19th 10:09 pm Scorpio
22nd 10:45 am Sagittarius
24th 10:43 pm Capricorn
27th 8:37 am Aquarius
29th 4:10 pm Pisces
31st 9:47 pm Aries

February 2017
3rd 1:50 am Taurus
5th 4:44 am Gemini
7th 7:03 am Cancer
9th 9:41 am Leo
11th 1:52 pm Virgo
13th 8:43 pm Libra
16th 6:40 am Scorpio
18th 6:52 pm Sagittarius
21st 7:07 am Capricorn
23rd 5:17 pm Aquarius
26th 12:24 am Pisces
28th 4:52 am Aries

March 2017
2nd 7:43 am Taurus
4th 10:06 am Gemini
6th 12:54 pm Cancer
8th 4:46 pm Leo
10th 10:07 pm Virgo
13th 5:28 am Libra
15th 3:10 pm Scorpio
18th 2:59 am Sagittarius
20th 3:30 pm Capricorn
23rd 2:28 am Aquarius
25th 10:06 am Pisces
27th 2:11 pm Aries
29th 3:48 pm Taurus
31st 4:41 pm Gemini

April 2017
2nd 6:27 pm Cancer
4th 10:13 pm Leo
7th 4:20 am Virgo
9th 12:34 pm Libra
11th 10:42 pm Scorpio
14th 10:26 am Sagittarius
16th 11:04 pm Capricorn
19th 10:51 am Aquarius
21st 7:42 pm Pisces
24th 12:32 am Aries
26th 1:56 am Taurus
28th 1:39 am Gemini
30th 1:48 am Cancer

May 2017
2nd 4:12 am Leo
4th 9:46 am Virgo
6th 6:20 pm Libra
9th 5:00 am Scorpio
11th 4:59 pm Sagittarius
14th 5:37 am Capricorn
16th 5:49 pm Aquarius
19th 3:52 am Pisces
21st 10:10 am Aries
23rd 12:33 pm Taurus
25th 12:16 pm Gemini
27th 11:25 am Cancer
29th 12:12 pm Leo
31st 4:16 pm Virgo

June 2017
3rd 12:04 am Libra
5th 10:46 am Scorpio
7th 10:59 pm Sagittarius
10th 11:36 am Capricorn
12th 11:45 pm Aquarius
15th 10:17 am Pisces
17th 5:54 pm Aries
19th 9:53 pm Taurus
21st 10:44 pm Gemini
23rd 10:07 pm Cancer
25th 10:07 pm Leo
28th 12:41 am Virgo
30th 7:02 am Libra

July 2017
2nd 4:59 pm Scorpio
5th 5:08 am Sagittarius
7th 5:44 pm Capricorn
10th 5:35 am Aquarius
12th 3:51 pm Pisces
14th 11:52 pm Aries
17th 5:44 am Taurus
19th 7:32 am Gemini
21st 8:10 am Cancer
23rd 8:34 am Leo
25th 10:33 am Virgo
27th 3:37 pm Libra
30th 12:23 am Scorpio

August 2017
1st 12:01 pm Sagittarius
4th 12:37 am Capricorn
6th 12:15 pm Aquarius
8th 9:56 pm Pisces
11th 5:22 am Aries
13th 10:40 am Taurus
15th 2:06 pm Gemini
17th 4:13 pm Cancer
19th 5:55 pm Leo
21st 8:25 pm Virgo
24th 1:05 am Libra
26th 8:53 am Scorpio
28th 7:47 pm Sagittarius
31st 8:18 am Capricorn

September 2017
2nd 8:06 pm Aquarius
5th 5:28 am Pisces
7th 12:02 pm Aries
9th 4:23 pm Taurus
11th 7:30 pm Gemini
13th 10:12 pm Cancer
16th 1:09 am Leo
18th 4:52 am Virgo
20th 10:06 am Libra
22nd 5:40 pm Scorpio
25th 4:01 am Sagittarius
27th 4:23 pm Capricorn
30th 4:40 am Aquarius

October 2017
2nd 2:26 pm Pisces
4th 8:40 pm Aries
6th 11:56 pm Taurus
9th 1:45 am Gemini
11th 3:38 am Cancer
13th 6:41 am Leo
15th 11:19 am Virgo
17th 5:35 pm Libra
20th 1:41 am Scorpio
22nd 11:56 am Sagittarius
25th 12:12 am Capricorn
27th 12:58 pm Aquarius
29th 11:46 pm Pisces

November 2017
1st 6:43 am Aries
3rd 9:47 am Taurus
5th 10:27 am Gemini
7th 10:45 am Cancer
9th 12:29 pm Leo
11th 4:41 pm Virgo
13th 11:26 pm Libra
16th 8:19 am Scorpio
18th 6:59 pm Sagittarius
21st 7:14 am Capricorn
23rd 8:14 pm Aquarius
26th 8:03 am Pisces
28th 4:30 pm Aries
30th 8:38 pm Taurus

December 2017
2nd 9:21 pm Gemini
4th 8:37 pm Cancer
6th 8:38 pm Leo
8th 11:09 pm Virgo
11th 5:01 am Libra
13th 1:58 pm Scorpio
16th 1:07 am Sagittarius
18th 1:33 pm Capricorn
21st 2:29 am Aquarius
23rd 2:41 pm Pisces
26th 12:27 am Aries
28th 6:23 am Taurus
30th 8:31 am Gemini

January 2018
1st 8:11 am Cancer
3rd 7:23 am Leo
5th 8:12 am Virgo
7th 12:14 pm Libra
9th 8:05 pm Scorpio
12th 7:04 am Sagittarius
14th 7:42 pm Capricorn
17th 8:32 am Aquarius
19th 8:26 pm Pisces
22nd 6:27 am Aries
24th 1:39 pm Taurus
26th 5:40 pm Gemini
28th 6:58 pm Cancer
30th 6:54 pm Leo

February 2018
1st 7:13 pm Virgo
3rd 9:47 pm Libra
6th 3:56 am Scorpio
8th 1:53 pm Sagittarius
11th 2:21 am Capricorn
13th 3:11 pm Aquarius
16th 2:42 am Pisces
18th 12:04 pm Aries
20th 7:12 pm Taurus
23rd 12:07 am Gemini
25th 3:06 am Cancer
27th 4:42 am Leo

March 2018
1st 5:58 am Virgo
3rd 8:21 am Libra
5th 1:23 pm Scorpio
7th 10:03 pm Sagittarius
10th 9:51 am Capricorn
12th 10:44 pm Aquarius
15th 10:12 am Pisces
17th 6:57 pm Aries
20th 1:07 am Taurus
22nd 5:30 am Gemini
24th 8:53 am Cancer
26th 11:45 am Leo
28th 2:30 pm Virgo
30th 5:52 pm Libra

April 2018
1st 10:57 pm Scorpio
4th 6:55 am Sagittarius
6th 6:01 pm Capricorn
9th 6:50 am Aquarius
11th 6:39 pm Pisces
14th 3:26 am Aries
16th 8:51 am Taurus
18th 12:03 pm Gemini
20th 2:27 pm Cancer
22nd 5:09 pm Leo
24th 8:40 pm Virgo
27th 1:13 am Libra
29th 7:11 am Scorpio

May 2018
1st 3:19 pm Sagittarius
4th 2:06 am Capricorn
6th 2:48 pm Aquarius
9th 3:10 am Pisces
11th 12:40 pm Aries
13th 6:15 pm Taurus
15th 8:44 pm Gemini
17th 9:48 pm Cancer
19th 11:11 pm Leo
22nd 2:03 am Virgo
24th 6:52 am Libra
26th 1:39 pm Scorpio
28th 10:29 pm Sagittarius
31st 9:26 am Capricorn

September 2018
2nd 8:01 am Gemini
4th 12:04 pm Cancer
6th 1:55 pm Leo
8th 2:30 pm Virgo
10th 3:21 pm Libra
12th 6:15 pm Scorpio
15th 12:45 am Sagittarius
17th 11:07 am Capricorn
19th 11:52 pm Aquarius
22nd 12:26 pm Pisces
24th 11:04 pm Aries
27th 7:16 am Taurus
29th 1:26 pm Gemini

January 2019
2nd 8:58 am Sagittarius
4th 6:55 pm Capricorn
7th 6:46 am Aquarius
9th 7:43 pm Pisces
12th 8:17 am Aries
14th 6:31 pm Taurus
17th 1:00 am Gemini
19th 3:44 am Cancer
21st 3:55 am Leo
23rd 3:22 am Virgo
25th 4:03 am Libra
27th 7:31 am Scorpio
29th 2:32 pm Sagittarius

May 2019
1st 10:23 am Aries
3rd 8:18 pm Taurus
6th 3:40 am Gemini
8th 9:07 am Cancer
10th 1:14 pm Leo
12th 4:22 pm Virgo
14th 6:51 pm Libra
16th 9:26 pm Scorpio
19th 1:21 am Sagittarius
21st 7:56 am Capricorn
23rd 5:49 pm Aquarius
26th 6:07 am Pisces
28th 6:31 pm Aries
31st 4:43 am Taurus

September 2019
2nd 11:35 pm Scorpio
5th 3:08 am Sagittarius
7th 10:37 am Capricorn
9th 9:23 pm Aquarius
12th 9:51 am Pisces
14th 10:32 pm Aries
17th 10:31 am Taurus
19th 8:57 pm Gemini
22nd 4:50 am Cancer
24th 9:19 am Leo
26th 10:37 am Virgo
28th 10:04 am Libra
30th 9:42 am Scorpio

June 2018
2nd 10:06 pm Aquarius
5th 10:53 am Pisces
7th 9:25 pm Aries
10th 4:04 am Taurus
12th 6:53 am Gemini
14th 7:20 am Cancer
16th 7:21 am Leo
18th 8:41 am Virgo
20th 12:29 pm Libra
22nd 7:10 pm Scorpio
25th 4:29 am Sagittarius
27th 3:52 pm Capricorn
30th 4:36 am Aquarius

October 2018
1st 6:00 pm Cancer
3rd 9:12 pm Leo
5th 11:19 pm Virgo
8th 1:10 am Libra
10th 4:09 am Scorpio
12th 9:53 am Sagittarius
14th 7:16 pm Capricorn
17th 7:35 am Aquarius
19th 8:20 pm Pisces
22nd 6:58 am Aries
24th 2:33 pm Taurus
26th 7:41 pm Gemini
28th 11:27 pm Cancer
31st 2:42 am Leo

February 2019
1st 12:47 am Capricorn
3rd 1:03 pm Aquarius
6th 2:02 am Pisces
8th 2:34 pm Aries
11th 1:28 am Taurus
13th 9:32 am Gemini
15th 2:03 pm Cancer
17th 3:22 pm Leo
19th 2:48 pm Virgo
21st 2:18 pm Libra
23rd 3:56 pm Scorpio
25th 9:19 pm Sagittarius
28th 6:48 am Capricorn

June 2019
2nd 11:48 am Gemini
4th 4:17 pm Cancer
6th 7:16 pm Leo
8th 9:45 pm Virgo
11th 12:29 am Libra
13th 4:03 am Scorpio
15th 9:03 am Sagittarius
17th 4:13 pm Capricorn
20th 2:00 am Aquarius
22nd 2:01 pm Pisces
25th 2:38 am Aries
27th 1:31 pm Taurus
29th 9:09 pm Gemini

October 2019
2nd 11:44 am Sagittarius
4th 5:43 pm Capricorn
7th 3:42 am Aquarius
9th 4:05 pm Pisces
12th 4:46 am Aries
14th 4:24 pm Taurus
17th 2:30 am Gemini
19th 10:42 am Cancer
21st 4:28 pm Leo
23rd 7:30 pm Virgo
25th 8:20 pm Libra
27th 8:30 pm Scorpio
29th 9:59 pm Sagittarius

July 2018
2nd 5:31 pm Pisces
5th 4:49 am Aries
7th 12:50 pm Taurus
9th 4:58 pm Gemini
11th 5:59 pm Cancer
13th 5:32 pm Leo
15th 5:31 pm Virgo
17th 7:42 pm Libra
20th 1:13 am Scorpio
22nd 10:12 am Sagittarius
24th 9:48 pm Capricorn
27th 10:41 am Aquarius
29th 11:28 pm Pisces

November 2018
2nd 5:48 am Virgo
4th 9:01 am Libra
6th 1:03 pm Scorpio
8th 6:59 pm Sagittarius
11th 3:54 am Capricorn
13th 3:45 pm Aquarius
16th 4:41 am Pisces
18th 3:55 pm Aries
20th 11:43 pm Taurus
23rd 4:11 am Gemini
25th 6:38 am Cancer
27th 8:35 am Leo
29th 11:08 am Virgo

March 2019
2nd 7:06 am Aquarius
5th 8:11 am Pisces
7th 8:27 pm Aries
10th 7:10 am Taurus
12th 3:48 pm Gemini
14th 9:49 pm Cancer
17th 12:57 am Leo
19th 1:41 am Virgo
21st 1:28 am Libra
23rd 2:16 am Scorpio
25th 6:06 am Sagittarius
27th 2:07 pm Capricorn
30th 1:46 am Aquarius

July 2019
2nd 1:24 am Cancer
4th 3:20 am Leo
6th 4:25 am Virgo
8th 6:07 am Libra
10th 9:29 am Scorpio
12th 3:05 pm Sagittarius
14th 11:05 pm Capricorn
17th 9:18 am Aquarius
19th 9:19 pm Pisces
22nd 10:02 am Aries
24th 9:42 pm Taurus
27th 6:29 am Gemini
29th 11:31 am Cancer
31st 1:19 pm Leo

November 2019
1st 2:38 am Capricorn
3rd 11:19 am Aquarius
5th 11:08 pm Pisces
8th 11:48 am Aries
10th 11:18 pm Taurus
13th 8:46 am Gemini
15th 4:15 pm Cancer
17th 9:57 pm Leo
20th 1:54 am Virgo
22nd 4:20 am Libra
24th 5:59 am Scorpio
26th 8:11 am Sagittarius
28th 12:33 pm Capricorn
30th 8:13 pm Aquarius

August 2018
1st 10:54 am Aries
3rd 7:51 pm Taurus
6th 1:32 am Gemini
8th 4:01 am Cancer
10th 4:18 am Leo
12th 3:59 am Virgo
14th 4:57 am Libra
16th 8:54 am Scorpio
18th 4:44 pm Sagittarius
21st 4:00 am Capricorn
23rd 4:55 pm Aquarius
26th 5:32 am Pisces
28th 4:35 pm Aries
31st 1:30 am Taurus

December 2018
1st 2:49 pm Libra
3rd 7:55 pm Scorpio
6th 2:49 am Sagittarius
8th 12:01 pm Capricorn
10th 11:39 pm Aquarius
13th 12:39 pm Pisces
16th 12:44 am Aries
18th 9:37 am Taurus
20th 2:35 pm Gemini
22nd 4:29 pm Cancer
24th 4:59 pm Leo
26th 5:50 pm Virgo
28th 8:23 pm Libra
31st 1:23 am Scorpio

April 2019
1st 2:48 pm Pisces
4th 2:56 am Aries
6th 1:06 pm Taurus
8th 9:15 pm Gemini
11th 3:31 am Cancer
13th 7:50 am Leo
15th 10:14 am Virgo
17th 11:23 am Libra
19th 12:41 pm Scorpio
21st 3:59 pm Sagittarius
23rd 10:50 pm Capricorn
26th 9:27 am Aquarius
28th 10:11 pm Pisces

August 2019
2nd 1:21 pm Virgo
4th 1:30 pm Libra
6th 3:32 pm Scorpio
8th 8:34 pm Sagittarius
11th 4:50 am Capricorn
13th 3:35 pm Aquarius
16th 3:49 am Pisces
18th 4:32 pm Aries
21st 4:37 am Taurus
23rd 2:33 pm Gemini
25th 9:05 pm Cancer
27th 11:53 pm Leo
29th 11:57 pm Virgo
31st 11:08 pm Libra

December 2019
3rd 7:10 am Pisces
5th 7:44 pm Aries
8th 7:29 am Taurus
10th 4:47 pm Gemini
12th 11:23 pm Cancer
15th 3:56 am Leo
17th 7:16 am Virgo
19th 10:05 am Libra
21st 12:58 pm Scorpio
23rd 4:34 pm Sagittarius
25th 9:45 pm Capricorn
28th 5:20 am Aquarius
30th 3:41 pm Pisces

January 2020
2nd 4:00 am Aries
4th 4:15 pm Taurus
7th 2:11 am Gemini
9th 8:43 am Cancer
11th 12:17 pm Leo
13th 2:07 pm Virgo
15th 3:44 pm Libra
17th 6:20 pm Scorpio
19th 10:41 pm Sagittarius
22nd 4:59 am Capricorn
24th 1:20 pm Aquarius
26th 11:44 pm Pisces
29th 11:50 am Aries

February 2020
1st 12:28 am Taurus
3rd 11:28 am Gemini
5th 7:03 pm Cancer
7th 10:45 pm Leo
9th 11:39 pm Virgo
11th 11:37 pm Libra
14th 12:37 am Scorpio
16th 4:07 am Sagittarius
18th 10:36 am Capricorn
20th 7:42 pm Aquarius
23rd 6:37 am Pisces
25th 6:47 pm Aries
28th 7:29 am Taurus

March 2020
1st 7:20 pm Gemini
4th 4:25 am Cancer
6th 9:28 am Leo
8th 10:48 am Virgo
10th 10:04 am Libra
12th 9:29 am Scorpio
14th 11:09 am Sagittarius
16th 4:25 pm Capricorn
19th 1:16 am Aquarius
21st 12:33 pm Pisces
24th 12:58 am Aries
26th 1:36 pm Taurus
29th 1:38 am Gemini
31st 11:43 am Cancer

April 2020
2nd 6:26 pm Leo
4th 9:18 pm Virgo
6th 9:17 pm Libra
8th 8:18 pm Scorpio
10th 8:36 pm Sagittarius
13th 12:05 am Capricorn
15th 7:37 am Aquarius
17th 6:29 pm Pisces
20th 7:00 am Aries
22nd 7:36 pm Taurus
25th 7:20 am Gemini
27th 5:27 pm Cancer
30th 1:06 am Leo

May 2020
2nd 5:35 am Virgo
4th 7:10 am Libra
6th 7:05 am Scorpio
8th 7:16 am Sagittarius
10th 9:39 am Capricorn
12th 3:38 pm Aquarius
15th 1:24 am Pisces
17th 1:35 pm Aries
20th 2:10 am Taurus
22nd 1:36 pm Gemini
24th 11:09 pm Cancer
27th 6:33 am Leo
29th 11:40 am Virgo
31st 2:38 pm Libra

June 2020
2nd 4:06 pm Scorpio
4th 5:18 pm Sagittarius
6th 7:45 pm Capricorn
9th 12:54 am Aquarius
11th 9:31 am Pisces
13th 9:03 pm Aries
16th 9:35 am Taurus
18th 8:59 pm Gemini
21st 6:02 am Cancer
23rd 12:33 pm Leo
25th 5:05 pm Virgo
27th 8:17 pm Libra
29th 10:48 pm Scorpio

July 2020
2nd 1:21 am Sagittarius
4th 4:48 am Capricorn
6th 10:08 am Aquarius
8th 6:12 pm Pisces
11th 5:06 am Aries
13th 5:33 pm Taurus
16th 5:19 am Gemini
18th 2:24 pm Cancer
20th 8:16 pm Leo
22nd 11:40 pm Virgo
25th 1:54 am Libra
27th 4:12 am Scorpio
29th 7:25 am Sagittarius
31st 11:58 am Capricorn

August 2020
2nd 6:11 pm Aquarius
5th 2:28 am Pisces
7th 1:04 pm Aries
10th 1:28 am Taurus
12th 1:45 pm Gemini
14th 11:35 pm Cancer
17th 5:38 am Leo
19th 8:21 am Virgo
21st 9:16 am Libra
23rd 10:16 am Scorpio
25th 12:49 pm Sagittarius
27th 5:37 pm Capricorn
30th 12:37 am Aquarius

September 2020
1st 9:34 am Pisces
3rd 8:22 pm Aries
6th 8:43 am Taurus
8th 9:27 pm Gemini
11th 8:22 am Cancer
13th 3:32 pm Leo
15th 6:38 pm Virgo
17th 6:57 pm Libra
19th 6:34 pm Scorpio
21st 7:32 pm Sagittarius
23rd 11:16 pm Capricorn
26th 6:08 am Aquarius
28th 3:33 pm Pisces

October 2020
1st 2:47 am Aries
3rd 3:12 pm Taurus
6th 4:02 am Gemini
8th 3:45 pm Cancer
11th 12:24 am Leo
13th 4:56 am Virgo
15th 5:54 am Libra
17th 5:06 am Scorpio
19th 4:43 am Sagittarius
21st 6:44 am Capricorn
23rd 12:16 pm Aquarius
25th 9:18 pm Pisces
28th 8:44 am Aries
30th 9:19 pm Taurus

November 2020
2nd 9:59 am Gemini
4th 9:45 pm Cancer
7th 7:18 am Leo
9th 1:30 pm Virgo
11th 4:10 pm Libra
13th 4:20 pm Scorpio
15th 3:48 pm Sagittarius
17th 4:35 pm Capricorn
19th 8:25 pm Aquarius
22nd 4:06 am Pisces
24th 3:04 pm Aries
27th 3:43 am Taurus
29th 4:16 pm Gemini

December 2020
2nd 3:33 am Cancer
4th 12:52 pm Leo
6th 7:46 pm Virgo
9th 12:01 am Libra
11th 1:59 am Scorpio
13th 2:39 am Sagittarius
15th 3:35 am Capricorn
17th 6:27 am Aquarius
19th 12:39 pm Pisces
21st 10:32 pm Aries
24th 10:55 am Taurus
26th 11:33 pm Gemini
29th 10:28 am Cancer
31st 6:58 pm Leo

January 2021
3rd 1:13 am Virgo
5th 5:42 am Libra
7th 8:54 am Scorpio
9th 11:15 am Sagittarius
11th 1:30 pm Capricorn
13th 4:44 pm Aquarius
15th 10:17 pm Pisces
18th 7:07 am Aries
20th 6:55 pm Taurus
23rd 7:43 am Gemini
25th 6:51 pm Cancer
28th 2:54 am Leo
30th 8:03 am Virgo

February 2021
1st 11:26 am Libra
3rd 2:15 pm Scorpio
5th 5:16 pm Sagittarius
7th 8:52 pm Capricorn
10th 1:20 am Aquarius
12th 7:23 am Pisces
14th 3:54 pm Aries
17th 3:11 am Taurus
19th 4:03 pm Gemini
22nd 3:52 am Cancer
24th 12:23 pm Leo
26th 5:08 pm Virgo
28th 7:17 pm Libra

March 2021
2nd 8:39 pm Scorpio
4th 10:43 pm Sagittarius
7th 2:20 am Capricorn
9th 7:41 am Aquarius
11th 2:44 pm Pisces
13th 11:44 pm Aries
16th 10:56 am Taurus
18th 11:47 pm Gemini
21st 12:17 pm Cancer
23rd 9:56 pm Leo
26th 3:25 am Virgo
28th 5:23 am Libra
30th 5:34 am Scorpio

April 2021
1st 5:59 am Sagittarius
3rd 8:13 am Capricorn
5th 1:03 pm Aquarius
7th 8:30 pm Pisces
10th 6:11 am Aries
12th 5:44 pm Taurus
15th 6:35 am Gemini
17th 7:25 pm Cancer
20th 6:10 am Leo
22nd 1:08 pm Virgo
24th 4:06 pm Libra
26th 4:19 pm Scorpio
28th 3:43 pm Sagittarius
30th 4:16 pm Capricorn

May 2021
2nd 7:31 pm Aquarius
5th 2:08 am Pisces
7th 11:52 am Aries
9th 11:46 pm Taurus
12th 12:43 pm Gemini
15th 1:30 am Cancer
17th 12:43 pm Leo
19th 8:59 pm Virgo
22nd 1:35 am Libra
24th 3:01 am Scorpio
26th 2:40 am Sagittarius
28th 2:24 am Capricorn
30th 4:04 am Aquarius

June 2021
1st 9:07 am Pisces
3rd 5:58 pm Aries
6th 5:46 am Taurus
8th 6:47 pm Gemini
11th 7:22 am Cancer
13th 6:22 pm Leo
16th 3:02 am Virgo
18th 8:53 am Libra
20th 11:58 am Scorpio
22nd 12:56 pm Sagittarius
24th 1:06 pm Capricorn
26th 2:09 pm Aquarius
28th 5:51 pm Pisces

July 2021
1st 1:21 am Aries
3rd 12:27 pm Taurus
6th 1:24 am Gemini
8th 1:50 pm Cancer
11th 12:20 am Leo
13th 8:30 am Virgo
15th 2:31 pm Libra
17th 6:38 pm Scorpio
19th 9:08 pm Sagittarius
21st 10:36 pm Capricorn
24th 12:12 am Aquarius
26th 3:30 am Pisces
28th 9:57 am Aries
30th 8:08 pm Taurus

August 2021
2nd 8:46 am Gemini
4th 9:17 pm Cancer
7th 7:31 am Leo
9th 2:56 pm Virgo
11th 8:08 pm Libra
14th 12:01 am Scorpio
16th 3:12 am Sagittarius
18th 5:58 am Capricorn
20th 8:49 am Aquarius
22nd 12:43 pm Pisces
24th 6:57 pm Aries
27th 4:26 am Taurus
29th 4:41 pm Gemini

September 2021
1st 5:25 am Cancer
3rd 3:58 pm Leo
5th 11:06 pm Virgo
8th 3:21 am Libra
10th 6:05 am Scorpio
12th 8:35 am Sagittarius
14th 11:34 am Capricorn
16th 3:23 pm Aquarius
18th 8:22 pm Pisces
21st 3:13 am Aries
23rd 12:38 pm Taurus
26th 12:36 am Gemini
28th 1:34 pm Cancer

October 2021
1st 12:53 am Leo
3rd 8:38 am Virgo
5th 12:41 pm Libra
7th 2:23 pm Scorpio
9th 3:25 pm Sagittarius
11th 5:15 pm Capricorn
13th 8:47 pm Aquarius
16th 2:22 am Pisces
18th 10:04 am Aries
20th 7:59 pm Taurus
23rd 7:57 am Gemini
25th 8:59 am Cancer
28th 9:07 am Leo
30th 6:09 pm Virgo

November 2021
1st 11:11 pm Libra
4th 12:52 am Scorpio
6th 12:52 am Sagittarius
8th 1:03 am Capricorn
10th 3:03 am Aquarius
12th 7:53 am Pisces
14th 3:48 pm Aries
17th 2:18 am Taurus
19th 2:32 pm Gemini
22nd 3:33 am Cancer
24th 3:58 pm Leo
27th 2:12 am Virgo
29th 8:55 am Libra

December 2021
1st 11:56 am Scorpio
3rd 12:13 pm Sagittarius
5th 11:32 am Capricorn
7th 11:49 am Aquarius
9th 2:53 pm Pisces
11th 9:46 pm Aries
14th 8:10 am Taurus
16th 8:42 pm Gemini
19th 9:41 am Cancer
21st 9:53 pm Leo
24th 8:24 am Virgo
26th 4:24 pm Libra
28th 9:16 pm Scorpio
30th 11:08 pm Sagittarius

January 2022
1st 11:02 pm Capricorn
3rd 10:44 pm Aquarius
6th 12:16 am Pisces
8th 5:26 am Aries
10th 2:46 pm Taurus
13th 3:08 am Gemini
15th 4:10 pm Cancer
18th 4:03 am Leo
20th 2:02 pm Virgo
22nd 10:02 pm Libra
25th 3:57 am Scorpio
27th 7:34 am Sagittarius
29th 9:09 am Capricorn
31st 9:43 am Aquarius

February 2022
2nd 11:00 am Pisces
4th 2:56 pm Aries
6th 10:52 pm Taurus
9th 10:26 am Gemini
11th 11:27 pm Cancer
14th 11:17 am Leo
16th 8:42 pm Virgo
19th 3:51 am Libra
21st 9:19 am Scorpio
23rd 1:29 pm Sagittarius
25th 4:27 pm Capricorn
27th 6:36 pm Aquarius

March 2022
1st 8:54 pm Pisces
4th 12:52 am Aries
6th 7:59 am Taurus
8th 6:39 pm Gemini
11th 7:24 am Cancer
13th 7:31 pm Leo
16th 4:59 am Virgo
18th 11:26 am Libra
20th 3:45 pm Scorpio
22nd 6:59 pm Sagittarius
24th 9:54 pm Capricorn
27th 12:55 am Aquarius
29th 4:32 am Pisces
31st 9:31 am Aries

April 2022
2nd 4:50 pm Taurus
5th 3:04 am Gemini
7th 3:30 pm Cancer
10th 3:59 am Leo
12th 2:07 pm Virgo
14th 8:46 pm Libra
17th 12:23 am Scorpio
19th 2:16 am Sagittarius
21st 3:52 am Capricorn
23rd 6:17 am Aquarius
25th 10:15 am Pisces
27th 4:10 pm Aries
30th 12:19 am Taurus

May 2022
2nd 10:46 am Gemini
4th 11:05 pm Cancer
7th 11:49 am Leo
9th 10:53 pm Virgo
12th 6:34 am Libra
14th 10:34 am Scorpio
16th 11:51 am Sagittarius
18th 12:03 pm Capricorn
20th 12:53 pm Aquarius
22nd 3:49 pm Pisces
24th 9:39 pm Aries
27th 6:22 am Taurus
29th 5:22 pm Gemini

June 2022
1st 5:49 am Cancer
3rd 6:38 pm Leo
6th 6:21 am Virgo
8th 3:22 pm Libra
10th 8:41 pm Scorpio
12th 10:31 pm Sagittarius
14th 10:14 pm Capricorn
16th 9:44 pm Aquarius
18th 11:01 pm Pisces
21st 3:37 am Aries
23rd 11:57 am Taurus
25th 11:13 pm Gemini
28th 11:53 am Cancer

July 2022
1st 12:39 am Leo
3rd 12:31 pm Virgo
5th 10:25 pm Libra
8th 5:15 am Scorpio
10th 8:34 am Sagittarius
12th 9:02 am Capricorn
14th 8:14 am Aquarius
16th 8:18 am Pisces
18th 11:17 am Aries
20th 6:22 pm Taurus
23rd 5:10 am Gemini
25th 5:53 pm Cancer
28th 6:36 am Leo
30th 6:10 pm Virgo

August 2022
2nd 4:05 am Libra
4th 11:46 am Scorpio
6th 4:38 pm Sagittarius
8th 6:39 pm Capricorn
10th 6:46 pm Aquarius
12th 6:45 pm Pisces
14th 8:43 pm Aries
17th 2:22 am Taurus
19th 12:05 pm Gemini
22nd 12:29 am Cancer
24th 1:09 pm Leo
27th 12:25 am Virgo
29th 9:45 am Libra
31st 5:11 pm Scorpio

September 2022
2nd 10:39 pm Sagittarius
5th 2:03 am Capricorn
7th 3:41 am Aquarius
9th 4:43 am Pisces
11th 6:47 am Aries
13th 11:39 am Taurus
15th 8:16 pm Gemini
18th 7:59 am Cancer
20th 8:37 pm Leo
23rd 7:53 am Virgo
25th 4:43 pm Libra
27th 11:14 pm Scorpio
30th 4:03 am Sagittarius

October 2022
2nd 7:38 am Capricorn
4th 10:21 am Aquarius
6th 12:47 pm Pisces
8th 3:57 pm Aries
10th 9:04 pm Taurus
13th 5:08 am Gemini
15th 4:10 pm Cancer
18th 4:44 am Leo
20th 4:25 pm Virgo
23rd 1:24 am Libra
25th 7:19 am Scorpio
27th 10:55 am Sagittarius
29th 1:22 pm Capricorn
31st 3:43 pm Aquarius

November 2022
2nd 6:46 pm Pisces
4th 11:07 pm Aries
7th 5:15 am Taurus
9th 1:37 pm Gemini
12th 12:22 am Cancer
14th 12:47 pm Leo
17th 1:03 am Virgo
19th 10:57 am Libra
21st 5:16 pm Scorpio
23rd 8:16 pm Sagittarius
25th 9:18 pm Capricorn
27th 10:07 pm Aquarius
30th 12:15 am Pisces

December 2022
2nd 4:41 am Aries
4th 11:38 am Taurus
6th 8:48 pm Gemini
9th 7:49 am Cancer
11th 8:08 pm Leo
14th 8:45 am Virgo
16th 7:49 pm Libra
19th 3:30 am Scorpio
21st 7:13 am Sagittarius
23rd 7:50 am Capricorn
25th 7:14 am Aquarius
27th 7:34 am Pisces
29th 10:36 am Aries
31st 5:08 pm Taurus

January 2023
3rd 2:44 am Gemini
5th 2:14 pm Cancer
8th 2:40 am Leo
10th 3:15 pm Virgo
13th 2:56 am Libra
15th 12:08 pm Scorpio
17th 5:33 pm Sagittarius
19th 7:12 pm Capricorn
21st 6:30 pm Aquarius
23rd 5:37 pm Pisces
25th 6:48 pm Aries
27th 11:42 pm Taurus
30th 8:34 am Gemini

February 2023
1st 8:11 pm Cancer
4th 8:48 am Leo
6th 9:14 pm Virgo
9th 8:46 am Libra
11th 6:34 pm Scorpio
14th 1:31 am Sagittarius
16th 4:59 am Capricorn
18th 5:35 am Aquarius
20th 4:56 am Pisces
22nd 5:14 am Aries
24th 8:29 am Taurus
26th 3:47 pm Gemini

March 2023
1st 2:40 am Cancer
3rd 3:15 pm Leo
6th 3:38 am Virgo
8th 2:44 pm Libra
11th 12:06 am Scorpio
13th 7:20 am Sagittarius
15th 12:06 pm Capricorn
17th 2:25 pm Aquarius
19th 3:13 pm Pisces
21st 4:02 pm Aries
23rd 6:42 pm Taurus
26th 12:41 am Gemini
28th 10:21 am Cancer
30th 10:31 pm Leo

April 2023
2nd 10:57 am Virgo
4th 9:51 pm Libra
7th 6:29 am Scorpio
9th 12:57 pm Sagittarius
11th 5:33 pm Capricorn
13th 8:42 pm Aquarius
15th 10:57 pm Pisces
18th 1:09 am Aries
20th 4:30 am Taurus
22nd 10:11 am Gemini
24th 6:58 pm Cancer
27th 6:29 am Leo
29th 6:59 pm Virgo

May 2023
2nd 6:09 am Libra
4th 2:32 pm Scorpio
6th 8:04 pm Sagittarius
8th 11:33 pm Capricorn
11th 2:05 am Aquarius
13th 4:39 am Pisces
15th 7:56 am Aries
17th 12:28 pm Taurus
19th 6:48 pm Gemini
22nd 3:28 am Cancer
24th 2:34 pm Leo
27th 3:05 am Virgo
29th 2:50 pm Libra
31st 11:45 pm Scorpio

June 2023
3rd 5:03 am Sagittarius
5th 7:31 am Capricorn
7th 8:42 am Aquarius
9th 10:14 am Pisces
11th 1:20 pm Aries
13th 6:31 pm Taurus
16th 1:45 am Gemini
18th 10:57 am Cancer
20th 10:04 pm Leo
23rd 10:34 am Virgo
25th 10:57 pm Libra
28th 8:55 am Scorpio
30th 2:59 pm Sagittarius

July 2023
2nd 5:21 pm Capricorn
4th 5:31 pm Aquarius
6th 5:33 pm Pisces
8th 7:19 pm Aries
10th 11:55 pm Taurus
13th 7:26 am Gemini
15th 5:13 pm Cancer
18th 4:39 am Leo
20th 5:12 pm Virgo
23rd 5:54 am Libra
25th 4:55 pm Scorpio
28th 12:24 am Sagittarius
30th 3:44 am Capricorn

August 2023
1st 3:58 am Aquarius
3rd 3:06 am Pisces
5th 3:19 am Aries
7th 6:24 am Taurus
9th 1:04 pm Gemini
11th 10:52 pm Cancer
14th 10:36 am Leo
16th 11:14 pm Virgo
19th 11:53 am Libra
21st 11:22 pm Scorpio
24th 8:07 am Sagittarius
26th 1:05 pm Capricorn
28th 2:32 pm Aquarius
30th 1:57 pm Pisces

September 2023
1st 1:26 am Aries
3rd 2:59 pm Taurus
5th 8:06 pm Gemini
8th 4:59 am Cancer
10th 4:36 pm Leo
13th 5:18 am Virgo
15th 5:44 pm Libra
18th 4:58 am Scorpio
20th 2:06 pm Sagittarius
22nd 8:20 pm Capricorn
24th 11:29 pm Aquarius
27th 12:18 am Pisces
29th 12:17 am Aries

October 2023
1st 1:18 am Taurus
3rd 5:03 am Gemini
5th 12:31 pm Cancer
7th 11:24 pm Leo
10th 12:01 pm Virgo
13th 12:22 am Libra
15th 11:04 am Scorpio
17th 7:36 pm Sagittarius
20th 1:55 am Capricorn
22nd 6:06 am Aquarius
24th 8:33 am Pisces
26th 10:02 am Aries
28th 11:45 am Taurus
30th 3:08 pm Gemini

November 2023
1st 9:30 pm Cancer
4th 7:20 am Leo
6th 7:38 pm Virgo
9th 8:07 am Libra
11th 6:39 pm Scorpio
14th 2:23 am Sagittarius
16th 7:42 am Capricorn
18th 11:28 am Aquarius
20th 2:29 pm Pisces
22nd 5:20 pm Aries
24th 8:29 pm Taurus
27th 12:40 am Gemini
29th 6:54 am Cancer

December 2023
1st 4:00 pm Leo
4th 3:50 am Virgo
6th 4:34 pm Libra
9th 3:35 am Scorpio
11th 11:11 am Sagittarius
13th 3:32 pm Capricorn
15th 5:56 pm Aquarius
17th 7:58 pm Pisces
19th 10:47 pm Aries
22nd 2:50 am Taurus
24th 8:15 am Gemini
26th 3:15 pm Cancer
29th 12:23 am Leo
31st 11:53 am Virgo

January 2024
3rd 12:47 am Libra
5th 12:39 pm Scorpio
7th 9:08 pm Sagittarius
10th 1:33 am Capricorn
12th 3:01 am Aquarius
14th 3:29 am Pisces
16th 4:49 am Aries
18th 8:12 am Taurus
20th 1:58 pm Gemini
22nd 9:51 pm Cancer
25th 7:36 am Leo
27th 7:11 pm Virgo
30th 8:04 am Libra

February 2024
1st 8:36 pm Scorpio
4th 6:28 am Sagittarius
6th 12:08 pm Capricorn
8th 1:59 pm Aquarius
10th 1:43 pm Pisces
12th 1:26 pm Aries
14th 3:02 pm Taurus
16th 7:39 pm Gemini
19th 3:25 am Cancer
21st 1:40 pm Leo
24th 1:37 am Virgo
26th 2:29 pm Libra
29th 3:09 am Scorpio

March 2024
2nd 1:55 pm Sagittarius
4th 9:15 pm Capricorn
7th 12:38 am Aquarius
9th 1:03 am Pisces
11th 12:19 am Aries
13th 12:28 am Taurus
15th 3:15 am Gemini
17th 9:40 am Cancer
19th 7:32 pm Leo
22nd 7:41 am Virgo
24th 8:37 pm Libra
27th 9:02 am Scorpio
29th 7:51 pm Sagittarius

April 2024
1st 4:05 am Capricorn
3rd 9:08 am Aquarius
5th 11:13 am Pisces
7th 11:25 am Aries
9th 11:24 am Taurus
11th 12:59 pm Gemini
13th 5:45 pm Cancer
16th 2:24 am Leo
18th 2:10 pm Virgo
21st 3:08 am Libra
23rd 3:19 pm Scorpio
26th 1:37 am Sagittarius
28th 9:37 am Capricorn
30th 3:19 pm Aquarius

May 2024
2nd 6:52 pm Pisces
4th 8:41 pm Aries
6th 9:42 pm Taurus
8th 11:20 pm Gemini
11th 3:13 am Cancer
13th 10:36 am Leo
15th 9:32 pm Virgo
18th 10:22 am Libra
20th 10:34 pm Scorpio
23rd 8:24 am Sagittarius
25th 3:36 pm Capricorn
27th 8:45 pm Aquarius
30th 12:33 am Pisces

June 2024
1st 3:28 am Aries
3rd 5:55 am Taurus
5th 8:36 am Gemini
7th 12:41 pm Cancer
9th 7:29 pm Leo
12th 5:38 am Virgo
14th 6:11 pm Libra
17th 6:37 am Scorpio
19th 4:31 pm Sagittarius
21st 11:08 pm Capricorn
24th 3:14 am Aquarius
26th 6:08 am Pisces
28th 8:52 am Aries
30th 12:00 pm Taurus

July 2024
2nd 3:50 pm Gemini
4th 8:51 pm Cancer
7th 3:56 am Leo
9th 1:47 pm Virgo
12th 2:06 am Libra
14th 2:52 pm Scorpio
17th 1:25 am Sagittarius
19th 8:14 am Capricorn
21st 11:43 am Aquarius
23rd 1:24 pm Pisces
25th 2:53 pm Aries
27th 5:22 pm Taurus
29th 9:28 pm Gemini

August 2024
1st 3:19 am Cancer
3rd 11:09 am Leo
5th 9:16 pm Virgo
8th 9:31 am Libra
10th 10:33 pm Scorpio
13th 9:59 am Sagittarius
15th 5:51 pm Capricorn
17th 9:45 pm Aquarius
19th 10:52 pm Pisces
21st 11:02 pm Aries
24th 12:00 am Taurus
26th 3:04 am Gemini
28th 8:47 am Cancer
30th 5:09 pm Leo

September 2024
2nd 3:48 am Virgo
4th 4:11 pm Libra
7th 5:18 am Scorpio
9th 5:25 pm Sagittarius
12th 2:37 am Capricorn
14th 7:53 am Aquarius
16th 9:39 am Pisces
18th 9:25 am Aries
20th 9:03 am Taurus
22nd 10:24 am Gemini
24th 2:50 pm Cancer
26th 10:47 pm Leo
29th 9:41 am Virgo

October 2024
1st 10:19 pm Libra
4th 11:22 am Scorpio
6th 11:34 pm Sagittarius
9th 9:38 am Capricorn
11th 4:31 pm Aquarius
13th 7:55 pm Pisces
15th 8:34 pm Aries
17th 8:00 pm Taurus
19th 8:07 pm Gemini
21st 10:50 pm Cancer
24th 5:24 am Leo
26th 3:47 pm Virgo
29th 4:29 am Libra
31st 5:29 pm Scorpio

November 2024
3rd 5:19 am Sagittarius
5th 3:17 pm Capricorn
7th 10:57 pm Aquarius
10th 3:59 am Pisces
12th 6:26 am Aries
14th 6:59 am Taurus
16th 7:09 am Gemini
18th 8:50 am Cancer
20th 1:51 pm Leo
22nd 11:01 pm Virgo
25th 11:19 am Libra
28th 12:20 am Scorpio
30th 11:53 am Sagittarius

December 2024
2nd 9:09 pm Capricorn
5th 4:21 am Aquarius
7th 9:49 am Pisces
9th 1:38 pm Aries
11th 3:55 pm Taurus
13th 5:22 pm Gemini
15th 7:22 pm Cancer
17th 11:39 pm Leo
20th 7:36 am Virgo
22nd 7:07 pm Libra
25th 8:06 am Scorpio
27th 7:46 pm Sagittarius
30th 4:37 am Capricorn

January 2025	**February 2025**	**March 2025**	**April 2025**
1st 10:50 am Aquarius	2nd 1:10 am Aries	1st 9:52 am Aries	1st 8:26 pm Gemini
3rd 3:21 pm Pisces	4th 3:33 am Taurus	3rd 12:37 am Taurus	3rd 10:50 pm Cancer
5th 7:01 pm Aries	6th 6:44 am Gemini	5th 12:29 pm Gemini	6th 4:34 am Leo
7th 10:11 pm Taurus	8th 11:04 am Cancer	7th 4:29 pm Cancer	8th 1:39 pm Virgo
10th 1:07 am Gemini	10th 5:01 pm Leo	9th 10:59 pm Leo	11th 1:12 am Libra
12th 4:24 am Cancer	13th 1:07 am Virgo	12th 7:55 am Virgo	13th 1:54 pm Scorpio
14th 9:12 am Leo	15th 11:44 am Libra	14th 6:59 pm Libra	16th 2:37 am Sagittarius
16th 4:45 pm Virgo	18th 12:19 am Scorpio	17th 7:30 am Scorpio	18th 2:11 pm Capricorn
19th 3:33 am Libra	20th 12:54 pm Sagittarius	19th 8:17 pm Sagittarius	20th 11:21 pm Aquarius
21st 4:19 pm Scorpio	22nd 11:08 pm Capricorn	22nd 7:28 am Capricorn	23rd 5:06 am Pisces
24th 4:28 am Sagittarius	25th 5:40 am Aquarius	24th 3:24 am Aquarius	25th 7:24 am Aries
26th 1:42 pm Capricorn	27th 8:47 am Pisces	26th 7:32 am Pisces	27th 7:17 am Taurus
28th 7:32 pm Aquarius		28th 8:36 am Aries	29th 6:35 am Gemini
30th 10:52 pm Pisces		30th 8:16 pm Taurus	
May 2025	**June 2025**	**July 2025**	**August 2025**
1st 7:23 am Cancer	2nd 2:59 am Virgo	1st 9:16 pm Libra	3rd 5:59 am Sagittarius
3rd 11:29 am Leo	4th 1:37 pm Libra	4th 9:32 am Scorpio	5th 5:04 pm Capricorn
5th 7:39 pm Virgo	7th 2:22 am Scorpio	6th 10:06 pm Sagittarius	8th 1:18 am Aquarius
8th 7:06 am Libra	9th 2:55 pm Sagittarius	9th 8:55 am Capricorn	10th 6:50 am Pisces
10th 7:58 pm Scorpio	12th 1:55 am Capricorn	11th 5:21 pm Aquarius	12th 10:33 am Aries
13th 8:34 am Sagittarius	14th 10:59 am Aquarius	13th 11:45 pm Pisces	14th 1:22 pm Taurus
15th 7:57 pm Capricorn	16th 6:08 pm Pisces	16th 4:32 am Aries	16th 4:01 pm Gemini
18th 5:29 am Aquarius	18th 11:08 pm Aries	18th 7:59 am Taurus	18th 7:05 pm Cancer
20th 12:28 pm Pisces	21st 1:53 am Taurus	20th 10:22 am Gemini	20th 11:17 pm Leo
22nd 4:26 pm Aries	23rd 2:57 am Gemini	22nd 12:27 pm Cancer	23rd 5:24 am Virgo
24th 5:38 pm Taurus	25th 3:44 am Cancer	24th 3:29 pm Leo	25th 2:08 pm Libra
26th 5:22 pm Gemini	27th 6:05 am Leo	26th 8:55 pm Virgo	28th 1:27 am Scorpio
28th 5:33 pm Cancer	29th 11:43 am Virgo	29th 5:43 am Libra	30th 2:04 pm Sagittarius
30th 8:17 pm Leo		31st 5:24 pm Scorpio	
September 2025	**October 2025**	**November 2025**	**December 2025**
2nd 1:44 am Capricorn	1st 7:51 pm Aquarius	2nd 3:39 pm Aries	2nd 3:13 am Taurus
4th 10:32 am Aquarius	4th 2:07 am Pisces	4th 4:16 pm Taurus	4th 2:48 am Gemini
6th 3:54 pm Pisces	6th 4:48 am Aries	6th 3:21 pm Gemini	6th 1:54 am Cancer
8th 6:37 pm Aries	8th 5:13 am Taurus	8th 3:07 pm Cancer	8th 2:48 am Leo
10th 8:04 pm Taurus	10th 5:12 am Gemini	10th 5:33 pm Leo	10th 7:20 am Virgo
12th 9:38 pm Gemini	12th 6:37 am Cancer	12th 11:52 pm Virgo	12th 4:03 pm Libra
15th 12:30 am Cancer	14th 10:47 am Leo	15th 9:43 am Libra	15th 3:51 am Scorpio
17th 5:20 am Leo	16th 6:05 pm Virgo	17th 9:44 pm Scorpio	17th 4:38 pm Sagittarius
19th 12:23 pm Virgo	19th 4:01 am Libra	20th 10:26 am Sagittarius	20th 4:52 am Capricorn
21st 9:41 pm Libra	21st 3:42 pm Scorpio	22nd 10:52 pm Capricorn	22nd 3:52 pm Aquarius
24th 8:59 am Scorpio	24th 4:19 am Sagittarius	25th 10:15 am Aquarius	25th 1:09 am Pisces
26th 9:37 pm Sagittarius	26th 4:53 pm Capricorn	27th 7:23 pm Pisces	27th 8:01 am Aries
29th 9:54 am Capricorn	29th 3:55 am Aquarius	30th 1:07 am Aries	29th 11:57 am Taurus
	31st 11:45 am Pisces		31st 1:14 pm Gemini
January 2026	**February 2026**	**March 2026**	**April 2026**
2nd 1:10 pm Cancer	1st 12:09 am Leo	2nd 12:34 pm Virgo	1st 2:51 am Libra
4th 1:44 pm Leo	3rd 3:21 am Virgo	4th 6:56 pm Libra	3rd 12:11 pm Scorpio
6th 4:57 pm Virgo	5th 9:32 am Libra	7th 4:01 am Scorpio	5th 11:31 pm Sagittarius
9th 12:06 am Libra	7th 7:13 pm Scorpio	9th 3:36 pm Sagittarius	8th 12:04 pm Capricorn
11th 10:55 am Scorpio	10th 7:21 am Sagittarius	12th 4:07 am Capricorn	10th 11:55 pm Aquarius
13th 11:34 pm Sagittarius	12th 7:44 pm Capricorn	14th 3:13 pm Aquarius	13th 8:55 am Pisces
16th 11:47 am Capricorn	15th 6:16 am Aquarius	16th 11:15 pm Pisces	15th 2:04 pm Aries
18th 10:18 pm Aquarius	17th 2:09 pm Pisces	19th 4:03 am Aries	17th 3:58 pm Taurus
21st 6:49 am Pisces	19th 7:39 pm Aries	21st 6:35 am Taurus	19th 4:18 pm Gemini
23rd 1:25 pm Aries	21st 11:31 pm Taurus	23rd 8:19 am Gemini	21st 5:01 pm Cancer
25th 6:05 pm Taurus	24th 2:29 am Gemini	25th 10:33 am Cancer	23rd 7:41 pm Leo
27th 8:55 pm Gemini	26th 5:11 am Cancer	27th 2:10 pm Leo	26th 1:04 am Virgo
29th 10:32 pm Cancer	28th 8:17 am Leo	29th 7:33 pm Virgo	28th 9:02 am Libra
			30th 7:02 pm Scorpio
May 2026	**June 2026**	**July 2026**	**August 2026**
3rd 6:33 am Sagittarius	2nd 1:19 am Capricorn	1st 7:32 pm Aquarius	2nd 8:36 pm Aries
5th 7:06 pm Capricorn	4th 1:45 pm Aquarius	4th 6:30 am Pisces	5th 2:35 am Taurus
8th 7:27 am Aquarius	7th 12:43 am Pisces	6th 3:06 pm Aries	7th 6:08 am Gemini
10th 5:39 pm Pisces	9th 8:33 am Aries	8th 8:30 pm Taurus	9th 7:46 am Cancer
13th 12:03 am Aries	11th 12:28 pm Taurus	10th 10:42 pm Gemini	11th 8:39 am Leo
15th 2:31 am Taurus	13th 1:07 pm Gemini	12th 10:47 pm Cancer	13th 10:18 am Virgo
17th 2:23 am Gemini	15th 12:15 pm Cancer	14th 10:35 pm Leo	15th 2:20 pm Libra
19th 1:46 am Cancer	17th 12:06 pm Leo	17th 12:07 am Virgo	17th 9:46 pm Scorpio
21st 2:48 am Leo	19th 2:37 pm Virgo	19th 4:56 am Libra	20th 8:29 am Sagittarius
23rd 6:57 am Virgo	21st 8:55 pm Libra	21st 1:34 pm Scorpio	22nd 8:59 pm Capricorn
25th 2:33 pm Libra	24th 6:43 am Scorpio	24th 1:07 am Sagittarius	25th 9:01 am Aquarius
28th 12:52 am Scorpio	26th 6:40 pm Sagittarius	26th 1:44 pm Capricorn	27th 7:03 pm Pisces
30th 12:44 pm Sagittarius	29th 7:18 am Capricorn	29th 1:46 am Aquarius	30th 2:38 am Aries
		31st 12:13 pm Pisces	

September 2026
1st 8:01 am Taurus
3rd 11:47 am Gemini
5th 2:30 pm Cancer
7th 4:50 pm Leo
9th 7:35 pm Virgo
11th 11:51 pm Libra
14th 6:44 am Scorpio
16th 4:41 pm Sagittarius
19th 4:54 am Capricorn
21st 5:14 pm Aquarius
24th 3:23 am Pisces
26th 10:23 am Aries
28th 2:40 pm Taurus
30th 5:26 pm Gemini

October 2026
2nd 7:54 pm Cancer
4th 10:54 pm Leo
7th 2:52 am Virgo
9th 8:10 am Libra
11th 3:21 pm Scorpio
14th 12:59 am Sagittarius
16th 12:56 pm Capricorn
19th 1:40 am Aquarius
21st 12:34 pm Pisces
23rd 7:53 pm Aries
25th 11:35 pm Taurus
28th 1:02 am Gemini
30th 2:05 am Cancer

November 2026
1st 4:18 am Leo
3rd 8:27 am Virgo
5th 2:38 pm Libra
7th 10:40 pm Scorpio
10th 8:35 am Sagittarius
12th 8:27 pm Capricorn
15th 9:23 am Aquarius
17th 9:19 pm Pisces
20th 5:52 am Aries
22nd 10:10 am Taurus
24th 11:10 am Gemini
26th 10:52 am Cancer
28th 11:21 am Leo
30th 2:12 pm Virgo

December 2026
2nd 8:03 pm Libra
5th 4:35 am Scorpio
7th 3:06 pm Sagittarius
10th 3:08 am Capricorn
12th 4:05 pm Aquarius
15th 4:35 am Pisces
17th 2:34 pm Aries
19th 8:29 pm Taurus
21st 10:27 pm Gemini
23rd 9:59 pm Cancer
25th 9:13 pm Leo
27th 10:13 pm Virgo
30th 2:26 am Libra

January 2027
1st 10:15 am Scorpio
3rd 8:57 pm Sagittarius
6th 9:17 am Capricorn
8th 10:11 pm Aquarius
11th 10:35 am Pisces
13th 9:13 pm Aries
16th 4:43 am Taurus
18th 8:33 am Gemini
20th 9:22 am Cancer
22nd 8:46 am Leo
24th 8:45 am Virgo
26th 11:12 am Libra
28th 5:21 pm Scorpio
31st 3:13 am Sagittarius

February 2027
2nd 3:32 pm Capricorn
5th 4:28 am Aquarius
7th 4:31 pm Pisces
10th 2:48 am Aries
12th 10:44 am Taurus
14th 3:58 pm Gemini
16th 6:38 pm Cancer
18th 7:31 pm Leo
20th 7:59 pm Virgo
22nd 9:44 pm Libra
25th 2:24 am Scorpio
27th 10:52 am Sagittarius

March 2027
1st 10:35 pm Capricorn
4th 11:31 am Aquarius
6th 11:25 pm Pisces
9th 9:02 am Aries
11th 4:16 pm Taurus
13th 9:30 pm Gemini
16th 1:10 am Cancer
18th 3:41 am Leo
20th 5:37 am Virgo
22nd 8:02 am Libra
24th 12:18 pm Scorpio
26th 7:43 pm Sagittarius
29th 6:32 am Capricorn
31st 7:19 pm Aquarius

April 2027
3rd 7:25 am Pisces
5th 4:48 pm Aries
7th 11:09 pm Taurus
10th 3:21 am Gemini
12th 6:32 am Cancer
14th 9:30 am Leo
16th 12:39 pm Virgo
18th 4:22 pm Libra
20th 9:21 pm Scorpio
23rd 4:37 am Sagittarius
25th 2:51 pm Capricorn
28th 3:23 am Aquarius
30th 3:51 pm Pisces

May 2027
3rd 1:43 am Aries
5th 7:53 am Taurus
7th 11:07 am Gemini
9th 12:59 pm Cancer
11th 3:01 pm Leo
13th 6:05 pm Virgo
15th 10:33 pm Libra
18th 4:33 am Scorpio
20th 12:27 pm Sagittarius
22nd 10:42 pm Capricorn
25th 11:04 am Aquarius
27th 11:55 pm Pisces
30th 10:39 am Aries

June 2027
1st 5:33 pm Taurus
3rd 8:43 pm Gemini
5th 9:39 pm Cancer
7th 10:13 pm Leo
10th 12:00 am Virgo
12th 3:57 am Libra
14th 10:17 am Scorpio
16th 6:53 pm Sagittarius
19th 5:35 am Capricorn
21st 5:59 pm Aquarius
24th 7:00 am Pisces
26th 6:35 pm Aries
29th 2:46 am Taurus

July 2027
1st 6:56 am Gemini
3rd 7:59 am Cancer
5th 7:41 am Leo
7th 7:57 am Virgo
9th 10:23 am Libra
11th 3:54 pm Scorpio
14th 12:33 am Sagittarius
16th 11:39 am Capricorn
19th 12:15 am Aquarius
21st 1:14 pm Pisces
24th 1:09 am Aries
26th 10:27 am Taurus
28th 4:10 pm Gemini
30th 6:25 pm Cancer

August 2027
1st 6:25 pm Leo
3rd 5:58 pm Virgo
5th 6:55 pm Libra
7th 10:52 pm Scorpio
10th 6:35 am Sagittarius
12th 5:34 pm Capricorn
15th 6:19 am Aquarius
17th 7:11 pm Pisces
20th 6:54 am Aries
22nd 4:32 pm Taurus
24th 11:26 pm Gemini
27th 3:21 am Cancer
29th 4:43 am Leo
31st 4:44 am Virgo

September 2027
2nd 5:07 am Libra
4th 7:44 am Scorpio
6th 2:01 pm Sagittarius
9th 12:12 am Capricorn
11th 12:49 pm Aquarius
14th 1:39 am Pisces
16th 12:56 pm Aries
18th 10:05 pm Taurus
21st 5:06 am Gemini
23rd 10:02 am Cancer
25th 1:00 pm Leo
27th 2:28 pm Virgo
29th 3:31 pm Libra

October 2027
1st 5:46 pm Scorpio
3rd 10:56 pm Sagittarius
6th 7:59 am Capricorn
8th 8:09 pm Aquarius
11th 9:01 am Pisces
13th 8:09 pm Aries
16th 4:37 am Taurus
18th 10:46 am Gemini
20th 3:25 pm Cancer
22nd 7:03 pm Leo
24th 9:54 pm Virgo
27th 12:21 am Libra
29th 3:23 am Scorpio
31st 8:24 am Sagittarius

November 2027
2nd 4:40 pm Capricorn
5th 4:13 am Aquarius
7th 5:08 pm Pisces
10th 4:38 am Aries
12th 12:58 pm Taurus
14th 6:15 pm Gemini
16th 9:39 pm Cancer
19th 12:27 am Leo
21st 3:25 am Virgo
23rd 6:52 am Libra
25th 11:10 am Scorpio
27th 5:01 pm Sagittarius
30th 1:18 am Capricorn

December 2027
2nd 12:25 pm Aquarius
5th 1:20 am Pisces
7th 1:30 pm Aries
9th 10:35 pm Taurus
12th 3:55 am Gemini
14th 6:24 am Cancer
16th 7:41 am Leo
18th 9:17 am Virgo
20th 12:13 pm Libra
22nd 5:00 pm Scorpio
24th 11:50 pm Sagittarius
27th 8:51 am Capricorn
29th 8:04 pm Aquarius

January 2028
1st 8:52 am Pisces
3rd 9:35 pm Aries
6th 7:55 am Taurus
8th 2:26 pm Gemini
10th 5:15 pm Cancer
12th 5:43 pm Leo
14th 5:40 pm Virgo
16th 6:51 pm Libra
18th 10:35 pm Scorpio
21st 5:23 am Sagittarius
23rd 3:01 pm Capricorn
26th 2:43 am Aquarius
28th 3:33 pm Pisces
31st 4:22 am Aries

February 2028
2nd 3:37 pm Taurus
4th 11:46 pm Gemini
7th 4:06 am Cancer
9th 5:13 am Leo
11th 4:35 am Virgo
13th 4:13 am Libra
15th 6:03 am Scorpio
17th 11:29 am Sagittarius
19th 8:45 pm Capricorn
22nd 8:43 am Aquarius
24th 9:43 pm Pisces
27th 10:22 am Aries
29th 9:41 pm Taurus

March 2028
3rd 6:48 am Gemini
5th 12:54 pm Cancer
7th 3:43 pm Leo
9th 3:59 pm Virgo
11th 3:22 pm Libra
13th 3:53 pm Scorpio
15th 7:33 pm Sagittarius
18th 3:26 am Capricorn
20th 2:56 pm Aquarius
23rd 3:59 am Pisces
25th 4:30 pm Aries
28th 3:24 am Taurus
30th 12:23 pm Gemini

April 2028
1st 7:14 pm Cancer
3rd 11:38 pm Leo
6th 1:36 am Virgo
8th 2:03 am Libra
10th 2:37 am Scorpio
12th 5:18 am Sagittarius
14th 11:44 am Capricorn
16th 10:11 pm Aquarius
19th 10:56 am Pisces
21st 11:26 pm Aries
24th 9:58 am Taurus
26th 6:15 pm Gemini
29th 12:37 am Cancer

May 2028
1st 5:23 am Leo
3rd 8:36 am Virgo
5th 10:34 am Libra
7th 12:16 pm Scorpio
9th 3:12 pm Sagittarius
11th 8:59 pm Capricorn
14th 6:26 am Aquarius
16th 6:38 pm Pisces
19th 7:12 am Aries
21st 5:48 pm Taurus
24th 1:35 am Gemini
26th 6:59 am Cancer
28th 10:55 am Leo
30th 2:01 pm Virgo

September 2028
2nd 11:33 pm Pisces
5th 12:15 pm Aries
8th 12:34 am Taurus
10th 11:24 am Gemini
12th 7:26 pm Cancer
14th 11:48 pm Leo
17th 12:52 am Virgo
19th 12:06 am Libra
20th 11:39 pm Scorpio
23rd 1:39 am Sagittarius
25th 7:33 am Capricorn
27th 5:20 pm Aquarius
30th 5:33 am Pisces

January 2029
2nd 2:35 am Leo
4th 5:27 am Virgo
6th 7:51 am Libra
8th 10:38 am Scorpio
10th 2:27 pm Sagittarius
12th 7:46 pm Capricorn
15th 3:05 am Aquarius
17th 12:47 pm Pisces
20th 12:38 am Aries
22nd 1:13 pm Taurus
25th 12:19 am Gemini
27th 8:05 am Cancer
29th 12:16 pm Leo
31st 1:54 pm Virgo

May 2029
1st 11:08 pm Capricorn
4th 5:00 am Aquarius
6th 2:41 pm Pisces
9th 2:49 am Aries
11th 3:30 pm Taurus
14th 3:23 am Gemini
16th 1:45 pm Cancer
18th 9:59 pm Leo
21st 3:33 am Virgo
23rd 6:23 am Libra
25th 7:14 am Scorpio
27th 7:37 am Sagittarius
29th 9:20 am Capricorn
31st 2:00 pm Aquarius

September 2029
2nd 9:30 pm Cancer
5th 4:53 am Leo
7th 8:22 am Virgo
9th 9:13 am Libra
11th 9:25 am Scorpio
13th 10:50 am Sagittarius
15th 2:41 pm Capricorn
17th 9:13 pm Aquarius
20th 5:59 am Pisces
22nd 4:35 pm Aries
25th 4:41 am Taurus
27th 5:33 pm Gemini
30th 5:27 am Cancer

June 2028
1st 4:47 pm Libra
3rd 7:44 pm Scorpio
5th 11:44 pm Sagittarius
8th 5:53 am Capricorn
10th 2:57 pm Aquarius
13th 2:40 am Pisces
15th 3:18 pm Aries
18th 2:25 am Taurus
20th 10:25 am Gemini
22nd 3:17 pm Cancer
24th 6:03 pm Leo
26th 7:58 pm Virgo
28th 10:10 pm Libra

October 2028
2nd 6:17 pm Aries
5th 6:22 am Taurus
7th 5:09 pm Gemini
10th 1:57 am Cancer
12th 7:53 am Leo
14th 10:38 am Virgo
16th 10:56 am Libra
18th 10:30 am Scorpio
20th 11:30 am Sagittarius
22nd 3:51 pm Capricorn
25th 12:22 am Aquarius
27th 12:06 pm Pisces
30th 12:51 am Aries

February 2029
2nd 2:40 pm Libra
4th 4:15 pm Scorpio
6th 7:51 pm Sagittarius
9th 1:52 am Capricorn
11th 10:08 am Aquarius
13th 8:19 pm Pisces
16th 8:07 am Aries
18th 8:48 pm Taurus
21st 8:44 am Gemini
23rd 5:53 pm Cancer
25th 11:00 pm Leo
28th 12:33 am Virgo

June 2029
2nd 10:23 pm Pisces
5th 9:50 am Aries
7th 10:26 pm Gemini
10th 10:13 am Gemini
12th 8:01 pm Cancer
15th 3:34 am Leo
17th 8:59 am Virgo
19th 12:35 pm Libra
21st 2:51 pm Scorpio
23rd 4:37 pm Sagittarius
25th 7:05 pm Capricorn
27th 11:34 pm Aquarius
30th 7:05 am Pisces

October 2029
2nd 2:14 pm Leo
4th 6:48 pm Virgo
6th 7:49 pm Libra
8th 7:09 pm Scorpio
10th 7:01 pm Sagittarius
12th 9:16 pm Capricorn
15th 2:52 am Aquarius
17th 11:38 am Pisces
19th 10:38 pm Aries
22nd 10:56 am Taurus
24th 11:45 pm Gemini
27th 11:57 am Cancer
29th 9:54 pm Leo

July 2028
1st 1:27 am Scorpio
3rd 6:24 am Sagittarius
5th 1:26 pm Capricorn
7th 10:49 pm Aquarius
10th 10:23 am Pisces
12th 11:04 pm Aries
15th 10:50 am Taurus
17th 7:46 pm Gemini
20th 1:02 am Cancer
22nd 3:17 am Leo
24th 3:56 am Virgo
26th 4:41 am Libra
28th 7:02 am Scorpio
30th 11:54 am Sagittarius

November 2028
1st 12:44 pm Taurus
3rd 10:58 pm Gemini
6th 7:24 am Cancer
8th 1:50 pm Leo
10th 5:59 pm Virgo
12th 7:59 pm Libra
14th 8:49 pm Scorpio
16th 10:06 pm Sagittarius
19th 1:42 am Capricorn
21st 8:56 am Aquarius
23rd 7:44 pm Pisces
26th 8:19 am Aries
28th 8:17 pm Taurus

March 2029
2nd 12:10 am Libra
4th 12:01 am Scorpio
6th 2:02 am Sagittarius
8th 7:19 am Capricorn
10th 3:49 pm Aquarius
13th 2:35 am Pisces
15th 2:39 pm Aries
18th 3:19 am Taurus
20th 3:37 pm Gemini
23rd 1:58 am Cancer
25th 8:44 am Leo
27th 11:30 am Virgo
29th 11:20 am Libra
31st 10:16 am Scorpio

July 2029
2nd 5:42 am Aries
5th 6:08 am Taurus
7th 6:04 pm Gemini
10th 3:42 am Cancer
12th 10:29 am Leo
14th 2:55 pm Virgo
16th 5:58 pm Libra
18th 8:34 pm Scorpio
20th 11:26 pm Sagittarius
23rd 3:08 am Capricorn
25th 8:21 am Aquarius
27th 3:48 pm Pisces
30th 1:55 am Aries

November 2029
1st 4:09 am Virgo
3rd 6:34 am Libra
5th 6:22 am Scorpio
7th 5:34 am Sagittarius
9th 6:17 am Capricorn
11th 10:09 am Aquarius
13th 5:49 pm Pisces
16th 4:37 am Aries
18th 5:05 pm Taurus
21st 5:48 am Gemini
23rd 5:42 pm Cancer
26th 3:50 am Leo
28th 11:15 am Virgo
30th 3:28 pm Libra

August 2028
1st 7:32 am Capricorn
4th 5:33 am Aquarius
6th 5:20 pm Pisces
9th 6:01 am Aries
11th 6:17 pm Taurus
14th 4:22 am Gemini
16th 10:55 am Cancer
18th 1:46 pm Leo
20th 2:00 pm Virgo
22nd 1:29 pm Libra
24th 2:12 pm Scorpio
26th 5:51 pm Sagittarius
29th 1:07 am Capricorn
31st 11:26 am Aquarius

December 2028
1st 6:09 am Gemini
3rd 1:42 pm Cancer
5th 7:20 pm Leo
7th 11:29 pm Virgo
10th 2:29 am Libra
12th 4:52 am Scorpio
14th 7:29 am Sagittarius
16th 11:34 am Capricorn
18th 6:20 pm Aquarius
21st 4:16 am Pisces
23rd 4:28 pm Aries
26th 4:46 am Taurus
28th 2:57 pm Gemini
30th 10:06 pm Cancer

April 2029
2nd 10:36 am Sagittarius
4th 2:09 pm Capricorn
6th 9:39 pm Aquarius
9th 8:19 am Pisces
11th 8:38 pm Aries
14th 9:18 am Taurus
16th 9:28 pm Gemini
19th 8:12 am Cancer
21st 4:14 pm Leo
23rd 8:43 pm Virgo
25th 9:55 pm Libra
27th 9:20 pm Scorpio
29th 9:03 pm Sagittarius

August 2029
1st 2:07 pm Taurus
4th 2:26 am Gemini
6th 12:32 pm Cancer
8th 7:09 pm Leo
10th 10:40 pm Virgo
13th 12:28 am Libra
15th 2:07 am Scorpio
17th 4:52 am Sagittarius
19th 9:17 am Capricorn
21st 3:29 pm Aquarius
23rd 11:33 pm Pisces
26th 9:42 am Aries
28th 9:46 pm Taurus
31st 10:28 am Gemini

December 2029
2nd 4:54 pm Scorpio
4th 4:53 pm Sagittarius
6th 5:12 pm Capricorn
8th 7:41 pm Aquarius
11th 1:43 am Pisces
13th 11:30 am Aries
15th 11:48 pm Taurus
18th 12:32 pm Gemini
21st 12:03 am Cancer
23rd 9:31 am Leo
25th 4:46 pm Virgo
27th 9:50 pm Libra
30th 12:55 am Scorpio

January 2030
1st 2:35 am Sagittarius
3rd 3:54 am Capricorn
5th 6:18 am Aquarius
7th 11:15 am Pisces
9th 7:46 pm Aries
12th 7:26 am Taurus
14th 8:15 pm Gemini
17th 7:45 am Cancer
19th 4:36 pm Leo
21st 10:50 pm Virgo
24th 3:13 am Libra
26th 6:36 am Scorpio
28th 9:32 am Sagittarius
30th 12:24 pm Capricorn

February 2030
1st 3:53 pm Aquarius
3rd 8:58 pm Pisces
6th 4:48 am Aries
8th 3:43 pm Taurus
11th 4:30 am Gemini
13th 4:28 pm Cancer
16th 1:27 am Leo
18th 6:58 am Virgo
20th 10:04 am Libra
22nd 12:18 pm Scorpio
24th 2:53 pm Sagittarius
26th 6:25 pm Capricorn
28th 11:07 pm Aquarius

March 2030
3rd 5:12 am Pisces
5th 1:17 pm Aries
7th 11:55 pm Taurus
10th 12:33 pm Gemini
13th 1:08 am Cancer
15th 10:58 am Leo
17th 4:49 pm Virgo
19th 7:18 pm Libra
21st 8:08 pm Scorpio
23rd 9:12 pm Sagittarius
25th 11:51 pm Capricorn
28th 4:37 am Aquarius
30th 11:30 am Pisces

April 2030
1st 8:22 pm Aries
4th 7:14 am Taurus
6th 7:50 pm Gemini
9th 8:46 am Cancer
11th 7:44 pm Leo
14th 2:49 am Virgo
16th 5:53 am Libra
18th 6:17 am Scorpio
20th 5:59 am Sagittarius
22nd 6:56 am Capricorn
24th 10:26 am Aquarius
26th 4:57 pm Pisces
29th 2:13 am Aries

May 2030
1st 1:34 pm Taurus
4th 2:16 am Gemini
6th 3:16 pm Cancer
9th 2:54 am Leo
11th 11:24 am Virgo
13th 3:57 pm Libra
15th 5:10 pm Scorpio
17th 4:40 pm Sagittarius
19th 4:23 pm Capricorn
21st 6:10 pm Aquarius
23rd 11:16 pm Pisces
26th 7:57 am Aries
28th 7:25 pm Taurus
31st 8:18 am Gemini

June 2030
2nd 9:11 pm Cancer
5th 8:49 am Leo
7th 6:04 pm Virgo
10th 12:07 am Libra
12th 2:56 am Scorpio
14th 3:25 am Sagittarius
16th 3:06 am Capricorn
18th 3:51 am Aquarius
20th 7:23 am Pisces
22nd 2:45 pm Aries
25th 1:41 am Taurus
27th 2:32 pm Gemini
30th 3:18 am Cancer

July 2030
2nd 2:33 pm Leo
4th 11:37 pm Virgo
7th 6:16 am Libra
9th 10:29 am Scorpio
11th 12:34 pm Sagittarius
13th 1:21 pm Capricorn
15th 2:14 pm Aquarius
17th 4:57 pm Pisces
19th 11:01 pm Aries
22nd 8:56 am Taurus
24th 9:29 pm Gemini
27th 10:14 am Cancer
29th 9:07 pm Leo

August 2030
1st 5:30 am Virgo
3rd 11:40 am Libra
5th 4:11 pm Scorpio
7th 7:24 pm Sagittarius
9th 9:40 pm Capricorn
11th 11:40 pm Aquarius
14th 2:39 am Pisces
16th 8:08 am Aries
18th 5:08 pm Taurus
21st 5:11 am Gemini
23rd 6:00 pm Cancer
26th 4:58 am Leo
28th 12:51 pm Virgo
30th 6:04 pm Libra

September 2030
1st 9:43 pm Scorpio
4th 12:49 am Sagittarius
6th 3:50 am Capricorn
8th 7:06 am Aquarius
10th 11:09 am Pisces
12th 4:59 pm Aries
15th 1:39 am Taurus
17th 1:14 pm Gemini
20th 2:10 am Cancer
22nd 1:40 pm Leo
24th 9:49 pm Virgo
27th 2:30 am Libra
29th 4:59 am Scorpio

October 2030
1st 6:49 am Sagittarius
3rd 9:13 am Capricorn
5th 12:46 pm Aquarius
7th 5:46 pm Pisces
10th 12:32 am Aries
12th 9:33 am Taurus
14th 9:00 pm Gemini
17th 9:57 am Cancer
19th 10:12 pm Leo
22nd 7:23 am Virgo
24th 12:37 pm Libra
26th 2:39 pm Scorpio
28th 3:11 pm Sagittarius
30th 3:59 pm Capricorn

November 2030
1st 6:25 pm Aquarius
3rd 11:15 pm Pisces
6th 6:37 am Aries
8th 4:20 pm Taurus
11th 4:02 am Gemini
13th 4:57 pm Cancer
16th 5:38 am Leo
18th 4:03 pm Virgo
20th 10:46 pm Libra
23rd 1:40 am Scorpio
25th 1:58 am Sagittarius
27th 1:29 am Capricorn
29th 2:07 am Aquarius

December 2030
1st 5:27 am Pisces
3rd 12:14 pm Aries
5th 10:13 pm Taurus
8th 10:19 am Gemini
10th 11:17 pm Cancer
13th 11:53 am Leo
15th 10:55 pm Virgo
18th 7:09 am Libra
20th 11:51 am Scorpio
22nd 1:20 pm Sagittarius
24th 12:55 pm Capricorn
26th 12:27 pm Aquarius
28th 1:58 pm Pisces
30th 7:07 pm Aries

January 2031
2nd 4:19 am Taurus
4th 4:27 pm Gemini
7th 5:31 am Cancer
9th 5:51 pm Leo
12th 4:38 am Virgo
14th 1:21 pm Libra
16th 7:31 pm Scorpio
18th 10:53 pm Sagittarius
20th 11:52 pm Capricorn
22nd 11:47 pm Aquarius
25th 12:31 am Pisces
27th 4:06 am Aries
29th 11:49 am Taurus
31st 11:16 pm Gemini

February 2031
3rd 12:19 pm Cancer
6th 12:33 am Leo
8th 10:44 am Virgo
10th 6:51 pm Libra
13th 1:09 am Scorpio
15th 5:39 am Sagittarius
17th 8:21 am Capricorn
19th 9:45 am Aquarius
21st 11:08 am Pisces
23rd 2:16 pm Aries
25th 8:47 pm Taurus
28th 7:10 am Gemini

March 2031
2nd 7:54 pm Cancer
5th 8:16 am Leo
7th 6:16 pm Virgo
10th 1:35 am Libra
12th 6:54 am Scorpio
14th 10:59 am Sagittarius
16th 2:17 pm Capricorn
18th 5:02 pm Aquarius
20th 7:48 pm Pisces
22nd 11:42 pm Aries
25th 6:05 am Taurus
27th 3:44 pm Gemini
30th 4:00 am Cancer

April 2031
1st 4:35 pm Leo
4th 3:01 am Virgo
6th 10:11 am Libra
8th 2:34 pm Scorpio
10th 5:23 pm Sagittarius
12th 7:45 pm Capricorn
14th 10:30 pm Aquarius
17th 2:09 am Pisces
19th 7:12 am Aries
21st 2:19 pm Taurus
23rd 11:59 pm Gemini
26th 11:57 am Cancer
29th 12:43 am Leo

May 2031
1st 11:54 am Virgo
3rd 7:48 pm Libra
6th 12:10 am Scorpio
8th 2:02 am Sagittarius
10th 2:56 am Capricorn
12th 4:23 am Aquarius
14th 7:31 am Pisces
16th 12:59 pm Aries
18th 8:55 pm Taurus
21st 7:08 am Gemini
23rd 7:10 pm Cancer
26th 7:59 am Leo
28th 7:54 pm Virgo
31st 5:01 am Libra

June 2031
2nd 10:23 am Scorpio
4th 12:23 pm Sagittarius
6th 12:25 pm Capricorn
8th 12:20 pm Aquarius
10th 1:56 pm Pisces
12th 6:32 pm Aries
15th 2:31 am Taurus
17th 1:13 pm Gemini
20th 1:32 am Cancer
22nd 2:22 pm Leo
25th 2:34 am Virgo
27th 12:44 pm Libra
29th 7:37 pm Scorpio

July 2031
1st 10:49 pm Sagittarius
3rd 11:09 pm Capricorn
5th 10:19 pm Aquarius
7th 10:27 pm Pisces
10th 1:28 am Aries
12th 8:25 am Taurus
14th 6:57 pm Gemini
17th 7:28 am Cancer
19th 8:18 pm Leo
22nd 8:21 am Virgo
24th 6:51 pm Libra
27th 2:55 am Scorpio
29th 7:45 am Sagittarius
31st 9:26 am Capricorn

August 2031
2nd 9:06 am Aquarius
4th 8:41 am Pisces
6th 10:21 am Aries
8th 3:47 pm Taurus
11th 1:21 am Gemini
13th 1:39 pm Cancer
16th 2:29 am Leo
18th 2:15 pm Virgo
21st 12:22 am Libra
23rd 8:35 am Scorpio
25th 2:29 pm Sagittarius
27th 5:46 pm Capricorn
29th 6:53 pm Aquarius
31st 7:08 pm Pisces

September 2031
2nd 8:28 pm Aries
5th 12:46 am Taurus
7th 9:04 am Gemini
9th 8:42 pm Cancer
12th 9:26 am Leo
14th 9:06 pm Virgo
17th 6:40 am Libra
19th 2:10 pm Scorpio
21st 7:54 pm Sagittarius
23rd 11:56 pm Capricorn
26th 2:27 am Aquarius
28th 4:09 pm Pisces
30th 6:18 am Aries

January 2032
2nd 4:51 am Virgo
4th 4:45 pm Libra
7th 2:02 am Scorpio
9th 7:24 am Sagittarius
11th 9:01 am Capricorn
13th 8:23 am Aquarius
15th 7:42 am Pisces
17th 9:07 am Aries
19th 2:07 pm Taurus
21st 10:48 pm Gemini
24th 10:03 am Cancer
26th 10:27 pm Leo
29th 11:01 am Virgo
31st 11:01 pm Libra

May 2032
1st 6:24 pm Aquarius
3rd 9:00 pm Pisces
5th 11:40 pm Aries
8th 3:13 am Taurus
10th 8:33 am Gemini
12th 4:31 pm Cancer
15th 3:16 am Leo
17th 3:40 pm Virgo
20th 3:32 am Libra
22nd 12:49 pm Scorpio
24th 6:50 pm Sagittarius
26th 10:13 pm Capricorn
29th 12:17 am Aquarius
31st 2:22 am Pisces

September 2032
1st 6:18 am Leo
3rd 6:52 pm Virgo
6th 7:33 am Libra
8th 7:22 pm Scorpio
11th 5:05 am Sagittarius
13th 11:34 am Capricorn
15th 2:31 pm Aquarius
17th 2:50 pm Pisces
19th 2:17 pm Aries
21st 2:54 pm Taurus
23rd 6:27 pm Gemini
26th 1:51 am Cancer
28th 12:37 pm Leo

January 2033
2nd 5:22 am Aquarius
4th 6:39 pm Pisces
6th 8:35 pm Aries
9th 12:07 am Taurus
11th 5:28 am Gemini
13th 12:30 pm Cancer
15th 9:24 pm Leo
18th 8:24 am Virgo
20th 9:07 pm Libra
23rd 9:44 am Scorpio
25th 7:44 pm Sagittarius
28th 1:35 am Capricorn
30th 3:42 am Aquarius

October 2031
2nd 10:29 am Taurus
4th 5:55 pm Gemini
7th 4:42 am Cancer
9th 5:14 pm Leo
12th 5:07 am Virgo
14th 2:34 pm Libra
16th 9:18 pm Scorpio
19th 1:56 am Sagittarius
21st 5:18 am Capricorn
23rd 8:07 am Aquarius
25th 10:55 am Pisces
27th 2:24 pm Aries
29th 7:26 pm Taurus

February 2032
3rd 9:15 am Virgo
5th 4:20 pm Sagittarius
7th 7:37 pm Capricorn
9th 7:50 pm Aquarius
11th 6:50 pm Pisces
13th 6:54 pm Aries
15th 10:03 pm Taurus
18th 5:19 am Gemini
20th 4:06 pm Cancer
23rd 4:37 am Leo
25th 5:10 pm Virgo
28th 4:48 am Libra

June 2032
2nd 5:26 am Aries
4th 9:59 am Taurus
6th 4:18 pm Gemini
9th 12:38 am Cancer
11th 11:12 am Leo
13th 11:30 pm Virgo
16th 11:52 am Libra
18th 10:00 pm Scorpio
21st 4:25 am Sagittarius
23rd 7:19 am Capricorn
25th 8:10 am Aquarius
27th 8:50 am Pisces
29th 10:57 am Aries

October 2032
1st 1:10 am Virgo
3rd 1:44 pm Libra
6th 1:07 am Scorpio
8th 10:36 am Sagittarius
10th 5:39 pm Capricorn
12th 10:02 pm Aquarius
15th 12:04 am Pisces
17th 12:45 am Aries
19th 1:38 am Taurus
21st 4:24 am Gemini
23rd 10:25 am Cancer
25th 8:05 pm Leo
28th 8:18 am Virgo
30th 8:55 pm Libra

February 2033
1st 3:50 am Pisces
3rd 4:04 am Aries
5th 6:07 am Taurus
7th 10:52 am Gemini
9th 6:17 pm Cancer
12th 3:54 am Leo
14th 3:16 pm Virgo
17th 3:58 am Libra
19th 4:50 pm Scorpio
22nd 3:55 am Sagittarius
24th 11:20 am Capricorn
26th 2:39 pm Aquarius
28th 2:57 pm Pisces

November 2031
1st 2:53 am Gemini
3rd 1:07 pm Cancer
6th 1:25 am Leo
8th 1:42 pm Virgo
10th 11:46 pm Libra
13th 6:30 am Scorpio
15th 10:14 am Sagittarius
17th 12:11 pm Capricorn
19th 1:49 pm Aquarius
21st 4:19 pm Pisces
23rd 8:27 pm Aries
26th 2:35 am Taurus
28th 10:48 am Gemini
30th 9:07 pm Cancer

March 2032
1st 2:57 pm Scorpio
3rd 10:51 pm Sagittarius
6th 3:45 am Capricorn
8th 5:43 am Aquarius
10th 5:49 am Pisces
12th 5:54 am Aries
14th 8:01 am Taurus
16th 1:41 pm Gemini
18th 11:15 pm Cancer
21st 11:23 am Leo
23rd 11:58 pm Virgo
26th 11:20 am Libra
28th 8:50 pm Scorpio
31st 4:17 am Sagittarius

July 2032
1st 3:27 pm Taurus
3rd 10:24 pm Gemini
6th 7:27 am Cancer
8th 6:17 pm Leo
11th 6:35 am Virgo
13th 7:19 pm Libra
16th 6:29 am Scorpio
18th 2:05 pm Sagittarius
20th 5:35 pm Capricorn
22nd 6:04 pm Aquarius
24th 5:30 pm Pisces
26th 6:03 pm Aries
28th 9:18 pm Taurus
31st 3:51 am Gemini

November 2032
2nd 7:59 am Scorpio
4th 4:41 pm Sagittarius
6th 11:05 pm Capricorn
9th 3:39 am Aquarius
11th 6:49 am Pisces
13th 9:08 am Aries
15th 11:21 am Taurus
17th 2:33 pm Gemini
19th 8:01 pm Cancer
22nd 4:40 am Leo
24th 4:17 pm Virgo
27th 5:01 am Libra
29th 4:19 pm Scorpio

March 2033
2nd 2:15 pm Aries
4th 2:34 pm Taurus
6th 5:34 pm Gemini
9th 12:01 am Cancer
11th 9:37 am Leo
13th 9:23 pm Virgo
16th 10:11 am Libra
18th 10:57 pm Scorpio
21st 10:21 am Sagittarius
23rd 7:00 pm Capricorn
26th 12:02 am Aquarius
28th 1:46 am Pisces
30th 1:31 am Aries

December 2031
3rd 9:12 am Leo
5th 9:50 pm Virgo
8th 8:56 am Libra
10th 4:43 pm Scorpio
12th 8:39 pm Sagittarius
14th 9:45 pm Capricorn
16th 9:46 pm Aquarius
18th 10:40 pm Pisces
21st 1:56 am Aries
23rd 8:13 am Taurus
25th 5:10 pm Gemini
28th 4:03 am Cancer
30th 4:11 pm Leo

April 2032
2nd 9:38 am Capricorn
4th 12:55 pm Aquarius
6th 2:39 pm Pisces
8th 3:57 pm Aries
10th 6:20 pm Taurus
12th 11:17 pm Gemini
15th 7:40 am Cancer
17th 7:04 pm Leo
20th 7:36 am Virgo
22nd 7:03 pm Libra
25th 4:07 am Scorpio
27th 10:39 am Sagittarius
29th 3:10 pm Capricorn

August 2032
2nd 1:13 pm Cancer
5th 12:29 am Leo
7th 12:54 pm Virgo
10th 1:42 am Libra
12th 1:31 pm Scorpio
14th 10:30 pm Sagittarius
17th 3:28 am Capricorn
19th 4:45 am Aquarius
21st 4:01 am Pisces
23rd 3:25 am Aries
25th 5:03 am Taurus
27th 10:11 am Gemini
29th 6:57 pm Cancer

December 2032
2nd 12:36 am Sagittarius
4th 5:56 am Capricorn
6th 9:24 am Aquarius
8th 12:10 pm Pisces
10th 3:07 pm Aries
12th 6:39 pm Taurus
14th 11:07 pm Gemini
17th 5:07 am Cancer
19th 1:29 pm Leo
22nd 12:35 am Virgo
24th 1:21 pm Libra
27th 1:20 am Scorpio
29th 10:07 am Sagittarius
31st 3:07 pm Capricorn

April 2033
1st 1:10 am Taurus
3rd 2:37 am Gemini
5th 7:22 am Cancer
7th 3:55 pm Leo
10th 3:30 am Virgo
12th 4:25 pm Libra
15th 4:59 am Scorpio
17th 4:03 pm Sagittarius
20th 12:53 am Capricorn
22nd 7:02 am Aquarius
24th 10:26 am Pisces
26th 11:42 am Aries
28th 12:02 pm Taurus
30th 1:04 pm Gemini

May 2033
2nd 4:31 pm Cancer
4th 11:39 pm Leo
7th 10:25 am Virgo
9th 11:13 pm Libra
12th 11:43 am Scorpio
14th 10:18 pm Sagittarius
17th 6:30 am Capricorn
19th 12:32 pm Aquarius
21st 4:44 pm Pisces
23rd 7:28 pm Aries
25th 9:14 pm Taurus
27th 11:03 pm Gemini
30th 2:19 am Cancer

June 2033
1st 8:30 am Leo
3rd 6:18 pm Virgo
6th 6:44 am Libra
8th 7:21 pm Scorpio
11th 5:48 am Sagittarius
13th 1:18 pm Capricorn
15th 6:24 pm Aquarius
17th 10:07 pm Pisces
20th 1:13 am Aries
22nd 4:06 am Taurus
24th 7:12 am Gemini
26th 11:15 am Cancer
28th 5:25 pm Leo

July 2033
1st 2:39 am Virgo
3rd 2:40 pm Libra
6th 3:29 am Scorpio
8th 2:19 pm Sagittarius
10th 9:43 pm Capricorn
13th 1:59 am Aquarius
15th 4:31 am Pisces
17th 6:43 am Aries
19th 9:32 am Taurus
21st 1:21 pm Gemini
23rd 6:27 pm Cancer
26th 1:19 am Leo
28th 10:38 am Virgo
30th 10:27 pm Libra

August 2033
2nd 11:25 am Scorpio
4th 11:02 pm Sagittarius
7th 7:08 am Capricorn
9th 11:25 am Aquarius
11th 1:05 pm Pisces
13th 1:54 pm Aries
15th 3:26 pm Taurus
17th 6:44 pm Gemini
20th 12:10 am Cancer
22nd 7:48 am Leo
24th 5:39 pm Virgo
27th 5:33 am Libra
29th 6:37 pm Scorpio

September 2033
1st 6:56 am Sagittarius
3rd 4:17 pm Capricorn
5th 9:36 pm Aquarius
7th 11:27 pm Pisces
9th 11:27 pm Aries
11th 11:28 pm Taurus
14th 1:13 am Gemini
16th 5:45 am Cancer
18th 1:24 pm Leo
20th 11:44 pm Virgo
23rd 11:56 am Libra
26th 1:00 am Scorpio
28th 1:34 pm Sagittarius
30th 11:59 pm Capricorn

October 2033
3rd 6:55 am Aquarius
5th 10:07 am Pisces
7th 10:32 am Aries
9th 9:52 am Taurus
11th 10:04 am Gemini
13th 12:54 pm Cancer
15th 7:26 pm Leo
18th 5:33 am Virgo
20th 5:58 pm Libra
23rd 7:03 am Scorpio
25th 7:25 pm Sagittarius
28th 6:05 am Capricorn
30th 2:11 pm Aquarius

November 2033
1st 7:09 pm Pisces
3rd 9:09 pm Aries
5th 9:10 pm Taurus
7th 8:54 pm Gemini
9th 10:19 pm Cancer
12th 3:10 am Leo
14th 12:11 pm Virgo
17th 12:22 am Libra
19th 1:28 pm Scorpio
22nd 1:32 am Sagittarius
24th 11:41 am Capricorn
26th 7:46 pm Aquarius
29th 1:44 am Pisces

December 2033
1st 5:27 am Aries
3rd 7:10 am Taurus
5th 7:49 am Gemini
7th 9:02 am Cancer
9th 12:45 pm Leo
11th 8:21 pm Virgo
14th 7:42 am Libra
16th 8:44 pm Scorpio
19th 8:46 am Sagittarius
21st 6:22 pm Capricorn
24th 1:35 am Aquarius
26th 7:05 am Pisces
28th 11:19 am Aries
30th 2:26 pm Taurus

January 2034
1st 4:42 pm Gemini
3rd 7:00 pm Cancer
5th 10:48 pm Leo
8th 5:36 am Virgo
10th 4:00 pm Libra
13th 4:45 am Scorpio
15th 5:04 pm Sagittarius
18th 2:45 am Capricorn
20th 9:18 am Aquarius
22nd 1:36 pm Pisces
24th 4:50 pm Aries
26th 7:50 pm Taurus
28th 10:59 pm Gemini
31st 2:39 am Cancer

February 2034
2nd 7:32 am Leo
4th 2:37 pm Virgo
7th 12:35 am Libra
9th 12:56 pm Scorpio
12th 1:37 am Sagittarius
14th 12:02 pm Capricorn
16th 6:53 pm Aquarius
18th 10:33 pm Pisces
21st 12:24 am Aries
23rd 1:57 am Taurus
25th 4:21 am Gemini
27th 8:18 am Cancer

March 2034
1st 2:10 pm Leo
3rd 10:09 pm Virgo
6th 8:25 am Libra
8th 8:37 pm Scorpio
11th 9:27 am Sagittarius
13th 8:49 pm Capricorn
16th 4:50 am Aquarius
18th 9:05 am Pisces
20th 10:27 am Aries
22nd 10:36 am Taurus
24th 11:18 am Gemini
26th 2:02 pm Cancer
28th 7:38 pm Leo
31st 4:11 am Virgo

April 2034
2nd 3:03 pm Libra
5th 3:25 am Scorpio
7th 4:15 pm Sagittarius
10th 4:09 am Capricorn
12th 1:29 pm Aquarius
14th 7:12 pm Pisces
16th 9:24 pm Aries
18th 9:16 pm Taurus
20th 8:42 pm Gemini
22nd 9:42 pm Cancer
25th 1:52 am Leo
27th 9:51 am Virgo
29th 8:55 pm Libra

May 2034
2nd 9:34 am Scorpio
4th 10:21 pm Sagittarius
7th 10:14 am Capricorn
9th 8:15 pm Aquarius
12th 3:26 am Pisces
14th 7:14 am Aries
16th 8:07 am Taurus
18th 7:30 am Gemini
20th 7:26 am Cancer
22nd 10:00 am Leo
24th 4:34 pm Virgo
27th 3:02 am Libra
29th 3:41 pm Scorpio

June 2034
1st 4:26 am Sagittarius
3rd 4:00 pm Capricorn
6th 1:52 am Aquarius
8th 9:38 am Pisces
10th 2:49 pm Aries
12th 5:18 pm Taurus
14th 5:48 pm Gemini
16th 5:55 pm Cancer
18th 7:41 pm Leo
21st 12:53 am Virgo
23rd 10:11 am Libra
25th 10:25 pm Scorpio
28th 11:08 am Sagittarius
30th 10:28 pm Capricorn

July 2034
3rd 7:44 am Aquarius
5th 3:03 pm Pisces
7th 8:33 pm Aries
10th 12:10 am Taurus
12th 2:09 am Gemini
14th 3:26 am Cancer
16th 5:32 am Leo
18th 10:11 am Virgo
20th 6:28 pm Libra
23rd 5:59 am Scorpio
25th 6:39 pm Sagittarius
28th 6:03 am Capricorn
30th 2:56 pm Aquarius

August 2034
1st 9:23 pm Pisces
4th 2:05 am Aries
6th 5:36 am Taurus
8th 8:23 am Gemini
10th 10:56 am Cancer
12th 2:10 pm Leo
14th 7:14 pm Virgo
17th 3:11 am Libra
19th 2:06 pm Scorpio
22nd 2:40 am Sagittarius
24th 2:27 pm Capricorn
26th 11:35 pm Aquarius
29th 5:35 am Pisces
31st 9:11 am Aries

September 2034
2nd 11:33 am Taurus
4th 1:45 pm Gemini
6th 4:40 pm Cancer
8th 8:54 pm Leo
11th 2:58 am Virgo
13th 11:19 am Libra
15th 10:05 pm Scorpio
18th 10:31 am Sagittarius
20th 10:51 pm Capricorn
23rd 8:53 am Aquarius
25th 3:23 pm Pisces
27th 6:33 pm Aries
29th 7:39 pm Taurus

October 2034
1st 8:21 pm Gemini
3rd 10:14 pm Cancer
6th 2:22 am Leo
8th 9:06 am Virgo
10th 6:13 pm Libra
13th 5:17 am Scorpio
15th 5:42 pm Sagittarius
18th 6:21 am Capricorn
20th 5:29 pm Aquarius
23rd 1:21 am Pisces
25th 5:17 am Aries
27th 6:05 am Taurus
29th 5:31 am Gemini
31st 5:41 am Cancer

November 2034
2nd 8:23 am Leo
4th 2:36 pm Virgo
7th 12:02 am Libra
9th 11:34 am Scorpio
12th 12:06 am Sagittarius
14th 12:45 pm Capricorn
17th 12:29 am Aquarius
19th 9:48 am Pisces
21st 3:27 pm Aries
23rd 5:20 pm Taurus
25th 4:44 pm Gemini
27th 3:46 pm Cancer
29th 4:41 pm Leo

December 2034
1st 9:15 pm Virgo
4th 5:53 am Libra
6th 5:28 pm Scorpio
9th 6:10 am Sagittarius
11th 6:40 pm Capricorn
14th 6:15 am Aquarius
16th 4:10 pm Pisces
18th 11:21 pm Aries
21st 3:06 am Taurus
23rd 3:51 am Gemini
25th 3:11 am Cancer
27th 3:16 am Leo
29th 6:11 am Virgo
31st 1:12 pm Libra

January 2035
2nd 11:59 pm Scorpio
5th 12:38 pm Sagittarius
8th 1:05 am Capricorn
10th 12:12 pm Aquarius
12th 9:39 pm Pisces
15th 5:06 am Aries
17th 10:08 am Taurus
19th 12:43 pm Gemini
21st 1:36 pm Cancer
23rd 2:17 pm Leo
25th 4:40 pm Virgo
27th 10:21 pm Libra
30th 7:50 am Scorpio

February 2035
1st 7:58 pm Sagittarius
4th 8:29 am Capricorn
6th 7:27 pm Aquarius
9th 4:10 am Pisces
11th 10:44 am Aries
13th 3:32 pm Taurus
15th 6:54 pm Gemini
17th 9:18 pm Cancer
19th 11:30 pm Leo
22nd 2:42 am Virgo
24th 8:09 am Libra
26th 4:43 pm Scorpio

March 2035
1st 4:07 am Sagittarius
3rd 4:38 pm Capricorn
6th 3:57 am Aquarius
8th 12:30 pm Pisces
10th 6:10 pm Aries
12th 9:44 pm Taurus
15th 12:19 am Gemini
17th 2:54 am Cancer
19th 6:10 am Leo
21st 10:40 am Virgo
23rd 4:55 pm Libra
26th 1:26 am Scorpio
28th 12:22 pm Sagittarius
31st 12:49 am Capricorn

April 2035
2nd 12:43 pm Aquarius
4th 9:57 pm Pisces
7th 3:34 am Aries
9th 6:11 am Taurus
11th 7:19 am Gemini
13th 8:40 am Cancer
15th 11:33 am Leo
17th 4:35 pm Virgo
19th 11:48 pm Libra
22nd 8:58 am Scorpio
24th 7:57 pm Sagittarius
27th 8:19 am Capricorn
29th 8:44 pm Aquarius

May 2035
2nd 7:04 am Pisces
4th 1:38 pm Aries
6th 4:22 pm Taurus
8th 4:38 pm Gemini
10th 4:29 pm Cancer
12th 5:51 pm Leo
14th 10:05 pm Virgo
17th 5:23 am Libra
19th 3:08 pm Scorpio
22nd 2:31 am Sagittarius
24th 2:56 pm Capricorn
27th 3:32 am Aquarius
29th 2:45 pm Pisces
31st 10:45 pm Aries

June 2035
3rd 2:40 am Taurus
5th 3:16 am Gemini
7th 2:24 am Cancer
9th 2:20 am Leo
11th 4:57 am Virgo
13th 11:12 am Libra
15th 8:47 pm Scorpio
18th 8:27 am Sagittarius
20th 8:59 pm Capricorn
23rd 9:29 am Aquarius
25th 8:58 pm Pisces
28th 6:01 am Aries
30th 11:31 am Taurus

July 2035
2nd 1:28 pm Gemini
4th 1:09 pm Cancer
6th 12:35 pm Leo
8th 1:52 pm Virgo
10th 6:34 pm Libra
13th 3:06 am Scorpio
15th 2:30 pm Sagittarius
18th 3:06 am Capricorn
20th 3:26 pm Aquarius
23rd 2:36 am Pisces
25th 11:48 am Aries
27th 6:17 pm Taurus
29th 9:48 pm Gemini
31st 10:55 pm Cancer

August 2035
2nd 11:04 pm Leo
5th 12:03 am Virgo
7th 3:37 am Libra
9th 10:48 am Scorpio
11th 9:25 pm Sagittarius
14th 9:52 am Capricorn
16th 10:09 pm Aquarius
19th 8:51 am Pisces
21st 5:25 pm Aries
23rd 11:46 pm Taurus
26th 4:01 am Gemini
28th 6:35 am Cancer
30th 8:11 am Leo

September 2035
1st 10:00 am Virgo
3rd 1:26 pm Libra
5th 7:43 pm Scorpio
8th 5:22 am Sagittarius
10th 5:28 pm Capricorn
13th 5:53 am Aquarius
15th 4:29 pm Pisces
18th 12:21 am Aries
20th 5:43 am Taurus
22nd 9:25 am Gemini
24th 12:19 pm Cancer
26th 3:04 pm Leo
28th 6:14 pm Virgo
30th 10:31 pm Libra

October 2035
3rd 4:49 am Scorpio
5th 1:52 pm Sagittarius
8th 1:33 am Capricorn
10th 2:12 pm Aquarius
13th 1:18 am Pisces
15th 9:08 am Aries
17th 1:38 pm Taurus
19th 4:03 pm Gemini
21st 5:54 pm Cancer
23rd 8:28 pm Leo
26th 12:23 am Virgo
28th 5:48 am Libra
30th 12:52 pm Scorpio

November 2035
1st 10:01 pm Sagittarius
4th 9:27 am Capricorn
6th 10:17 pm Aquarius
9th 10:14 am Pisces
11th 6:58 pm Aries
13th 11:37 pm Taurus
16th 1:10 am Gemini
18th 1:31 am Cancer
20th 2:36 am Leo
22nd 5:46 am Virgo
24th 11:25 am Libra
26th 7:19 pm Scorpio
29th 5:05 am Sagittarius

December 2035
1st 4:37 pm Capricorn
4th 5:28 am Aquarius
6th 6:07 pm Pisces
9th 4:14 am Aries
11th 10:11 am Taurus
13th 12:11 pm Gemini
15th 11:51 am Cancer
17th 11:22 am Leo
19th 12:43 pm Virgo
21st 5:09 pm Libra
24th 12:51 am Scorpio
26th 11:05 am Sagittarius
28th 10:59 pm Capricorn
31st 11:49 am Aquarius

January 2036
3rd 12:35 am Pisces
5th 11:38 am Aries
7th 7:18 pm Taurus
9th 10:56 pm Gemini
11th 11:23 pm Cancer
13th 10:31 pm Leo
15th 10:26 pm Virgo
18th 12:58 am Libra
20th 7:11 am Scorpio
22nd 4:57 pm Sagittarius
25th 5:02 am Capricorn
27th 5:56 pm Aquarius
30th 6:26 am Pisces

February 2036
1st 5:29 pm Aries
4th 2:03 am Taurus
6th 7:25 am Gemini
8th 9:41 am Cancer
10th 9:55 am Leo
12th 9:46 am Virgo
14th 11:41 am Libra
16th 3:36 pm Scorpio
18th 11:59 pm Sagittarius
21st 11:35 am Capricorn
24th 12:32 am Aquarius
26th 12:50 pm Pisces
28th 11:19 pm Aries

March 2036
2nd 7:32 am Taurus
4th 1:29 pm Gemini
6th 5:14 pm Cancer
8th 7:14 pm Leo
10th 8:20 pm Virgo
12th 9:53 pm Libra
15th 1:31 am Scorpio
17th 8:32 am Sagittarius
19th 7:10 pm Capricorn
22nd 7:55 am Aquarius
24th 8:17 pm Pisces
27th 6:22 am Aries
29th 1:43 pm Taurus
31st 6:56 pm Gemini

April 2036
2nd 10:47 pm Cancer
5th 1:49 am Leo
7th 4:26 am Virgo
9th 7:14 am Libra
11th 11:15 am Scorpio
13th 5:45 pm Sagittarius
16th 3:31 am Capricorn
18th 3:53 pm Aquarius
21st 4:29 am Pisces
23rd 2:45 pm Aries
25th 9:39 pm Taurus
28th 1:48 am Gemini
30th 4:34 am Cancer

May 2036
2nd 7:10 am Leo
4th 10:18 am Virgo
6th 2:14 pm Libra
8th 7:19 pm Scorpio
11th 2:15 am Sagittarius
13th 11:48 am Capricorn
15th 11:51 pm Aquarius
18th 12:41 pm Pisces
20th 11:39 pm Aries
23rd 6:56 am Taurus
25th 10:40 am Gemini
27th 12:17 pm Cancer
29th 1:31 pm Leo
31st 3:46 pm Virgo

June 2036
2nd 7:43 pm Libra
5th 1:33 am Scorpio
7th 9:19 am Sagittarius
9th 7:13 pm Capricorn
12th 7:13 am Aquarius
14th 8:13 pm Pisces
17th 7:59 am Aries
19th 4:22 pm Taurus
21st 8:42 pm Gemini
23rd 9:59 pm Cancer
25th 10:05 pm Leo
27th 10:47 pm Virgo
30th 1:32 am Libra

July 2036
2nd 6:59 am Scorpio
4th 3:09 pm Sagittarius
7th 1:36 am Capricorn
9th 1:48 pm Aquarius
12th 2:50 am Pisces
14th 3:05 pm Aries
17th 12:40 am Taurus
19th 6:24 am Gemini
21st 8:32 am Cancer
23rd 8:28 am Leo
25th 8:05 am Virgo
27th 9:13 am Libra
29th 1:17 pm Scorpio
31st 8:50 pm Sagittarius

August 2036
3rd 7:26 am Capricorn
5th 7:53 pm Aquarius
8th 8:53 am Pisces
10th 9:07 pm Aries
13th 7:20 am Taurus
15th 2:28 pm Gemini
17th 6:11 pm Cancer
19th 7:09 pm Leo
21st 6:48 pm Virgo
23rd 6:57 pm Libra
25th 9:27 pm Scorpio
28th 3:38 am Sagittarius
30th 1:36 pm Capricorn

September 2036
2nd 2:04 am Aquarius
4th 3:02 pm Pisces
7th 2:56 am Aries
9th 12:57 pm Taurus
11th 8:38 pm Gemini
14th 1:46 am Cancer
16th 4:24 am Leo
18th 5:13 am Virgo
20th 5:36 am Libra
22nd 7:18 am Scorpio
24th 12:06 pm Sagittarius
26th 8:54 pm Capricorn
29th 8:56 am Aquarius

October 2036
1st 9:54 pm Pisces
4th 9:34 am Aries
6th 6:55 pm Taurus
9th 2:05 am Gemini
11th 7:27 am Cancer
13th 11:16 am Leo
15th 1:41 pm Virgo
17th 3:21 pm Libra
19th 5:28 pm Scorpio
21st 9:42 pm Sagittarius
24th 5:26 am Capricorn
26th 4:42 pm Aquarius
29th 5:39 am Pisces
31st 5:26 pm Aries

November 2036
3rd 2:26 am Taurus
5th 8:39 am Gemini
7th 1:05 pm Cancer
9th 4:38 pm Leo
11th 7:48 pm Virgo
13th 10:49 pm Libra
16th 2:12 am Scorpio
18th 6:59 am Sagittarius
20th 2:25 pm Capricorn
23rd 1:03 am Aquarius
25th 1:49 pm Pisces
28th 2:08 am Aries
30th 11:31 am Taurus

December 2036
2nd 5:24 pm Gemini
4th 8:42 pm Cancer
6th 10:52 pm Leo
9th 1:12 am Virgo
11th 4:22 am Libra
13th 8:44 am Scorpio
15th 2:38 pm Sagittarius
17th 10:39 pm Capricorn
20th 9:10 am Aquarius
22nd 9:46 pm Pisces
25th 10:32 am Aries
27th 9:00 pm Taurus
30th 3:40 am Gemini

January 2037
1st 6:47 am Cancer
3rd 7:47 am Leo
5th 8:26 am Virgo
7th 10:12 am Libra
9th 2:07 pm Scorpio
11th 8:32 pm Sagittarius
14th 5:22 am Capricorn
16th 4:22 pm Aquarius
19th 4:55 am Pisces
21st 5:53 pm Aries
24th 5:21 am Taurus
26th 1:32 pm Gemini
28th 5:48 pm Cancer
30th 6:54 pm Leo

February 2037
1st 6:30 pm Virgo
3rd 6:29 pm Libra
5th 8:39 pm Scorpio
8th 2:08 am Sagittarius
10th 11:03 am Capricorn
12th 10:33 pm Aquarius
15th 11:19 am Pisces
18th 12:12 am Aries
20th 11:59 am Taurus
22nd 9:26 pm Gemini
25th 3:29 am Cancer
27th 6:01 am Leo

March 2037
1st 5:59 am Virgo
3rd 5:12 am Libra
5th 5:42 am Scorpio
7th 9:23 am Sagittarius
9th 5:10 pm Capricorn
12th 4:28 am Aquarius
14th 5:25 pm Pisces
17th 6:12 am Aries
19th 5:44 pm Taurus
22nd 3:26 am Gemini
24th 10:41 am Cancer
26th 2:59 pm Leo
28th 4:32 pm Virgo
30th 4:23 pm Libra

April 2037
1st 4:25 pm Scorpio
3rd 6:42 pm Sagittarius
6th 12:54 am Capricorn
8th 11:11 am Aquarius
10th 11:56 pm Pisces
13th 12:41 pm Aries
15th 11:51 pm Taurus
18th 8:59 am Gemini
20th 4:13 pm Cancer
22nd 9:26 pm Leo
25th 12:32 am Virgo
27th 1:51 am Libra
29th 2:47 am Scorpio

May 2037
1st 4:53 am Sagittarius
3rd 10:02 am Capricorn
5th 7:07 pm Aquarius
8th 7:15 am Pisces
10th 7:59 pm Aries
13th 7:04 am Taurus
15th 3:37 pm Gemini
17th 9:59 pm Cancer
20th 2:48 am Leo
22nd 6:22 am Virgo
24th 8:59 am Libra
26th 11:14 am Scorpio
28th 2:13 pm Sagittarius
30th 7:23 pm Capricorn

June 2037
2nd 3:47 am Aquarius
4th 3:14 pm Pisces
7th 3:55 am Aries
9th 3:16 pm Taurus
11th 11:47 pm Gemini
14th 5:25 am Cancer
16th 9:06 am Leo
18th 11:51 am Virgo
20th 2:28 pm Libra
22nd 5:32 pm Scorpio
24th 9:40 pm Sagittarius
27th 3:39 am Capricorn
29th 12:10 pm Aquarius

July 2037
1st 11:17 pm Pisces
4th 11:52 am Aries
6th 11:46 pm Taurus
9th 8:54 am Gemini
11th 2:35 pm Cancer
13th 5:28 pm Leo
15th 6:53 pm Virgo
17th 8:19 pm Libra
19th 10:55 pm Scorpio
22nd 3:29 am Sagittarius
24th 10:20 am Capricorn
26th 7:29 pm Aquarius
29th 6:43 am Pisces
31st 7:16 pm Aries

August 2037
3rd 7:38 am Taurus
5th 5:49 pm Gemini
8th 12:28 am Cancer
10th 3:32 am Leo
12th 4:10 am Virgo
14th 4:08 am Libra
16th 5:17 am Scorpio
18th 9:02 am Sagittarius
20th 3:56 pm Capricorn
23rd 1:39 am Aquarius
25th 1:16 pm Pisces
28th 1:52 am Aries
30th 2:24 pm Taurus

September 2037
2nd 1:30 am Gemini
4th 9:35 am Cancer
6th 1:54 pm Leo
8th 2:54 pm Virgo
10th 2:12 pm Libra
12th 1:53 pm Scorpio
14th 3:59 pm Sagittarius
16th 9:50 pm Capricorn
19th 7:22 am Aquarius
21st 7:15 pm Pisces
24th 7:57 am Aries
26th 8:22 pm Taurus
29th 7:41 am Gemini

October 2037
1st 4:52 pm Cancer
3rd 10:51 pm Leo
6th 1:19 am Virgo
8th 1:13 am Libra
10th 12:25 am Scorpio
12th 1:11 am Sagittarius
14th 5:23 am Capricorn
16th 1:47 pm Aquarius
19th 1:24 am Pisces
21st 2:10 pm Aries
24th 2:24 am Taurus
26th 1:19 pm Gemini
28th 10:34 pm Cancer
31st 5:32 am Leo

November 2037
2nd 9:41 am Virgo
4th 11:13 am Libra
6th 11:18 am Scorpio
8th 11:51 am Sagittarius
10th 2:53 pm Capricorn
12th 9:49 pm Aquarius
15th 8:30 am Pisces
17th 9:07 pm Aries
20th 9:20 am Taurus
22nd 7:49 pm Gemini
25th 4:18 am Cancer
27th 10:56 am Leo
29th 3:43 pm Virgo

December 2037
1st 6:43 pm Libra
3rd 8:26 pm Scorpio
5th 10:03 pm Sagittarius
8th 1:09 am Capricorn
10th 7:13 am Aquarius
12th 4:48 pm Pisces
15th 4:57 am Aries
17th 5:21 pm Taurus
20th 3:53 am Gemini
22nd 11:45 am Cancer
24th 5:16 pm Leo
26th 9:11 pm Virgo
29th 12:13 am Libra
31st 2:58 am Scorpio

January 2038
2nd 6:04 am Sagittarius
4th 10:17 am Capricorn
6th 4:36 pm Aquarius
9th 1:39 am Pisces
11th 1:14 pm Aries
14th 1:49 am Taurus
16th 12:59 pm Gemini
18th 9:06 pm Cancer
21st 1:57 am Leo
23rd 4:30 am Virgo
25th 6:10 am Libra
27th 8:19 am Scorpio
29th 11:51 am Sagittarius
31st 5:12 pm Capricorn

February 2038
3rd 12:29 am Aquarius
5th 9:51 am Pisces
7th 9:13 pm Aries
10th 9:49 am Taurus
12th 9:48 pm Gemini
15th 7:01 am Cancer
17th 12:22 pm Leo
19th 2:22 pm Virgo
21st 2:37 pm Libra
23rd 3:04 pm Scorpio
25th 5:26 pm Sagittarius
27th 10:38 pm Capricorn

March 2038
2nd 6:36 am Aquarius
4th 4:40 pm Pisces
7th 4:16 am Aries
9th 4:50 pm Taurus
12th 5:18 am Gemini
14th 3:47 pm Cancer
16th 10:36 pm Leo
19th 1:22 am Virgo
21st 1:17 am Libra
23rd 12:25 am Scorpio
25th 1:01 am Sagittarius
27th 4:44 am Capricorn
29th 12:06 pm Aquarius
31st 10:26 pm Pisces

April 2038
3rd 10:25 am Aries
5th 11:02 pm Taurus
8th 11:30 am Gemini
10th 10:40 pm Cancer
13th 6:57 am Leo
15th 11:22 am Virgo
17th 12:19 pm Libra
19th 11:26 am Scorpio
21st 10:56 am Sagittarius
23rd 12:56 pm Capricorn
25th 6:45 pm Aquarius
28th 4:21 am Pisces
30th 4:20 pm Aries

May 2038
3rd 5:03 am Taurus
5th 5:19 pm Gemini
8th 4:21 am Cancer
10th 1:15 pm Leo
12th 7:06 pm Virgo
14th 9:43 pm Libra
16th 10:00 pm Scorpio
18th 9:44 pm Sagittarius
20th 10:55 pm Capricorn
23rd 3:15 am Aquarius
25th 11:30 am Pisces
27th 10:53 pm Aries
30th 11:32 am Taurus

June 2038
1st 11:39 pm Gemini
4th 10:12 am Cancer
6th 6:42 pm Leo
9th 12:54 am Virgo
11th 4:44 am Libra
13th 6:36 am Scorpio
15th 7:35 am Sagittarius
17th 9:09 am Capricorn
19th 12:54 pm Aquarius
21st 7:59 pm Pisces
24th 6:25 am Aries
26th 6:49 pm Taurus
29th 6:58 am Gemini

July 2038
1st 5:12 pm Cancer
4th 12:56 am Leo
6th 6:25 am Virgo
8th 10:13 am Libra
10th 12:57 pm Scorpio
12th 3:18 pm Sagittarius
14th 6:04 pm Capricorn
16th 10:17 pm Aquarius
19th 4:59 am Pisces
21st 2:40 pm Aries
24th 2:42 am Taurus
26th 3:04 pm Gemini
29th 1:31 am Cancer
31st 8:50 am Leo

August 2038
2nd 1:18 pm Virgo
4th 4:03 pm Libra
6th 6:19 pm Scorpio
8th 9:06 pm Sagittarius
11th 12:57 am Capricorn
13th 6:14 am Aquarius
15th 1:23 pm Pisces
17th 10:53 pm Aries
20th 10:37 am Taurus
22nd 11:16 pm Gemini
25th 10:25 am Cancer
27th 6:09 pm Leo
29th 10:13 pm Virgo
31st 11:48 pm Libra

September 2038
3rd 12:43 am Scorpio
5th 2:36 am Sagittarius
7th 6:27 am Capricorn
9th 12:27 pm Aquarius
11th 8:26 pm Pisces
14th 6:17 am Aries
16th 5:59 pm Taurus
19th 6:48 am Gemini
21st 6:48 pm Cancer
24th 3:43 am Leo
26th 8:27 am Virgo
28th 9:45 am Libra
30th 9:29 am Scorpio

October 2038
2nd 9:46 am Sagittarius
4th 12:19 pm Capricorn
6th 5:54 pm Aquarius
9th 2:15 am Pisces
11th 12:40 pm Aries
14th 12:35 am Taurus
16th 1:23 pm Gemini
19th 1:53 am Cancer
21st 12:04 pm Leo
23rd 6:21 pm Virgo
25th 8:38 pm Libra
27th 8:19 pm Scorpio
29th 7:31 pm Sagittarius
31st 8:21 pm Capricorn

November 2038
3rd 12:22 am Aquarius
5th 7:59 am Pisces
7th 6:31 pm Aries
10th 6:42 am Taurus
12th 7:28 pm Gemini
15th 7:51 am Cancer
17th 6:36 pm Leo
20th 2:21 am Virgo
22nd 6:26 am Libra
24th 7:24 am Scorpio
26th 6:51 am Sagittarius
28th 6:47 am Capricorn
30th 9:08 am Aquarius

December 2038
2nd 3:08 pm Pisces
5th 12:51 am Aries
7th 12:59 pm Taurus
10th 1:48 am Gemini
12th 1:50 pm Cancer
15th 12:12 am Leo
17th 8:18 am Virgo
19th 1:43 pm Libra
21st 4:32 pm Scorpio
23rd 5:29 pm Sagittarius
25th 5:59 pm Capricorn
27th 7:42 pm Aquarius
30th 12:16 am Pisces

January 2039
1st 8:35 am Aries
3rd 8:08 pm Taurus
6th 8:59 am Gemini
8th 8:53 pm Cancer
11th 6:34 am Leo
13th 1:54 pm Virgo
15th 7:13 pm Libra
17th 10:57 pm Scorpio
20th 1:33 am Sagittarius
22nd 3:35 am Capricorn
24th 6:04 am Aquarius
26th 10:19 am Pisces
28th 5:35 pm Aries
31st 4:15 am Taurus

February 2039
2nd 4:56 pm Gemini
5th 5:07 am Cancer
7th 2:39 pm Leo
9th 9:05 pm Virgo
12th 1:14 am Libra
14th 4:19 am Scorpio
16th 7:15 am Sagittarius
18th 10:30 am Capricorn
20th 2:22 pm Aquarius
22nd 7:26 pm Pisces
25th 2:39 am Aries
27th 12:42 pm Taurus

March 2039
2nd 1:09 am Gemini
4th 1:45 pm Cancer
6th 11:53 pm Leo
9th 6:15 am Virgo
11th 9:28 am Libra
13th 11:08 am Scorpio
15th 12:54 pm Sagittarius
17th 3:51 pm Capricorn
19th 8:23 pm Aquarius
22nd 2:31 am Pisces
24th 10:28 am Aries
26th 8:36 pm Taurus
29th 8:52 am Gemini
31st 9:50 pm Cancer

April 2039
3rd 8:57 am Leo
5th 4:15 pm Virgo
7th 7:36 pm Libra
9th 8:24 pm Scorpio
11th 8:39 pm Sagittarius
13th 10:05 pm Capricorn
16th 1:48 am Aquarius
18th 8:06 am Pisces
20th 4:44 pm Aries
23rd 3:24 am Taurus
25th 3:45 pm Gemini
28th 4:49 am Cancer
30th 4:43 pm Leo

May 2039
3rd 1:25 am Virgo
5th 5:58 am Libra
7th 7:09 am Scorpio
9th 6:42 am Sagittarius
11th 6:38 am Capricorn
13th 8:40 am Aquarius
15th 1:51 pm Pisces
17th 10:18 pm Aries
20th 9:19 am Taurus
22nd 9:55 pm Gemini
25th 10:57 am Cancer
27th 11:05 pm Leo
30th 8:46 am Virgo

June 2039
1st 2:55 pm Libra
3rd 5:30 pm Scorpio
5th 5:38 pm Sagittarius
7th 5:04 pm Capricorn
9th 5:44 pm Aquarius
11th 9:15 pm Pisces
14th 4:32 am Aries
16th 3:14 pm Taurus
19th 3:56 am Gemini
21st 4:55 pm Cancer
24th 4:47 am Leo
26th 2:38 pm Virgo
28th 9:46 pm Libra

July 2039
1st 1:57 am Scorpio
3rd 3:35 am Sagittarius
5th 3:46 am Capricorn
7th 4:07 am Aquarius
9th 6:27 am Pisces
11th 12:16 pm Aries
13th 10:00 pm Taurus
16th 10:27 am Gemini
18th 11:23 pm Cancer
21st 10:55 am Leo
23rd 8:13 pm Virgo
26th 3:17 am Libra
28th 8:16 am Scorpio
30th 11:21 am Sagittarius

August 2039
1st 1:01 pm Capricorn
3rd 2:13 pm Aquarius
5th 4:26 pm Pisces
7th 9:19 pm Aries
10th 5:55 am Taurus
12th 5:47 pm Gemini
15th 6:43 am Cancer
17th 6:09 pm Leo
20th 2:51 am Virgo
22nd 9:05 am Libra
24th 1:37 pm Scorpio
26th 5:09 pm Sagittarius
28th 8:01 pm Capricorn
30th 10:35 pm Aquarius

September 2039
2nd 1:41 am Pisces
4th 6:35 am Aries
6th 2:33 pm Taurus
9th 1:48 am Gemini
11th 2:41 pm Cancer
14th 2:27 am Leo
16th 11:07 am Virgo
18th 4:35 pm Libra
20th 7:59 pm Scorpio
22nd 10:38 pm Sagittarius
25th 1:28 am Capricorn
27th 4:51 am Aquarius
29th 9:08 am Pisces

October 2039
1st 2:53 pm Aries
3rd 10:59 pm Taurus
6th 9:53 am Gemini
8th 10:42 pm Cancer
11th 11:02 am Leo
13th 8:27 pm Virgo
16th 2:02 am Libra
18th 4:39 am Scorpio
20th 5:55 am Sagittarius
22nd 7:25 am Capricorn
24th 10:14 am Aquarius
26th 2:53 pm Pisces
28th 9:32 pm Aries
31st 6:21 am Taurus

November 2039
2nd 5:24 pm Gemini
5th 6:08 am Cancer
7th 6:57 pm Leo
10th 5:31 am Virgo
12th 12:17 pm Libra
14th 3:16 pm Scorpio
16th 3:50 pm Sagittarius
18th 3:48 pm Capricorn
20th 4:56 pm Aquarius
22nd 8:31 pm Pisces
25th 3:07 am Aries
27th 12:30 pm Taurus
30th 12:02 am Gemini

December 2039
2nd 12:48 pm Cancer
5th 1:41 am Leo
7th 1:05 pm Virgo
9th 9:26 pm Libra
12th 1:57 am Scorpio
14th 3:13 am Sagittarius
16th 2:41 am Capricorn
18th 2:20 am Aquarius
20th 4:04 am Pisces
22nd 9:17 am Aries
24th 6:17 pm Taurus
27th 6:05 am Gemini
29th 7:02 pm Cancer

January 2040
1st 7:43 am Leo
3rd 7:09 pm Virgo
6th 4:24 am Libra
8th 10:40 am Scorpio
10th 1:42 pm Sagittarius
12th 2:11 pm Capricorn
14th 1:39 pm Aquarius
16th 2:06 pm Pisces
18th 5:31 pm Aries
21st 1:07 am Taurus
23rd 12:25 pm Gemini
26th 1:27 am Cancer
28th 2:01 pm Leo
31st 12:57 am Virgo

May 2040
2nd 8:18 pm Aquarius
4th 11:31 pm Pisces
7th 4:27 am Aries
9th 11:27 am Taurus
11th 8:47 pm Gemini
14th 8:20 am Cancer
16th 9:05 pm Leo
19th 9:07 am Virgo
21st 6:22 pm Libra
23rd 11:54 pm Scorpio
26th 2:14 am Sagittarius
28th 2:48 am Capricorn
30th 3:18 am Aquarius

September 2040
2nd 10:30 pm Leo
5th 10:32 am Virgo
7th 8:51 pm Libra
10th 5:16 am Scorpio
12th 11:45 am Sagittarius
14th 4:03 pm Capricorn
16th 6:15 pm Aquarius
18th 7:11 pm Pisces
20th 8:26 pm Aries
22nd 11:48 pm Taurus
25th 6:44 am Gemini
27th 5:18 pm Cancer
30th 5:52 am Leo

January 2041
1st 10:41 pm Capricorn
3rd 10:25 pm Aquarius
5th 10:11 pm Pisces
7th 11:59 pm Aries
10th 5:01 am Taurus
12th 1:22 pm Gemini
15th 12:06 am Cancer
17th 12:08 pm Leo
20th 12:44 am Virgo
22nd 1:02 pm Libra
24th 11:33 pm Scorpio
27th 6:39 am Sagittarius
29th 9:47 am Capricorn
31st 9:49 am Aquarius

May 2041
1st 10:06 pm Gemini
4th 5:26 am Cancer
6th 3:53 pm Leo
9th 4:14 am Virgo
11th 4:14 pm Libra
14th 1:59 am Scorpio
16th 8:50 am Sagittarius
18th 1:15 pm Capricorn
20th 4:13 pm Aquarius
22nd 6:44 pm Pisces
24th 9:35 pm Aries
27th 1:22 am Taurus
29th 6:40 am Gemini
31st 2:08 pm Cancer

February 2040
2nd 9:57 am Libra
4th 4:54 pm Scorpio
6th 9:31 pm Sagittarius
8th 11:47 pm Capricorn
11th 12:28 am Aquarius
13th 1:04 am Pisces
15th 3:34 am Aries
17th 9:40 am Taurus
19th 7:51 pm Gemini
22nd 8:35 am Cancer
24th 9:12 pm Leo
27th 7:48 am Virgo
29th 4:01 pm Libra

June 2040
1st 5:18 am Pisces
3rd 9:52 am Aries
5th 5:19 pm Taurus
8th 3:18 am Gemini
10th 3:08 pm Cancer
13th 3:55 am Leo
15th 4:19 pm Virgo
18th 2:41 am Libra
20th 9:35 am Scorpio
22nd 12:46 pm Sagittarius
24th 1:11 pm Capricorn
26th 12:35 pm Aquarius
28th 12:58 pm Pisces
30th 4:05 pm Aries

October 2040
2nd 5:58 pm Virgo
5th 3:59 am Libra
7th 11:36 am Scorpio
9th 5:16 pm Sagittarius
11th 9:28 pm Capricorn
14th 12:32 am Aquarius
16th 2:54 am Pisces
18th 5:27 am Aries
20th 9:24 am Taurus
22nd 3:59 pm Gemini
25th 1:46 am Cancer
27th 1:55 pm Leo
30th 2:17 am Virgo

February 2041
2nd 8:44 am Pisces
4th 8:49 am Aries
6th 12:03 pm Taurus
8th 7:18 pm Gemini
11th 5:54 am Cancer
13th 6:13 pm Leo
16th 6:50 am Virgo
18th 6:55 pm Libra
21st 5:41 am Scorpio
23rd 2:01 pm Sagittarius
25th 6:57 pm Capricorn
27th 8:32 pm Aquarius

June 2041
3rd 12:09 am Leo
5th 12:14 pm Virgo
8th 12:37 am Libra
10th 10:57 am Scorpio
12th 5:51 pm Sagittarius
14th 9:29 pm Capricorn
16th 11:10 pm Aquarius
19th 12:31 am Pisces
21st 2:57 am Aries
23rd 7:11 am Taurus
25th 1:25 pm Gemini
27th 9:36 pm Cancer
30th 7:47 am Leo

March 2040
2nd 10:19 pm Scorpio
5th 3:08 am Sagittarius
7th 6:35 am Capricorn
9th 8:53 am Aquarius
11th 10:46 am Pisces
13th 1:40 pm Aries
15th 7:12 pm Taurus
18th 4:21 am Gemini
20th 4:28 pm Cancer
23rd 5:11 am Leo
25th 3:59 pm Virgo
27th 11:47 pm Libra
30th 5:05 am Scorpio

July 2040
2nd 10:54 pm Taurus
5th 9:01 am Gemini
7th 9:11 pm Cancer
10th 10:01 am Leo
12th 10:26 pm Virgo
15th 9:23 am Libra
17th 5:39 pm Scorpio
19th 10:24 pm Sagittarius
21st 11:50 pm Capricorn
23rd 11:15 pm Aquarius
25th 10:41 pm Pisces
28th 12:15 am Aries
30th 5:35 am Taurus

November 2040
1st 12:36 pm Libra
3rd 7:54 pm Scorpio
6th 12:31 am Sagittarius
8th 3:29 am Capricorn
10th 5:54 am Aquarius
12th 8:37 am Pisces
14th 12:17 pm Aries
16th 5:26 pm Taurus
19th 12:37 am Gemini
21st 10:14 am Cancer
23rd 10:02 pm Leo
26th 10:38 am Virgo
28th 9:49 pm Libra

March 2041
1st 8:05 pm Pisces
3rd 7:40 pm Aries
5th 9:26 pm Taurus
8th 2:58 am Gemini
10th 12:28 pm Cancer
13th 12:33 am Leo
15th 1:13 pm Virgo
18th 1:02 am Libra
20th 11:19 am Scorpio
22nd 7:40 pm Sagittarius
25th 1:33 am Capricorn
27th 4:47 am Aquarius
29th 5:57 am Pisces
31st 6:24 am Aries

July 2041
2nd 7:46 pm Virgo
5th 8:27 am Libra
7th 7:42 pm Scorpio
10th 3:31 am Sagittarius
12th 7:21 am Capricorn
14th 8:17 am Aquarius
16th 8:15 am Pisces
18th 9:14 am Aries
20th 12:39 pm Taurus
22nd 6:57 pm Gemini
25th 3:44 am Cancer
27th 2:23 pm Leo
30th 2:29 am Virgo

April 2040
1st 8:51 am Sagittarius
3rd 11:57 pm Capricorn
5th 2:51 pm Aquarius
7th 6:00 pm Pisces
9th 10:05 pm Aries
12th 4:08 am Taurus
14th 1:00 pm Gemini
17th 12:38 am Cancer
19th 1:23 pm Leo
22nd 12:46 am Virgo
24th 8:59 am Libra
26th 1:53 pm Scorpio
28th 4:31 pm Sagittarius
30th 6:15 pm Capricorn

August 2040
1st 2:59 pm Gemini
4th 3:07 am Cancer
6th 3:59 pm Leo
9th 4:12 am Virgo
11th 3:01 pm Libra
13th 11:51 pm Scorpio
16th 5:59 am Sagittarius
18th 9:05 am Capricorn
20th 9:41 am Aquarius
22nd 9:21 am Pisces
24th 10:09 am Aries
26th 2:04 pm Taurus
28th 10:09 pm Gemini
31st 9:40 am Cancer

December 2040
1st 5:46 am Scorpio
3rd 10:09 am Sagittarius
5th 11:56 am Capricorn
7th 12:46 pm Aquarius
9th 2:17 pm Pisces
11th 5:42 pm Aries
13th 11:31 pm Taurus
16th 7:39 am Gemini
18th 5:46 pm Cancer
21st 5:32 am Leo
23rd 6:11 pm Virgo
26th 6:11 am Libra
28th 3:31 pm Scorpio
30th 8:55 pm Sagittarius

April 2041
2nd 7:58 am Taurus
4th 12:21 pm Gemini
6th 8:29 pm Cancer
9th 7:47 am Leo
11th 8:23 pm Virgo
14th 8:09 am Libra
16th 5:56 pm Scorpio
19th 1:28 am Sagittarius
21st 6:58 am Capricorn
23rd 10:44 am Aquarius
25th 1:13 pm Pisces
27th 3:10 pm Aries
29th 5:42 pm Taurus

August 2041
1st 3:18 am Libra
4th 3:19 pm Scorpio
6th 12:28 am Sagittarius
8th 5:29 pm Capricorn
10th 6:48 pm Aquarius
12th 6:09 pm Pisces
14th 5:44 pm Aries
16th 7:32 pm Taurus
19th 12:44 am Gemini
21st 9:17 am Cancer
23rd 8:15 pm Leo
26th 8:33 am Virgo
28th 9:21 pm Libra
31st 9:35 am Scorpio

September 2041
2nd 7:44 pm Sagittarius
5th 2:21 am Capricorn
7th 5:06 am Aquarius
9th 5:04 am Pisces
11th 4:13 am Aries
13th 4:41 am Taurus
15th 8:12 am Gemini
17th 3:34 pm Cancer
20th 2:11 am Leo
22nd 2:35 pm Virgo
25th 3:19 am Libra
27th 3:16 pm Scorpio
30th 1:32 am Sagittarius

October 2041
2nd 9:09 am Capricorn
4th 1:34 pm Aquarius
6th 3:09 pm Pisces
8th 3:09 pm Aries
10th 3:24 pm Taurus
12th 5:44 pm Gemini
14th 11:32 pm Cancer
17th 9:05 am Leo
19th 9:14 pm Virgo
22nd 9:57 am Libra
24th 9:34 pm Scorpio
27th 7:12 am Sagittarius
29th 2:37 pm Capricorn
31st 7:47 pm Aquarius

November 2041
2nd 10:54 pm Pisces
5th 12:34 am Aries
7th 1:51 am Taurus
9th 4:11 am Gemini
11th 9:02 am Cancer
13th 5:22 pm Leo
16th 4:50 am Virgo
18th 5:35 pm Libra
21st 5:12 am Scorpio
23rd 2:16 pm Sagittarius
25th 8:41 pm Capricorn
28th 1:10 am Aquarius
30th 4:33 am Pisces

December 2041
2nd 7:25 am Aries
4th 10:15 am Taurus
6th 1:42 pm Gemini
8th 6:44 pm Cancer
11th 2:25 am Leo
13th 1:09 pm Virgo
16th 1:49 am Libra
18th 1:54 pm Scorpio
20th 11:07 pm Sagittarius
23rd 4:52 am Capricorn
25th 8:05 am Aquarius
27th 10:16 am Pisces
29th 12:45 am Aries
31st 4:15 pm Taurus

January 2042
2nd 8:56 pm Gemini
5th 3:01 am Cancer
7th 10:59 am Leo
9th 9:25 pm Virgo
12th 9:54 am Libra
14th 10:34 pm Scorpio
17th 8:44 am Sagittarius
19th 2:54 pm Capricorn
21st 5:31 pm Aquarius
23rd 6:18 pm Pisces
25th 7:12 pm Aries
27th 9:42 pm Taurus
30th 2:26 am Gemini

February 2042
1st 9:19 am Cancer
3rd 6:08 pm Leo
6th 4:50 am Virgo
8th 5:14 pm Libra
11th 6:13 am Scorpio
13th 5:29 pm Sagittarius
16th 1:01 am Capricorn
18th 4:22 am Aquarius
20th 4:48 am Pisces
22nd 4:22 am Aries
24th 5:05 am Taurus
26th 8:23 am Gemini
28th 2:48 pm Cancer

March 2042
2nd 11:59 pm Leo
5th 11:13 am Virgo
7th 11:46 pm Libra
10th 12:42 pm Scorpio
13th 12:34 am Sagittarius
15th 9:29 am Capricorn
17th 2:29 pm Aquarius
19th 3:57 pm Pisces
21st 3:28 pm Aries
23rd 3:02 pm Taurus
25th 4:33 pm Gemini
27th 9:23 pm Cancer
30th 5:51 am Leo

April 2042
1st 5:09 pm Virgo
4th 5:54 am Libra
6th 6:43 pm Scorpio
9th 6:26 am Sagittarius
11th 3:56 pm Capricorn
13th 10:22 pm Aquarius
16th 1:34 am Pisces
18th 2:18 am Aries
20th 2:05 am Taurus
22nd 2:43 am Gemini
24th 5:58 am Cancer
26th 12:58 pm Leo
28th 11:35 pm Virgo

May 2042
1st 12:18 pm Libra
4th 1:04 am Scorpio
6th 12:21 pm Sagittarius
8th 9:29 pm Capricorn
11th 4:17 am Aquarius
13th 8:43 am Pisces
15th 11:06 am Aries
17th 12:10 pm Taurus
19th 1:13 pm Gemini
21st 3:50 pm Cancer
23rd 9:34 pm Leo
26th 7:06 am Virgo
28th 7:26 pm Libra
31st 8:12 am Scorpio

June 2042
2nd 7:15 pm Sagittarius
5th 3:41 am Capricorn
7th 9:47 am Aquarius
9th 2:14 pm Pisces
11th 5:31 pm Aries
13th 7:59 pm Taurus
15th 10:17 pm Gemini
18th 1:24 am Cancer
20th 6:46 am Leo
22nd 3:27 pm Virgo
25th 3:14 am Libra
27th 4:03 pm Scorpio
30th 3:16 am Sagittarius

July 2042
2nd 11:22 am Capricorn
4th 4:34 pm Aquarius
6th 8:01 pm Pisces
8th 10:52 pm Aries
11th 1:49 am Taurus
13th 5:12 am Gemini
15th 9:26 am Cancer
17th 3:20 pm Leo
19th 11:50 pm Virgo
22nd 11:12 am Libra
25th 12:06 am Scorpio
27th 11:52 am Sagittarius
29th 8:21 pm Capricorn

August 2042
1st 1:13 am Aquarius
3rd 3:36 am Pisces
5th 5:11 am Aries
7th 7:17 am Taurus
9th 10:41 am Gemini
11th 3:40 pm Cancer
13th 10:27 pm Leo
16th 7:25 am Virgo
18th 6:45 pm Libra
21st 7:41 am Scorpio
23rd 8:07 pm Sagittarius
26th 5:38 am Capricorn
28th 11:09 am Aquarius
30th 1:18 pm Pisces

September 2042
1st 1:46 pm Aries
3rd 2:20 pm Taurus
5th 4:30 pm Gemini
7th 9:05 pm Cancer
10th 4:16 am Leo
12th 1:53 pm Virgo
15th 1:31 am Libra
17th 2:28 pm Scorpio
20th 3:17 am Sagittarius
22nd 1:56 pm Capricorn
24th 8:54 pm Aquarius
26th 11:59 pm Pisces
29th 12:23 am Aries
30th 11:52 pm Taurus

October 2042
3rd 12:22 am Gemini
5th 3:26 am Cancer
7th 9:54 am Leo
9th 7:38 pm Virgo
12th 7:38 am Libra
14th 8:39 pm Scorpio
17th 9:24 am Sagittarius
19th 8:36 pm Capricorn
22nd 4:59 am Aquarius
24th 9:49 am Pisces
26th 11:27 am Aries
28th 11:07 am Taurus
30th 10:39 am Gemini

November 2042
1st 12:02 pm Cancer
3rd 4:53 pm Leo
6th 1:46 am Virgo
8th 1:43 pm Libra
11th 2:49 am Scorpio
13th 3:19 pm Sagittarius
16th 2:15 am Capricorn
18th 11:05 am Aquarius
20th 5:20 pm Pisces
22nd 8:48 pm Aries
24th 9:55 pm Taurus
26th 9:54 pm Gemini
28th 10:35 pm Cancer

December 2042
1st 1:56 am Leo
3rd 9:19 am Virgo
5th 8:32 pm Libra
8th 9:35 am Scorpio
10th 9:59 pm Sagittarius
13th 8:22 am Capricorn
15th 4:34 pm Aquarius
17th 10:55 pm Pisces
20th 3:30 am Aries
22nd 6:20 am Taurus
24th 7:52 am Gemini
26th 9:15 am Cancer
28th 12:12 pm Leo
30th 6:25 pm Virgo

January 2043
2nd 4:31 am Libra
4th 5:13 pm Scorpio
7th 5:46 am Sagittarius
9th 3:58 pm Capricorn
11th 11:22 pm Aquarius
14th 4:42 am Pisces
16th 8:49 am Aries
18th 12:14 pm Taurus
20th 3:08 pm Gemini
22nd 5:59 pm Cancer
24th 9:48 pm Leo
27th 3:54 am Virgo
29th 1:15 pm Libra

February 2043
1st 1:25 am Scorpio
3rd 2:10 pm Sagittarius
6th 12:52 am Capricorn
8th 8:12 am Aquarius
10th 12:36 pm Pisces
12th 3:22 pm Aries
14th 5:45 pm Taurus
16th 8:34 pm Gemini
19th 12:16 am Cancer
21st 5:18 am Leo
23rd 12:14 pm Virgo
25th 9:40 pm Libra
28th 9:29 am Scorpio

March 2043
2nd 10:20 pm Sagittarius
5th 9:50 am Capricorn
7th 6:02 pm Aquarius
9th 10:34 pm Pisces
12th 12:27 am Aries
14th 1:17 am Taurus
16th 2:38 am Gemini
18th 5:40 am Cancer
20th 11:01 am Leo
22nd 6:49 pm Virgo
25th 4:53 am Libra
27th 4:47 pm Scorpio
30th 5:38 am Sagittarius

April 2043
1st 5:44 pm Capricorn
4th 3:13 am Aquarius
6th 8:56 am Pisces
8th 11:11 am Aries
10th 11:18 am Taurus
12th 11:06 am Gemini
14th 12:27 pm Cancer
16th 4:43 pm Leo
19th 12:24 am Virgo
21st 10:56 am Libra
23rd 11:13 pm Scorpio
26th 12:02 pm Sagittarius
29th 12:18 am Capricorn

May 2043
1st 10:40 am Aquarius
3rd 5:56 pm Pisces
5th 9:35 pm Aries
7th 10:16 pm Taurus
9th 9:33 pm Gemini
11th 9:29 pm Cancer
14th 12:04 am Leo
16th 6:33 am Virgo
18th 4:45 pm Libra
21st 5:12 am Scorpio
23rd 6:04 pm Sagittarius
26th 6:07 am Capricorn
28th 4:38 pm Aquarius
31st 12:51 am Pisces

June 2043
2nd 6:05 am Aries
4th 8:16 am Taurus
6th 8:18 am Gemini
8th 7:57 am Cancer
10th 9:20 am Leo
12th 2:17 pm Virgo
14th 11:24 pm Libra
17th 11:31 am Scorpio
20th 12:23 am Sagittarius
22nd 12:12 pm Capricorn
24th 10:15 pm Aquarius
27th 6:24 am Pisces
29th 12:25 pm Aries

July 2043
1st 4:03 pm Taurus
3rd 5:34 pm Gemini
5th 6:06 pm Cancer
7th 7:25 pm Leo
9th 11:26 pm Virgo
12th 7:20 am Libra
14th 6:42 pm Scorpio
17th 7:27 am Sagittarius
19th 7:12 pm Capricorn
22nd 4:47 am Aquarius
24th 12:11 pm Pisces
26th 5:48 pm Aries
28th 9:53 pm Taurus
31st 12:36 am Gemini

August 2043
2nd 2:32 am Cancer
4th 4:48 am Leo
6th 8:54 am Virgo
8th 4:07 pm Libra
11th 2:42 am Scorpio
13th 3:13 pm Sagittarius
16th 3:12 am Capricorn
18th 12:46 pm Aquarius
20th 7:31 pm Pisces
23rd 12:05 am Aries
25th 3:21 am Taurus
27th 6:05 am Gemini
29th 8:53 am Cancer
31st 12:22 pm Leo

September 2043
2nd 5:22 pm Virgo
5th 12:46 am Libra
7th 10:58 am Scorpio
9th 11:14 pm Sagittarius
12th 11:35 am Capricorn
14th 9:47 pm Aquarius
17th 4:40 am Pisces
19th 8:29 am Aries
21st 10:27 am Taurus
23rd 11:57 am Gemini
25th 2:15 pm Cancer
27th 6:10 pm Leo
30th 12:09 am Virgo

October 2043
2nd 8:20 am Libra
4th 6:42 pm Scorpio
7th 6:50 am Sagittarius
9th 7:30 pm Capricorn
12th 6:42 am Aquarius
14th 2:37 pm Pisces
16th 6:46 pm Aries
18th 8:00 pm Taurus
20th 8:02 pm Gemini
22nd 8:45 pm Cancer
24th 11:43 pm Leo
27th 5:42 am Virgo
29th 2:31 pm Libra

November 2043
1st 1:25 am Scorpio
3rd 1:39 pm Sagittarius
6th 2:23 am Capricorn
8th 2:20 pm Aquarius
10th 11:45 pm Pisces
13th 5:19 am Aries
15th 7:08 am Taurus
17th 6:37 am Gemini
19th 5:51 am Cancer
21st 7:00 am Leo
23rd 11:40 am Virgo
25th 8:07 pm Libra
28th 7:21 am Scorpio
30th 7:50 pm Sagittarius

December 2043
3rd 8:29 am Capricorn
5th 8:31 pm Aquarius
8th 6:52 am Pisces
10th 2:10 pm Aries
12th 5:42 pm Taurus
14th 6:05 pm Gemini
16th 5:04 pm Cancer
18th 4:54 pm Leo
20th 7:43 pm Virgo
23rd 2:43 am Libra
25th 1:24 pm Scorpio
28th 1:58 am Sagittarius
30th 2:35 pm Capricorn

January 2044
2nd 2:16 am Aquarius
4th 12:29 pm Pisces
6th 8:36 pm Aries
9th 1:49 am Taurus
11th 4:02 am Gemini
13th 4:12 am Cancer
15th 4:08 am Leo
17th 5:56 am Virgo
19th 11:17 am Libra
21st 8:40 pm Scorpio
24th 8:48 am Sagittarius
26th 9:27 pm Capricorn
29th 8:52 am Aquarius
31st 6:25 pm Pisces

February 2044
3rd 2:00 am Aries
5th 7:36 am Taurus
7th 11:10 am Gemini
9th 1:05 pm Cancer
11th 2:22 pm Leo
13th 4:33 pm Virgo
15th 9:13 pm Libra
18th 5:21 am Scorpio
20th 4:37 pm Sagittarius
23rd 5:12 am Capricorn
25th 4:46 pm Aquarius
28th 1:56 am Pisces

March 2044
1st 8:34 am Aries
3rd 1:12 pm Taurus
5th 4:34 pm Gemini
7th 7:18 pm Cancer
9th 10:02 pm Leo
12th 1:31 am Virgo
14th 6:43 am Libra
16th 2:28 pm Scorpio
19th 1:02 am Sagittarius
21st 1:23 pm Capricorn
24th 1:23 am Aquarius
26th 10:55 am Pisces
28th 5:09 pm Aries
30th 8:39 pm Taurus

April 2044
1st 10:43 pm Gemini
4th 12:42 am Cancer
6th 3:40 am Leo
8th 8:10 am Virgo
10th 2:27 pm Libra
12th 10:43 pm Scorpio
15th 9:07 am Sagittarius
17th 9:17 pm Capricorn
20th 9:42 am Aquarius
22nd 8:09 pm Pisces
25th 2:59 am Aries
27th 6:12 am Taurus
29th 7:06 am Gemini

May 2044
1st 7:34 am Cancer
3rd 9:22 am Leo
5th 1:35 pm Virgo
7th 8:24 pm Libra
10th 5:26 am Scorpio
12th 4:13 pm Sagittarius
15th 4:22 am Capricorn
17th 5:01 pm Aquarius
20th 4:24 am Pisces
22nd 12:32 pm Aries
24th 4:34 pm Taurus
26th 5:20 pm Gemini
28th 4:44 pm Cancer
30th 4:56 pm Leo

June 2044
1st 7:43 pm Virgo
4th 1:55 am Libra
6th 11:08 am Scorpio
8th 10:21 pm Sagittarius
11th 10:39 am Capricorn
13th 11:19 pm Aquarius
16th 11:10 am Pisces
18th 8:31 pm Aries
21st 2:04 am Taurus
23rd 3:51 am Gemini
25th 3:20 am Cancer
27th 2:37 am Leo
29th 3:52 am Virgo

July 2044
1st 8:34 am Libra
3rd 4:59 pm Scorpio
6th 4:11 am Sagittarius
8th 4:39 pm Capricorn
11th 5:12 am Aquarius
13th 4:56 pm Pisces
16th 2:47 am Aries
18th 9:37 am Taurus
20th 1:01 pm Gemini
22nd 1:42 pm Cancer
24th 1:17 pm Leo
26th 1:48 pm Virgo
28th 5:04 pm Libra
31st 12:07 am Scorpio

August 2044
2nd 10:36 am Sagittarius
4th 10:59 pm Capricorn
7th 11:29 am Aquarius
9th 10:49 pm Pisces
12th 8:18 am Aries
14th 3:27 pm Taurus
16th 8:02 pm Gemini
18th 10:17 pm Cancer
20th 11:10 pm Leo
23rd 12:09 am Virgo
25th 2:53 am Libra
27th 8:44 am Scorpio
29th 6:09 pm Sagittarius

September 2044
1st 6:09 am Capricorn
3rd 6:40 pm Aquarius
6th 5:47 am Pisces
8th 2:33 pm Aries
10th 8:59 pm Taurus
13th 1:32 am Gemini
15th 4:40 am Cancer
17th 7:00 am Leo
19th 9:18 am Virgo
21st 12:36 pm Libra
23rd 6:05 pm Scorpio
26th 2:39 am Sagittarius
28th 2:05 pm Capricorn

October 2044
1st 2:42 am Aquarius
3rd 2:02 pm Pisces
5th 10:30 pm Aries
8th 3:59 am Taurus
10th 7:25 am Gemini
12th 10:03 am Cancer
14th 12:48 pm Leo
16th 4:15 pm Virgo
18th 8:46 pm Libra
21st 2:51 am Scorpio
23rd 11:14 am Sagittarius
25th 10:14 pm Capricorn
28th 10:54 am Aquarius
30th 10:56 pm Pisces

November 2044
2nd 7:56 am Aries
4th 1:08 pm Taurus
6th 3:28 pm Gemini
8th 4:38 pm Cancer
10th 6:21 pm Leo
12th 9:41 pm Virgo
15th 2:37 am Libra
17th 10:02 am Scorpio
19th 6:57 pm Sagittarius
22nd 5:55 am Capricorn
24th 6:34 pm Aquarius
27th 7:15 am Pisces
29th 5:29 pm Aries

December 2044
1st 11:35 pm Taurus
4th 1:50 am Gemini
6th 1:54 am Cancer
8th 1:56 am Leo
10th 3:45 am Virgo
12th 8:21 am Libra
14th 3:44 pm Scorpio
17th 1:21 am Sagittarius
19th 12:41 pm Capricorn
22nd 1:20 am Aquarius
24th 2:16 pm Pisces
27th 1:37 am Aries
29th 9:22 am Taurus
31st 12:53 pm Gemini

January 2045	**February 2045**	**March 2045**	**April 2045**
2nd 1:13 pm Cancer	2nd 11:25 pm Virgo	2nd 10:38 am Virgo	3rd 12:53 am Scorpio
4th 12:20 pm Leo	5th 11:32 am Libra	4th 11:32 am Libra	5th 6:45 am Sagittarius
6th 12:25 pm Virgo	7th 5:05 am Scorpio	6th 2:42 pm Scorpio	7th 4:09 pm Capricorn
8th 3:11 pm Libra	9th 1:25 pm Sagittarius	8th 9:29 pm Sagittarius	10th 4:23 am Aquarius
10th 9:30 pm Scorpio	12th 12:54 am Capricorn	11th 7:58 am Capricorn	12th 5:06 pm Pisces
13th 7:02 am Sagittarius	14th 1:47 am Aquarius	13th 8:42 am Aquarius	15th 3:52 am Aries
15th 6:45 pm Capricorn	17th 2:25 am Pisces	16th 9:19 am Pisces	17th 11:36 am Taurus
18th 7:31 am Aquarius	19th 1:39 pm Aries	18th 8:06 pm Aries	19th 4:46 pm Gemini
20th 8:20 pm Pisces	21st 10:46 pm Taurus	21st 4:28 am Taurus	21st 8:26 pm Cancer
23rd 7:58 am Aries	24th 5:13 am Gemini	23rd 10:39 am Gemini	23rd 11:30 pm Leo
25th 4:59 pm Taurus	26th 8:54 am Cancer	25th 3:01 pm Cancer	26th 2:29 am Virgo
27th 10:21 pm Gemini	28th 10:18 am Leo	27th 5:55 pm Leo	28th 5:44 am Libra
30th 12:14 am Cancer		29th 7:52 pm Virgo	30th 9:51 am Scorpio
31st 11:57 pm Leo		31st 9:44 pm Libra	

May 2045	**June 2045**	**July 2045**	**August 2045**
2nd 3:51 pm Sagittarius	1st 8:42 am Capricorn	1st 3:15 am Aquarius	2nd 11:06 am Aries
5th 12:43 am Capricorn	3rd 8:13 am Aquarius	3rd 4:12 pm Pisces	4th 9:45 pm Taurus
7th 12:26 pm Aquarius	6th 9:08 am Pisces	6th 4:40 am Aries	7th 5:02 am Gemini
10th 1:18 am Pisces	8th 9:04 pm Aries	8th 2:27 pm Taurus	9th 8:36 am Cancer
12th 12:31 pm Aries	11th 5:41 am Taurus	10th 8:16 pm Gemini	11th 9:19 am Leo
14th 8:19 pm Taurus	13th 10:22 am Gemini	12th 10:28 pm Cancer	13th 8:48 am Virgo
17th 12:46 am Gemini	15th 12:09 pm Cancer	14th 10:33 pm Leo	15th 8:56 am Libra
19th 3:13 am Cancer	17th 12:48 pm Leo	16th 10:27 pm Virgo	17th 11:30 am Scorpio
21st 5:12 am Leo	19th 2:04 pm Virgo	18th 11:54 pm Libra	19th 5:38 pm Sagittarius
23rd 7:51 am Virgo	21st 5:05 pm Libra	21st 4:06 am Scorpio	22nd 3:22 am Capricorn
25th 11:39 am Libra	23rd 10:22 pm Scorpio	23rd 11:26 am Sagittarius	24th 3:32 pm Aquarius
27th 4:48 pm Scorpio	26th 5:53 am Sagittarius	25th 9:30 pm Capricorn	27th 4:33 am Pisces
29th 11:38 pm Sagittarius	28th 3:34 pm Capricorn	28th 9:32 am Aquarius	29th 4:56 pm Aries
		30th 10:30 pm Pisces	

September 2045	**October 2045**	**November 2045**	**December 2045**
1st 3:40 am Taurus	2nd 11:22 pm Cancer	1st 8:54 am Leo	2nd 8:37 pm Libra
3rd 11:53 am Gemini	5th 3:09 am Leo	3rd 12:03 pm Virgo	5th 12:22 am Scorpio
5th 5:03 pm Cancer	7th 5:03 am Virgo	5th 2:28 pm Libra	7th 5:15 am Sagittarius
7th 7:19 pm Leo	9th 5:56 am Libra	7th 4:54 pm Scorpio	9th 12:14 pm Capricorn
9th 7:37 pm Virgo	11th 7:17 am Scorpio	9th 8:42 pm Sagittarius	11th 10:04 pm Aquarius
11th 7:31 pm Libra	13th 10:55 am Sagittarius	12th 3:22 am Capricorn	14th 10:24 am Pisces
13th 8:54 pm Scorpio	15th 6:15 pm Capricorn	14th 1:35 pm Aquarius	16th 11:13 pm Aries
16th 1:30 am Sagittarius	18th 5:20 am Aquarius	17th 2:15 am Pisces	19th 9:51 am Taurus
18th 10:06 am Capricorn	20th 6:15 pm Pisces	19th 2:41 pm Aries	21st 4:49 pm Gemini
20th 9:58 pm Aquarius	23rd 6:24 am Aries	22nd 12:31 am Taurus	23rd 8:27 pm Cancer
23rd 10:59 am Pisces	25th 4:07 pm Taurus	24th 7:07 am Gemini	25th 10:13 pm Leo
25th 11:08 pm Aries	27th 11:20 pm Gemini	26th 11:22 am Cancer	27th 11:39 pm Virgo
28th 9:21 am Taurus	30th 4:44 am Cancer	28th 2:29 pm Leo	30th 2:01 am Libra
30th 5:26 pm Gemini		30th 5:26 pm Virgo	

January 2046	**February 2046**	**March 2046**	**April 2046**
1st 5:57 am Scorpio	2nd 1:38 am Capricorn	1st 7:19 am Capricorn	2nd 1:09 pm Pisces
3rd 11:46 am Sagittarius	4th 12:26 pm Aquarius	3rd 6:17 pm Aquarius	5th 2:06 am Aries
5th 7:41 pm Capricorn	7th 12:50 am Pisces	6th 6:59 am Pisces	7th 1:50 pm Taurus
8th 5:51 am Aquarius	9th 1:48 pm Aries	8th 7:55 pm Aries	9th 11:47 pm Gemini
10th 6:02 pm Pisces	12th 1:57 am Taurus	11th 7:58 am Taurus	12th 7:42 am Cancer
13th 7:03 am Aries	14th 11:35 am Gemini	13th 6:13 pm Gemini	14th 1:12 pm Leo
15th 6:40 pm Taurus	16th 5:34 pm Cancer	16th 1:42 am Cancer	16th 4:04 pm Virgo
18th 2:55 am Gemini	18th 7:54 pm Leo	18th 5:50 am Leo	18th 4:51 pm Libra
20th 7:14 am Cancer	20th 7:48 pm Virgo	20th 6:58 am Virgo	20th 4:59 pm Scorpio
22nd 8:35 am Leo	22nd 7:06 pm Libra	22nd 6:25 am Libra	22nd 6:27 pm Sagittarius
24th 8:38 am Virgo	24th 7:49 pm Scorpio	24th 6:09 am Scorpio	24th 11:08 pm Capricorn
26th 9:11 am Libra	26th 11:39 pm Sagittarius	26th 8:17 am Sagittarius	27th 7:57 am Aquarius
28th 11:45 am Scorpio		28th 2:21 pm Capricorn	29th 8:01 pm Pisces
30th 5:13 pm Sagittarius		31st 12:30 am Aquarius	

May 2046	**June 2046**	**July 2046**	**August 2046**
2nd 8:56 am Aries	1st 4:12 am Taurus	3rd 4:13 am Cancer	1st 5:18 pm Leo
4th 8:29 pm Taurus	3rd 1:17 pm Gemini	5th 7:53 am Leo	3rd 6:32 pm Virgo
7th 5:51 am Gemini	5th 7:48 pm Cancer	7th 10:12 am Virgo	5th 7:11 pm Libra
9th 1:10 pm Cancer	8th 12:27 am Leo	9th 12:17 pm Libra	7th 8:48 pm Scorpio
11th 6:45 pm Leo	10th 3:58 am Virgo	11th 3:03 pm Scorpio	10th 12:34 am Sagittarius
13th 10:37 pm Virgo	12th 6:50 am Libra	13th 7:09 pm Sagittarius	12th 6:59 am Capricorn
16th 12:55 am Libra	14th 9:31 am Scorpio	16th 1:04 am Capricorn	14th 3:55 pm Aquarius
18th 2:23 am Scorpio	16th 12:46 pm Sagittarius	18th 9:16 am Aquarius	17th 2:54 am Pisces
20th 4:25 am Sagittarius	18th 5:41 pm Capricorn	20th 7:52 pm Pisces	19th 3:16 pm Aries
22nd 8:43 am Capricorn	21st 1:19 am Aquarius	23rd 8:14 am Aries	22nd 3:55 am Taurus
24th 4:33 pm Aquarius	23rd 11:58 am Pisces	25th 8:39 pm Taurus	24th 3:10 pm Gemini
27th 3:47 am Pisces	26th 12:30 am Aries	28th 6:59 am Gemini	26th 11:20 pm Cancer
29th 4:31 pm Aries	28th 12:31 pm Taurus	30th 1:50 pm Cancer	29th 3:40 am Leo
	30th 9:59 pm Gemini		31st 4:49 am Virgo

September 2046
2nd 4:25 am Libra
4th 4:27 am Scorpio
6th 6:48 am Sagittarius
8th 12:33 pm Capricorn
10th 9:39 pm Aquarius
13th 9:05 am Pisces
15th 9:36 pm Aries
18th 10:13 am Taurus
20th 9:55 pm Gemini
23rd 7:21 am Cancer
25th 1:17 pm Leo
27th 3:34 pm Virgo
29th 3:18 pm Libra

January 2047
3rd 1:43 am Aries
5th 2:17 pm Taurus
8th 1:38 am Gemini
10th 10:12 am Cancer
12th 3:53 pm Leo
14th 7:28 pm Virgo
16th 10:05 pm Libra
19th 12:40 am Scorpio
21st 3:55 am Sagittarius
23rd 8:23 am Capricorn
25th 2:37 pm Aquarius
27th 11:07 pm Pisces
30th 10:03 am Aries

May 2047
2nd 4:11 am Leo
4th 10:11 am Virgo
6th 12:34 pm Libra
8th 12:26 pm Scorpio
10th 11:43 am Sagittarius
12th 12:34 pm Capricorn
14th 4:45 pm Aquarius
17th 12:55 am Pisces
19th 12:11 pm Aries
22nd 12:50 am Taurus
24th 1:14 pm Gemini
27th 12:27 am Cancer
29th 9:48 am Leo
31st 4:37 pm Virgo

September 2047
1st 3:40 am Aquarius
3rd 10:44 am Pisces
5th 7:49 pm Aries
8th 7:04 am Taurus
10th 7:44 pm Gemini
13th 7:48 am Cancer
15th 4:53 pm Leo
17th 9:59 pm Virgo
19th 11:47 pm Libra
22nd 12:08 am Scorpio
24th 12:59 am Sagittarius
26th 3:50 am Capricorn
28th 9:14 am Aquarius
30th 4:59 pm Pisces

January 2048
2nd 8:43 pm Leo
5th 5:04 am Virgo
7th 11:09 am Libra
9th 3:03 pm Scorpio
11th 5:10 pm Sagittarius
13th 6:20 pm Capricorn
15th 7:56 pm Aquarius
17th 11:30 pm Pisces
20th 6:22 am Aries
22nd 4:49 pm Taurus
25th 5:28 am Gemini
27th 5:50 pm Cancer
30th 4:00 am Leo

October 2046
1st 2:25 pm Scorpio
3rd 3:09 pm Sagittarius
5th 7:20 pm Capricorn
8th 3:36 am Aquarius
10th 2:59 pm Pisces
13th 3:40 am Aries
15th 4:09 pm Taurus
18th 3:40 am Gemini
20th 1:33 pm Cancer
22nd 8:51 pm Leo
25th 12:54 am Virgo
27th 1:58 am Libra
29th 1:28 am Scorpio
31st 1:30 am Sagittarius

February 2047
1st 10:32 pm Taurus
4th 10:33 am Gemini
6th 7:56 pm Cancer
9th 1:40 am Leo
11th 4:19 am Virgo
13th 5:23 am Libra
15th 6:34 am Scorpio
17th 9:16 am Sagittarius
19th 2:12 pm Capricorn
21st 9:24 pm Aquarius
24th 6:38 am Pisces
26th 5:40 pm Aries

June 2047
2nd 8:31 pm Libra
4th 9:57 pm Scorpio
6th 10:11 pm Sagittarius
8th 10:59 pm Capricorn
11th 2:12 am Aquarius
13th 8:58 am Pisces
15th 7:16 pm Aries
18th 7:39 am Taurus
20th 8:02 pm Gemini
23rd 6:52 am Cancer
25th 3:33 pm Leo
27th 10:01 pm Virgo
30th 2:26 am Libra

October 2047
3rd 2:42 am Aries
5th 2:06 pm Taurus
8th 2:48 am Gemini
10th 3:25 pm Cancer
13th 1:47 am Leo
15th 8:08 am Virgo
17th 10:28 am Libra
19th 10:17 am Scorpio
21st 9:44 am Sagittarius
23rd 10:52 am Capricorn
25th 3:03 pm Aquarius
27th 10:33 pm Pisces
30th 8:38 am Aries

February 2048
1st 11:27 am Virgo
3rd 4:41 pm Libra
5th 8:32 pm Scorpio
7th 11:37 pm Sagittarius
10th 2:22 am Capricorn
12th 5:18 am Aquarius
14th 9:22 am Pisces
16th 3:46 am Aries
19th 1:21 am Taurus
21st 1:35 pm Gemini
24th 2:16 am Cancer
26th 12:44 pm Leo
28th 7:47 pm Virgo

November 2046
2nd 4:13 am Capricorn
4th 10:58 am Aquarius
6th 9:33 pm Pisces
9th 10:09 am Aries
11th 10:36 pm Taurus
14th 9:40 am Gemini
16th 7:03 pm Cancer
19th 2:32 am Leo
21st 7:45 am Virgo
23rd 10:33 am Libra
25th 11:34 am Scorpio
27th 12:17 pm Sagittarius
29th 2:33 pm Capricorn

March 2047
1st 6:04 am Taurus
3rd 6:35 pm Gemini
6th 5:10 am Cancer
8th 12:04 pm Leo
10th 3:01 pm Virgo
12th 3:18 pm Libra
14th 2:54 pm Scorpio
16th 3:53 pm Sagittarius
18th 7:46 pm Capricorn
21st 2:55 am Aquarius
23rd 12:43 pm Pisces
26th 12:13 am Aries
28th 12:39 pm Taurus
31st 1:18 am Gemini

July 2047
2nd 5:08 am Scorpio
4th 6:51 am Sagittarius
6th 8:42 am Capricorn
8th 12:00 pm Aquarius
10th 6:02 pm Pisces
13th 3:23 am Aries
15th 3:16 pm Taurus
18th 3:44 am Gemini
20th 2:34 pm Cancer
22nd 10:40 pm Leo
25th 4:11 am Virgo
27th 7:53 am Libra
29th 10:41 am Scorpio
31st 1:20 pm Sagittarius

November 2047
1st 8:24 pm Taurus
4th 9:05 am Gemini
6th 9:48 pm Cancer
9th 8:59 am Leo
11th 4:56 pm Virgo
13th 8:52 pm Libra
15th 9:31 pm Scorpio
17th 8:41 pm Sagittarius
19th 8:31 pm Capricorn
21st 10:54 pm Aquarius
24th 4:58 am Pisces
26th 2:33 pm Aries
29th 2:28 am Taurus

March 2048
1st 11:55 pm Libra
4th 2:31 am Scorpio
6th 4:58 am Sagittarius
8th 8:05 am Capricorn
10th 12:09 pm Aquarius
12th 5:23 pm Pisces
15th 12:21 am Aries
17th 9:45 am Taurus
19th 9:39 pm Gemini
22nd 10:34 am Cancer
24th 9:52 pm Leo
27th 5:29 am Virgo
29th 9:19 am Libra
31st 10:47 am Scorpio

December 2046
1st 8:04 pm Aquarius
4th 5:25 am Pisces
6th 5:31 pm Aries
9th 6:03 am Taurus
11th 4:59 pm Gemini
14th 1:40 am Cancer
16th 8:14 am Leo
18th 1:08 pm Virgo
20th 4:38 pm Libra
22nd 7:08 pm Scorpio
24th 9:22 pm Sagittarius
27th 12:30 am Capricorn
29th 5:51 am Aquarius
31st 2:20 pm Pisces

April 2047
2nd 12:45 pm Cancer
4th 9:11 pm Leo
7th 1:33 am Virgo
9th 2:23 am Libra
11th 1:26 am Scorpio
13th 12:59 am Sagittarius
15th 3:05 am Capricorn
17th 8:56 am Aquarius
19th 6:22 pm Pisces
22nd 6:05 am Aries
24th 6:41 pm Taurus
27th 7:13 am Gemini
29th 6:48 pm Cancer

August 2047
2nd 4:28 pm Capricorn
4th 8:45 pm Aquarius
7th 2:59 am Pisces
9th 11:51 am Aries
11th 11:18 pm Taurus
14th 11:52 am Gemini
16th 11:12 pm Cancer
19th 7:24 am Leo
21st 12:13 pm Virgo
23rd 2:43 pm Libra
25th 4:26 pm Scorpio
27th 6:43 pm Sagittarius
29th 10:22 pm Capricorn

December 2047
1st 3:14 pm Gemini
4th 3:41 am Cancer
6th 2:48 pm Leo
8th 11:35 pm Virgo
11th 5:11 am Libra
13th 7:38 am Scorpio
15th 7:56 am Sagittarius
17th 7:46 am Capricorn
19th 9:03 am Aquarius
21st 1:26 pm Pisces
23rd 9:40 pm Aries
26th 9:06 am Taurus
28th 9:56 pm Gemini
31st 10:11 am Cancer

April 2048
2nd 11:43 am Sagittarius
4th 1:41 pm Capricorn
6th 5:31 pm Aquarius
8th 11:25 pm Pisces
11th 7:15 am Aries
13th 5:08 pm Taurus
16th 5:01 am Gemini
18th 6:03 pm Cancer
21st 6:08 am Leo
23rd 2:59 pm Virgo
25th 7:41 pm Libra
27th 9:02 pm Scorpio
29th 8:54 pm Sagittarius

May 2048
1st 9:14 pm Capricorn
3rd 11:37 pm Aquarius
6th 4:51 am Pisces
8th 12:55 pm Aries
10th 11:21 pm Taurus
13th 11:31 am Gemini
16th 12:34 am Cancer
18th 1:02 pm Leo
20th 11:03 pm Virgo
23rd 5:14 am Libra
25th 7:41 am Scorpio
27th 7:40 am Sagittarius
29th 7:05 am Capricorn
31st 7:51 am Aquarius

September 2048
2nd 3:12 am Cancer
4th 3:14 pm Leo
7th 12:33 am Virgo
9th 6:56 am Libra
11th 11:19 am Scorpio
13th 2:44 pm Sagittarius
15th 5:49 pm Capricorn
17th 8:50 pm Aquarius
20th 12:16 am Pisces
22nd 5:00 am Aries
24th 12:13 pm Taurus
26th 10:35 pm Gemini
29th 11:14 am Cancer

January 2049
1st 3:59 am Sagittarius
3rd 4:07 am Capricorn
5th 3:23 am Aquarius
7th 3:49 am Pisces
9th 7:17 am Aries
11th 2:48 pm Taurus
14th 1:54 am Gemini
16th 2:47 pm Cancer
19th 3:36 am Leo
21st 3:11 pm Virgo
24th 12:58 am Libra
26th 8:21 am Scorpio
28th 12:55 pm Sagittarius
30th 2:43 pm Capricorn

May 2049
1st 1:51 am Taurus
3rd 10:14 am Gemini
5th 9:15 pm Cancer
8th 9:54 am Leo
10th 10:02 pm Virgo
13th 7:28 am Libra
15th 1:20 pm Scorpio
17th 4:13 pm Sagittarius
19th 5:30 pm Capricorn
21st 6:41 pm Aquarius
23rd 9:04 pm Pisces
26th 1:28 am Aries
28th 8:13 am Taurus
30th 5:21 pm Gemini

September 2049
1st 8:22 pm Scorpio
4th 3:25 am Sagittarius
6th 7:48 am Capricorn
8th 9:36 am Aquarius
10th 9:51 am Pisces
12th 10:21 am Aries
14th 1:07 pm Taurus
16th 7:40 pm Gemini
19th 6:04 am Cancer
21st 6:39 pm Leo
24th 7:00 am Virgo
26th 5:36 pm Libra
29th 2:09 am Scorpio

June 2048
2nd 11:29 am Pisces
4th 6:42 pm Aries
7th 5:05 am Taurus
9th 5:30 pm Gemini
12th 6:33 am Cancer
14th 6:56 pm Leo
17th 5:24 am Virgo
19th 12:53 pm Libra
21st 4:58 pm Scorpio
23rd 6:11 pm Sagittarius
25th 5:55 pm Capricorn
27th 5:57 pm Aquarius
29th 8:07 pm Pisces

October 2048
1st 11:42 pm Leo
4th 9:25 am Virgo
6th 3:34 pm Libra
8th 6:57 pm Scorpio
10th 9:04 pm Sagittarius
12th 11:16 pm Capricorn
15th 2:20 am Aquarius
17th 6:37 am Pisces
19th 12:25 pm Aries
21st 8:14 pm Taurus
24th 6:34 am Gemini
26th 7:02 pm Cancer
29th 7:54 am Leo
31st 6:37 pm Virgo

February 2049
1st 2:46 pm Aquarius
3rd 2:48 pm Pisces
5th 4:54 pm Aries
7th 10:45 pm Taurus
10th 8:46 am Gemini
12th 9:27 pm Cancer
15th 10:17 am Leo
17th 9:30 pm Virgo
20th 6:38 am Libra
22nd 1:51 pm Scorpio
24th 7:12 pm Sagittarius
26th 10:36 pm Capricorn

June 2049
2nd 4:34 am Cancer
4th 5:11 pm Leo
7th 5:43 am Virgo
9th 4:12 pm Libra
11th 11:12 pm Scorpio
14th 2:31 am Sagittarius
16th 3:14 am Capricorn
18th 3:03 am Aquarius
20th 3:51 am Pisces
22nd 7:09 am Aries
24th 1:42 pm Taurus
26th 11:17 pm Gemini
29th 10:57 am Cancer

October 2049
1st 8:48 am Sagittarius
3rd 1:39 pm Capricorn
5th 4:46 pm Aquarius
7th 6:34 pm Pisces
9th 8:10 pm Aries
11th 11:07 pm Taurus
14th 4:57 am Gemini
16th 2:20 pm Cancer
19th 2:25 am Leo
21st 2:52 pm Virgo
24th 1:33 am Libra
26th 9:32 am Scorpio
28th 3:09 pm Sagittarius
30th 7:09 pm Capricorn

July 2048
2nd 1:49 am Aries
4th 11:22 am Taurus
6th 11:40 pm Gemini
9th 12:42 pm Cancer
12th 12:48 am Leo
14th 10:58 am Virgo
16th 6:47 pm Libra
19th 12:04 am Scorpio
21st 2:55 am Sagittarius
23rd 3:58 am Capricorn
25th 4:28 am Aquarius
27th 6:04 am Pisces
29th 10:31 am Aries
31st 6:51 pm Taurus

November 2048
3rd 1:33 am Libra
5th 4:51 am Scorpio
7th 5:55 am Sagittarius
9th 6:32 am Capricorn
11th 8:14 am Aquarius
13th 12:01 pm Pisces
15th 6:15 pm Aries
18th 2:53 am Taurus
20th 1:40 pm Gemini
23rd 2:09 am Cancer
25th 3:09 pm Leo
28th 2:49 am Virgo
30th 11:13 am Libra

March 2049
1st 12:18 am Aquarius
3rd 1:20 am Pisces
5th 3:21 am Aries
7th 8:12 am Taurus
9th 4:58 pm Gemini
12th 4:59 am Cancer
14th 5:50 pm Leo
17th 5:03 am Virgo
19th 1:36 pm Libra
21st 7:52 pm Scorpio
24th 12:35 am Sagittarius
26th 4:16 am Capricorn
28th 7:08 am Aquarius
30th 9:38 am Pisces

July 2049
1st 11:39 pm Leo
4th 12:17 pm Virgo
6th 11:32 pm Libra
9th 7:56 am Scorpio
11th 12:37 pm Sagittarius
13th 1:57 pm Capricorn
15th 1:22 pm Aquarius
17th 12:52 pm Pisces
19th 2:31 pm Aries
21st 7:48 pm Taurus
24th 4:57 am Gemini
26th 4:47 pm Cancer
29th 5:37 am Leo
31st 6:09 pm Virgo

November 2049
1st 10:13 pm Aquarius
4th 12:57 am Pisces
6th 3:57 am Aries
8th 8:02 am Taurus
10th 2:11 pm Gemini
12th 11:07 pm Cancer
15th 10:38 am Leo
17th 11:13 pm Virgo
20th 10:30 am Libra
22nd 6:46 pm Scorpio
24th 11:47 pm Sagittarius
27th 2:28 am Capricorn
29th 4:13 am Aquarius

August 2048
3rd 6:33 am Gemini
5th 7:33 pm Cancer
8th 7:28 am Leo
10th 5:02 pm Virgo
13th 12:16 am Libra
15th 5:35 am Scorpio
17th 9:23 am Sagittarius
19th 11:55 am Capricorn
21st 1:44 pm Aquarius
23rd 3:56 pm Pisces
25th 8:02 pm Aries
28th 3:25 am Taurus
30th 2:20 pm Gemini

December 2048
2nd 3:40 pm Scorpio
4th 4:54 pm Sagittarius
6th 4:34 pm Capricorn
8th 4:33 pm Aquarius
10th 6:38 pm Pisces
12th 11:55 pm Aries
15th 8:36 am Taurus
17th 7:53 pm Gemini
20th 8:34 am Cancer
22nd 9:29 pm Leo
25th 9:24 am Virgo
27th 7:01 pm Libra
30th 1:16 am Scorpio

April 2049
1st 12:42 pm Aries
3rd 5:43 pm Taurus
6th 1:51 am Gemini
8th 1:09 pm Cancer
11th 1:56 am Leo
13th 1:31 pm Virgo
15th 10:11 pm Libra
18th 3:47 am Scorpio
20th 7:19 am Sagittarius
22nd 9:55 am Capricorn
24th 12:30 pm Aquarius
26th 3:39 pm Pisces
28th 7:52 pm Aries

August 2049
3rd 5:31 am Libra
5th 2:48 pm Scorpio
7th 9:04 pm Sagittarius
9th 11:55 pm Capricorn
12th 12:07 am Aquarius
13th 11:23 pm Pisces
15th 11:54 pm Aries
18th 3:37 am Taurus
20th 11:32 am Gemini
22nd 10:56 pm Cancer
25th 11:46 am Leo
28th 12:09 am Virgo
30th 11:08 am Libra

December 2049
1st 6:19 am Pisces
3rd 9:43 am Aries
5th 2:52 pm Taurus
7th 10:01 pm Gemini
10th 7:17 am Cancer
12th 6:36 pm Leo
15th 7:11 am Virgo
17th 7:14 pm Libra
20th 4:37 am Scorpio
22nd 10:12 am Sagittarius
24th 12:24 pm Capricorn
26th 12:45 pm Aquarius
28th 1:09 pm Pisces
30th 3:21 pm Aries

January 2050
1st 8:20 pm Taurus
4th 4:08 am Gemini
6th 2:09 pm Cancer
9th 1:42 am Leo
11th 2:14 pm Virgo
14th 2:42 am Libra
16th 1:21 pm Scorpio
18th 8:28 pm Sagittarius
20th 11:33 pm Capricorn
22nd 11:39 pm Aquarius
24th 10:45 pm Pisces
26th 11:07 pm Aries
29th 2:33 am Taurus
31st 9:43 am Gemini

February 2050
2nd 7:59 pm Cancer
5th 7:57 am Leo
7th 8:31 pm Virgo
10th 8:55 am Libra
12th 8:09 pm Scorpio
15th 4:45 am Sagittarius
17th 9:37 am Capricorn
19th 10:54 am Aquarius
21st 10:06 am Pisces
23rd 9:26 am Aries
25th 11:06 am Taurus
27th 4:36 pm Gemini

March 2050
2nd 2:02 am Cancer
4th 1:59 pm Leo
7th 2:40 am Virgo
9th 2:50 pm Libra
12th 1:50 am Scorpio
14th 10:54 am Sagittarius
16th 5:09 pm Capricorn
18th 8:13 pm Aquarius
20th 8:48 pm Pisces
22nd 8:33 pm Aries
24th 9:30 pm Taurus
27th 1:30 am Gemini
29th 9:28 am Cancer
31st 8:43 pm Leo

April 2050
3rd 9:21 am Virgo
5th 9:26 pm Libra
8th 7:55 am Scorpio
10th 4:25 pm Sagittarius
12th 10:47 pm Capricorn
15th 2:55 am Aquarius
17th 5:07 am Pisces
19th 6:17 am Aries
21st 7:52 am Taurus
23rd 11:27 am Gemini
25th 6:17 pm Cancer
28th 4:31 am Leo
30th 4:50 pm Virgo

May 2050
3rd 5:01 am Libra
5th 3:17 pm Scorpio
7th 11:02 pm Sagittarius
10th 4:30 am Capricorn
12th 8:20 am Aquarius
14th 11:09 am Pisces
16th 1:37 pm Aries
18th 4:30 pm Taurus
20th 8:46 pm Gemini
23rd 3:24 am Cancer
25th 12:55 pm Leo
28th 12:50 am Virgo
30th 1:13 pm Libra

June 2050
1st 11:50 pm Scorpio
4th 7:20 am Sagittarius
6th 11:52 am Capricorn
8th 2:30 pm Aquarius
10th 4:35 pm Pisces
12th 7:11 pm Aries
14th 10:59 pm Taurus
17th 4:20 am Gemini
19th 11:34 am Cancer
21st 9:03 pm Leo
24th 8:41 am Virgo
26th 9:18 pm Libra
29th 8:39 am Scorpio

July 2050
1st 4:45 pm Sagittarius
3rd 9:05 pm Capricorn
5th 10:42 pm Aquarius
7th 11:23 pm Pisces
10th 12:52 am Aries
12th 4:21 am Taurus
14th 10:13 am Gemini
16th 6:16 pm Cancer
19th 4:12 am Leo
21st 3:52 pm Virgo
24th 4:37 am Libra
26th 4:44 pm Scorpio
29th 2:01 am Sagittarius
31st 7:12 am Capricorn

August 2050
2nd 8:46 am Aquarius
4th 8:27 am Pisces
6th 8:25 am Aries
8th 10:29 am Taurus
10th 3:41 pm Gemini
12th 11:53 pm Cancer
15th 10:20 am Leo
17th 10:15 pm Virgo
20th 11:01 am Libra
22nd 11:32 pm Scorpio
25th 9:58 am Sagittarius
27th 4:39 pm Capricorn
29th 7:19 pm Aquarius
31st 7:09 pm Pisces

September 2050
2nd 6:14 pm Aries
4th 6:45 pm Taurus
6th 10:22 pm Gemini
9th 5:41 am Cancer
11th 4:03 pm Leo
14th 4:13 am Virgo
16th 4:58 pm Libra
19th 5:22 am Scorpio
21st 4:15 pm Sagittarius
24th 12:16 am Capricorn
26th 4:37 am Aquarius
28th 5:47 am Pisces
30th 5:16 am Aries

October 2050
2nd 5:06 am Taurus
4th 7:13 am Gemini
6th 12:57 pm Cancer
8th 10:25 pm Leo
11th 10:26 am Virgo
13th 11:13 pm Libra
16th 11:18 am Scorpio
18th 9:48 pm Sagittarius
21st 6:05 am Capricorn
23rd 11:40 am Aquarius
25th 2:34 pm Pisces
27th 3:34 pm Aries
29th 4:01 pm Taurus
31st 5:39 pm Gemini

November 2050
2nd 10:05 pm Cancer
5th 6:11 am Leo
7th 5:33 pm Virgo
10th 6:18 am Libra
12th 6:17 pm Scorpio
15th 4:09 am Sagittarius
17th 11:40 am Capricorn
19th 5:07 pm Aquarius
21st 8:53 pm Pisces
23rd 11:27 pm Aries
26th 1:28 am Taurus
28th 3:55 am Gemini
30th 8:06 am Cancer

December 2050
2nd 3:13 pm Leo
5th 1:40 am Virgo
7th 2:14 pm Libra
10th 2:29 am Scorpio
12th 12:13 pm Sagittarius
14th 6:53 pm Capricorn
16th 11:09 pm Aquarius
19th 2:15 am Pisces
21st 5:08 am Aries
23rd 8:21 am Taurus
25th 12:12 pm Gemini
27th 5:15 pm Cancer
30th 12:21 am Leo

APPENDIX B
Rising Signs Chart

To use this chart to find your rising sign, find your birthday in the left-hand column. If it falls between two dates, use the date above it. Slide across the date to line up with your time of birth. The result is your rising sign.

The first chart is for those born before noon, and the second is for those born after noon.

	1 AM	2 AM	3 AM	4 AM	5 AM	6 AM	7 AM	8 AM	9 AM	10 AM	11 AM	12 NOON
Jan 1	Lib	Sc	Sc	Sc	Sag	Sag	Cap	Cap	Aq	Aq	Pis	Ar
Jan 9	Lib	Sc	Sc	Sag	Sag	Sag	Cap	Cap	Aq	Pis	Ar	Tau
Jan 17	Sc	Sc	Sc	Sag	Sag	Cap	Cap	Aq	Aq	Pis	Ar	Tau
Jan 25	Sc	Sc	Sag	Sag	Sag	Cap	Cap	Aq	Pis	Ar	Tau	Tau
Feb 2	Sc	Sc	Sag	Sag	Cap	Cap	Aq	Pis	Pis	Ar	Tau	Gem
Feb 10	Sc	Sag	Sag	Sag	Cap	Cap	Aq	Pis	Ar	Tau	Tau	Gem
Feb 18	Sc	Sag	Sag	Cap	Cap	Aq	Pis	Pis	Ar	Tau	Gem	Gem
Feb 26	Sag	Sag	Sag	Cap	Aq	Aq	Pis	Ar	Tau	Tau	Gem	Gem
Mar 6	Sag	Sag	Cap	Cap	Aq	Pis	Pis	Ar	Tau	Gem	Gem	Can
Mar 14	Sag	Cap	Cap	Aq	Aq	Pis	Ar	Tau	Tau	Gem	Gem	Can
Mar 22	Sag	Cap	Cap	Aq	Pis	Ar	Ar	Tau	Gem	Gem	Can	Can
Mar 30	Cap	Cap	Aq	Pis	Pis	Ar	Tau	Tau	Gem	Can	Can	Can
Apr 7	Cap	Cap	Aq	Pis	Ar	Ar	Tau	Gem	Gem	Can	Can	Leo
Apr 14	Cap	Aq	Aq	Pis	Ar	Tau	Tau	Gem	Gem	Can	Can	Leo
Apr 22	Cap	Aq	Pis	Ar	Ar	Tau	Gem	Gem	Gem	Can	Leo	Leo
Apr 30	Aq	Aq	Pis	Ar	Tau	Tau	Gem	Can	Can	Can	Leo	Leo
May 8	Aq	Pis	Ar	Ar	Tau	Gem	Gem	Can	Can	Leo	Leo	Leo
May 16	Aq	Pis	Ar	Tau	Gem	Gem	Can	Can	Can	Leo	Leo	Vir
May 24	Pis	Ar	Ar	Tau	Gem	Gem	Can	Can	Leo	Leo	Leo	Vir
June 1	Pis	Ar	Tau	Gem	Gem	Can	Can	Can	Leo	Leo	Vir	Vir
June 9	Ar	Ar	Tau	Gem	Gem	Can	Can	Leo	Leo	Leo	Vir	Vir
June 17	Ar	Tau	Gem	Gem	Can	Can	Can	Leo	Leo	Vir	Vir	Vir
June 25	Tau	Tau	Gem	Gem	Can	Can	Leo	Leo	Leo	Vir	Vir	Lib
July 3	Tau	Gem	Gem	Can	Can	Can	Leo	Leo	Vir	Vir	Vir	Lib
July 11	Tau	Gem	Gem	Can	Can	Leo	Leo	Leo	Vir	Vir	Lib	Lib
July 18	Gem	Gem	Can	Can	Can	Leo	Leo	Vir	Vir	Vir	Lib	Lib
July 26	Gem	Gem	Can	Can	Leo	Leo	Vir	Vir	Vir	Lib	Lib	Lib
Aug 3	Gem	Can	Can	Can	Leo	Leo	Vir	Vir	Vir	Lib	Lib	Sc
Aug 11	Gem	Can	Can	Leo	Leo	Leo	Vir	Vir	Lib	Lib	Lib	Sc
Aug 18	Can	Can	Can	Leo	Leo	Vir	Vir	Vir	Lib	Lib	Sc	Sc
Aug 27	Can	Can	Leo	Leo	Leo	Vir	Vir	Lib	Lib	Lib	Sc	Sc
Sept 4	Can	Can	Leo	Leo	Leo	Vir	Vir	Vir	Lib	Lib	Sc	Sc
Sept 12	Can	Leo	Leo	Leo	Vir	Vir	Lib	Lib	Lib	Sc	Sc	Sag
Sept 20	Leo	Leo	Leo	Vir	Vir	Vir	Lib	Lib	Sc	Sc	Sc	Sag
Sept 28	Leo	Leo	Leo	Vir	Vir	Lib	Lib	Lib	Sc	Sc	Sag	Sag
Oct 6	Leo	Leo	Vir	Vir	Vir	Lib	Lib	Sc	Sc	Sc	Sag	Sag
Oct 14	Leo	Vir	Vir	Vir	Lib	Lib	Lib	Sc	Sc	Sag	Sag	Cap
Oct 22	Leo	Vir	Vir	Lib	Lib	Lib	Sc	Sc	Sc	Sag	Sag	Cap
Oct 30	Vir	Vir	Vir	Lib	Lib	Sc	Sc	Sc	Sag	Sag	Cap	Cap
Nov 7	Vir	Vir	Lib	Lib	Lib	Sc	Sc	Sc	Sag	Sag	Cap	Cap
Nov 15	Vir	Vir	Lib	Lib	Sc	Sc	Sc	Sag	Sag	Cap	Cap	Aq
Nov 23	Vir	Lib	Lib	Lib	Sc	Sc	Sag	Sag	Sag	Cap	Cap	Aq
Dec 1	Vir	Lib	Lib	Sc	Sc	Sc	Sag	Sag	Cap	Cap	Aq	Aq
Dec 9	Lib	Lib	Lib	Sc	Sc	Sag	Sag	Sag	Cap	Cap	Aq	Pis
Dec 18	Lib	Lib	Sc	Sc	Sc	Sag	Sag	Cap	Cap	Aq	Aq	Pis
Dec 28	Lib	Lib	Sc	Sc	Sag	Sag	Sag	Cap	Aq	Aq	Pis	Ar

	1	2	3	4	5	6	7	8	9	10	11	12
	PM	PM	PM	PM	PM	PM	PM	PM	PM	PM	PM	MIDNIGHT
Jan 1	Tau	Gem	Gem	Can	Can	Can	Leo	Leo	Vir	Vir	Vir	Lib
Jan 9	Tau	Gem	Gem	Can	Can	Leo	Leo	Leo	Vir	Vir	Vir	Lib
Jan 17	Gem	Gem	Can	Can	Can	Leo	Leo	Vir	Vir	Vir	Lib	Lib
Jan 25	Gem	Gem	Can	Can	Leo	Leo	Leo	Vir	Vir	Lib	Lib	Lib
Feb 2	Gem	Can	Can	Can	Leo	Leo	Vir	Vir	Vir	Lib	Lib	Sc
Feb 10	Gem	Can	Can	Leo	Leo	Leo	Vir	Vir	Lib	Lib	Lib	Sc
Feb 18	Can	Can	Can	Leo	Leo	Vir	Vir	Vir	Lib	Lib	Sc	Sc
Feb 26	Can	Can	Leo	Leo	Leo	Vir	Vir	Lib	Lib	Lib	Sc	Sc
Mar 6	Can	Leo	Leo	Leo	Vir	Vir	Vir	Lib	Lib	Sc	Sc	Sc
Mar 14	Can	Leo	Leo	Vir	Vir	Vir	Lib	Lib	Lib	Sc	Sc	Sag
Mar 22	Leo	Leo	Leo	Vir	Vir	Lib	Lib	Lib	Sc	Sc	Sc	Sag
Mar 30	Leo	Leo	Vir	Vir	Vir	Lib	Lib	Sc	Sc	Sc	Sag	Sag
Apr 7	Leo	Leo	Vir	Vir	Lib	Lib	Lib	Sc	Sc	Sc	Sag	Sag
Apr 14	Leo	Vir	Vir	Vir	Lib	Lib	Sc	Sc	Sc	Sag	Sag	Cap
Apr 22	Leo	Vir	Vir	Lib	Lib	Lib	Sc	Sc	Sc	Sag	Sag	Cap
Apr 30	Vir	Vir	Vir	Lib	Lib	Sc	Sc	Sc	Sag	Sag	Cap	Cap
May 8	Vir	Vir	Lib	Lib	Lib	Sc	Sc	Sag	Sag	Sag	Cap	Cap
May 16	Vir	Vir	Lib	Lib	Sc	Sc	Sc	Sag	Sag	Cap	Cap	Aq
May 24	Vir	Lib	Lib	Lib	Sc	Sc	Sag	Sag	Sag	Cap	Cap	Aq
June 1	Vir	Lib	Lib	Sc	Sc	Sc	Sag	Sag	Cap	Cap	Aq	Aq
June 9	Lib	Lib	Lib	Sc	Sc	Sag	Sag	Sag	Cap	Cap	Aq	Pis
June 17	Lib	Lib	Sc	Sc	Sc	Sag	Sag	Cap	Cap	Aq	Aq	Pis
June 25	Lib	Lib	Sc	Sc	Sag	Sag	Sag	Cap	Cap	Aq	Pis	Ar
July 3	Lib	Sc	Sc	Sc	Sag	Sag	Cap	Cap	Aq	Aq	Pis	Ar
July 11	Lib	Sc	Sc	Sag	Sag	Sag	Cap	Cap	Aq	Pis	Ar	Tau
July 18	Sc	Sc	Sc	Sag	Sag	Cap	Cap	Aq	Aq	Pis	Ar	Tau
July 26	Sc	Sc	Sag	Sag	Sag	Cap	Cap	Aq	Pis	Ar	Tau	Tau
Aug 3	Sc	Sc	Sag	Sag	Cap	Cap	Aq	Aq	Pis	Ar	Tau	Gem
Aug 11	Sc	Sag	Sag	Sag	Cap	Cap	Aq	Pis	Ar	Tau	Tau	Gem
Aug 18	Sc	Sag	Sag	Cap	Cap	Aq	Pis	Pis	Ar	Tau	Gem	Gem
Aug 27	Sag	Sag	Sag	Cap	Cap	Aq	Pis	Ar	Tau	Tau	Gem	Gem
Sept 4	Sag	Sag	Cap	Cap	Aq	Pis	Pis	Ar	Tau	Gem	Gem	Can
Sept 12	Sag	Sag	Cap	Aq	Aq	Pis	Ar	Tau	Tau	Gem	Gem	Can
Sept 20	Sag	Cap	Cap	Aq	Pis	Pis	Ar	Tau	Gem	Gem	Can	Can
Sept 28	Cap	Cap	Aq	Aq	Pis	Ar	Tau	Tau	Gem	Gem	Can	Can
Oct 6	Cap	Cap	Aq	Pis	Ar	Ar	Tau	Gem	Gem	Can	Can	Leo
Oct 14	Cap	Aq	Aq	Pis	Ar	Tau	Tau	Gem	Gem	Can	Can	Leo
Oct 22	Cap	Aq	Pis	Ar	Ar	Tau	Gem	Gem	Can	Can	Leo	Leo
Oct 30	Aq	Aq	Pis	Ar	Tau	Tau	Gem	Can	Can	Can	Leo	Leo
Nov 7	Aq	Aq	Pis	Ar	Tau	Tau	Gem	Can	Can	Can	Leo	Leo
Nov 15	Aq	Pis	Ar	Tau	Gem	Gem	Can	Can	Can	Leo	Leo	Vir
Nov 23	Pis	Ar	Ar	Tau	Gem	Gem	Can	Can	Leo	Leo	Leo	Vir
Dec 1	Pis	Ar	Tau	Gem	Gem	Can	Can	Can	Leo	Leo	Vir	Vir
Dec 9	Ar	Tau	Tau	Gem	Gem	Can	Can	Leo	Leo	Leo	Vir	Vir
Dec 18	Ar	Tau	Gem	Gem	Can	Can	Can	Leo	Leo	Vir	Vir	Vir
Dec 28	Tau	Tau	Gem	Gem	Can	Can	Leo	Leo	Vir	Vir	Vir	Lib

About the Author

Stacy Dicker, PhD, is a clinical psychologist in private practice. She has been seeing psychotherapy clients for more than twenty years, and taught courses on eating disorders and adult psychotherapy to upper-level psychology majors at the University of Colorado, Boulder, for nearly ten years.

Her interest in astrology was first sparked by Linda Goodman's famous book *Love Signs* more than thirty years ago. A longtime student of astrology, Stacy has benefited tremendously from using this wise, ancient, and ultimately credible archetypal system to help herself and her clients develop more compassion for their own and others' natures. The blend of astrology and psychology led her to significantly change her attitude toward her own highly earthy nature—which was no small feat.

Stacy has been a music person since childhood. She has played numerous instruments over the course of her life, starting with piano, and most recently, the drums. Whether listening to it or playing it, music has always been an integral part of her life. Nothing—besides dogs—makes her happier than when she gets to see her favorite bands perform live. She is a huge fan of meaningful connection and good communication, loves to travel with her husband, Jeremy, and has been known to make a game of *Cards Against Humanity* go on way too long.

Visit Stacy's website at www.psychstrology.com to learn more about her book, programs, and services.

Made in the USA
Coppell, TX
22 June 2023

18425707R00177